Advances in Differential Dynamical Systems with Applications to Economics and Biology, 2nd Edition

Advances in Differential Dynamical Systems with Applications to Economics and Biology, 2nd Edition

Guest Editors

Mihaela Neamțu
Eva Kaslik
Anca Rădulescu

MDPI

Basel • Beijing • Wuhan • Barcelona • Belgrade • Novi Sad • Cluj • Manchester

Guest Editors

Mihaela Neamţu
Faculty of Economics and Business Administration
West University of Timişoara
Timişoara
Romania

Eva Kaslik
Faculty of Mathematics and Computer Science
West University of Timișoara
Timişoara
Romania

Anca Rădulescu
Department of Mathematics
State University of New York at New Paltz
New Paltz, NY
USA

Editorial Office

MDPI AG
Grosspeteranlage 5
4052 Basel, Switzerland

This is a reprint of the Special Issue, published open access by the journal *Mathematics* (ISSN 2227-7390), freely accessible at: https://www.mdpi.com/si/mathematics/Differ_Dyn_Syst_II.

For citation purposes, cite each article independently as indicated on the article page online and as indicated below:

Lastname, A.A.; Lastname, B.B. Article Title. *Journal Name* **Year**, *Volume Number*, Page Range.

ISBN 978-3-7258-3711-3 (Hbk)
ISBN 978-3-7258-3712-0 (PDF)
https://doi.org/10.3390/books978-3-7258-3712-0

Contents

About the Editors

Mihaela Neamțu

Mihaela Neamțu, Ph.D., is a Full Professor in the Faculty of Economics and Business Administration at the West University of Timişoara, Romania. She received both her B.S. degree and Ph.D. degree in mathematics in 1994 and 2001, respectively. She received her habilitation in mathematics from this same university in 2019. Her current field of research is nonlinear dynamics, economic modeling, differential equations, stability analysis, biomathematics, numerical simulation, and mathematical modeling. She has been the director and investigator of several national and international projects. Professor Neamțu is the author or co-author of five books and various scientific papers published in peer-reviewed scholarly journals. She has been the director of two national projects and a member of more than 14 national and international projects. She is a member of the Romanian Mathematical Society (R.M.S.). Professor Neamțu has been a visiting scientist at Nottingham Trent University, UK; the University of Perpignan Via Domitia and Universitatea La Rochelle, France.

Eva Kaslik

Eva Kaslik, Ph.D., is a Full Professor in the Department of Mathematics and Computer Science at the West University of Timişoara, Romania. She received her B.S. degree in pure Mathematics and M.S. in Applied Mathematics in 2002 and 2004, respectively. She received her Ph.D. Degree in 2006 from Université Paris Nord, France, and the West University of Timişoara, and received a habilitation in mathematics from the West University of Timişoara, in 2015. She has been the director of two national projects and one international project, a member of the Management Committee of the EU-funded program COST Action CA15225, and a member of more than 10 national and international projects. Professor Kaslik has been invited to give talks and presentations at more than 30 national and international conferences. Her current field of research is qualitative and quantitative analysis of systems of fractional-order differential equations and systems of delay differential equations with distributed delays and their applications in neuroscience, medicine, biology, and economy.

Anca Rădulescu

Anca Rădulescu, Ph.D., is an Associate Professor in the Department of Mathematics at the State University of New York at New Paltz, USA. She received her B.S. from the University of Bucharest in 1998 and her Ph.D. in mathematics from Stony Brook University in 2005. She was a Visiting Assistant Professor at the City University of New York, Brooklyn College, and an Instructor at the University of Colorado Boulder, USA. Since 2014, Dr. Rădulescu has worked with the State University of New York at New Paltz. She has been an invited speaker and served as co-organizer and session chair at many international conferences in her research field. Her main research interest is problems from complex dynamics that have applications to various fields in the natural sciences. Part of her work is purely theoretical, focused on identifying and understanding new phenomena in discrete random complex dynamics and complex dynamic networks. The other part centers around using dynamical systems methods and results to derive and analyze models in a variety of fields, among which mathematical neuroscience, medicine epidemiology, climate, and the environment.

mathematics

MDPI

Article

Dynamics of a Four-Dimensional Economic Model

Gheorghe Moza [1,*], Oana Brandibur [2] and Ariana Găină [2]

[1] Department of Mathematics, Politehnica University of Timisoara, 300006 Timisoara, Romania
[2] Department of Mathematics, West University of Timisoara, 300223 Timisoara, Romania
* Correspondence: gheorghe.moza@upt.ro

Abstract: The interdependency between interest rates, investment demands and inflation rates in a given economy has a continuous dynamics. We propose a four-dimensional model which describes these interactions by imposing a control law on the interest rate. By a qualitative analysis based on tools from dynamical systems theory, we obtain in the new model that the three economic indicators can be stabilized to three equilibrium states.

Keywords: dynamical systems; bifurcation diagrams; economic models; local dynamics

MSC: 37G10; 34C23; 37N40

1. Introduction

Many economic and financial phenomena are modeled by dynamical systems based on differential or difference Equations [1–5]. Financial exhibition can be seen as an elective, flexible and active inquiry field that can be used to modify the functions of any investigation method, strategy or inquiry center. According to [6], financial demonstration may be thought as a multi-discipline research strategy that encourages the consideration of a variety of socio-economic-political concerns which can have a negative impact on society anywhere and at any time. However, it shall be asserted that financial demonstration has become an essential technical-theoretical explanatory instrument for future academics, financial experts, strategy builders and transnational educators. The importance of "stabilizing an unsteady economy" through adequate macroeconomic stabilization measures implemented by government and central bank is highlighted. It is vital to understand how business emergencies arise and how they can be managed in order to be proficient in these tactics. As a result, studying dynamic nonlinear macroeconomic models could provide new insights in this area.

Various models and methods for examining economic indicators of an economy can be found in the literature. Modeling principles in economic environments is presented in [7]. A book dealing with economic models based on ordinary and partially differential equations is [8], where the following three topics of financial engineering are covered: control and stabilization in financial models, state estimation and forecasting and validation by statistical methods of decision-making tools. A macroeconomic model applied to three national economies is presented in [9], where approach is based on three main tools: the state-space modeling from control theory, fractional calculus and orthogonal distance fitting method. A model for studying the perspective of annual flow of inheritance (in level or as a share of national income) in a two-sector economy with one pure consumption good and one capital good was recently presented in [10]. Using tools from dynamical systems theory, two endogenous behaviors, which can operate independently or together, are obtained. It is shown that theoretical results provided by the model are consistent with some empirical data. In a recent paper [11], a deep learning method for matching the production of wind energy with consumers' needs is presented. A neural ordinary differential equation is used to model the wind speed continuously. A mathematical model based on differential

Citation: Moza, G.; Brandibur, O.; Găină, A. Dynamics of a Four-Dimensional Economic Model. *Mathematics* **2023**, *11*, 797. https://doi.org/10.3390/math11040797

Academic Editor: Huaizhong Zhao

Received: 20 December 2022
Revised: 1 February 2023
Accepted: 1 February 2023
Published: 4 February 2023

equations for studying epidemic and economic consequences of COVID-19 is presented in [12]. The model deals mainly with interactions between the disease transmission, the pandemic management, and the economic growth. A macroeconomic development model, known as the Grossman–Helpman model of endogenous product cycles, is presented in [13], where the stabilization problem is studied by a method based on optimal control.

A three-dimensional (3D) model to study the interactions of three macroeconomic indicators in a given economy is presented in [14]. This model is based on three ordinary differential equations and was designed to describe the relationships between three financial instruments: the interest rate $x(t)$, the investment demand $y(t)$ and the inflation rate $z(t)$. By studying the local behavior of the model around one of its equilibrium points, conditions to stabilize the economy around this steady state have been obtained in [14]. The finance system is an essential component of our economy that consist of interactions between the institutional units and markets, generally in a complex manner for the purpose of economic growth in investment and the demand of commercials. When an inflation occurs and a chaotic phenomenon appears in the finance system, the interest rate must be adjusted and controlled, regarding our model, it is possible by introducing a control function. The control of finance system goes to a quick and effective revival of the economy. This method is used when an economic crisis occurs. In order to find more economically relevant steady states to which the 3D model could be stabilized, we apply a control function to the model and study the resulting four-dimensional (4D) system. In addition, we consider in this work that $x(t)$ is the *real* interest rate, which is defined as the difference between the nominal interest rate and the inflation rate, thus, $x(t)$ may take positive or negative values.

A generalization to fractional order version of the 3D model is reported in [15], while in [16] the generalized model is studied in a new framework with delay. Moreover, Ref. [16] investigates by numerical simulations the effect of time delay to chaos in the model, while methods to suppress chaos in the model were presented in [17]. Fractional-order dynamical models and their bifurcations [18–23] are promising tools for studying economic models.

The paper is organized as follows: after the introduction, Section 2 describes the model to be studied and presents a local analysis of its behavior, where equilibrium points are characterized in terms of their type and stability properties. The occurrence of transcritical and pitchfork bifurcations when the system's parameters vary is particularly pointed out. Section 3 provides bifurcation diagrams for several combinations of parameters, revealing the complex behavior of the system.

2. Local Analysis of the Model

The 3D system studied in [14] is given by

$$\dot{x} = z + x(y - a),\ \dot{y} = -x^2 - by + 1,\ \dot{z} = -x - cz, \tag{1}$$

where $\dot{x} = \frac{dx}{dt}$ denotes the usual derivative with respect to time. The system has been studied in the first octant given by $x \geq 0$, $y \geq 0$ and $z \geq 0$, where $x = x(t)$ is the real interest rate, $y = y(t)$ the investment demand, $z = z(t)$ the inflation rate, $a \in \mathbb{R}$ the amount (of money) saved, $b \geq 0$ the cost per investment, $c > 0$ the elasticity of the demand on the commercial market.

We propose in this work to apply a feedback control function $u(t)$ to the first equation of (1) in the form

$$\dot{x}(t) = z(t) + x(t)(y(t) - a) - u(t), \tag{2}$$

where $u(t) = u(0)e^{\int_0^t (m - dx(t))dt}$, with $m, d \in \mathbb{R}$ and $d \neq 0$. Then, u satisfies the equation $\dot{u} = u(m - dx)$, which, together with (2), lead to a new four-dimensional (4D) system, given by

$$\dot{X} = F(X, \mu), \tag{3}$$

where $X = \begin{pmatrix} x & y & z & u \end{pmatrix}^T$, $F(X,\mu) = \begin{pmatrix} f_1 & f_2 & f_3 & f_4 \end{pmatrix}^T$, respectively,

$$f_1 = z + x(y-a) - u,\ f_2 = -x^2 - by + 1,\ f_3 = -x - cz \text{ and } f_4 = u(m - dx).$$

The parameter vector is $\mu = (a, b, c, d, m)$; T stands for the transpose here.
Therefore, the four-dimensional system of differential equations to be studied is

$$\begin{cases} \dot{x} = z + x(y-a) - u \\ \dot{y} = -x^2 - by + 1 \\ \dot{z} = -x - cz \\ \dot{u} = u(m - dx) \end{cases}.$$

The model (3) presents economic relevance whenever its state variables lie in the set

$$\Sigma = \{\, (x, y, z, u) | x \in \mathbb{R}, y \geq 0, z \geq 0, u \in \mathbb{R}\}.$$

The new differential equation in $\dot{u}(t)$ leads in general to a different behavior of all state variables in the 4D model compared to the 3D model. In what follows, a qualitative analysis of the new model is investigated by well-known tools from the dynamical systems theory, providing several bifurcation diagrams which describe the local dynamics of the model around its equilibrium points.

The control introduced in this work by (2) is far from being unique. More other different control laws can be proposed. They can be designed as equations of type (2) or other types of constraints applied to one or more of the basis equations of the model. Their final role is to determine different behaviors of the transformed 3D model, which have economic relevance and are desirable in an economy.

Remark 1. *The hyperplane $u = 0$ is invariant with respect to the flow of (3). The model (3) with $u = 0$ and $x(t) \geq 0$ was studied in [14].*

Our next step is to determine the equilibrium points (x^*, y^*, z^*, u^*) of system (3), which are the solutions of the algebraic system

$$\begin{cases} z + x(y-a) - u = 0 \\ -x^2 - by + 1 = 0 \\ -x - cz = 0 \\ u(m - dx) = 0 \end{cases}.$$

The system (3) has four isolated equilibrium points: $P_1 = \left(0, \frac{1}{b}, 0, 0\right)$ for all $a, m \in \mathbb{R}$, $b > 0$, $c > 0$ and $d \neq 0$, the pair $P_2 = \left(\sqrt{\alpha}, \frac{ac+1}{c}, -\frac{1}{c}\sqrt{\alpha}, 0\right)$ and $P_3 = \left(-\sqrt{\alpha}, \frac{ac+1}{c}, \frac{1}{c}\sqrt{\alpha}, 0\right)$ for all $a, m \in \mathbb{R}$, $b \geq 0$, $c > 0$, $d \neq 0$ and $\alpha = \frac{1}{c}(c - b - abc) \geq 0$, respectively, $P_4 = \left(x_4, \frac{1-x_4^2}{b}, -\frac{x_4}{c}, x_4\frac{c-b-cx_4^2-abc}{bc}\right)$, where $x_4 = \frac{m}{d}$, for all $a, m \in \mathbb{R}$, $b > 0$, $c > 0$ and $d \neq 0$.

Remark 2. *Since $x(t)$ may be positive or negative in (3), three different equilibrium points $(P_1, P_3$ and $P_4)$ with economic relevance arise in the 4D model (3), while in the 3D model (1) only one equilibrium presented economic relevance and was studied in [14]. Notice that P_4 coincides with P_1 if $m = 0$, respectively, P_2 and P_3 collide to P_1 on $\alpha = 0$ and $b > 0$.*

In addition, the system has two more non-isolated equilibria for $b = 0$, that is, $Q_y = \left(1, y, -\frac{1}{c}, y - a - \frac{1}{c}\right)$ if $m = d \neq 0$, respectively, $S_y = \left(-1, y, \frac{1}{c}, -y + a + \frac{1}{c}\right)$ if $m = -d \neq 0$.

If P is a saddle equilibrium point, denote by (n_s, n_u) the dimensions of its stable and unstable manifolds. For $b > 0$, denote by $\beta_1 = \frac{1}{2b}(1 - ab - bc)$.

Theorem 1. *Assume $m > 0$. Then:*

(a) *if $\alpha > 0$, the equilibrium point P_1 is a saddle with $(n_s, n_u) = (2,2)$;*
(b) *if $\alpha < 0$ and $\beta_1 < 0$, the equilibrium point P_1 is a saddle with $(n_s, n_u) = (3,1)$;*
(c) *if $\alpha < 0$ and $\beta_1 > 0$, the equilibrium point P_1 is a saddle with $(n_s, n_u) = (1,3)$.*

The next result gives us a characterization of the nature of the equilibrium point P_1 for the case when the parameter m involved in the differential equation of system (3) describing the control function u is negative. Moreover, the dimensions of the stable and unstable manifolds are established, respectively.

Theorem 2. *Assume $m < 0$. Then,*

(a) *P_1 is a saddle with $(n_s, n_u) = (3,1)$ if $\alpha > 0$, respectively, $(n_s, n_u) = (2,2)$ if $\alpha < 0$ and $\beta_1 > 0$;*
(b) *P_1 is an attractor whenever $\alpha < 0$ and $\beta_1 < 0$;*
(c) *if $0 < c < 1$, a Hopf bifurcation occurs at P_1 on $(H) : 1 - ab - bc = 0$.*

Proof. The eigenvalues associated with the equilibrium point P_1 are $-b$, m and $\lambda^{\pm}_{p_1} = \beta_1 \pm \sqrt{\Delta_1}$, where $\beta_1 = \frac{1}{2b}(1 - ab - bc)$ and $\Delta_1 = \frac{(1-ab+bc)^2}{4b^2} - 1$. Since $\lambda^{+}_{p_1}\lambda^{-}_{p_1} = -\frac{c-b-abc}{b}$ and $\lambda^{+}_{p_1} + \lambda^{-}_{p_1} = \frac{1-ab-bc}{b}$, the proofs of the above theorems follow (except the point c) of the last theorem.

For the case (c), assume β_1 is the bifurcation parameter. A necessary condition to have Hopf bifurcation at P_1 is $\Delta_1 < 0$, which is equivalent to $-(1+c) < \beta_1 < 1 - c$. It follows that β_1 can cross 0 from negative to positive values if and only if $0 < c < 1$. At $\beta_1 = 0$ the obtained eigenvalues $\pm i\sqrt{1-c^2}$ are purely complex. Since $\left.\frac{\partial\left(Re\left(\lambda^{\pm}_{p_1}\right)\right)}{\partial\beta_1}\right|_{\beta_1=0} = 1$ if $\Delta_1 < 0$, a Hopf bifurcation occurs on H. The bifurcation is non-degenerate if the first Lyapunov coefficient $l_1(0)$ is nonzero, in which case a limit cycle (stable or unstable) arises around the equilibrium P_1 when β_1 crosses 0. If $l_1(0) = 0$, the bifurcation becomes degenerate and more limit cycles may arise around P_1 when β_1 crosses 0. □

In the following we study how the equilibrium point P_4 bifurcates from the equilibrium point P_1 when the parameter m crosses 0, respectively, how equilibrium points P_2 and P_3 are born from P_1 when parameter α increases from 0. We will show that the equilibrium points bifurcate from P_1 through transcritical, respectively, pitchfork bifurcations.

Theorem 3. *Assume $b > 0$. The system undergoes a transcritical bifurcation at $m = 0$ if $\alpha \neq 0$ and $\beta_1 \neq 0$, respectively, a pitchfork bifurcation at $\alpha = 0$ if $m \neq 0$ and $c \neq \pm 1$.*

Proof. If $m = 0$, $\alpha \neq 0$ and $\beta_1 \neq 0$, the eigenvalues of P_1 are $-b$, 0 and $\lambda^{\pm}_{p_1}$, with $Re\left(\lambda^{\pm}_{p_1}\right) \neq 0$; if $\lambda^{\pm}_{p_1}$ are real, this follows from $\lambda^{+}_{p_1}\lambda^{-}_{p_1} = -\frac{\alpha c}{b} \neq 0$. To prove the transcritical bifurcation, we will use Sotomayor's theorem [23]. Denote by $\mu_0 = (a, b, c, d, 0)$. The Jacobian matrix $J_0 = DF(P_1, \mu_0)$ of the vector field F, expressed at P_1 and $\mu = \mu_0$, has an eigenvalue $\lambda = 0$ with a corresponding eigenvector $v = \begin{pmatrix} -bc & 0 & b & -c\alpha \end{pmatrix}^T$. The value $\lambda = 0$ is also an eigenvalue for the transpose matrix J_0^T, which has a corresponding eigenvector $w = \begin{pmatrix} 0 & 0 & 0 & 1 \end{pmatrix}^T$; T stands for the transpose here.

It is clear that $w^T \cdot F_m(P_1, \mu_0) = 0$ and $w^T \cdot [DF_m(P_1, \mu_0) \cdot v] = -c\alpha \neq 0$, where $F_m = \frac{\partial F}{\partial m} = \begin{pmatrix} 0 & 0 & 0 & u \end{pmatrix}^T$; DF_m is the Jacobian matrix of the vector field F_m. It remains to determine $D^2F(P_1, \mu_0)(v, v)$, where, by definition $D^2F = \begin{pmatrix} d^2f_1 & d^2f_2 & d^2f_3 & d^2f_4 \end{pmatrix}^T$. For a real-valued function $f : V \subset \mathbb{R}^4 \to \mathbb{R}$, $x \mapsto f(x)$, $x = (x_1, x_2, x_3, x_4)$, V open, and a vector $v = (v_1, v_2, v_3, v_4)$, $d^2f(v, v) = \sum_{i,j=1}^{4} \frac{\partial^2 f}{\partial x_i x_j} v_i v_j$ denotes the differential of second order applied to the pair (v, v). Taking into account the expression of w, one needs to determine only $d^2 f_4(v, v)$ at (P_1, μ_0), which is $-2dv_1v_4 = -2bc^2 d\alpha$. Finally, $w^T \cdot \left[D^2F(P_1, \mu_0)(v, v)\right] = -2bc^2 d\alpha \neq 0$.

For the pitchfork bifurcation at $\alpha = 0$, we observe first that $\Sigma := \{u = 0\}$ is an invariant manifold of the system (3). Since $P_{2,3} \in \Sigma$ for all $\alpha \geq 0$, the bifurcation takes place on Σ and can be studied by restricting the system (3) to Σ. Translating first P_1 to the origin $O(0,0,0)$ by $y \to y - \frac{1}{b}$, the system (3) restricted to Σ reads

$$\dot{Y} = G(Y, \mu), \tag{4}$$

where $Y = \begin{pmatrix} x & y & z \end{pmatrix}^T$, $G(Y, \mu) = \begin{pmatrix} g_1 & g_2 & g_3 \end{pmatrix}^T$, respectively,

$$g_1 = z + x(y - a + 1/b),\ g_2 = -x^2 - by \text{ and } g_3 = -x - cz.$$

$P_2' = \left(-\sqrt{\alpha}, \frac{ac+1}{c} - \frac{1}{b}, \frac{1}{c}\sqrt{\alpha}\right)$ and $P_3' = \left(\sqrt{\alpha}, \frac{ac+1}{c} - \frac{1}{b}, -\frac{1}{c}\sqrt{\alpha}\right)$, $a \in \mathbb{R}$, $b > 0$, $c > 0$ and $\alpha = \frac{1}{c}(c - b - abc) \geq 0$, become equilibrium points of the system (4).

The stability of the equilibrium O in the system (4) has been studied in [14]. In addition to the results from [14], we show that the points P_2' and P_3' are born from O when α crosses 0 from negative to positive values by a bifurcation of type nondegenerate pitchfork. This bifurcation was not studied in [14].

Consider α the bifurcation parameter with $m \neq 0$ and $c \neq \pm 1$. P_2' and P_3' collide to O at $\alpha = 0$. The eigenvalues of O in (4) at $\alpha = 0$ are 0, $-b$ and $\frac{1}{c} - c$, with the corresponding eigenvector to 0 given by $v = \begin{pmatrix} -c & 0 & 1 \end{pmatrix}^T$.

The system (4) is $\mathbb{Z}_2$-equivariant with the symmetry $R(Y) = \begin{pmatrix} -x & y & -z \end{pmatrix}^T$. Indeed, $R(R(Y)) = Y$ and $R \circ G(Y, \mu) = G \circ R(Y, \mu)$. In other words, the system (4) remains unchanged by applying the transformation $(x, y, z) \overset{R}{\mapsto} (-x, y, -z)$. Notice that, we can write $\mathbb{R}^3 = X^+ \oplus X^-$, where $X^+ = \{(0, y, 0), y \in \mathbb{R}\}$ and $X^- = \{(x, 0, z), x, z \in \mathbb{R}\}$, such that $R(Y) = Y$ if $Y \in X^+$ and $R(Y) = -Y$ if $Y \in X^-$. With these notations, it follows that $v \in X^-$; when needed, we write a vector $\begin{pmatrix} x & y & z \end{pmatrix}^T$ as (x, y, z).

Thus, applying a result from [24] page 284, the system (4) undergoes a pitchfork bifurcation at $\alpha = 0$, which can be degenerate or not. To determine which is the case, we proceed as it follows. Find first the normal form of (4). To this end, consider the transformation $Z = P^{-1}Y$, where $P = \begin{pmatrix} v_1 & v_2 & v_3 \end{pmatrix}$ is a column matrix containing the eigenvectors corresponding to the eigenvalues 0, $-b$ and $\frac{1}{c} - c$ of O at $\alpha = 0$, that is, $v_1 = \begin{pmatrix} -c & 0 & 1 \end{pmatrix}^T$, $v_2 = \begin{pmatrix} 0 & 1 & 0 \end{pmatrix}^T$ and $v_3 = \begin{pmatrix} -1 & 0 & c \end{pmatrix}^T$, and $Z = \begin{pmatrix} z_1 & z_2 & z_3 \end{pmatrix}^T$. The system (4) in the new variables z_1, z_2 and z_3 reads

$$\dot{z}_1 = k(z_3 + cz_1)z_2,\ \dot{z}_2 = -bz_2 - c^2z_1^2 - 2cz_1z_3 - z_3^2,\ \dot{z}_3 = -\frac{1}{k}z_3 - kz_1z_2 - \frac{k}{c}z_2z_3, \tag{5}$$

where $k = \frac{c}{c^2-1}$. Since the eigenvalues of O in (4) at $\alpha = 0$ are 0, $-b$ and $\frac{1}{c} - c$ (in this order), we consider the extended system of dimension 4 formed by $\dot{\alpha} = 0$ and the three equations from (5). The new system has at $\alpha = 0$ the eigenvalues $0, 0, -b$ and $\frac{1}{c} - c$, thus, applying the Center Manifold Theorem, there exists a two-dimensional center manifold W_c^α of class C^∞ of the form $z_2 = h_2(z_1, \alpha)$ and $z_3 = h_3(z_1, \alpha)$, $h_2, h_3 \in C^\infty$, which locally (in cubic terms) can be expressed by

$$z_2 = \sum_{i+j\leq 3} c_{ij} z_1^i \alpha^j \text{ and } z_3 = \sum_{i+j\leq 3} d_{ij} z_1^i \alpha^j.$$

Using the method of undetermined coefficients, we found $c_{20} = \frac{-c^2}{b}$, $d_{30} = \frac{c^4}{b(c^2-1)^2}$, while the other coefficients are all 0. Therefore, the system (5) on the center manifold W_c^α is of the form

$$\dot{z}_1 = \beta(\alpha)z_1 + \sigma_0 z_1^3 + \ldots$$

where $\beta(\alpha)$ is a smooth function of α with $\beta(0) = 0$ and $\sigma_0 = \frac{c^4}{b(1-c^2)} \neq 0$, thus, the pitchfork bifurcation is non-degenerate. To find the function $\beta(\alpha)$, higher order terms are needed in the expressions of $h_2(z_1, \alpha)$ and $h_3(z_1, \alpha)$.

We notice that the coefficient σ_0 could be obtained without considering the extended system, by finding the 1−dimensional center manifold W_c directly in the system (5) and then the restriction of (5) on W_c. In this case, W_c is given locally by $z_2 = \sum_{i=1}^{3} c_i z_1^i$ and $z_3 = \sum_{i=1}^{3} d_i z_1^i$. Applying the method of undetermined coefficients, one can show $c_2 = -\frac{c^2}{b}$ and $d_3 = \frac{1}{b}\frac{c^4}{(c^2-1)^2}$, while the other coefficients are 0. These lead to $\dot{z}_1 = \sigma_0 z_1^3 + \dots$. The advantage of using the extended system is that $\beta(\alpha)$ may also be determined. □

Remark 3. *The Sotomayor's theorem for pitchfork bifurcation gives no answer to the problem because* $D^3F = \begin{pmatrix} 0 & 0 & 0 & 0 \end{pmatrix}^T$.

The local behavior of the system (3) at $P_{2,3}$. The characteristic polynomial at P_2 and P_3 with $\alpha > 0$ is $P(\lambda) = (\lambda - m \pm d\sqrt{\alpha})Q(\lambda)$, where

$$Q(\lambda) = \lambda^3 + s_2\lambda^2 + s_1\lambda + 2c\alpha,$$

$s_2 = \frac{1}{c}(c^2 + bc - 1)$ and $s_1 = \frac{1}{c}(bc^2 + 2c\alpha - b)$; " + " corresponds to P_2 and " − " to P_3. Denote by λ_1, λ_2 and λ_3 the roots of $Q(\lambda)$, respectively, $\lambda_4^{P_2} = m - d\sqrt{\alpha}$ and $\lambda_4^{P_3} = m + d\sqrt{\alpha}$. Since the roots of $Q(\lambda)$ satisfy $\lambda_1\lambda_2\lambda_3 < 0$, $P_{2,3}$ are saddles or attractors. Denote by $s_3 = s_2 s_1 - 2c\alpha$. By Routh–Hurwitz conditions, λ_1, λ_2 and λ_3 have negative real parts if and only if

$$s_2 > 0 \text{ and } s_3 > 0, \tag{6}$$

which are equivalent to $c(b + c) > 1$ and $b(1 - bc)(2ac + 3) + bc^3(b + c) - 2c > 0$. We notice that (6) are satisfied at least for $\alpha > 0$ sufficiently small and $c^2 > 1$. The results are summarized in the next Theorem 4. The attractors P_2 and P_3 with orbits converging to them are illustrated in Figure 1.

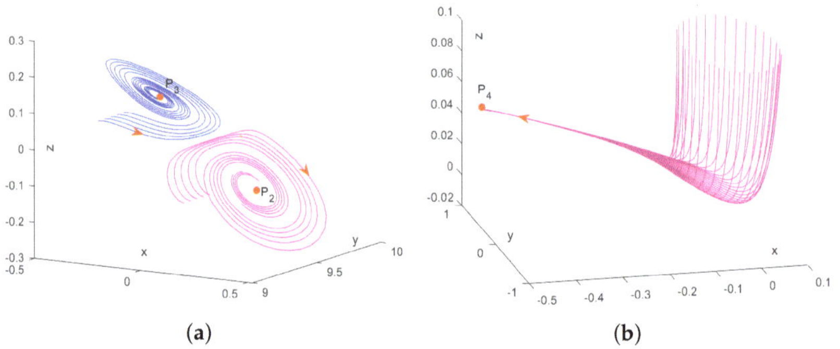

Figure 1. (**a**) Orbits around the attractors P_2 and P_3 in the system (3) projected in the xyz space. The parameters are $a = 9$, $b = 0.1$, $c = 2$, $m = d = -1$. The starting points for P_2 are $(0.2,\ 9 + i/2,\ -0.1,\ 0.05)$, while for P_3 they are $(-0.2,\ 9 + i/2,\ 0.1,\ 0.05)$, for $i = 0, 1, 2, 3, 4$. (**b**) Orbits around the attractor P_4 for $a = b = 1$, $c = 10$, $m = 0.1$ and $d = -0.2$.

Theorem 4. *Assume $\alpha > 0$. Then, P_2 and P_3 are attractors if (6) is satisfied and $\lambda_4^{P_2} < 0$ for P_2, respectively, $\lambda_4^{P_3} < 0$ for P_3. In the other cases with $\lambda_4^{P_{2,3}} \neq 0$, P_2 and P_3 are saddles.*

The local behavior of the system (3) at P_4. The characteristic polynomial at P_4 is

$$S(\lambda) = \lambda^4 + m_3\lambda^3 + m_2\lambda^2 + m_1\lambda + m_0,$$

where $m_3 = a + b + c - \frac{1}{b} + \frac{m^2}{bd^2}$, $m_2 = -\frac{c}{b}\alpha + \frac{m_0}{bc} + \frac{3b+c}{bd^2}m^2 - 2b\beta_1$, $m_1 = -c\frac{b+m}{b}\alpha + \frac{1}{c}m_0 + cm^2\frac{3b+m}{bd^2}$ and $m_0 = cm\frac{m^2-d^2\alpha}{d^2}$; $\alpha = \frac{1}{c}(c - b - abc)$ and $\beta_1 = \frac{1}{2b}(1 - ab - bc)$.

Remark 4. *Denote by $\beta_2 = bc + bm + cm$ and $\beta_3 = b + c + m$. Then m_1 and m_2 can be written in the forms*

$$m_1 = a\beta_2 + N_1 \text{ and } m_2 = a\beta_3 + N_2, \tag{7}$$

where $N_1 = m^2\frac{2bc+\beta_2}{bd^2} + (b-c)\frac{\beta_2}{bc}$ and $N_2 = m^2\frac{2b+\beta_3}{bd^2} + \frac{1}{bc}(b-c)m + \frac{c}{b}(b^2-1)$.

For $c > 0$ arbitrary fixed, define the following curves lying in the ba−parametric plane: $A = \{(b,a), \alpha = 0, b > 0\}$, $H = \{(b,a), \beta_1 = 0, b > 0\}$, $S_2 = \{(b,a), s_2 = 0, b > 0\}$, $S_3 = \{(b,a), s_3 = 0, b > 0\}$, $L_1 = \left\{(b,a), \lambda_4^{P_2} = 0, b > 0\right\}$, $L_2 = \left\{(b,a), \lambda_4^{P_3} = 0, b > 0\right\}$ and $M_i = \{(b,a), m_i = 0, b > 0\}$, $i = 1,2,3$. Notice that b corresponds to the x-axis, while a to the y-axis, and all curves are included in the region $b > 0$.

Theorem 5. *If $m_0 < 0$, then P_4 is a saddle. Assume $m_0 > 0$. Then,*

(a) P_4 is a saddle or an attractor for all $d > 0$ and $m \neq 0$.

(b) P_4 is an attractor if and only if $m_3 > 0$, $k_0 = m_3m_2 - m_1 > 0$ and $k_1 = (m_3m_2 - m_1)m_1 - m_3^2m_0 > 0$. In particular, if $\alpha < 0$, $\beta_1 < 0$, $b(b+c)(a+b) > c$ and $m > 0$ sufficiently small, P_4 is an attractor, as shown in Figure 1.

Proof. It is clear that P_4 is a saddle if $m_0 < 0$, since the product of its eigenvalues is negative.

(a) Let further be $m_0 > 0$. Assume first $m > 0$, thus, $m^2 > \alpha d^2$. It is clear that $m_1 > 0$ if $\alpha \le 0$, thus,

$$E_2 = \lambda_1\lambda_2(\lambda_3 + \lambda_4) + \lambda_2\lambda_3\lambda_4 = -m_1 < 0.$$

Let $\alpha > 0$. Then, $m^2 > \alpha d^2$ yields $m_1 > 2c\alpha + \frac{1}{c}m_0 > 0$, thus, $E_2 < 0$.
Secondly, assume $m < 0$. Then $m^2 < \alpha d^2$ and $\alpha > 0$ follow from $m_0 > 0$. For an arbitrary fixed $b > 0$, denote by $(b, a_{l_2}) \in L_2$, $(b, a_{m_1}) \in M_1$, $(b, a_{m_2}) \in M_2$ and $(b, a_{m_3}) \in M_3$ four points from the corresponding curves. Then,

$$a_{m_1} = -\frac{N_1}{\beta_2},\ a_{m_2} = -\frac{N_2}{\beta_3},\ a_{l_2} - a_{m_1} = \frac{2cm^2}{d^2\beta_2} \text{ and } a_{m_2} - a_{m_1} = N_3, \tag{8}$$

where $N_3 = \left(1 - c^2\right)\frac{b}{c\beta_3} + 2m^2\frac{c^2-bm}{d^2\beta_2\beta_3}$. Notice that $a_{m_3} = \frac{1}{b} - c - b - \frac{m^2}{bd^2}$ and $a_{l_2} = \frac{1}{b} - \frac{1}{c} - \frac{m^2}{bd^2}$. More cases need to be considered further.

(a1) Assume $\beta_2 \le 0$. The curve L_2 is given by

$$a = a_{l_2}, \tag{9}$$

with $b > 0$ and $c > 0$. One can show that $m_0 > 0$ is equivalent to $a < a_{l_2}$. If $\beta_2 = 0$, then $m_1 = \frac{2b^2c^3}{d^2(b+c)^2} > 0$, thus, $E_2 = -m_1 < 0$. If $\beta_2 < 0$, then, from $m_1 = a\beta_2 + N_1$ and $a < a_{l_2}$, one gets $m_1 > \frac{2c}{d^2}m^2$, which leads to $E_2 < 0$.

(a2) Assume $\beta_2 > 0$ and $0 < c \le 1$. Then $\beta_3 > 0$ as well. Since $m_1|_{L_2} = \frac{2cm^2}{d^2} \neq 0$ and $m_2|_{M_1} = -N_3\beta_3 \neq 0$, it follows that $L_2 \cap M_1 = \emptyset$ and $M_2 \cap M_1 = \emptyset$; we denoted as usual by $m_1|_{L_2} = m_1(b,a)$ for $(b,a) \in L_2$. From (8), one get $a_{l_2} > a_{m_1}$ and $a_{m_2} > a_{m_1}$, since $N_3 > 0$ if $0 < c \le 1$.

For $b > 0$, denote by $M_1^+ = \{(b,a), m_1 > 0, m_0 \geq 0\}$ and $M_1^- = \{(b,a), m_1 \leq 0, m_0 \geq 0\}$, the two regions from $m_0 \geq 0$ corresponding to $m_1 > 0$, respectively, $m_1 \leq 0$. Then $E_2 = -m_1 < 0$ on the region M_1^+. Notice that $L_2 \subset M_1^+$, because $m_1|_{L_2} = \frac{2cm^2}{d^2} > 0$ and $L_2 \cap M_1 = \emptyset$.
If $m_1 \leq 0$, which is equivalent to $a \leq a_{m_1}$, one can show

$$m_2 \leq -N_3\beta_3 < 0,$$

whenever $0 < c \leq 1$. It follows that

$$E_3 = \lambda_1(\lambda_2 + \lambda_3 + \lambda_4) + \lambda_2(\lambda_3 + \lambda_4) + \lambda_3\lambda_4 = m_2 < 0,$$

on M_1^-. Therefore, $E_2 < 0$ or $E_3 < 0$ on $m_0 > 0$, whenever $\beta_2 > 0$ and $0 < c \leq 1$.

(a3) Assume $\beta_2 > 0$ and $c > 1$, thus, $\beta_3 > 0$. Since

$$m_1|_{L_2} = \frac{2cm^2}{d^2} \neq 0,\ m_2|_{L_2} > \frac{b}{c}\left(c^2 - 1\right) \neq 0 \text{ and } m_3|_{L_2} = b + c - \frac{1}{c} \neq 0,$$

it follows that $L_2 \cap M_1 = \emptyset$, $L_2 \cap M_2 = \emptyset$ and $L_2 \cap M_3 = \emptyset$. Notice that $a_{l_2} - a_{m_2} = \frac{bd^2(c^2-1)+2cm^2}{cd^2\beta_3} > 0$.
In the region $b > 0$, denote by $M_2^+ = \{(b,a), m_2 \geq 0, m_0 \geq 0\}$ and $M_2^- = \{(b,a), m_2 < 0, m_0 \geq 0\}$. Then $E_3 = m_2 < 0$ on the region M_2^-. Notice that $L_2 \subset M_2^+$, because $m_2|_{L_2} > \frac{b}{c}(c^2 - 1) > 0$ and $L_2 \cap M_2 = \emptyset$.
Assume further $m_2 \geq 0$. If $m_1 > 0$, then $E_2 = -m_1 < 0$. It remains the case $m_1 \leq 0$. We notice that M_2 may intersect M_1 in the region $m_0 \geq 0$, since

$$m_2|_{M_1} = 2m^2\frac{bm - c^2}{d^2\beta_2} + \frac{b}{c}\left(c^2 - 1\right),$$

may be zero. The inequalities $m_2 \geq 0$ and $m_1 \leq 0$ yield $-\frac{N_2}{\beta_3} \leq a \leq -\frac{N_1}{\beta_2}$, thus, $N_2\beta_2 > N_1\beta_3$, which, in turns, leads to

$$\frac{m^2}{d^2} < \frac{\beta_2 b(c^2 - 1)}{2c(c^2 - bm)}. \tag{10}$$

Then, $-\frac{N_2}{\beta_3} \leq a$ and (10) yield

$$m_3 > \frac{-bcm(b + c) + c^2(c^2 - 1) + bc + mb}{c(c^2 - bm)},$$

which implies $m_3 > 0$, because $bc + mb > -mc > 0$ follows from $\beta_2 > 0$ and $m < 0$. Therefore,

$$E_4 = \lambda_1 + \lambda_2 + \lambda_3 + \lambda_4 = -m_3 < 0.$$

It follows that, $E_2 < 0$ or $E_3 < 0$ or $E_4 < 0$ whenever $m_0 > 0$, if $c > 0$, $d > 0$ and $m \neq 0$, which, in turn, imply that at least one eigenvalue λ_i has $Re(\lambda_i) < 0$. This confirms the proof.

(b) The result follows from Routh–Hurwitz conditions for $S(\lambda)$, which are $m_0 > 0$, $m_3 > 0$, $m_3m_2 > m_1$ and $k_1 > 0$. For the particular case, we write the expression k_1 as a polynomial in m,

$$k_1(m) = \sum_{i=1}^{8} c_i' m^i + \alpha\beta_1(b(b + c)(a + b) - c)\frac{2c}{b}$$

for some coefficients c_i', thus, $k_1 > 0$. The condition $m_3 m_2 > m_1$ follows from $k_1 > 0$ and $m_1 > 0$.

□

Example 1. *The equilibrium point P_4 does not exist in the 3D model. This happens due to the control function $u(t)$, defined by the two constraints in the new 4D model. When P_4 is an attractor and $P_4 \in \Sigma$, the three state variables, namely the real interest rate $x = x(t)$, the investment demand $y = y(t)$ and the inflation rate $z = z(t)$, can be stabilized at least locally around three fixed values $\frac{m}{d}$, $\frac{d^2-m^2}{bd^2}$ and $-\frac{m}{cd}$, respectively, which are economically relevant if $md < 0$ and $d^2 > m^2$. This scenario does not arise in the 3D model since P_4 is not a steady state of the model.*

3. Bifurcation Diagrams

Denote by R the region

$$R = \{(b,a), b \geq 0\}.$$

The curve A has a unique branch of the form $a = \frac{1}{b} - \frac{1}{c}$ lying in R, for all $c > 0$ arbitrary fixed, which splits the region R into two parts: $\alpha > 0$ in the region from R that contains the origin $(0,0)$, and $\alpha < 0$ in the other region, as shown in Figures 2–5.

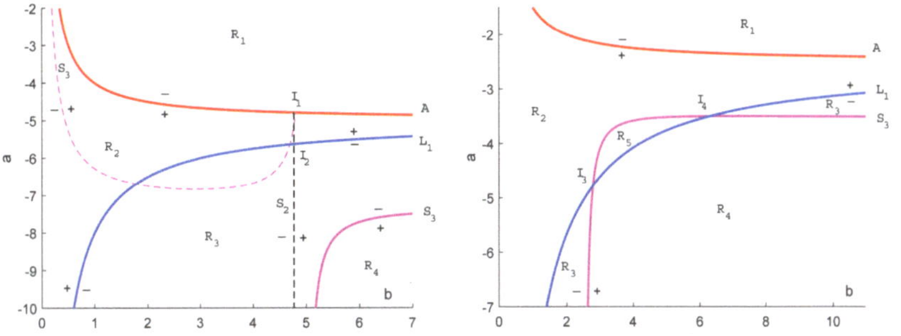

(a) (b)

Figure 2. Bifurcation diagrams of the system (3) for $0 < c < 1$ and (**a**) $0 < m < c_0 d$, respectively, (**b**) $m > c_0 d > 0$, where $c_0 = \frac{c+1}{c\sqrt{2}}\sqrt{1-c^2}$.

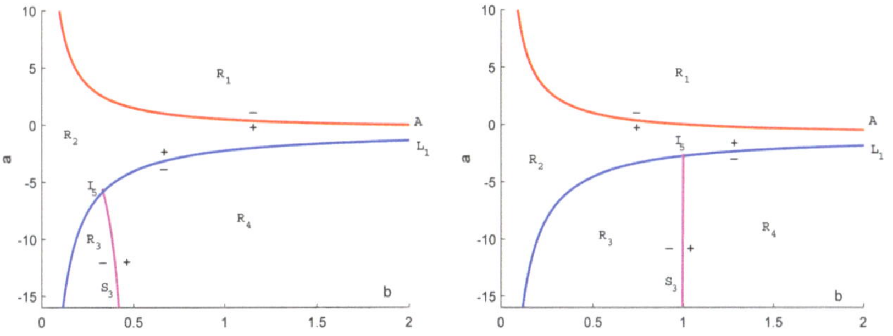

(a) (b)

Figure 3. Bifurcation diagrams of the system (3) for $m > 0$, $d > 0$ and (**a**) $c > 1$, respectively, (**b**) $c = 1$.

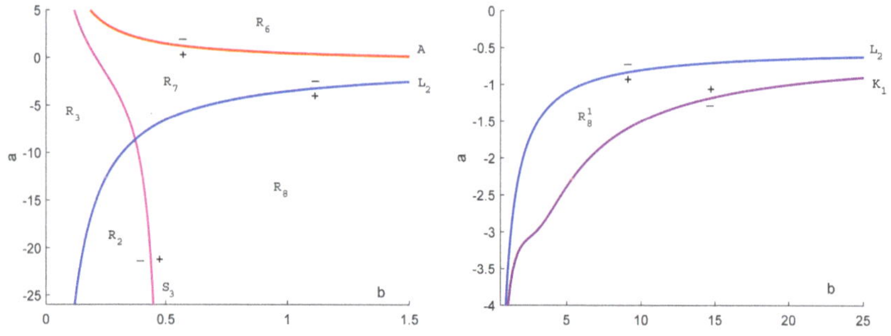

(**a**) (**b**)

Figure 4. Bifurcation diagrams of the system (3) for $m < 0, d > 0$ and $c > 1$, (**a**,**b**). A region R_8^1 where P_4 is an attractor is presented in (**b**).

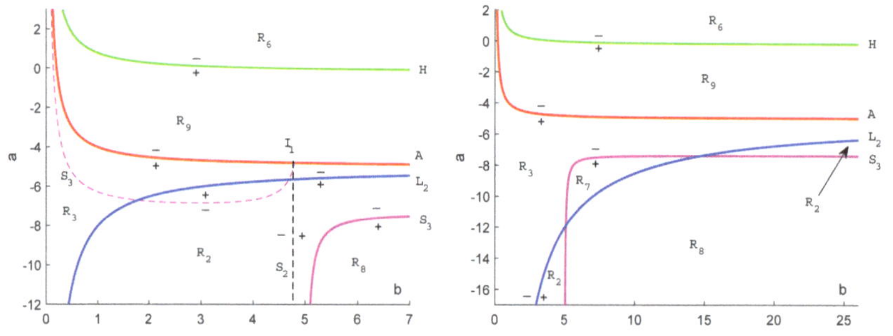

(**a**) (**b**)

Figure 5. Bifurcation diagrams of the system (3) for $0 < c < 1$, $d > 0$ and (**a**) $-c_0 d < m < 0$, respectively, (**b**) $m < -c_0 d < 0$.

S_2 is the vertical line $b = \frac{1}{c} - c$, thus, $s_2 < 0$ on the left of S_2 and $s_2 > 0$ on the right of S_2, for all $c > 0$ arbitrary fixed. If $c = 1$, $s_2 = b$. If $c > 1$, the curve S_2 lies on $b < 0$, thus, it is outside the region of interest. However, the sign of s_2 is important if $c > 1$ as well.

If $c \neq 1$, the curve S_3 has in R two branches asymptotically to the vertical line $b = \frac{1}{c}$ (on the left and right of the line) given by $s_3 = 2b\frac{1-bc}{c}a + \left(c - \frac{3}{c}\right)b^2 + \left(\frac{3}{c^2} + c^2\right)b - \frac{2}{c} = 0$. Notice that $s_3 = \frac{c^2-1}{c} \neq 0$ if $b = \frac{1}{c}$. It follows that $s_3 < 0$ in the region from R that contains $(0,0)$. The sign of s_3 changes when (b,a) crosses a branch of S_3, as shown in Figures 2–5. Notice that a branch of the curve S_3 may lie on $\alpha < 0$, especially if $c > 1$, and this branch is not taken into account (it is not depicted in Figures 3 and 4) because $P_{2,3}$ do not exist on $\alpha < 0$.

If $c = 1$, then $s_3 = 2(1-b)(b + ab - 1)$, thus, S_3 has two branches in R as well: one is the vertical line $b = 1$ and the other is the curve A, as shown in Figure 3b. It is clear that $s_3 < 0$ in the region from R that contains $(0,0)$.

If $0 < c < 1$, the curves A, S_2 and S_3 intersect at the same point $I_1 = (b_1, a_1)$, with $b_1 = \frac{1}{c} - c > 0$ and $a_1 = \frac{2c^2-1}{c-c^3}$. If in addition $md > 0$, then $L_1 \cap S_2 = \{I_2\}$, $I_2 = (b_2, a_2)$, where $b_2 = b_1$ and $a_2 = a_1 - \frac{m^2 c}{d^2(1-c^2)}$, thus, $a_2 < a_1$. If $md < 0$, then $L_2 \cap S_2 = \{I_2\}$.

Since $m_0 = cm\frac{m^2-d^2\alpha}{d^2}$, $\lambda_4^{P_2} = m - d\sqrt{\alpha}$ and $\lambda_4^{P_3} = m + d\sqrt{\alpha}$, by Theorem 5, the curves $L_1 : \lambda_4^{P_2} = 0$ and $L_2 : \lambda_4^{P_3} = 0$ devide the region R into two disjoint subregions (on the left and right of L_1, and the same for L_2), as shown in Figures 2–5. On one subregion P_4 is a saddle, while on the other P_4 is a saddle or an attractor.

The following theorem clarifies the intersection of the bifurcation curves L_1 and S_3. Since $\lambda_4^{P_2}$ has constant sign on $\alpha > 0$ if $md < 0$, only the case $md > 0$ is needed. We assume further $m > 0$ and $d > 0$. The case $m < 0$ and $d < 0$ is similar.

Theorem 6. *Assume $m > 0$ and $d > 0$. The following assertions are true.*

(1) *If $0 < c < 1$ and $b > \frac{1}{c}$, the intersection $L_1 \cap S_3$ on $\alpha > 0$ has zero points if $0 < m < dc_0$, one point if $m = dc_0$, respectively, two points if $m > dc_0$, where $c_0 = \frac{c+1}{c\sqrt{2}}\sqrt{1-c^2}$.*

(2) *If $0 < c < 1$ and $0 < b \le \frac{1}{c}$, then either $s_2 < 0$ or $s_3 < 0$ on $\alpha > 0$.*

(3) *If $c \ge 1$, the intersection $L_1 \cap S_3$ has a single point on $\alpha > 0$ and $b > 0$.*

Proof. Since $\lambda_4^{P_2} = m - d\sqrt{\alpha}$, the curve L_1 is defined only on $\alpha > 0$ and is given by $a = \frac{1}{b} - \frac{1}{c} - \frac{m^2}{bd^2}$, with $b > 0$. The intersection $L_1 \cap S_3$ satisfies $s_3 = 0$ and $\lambda_4^{P_2} = 0$, which lead to an equation in b of the form

$$\left(c - \frac{1}{c}\right)b^2 + \left(\frac{2m^2}{d^2} + \frac{1}{c^2} + c^2 - 2\right)b - \frac{2m^2}{cd^2} = 0. \tag{11}$$

(1) By $w = b - \frac{1}{c}$, (11) reads $p_0w^2 + p_1w + p_0 = 0$, where $p_0 = c - \frac{1}{c}$ and $p_1 = \frac{2m^2}{d^2} - \frac{1}{c^2} + c^2$. Its roots $w_{1,2}$ satisfy $w_1w_2 = 1$. Thus, $w_1 > 0$ and $w_2 > 0$ iff $w_1 + w_2 > 0$ and $\Delta > 0$ (the discriminant). Since $p_0 < 0$, the inequalities lead to $p_1 > 0$ and $\Delta = (p_1 - 2p_0)(p_1 + 2p_0) > 0$, that is, $p_1 > 0$ and $p_1 + 2p_0 > 0$. However, $p_1 + 2p_0 = 2\left(\frac{m^2}{d^2} - c_0^2\right) > 0$, where $c_0 = \frac{c+1}{c\sqrt{2}}\sqrt{1-c^2} > 0$, and $m > 0$, lead to $m > dc_0$. Moreover, $p_1 + 2p_0 > 0$ leads to $\frac{2m^2}{d^2} > 2c_0^2 > \frac{1}{c^2} - c^2 > 0$, which, in turn, leads to $p_1 > 0$. Therefore, $w_1 > 0$ and $w_2 > 0$ iff $m > dc_0$. In this case $L_1 \cap S_3 = \{I_3, I_4\}$, where $I_i = (b_i, a_i)$, $a_i = \frac{1}{b_i} - \frac{1}{c} - \frac{m^2}{b_id^2}$, $i = 3, 4$, respectively, $b_3 = w_1 + \frac{1}{c}$ and $b_4 = w_2 + \frac{1}{c}$. It is clear that $I_3 = I_4$ if $m = dc_0$. If $0 < m < dc_0$ and $p_1 > 0$, then $\Delta < 0$, thus $L_1 \cap S_3$ is the empty set.

(2) If $0 < b < \frac{1}{c} - c$, then $s_2 < 0$. If $b = \frac{1}{c} - c$, then $s_2 = 0$ and $s_3 = -2c\alpha < 0$ on $\alpha > 0$, while, $s_3 = \frac{c^2-1}{c} < 0$ if $b = \frac{1}{c}$. Let $\frac{1}{c} - c < b < \frac{1}{c}$ and $\alpha > 0$. Then $s_2 > 0$ and

$$s_3 = 2\alpha\frac{bc-1}{c} - \frac{b}{c}s_2\left(1 - c^2\right) < 0.$$

(3) Assume $c > 1$. Then, the roots $b_{5,6}$ of (11) satisfy $b_5b_6 < 0$, thus, $b_5 > 0$ and $b_6 < 0$; notice that the discriminant of Equation (11) is positive. It follows that $L_1 \cap S_3 = \{I_5\}$, where $I_5 = (b_5, a_5)$ and $a_5 = \frac{1}{b_5} - \frac{1}{c} - \frac{m^2}{b_5d^2}$. If $c = 1$, then $L_1 \cap S_3 = \{I_5\}$, where $I_5 = \left(1, -\frac{m^2}{d^2}\right)$.

The theorem is now proved. □

A similar result can be obtained for the intersection of the curve L_2 with S_3. Since $\lambda_4^{P_3} = m + d\sqrt{\alpha}$ has constant sign on $\alpha > 0$ if $md > 0$, only the case $md < 0$ is needed. We present the result for $m < 0$ and $d > 0$, while the remaining case $m > 0$ and $d < 0$ can be treated similarly. A proof of the next theorem can be obtained as above.

Theorem 7. *Assume $m < 0$ and $d > 0$. The following assertions are true.*

(1) *If $0 < c < 1$ and $b > \frac{1}{c}$, the intersection $L_2 \cap S_3$ on $\alpha > 0$ has zero points if $-dc_0 < m < 0$, one point if $m = -dc_0$, respectively, two points if $m < -dc_0 < 0$.*

(2) *If $0 < c < 1$ and $0 < b \le \frac{1}{c}$, then either $s_2 < 0$ or $s_3 < 0$ on $\alpha > 0$.*

(3) *If $c \ge 1$, the intersection $L_2 \cap S_3$ has a single point on $\alpha > 0$ and $b > 0$.*

Remark 5. *For $d > 0$ and $m \in \mathbb{R}$ we obtain:*

(1) *If $m > 0$ and $d > 0$, then $\lambda_4^{P_3} = m + d\sqrt{\alpha} > 0$ and $m_0 = cm\frac{\lambda_4^{P_2}\lambda_4^{P_3}}{d^2}$ has the same sign as $\lambda_4^{P_2}$ on $\alpha > 0$, and $m_0 > 0$ if $\alpha \leq 0$. The curves $\{m_0 = 0\}$ and L_1 coincide.*

(2) *If $m < 0$ and $d > 0$, then $\lambda_4^{P_2} = m - d\sqrt{\alpha} < 0$ and m_0 has the same sign as $\lambda_4^{P_3}$ on $\alpha > 0$, and $m_0 < 0$ if $\alpha \leq 0$. The curve $\{m_0 = 0\}$ coincides to L_2 in this case.*

Remark 6. *In the following cases, we will determine the bifurcation diagrams of the system (3) when $m > 0$ and $d > 0$, respectively, $m < 0$ and $d > 0$. One can proceed similarly in other cases.*

Case 1. Assume first $0 < c < 1$, $m > 0$ and $d > 0$. Notice that $\lambda_4^{P_3} > 0$, whenever P_3 exists, and $\{m_0 = 0\}$ coincides to L_1. Based on Theorem 6, two main bifurcation diagrams arise to describe the system's dynamics, as shown in Figure 2a,b. The bifurcation curves in the two diagrams are illustrated in Matlab: Figure 2a uses $c = 0.2$, $m = 1$ and $d = 0.5$, while Figure 2b $c = 0.4$, $m = 2.7$ and $d = 1$.

Case 2. Assume $c > 1$, $m > 0$ and $d > 0$. Then S_2 lies on $b < 0$ and $s_2 > 0$ on $b > 0$. By Theorem 6, $L_1 \cap S_3 = \{I_5\}$ in the region $\alpha > 0$ from R. One can show $A \cap S_3 = \emptyset$ on $b > 0$ and $\beta_1 < 0$ in the region R where $\alpha < 0$. As in case 1, $\lambda_4^{P_3} > 0$ on $\alpha > 0$ and $\{m_0 = 0\}$ coincides to L_1. In particular, if $c = 1$, then $s_2 = b > 0$ and $s_3 = 2(b-1)\alpha$. Two main bifurcation diagrams emerge in this case, which are depicted in Figure 3a,b. The curves are illustrated for $c = 2$, $m = 1$ and $d = 0.6$ in Figure 3a, respectively, $c = 1$, $m = 1$ and $d = 0.6$ in Figure 3b.

Case 3. Assume $c > 1$, $m < 0$ and $d > 0$. The curve L_2 is given by the same expression as L_1. The curve $\{m_0 = 0\}$ coincides to L_2 in this case; $\lambda_4^{P_2} < 0$ whenever P_2 exists. Furthermore, $sign(m_0) = sign\left(\lambda_4^{P_3}\right)$ on $\alpha > 0$ and $m_0 < 0$ if $\alpha \leq 0$, respectively, $\beta_1 < 0$ in the region R where $\alpha < 0$. Using Theorem 7, a bifurcation diagram is presented in Figure 4a. Figure 4b presents a region R_8^1 where P_4 is an attractor, in a typical case $m = -1$, $d = 0.5$ and $c = 2$. The strip R_8^1 is quite large, it extends to infinity along the horizontal axis when $b > 0$ is large. We denoted by K_1 the curve $\{(b, a), k_1 = 0\}$.

Case 4. Assume $0 < c < 1$, $m < 0$ and $d > 0$, thus, $\lambda_4^{P_2} < 0$ if $\alpha > 0$. By Theorem 7, two main bifurcation diagrams arise to describe the system's dynamics, as shown in Figure 5a,b. Figure 5a is illustrated for $c = 0.2$, $m = -1$ and $d = 0.5$, while Figure 5b for $c = 0.2$, $m = -3$ and $d = 0.5$.

Remark 7. *The type of the equilibria P_1, $P_{2,3}$ and P_4 as they appear in different regions from the above bifurcation diagrams presented in Figures 2–5, are described in Table 1.*

Table 1. The type of the equilibria P_1, P_2, P_3 and P_4 on different regions from bifurcation diagrams; s stands for saddle, while a for attractor.

	R_1	R_2	R_3	R_4	R_5	R_6	R_7	R_8	R_9
P_1	s	s	s	s	s	a	s	s	s
P_2	—	s	s	a	a	—	a	s	—
P_3	—	s	s	s	s	—	a	a	—
P_4	a, s	a, s	s	s	a, s	s	s	a, s	s

The different behavior of P_1 as an attractor on the region R_6 is presented in Figure 6, while the two possible states of P_4 as an attractor or saddle are depicted in Figure 7.

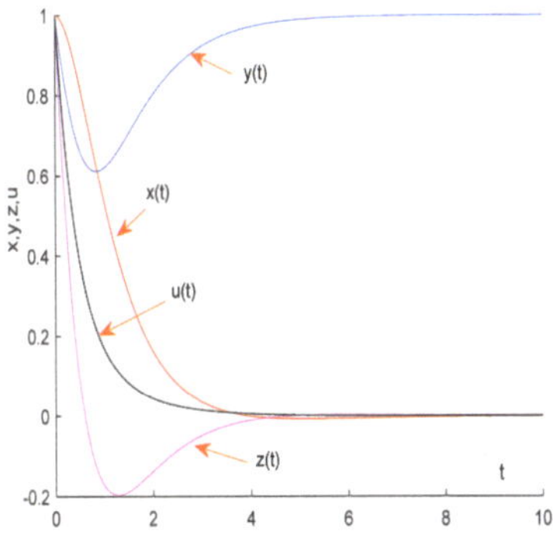

Figure 6. The time series of the four variables around the attractor P_1 in the system (3). The parameters are $a = 1, b = 1, c = 2, m = -1$ and $d = 1$. The starting point of these series is $(1, 1, 1, 1)$.

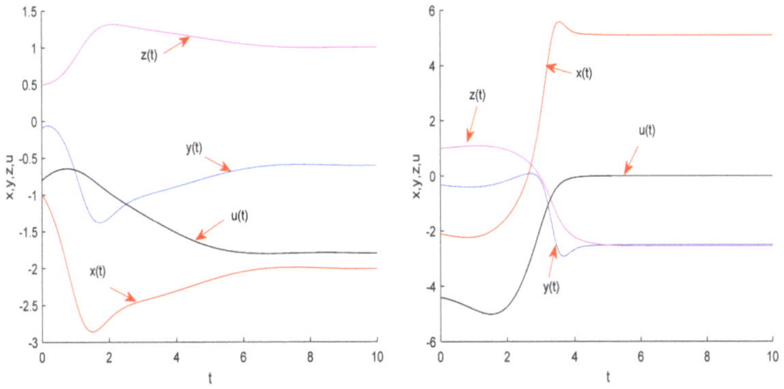

Figure 7. (**Left**). The time series of the four variables when P_4 is an attractor within the region R_8. The parameters are $a = -2, b = 5, c = 2, m = -1, d = 0.5$ and $P_4(-2, -0.6, 1, -1.8)$. The starting point of these series is $(-1, -0.1, -0.5, -0.8)$. One may notice that the four series converge correspondingly to the four coordinates of P_4 as t increases, that is, $x(t) \to -2, y(t) \to -0.6, z(t) \to 1$, and $u(t) \to -1.8$. (**Right**). The time series of the four variables when P_4 is a saddle within the region R_8. The parameters are $a = -3, b = 10, c = 2, m = -1, d = 0.5$ and $P_4(-2, -0.3, 1, -4.4)$. The starting point of these series is $(-2.1, -0.3, 1, -4.4)$. One may notice that the four series do not converge correspondingly to the four coordinates of P_4 as t increases.

4. Conclusions

An economic model based on differential equations with four variables, the real interest rate, the investment demand, the inflation rate and a control function of the system, has been investigated. The model builds upon a three-dimensional model studied earlier in [14], to which a new variable and equation related to the real interest rate are added. A qualitative analysis has been performed and more bifurcation diagrams were obtained for understanding its local behavior, which undergoes three bifurcations: transcritical, pitchfork and Hopf. Bifurcation diagrams are used to illustrate how the dynamics of the 4D system alters with the increasing value of the parameters m and c. The occurrence of Hopf bifurcation means that the system's equilibrium points can evolve into predictable economic cycle.

The system (3) proposed in this work has three equilibrium points with economic relevance, P_1, P_3 and P_4, while the initial system studied in [14], which corresponds to $u = 0$ in (3), has only one steady state with economic relevance, the point P_1. Thus, the control function u proposed in this work increases the relevance of the initial model. This could lead to a better understanding of economical prediction for more complex financial phenomena and also explain complex and dynamic behaviour of various economic systems. When the control function is null, we notice that the saving amount variable a is inversely proportional with the fluctuation of the system, meaning the smaller the saving amount is, the bigger the fluctuation of the system is, so the saving amount has to keep a balance because a too small saving amount means chaotic phenomenon and a too large saving amount means a slow economy. When the control function is different from zero, the Routh-Hurwitz criterion is used to study the properties of the asymptotic stability of the economic model with control. This control function can improve the economic vigor and become a necessary condition, in order to make the economy develop well. Numerical simulations are provided using Matlab in order to illustrate the effectiveness of the proposed approaches.

Author Contributions: Conceptualization, G.M.; methodology, G.M.; software, G.M.; validation, G.M., O.B. and A.G.; formal analysis, G.M.; investigation, G.M., O.B. and A.G.; resources, G.M.; data curation, G.M.; writing—original draft preparation, G.M., O.B. and A.G.; writing—review and editing, G.M., O.B. and A.G.; visualization, G.M.; supervision, G.M.; project administration, G.M.; funding acquisition, G.M. All authors have read and agreed to the published version of the manuscript.

Funding: This research was funded by Horizon2020-2017-RISE-777911 project.

Institutional Review Board Statement: Not applicable.

Informed Consent Statement: Not applicable.

Data Availability Statement: Not applicable.

Conflicts of Interest: The authors declare no conflict of interest.

References

1. Angeli, D.; Rishi, A.; Rawlings, J. On average performance and stability of economic model predictive control. *IEEE Trans. Autom. Control* **2011**, *57*, 1615–1626. [CrossRef]
2. Aizawa, H.; Ikeda, K.; Osawa, M.; Gaspar, J.M. Breaking and sustaining bifurcations in S_N -invariant equidistant economy. *Int. J. Bifurc. Chaos* **2020**, *30*, 2050240. [CrossRef]
3. Danca, M.F. Coexisting hidden and self-excited attractors in an economic model of integer or fractional order. *Int. J. Bifurc. Chaos* **2021**, *31*, 2150062. [CrossRef]
4. Guerrini, L. Bifurcation analysis of an economic model. *Int. J. Math. Anal.* **2012**, *6*, 2779–2787.
5. Medio, A.; Pireddu, M.; Zanolin, F. Chaotic dynamics for maps in one and two dimensions: A geometrical method and applications to economics. *Int. J. Bifurc. Chaos* **2009**, *19*, 3283–3309. [CrossRef]
6. Minsky, H. *Stabilizing an Unstable Economy: A Twentieth Century Fund Report*; Yale University Press: London, UK, 1986.
7. Romer, D. *Advanced Macroeconomics*; McGraw-Hill: New York, NY, USA, 2012.
8. Rigatos, G. *State-Space Approaches for MODELLING and control in Financial Engineering*; Springer: Cham, Switzerland, 2017.
9. Skovranek, T.; Podlubny, I.; Petras, I. Modeling of the national economies in state-space: A fractional calculus approach. *Econ. Model.* **2012**, *29*, 1322–1327. [CrossRef]
10. Pelgrin, F.; Venditti, A. On the long-run fluctuations of inheritance in two-sector OLG models. *J. Math. Econ.* **2022**, *101*, 102670. [CrossRef]
11. Ye, R.; Li, X.; Ye, Y.; Zhang, B. DynamicNet: A time-variant ODE network for multi-step wind speed prediction. *Neural Netw.* **2022**, *152*, 118–139. [CrossRef] [PubMed]
12. Bai, J.; Wang, X.; Wang, J. An epidemic-economic model for COVID-19. *Math. Biosci. Eng.* **2022**, *19*, 9658–9696. [CrossRef] [PubMed]
13. Rigatos, G.; Siano, P.; Ghosh, T.; Sarno, D. A nonlinear optimal control approach to stabilization of a macroeconomic development model. *Quant. Financ. Econ.* **2018**, *2*, 373–387. [CrossRef]
14. Ma, J.; Chen, Y. Study for the bifurcation topological structure and the global complicated character of a kind of nonlinear finance system. *Appl. Math. Mech.* **2001**, *22*, 1240–1251. [CrossRef]
15. Chen, W.C. Nonlinear dynamics and chaos in a fractional-order financial system. *Chaos Solitons Fractals* **2008**, *36*, 1305–1314. [CrossRef]
16. Zhen, W.; Xia, H.; Guodong, S. Analysis of nonlinear dynamics and chaos in a fractional order financial system with time delay. *Comput. Math. Appl.* **2011**, *62*, 1531–1539.
17. Jajarmi, A.; Hajipour, M.; Baleanu, D. New aspects of the adaptive synchronization and hyperchaos suppression of a financial model. *Chaos Solitons Fractals* **2017**, *99*, 285–296. [CrossRef]

18. Alidousti, J.; Ghahfarokhi, M.M. Stability and bifurcation for time delay fractional predator prey system by incorporating the dispersal of prey. *Appl. Math. Model.* **2019**, *72*, 385–402. [CrossRef]
19. Alidousti, J. Stability and bifurcation analysis for a fractional prey-predator scavenger model. *Appl. Math. Model.* **2020**, *81*, 342–355. [CrossRef]
20. Huang, C.; Wang, J.; Chen, X.; Cao, J. Bifurcations in a fractional-order BAM neural network with four different delays. *Neural Netw.* **2021**, *141*, 344–354. [CrossRef] [PubMed]
21. Huang, C.; Liu, H.; Chen, X.; Zhang, M.; Ding, L.; Cao, J.; Alsaedi, A. Dynamic optimal control of enhancing feedback treatment for a delayed fractional order predator-prey model. *Phys. A Stat. Mech. Appl.* **2020**, *554*, 124136. [CrossRef]
22. Xu, C.; Liu, Z.; Liao, M.; Yao, L. Theoretical analysis and computer simulations of a fractional order bank data model incorporating two unequal time delays. *Expert Syst. Appl.* **2022**, *199*, 116859. [CrossRef]
23. Perko, L. *Differential Equations and Dynamical Systems*, 3rd ed.; Springer: New York, NY, USA, 2001.
24. Kuznetsov, Y.A. *Elements of Applied Bifurcation Theory*, 3rd ed.; Springer: New York, NY, USA, 2004.

mathematics MDPI

Article

Stochastic Dynamics of a Virus Variant Epidemic Model with Double Inoculations

Hui Chen †, Xuewen Tan *,†, Jun Wang, Wenjie Qin and Wenhui Luo

Department of Mathematics, Yunnan Minzu University, 2929, Yuehua Street, Chenggong District, Kunming 650500, China
* Correspondence: tanxw0910@ymu.edu.cn; Tel.: +86-182-8877-1233
† These authors contributed equally to this work.

Abstract: In this paper, we establish a random epidemic model with double vaccination and spontaneous variation of the virus. Firstly, we prove the global existence and uniqueness of positive solutions for a stochastic epidemic model. Secondly, we prove the threshold R_0^* can be used to control the stochastic dynamics of the model. If $R_0^* < 0$, the disease will be extinct with probability 1; whereas if $R_0^* > 0$, the disease can almost certainly continue to exist, and there is a unique stable distribution. Finally, we give some numerical examples to verify our theoretical results. Most of the existing studies prove the stochastic dynamics of the model by constructing Lyapunov functions. However, the construction of a Lyapunov function of higher-order models is extremely complex, so this method is not applicable to all models. In this paper, we use the definition method suitable for more models to prove the stationary distribution. Most of the stochastic infectious disease models studied now are second-order or third-order, and cannot accurately describe infectious diseases. In order to solve this kind of problem, this paper adopts a higher price five-order model.

Keywords: epidemic model; vaccine inoculation; extinction; stationary distribution

MSC: 92-10; 92B05

Citation: Chen, H.; Tan, X.; Wang, J.; Qin, W.; Luo, W. Stochastic Dynamics of a Virus Variant Epidemic Model with Double Inoculations. *Mathematics* **2023**, *11*, 1712. https://doi.org/10.3390/math11071712

Academic Editors: Mihaela Neamţu, Eva Kaslik and Anca Rădulescu

Received: 20 February 2023
Revised: 26 March 2023
Accepted: 27 March 2023
Published: 3 April 2023

1. Introduction

Infectious diseases have become the greatest enemy of human health. When an infectious disease appears and prevails in an area, the primary task is to make every effort to prevent the spread of the disease. Vaccination is one of the important preventive measures. Through vaccination, smallpox was eliminated in the world at the end of the 1970s. This is a great victory for human beings in the fight against infectious diseases, an important milestone in the history of preventive medicine, and a great achievement of vaccination for human beings. In mathematical epidemiology, the control and eradication of infectious diseases are urgent problems, and have greatly attracted the interest of researchers in many fields. Now scholars have proposed and extensively discussed various types of optimizing models and their influencing factors, such as vaccination, time delay, impulse, media reports, etc. [1–4]. However, as a disease progresses, a virus can mutate as it spreads, allowing the disease to spiral out of control. Cai et al. analyzed the stability of the infectious disease model of virus mutation of inoculation, but only considered the condition that the inoculated individual was completely effective against the virus at a certain stage [5,6]. Baba and Bilgen et al. considered the problem of double-inoculation infectious diseases, which had an adverse effect on the two viruses respectively, but did not consider the conversion between patients infected with the two viruses [7,8]. Therefore, on the basis of the research on the problem of virus mutated infectious disease, considering the situation of two kinds of vaccination for susceptible people, a kind of virus mutated infectious disease model with double vaccination was proposed.

Taking into account the important role of vaccination in preventing the occurrence of infectious diseases, we assume that the first type of vaccinated people are fully immune to the premutation virus and partially resistant to the post mutation virus, whereas the second are fully immune to the postmutation virus and partially resistant to the premutation virus. In addition, the two types of the infected are infectious, and the disease is not fatal before the virus mutation, whereas it is fatal after the virus mutation. Based on the above assumptions, a model was established as follows:

$$\begin{cases} \dot{S}(t) = \Lambda - \beta_1 S(t) I_1(t) - \beta_2 S(t) I_2(t) - \lambda S(t) \\ \dot{V_1}(t) = \varphi_1 S(t) - k_1 I_2(t) V_1(t) - a V_1(t) \\ \dot{V_2}(t) = \varphi_2 S(t) - k_2 I_1(t) V_2(t) - a V_2(t) \\ \dot{I_1}(t) = \beta_1 S(t) I_1(t) + k_2 I_1(t) V_2(t) - \alpha_1 I_1(t) \\ \dot{I_2}(t) = \beta_2 S(t) I_2(t) + k_1 I_2(t) V_1(t) + \varepsilon I_1(t) - \alpha_2 I_2(t) \\ \dot{R}(t) = \gamma_1 I_1(t) + \gamma_2 I_2(t) - a R(t), \end{cases} \tag{1}$$

where $S(t), V_1(t), V_2(t), I_1(t), I_2(t)$, and $R(t)$, respectively, represent the number at the time t of the susceptible, those vaccinated to the first and to the second types of vaccines, the infected before and after virus mutation, and the recovered. Λ is the input rate of the population. β_1 and β_2 are the infection coefficients, respectively, before and after virus mutation. a is the natural mortality of the population. φ_1 and φ_2 are the vaccination rates of the first and the second vaccines. k_1 and k_2 are the infection rates of the infected with the first type of people vaccinated after virus mutation, and the second before virus mutation, respectively. γ_1 and γ_2 are the recovery rates of the infected, respectively, before and after the virus mutation. ε is the ratio of the infected before the virus mutation to the infected after virus mutation in number. δ is the mortality rate of the infected after virus mutation. In addition, $\lambda := a + \varphi_1 + \varphi_2; \alpha_1 := a + \gamma_1 + \varepsilon; \alpha_2 := a + \gamma_2 + \varepsilon$.

According to the biological significance of the model, it is assumed that all parameters are positive, and the dynamic behavior of population R does not affect other populations. Thus, the following model is considered:

$$\begin{cases} \dot{S}(t) = \Lambda - \beta_1 S(t) I_1(t) - \beta_2 S(t) I_2(t) - \lambda S(t) \\ \dot{V_1}(t) = \varphi_1 S(t) - k_1 I_2(t) V_1(t) - a V_1(t) \\ \dot{V_2}(t) = \varphi_2 S(t) - k_2 I_1(t) V_2(t) - a V_2(t) \\ \dot{I_1}(t) = \beta_1 S(t) I_1(t) + k_2 I_1(t) V_2(t) - \alpha_1 I_1(t) \\ \dot{I_2}(t) = \beta_2 S(t) I_2(t) + k_1 I_2(t) V_1(t) + \varepsilon I_1(t) - \alpha_2 I_2(t). \end{cases} \tag{2}$$

Model (2) has a basic reproduction number R_0, where

$$R_0 = \max\{R_1, R_2\}, R_1 = \frac{\beta_1 \Lambda}{\alpha_1 \lambda} + \frac{k_2 \varphi_2 \Lambda}{a \alpha_1 \lambda}, R_2 = \frac{\beta_2 \Lambda}{\alpha_2 \lambda} + \frac{k_1 \varphi_1 \Lambda}{a \alpha_2 \lambda};$$

it also has a disease-free equilibrium

$$E_0(S_0, V_1^0, V_2^0, 0, 0) = E_0(\frac{\Lambda}{\lambda}, \frac{\varphi_1 \Lambda}{a\lambda}, \frac{\varphi_2 \Lambda}{a\lambda}, 0, 0).$$

Moreover, when $R_2 > 0$, model (2) has a boundary equilibrium point

$$E_2(\widetilde{S}, \widetilde{V_1}, \widetilde{V_2}, \widetilde{I_1}, \widetilde{I_2}) = E_2(\frac{\Lambda}{\beta_2 \widetilde{I_2} + \lambda}, \frac{\varphi_1 \Lambda}{(k_1 \widetilde{I_2} + a)(\beta_2 \widetilde{I_2} + \lambda)}, \frac{\varphi_2 \Lambda}{a(\beta_2 \widetilde{I_2} + \lambda)}, \widetilde{I_1}, \widetilde{I_2}),$$

where the disease will disappear before the virus mutation, and after the virus mutation it will spread; when I_1^* and $I_2^* > 0$, both before and after the virus mutates, model (2) has an endemic disease balance point $E_3(S^*, V_1^*, V_2^*, I_1^*, I_2^*)$, where

$$S^* = \frac{\Lambda}{\beta_1 I_1^* + \beta_2 I_2^* + \lambda},$$
$$V_1^* = \frac{\varphi_1 \Lambda}{(k_1 I_2^* + a)(\beta_1 I_1^* + \beta_2 I_2^* + \lambda)},$$
$$V_2^* = \frac{\varphi_2 \Lambda}{(k_2 I_1^* + a)(\beta_1 I_1^* + \beta_2 I_2^* + \lambda)}.$$

On the other hand, environmental change has a key impact on the development of epidemics [9]. For disease transmission, because of the unpredictability of human contact, the growth and spread of epidemics are essentially random, so population numbers are constantly disturbed [10,11]. Therefore, in epidemic dynamics, stochastic differential equation (SDE) models may be a more appropriate approach to modeling epidemics in many situations. Many real stochastic epidemic models can be derived based on their deterministic formulas [9,12–23]. Assuming that the coefficients of model (2) are affected by random noise that can be represented by Brownian motion, model (2) becomes:

$$\begin{cases} dS(t) = (\Lambda - \beta_1 S I_1 - \beta_2 S I_2 - \lambda S)dt + \sigma_1 S dB_1(t) \\ dV_1(t) = (\varphi_1 S - k_1 I_2 V_1 - a V_1)dt + \sigma_2 V_1 dB_2(t) \\ dV_2(t) = (\varphi_2 S - k_2 I_1 V_2 - a V_2)dt + \sigma_3 V_2 dB_3(t) \\ dI_1(t) = (\beta_1 S I_1 + k_2 I_1 V_2 - \alpha_1 I_1)dt + \sigma_4 I_1 dB_4(t) \\ dI_2(t) = (\beta_2 S I_2 + k_1 I_2 V_1 + \varepsilon I_1 - \alpha_2 I_2)dt + \sigma_5 I_2 dB_5(t), \end{cases} \tag{3}$$

where $\sigma_i (i = 1,2,3,4,5)$ represents the intensities of the white noises, and $B_i(t)(i = 1,2,3,4,5)$ are mutually independent standard Brownian motions. However, the groups S, V_1, V_2, I_1, and I_2 are usually subject to the same random factors such as temperature, humidity, etc., in reality. As a result, it is more reasonable to assume that the five classes of random perturbance noises are uncorrelated. If we set $B_i(t) = B(t)(i = 1,2,3,4,5)$, then model (3) becomes:

$$\begin{cases} dS(t) = (\Lambda - \beta_1 S I_1 - \beta_2 S I_2 - \lambda S)dt + \sigma_1 S dB(t) \\ dV_1(t) = (\varphi_1 S - k_1 I_2 V_1 - a V_1)dt + \sigma_2 V_1 dB(t) \\ dV_2(t) = (\varphi_2 S - k_2 I_1 V_2 - a V_2)dt + \sigma_3 V_2 dB(t) \\ dI_1(t) = (\beta_1 S I_1 + k_2 I_1 V_2 - \alpha_1 I_1)dt + \sigma_4 I_1 dB(t) \\ dI_2(t) = (\beta_2 S I_2 + k_1 I_2 V_1 + \varepsilon I_1 - \alpha_2 I_2)dt + \sigma_5 I_2 dB(t). \end{cases} \tag{4}$$

Let $(\Omega, \mathcal{F}, \{\mathcal{F}_t\}_{t\geq 0}, \mathbb{P})$ be a complete probability space with the filtration $\{\mathcal{F}_t\}_{t\geq 0}$ satisfying the usual condition (i.e., $\{\mathcal{F}_t\}_{t\geq 0}$ is increasing and right continuous whereas $\mathcal{F}_0$ contains all $\mathbb{P}$-null sets). Throughout this paper, $a \wedge b := \min\{a, b\}$, $a \vee b := \max\{a, b\}$ and $R_+^{5,\circ} := \{(u, v, w, x, y) : u, v, w, x, y > 0\}$ are denoted.

First, we prove the global existence and uniqueness of the positive solution of model (4). Similar to a deterministic model, we introduce a threshold value R_0^*, able to be calculated from the coefficients. We show that if $R_0^* < 0$, $I(t), I(t) = I_1(t) + I_2(t)$ will be extinct with probability 1, and $S(t), V_1(t), V_2(t)$ will weakly converge to their unique invariant probability measures $\mu_1^*, \mu_2^*, \mu_3^*$, respectively. If $R_0^* > 0$, then coexistence occurs, and all positive solutions of model (4) are converged to the unique variational probability measure μ^* in the total variational norm.

Most of the existing studies use the method of constructing the Lyapunov function to prove the existence of the stationary distribution of the solution of model (4). However, this method is not applicable to all models. In this paper, the definition method applicable to more models is used to prove the stationary distribution [24–27]. Moreover, most of the stochastic infectious disease models studied now are second order or third order. Therefore, in order to depict infectious diseases more accurately, we have established a fifth-order model–a double inoculation and random infectious disease model of spontaneous virus mutation, considering two kinds of vaccination for susceptible people on the basis of the research on infectious diseases of virus mutation.

The main structure of this paper is as follows: In Section 2 we prove the global existence and uniqueness of the positive solution of model (4). In Sections 3 and 4, we are devoted to the proof of extinction and coexistence, respectively. In Section 5, we provide an example to support our findings. In Section 6, the main results are discussed and summarized briefly.

2. Existence and Uniqueness of the Global Solutions

Theorem 1. *For any given value $(S(0), V_1(0), V_2(0), I_1(0), I_2(0))$, there is a unique solution $(S(t), V_1(t), V_2(t), I_1(t), I_2(t))$ to model (4) on $t \geq 0$ and the solution will remain in $R_+^{5,\circ}$ with probability 1, i.e., $(S(t), V_1(t), V_2(t), I_1(t), I_2(t))$ in $R_+^{5,\circ}$ for all $t \geq 0$ almost surely.*

Proof of Theorem 1. Since the coefficients of model (4) satisfy local Lipschitz and linear growth conditions, it can be seen from the existence and uniqueness theorem of solutions of stochastic differential equations that for any $(S(0), V_1(0), V_2(0), I_1(0), I_2(0)) \in R_+^{5,\circ}$, model (4) has a locally unique solution $(S(t), V_1(t), V_2(t), I_1(t), I_2(t))$. To prove the global nature of the solution, we only need to prove that $\tau_e = +\infty$, where τ_e is the explosion time.

Let $k_0 > 0$ be a sufficiently large positive number, so that for each $t \geq 0$, $S(t)$, $V_1(t)$, $V_2(t)$, $I_1(t)$, $I_2(t)$ fall in the interval $[\frac{1}{k_0}, k_0]$. For each integer $k > k_0$, define the stop time τ_e as follows:

$$\tau_k = inf\{t \in [0, \tau_e] : S(t) \notin (\frac{1}{k}, k), or V_1(t) \notin (\frac{1}{k}, k), or V_2(t) \notin (\frac{1}{k}, k), or I_1(t) \notin (\frac{1}{k}, k), or I_2(t) \notin (\frac{1}{k}, k)\},$$

where $inf\emptyset = \infty$. Obviously, when $k \to \infty$, τ_k increases monotonously.

Let $\tau_\infty = \lim_{k\to+\infty} \tau_k$, then $\tau_\infty \leq \tau_e$. So we just have to prove $\tau_\infty = \infty$. Supposing that $\tau_\infty \neq \infty$, then there are constants $T > 0$ and $\varepsilon_1 \in (0,1)$ such that $P\{\tau_\infty \leq T\} > \varepsilon_1$. Further, there is an integer $k_1 \leq k_0$ that makes

$$P\{\tau_k \leq T\} \geq \varepsilon_1 \quad for\ all \quad k \geq k_1. \tag{5}$$

Define C^5 function: $V : R_+^{5,\circ} \to R_+$ by $V(N(t)) = N(t) - 1 - lnN(t)$, where $N(t) := S(t) + V_1(t) + V_2(t) + I_1(t) + I_2(t)$. Obviously, function $V(N(t))$ is a non-negative function. If $(S(t), V_1(t), V_2(t), I_1(t), I_2(t)) \in R_+^{5,\circ}$, according to $It\hat{o}'s$ formula, there is a positive number $G := \Lambda + a + \gamma_1 + \gamma_2 + \delta + \frac{1}{2}(\sigma_1^2 + \sigma_2^2 + \sigma_3^2 + \sigma_4^2 + \sigma_5^2)$, so that

$$\begin{aligned}
dV &= LVdt + (1 - \frac{1}{N})(\sigma_1 S + \sigma_2 V_1 + \sigma_3 V_2 + \sigma_4 I_1 + \sigma_5 I_2)dB(t),\\
LV &= (1 - \frac{1}{N})[\Lambda - aN - \gamma_1 I_1 - (\gamma_2 + \delta)I_2] + \frac{1}{2N^2}(\sigma_1^2 S^2 + \sigma_2^2 V_1^2 + \sigma_3^2 V_2^2 + \sigma_4^2 I_1^2 + \sigma_5^2 I_2^2)\\
&= \Lambda - aN - \gamma_1 I_1 - (\gamma_2 + \delta)I_2 - \frac{\Lambda}{N} + a + \frac{\gamma_1 I_1}{N} + \frac{(\gamma_2 + \delta)I_2}{N}\\
&+ \frac{1}{2N^2}(\sigma_1^2 S^2 + \sigma_2^2 V_1^2 + \sigma_3^2 V_2^2 + \sigma_4^2 I_1^2 + \sigma_5^2 I_2^2)\\
&\leq \Lambda + a + \gamma_1 + \gamma_2 + \delta + \frac{1}{2}(\sigma_1^2 + \sigma_2^2 + \sigma_3^2 + \sigma_4^2 + \sigma_5^2)\\
&:= G,\\
dV &\leq Gdt + (1 - \frac{1}{N})(\sigma_1 S + \sigma_2 V_1 + \sigma_3 V_2 + \sigma_4 I_1 + \sigma_5 I_2)dB(t).
\end{aligned}$$

Integrate both sides of the above inequality from 0 to $\tau_k \wedge T$ at the same time, we get

$$\int_0^{\tau_k \wedge T} dV \leq \int_0^{\tau_k \wedge T} Gdt + \int_0^{\tau_k \wedge T} (1 - \frac{1}{N})(\sigma_1 S + \sigma_2 V_1 + \sigma_3 V_2 + \sigma_4 I_1 + \sigma_5 I_2) dB(t),$$

moreover, then we take the expectation, and obtain

$$EV(N(\tau_k \wedge T)) \leq V(N(0)) + GE(\tau_k \wedge T) \leq V(N(0)) + GT. \tag{6}$$

Set $\Omega_k = \{\tau_k \leq T\}$ for $k \geq k_1$ and by (5), we have $P(\Omega_k) \geq \varepsilon_1$. Noting that for every $\omega \in \Omega_k$, there is $S(\tau_k, \omega)$ or $V_1(\tau_k, \omega)$ or $V_2(\tau_k, \omega)$ or $I_1(\tau_k, \omega)$ or $I_2(\tau_k, \omega)$, being equal to either k or $\frac{1}{k}$, and hence

$$V((N(\tau_k, \omega)) \geq min\{k - 1 - lnk, \frac{1}{k} - 1 + lnk\}.$$

It then follows from (6) that

$$V(N(0)) + GT \geq E[1_{\Omega_k}(\omega) V(N(\omega))] \geq \varepsilon_1 min\{k - 1 - lnk, \frac{1}{k} - 1 + lnk\},$$

where 1_{Ω_k} is the indicator function of Ω_k. Letting $k \to \infty$, we obtain the following contradiction:

$$\infty > V(N(0)) + GT = \infty.$$

So we must have $\tau_\infty = \infty$ a.s. This completes the proof of Theorem 1. □

3. Extinction of Disease

For the infectious disease model, we always care about whether the disease will disappear. In this section, we first define a threshold value R_0^*, and the stochastic extinction of the disease when $R_0^* < 0$ is then proved in the model (4).

To obtain further properties of the solution, we case on the boundary of the first equation of model (4):

$$d\overline{S}(t) = [\Lambda - \lambda \overline{S}(t)]dt + \sigma_1 \overline{S}(t) dB(t) \tag{7}$$

so we have,

$$\frac{1}{t} \int_0^t \overline{S}(\tau) d\tau = \frac{\overline{S}(0) - \overline{S}(t)}{\lambda t} + \frac{\Lambda}{\lambda} + \frac{\sigma_1}{\lambda t} \int_0^t \overline{S}(\tau) dB(\tau).$$

For the given initial value u, let $\overline{S}(t)$ be the solution to model (7). According to the comparison theorem, $S_{u,v,w,x,y} \leq \overline{S}(t)\ \forall t \geq 0$. By solving the Fokker–Planck equation, the process $\overline{S}(t)$ has unique stationary distribution with density $f_1^*(x)$, and by the strong law of large numbers, we have

$$\lim_{t \to \infty} \frac{1}{t} \int_0^t \overline{S}(\tau) d\tau = \int_0^\infty x f_1^*(x) dx = \frac{\Lambda}{\lambda}. \tag{8}$$

For other equations of model (4), we use the same method to obtain:

$$d\overline{V}_1(t) = [\varphi_1 \overline{S}(t) - a\overline{V}_1(t)]dt + \sigma_2 \overline{V}_1(t) dB(t),$$

we have

$$\lim_{t \to \infty} \frac{1}{t} \int_0^t \overline{V}_1(\tau) d\tau = \int_0^\infty x f_2^*(x) dx = \frac{\varphi_1 \Lambda}{a\lambda}, \tag{9}$$

then similarly

$$d\overline{V}_2(t) = [\varphi_2 \overline{S}(t) - a\overline{V}_2(t)]dt + \sigma_3 \overline{V}_2(t) dB(t),$$

therefore

$$\lim_{t\to\infty}\frac{1}{t}\int_0^t \overline{V}_2(\tau)d\tau = \int_0^\infty x f_3^*(x)dx = \frac{\varphi_2\Lambda}{a\lambda}, \tag{10}$$

where $f_2^*(x), f_3^*(x)$ have the same definition as above.

To proceed, we define the threshold as follows:

$$R_0^* = \frac{(\beta_1+\beta_2)\Lambda}{\lambda} + \frac{k_1\varphi_1\Lambda}{a\lambda} + \frac{k_2\varphi_2\Lambda}{a\lambda} + \varepsilon - \alpha,$$

where $\alpha = \alpha_1 \wedge \alpha_2$.

Theorem 2. *If $R_0^* < 0$, then for any initial value $(S(0), V_1(0), V_2(0), I_1(0), I_2(0)) = (u,v,w,x,y) \in R_+^{5,\circ}$, $\limsup_{t\to\infty}\frac{lnI_{u,v,w,x,y}(t)}{t} \le R_0^*$ a.s., and the distribution of $Su,v,w,x,y(t)$, $V_{1_{u,v,w,x,y}}(t)$, $V_{2_{u,v,w,x,y}}(t)$ converge weakly to the unique invariant probability measures $\mu_1^*, \mu_2^*, \mu_3^*$ with the densities f_1^*, f_2^*, f_3^*, respectively.*

Proof of Theorem 2. Considering a Lyapunov function $I(t)$, defined by $I(t) = I_1(t) + I_2(t)$. Applying $It\hat{o}'s$ formula to $I(t)$, we have

$$\begin{aligned}
dlnI(t) = {}& [\frac{1}{I(t)}(\beta_1 S(t)I_1(t) + k_2 I_1(t)V_2(t) - \alpha_1 I_1(t) + \beta_2 S(t)I_2(t) + k_1 I_2(t)V_1(t) \\
& + \varepsilon I_1(t) - \alpha_2 I_2(t)) - \frac{\sigma_4^2 I_1(t)^2 + \sigma_5^2 I_2(t)^2}{2I^2(t)}]dt + \frac{\sigma_4 I_1(t) + \sigma_5 I_2(t)}{I(t)}dB(t) \\
\le {}& [(\beta_1+\beta_2)S(t) + \frac{k_2 I_1(t)}{I(t)}V_2(t) + \frac{k_1 I_2(t)}{I(t)}V_1(t) + \varepsilon\frac{I_1(t)}{I(t)} - \alpha]dt + \frac{\sigma_4 I_1(t) + \sigma_5 I_2(t)}{I(t)}dB(t) \\
\le {}& [(\beta_1+\beta_2)\overline{S}(t) + k_1\overline{V}_1(t) + k_2\overline{V}_2(t) + \varepsilon - \alpha]dt + (\sigma_4+\sigma_5)dB(t),
\end{aligned}$$

where $\alpha = \alpha_1 \wedge \alpha_2$.

Then integral from 0 to t at both ends of inequality

$$\begin{aligned}
lnI(t) - lnI(0) \le {}& (\beta_1+\beta_2)\int_0^t \overline{S}(\tau)d\tau + k_1\int_0^t \overline{V}_1(\tau)d\tau + k_2\int_0^t \overline{V}_2(\tau)d\tau \\
& + (\varepsilon-\alpha)t + (\sigma_4+\sigma_5)\int_0^t dB(\tau).
\end{aligned} \tag{11}$$

It finally follows from (11) by dividing t on the both sides and let $t \to \infty$ that,

$$\limsup_{t\to\infty}\frac{1}{t}\ln I(t) = \frac{(\beta_1+\beta_2)\Lambda}{\lambda} + \frac{k_1\varphi_1\Lambda}{a\lambda} + \frac{k_2\varphi_2\Lambda}{a\lambda} + \varepsilon - \alpha = R_0^* < 0. \tag{12}$$

Hence, $I(t)$ converges almost surely to 0 at an exponential rate.

For any $\varepsilon_1 > 0$, it follows from (12) that there exists $t_0 > 0$ such that $P(\Omega_{\varepsilon_1}) > 1 - \varepsilon_1$ where

$$\Omega_{\varepsilon_1} = \{lnI(t) \le R_0^* t\} = \{I(t) \le e^{R_0^* t}, \forall t \ge t_0\}.$$

Case 1. $S_{u,v,w,x,y}(t)$ converges weakly to the unique invariant probability measure μ_1^* with the density f_1^*.

We can choose that t_0 satisfying $-\frac{2\beta}{R_0^*}exp\{R_0^*\} < \varepsilon_1$. Let $\overline{S}(t)$ be the solution of (7). Supposing $\overline{S}(t_0) = S(t_0)$, then we can obtain $P\{S_{u,v,w,x,y}(t) \le \overline{S}(t)\} = 1$ by the comparison theorem. In view of the $It\hat{o}'s$ formula, for almost all $\omega \in \Omega_{\varepsilon_1}$ we have

$$
\begin{aligned}
0 \le ln\overline{S}(t) - lnS(t) &= \Lambda \int_{t_0}^{t} (\frac{1}{\overline{S}(\tau)} - \frac{1}{S(\tau)})d\tau + \int_{t_0}^{t} (\beta_1 I_1(\tau) + \beta_2 I_2(\tau))d\tau \\
&\le \beta \int_{t_0}^{t} I(\tau)d(\tau) \le \beta \int_{t_0}^{t} e^{R_0^* \tau} d\tau = -\frac{\beta}{R_0^*}(e^{R_0^* t_0} - e^{R_0^* t}) < \varepsilon_1,
\end{aligned}
$$

where $\beta = \beta_1 \vee \beta_2$. As a result, for any $t \ge t_0$ we have

$$
P\{|\ln S(t) - \ln \overline{S}(t)| \le \varepsilon_1\} > 1 - \varepsilon_1 \Leftrightarrow P\{|\ln S(t) - \ln \overline{S}(t)| > \varepsilon_1\} < \varepsilon_1. \tag{13}
$$

Now let us make an equivalent statement, that is, the distribution of $lnS(t)$ is weakly convergent to ν_1^* is equivalent to the distribution of $S(t)$ is weakly convergent to μ_1^*. By the Portmanteau theorem, it is sufficient to prove that for any $g(\cdot) : R \to R$ satisfying $|g(x) - g(y)| \le |x - y|$ and $|g(x)| < 1 \; \forall x, y \in R$, we have

$$
Eg(lnS_{u,v,w,x,y}(t)) \to \overline{g}_1 := \int_R g(x)\nu_1^*(dx) = \int_0^\infty g(lnx)\mu_1^*(dx).
$$

Because the diffusion of model (4) is non-degenerate, the distribution of $\overline{S}$ converges weakly to μ_1^* as $t \to \infty$. Therefore

$$
\lim_{t\to\infty} Eg(ln\overline{S}(t)) = \overline{g}_1, \tag{14}
$$

such that

$$
\begin{aligned}
|Eg_1(lnS(t)) - \overline{g}_1| &= |Eg(lnS(t)) - Eg_1(ln\overline{S}(t)) + Eg_1(ln\overline{S}(t)) - \overline{g}_1| \\
&\le E|lnS(t) - ln\overline{S}(t)| + E|g_1(ln\overline{S}(t)) - \overline{g}_1| \\
&\le \{|lnS(t) - ln\overline{S}(t)| < \varepsilon_1\}P\{|lnS(t) - ln\overline{S}(t)| < \varepsilon_1\} \\
&+ \{|lnS(t) - ln\overline{S}(t)| \ge \varepsilon_1\}P\{|lnS(t) - ln\overline{S}(t)| > \varepsilon_1\} \\
&\le \varepsilon_1 P\{|lnS(t) - ln\overline{S}(t)| < \varepsilon_1\} + 2\varepsilon_1 P\{|lnS(t) - ln\overline{S}(t)| > \varepsilon_1\}.
\end{aligned} \tag{15}
$$

Applying (13) and (14) to (15), we can obtain

$$
\limsup_{t\to\infty} |Eg(lnS(t)) - \overline{g}_1| \le 3\varepsilon_1.
$$

Case 2. $V_{1u,v,w,x,y}(t)$ converges weakly to the unique invariant probability measure μ_2^* with the density f_2^*.

Similar to Case 1, we can choose t_0 satisfying $-\frac{2k_1}{R_0^*}exp\{R_0^*\} < \varepsilon_1$. Then, we can get

$$
\begin{aligned}
ln\overline{V}_1(t) - lnV_1(t) &= \varphi_1 \int_{t_0}^{t} (\frac{\overline{S}(\tau)}{\overline{V}_1(\tau)} - \frac{S(\tau)}{V_1(\tau)})d\tau + k_1 \int_{t_0}^{t} I_2(\tau)d\tau \le k_1 \int_{t_0}^{t} I(\tau)d(\tau) \\
&\le k_1 \int_{t_0}^{t} e^{R_0^* \tau} d\tau = -\frac{k_1}{R_0^*}(e^{R_0^* t_0} - e^{R_0^* t}) < \varepsilon_1.
\end{aligned}
$$

As a result, for any $t \ge t_0$ we have

$$
P\{|\ln V_1(t) - \ln \overline{V}_1(t)| \le \varepsilon_1\} > 1 - \varepsilon_1 \Leftrightarrow P\{|\ln V_1(t) - \ln \overline{V_1}(t)| > \varepsilon_1\} < \varepsilon_1, \tag{16}
$$

then we have

$$
Eg(lnV_{1u,v,w,x,y}(t)) \to \overline{g}_2 := \int_R g(x)\nu_2^*(dx) = \int_0^\infty g(lnx)\mu_2^*(dx).
$$

Thus

$$
\lim_{t\to\infty} Eg(ln\overline{V}_{1v}(t)) = \overline{g}_2, \tag{17}
$$

such that

$$\begin{aligned}|Eg_1(lnS(t)) - \overline{g}_1| &= |Eg(lnS(t)) - Eg_1(ln\overline{S}(t)) + Eg_1(ln\overline{S}(t)) - \overline{g}_1| \\ &\leq \varepsilon_1 P\{|lnS(t) - ln\overline{S}(t)| < \varepsilon_1\} + 2\varepsilon_1 P\{|lnS(t) - ln\overline{S}(t)| > \varepsilon_1\}.\end{aligned} \tag{18}$$

Applying (16) and (17) to (18), we can obtain

$$\limsup_{t\to\infty} |Eg(lnV_{1u,v,w,x,y}(t)) - \overline{g}_2| \leq 3\varepsilon_1.$$

Case 3. $V_{2u,v,w,x,y}(t)$ converges weakly to the unique invariant probability measure μ_3^* with the density f_3^*.

The proof method is the same as above. Since ε_1 is taken arbitrarily, we obtain the desired conclusion. The proof is completed. □

4. Stationary Distribution

Now we focus on the case $R_0^* > 0$. Let $P(t,(u,v,w,x,y),\cdot)$ be the transition probability of $(S_{u,v,w,x,y}(t), V_{1u,v,w,x,y}(t), V_{2u,v,w,x,y}(t), I_{1u,v,w,x,y}(t), I_{2u,v,w,x,y}(t))$. Because the diffusion of model (4) is degenerate, i.e., $B_1(t) = B_2(t) = B_3(t) = B_4(t) = B_5(t) = B(t)$, we have to change the model to Stratonovich's form in order to obtain properties of $P(t,(u,v,w,x,y),\cdot)$,

$$\begin{cases} dS(t) = (\Lambda - c_1S(t) - \beta_1S(t)I_1(t) - \beta_2S(t)I_2(t))dt + \sigma_1S(t)\circ dB(t) \\ dV_1(t) = (-c_2V_1(t) + \varphi_1S(t) - k_1I_2(t)V_1(t))dt + \sigma_2V_1(t)\circ dB(t) \\ dV_2(t) = (-c_3V_2(t) + \varphi_2S(t) - k_2I_1(t)V_2(t))dt + \sigma_3V_2(t)\circ dB(t) \\ dI_1(t) = (-c_4I_1(t) + \beta_1S(t)I_1(t) + k_2I_1(t)V_2(t))dt + \sigma_4I_1(t)\circ dB(t) \\ dI_2(t) = (-c_5I_2(t) + \beta_2S(t)I_2(t) + k_1I_2(t)V_1(t) + \varepsilon I_1(t))dt + \sigma_5I_2(t)\circ dB(t), \end{cases}$$

where

$$c_1 = \lambda + \frac{\sigma_1^2}{2}; c_2 = a + \frac{\sigma_2^2}{2}; c_3 = a + \frac{\sigma_3^2}{2}; c_4 = \alpha_1 + \frac{\sigma_4^2}{2}; c_5 = \alpha_2 + \frac{\sigma_5^2}{2}.$$

Let

$$A(u,v,w,x,y) = \begin{pmatrix} \Lambda - c_1u - \beta_1ux - \beta_2uy \\ -c_2v + \varphi_1u - k_1vy \\ -c_3w + \varphi_2u - k_2wx \\ -c_4x + \beta_1ux + k_2wx \\ -c_5y + \beta_2uy + k_1vy + \varepsilon x \end{pmatrix}, B = \begin{pmatrix} \sigma_1u \\ \sigma_2v \\ \sigma_3w \\ \sigma_4x \\ \sigma_5y \end{pmatrix},$$

to proceed, we first recall the notion of Lie bracket. If $X(a_1,a_2,\cdots,a_n) = (X_1,X_2,\cdots,X_n)^\top$ and $Y(a_1,a_2,\cdots,a_n) = (Y_1,Y_2,\cdots,Y_n)^\top$ are two vector fields on R^n then the Lie bracket $[X,Y]$is a vector field given by

$$[X,Y]_i(a_1,a_2,\cdots,a_n) = \sum_{j=1}^{n}(X_j\frac{\partial Y_i}{\partial x_i}(a_1,a_2,\cdots,a_n) - Y_j\frac{\partial X_i}{\partial x_i}(a_1,a_2,\cdots,a_n)),$$

where $i = 1,2,\cdots,n$.

Using $\mathcal{L}(u,v,w,x,y)$ to represent the Lie algebra generated by $A(u,v,w,x,y)$, $B(u,v,w,x,y)$ and $\mathcal{L}_0(u,v,w,x,y)$ the ideal in $\mathcal{L}(u,v,w,x,y)$ generated by B. We have the following theorem.

Theorem 3. *The ideal $\mathcal{L}_0(u,v,w,x,y)$ in $\mathcal{L}(u,v,w,x,y)$ generated by $B(u,v,w,x,y)$ satisfies $dim\mathcal{L}_0(u,v,w,x,y) = 5$ at every $(u,v,w,x,y) \in R_+^{5,\circ}$. In other words, the set of vectors $B,[A,B],[B,[A,B]],[B,[B,[A,B]],\cdots$ spans R^5 at every $(u,v,w,x,y) \in R_+^{5,\circ}$. As a result, the transition probability $P(t,(u,v,w,x,y),\cdot)$ has smooth density $p(t,u,v,w,x,y,u',v',w',x',y')$.*

Proof of Theorem 3. By direct calculation,

$$C = [\ A, B\ ] = \begin{pmatrix} \sigma_1\Lambda + \sigma_4\beta_1 ux + \sigma_5\beta_2 uy \\ -\sigma_1\varphi_1 u + \sigma_2\varphi_1 u + \sigma_5 k_1 vy \\ -\sigma_1\varphi_2 u + \sigma_3\varphi_1 u + \sigma_4 k_2 wy \\ -\sigma_1\beta_1 ux - \sigma_3 k_2 wx \\ -\sigma_1\beta_2 uy - \sigma_2 k_1 vy - \sigma_4\varepsilon x + \sigma_5\varepsilon x \end{pmatrix},$$

$$D = [\ B, C\ ] = \begin{pmatrix} -\sigma_1^2\Lambda + \sigma_4^2\beta_1 ux + \sigma_5^2\beta_2 uy \\ -(\sigma_1 - \sigma_2)^2\varphi_1 u + \sigma_5^2 k_1 vy \\ -(\sigma_1 - \sigma_3)^2\varphi_2 u + \sigma_4^2 k_2 wx \\ -\sigma_1^2\beta_1 ux - \sigma_3^2 k_2 wx \\ -\sigma_1^2\beta_2 uy - \sigma_2^2 k_1 vy - (\sigma_4 - \sigma_5)^2\varepsilon x \end{pmatrix},$$

$$E = [\ C, D\ ] = \begin{pmatrix} e_{11} \\ e_{21} \\ e_{31} \\ e_{41} \\ e_{51} \end{pmatrix}, F = [\ D, E\ ] = \begin{pmatrix} f_{11} \\ f_{21} \\ f_{31} \\ f_{41} \\ f_{51} \end{pmatrix},$$

where elements in matrices E and F are shown in Appendix A.

Consequently,

$$det(B, C, D, E, F) \neq 0,$$

which means that $B; [A, B]; [B, C]; [C, D]; [D, E]$ are linearly independent. As a result, $B; [A, B]; [B, C]; [C, D]; [D, E]$ span $\mathbb{R}^5$for all $(u, v, w, x, y) \in \mathbb{R}_+^{5,\circ}$. Theorem 3 is proved. □

In view of the Hormander Theorem, the transition probability function $\mathcal{P}(t, u_0, v_0, w_0, x_0, y_0, \cdot)$ has a density $k(t, u, v, w, x, y, u_0, v_0, w_0, x_0, y_0)$ and $k \in C^5((0, \infty), \mathbb{R}_+^{5,\circ}, \mathbb{R}_+^{5,\circ}, \mathbb{R}_+^{5,\circ}, \mathbb{R}_+^{5,\circ}, \mathbb{R}_+^{5,\circ})$. Now we check the kernel k is positive. A fixed point $(u_0, v_0, w_0, x_0, y_0) \in \mathbb{R}_+^{5,\circ}$ and a function ϕ, considering the following model of integral equations:

$$\begin{cases} u_\phi(t) = u_0 + \int_0^t [\sigma_1\phi u_\phi + f_1(u_\phi, v_\phi, w_\phi, x_\phi, y_\phi)]d\tau \\ v_\phi(t) = v_0 + \int_0^t [\sigma_2\phi v_\phi + f_2(u_\phi, v_\phi, w_\phi, x_\phi, y_\phi)]d\tau \\ w_\phi(t) = w_0 + \int_0^t [\sigma_3\phi w_\phi + f_3(u_\phi, v_\phi, w_\phi, x_\phi, y_\phi)]d\tau \\ x_\phi(t) = x_0 + \int_0^t [\sigma_4\phi x_\phi + f_4(u_\phi, v_\phi, w_\phi, x_\phi, y_\phi)]d\tau \\ y_\phi(t) = y_0 + \int_0^t [\sigma_5\phi y_\phi + f_5(u_\phi, v_\phi, w_\phi, x_\phi, y_\phi)]d\tau, \end{cases} \quad (19)$$

where

$$f_1 = \Lambda - c_1 u - \beta_1 ux - \beta_2 uy; \qquad f_2 = -c_2 v + \varphi_1 u - k_1 vy;$$
$$f_3 = -c_3 w + \varphi_2 u - k_2 wx; \qquad f_4 = -c_4 x + \beta_1 ux + k_2 wx;$$
$$f_5 = -c_5 y + \beta_2 uy + k_1 vy + \varepsilon x.$$

Let $D_{u_0,v_0,w_0,x_0,y_0;\phi}$ be the *Frechét* derivative of the function h. If for some ϕ the derivative $D_{u_0,v_0,w_0,x_0,y_0;\phi}$ has rank 5, then $k(T, u, v, w, x, y, u_0, v_0, w_0, x_0, y_0) > 0$ for $u = u_\phi(T)$, $v = v_\phi(T)$, $w = w_\phi(T)$, $x = x_\phi(T)$, and $y = y_\phi(T)$. The derivative $D_{u_0,v_0,w_0,x_0,y_0;\phi}$ can be found by means of the perturbation method for ODEs.

Namely, let

$$\Gamma(t) = f'(u_\phi(t), v_\phi(t), w_\phi(t), x_\phi(t), y_\phi(t)),$$

where f' is the Jacobian of $f = [f_1, f_2, f_3, f_4, f_5]^\top$ and let $Q(t, t_0)$, for $T \geq t \geq t_0 \geq 0$, be a matrix function such that

$$Q(t_0, t_0) = I; \frac{\partial Q(t, t_0)}{\partial t} = \Gamma(t) Q(t, t_0),$$

and

$$\mathbf{v} = [\sigma_1, \sigma_2, \sigma_3, \sigma_,4, \sigma_5]^\top,$$

then $D_{u_0,v_0,w_0,x_0,y_0;\phi} h = \int_0^T Q(T, s) g(s) h(s) ds$.

Theorem 4. *For any $(u_0, v_0, w_0, x_0, y_0) \in \mathbb{R}_+^{5,\circ}$ and $(u, v, w, x, y) \in \mathbb{R}_+^{5,\circ}$, there exists $T > 0$ such that $k(T, u, v, w, x, y, u_0, v_0, w_0, x_0, y_0) > 0$.*

Proof of Theorem 4. First, we check that the rank of $D_{u_0,v_0,w_0,x_0,y_0;\phi}$ is 5. Let $\varepsilon_1 \in (0, T)$ and $h(t) = 1_{[T-\varepsilon_1,T]}, t \in (0, T)$. Since

$$Q(T, s) = Id + \Gamma(T)(s - T) + \frac{1}{2}\Gamma^2(T)(s - T)^2 + \frac{1}{6}\Gamma^3(T)(s - T)^3 + \frac{1}{24}\Gamma^4(T)(s - T)^4 + o((s - T)^4),$$

we obtain

$$D_{u_0,v_0,w_0,x_0,y_0;\phi} h = \varepsilon_1 \mathbf{v} - \frac{1}{2}\varepsilon_1^2 \Gamma(T)\mathbf{v} + \frac{1}{6}\varepsilon_1^3 \Gamma^2(T)\mathbf{v} - \frac{1}{24}\varepsilon_1^4 \Gamma^3(T)\mathbf{v} + \frac{1}{120}\varepsilon_1^5 \Gamma^4(T)\mathbf{v} + o(\varepsilon_1^5).$$

Directly calculated

$$\Gamma(T)\mathbf{v} = \begin{pmatrix} \sigma_1 a_{11} + \sigma_4 a_{14} + \sigma_5 a_{15} \\ \sigma_1 a_{21} + \sigma_2 a_{22} + \sigma_5 a_{25} \\ \sigma_1 a_{31} + \sigma_3 a_{33} + \sigma_4 a_{34} \\ \sigma_1 a_{41} + \sigma_3 a_{43} + \sigma_4 a_{44} \\ \sigma_1 a_{51} + \sigma_2 a_{52} + \sigma_4 a_{54} + \sigma_5 a_{55} \end{pmatrix}; \Gamma^2(T)\mathbf{v} = \begin{pmatrix} \sigma_1 b_{11} + \sigma_2 b_{12} + \sigma_3 b_{13} + \sigma_4 b_{14} + \sigma_5 b_{15} \\ \sigma_1 b_{21} + \sigma_2 b_{22} + \sigma_4 b_{24} + \sigma_5 b_{25} \\ \sigma_1 b_{31} + \sigma_3 a_{33} + \sigma_4 b_{34} + \sigma_5 b_{35} \\ \sigma_1 b_{41} + \sigma_3 b_{43} + \sigma_4 b_{44} + \sigma_5 b_{45} \\ \sigma_1 b_{51} + \sigma_2 b_{52} + \sigma_3 b_{53} + \sigma_4 b_{54} + \sigma_5 b_{55} \end{pmatrix};$$

$$\Gamma^3(T)\mathbf{v} = \begin{pmatrix} \sigma_1 c_{11} + \sigma_2 c_{12} + \sigma_3 c_{13} + \sigma_4 c_{14} + \sigma_5 c_{15} \\ \sigma_1 c_{21} + \sigma_2 c_{22} + \sigma_3 c_{23} + \sigma_4 c_{24} + \sigma_5 c_{25} \\ \sigma_1 c_{31} + \sigma_2 c_{32} + \sigma_3 c_{33} + \sigma_4 c_{34} + \sigma_5 c_{35} \\ \sigma_1 c_{41} + \sigma_2 c_{42} + \sigma_3 c_{43} + \sigma_4 c_{44} + \sigma_5 c_{45} \\ \sigma_1 c_{51} + \sigma_2 c_{52} + \sigma_3 c_{53} + \sigma_4 c_{54} + \sigma_5 c_{55} \end{pmatrix}; \Gamma^4(T)\mathbf{v} = \begin{pmatrix} \sigma_1 d_{11} + \sigma_2 d_{12} + \sigma_3 d_{13} + \sigma_4 d_{14} + \sigma_5 d_{15} \\ \sigma_1 d_{21} + \sigma_2 d_{22} + \sigma_3 d_{23} + \sigma_4 d_{24} + \sigma_5 d_{25} \\ \sigma_1 d_{31} + \sigma_2 d_{32} + \sigma_3 d_{33} + \sigma_4 d_{34} + \sigma_5 d_{35} \\ \sigma_1 d_{41} + \sigma_2 d_{42} + \sigma_3 d_{43} + \sigma_4 d_{44} + \sigma_5 d_{45} \\ \sigma_1 d_{51} + \sigma_2 d_{52} + \sigma_3 d_{53} + \sigma_4 d_{54} + \sigma_5 d_{55} \end{pmatrix},$$

where elements in matrices $\Gamma(T), \Gamma^2(T), \Gamma^3(T)$, and $\Gamma^4(T)$ are shown in Appendix B.

Therefore, it follows that $\mathbf{v}, \Gamma(T)\mathbf{v}, \Gamma^2(T)\mathbf{v}, \Gamma^3(T)\mathbf{v}, \Gamma^4(T)\mathbf{v}$ are linearly independent and the derivative $D_{u_0,v_0,w_0,x_0,y_0;\phi}$ has rank 5.

Putting

$$r_1 = -\frac{\sigma_2}{\sigma_1}, r_2 = -\frac{\sigma_3}{\sigma_1}, r_3 = -\frac{\sigma_4}{\sigma_1}, r_4 = -\frac{\sigma_5}{\sigma_1},$$

and

$$\overline{v}_\phi = u_\phi^{r_1}(t) v_\phi(t), \overline{w}_\phi = u_\phi^{r_2}(t) w_\phi(t), \overline{x}_\phi = u_\phi^{r_3}(t) x_\phi(t), \overline{y}_\phi = u_\phi^{r_4}(t) y_\phi(t),$$

we have an equivalent model of model (19)

$$\begin{cases} \dot{u}_\phi(t) = \sigma_1 \phi(t) u_\phi(t) + g_1(u_\phi(t), \overline{v}_\phi(t), \overline{w}_\phi(t), \overline{x}_\phi(t), \overline{y}_\phi(t)) \\ \dot{\overline{v}}_\phi(t) = g_2(u_\phi(t), \overline{v}_\phi(t), \overline{w}_\phi(t), \overline{x}_\phi(t), \overline{y}_\phi(t)) \\ \dot{\overline{w}}_\phi(t) = g_3(u_\phi(t), \overline{v}_\phi(t), \overline{w}_\phi(t), \overline{x}_\phi(t), \overline{y}_\phi(t)) \\ \dot{\overline{x}}_\phi(t) = g_4(u_\phi(t), \overline{v}_\phi(t), \overline{w}_\phi(t), \overline{x}_\phi(t), \overline{y}_\phi(t)) \\ \dot{\overline{y}}_\phi(t) = g_5(u_\phi(t), \overline{v}_\phi(t), \overline{w}_\phi(t), \overline{x}_\phi(t), \overline{y}_\phi(t)) \end{cases} \quad (20)$$

where

$$\begin{aligned}
g_1(u,\overline{v},\overline{w},\overline{x},\overline{y}) &= \Lambda - c_1 u - \beta_1 \overline{x} u^{1-r_3} - \beta_2 \overline{y} u^{1-r_4};\\
g_2(u,\overline{v},\overline{w},\overline{x},\overline{y}) &= u^{-r_1}\overline{v}[-(c_1r_1+c_2)u^{r_1} + \Lambda r_1 u^{r_1-1} + \varphi_1 u^{2r_1+1}\overline{v}^{-1}\\
&\quad - \beta_1 r_1 \overline{x} u^{r_1-r_3} - (\beta_2 r_1 + k_1)\overline{y} u^{r_1-r_4}];\\
g_3(u,\overline{v},\overline{w},\overline{x},\overline{y}) &= u^{-r_2}\overline{w}[-(c_1r_2+c_3)u^{r_2} + \Lambda r_2 u^{r_2-1} + \varphi_2 u^{2r_2+1}\overline{w}^{-1}\\
&\quad - \beta_2 r_2 \overline{y} u^{r_2-r_4} - (\beta_1 r_2 + k_2)\overline{x} u^{r_2-r_3}];\\
g_4(u,\overline{v},\overline{w},\overline{x},\overline{y}) &= u^{-r_3}\overline{x}[-c_1 + \Lambda r_3 u^{r_3-1} - c_4 u^{r_3} + \beta_1 u^{r_3+1} - \beta_1 r_3 \overline{x}\\
&\quad - \beta_2 r_3 \overline{y} u^{r_3-r_4} + k_2 \overline{w} u^{r_3-r_2}];\\
g_5(u,\overline{v},\overline{w},\overline{x},\overline{y}) &= u^{-r_4}\overline{y}[-(c_1r_4+c_5)u^{r_4} + \Lambda r_4 u^{r_4-1} + \beta_2 u^{r_4+1} - \beta_2 \overline{y}\\
&\quad + k_1 \overline{v} u^{r_4-r_1} - (\beta_1 r_4 - \varepsilon u^{r_4})\overline{x} u^{r_4-r_3}].
\end{aligned}$$

For any $u_0, u_1, \overline{v}_0, \overline{w}_0, \overline{x}_0, \overline{y}_0, \overline{v}_1, \overline{w}_1, \overline{x}_1, \overline{y}_1 > 0$ and suppose that $u_0 < u_1$ and let $\rho_1 = sup\{|g_1|, |g_2|, |g_3|, |g_4|, |g_5| : u_0 \le u \le u_1, |\overline{v} - \overline{v}_0| \le \varepsilon_1, |\overline{w} - \overline{w}_0| \le \varepsilon_1, |\overline{x} - \overline{x}_0| \le \varepsilon_1, |\overline{y} - \overline{y}_0| \le \varepsilon_1, \}$.

We choose $\phi(t) \equiv \rho_2$ with $(\frac{\sigma_1\rho_2 u_1}{\rho_1}) + 1)\varepsilon_1 \ge u_1 - u_0$. It is easy to check that with this control, there is $0 \le T \le \varepsilon_1/\rho_1$ such that

$$\begin{aligned}
&u_\phi(T, u_0, \overline{v}_0, \overline{w}_0, \overline{x}_0, \overline{y}_0) = u_1, && |\overline{v}_\phi(T, u_0, \overline{v}_0, \overline{w}_0, \overline{x}_0, \overline{y}_0) - \overline{v}_0| < \varepsilon_1,\\
&|\overline{w}_\phi(T, u_0, \overline{v}_0, \overline{w}_0, \overline{x}_0, \overline{y}_0) - \overline{w}_0| < \varepsilon_1, && |\overline{x}_\phi(T, u_0, \overline{v}_0, \overline{w}_0, \overline{x}_0, \overline{y}_0) - \overline{x}_0| < \varepsilon_1,\\
&|\overline{y}_\phi(T, u_0, \overline{v}_0, \overline{w}_0, \overline{x}_0, \overline{y}_0) - \overline{y}_0| < \varepsilon_1.
\end{aligned}$$

If $u_0 > u_1$,we can construct $\phi(t)$ similarly.

By choosing u_0 to be sufficiently large, for any $\overline{v}_0 \le \overline{v} \le \overline{v}_1, \overline{w}_0 \le \overline{w} \le \overline{w}_1, \overline{x}_0 \le \overline{x} \le \overline{x}_1, \overline{y}_0 \le \overline{y} \le \overline{y}_1$, there is a $\rho_3 > 0$ such that $g_1, g_2, g_3, g_4, g_5 > \rho_3$. This property, combined with (20), implies the existence of a feedback control ϕ and $T > 0$ satisfying that for any $0 \le t \le T$ we have

$$\begin{aligned}
&\overline{v}_\phi(T, u_0, \overline{v}_0, \overline{w}_0, \overline{x}_0, \overline{y}_0) = \overline{v}_1, && \overline{w}_\phi(T, u_0, \overline{v}_0, \overline{w}_0, \overline{x}_0, \overline{y}_0) = \overline{w}_1,\\
&\overline{x}_\phi(T, u_0, \overline{v}_0, \overline{w}_0, \overline{x}_0, \overline{y}_0) = \overline{x}_1, && \overline{y}_\phi(T, u_0, \overline{v}_0, \overline{w}_0, \overline{x}_0, \overline{y}_0) = \overline{y}_1,\\
&\overline{u}_\phi(t, u_0, \overline{v}_0, \overline{w}_0, \overline{x}_0, \overline{y}_0) = u_0.
\end{aligned}$$

This completes the proof. □

We construct a function $V : \mathbb{R}_+^{5,\circ} \to [1, \infty)$ satisfying that

$$\begin{aligned}
&EV(S_{u,v,w,x,y}(t^*), V_{1u,v,w,x,y}(t^*), V_{2u,v,w,x,y}(t^*), I_{1u,v,w,x,y}(t^*), I_{1u,v,w,x,y}(t^*))\\
&\quad \le V(u,v,w,x,y) - \kappa_1 V^\gamma(u,v,w,x,y) + \kappa_2 1_{\{(u,v,w,x,y)\in K\}}
\end{aligned}$$

for some petite set K and some $\gamma \in (0,1), \kappa_1, \kappa_2 > 0, t^* > 1$. If there exists a measure ψ with $\psi(\mathbb{R}_+^{5,\circ}) > 0$ and the probability distribution $\nu(\cdot)$ is concentrated on $\mathbb{N}$ so that for any $(u,v,w,x,y) \in K, Q \in \mathcal{B}(\mathbb{R}_+^{5,\circ})$

$$\mathcal{K}(u,v,w,x,y,Q) := \sum_{n=1}^{\infty} P(nt^*, u,v,w,x,y,Q)\nu(n) \ge \psi(Q),$$

then set K is called to be petite with respect to the Markov chain $S_{u,v,w,x,y}(t^*), V_{1u,v,w,x,y}(t^*), V_{2u,v,w,x,y}(t^*), I_{1u,v,w,x,y}(t^*), I_{1u,v,w,x,y}(t^*), n \in \mathbb{N}$. We must also prove that Markov chain $S_{u,v,w,x,y}(t^*), V_{1u,v,w,x,y}(t^*), V_{2u,v,w,x,y}(t^*), I_{1u,v,w,x,y}(t^*), I_{1u,v,w,x,y}(t^*), n \in \mathbb{N}$ is irreducible and aperiodic. The definitions and properties of irreducible sets, aperiodic sets, and small sets refer to [28] or [29]. The estimation of convergence rate is divided into the following theorems and propositions.

Theorem 5. *Let* $U(u,v,w,x,y) = (u+v+w+x+y)^{1+p^*} + u^{-\frac{p^*}{2}}$*.There exists positive constants* M_1, M_2 *such that*

$$e^{M_1 t} E(S, V_1, V_2, I_1, I_2) \leq U(u,v,w,x,y) + \frac{M_2(e^{M_1 t} - 1)}{M_1}.$$

Proof of Theorem 5. Considering the Lyapunov function $U(u,v,w,x,y) = (u+v+w+x+y)^{1+p^*} + u^{-\frac{p^*}{2}}$. By directly calculating the differential operator $LU(u,v,w,x,y)$ related to model (4), we obtain

$$\begin{aligned}
LU &= (1+p^*)(u+v+w+x+y)^{p^*}[\Lambda - a(u+v+w+x+y) - \gamma_1 x - (\gamma_2+\delta)y] \\
&\quad - \frac{p^*}{2}u^{-\frac{p^*}{2}-1}(\Lambda - \beta_1 ux - \beta_2 uy - \lambda u) + \frac{p^*(1+p^*)}{2}(u+v+w+x+y)^{p^*-1} \\
&\quad (\sigma_1 u + \sigma_2 v + \sigma_3 w + \sigma_4 x + \sigma_5 y)^2 + \frac{p^*(2+p^*)}{8}\sigma_1^2 u^{-\frac{p^*}{2}} \\
&= 2\Lambda(1+p^*)(u+v+w+x+y)^{p^*} - (1+p^*)(u+v+w+x+y)^{p^*-1} \\
&\quad [(a - \frac{p^*}{2}\sigma_1^2)u^2 + (a - \frac{p^*}{2}\sigma_2^2)v^2 + (a - \frac{p^*}{2}\sigma_3^2)w^2 + (a+\gamma_1 - \frac{p^*}{2}\sigma_4^2)x^2 \\
&\quad + (a+\gamma_2+\delta - \frac{p^*}{2}\sigma_5^2)y^2 + (2a - p^*\sigma_1\sigma_2)uv + (2a - p^*\sigma_1\sigma_3)uw \\
&\quad + (2a+\gamma_1 - p^*\sigma_1\sigma_4)ux + (2a+\gamma_2+\delta - p^*\sigma_1\sigma_5)uy + (2a - p^*\sigma_2\sigma_3)vw \\
&\quad + (2a+\gamma_1 - p^*\sigma_2\sigma_4)vx + (2a+\gamma_2+\delta - p^*\sigma_2\sigma_5)vy + (2a+\gamma_1 - p^*\sigma_3\sigma_4)wx \\
&\quad + (2a+\gamma_2+\delta - p^*\sigma_3\sigma_5)wy + (2a+\gamma_1+\gamma_2+\delta - p^*\sigma_4\sigma_5)xy] - \frac{p^*}{2}\Lambda u^{-\frac{p^*}{2}-1} \\
&\quad + \frac{p^*}{2}\beta_1 u^{-\frac{p^*}{2}}x + \frac{p^*}{2}\beta_2 u^{-\frac{p^*}{2}}y + \frac{p^*}{2}[\frac{(2+p^*)+\sigma_1^2}{4} + a + \varphi_1 + \varphi_2]u^{-\frac{p^*}{2}}.
\end{aligned} \tag{21}$$

By Young's inequality, we have

$$\begin{aligned}
u^{-\frac{p^*}{2}}x &\leq \frac{3p^*}{4+3p^*}u^{-\frac{4+3p^*}{6}} + \frac{4}{4+3p^*}x^{\frac{4+3p^*}{4}}; \\
u^{-\frac{p^*}{2}}y &\leq \frac{3p^*}{4+3p^*}u^{-\frac{4+3p^*}{6}} + \frac{4}{4+3p^*}y^{\frac{4+3p^*}{4}}.
\end{aligned} \tag{22}$$

Choose a number M_1 satisfying

$$0 < M_1 < \min\{a - \frac{p^*}{2}\sigma_1^2, a - \frac{p^*}{2}\sigma_2^2, a - \frac{p^*}{2}\sigma_3^2, a+\gamma_1 - \frac{p^*}{2}\sigma_4^2, a+\gamma_2+\delta - \frac{p^*}{2}\sigma_5^2\}.$$

From (21) and (22),we obtain

$$M_2 = \sup_{u,v,w,x,y \in \mathbb{R}_+^4} \{LU(u,v,w,x,y) + M_1 U(u,v,w,x,y)\} < \infty.$$

As a result,

$$LU(u+v+w+x+y) \leq M_2 - M_1 U(u+v+w+x+y). \tag{23}$$

For $n \in \mathbb{N}$, define the stopping time $\eta_n = inf\{t \geq 0 : U(S, V_1, V_2, I_1, I_2) \geq n\}$, then $It\hat{o}'s$ formula and (23) yield that

$$\begin{aligned}
&E(e^{M_1(t\wedge\eta_n)})U(S(t\wedge\eta_n), V_1(t\wedge\eta_n), V_2(t\wedge\eta_n), I_1(t\wedge\eta_n), I_2(t\wedge\eta_n)) \\
&\leq U(u,v,w,x,y) + E\int_0^{t\wedge\eta_n} e^{M_1 t}[LU(S, V_1, V_2, I_1, I_2) + M_1 U(S, V_1, V_2, I_1, I_2)]dt \\
&\leq U(u,v,w,x,y) + \frac{M_2(e^{M_1(t\wedge\eta_n)} - 1)}{M_1}.
\end{aligned}$$

By letting $n \to \infty$, we obtain from Fatou's lemma that

$$\begin{aligned}
&E(e^{M_1(t\wedge\eta_n)})U(S(t\wedge\eta_n), V_1(t\wedge\eta_n), V_2(t\wedge\eta_n), I_1(t\wedge\eta_n), I_2(t\wedge\eta_n)) \\
&\leq U(u,v,w,x,y) + \frac{M_2(e^{M_1 t} - 1)}{M_1}.
\end{aligned}$$

The Theorem 5 is proved. □

Theorem 6. *For any $t \geq 1$ and $A \in \mathcal{F}$ we have*

$$\begin{aligned}
E[lnI_1(t)]_-^2 1_A &\leq ([lnx]_-^2 + c_4^2 t^2 + 2c_4 t[lnx]_-)P(A); \\
E[lnI_2(t)]_-^2 1_A &\leq ([lny]_-^2 + c_5^2 t^2 + 2c_5 t[lny]_-)P(A),
\end{aligned}$$

where $[lnx]_- = 0 \vee (-lnx)$.

Proof of Theorem 6. We have

$$\begin{aligned}
-lnI_1(t) &= -lnI_1(0) - \int_0^t (\beta_1 S + k_2 V_2)dt + (\alpha_1 + \frac{\sigma_4^2}{2})t - \sigma_4 B(t) \\
&\leq -lnx + (\alpha_1 + \frac{\sigma_4^2}{2})t = -lnx + c_4 t,
\end{aligned}$$

where $c_4 = \alpha_1 + \frac{\sigma_4^2}{2}; c_5 = \alpha_2 + \frac{\sigma_5^2}{2}$, thus

$$[lnI_1(t)]_- \leq [lnx]_- + c_4 t.$$

This implies that

$$[lnI_1(t)]_-^2 1_A \leq ([lnx]_-^2 + c_4^2 t^2 + 2c_4 t[lnx]_-)1_A,$$

taking expectation both sides and using the estimate above, we obtain

$$E[lnI_1(t)]_-^2 1_A \leq ([lnx]_-^2 + c_4^2 t^2 + 2c_4 t[lnx]_-)P(A).$$

Similarly, we have

$$E[lnI_2(t)]_-^2 1_A \leq ([lny]_-^2 + c_5^2 t^2 + 2c_5 t[lny]_-)P(A),$$

where $c_5 = \alpha_2 + \frac{\sigma_5^2}{2}$. The Theorem 6 is proved. □

Choose $\varepsilon_1 \in (0,1)$ satisfying

$$\begin{aligned}
&-\frac{4R_0^* t}{3}(1-\varepsilon_1) + 2c_4 < -R_0^*; \qquad -\frac{4R_0^* t}{3}(1-\varepsilon_1) + 2c_5 < -R_0^*, \\
&-\frac{4R_0^* t}{3}(1-\varepsilon_1) + 4c_4\varepsilon_1 < -\frac{R_0^*}{2}; \quad -\frac{4R_0^* t}{3}(1-\varepsilon_1) + 4c_5\varepsilon_1 < -\frac{R_0^*}{2}.
\end{aligned} \tag{24}$$

Choose H so large that

$$\begin{aligned}
&(\beta_1+k_2)H-2c_4\geq 2+R_0^*; && (\beta_2+k_1)H-2c_5\geq 2+R_0^*,\\
&exp\{-\frac{(\beta_1+k_2)H-2c_4}{2\sigma_4^2}\}<\frac{\varepsilon_1}{2}; && exp\{-\frac{(\beta_2+k_1)H-2c_5}{2\sigma_5^2}\}<\frac{\varepsilon_1}{2},\\
&exp\{-\frac{R_0^*[(\beta_1+k_2)H-c_4]}{4\sigma_4^2}\}<\frac{\varepsilon_1}{2}; && exp\{-\frac{R_0^*[(\beta_2+k_1)H-c_5]}{4\sigma_5^2}\}<\frac{\varepsilon_1}{2}.
\end{aligned} \tag{25}$$

Theorem 7. *For ε_1 and H chosen as above, there is $M\in(0,1)$ and $T^*>1$ such that*

$$\begin{aligned}
&\mathbb{P}\{lnx+\frac{2R_0^*t}{3}\leq lnI_1(t)<0;\\
&\mathbb{P}\{lny+\frac{2R_0^*t}{3}\leq lnI_2(t)<0,
\end{aligned}$$

for all $u,v,w\in[0,H];x,y\in(0,M);t\in[T^*,2T^*]\}\geq 1-\varepsilon_1$.

Proof of Theorem 7. Let $\tilde{S}_u(t),\tilde{V}_{1v}(t),\tilde{V}_{2w}(t)$ be the solution with initial value u,v,w to

$$\begin{aligned}
d\tilde{S}(t)&=[\Lambda-(\beta_3\theta_1+\lambda)\tilde{S}]dt+\sigma_1\tilde{S}dB(t);\\
d\tilde{V_1}(t)&=[\varphi_1\tilde{S}-(\beta_4\theta_2+a)\tilde{V_1}]dt+\sigma_2\tilde{V_1}dB(t);\\
d\tilde{V_2}(t)&=[\varphi_2\tilde{S}-(\beta_5\theta_3+a)\tilde{V_1}]dt+\sigma_3\tilde{V_2}dB(t).
\end{aligned} \tag{26}$$

Calculated,

$$\begin{aligned}
&\mathbb{P}\{\lim_{t\to\infty}\frac{1}{t}\int_0^t\tilde{S}_u(\tau)d\tau=\frac{\Lambda}{\beta_3\theta_1+\lambda}\}=1;\forall u\in[0,\infty);\\
&\mathbb{P}\{\lim_{t\to\infty}\frac{1}{t}\int_0^t\tilde{V}_{1v}(\tau)d\tau=\frac{\varphi_1\Lambda}{(\beta_3\theta_1+\lambda)(\beta_4\theta_2+a)}\}=1;\forall v\in[0,\infty);\\
&\mathbb{P}\{\lim_{t\to\infty}\frac{1}{t}\int_0^t\tilde{V}_{2w}(\tau)d\tau=\frac{\varphi_2\Lambda}{(\beta_3\theta_1+\lambda)(\beta_5\theta_3+a)}\}=1;\forall w\in[0,\infty).
\end{aligned}$$

In view of the strong law of large numbers for martingales, $\mathbb{P}\{\lim_{t\to\infty}\frac{B(t)}{t}=0\}=1$. Hence, there exists $T^*>1$, such that

$$\begin{aligned}
&\mathbb{P}\{\frac{\sigma_1B(t)}{t}\geq-\frac{R_0^*}{12};\forall t\geq T^*\}\geq 1-\frac{\varepsilon_1}{3};\\
&\mathbb{P}\{\frac{\sigma_2B(t)}{t}\geq-\frac{R_0^*}{12};\forall t\geq T^*\}\geq 1-\frac{\varepsilon_1}{3};\\
&\mathbb{P}\{\frac{\sigma_3B(t)}{t}\geq-\frac{R_0^*}{12};\forall t\geq T^*\}\geq 1-\frac{\varepsilon_1}{3},
\end{aligned} \tag{27}$$

and

$$\begin{aligned}
&\mathbb{P}\{\frac{1}{t}\int_0^t\tilde{S}_0(\tau)d\tau\geq\frac{\Lambda}{\beta_3\theta_1+\lambda}-\frac{R_0^*}{12\beta};\forall t\geq T^*\}\geq 1-\frac{\varepsilon_1}{3};\\
&\mathbb{P}\{\frac{1}{t}\int_0^t\tilde{V}_{10}(\tau)d\tau\geq\frac{\varphi_1\Lambda}{(\beta_3\theta_1+\lambda)(\beta_4\theta_2+a)}-\frac{R_0^*}{12k_1};\forall t\geq T^*\}\geq 1-\frac{\varepsilon_1}{3};\\
&\mathbb{P}\{\frac{1}{t}\int_0^t\tilde{V}_{20}(\tau)d\tau\geq\frac{\varphi_2\Lambda}{(\beta_3\theta_1+\lambda)(\beta_5\theta_3+a)}-\frac{R_0^*}{12k_2};\forall t\geq T^*\}\geq 1-\frac{\varepsilon_1}{3},
\end{aligned} \tag{28}$$

where $\beta=\beta_1\wedge\beta_2$. By the uniqueness of solutions to (26), we obtain

$$\begin{aligned}
&\mathbb{P}\{\tilde{S}_0(t)\leq\tilde{S}_u(t);\forall t\geq 0\}=1;\forall u\geq 0;\\
&\mathbb{P}\{\tilde{V}_{10}(t)\leq\tilde{V}_{1v}(t);\forall t\geq 0\}=1;\forall v\geq 0;\\
&\mathbb{P}\{\tilde{V}_{20}(t)\leq\tilde{V}_{2w}(t);\forall t\geq 0\}=1;\forall w\geq 0.
\end{aligned}$$

Similar to (8)–(10), it can be shown that there exists $M \in (0,\theta), \theta = \max\{\theta_1, \theta_2, \theta_3\}$,

$$\mathbb{P}\{\xi_{u,v,w,x,y} \le 2T^*\} \le \frac{\varepsilon_1}{3}, \forall x, y \le M; u, v, w \in [0, H], \tag{29}$$

where $\xi_{u,v,w,x,y} = inf\{t \ge 0 : I_1, I_2 \ge 0\}$.

Observe also that

$$\begin{aligned} &\mathbb{P}\{S \ge \tilde{S}_u(t); \forall t \ge \xi_{u,v,w,x,y}\} = 1; \\ &\mathbb{P}\{V_1 \ge \tilde{V}_{1v}(t); \forall t \ge \xi_{u,v,w,x,y}\} = 1; \\ &\mathbb{P}\{V_2 \ge \tilde{V}_{2w}(t); \forall t \ge \xi_{u,v,w,x,y}\} = 1, \end{aligned} \tag{30}$$

which we have from the comparison theorem. From (27)–(30) we can be show that with probability greater than $1 - \varepsilon_1$, for all $t \in [T^*, 2T^*]$,

$$\begin{aligned} ln\theta &\ge lnI_1(t) = lnx + \beta_1 \int_0^t S(\tau)d\tau + k_2 \int_0^t V_2(\tau)d\tau - c_4 t + \sigma_4 B(t) \\ &\ge lnx + \frac{\beta_1 \Lambda t}{\beta_3\theta_1 + \lambda} - \frac{R_0^* t}{12} + \frac{\varphi_2 \Lambda t}{(\beta_3\theta_1 + \lambda)(\beta_5\theta_3 + a)} - \frac{R_0^* t}{12} - c_4 t - \frac{R_0^* t}{12} \\ &\ge lnx + \frac{2R_0^* t}{3}, \\ ln\theta &\ge lnI_2(t) = lny + \beta_2 \int_0^t S(\tau)d\tau + k_1 \int_0^t V_1(\tau)d\tau + \varepsilon \int_0^t \frac{I_1(\tau)}{I_2(\tau)} d\tau - c_5 t + \sigma_5 B(t) \\ &\ge lny + \frac{\beta_2 \Lambda t}{\beta_3\theta_1 + \lambda} - \frac{R_0^* t}{12} + \frac{\varphi_1 \Lambda t}{(\beta_3\theta_1 + \lambda)(\beta_4\theta_2 + a)} - \frac{R_0^* t}{12} - c_5 t - \frac{R_0^* t}{12} \\ &\ge lny + \frac{2R_0^* t}{3}. \end{aligned}$$

The proof is completed. □

Proposition 1. *Assuming $R_0^* > 0$. Let $M \in (0,1)$, H so large and $T^* > 1$. There exists $M_3, M_4 > 0$ independent of T^*, such that*

$$\begin{aligned} E[lnI_1(t)]_-^2 &\le [lnx]_-^2 - R_0^* t [lnx]_- + M_3 t^2, \\ E[lnI_2(t)]_-^2 &\le [lny]_-^2 - R_0^* t [lny]_- + M_4 t^2, \end{aligned}$$

for any $x, y \in (0, \infty), 0 \le u, v, w \le H, t \in [T^*, 2T^*]$.

Proof of Proposition 1. First, considering $x, y \in (0, M], 0 \le u, v, w \le H$, we have

$$P(\Omega_1) \ge 1 - \varepsilon_1, P(\Omega_2) \ge 1 - \varepsilon_1,$$

where

$$\begin{aligned} \Omega_1 &= \{lnx + \frac{2R_0^* t}{3} \le lnI_1(t) < 0; \forall t \in [T^*, 2T^*]\}, \\ \Omega_2 &= \{lny + \frac{2R_0^* t}{3} \le lnI_2(t) < 0; \forall t \in [T^*, 2T^*]\}. \end{aligned}$$

In Ω_1, Ω_2 we have

$$-lnx - \frac{2R_0^* t}{3} \ge -lnI_1(t) > 0; -lny - \frac{2R_0^* t}{3} \ge -lnI_2(t) > 0,$$

thus for any $t \in [T^*, 2T^*]$,

$$0 \le [lnI_1(t)]_- \le [lnx]_- - \frac{2R_0^* t}{3}; 0 \le [lnI_2(t)]_- \le [lny]_- - \frac{2R_0^* t}{3},$$

as a result,

$$[lnI_1(t)]_-^2 \le [lnx]_-^2 - \frac{4R_0^* t}{3}[lnx]_- + \frac{4R_0^{*2}t^2}{9};$$
$$[lnI_2(t)]_-^2 \le [lny]_-^2 - \frac{4R_0^* t}{3}[lny]_- + \frac{4R_0^{*2}t^2}{9},$$

which imply that

$$\begin{aligned} E[1_{\Omega_1}[lnI_1(t)]_-^2] &\le P(\Omega_1)[lnx]_-^2 - \frac{4R_0^* t}{3}P(\Omega_1)[lnx]_- + \frac{4R_0^{*2}t^2}{9}P(\Omega_1); \\ E[1_{\Omega_2}[lnI_2(t)]_-^2] &\le P(\Omega_2)[lny]_-^2 - \frac{4R_0^* t}{3}P(\Omega_2)[lny]_- + \frac{4R_0^{*2}t^2}{9}P(\Omega_2). \end{aligned} \tag{31}$$

In $\Omega_1^c = \Omega - \Omega_1; \Omega_2^c = \Omega - \Omega_2$, we have from Theorem 6 that

$$\begin{aligned} E[1_{\Omega_1^c}[lnI_1(t)]_-^2] &\le P(\Omega_1^c)[lnx]_-^2 - 2c_4 t P(\Omega_1^c)[lnx]_- + c_4^2 t^2 P(\Omega_1^c); \\ E[1_{\Omega_2^c}[lnI_2(t)]_-^2] &\le P(\Omega_2^c)[lny]_-^2 - 2c_5 t P(\Omega_2^c)[lny]_- + c_5^2 t^2 P(\Omega_2^c), \end{aligned} \tag{32}$$

adding (31) and (32) side by side, we obtain

$$E[lnI_1(t)]_-^2 \le [lnx]_-^2 + (-\frac{4R_0^*}{3}(1-\varepsilon_1) + 2c_4)t[lnx]_- + (\frac{4R_0^{*2}}{9} + c_4^2)t^2;$$
$$E[lnI_2(t)]_-^2 \le [lny]_-^2 + (-\frac{4R_0^*}{3}(1-\varepsilon_1) + 2c_5)t[lny]_- + (\frac{4R_0^{*2}}{9} + c_5^2)t^2,$$

in view of (24) we deduce

$$E[lnI_1(t)]_-^2 \le [lnx]_-^2 - R_0^* t[lnx]_- + (\frac{4R_0^{*2}}{9} + c_4^2)t^2;$$
$$E[lnI_2(t)]_-^2 \le [lny]_-^2 - R_0^* t[lny]_- + (\frac{4R_0^{*2}}{9} + c_5^2)t^2.$$

Now, for $x, y \in ([M, \infty)$ and $0 \le u, v, w \le H$, we have form Theorem 6 that

$$E[lnI_1(t)]_-^2 \le [lnx]_-^2 - R_0^* t[lnx]_- + M_3 t^2;$$
$$E[lnI_2(t)]_-^2 \le [lny]_-^2 - R_0^* t[lny]_- + M_4 t^2.$$

Letting M_3, M_4 sufficiently large, such that $M_3 > \frac{4R_0^{*2}}{9} + c_4^2, M_4 > \frac{4R_0^{*2}}{9} + c_5^2$, then the proof is completed. □

Proposition 2. *Assuming $R_0^* > 0$. There exist $M_7, M_8 > 0$ such that*

$$E[lnI_1(2T^*)]_-^2 \le [lnx]_-^2 - \frac{R_0^* T^*}{2}[lnx]_- + M_7 T^{*2},$$
$$E[lnI_2(2T^*)]_-^2 \le [lny]_-^2 - \frac{R_0^* T^*}{2}[lny]_- + M_8 T^{*2},$$

for $x, y \in (0, \infty); u, v, w > H$.

Proof of Proposition 2. First, considering $x, y \le exp\{-\frac{R_0^* T^*}{2}\}$. Defined the stopping time

$$\xi_{u,v,w,x,y} = T^* \wedge inf\{t > 0 : S, V_1, V_2 \le H\}.$$

Let

$$\Omega_3 = \{\sigma_4 B(t) - \frac{(\beta_1 + k_2)H - 2c_4}{2} T^* \leq 1\},$$
$$\Omega_4 = \{\sigma_5 B(t) - \frac{(\beta_2 + k_1)H - 2c_5}{2} T^* \leq 1\},$$
$$\Omega_5 = \{\sigma_4 B(t) - [(\beta_1 + k_2)H - c_4]t \leq \frac{R_0^*}{8}; \forall t \in [0, 2T^*]\},$$
$$\Omega_6 = \{\sigma_5 B(t) - [(\beta_2 + k_1)H - c_5]t \leq \frac{R_0^*}{8}; \forall t \in [0, 2T^*]\}.$$

By the exponential martingale inequality,

$$P(\Omega_3) \geq 1 - exp\{-\frac{(\beta_1 + k_2)H - 2c_4}{2\sigma_4^2}\} \geq 1 - \frac{\varepsilon_1}{2},$$
$$P(\Omega_4) \geq 1 - exp\{-\frac{(\beta_2 + k_1)H - 2c_5}{2\sigma_5^2}\} \geq 1 - \frac{\varepsilon_1}{2},$$
$$P(\Omega_5) \geq 1 - exp\{-\frac{R_0^*[(\beta_1 + k_2)H - c_4]}{4\sigma_4^2}\} \geq 1 - \frac{\varepsilon_1}{2},$$
$$P(\Omega_6) \geq 1 - exp\{-\frac{R_0^*[(\beta_2 + k_1)H - c_5]}{4\sigma_5^2}\} \geq 1 - \frac{\varepsilon_1}{2}.$$

Let

$$\Omega_7 = \Omega_3 \cap \{\xi_{u,v,w,x,y} = T^*\}; \Omega_8 = \Omega_4 \cap \{\xi_{u,v,w,x,y} = T^*\},$$
$$\Omega_9 = \{-lnI_1(t) \leq -lnx + \frac{R_0^*}{8}\} \cap \{\xi_{u,v,w,x,y} < T^*\};$$
$$\Omega_{10} = \{-lnI_2(t) \leq -lny + \frac{R_0^*}{8}\} \cap \{\xi_{u,v,w,x,y} < T^*\},$$
$$\Omega_{11} = \Omega - (\Omega_7 \cup \Omega_9); \Omega_{12} = \Omega - (\Omega_8 \cup \Omega_{10}).$$

If $x_1 \in \Omega_7, y_1 \in \Omega_8$, we have

$$\begin{aligned}
-lnI_1(2T^*) &= -lnx - \int_0^{2T^*} (\beta_1 S + k_2 V_2 - c_4)dt + \sigma_4 B(2T^*) \\
&\leq -lnx - \int_0^{T^*} (\beta_1 S + k_2 V_2 - c_4)dt - \int_0^{T^*} c_4 dt + \sigma_4 B(2T^*) \\
&\leq -lnx - T^*[(\beta_1 + k_2)H - 2c_4] + \sigma_4 B(2T^*) \\
&\leq -lnx - \frac{T^*[(\beta_1 + k_2)H - 2c_4]}{2} + 1 \\
&\leq -lnx - \frac{R_0^* T^*}{2},
\end{aligned}$$

similarly,

$$-lnI_2(2T^*) \leq -lny - \frac{R_0^* T^*}{2}.$$

If $x < exp\{-\frac{R_0^* T^*}{2}\}; y < exp\{-\frac{R_0^* T^*}{2}\}$, therefore

$$[lnI_1(2T^*)]_- \leq -\frac{R_0^* T^*}{2} + [lnx]_-,$$
$$[lnI_2(2T^*)]_- \leq -\frac{R_0^* T^*}{2} + [lny]_-.$$

Squaring and then multiplying by $1_{\Omega_7}, 1_{\Omega_8}$ and then taking expectation both sides, we yield

$$E[lnI_1(2T^*)]_-^2 1_{\Omega_7} \le [lnx]_-^2 P(\Omega_7) - R_0^* T^*[lnx]\_P(\Omega_7) + \frac{R_0^{*2}T^{*2}}{4},$$
$$E[lnI_2(2T^*)]_-^2 1_{\Omega_8} \le [lny]_-^2 P(\Omega_7) - R_0^* T^*[lny]\_P(\Omega_8) + \frac{R_0^{*2}T^{*2}}{4}. \quad (33)$$

If $x_1 \in \Omega_9$, then

$$\begin{aligned}-ln_1(\xi_{u,v,w,x,y}) &= -lnx - \int_0^{\xi_{u,v,w,x,y}} (\beta_1 S + k_2 V_2 - c_4)dt + \sigma_4 B(\xi_{u,v,w,x,y}) \\ &\le -lnx - [(\beta_1 + k_2)H - c_4]\xi_{u,v,w,x,y} + \sigma_4 B(\xi_{u,v,w,x,y}) \\ &\le -lnx + \frac{R_0^*}{8},\end{aligned}$$

similarly, $y_1 \in \Omega_{10}$, we have

$$-ln_2(\xi_{u,v,w,x,y}) \le -lny + \frac{R_0^*}{8},$$

as a result,

$$\Omega_4 \cap \{\xi_{u,v,w,x,y} < T^*\} \subset \Omega_9; \Omega_6 \cap \{\xi_{u,v,w,x,y} < T^*\} \subset \Omega_{10},$$

hence,

$$\begin{aligned}P(\Omega_{11}) &= P(\Omega_{11} \cap \{\xi_{u,v,w,x,y} < T^*\}) + P(\Omega_{11} \cap \{\xi_{u,v,w,x,y} = T^*\}) \\ &\le P(\Omega_3^c) + P(\Omega_5^c) \le \varepsilon_1, \\ P(\Omega_{12}) &= P(\Omega_{12} \cap \{\xi_{u,v,w,x,y} < T^*\}) + P(\Omega_{12} \cap \{\xi_{u,v,w,x,y} = T^*\}) \\ &\le P(\Omega_4^c) + P(\Omega_6^c) \le \varepsilon_1.\end{aligned}$$

Let $t < T^*; u', v', w' > 0$ and $-lnx' \le -lnx + \frac{R_0^*}{8} \le 0; -lny' - lny + \frac{R_0^*}{8} \le 0$. In view of Proposition and the strong Markov property, we can estimate the conditional expectation

$$\begin{aligned}&E[lnI_1(2T^*)]_-^2 | \xi_{u,v,w,x,y} = t, I_1 = x', S(\xi) = u', V_1(\xi) = v', V_2(\xi) = w'| \\ &\le [lnx']_-^2 - R_0^*(2T^* - t)[lnx']\_ + M_3(2T^* - t)^2 \\ &\le [lnx']_-^2 - R_0^* T^*[lnx']\_ + 4M_3 T^{*2} \\ &\le (-lnx + \frac{R_0^*}{8})^2 - R_0^* T^*(-lnx) + 4M_3 T^{*2} \\ &\le (-lnx)^2 - (R_0^* T^* - \frac{R_0^*}{4})(-lnx) + 4M_3 T^{*2} + \frac{R_0^{*2}}{64} \\ &\le [lnx]_-^2 - \frac{3R_0^* T^*}{4}[lnx]\_ + 4M_3 T^{*2} + \frac{R_0^{*2}}{64}, \\ &E[lnI_2(2T^*)]_-^2 | \xi_{u,v,w,x,y} = t, I_2 = y', S(\xi) = u', V_1(\xi) = v', V_2(\xi) = w'| \\ &\le [lny]_-^2 - \frac{3R_0^* T^*}{4}[lny]\_ + 4M_4 T^{*2} + \frac{R_0^{*2}}{64}.\end{aligned}$$

As a result,

$$E[lnI_1(2T^*)]_-^2 1_{\Omega_9} \le [lnx]_-^2 P(\Omega_9) - \frac{3R_0^* T^*}{4}[lnx]\_P(\Omega_9) + 4M_3 T^{*2} + \frac{R_0^{*2}}{64},$$
$$E[lnI_2(2T^*)]_-^2 1_{\Omega_{10}} \le [lny]_-^2 P(\Omega_{10}) - \frac{3R_0^* T^*}{4}[lny]\_P(\Omega_{10}) + 4M_4 T^{*2} + \frac{R_0^{*2}}{64}, \quad (34)$$

in view of Theorem 6,

$$E[lnI_1(2T^*)]_-^2 1_{\Omega_{11}} \le [lnx]_-^2 P(\Omega_{11}) + 4c_4 T^*[lnx]\_P(\Omega_{11}) + 4c_4 T^{*2},$$
$$E[lnI_2(2T^*)]_-^2 1_{\Omega_{12}} \le [lny]_-^2 P(\Omega_{12}) + 4c_5 T^*[lny]\_P(\Omega_{12}) + 4c_5 T^{*2}, \quad (35)$$

adding side by side (33)–(35), for some $M_5, M_6 > 0$, we have

$$E[lnI_1(2T^*)]_-^2 \le [lnx]_-^2 - T^*(\frac{3R_0^*}{4}(1-\varepsilon_1) + 4c_4\varepsilon_1) + M_5 T^{*2}$$
$$\le [lnx]_-^2 - \frac{R_0^* T^*}{2} + M_5 T^*;$$

$$E[lnI_2(2T^*)]_-^2 \le [lny]_-^2 - T^*(\frac{3R_0^*}{4}(1-\varepsilon_1) + 4c_5\varepsilon_1) + M_6 T^{*2}$$
$$\le [lny]_-^2 - \frac{R_0^* T^*}{2} + M_6 T^*.$$

We note that, if $x, y \ge exp\{-\frac{R_0^* T^*}{2}\}$, then

$$-lnx \le \frac{R_0^* T^*}{2}; -lny + \frac{R_0^* T^*}{2},$$

therefore, it follows from Theorem 6 that

$$E[lnI_1(2T^*)]_-^2 \le (\frac{R_0^*}{4} + c_4 R_0^* + 4c_4^2)T^{*2};$$
$$E[lnI_2(2T^*)]_-^2 \le (\frac{R_0^*}{4} + c_5 R_0^* + 4c_5^2)T^{*2}.$$

Let $M_7 = M_5 \vee (\frac{R_0^*}{4} + c_4 R_0^* + 4c_4^2); M_8 = M_6 \vee \frac{R_0^*}{4} + c_5 R_0^* + 4c_5^2$, for any $u, v, w \ge H$; $x, y \in (0, \infty)$, we have

$$E[lnI_1(2T^*)]_-^2 \le [lnx]_-^2 - \frac{R_0^* T^*}{2}[lnx]_- + M_7 T^{*2},$$
$$E[lnI_2(2T^*)]_-^2 \le [lny]_-^2 - \frac{R_0^* T^*}{2}[lny]_- + M_8 T^{*2}.$$

The proof is completed. □

Theorem 8. *Let $R_0^* > 0$, there exists an invariant probability measure π^* such that*
(a) $\lim_{t\to\infty} t^{q^*}||P(t,(u,v,w,x,y),\cdot) - \pi^*(\cdot)|| = 0; \forall (u,v,w,x,y) \in R_+^{5,\circ}$,
(b) $\lim_{t\to\infty} \frac{1}{t}\int_0^t h(S,V_1,V_2,I_1,I_2)ds = \int_{R_+^{5,\circ}} h(u,v,w,x,y)\pi^*(du,dv,dw,dx,dy) = 1$,
where $||\cdot||$ is the total variation norm, q^* is any positive number and $P(t,u,v,w,x,y,\cdot)$ is the transition probability of $(S(t), V_1(t), V_2(t), I_1(t), I_2(t))$.

Proof of Theorem 8. By virtue of Theorem 7, there are $h_1, H_1 > 0$ satisfying

$$EU(S(2T^*), V_1(2T^*), V_2(2T^*), I_1(2T^*), I_2(2T^*)) \le (1-h_1)U(u,v,w,x,y) + H_1. \quad (36)$$

Let

$$V = U(u,v,w,x,y) + [lnx]_-^2 + [lny]_-^2,$$

in view of Proposition 1, Proposition 2, and (26), there is a compact set $K \subseteq R_+^{5,\circ}, h_2, H_2 > 0$ satisfying

$$EV \le V - h_2\sqrt{V} + H_2 1_{\{(u,v,w,x,y)\in k\}}; \forall (u,v,w,x,y) \in R_+^{5,\circ}. \quad (37)$$

Applying (37) and Theorem 3.6 in [30], we obtain that

$$n||P(2nT^*, (u,v,w,x,y) - \pi^*)|| \to 0; n \to \infty, \tag{38}$$

for some invariant probability measure π^* the Markov chain $(S(2nT^*), V_1(2nT^*), V_2(2nT^*), I_1(2nT^*), I_2(2nT^*))$. Let $\tau_{\mathcal{K}} = inf\{n \in \mathbb{N} : (S(2nT^*), V_1(2nT^*), V_2(2nT^*), I_1(2nT^*), I_2(2nT^*)) \in \mathcal{K}\}$. It is shown in the proof of Theorem 3.6 in [30] that (37) implies $E_{\tau_{\mathcal{K}}} < \infty$. In view of [31], the Markov process $(S_{u,v,w,x,y}(t), V_{1u,v,w,x,y}(t), V_{2u,v,w,x,y}(t), I_{1u,v,w,x,y}(t), I_{2u,v,w,x,y}(t))$ has an invariant probability measure ϕ_*. As a result, ϕ_* is also an invariant probability measure of the Markov chain $(S(2nT^*), V_1(2nT^*), V_2(2nT^*), I_1(2nT^*), I_2(2nT^*))$. In light of (38), we must have $\phi_* = \phi^*$, then, ϕ^* is an invariant measure of the Markov process $(S(t), V_1(t), V_2(t), I_1(t), I_2(t))$.

In the proofs, we use the function $[Iny]_-^2$ for the sake of simplicity. In fact, we can treat $[Iny]_-^{1+q}$ for any small $q \in (0,1)$ in the same manner. For more details, we can refer to [24] or [25]. □

5. Numerical Examples

By using the Milstein method mentioned in Higham [32], model (4) can be rewritten as the following discretization equations:

$$\begin{cases} S_{k+1} = S_k + (\Lambda - \beta_1 S_k I_{1k} - \beta_2 S_k I_{2k} - \lambda S_k)\triangle t + \sigma_1 S_k \sqrt{\triangle t}\xi k + \frac{\sigma_1^2}{2} S_k(\triangle t\xi_k^2 - \triangle t) \\ V_{1k+1} = V_{1k} + (\varphi_1 S_k - k_1 I_{2k} V_k 1 - a V_{1k})\triangle t + \sigma_2 V_{1k}\sqrt{\triangle t}\xi k + \frac{\sigma_2^2}{2} V_{1k}(\triangle t\xi_k^2 - \triangle t) \\ V_{2k+1} = V_{2k} + (\varphi_2 S_k - k_2 I_{1k} V_{2k} - a V_{2k})\triangle t + \sigma_3 V_{2k}\sqrt{\triangle t}\xi k + \frac{\sigma_3^2}{2} V_{2k}(\triangle t\xi_k^2 - \triangle t) \\ I_{1k+1} = I_{1k} + (\beta_1 S_k I_{1k} + k_2 I_{1k} V_{2k} - \alpha_1 I_{1k})\triangle t + \sigma_4 I_{1k}\sqrt{\triangle t}\xi k + \frac{\sigma_4^2}{2} I_{1k}(\triangle t\xi_k^2 - \triangle t) \\ I_{2k+1} = I_{2k} + (\beta_2 S_k I_{2k} + k_1 I_{2k} V_{1k} + \varepsilon I_{1k} - \alpha_1 I_{2k})\triangle t + \sigma_5 I_{2k}\sqrt{\triangle t}\xi k + \frac{\sigma_5^2}{2} I_{2k}(\triangle t\xi_k^2 - \triangle t) \end{cases}$$

where $\xi_k, k = 1, 2, \cdots, n$ are Gaussian random variables. The following figures are drawn using MATLAB based on some numerical examples.

Example 1. *Consider (4) with parameters* $\Lambda = 15$; $a = 0.2$; $\beta_1 = 0.15$; $\beta_2 = 0.15$; $\gamma_1 = 0.5$; $\gamma_2 = 0.15$; $\varphi_1 = 0.4$; $\varphi_2 = 0.4$; $\varepsilon = 0.8$; $\delta = 0.01$; $k1 = 0.7$; $k2 = 0.5$; $\lambda = a + \varphi_1 + \varphi_2 = 1$; $\alpha_1 = a + \gamma_1 + \varepsilon = 1.5$; $\alpha_2 = a + \gamma_2 + \delta = 0.36$; $\sigma_1 = 0.5$; $\sigma_2 = 1$; $\sigma_3 = 0.8$; $\sigma_4 = 0.5$; $\sigma_5 = 0.5$. *Directing calculations show that* $R_0^* = 40.94 > 0$ *which satisfy the conditions in Theorem 8, then the disease is almost surely persistent (see Figures 1–5). Furthermore,the histograms of the probability density function of* $S(t)$,$V_1(t)$,$V_2(t)$,$I_1(t)$,$I_2(t)$, *for model (4) are shown in Figures 6–10, where Figure 11 represents the phase diagram of* $(V_1(t), I_1(t))$, *respectively.*

Example 2. *Let parameters* $\Lambda = 1$; $a = 0.5$; $\beta_1 = 0.15$; $\beta_2 = 0.22$; $\gamma_1 = 0.35$; $\gamma_2 = 0.25$; $\varphi_1 = 0.5$; $\varphi_2 = 0.4$; $\varepsilon = 0.54$; $\delta = 0.3$; $k1 = 0.2$; $k2 = 0.15$; $\lambda = a + \varphi_1 + \varphi_2 = 1.4$; $\alpha_1 = a + \gamma_1 + \varepsilon = 1.39$; $\alpha_2 = a + \gamma_2 + \delta = 1.05$; $\sigma_1 = 0.8$; $\sigma_2 = 0.6$; $\sigma_3 = 0.6$; $\sigma_4 = 0.5$; $\sigma_5 = 0.5$. *Directing calculations show that* $R_0^* = -0.03 < 0$, *which satisfy the conditions in Theorem 2, then the disease is almost certainly extinct (see Figures 12 and 13). In addition,* $S(t)$, $V_1(t)$, $V_2(t)$ *are weakly convergent to the unique invariant probability measure* $\mu_1^*, \mu_2^*, \mu_3^*$ *(see Figures 14–16).*

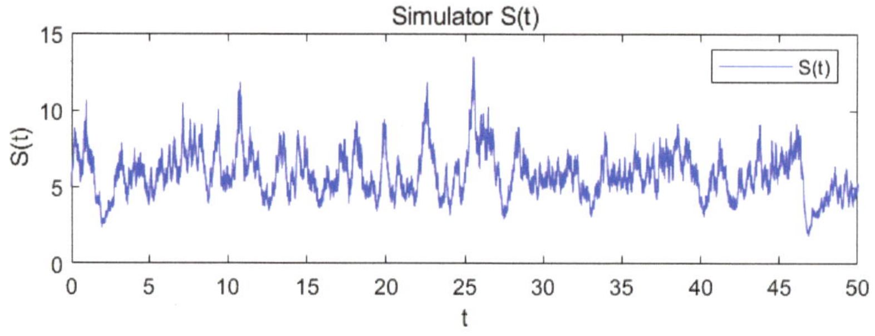

Figure 1. Sample path of S(t).

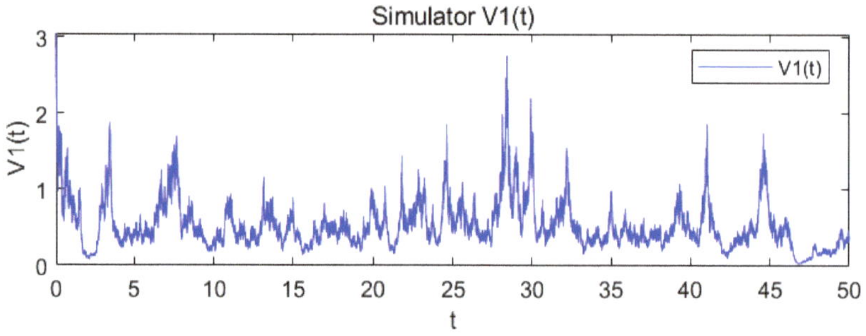

Figure 2. Sample path of V1(t).

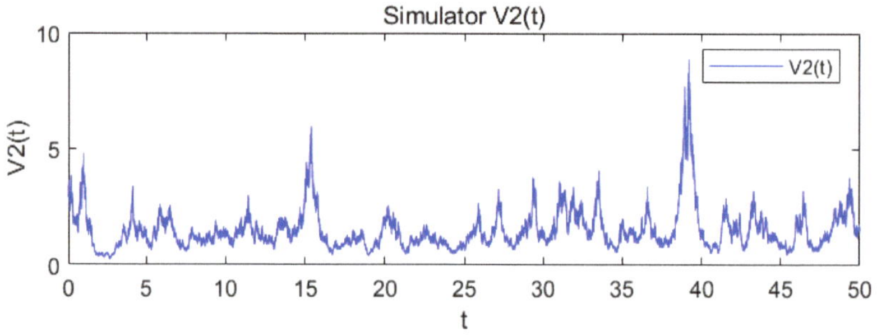

Figure 3. Sample path of V2(t).

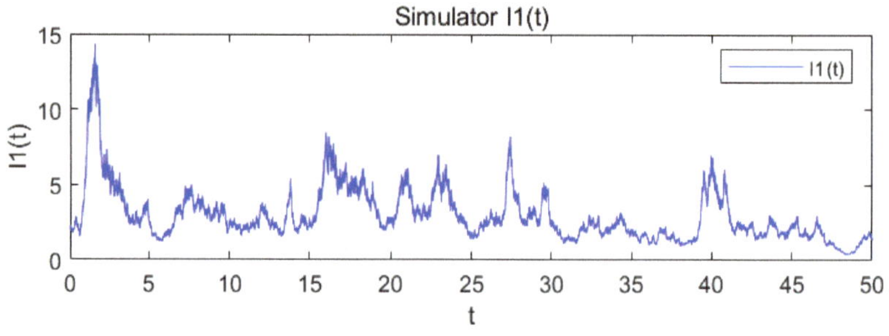

Figure 4. Sample path of I1(t).

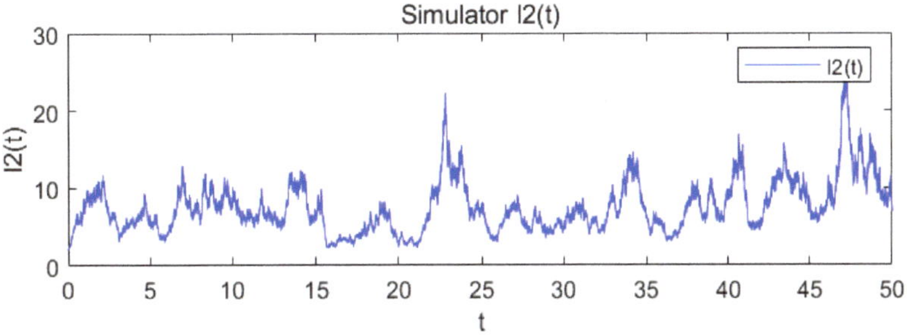

Figure 5. Sample path of I2(t).

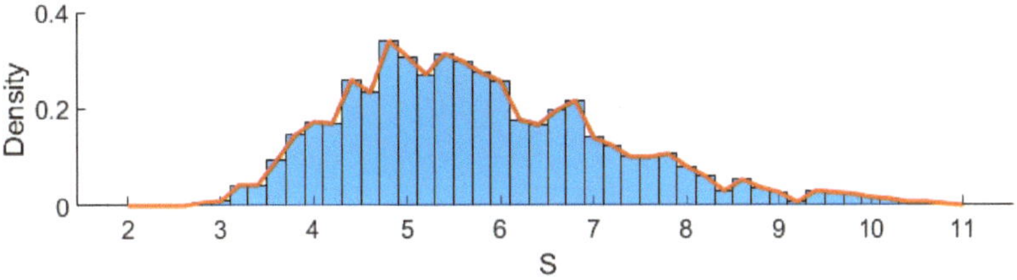

Figure 6. Histogram of the probability density function of S(t).

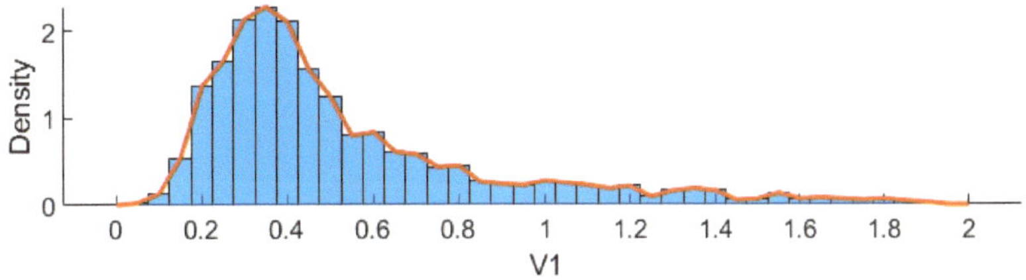

Figure 7. Histogram of the probability density function of V1(t).

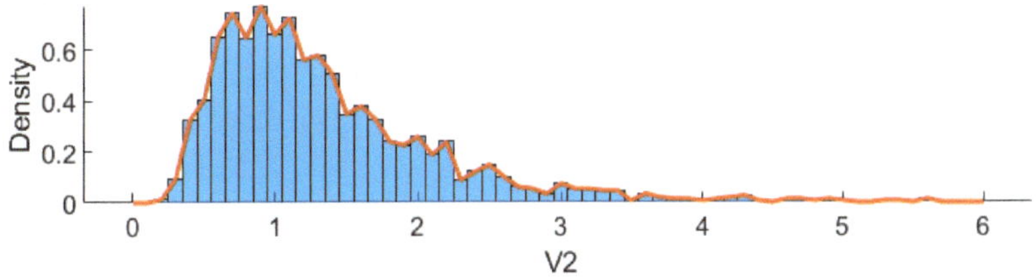

Figure 8. Histogram of the probability density function of V2(t).

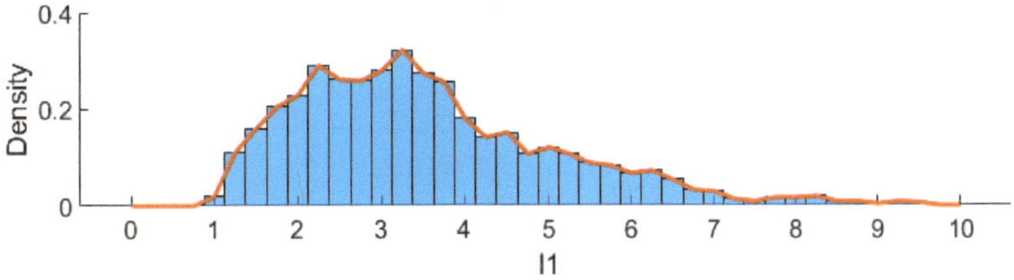

Figure 9. Histogram of the probability density function of I1(t).

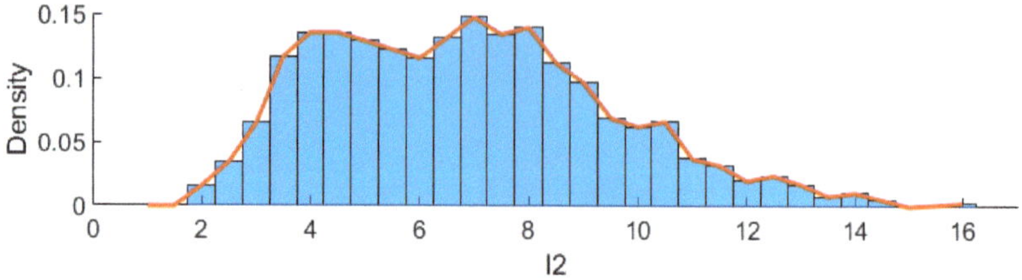

Figure 10. Histogram of the probability density function of I2(t).

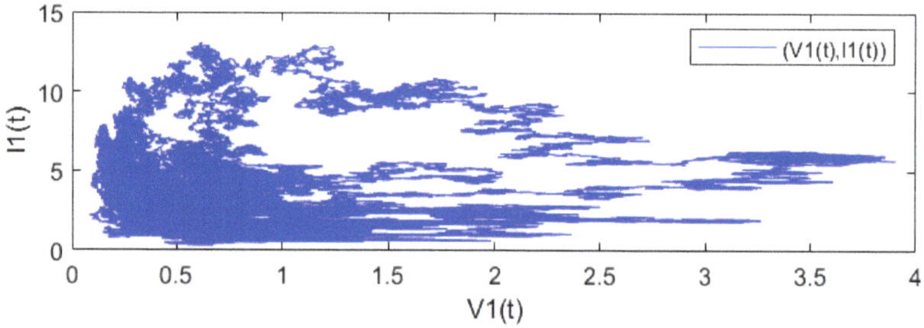

Figure 11. Phase portrait of model (4).

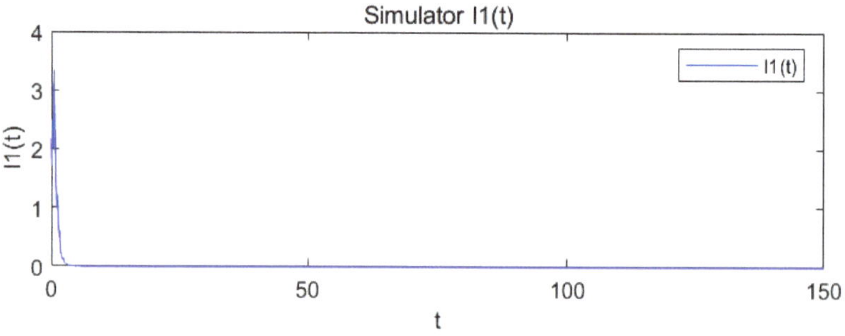

Figure 12. Sample path of I1(t).

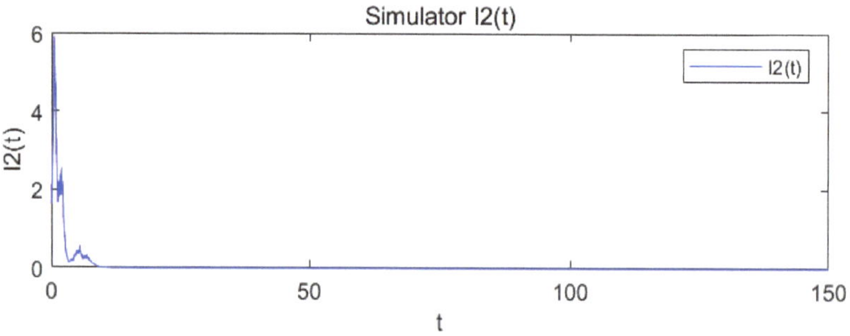

Figure 13. Sample path of I2(t).

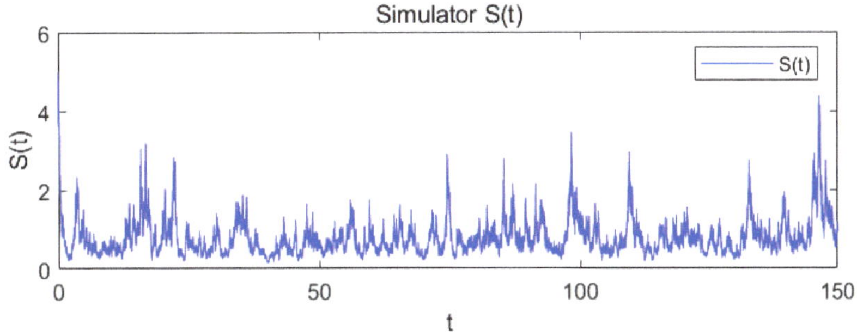

Figure 14. Sample path of S(t).

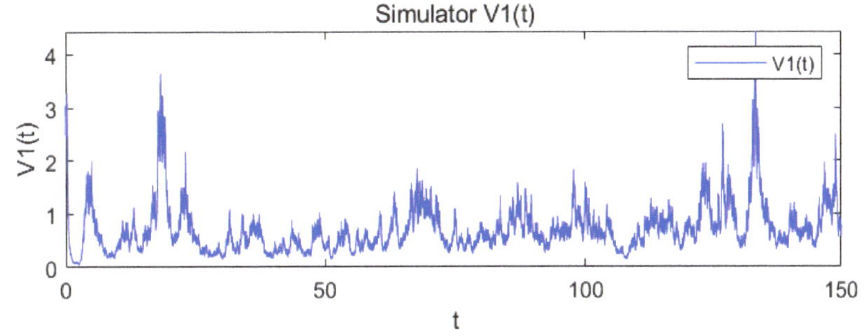

Figure 15. Sample path of V1(t).

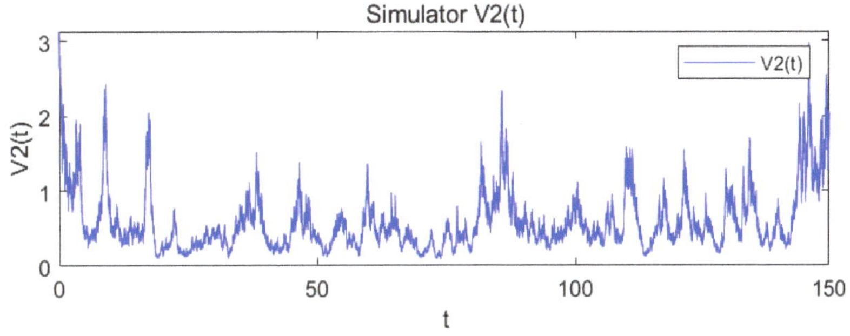

Figure 16. Sample path of V2(t).

6. Conclusions and Discussion

The main purpose of this paper is to study the global existence and uniqueness of the solution of model (4) and the extinction and stationary distribution of the disease by introducing a threshold R_0^*. If $R_0^* < 0$, the number of infected individuals $I(t)(I(t) = I_1(t) + I_2(t))$ tends to zero at an exponential rate, whereas the distribution of susceptible population $S(t)$, vaccinated of the first type $V_1(t)$ and vaccinated of the second type $V_2(t)$ converge weakly to the boundary distribution. On the other hand, if $R_0^* > 0$, the existence and uniqueness of the invariant probability measure and the convergence of the total variation norm of the transition probability to the invariant measure are obtained. In addition, the support of the invariant probability measure is described. Then, we obtain that the disease can almost certainly continue to exist, and there is an independent stable distribution. Finally, numerical simulation is carried out to verify our theoretical results.

In addition, most of the existing literature uses the method of constructing a Lyapunov function to prove the existence of stationary distribution of the solution of the random model (4). However, this approach does not work for all models. In this paper, the stationary distribution is proved using a definition that applies to more models. Most of the stochastic epidemic models studied so far are second-order or third-order models. However, as the disease progresses, the virus can mutate as it spreads, allowing the disease to spiral out of control. Therefore, in order to describe the infectious disease more accurately, considering the situation of two kinds of vaccinations for susceptible people, a fifth-order model was established–a class of virus mutation infectious disease model with double vaccinations. I sincerely hope that in the future we can build more complete models of infectious diseases to make greater progress.

Author Contributions: Formal analysis, H.C. and J.W.; funding acquisition, X.T.; software, W.Q. and W.L. All authors contributed equally and significantly in this paper. All authors have read and agreed to the published version of the manuscript.

Funding: This work is supported by National Natural Science Foundation of China (Nos. 12261104, 12126363).

Data Availability Statement: Data sharing is not applicable to this article as no data sets were generated or analyzed during the current study.

Conflicts of Interest: The authors declare that they have no competing interests.

Appendix A

$$
\begin{aligned}
e_{11} = {} & \sigma_1\sigma_4\beta_1(\sigma_4\Lambda x + \sigma_1\Lambda x - \sigma_4\beta_1u^2x + \sigma_1\beta_1u^2x) + \sigma_1\sigma_5\beta_2(\sigma_5\Lambda y + \sigma_1\Lambda y - \beta_2u^2y) - \sigma_2\sigma_5k_1\beta_2uvy \\
& - \sigma_3\sigma_4k_2\beta_1(\sigma_4 - \sigma_3)uwx - (\sigma_4 - \sigma_5^2)\beta_2\varepsilon ux; \\
e_{21} = {} & -\sigma_1(\sigma_1 - \sigma_2)^2\varphi_1\Lambda + \sigma_1\sigma_4^2\beta_1\varphi_1ux + \sigma_1\sigma_5^2\beta_2\varphi_1uy - \sigma_1\sigma_5^2k_1\varphi_1uy - \sigma_1\sigma_5^2\beta_2k_1uvy + \sigma_1^2\sigma_2\varphi_1\Lambda \\
& + \sigma_1^2\sigma_5\beta_2k_1uvy - \sigma_1^3\varphi_1\Lambda - \sigma_2\sigma_4^2\beta_1\varphi_1ux - \sigma_2\sigma_5^2\beta_2\varphi_1uy + \sigma_2\sigma_5^2k_1\varphi_1uy - \sigma_2\sigma_5^2k_1^2v^2y + \sigma_2^2\sigma_5k_1^2v^2y \\
& - \sigma_4(\sigma_1 - \sigma_2)^2\beta_1\varphi_1ux - \sigma_4\sigma_5^2k_1\varepsilon ux - \sigma_5(\sigma_1 - \sigma_2)^2\beta_2\varphi_1uy + \sigma_5(\sigma_1 - \sigma_2)^2k_1\varphi_1uy \\
& + \sigma_5(\sigma_4 - \sigma_5)^2k_1\varepsilon vx + \sigma_5^3k_1\varepsilon vx; \\
e_{31} = {} & -\sigma_1(\sigma_1 - \sigma_3)^2\varphi_2\Lambda + \sigma_1\sigma_4^2\beta_1\varphi_2ux - \sigma_1\sigma_4^2k_2\varphi_2ux - \sigma_1\sigma_4^2\beta_1k_2uwx + \sigma_1\sigma_5^2\beta_2\varphi_2uy + \sigma_1^2\sigma_3\varphi_2\Lambda \\
& + \sigma_1^2\sigma_4\beta_1k_2uwx - \sigma_1^3\varphi_2\Lambda - \sigma_3\sigma_4^2\beta_1\varphi_2ux + \sigma_3\sigma_4^2k_2\varphi_2ux - \sigma_3\sigma_4^2k_2^2w^2x - \sigma_3\sigma_5^2\beta_2\varphi_2uy + \sigma_3^2\sigma_4k_2^2w^2x \\
& - \sigma_4(\sigma_1 - \sigma_3)^2\beta_1\varphi_2ux + \sigma_4(\sigma_1 - \sigma_3)^2k_2\varphi_2ux - \sigma_5(\sigma_1 - \sigma_3)^2\beta_2\varphi_2uy;
\end{aligned}
$$

$$
\begin{aligned}
e_{41} = {} & \sigma_1\sigma_3^2k_2\varphi_2ux + \sigma_1\sigma_4^2\beta_1^2ux^2 + \sigma_1\sigma_5^2\beta_1\beta_2uxy - \sigma_1^2\sigma_4\beta_1^2ux^2 - \sigma_1^2\sigma_5\beta_1\beta_2uxy - 2\sigma_1^3\beta_1\Lambda x \\
& + \sigma_3(\sigma_1 - \sigma_3)^2k_2\varphi_2ux - \sigma_3\sigma_4^2k_2^2wx^2 - \sigma_3^2\sigma_4k_2^2wx^2 - \sigma_3^3k_2\varphi_2ux; \\
e_{51} = {} & \sigma_1\sigma_2^2k_1\varphi_1uy + \sigma_1\sigma_4^2\beta_1\beta_2uxy + \sigma_1\sigma_5^2\beta_2^2uy^2 + \sigma_1(\sigma_4 - \sigma_5)^2\beta_1\varepsilon ux - \sigma_1(\sigma_4 - \sigma_5)^2\beta_2\varepsilon ux \\
& - \sigma_1^2\sigma_4\beta_1\beta_2uxy - \sigma_1^2\sigma_4\beta_1\varepsilon ux + \sigma_1^2\sigma_4\beta_2\varepsilon ux - \sigma_1^2\sigma_5\beta_2^2uy^2 + \sigma_1^2\sigma_5\beta_1\varepsilon ux - \sigma_1^2\sigma_5\beta_2\varepsilon ux - 2\sigma_1^3\beta_2\Lambda y \\
& - \sigma_2(\sigma_1 - \sigma_2)^2k_1\varphi_1uy - \sigma_2(\sigma_4 - \sigma_5)^2k_1\varepsilon vx + \sigma_2\sigma_5^2k_1^2vy^2 + \sigma_2^2\sigma_4k_1\varepsilon vx - \sigma_2^2\sigma_5k_1^2vy^2 \\
& - \sigma_2^2\sigma_5k_1\varepsilon vx - \sigma_2^3k_1\varphi_2uy + \sigma_3(\sigma_4 - \sigma_5)^2k_2\varepsilon wx - \sigma_3^2\sigma_4k_2\varepsilon wx + \sigma_3^2\sigma_5k_2\varepsilon wx;
\end{aligned}
$$

$$f_{11} = (-\sigma_1^2\Lambda + \sigma_4^2\beta_1 ux + \sigma_5^2\beta_2 uy)[2\sigma_1\sigma_4\beta_1^2 ux(\sigma_1 - \sigma_4) - 2\sigma_1\sigma_5\beta_2^2 uy - \sigma_2\sigma_5 k_1\beta_2 vy$$
$$- \sigma_3\sigma_4 k_2\beta_1 wx(\sigma_4 - \sigma_3) - \sigma_4\sigma_5\beta_2\varepsilon x + \sigma_5^2\beta_2\varepsilon x] - \sigma_2\sigma_5 k_1\beta_2 uy[-(\sigma_1 - \sigma_2)^2\varphi_1 u + \sigma_5^2 k_1 vy]$$
$$- \sigma_3\sigma_4 k_2\beta_1 ux(\sigma_4 - \sigma_3)[-(\sigma_1 - \sigma_2)^2\varphi_2 u + \sigma_4^2 k_2 wx] - (\sigma_1^2\beta_1 ux + \sigma_3^2 k_2 wx)[\sigma_1\sigma_4\beta_1(\Lambda(\sigma_1 + \sigma_4)$$
$$+ \beta_1 u^2(\sigma_1 - \sigma_4)) - \sigma_3\sigma_4 k_2\beta_1 uw(\sigma_4 - \sigma_3) + \sigma_5\beta_2\varepsilon u(\sigma_5 - \sigma_4)] - [\sigma_1^2\beta_1 uy + \sigma_2^2 k_1 vy + (\sigma_4 - \sigma_5)^2\varepsilon x]$$
$$[\sigma_1\sigma_5\beta_2(\Lambda(\sigma_1 + \sigma_5) - \beta_2 u^2) - \sigma_2\sigma_5 k_1\beta_2 uv] - e_{11}(\sigma_4^2\beta_1 x + \sigma_5^2\beta_2 y) - e_{41}\sigma_4^2\beta_1 u - e_{51}\sigma_5^2\beta_2 u;$$
$$f_{21} = [-(\sigma_1 - \sigma_2)^2\varphi_1 u + \sigma_5^2 k_1 vy][\sigma_1\sigma_4^2\beta_1\varphi_1 x + \sigma_1\sigma_5\beta_2 k_1 vy(\sigma_1 - \sigma_5) - \sigma_2\sigma_4^2\beta_1\varphi_1 x$$
$$- \sigma_4(\sigma_1 - \sigma_2)^2\beta_1\varphi_1 x - \sigma_4\sigma_5^2 k_1\varepsilon x + (k_1 - \beta_2)(\sigma_5^2\varphi_1 y(\sigma_2\sigma_5 - \sigma_1\sigma_5 + (\sigma_1 - \sigma_2)^2))]$$
$$+ [-(\sigma_1 - \sigma_2)^2\varphi_1 u + \sigma_5^2 k_1 vy][\sigma_1\sigma_5\beta_2 k_1 uy(\sigma_1 - \sigma_5) + 2\sigma_1\sigma_5 k_1^2 vy(\sigma_2 - \sigma_5) + \sigma_5 k_1\varepsilon x(\sigma_4^2 - 2\sigma_4\sigma_5$$
$$+ 2\sigma_5^2)] - (\sigma_1^2\beta_1 ux + \sigma_3^2 k_2 wx)[\sigma_4(\sigma_1 - \sigma_2)\beta_1\varphi_1 u(\sigma_4 - \sigma_1 + \sigma_2) - \sigma_4\sigma_5^2 k_1\varepsilon u$$
$$+ \sigma_5 k_1\varepsilon v(\sigma_4^2 - 2\sigma_4\sigma_5 + 2\sigma_5^2) - (\sigma_1^2\beta_2 uy + \sigma_2^2 k_1 vy + (\sigma_4 - \sigma_5)^2\varepsilon x)][\sigma_1\sigma_5\beta_2 k_1 uv(\sigma_1 - \sigma_5)$$
$$+ \sigma_2\sigma_5 k_1^2 v^2(\sigma_2 - \sigma_5) + \varphi_1 u(k_1 - \beta_2)(-\sigma_1\sigma_5^2 + \sigma_2\sigma_5^2 + \sigma_5(\sigma_1 - \sigma_2)^2)] + e_{11}(\sigma_1 - \sigma_2)^2\varphi_1$$
$$- \sigma_5^2 k_1 y(e_{21} + e_{51});$$
$$f_{31} = (-\sigma_1^2\Lambda + \sigma_4^2\beta_1 ux + \sigma_5^2\beta_2 uy)[\sigma_1\sigma_4^2 k_1\varepsilon x + \sigma_4^2 k_2\varphi_2 x(\sigma_3 - \sigma_1) + \sigma_1\sigma_4\beta_1 k_2 wx(\sigma_1 - \sigma_4)$$
$$+ \sigma_5\beta_2\varphi_2 y(\sigma_1\sigma_5 - \sigma_3\sigma_5 - (\sigma_1 - \sigma_3)^2) - \sigma_4\beta_1\varphi_2 x(\sigma_3\sigma_4 + (\sigma_1 - \sigma_3)^2) + \sigma_4(\sigma_1 - \sigma_3)^2 k_2\varphi_2 x]$$
$$+ [-(\sigma_1 - \sigma_3)^2\varphi_2 u + \sigma_4^2 k_2 wx][\sigma_1\sigma_4\beta_1 k_2 ux(\sigma_1 - \sigma_4) + 2\sigma_3\sigma_4 k_2^2 wx(\sigma_3 - \sigma_4)]$$
$$- (\sigma_1^2\beta_1 ux + \sigma_3^2 k_2 wx)[\sigma_4\varphi_2 u(k_2 - \beta_1)(-\sigma_1\sigma_4 + \sigma_3\sigma_4 + (\sigma_1 - \sigma_3)^2) + \sigma_1\sigma_4\beta_1 k_2 uw(\sigma_1 - \sigma_4)$$
$$+ \sigma_3\sigma_4 k_2^2 w^2(\sigma_3 - \sigma_4)] - [\sigma_1^2\beta_2 uy + \sigma_2^2 k_1 vy + (\sigma_4 - \sigma_5)^2\varepsilon x][\sigma_5\beta_2\varphi_2 u(\sigma_1\sigma_5 - \sigma_3\sigma_5 - (\sigma_1 - \sigma_3)^2)]$$
$$+ e_{11}(\sigma_1 - \sigma_3)^2\varphi_2 - \sigma_4^2 k_2(e_{31} x + e_{41} w);$$
$$f_{41} = (-\sigma_1^2\Lambda + \sigma_4^2\beta_1 ux + \sigma_5^2\beta_2 uy)[\sigma_3 k_2\varphi_2 x(\sigma_1^2 - \sigma_1\sigma_3) + \sigma_1\sigma_4\beta_1^2 x^2(\sigma_4 - \sigma_1) + \sigma_1\sigma_5\beta_1\beta_2 xy(\sigma_5 - \sigma_1)]$$
$$+ [-(\sigma_1 - \sigma_3)^2\varphi_2 u + \sigma_4^2 k_2 wx][-\sigma_3\sigma_4 k_2^2 x^2(\sigma_3 + \sigma_4)] - (\sigma_1^2\beta_1 ux + \sigma_3^2 k_2 wx)[\sigma_3 k_2\varphi_2 u(\sigma_1^2 - \sigma_1\sigma_3)$$
$$+ 2\sigma_1\sigma_4\beta_1^2 ux(\sigma_4 - \sigma_1) + \sigma_1\sigma_5\beta_1\beta_2 uy(\sigma_5 - \sigma_1) - \sigma_3\sigma_4 k_2^2 wx(\sigma_3 + \sigma_4) - 2\sigma_1^3\beta_1\Lambda]$$
$$- [\sigma_1^2\beta_2 uy + \sigma_2^2 k_1 vy + (\sigma_4 - \sigma_5)^2\varepsilon x][\sigma_1\sigma_5\beta_1\beta_2 ux(\sigma_5 - \sigma_1)] + e_{11}\sigma_1^2\beta_1 x + e_{31}\sigma_3^2 k_2 x$$
$$+ e_{41}(\sigma_1^2\beta_1 u + \sigma_3^2 k_2 w);$$

$$f_{51} = (-\sigma_1^2\Lambda + \sigma_4^2\beta_1 ux + \sigma_5^2 uy)[\sigma_1\sigma_2^2 k_1\varphi_1 y + \sigma_1\sigma_4\beta_1\beta_2 ux(\sigma_4 - \sigma_1) + 2\sigma_1\sigma_5\beta_2^2 uy(\sigma_5 - \sigma_1) - 2\sigma_1^3\beta_2\Lambda$$
$$- \sigma_2 k_1\varphi_1 u(\sigma_1^2 - 2\sigma_1\sigma_2) + 2\sigma_2\sigma_5 k_1^2 vy(\sigma_5 - \sigma_2)] + [-(\sigma_1 - \sigma_2)^2\varphi_1 u + \sigma_5^2 k_1 vy][\sigma_2 k_1\varepsilon x(-(\sigma_4 - \sigma_5)^2$$
$$+ \sigma_2\sigma_5 - \sigma_2\sigma_5) + \sigma_2\sigma_5 k_1^2 y^2(\sigma_5 - \sigma_2)] + [-(\sigma_1 - \sigma_3)^2\varphi_2 u + \sigma_4^2 k_2 wx][\sigma_3 k_2\varepsilon x((\sigma_4 - \sigma_5)^2$$
$$- \sigma_3\sigma_4 + \sigma_3\sigma_5)] - (\sigma_1^2\beta_1 ux + \sigma_3^2 k_2 wx)[\sigma_1\sigma_4\beta_1\beta_2 uy(\sigma_4 - \sigma_1) + \sigma_1\varepsilon u((\sigma_4 - \sigma_5)^2 - \sigma_1\sigma_4 + \sigma_1\sigma_5)$$
$$+ \sigma_2 k_1\varepsilon v(-(\sigma_4 - \sigma_5)^2 + \sigma_2\sigma_4 - \sigma_2\sigma_5) + \sigma_3 k_2\varepsilon w((\sigma_4 0\sigma_5)^2 - \sigma_3\sigma_4 + \sigma_3\sigma_5)]$$
$$- [\sigma_1^2\beta_2 uy + \sigma_2^2 k_1 vy + (\sigma_4 - \sigma_5)^2\varepsilon x][\sigma_2 k_1\varphi_1 u(3\sigma_1\sigma_2 - \sigma_1^2 - \sigma_2^2) + \sigma_1\sigma_4\beta_1\beta_2 ux(\sigma_4 - \sigma_1)$$
$$+ 2\sigma_1\sigma_5\beta_2^2 uy(\sigma_5 - \sigma_1) + 2\sigma_2\sigma_5 k_1^2 vy(\sigma_5 - \sigma_2) - \sigma_2^3 k_1\varphi_2 u] + e_{21}\sigma_2^2 k_1 y + e_{41}(\sigma_4 - \sigma_5)^2$$
$$+ (\sigma_1^2\beta_2 u + \sigma_2^2 k_1 v)(e_{11} + e_{51}).$$

Appendix B

$a_{11} = -c_1 - \beta_1 x - \beta_2 y + \sigma_1 \phi;$ $a_{14} = -\beta_1 u;$
$a_{15} = -\beta_2 y;$ $a_{21} = -c_2 - k_1 y + \sigma_2 \phi;$
$a_{25} = -k_1 v;$ $a_{31} = \varphi_2;$
$a_{33} = -c_3 - k_2 x;$ $a_{34} = -k_2 w;$
$a_{41} = \beta_1 x;$ $a_{43} = \beta_1 x;$
$a_{43} = k_2 x;$ $a_{44} = \beta_1 u + k_2 w;$
$a_{51} = \beta_1 y;$ $a_{52} = k_1 y;$
$a_{54} = \varepsilon;$ $a_{55} = -c_5 + \beta_2 u + k_1 v,$
$b_{11} = a_{11}^2 + a_{14}a_{41} + a_{15}a_{51};$ $b_{12} = a_{15}a_{52};$
$b_{13} = a_{14}a_{43};$ $b_{14} = a_{11}a_{14} + a_{14}a_{44} + a_{15}a_{54};$
$b_{15} = a_{11}a_{15} + a_{15}a_{55};$ $b_{21} = a_{11}a_{21} + a_{21}a_{22} + a_{25}a_{51};$
$b_{22} = a_{22}^2 + a_{25}a_{52};$ $b_{24} = a_{14}a_{21} + a_{25}a_{54};$
$b_{25} = a_{15}a_{21} + a_{25}a_{55};$ $b_{31} = a_{11}a_{31} + a_{31}a_{33} + a_{34}a_{41};$
$b_{33} = a_{33}^2 + a_{34}a_{43};$ $b_{34} = a_{14}a_{31} + a_{33}a_{34} + a_{34}a_{44};$
$b_{35} = a_{15}a_{31};$ $b_{41} = a_{11}a_{41} + a_{31}a_{43} + a_{41}a_{44};$
$b_{43} = a_{33}a_{43} + a_{43}a_{44};$ $b_{44} = a_{14}a_{41} + a_{34}a_{43} + a_{44}^2;$
$b_{45} = a_{15}a_{41};$ $b_{51} = a_{11}a_{51} + a_{21}a_{52} + a_{41}a_{54} + a_{51}a_{55};$
$b_{52} = a_{22}a_{52} + a_{52}a_{55};$ $b_{53} = a_{43}a_{54};$
$b_{54} = a_{14}a_{51} + a_{44}a_{54} + a_{54}a_{55};$ $b_{55} = a_{15}a_{51} + a_{25}a_{52} + a_{55}^2,$
$c_{11} = a_{11}b_{11} + a_{21}b_{12} + a_{31}b_{13} + a_{41}b_{14} + a_{51}b_{15};$ $c_{12} = a_{52}b_{15};$
$c_{13} = a_{33}b_{13} + a_{43}b_{14};$ $c_{14} = a_{14}b_{11} + a_{34}b_{13} + a_{44}b_{14} + a_{54}b_{15};$
$c_{15} = a_{15}b_{11} + a_{25}b_{12} + a_{55}b_{15};$ $c_{21} = a_{11}b_{21} + a_{22}b_{22} + a_{41}b_{24} + a_{51}b_{25};$
$c_{22} = a_{52}b_{25};$ $c_{23} = a_{43}b_{24};$
$c_{24} = a_{14}b_{21} + a_{44}b_{24} + a_{54}b_{25};$ $c_{25} = a_{15}b_{21} + a_{25}b_{22} + a_{55}b_{25};$
$c_{31} = a_{11}b_{31} + a_{31}b_{33} + a_{41}b_{34} + a_{51}b_{35};$ $c_{32} = a_{52}b_{35};$
$c_{33} = a_{33}b_{33} + a_{43}b_{34};$ $c_{34} = a_{14}b_{31} + a_{34}b_{33} + a_{44}b_{34} + a_{54}b_{35};$
$c_{35} = a_{15}b_{31} + a_{55}b_{35};$ $c_{41} = a_{11}b_{41} + a_{31}b_{43} + a_{41}b_{44} + a_{51}b_{55};$
$c_{42} = a_{52}b_{45};$ $c_{43} = a_{33}b_{43} + a_{43}b_{44};$

$$c_{44} = a_{14}b_{41} + a_{34}b_{43} + a_{44}b_{44} + a_{54}b_{45}; \quad c_{45} = a_{15}b_{41} + a_{55}b_{45};$$
$$c_{51} = a_{11}b_{51} + a_{21}b_{52} + a_{31}b_{53} + a_{41}b_{54} + a_{51}b_{55}; \quad c_{52} = a_{52}b_{55};$$
$$c_{53} = a_{33}b53 + a_{43}b_{54}; \quad c_{54} = a_{14}b_{51} + a_{34}b_{53} + a_{44}b_{54} + a_{54}b_{55};$$
$$c_{55} = a_{15}b_{51} + a_{25}b_{52} + a_{55}b_{55};$$
$$d_{11} = b_{11}^2 + b_{12}b_{21} + b_{13}b_{31} + b_{14}b_{41} + b_{15}b_{51}; \quad d_{12} = b_{11}b_{12} + b_{12}b_{22} + b_{15}b_{52};$$
$$d_{13} = b_{11}b_{13} + b_{13}b_{33} + b_{14}b_{43} + b_{15}b_{53}; \quad d_{14} = b_{11}b_{14} + b_{12}b_{24} + b_{13}b_{34} + b_{14}b_{44} + b_{15}b_{54};$$
$$d_{15} = b_{11}b_{15} + b_{12}b_{25} + b_{13}b_{35} + b_{14}b_{45} + b_{15}b_{55}; \quad d_{21} = b_{11}b_{21} + b_{21}b_{22} + b_{24}b_{41} + b_{25}b_{51};$$
$$d_{22} = b_{12}b_{21} + b_{22}^2 + b_{25}b_{52}; \quad d_{23} = b_{13}b_{21} + b_{24}b_{43} + b_{25}b_{53};$$
$$d_{24} = b_{14}b_{21} + b_{22}b_{24} + b_{24}b_{44} + b_{25}b_{54}; \quad d_{25} = b_{15}b_{21} + b_{22}b_{25} + b_{24}b_{45} + b_{25}b_{55};$$
$$d_{31} = b_{11}b_{31} + b_{31}b_{33} + b_{34}b_{41} + b_{35}b_{51}; \quad d_{32} = b_{12}b_{31} + b_{35}b_{52};$$
$$d_{33} = b_{13}b_{31} + b_{33}^2 + b_{34}b_{43} + b_{35}b_{53}; \quad d_{34} = b_{14}b_{31} + b_{33}b_{34} + b_{34}b_{44} + b_{35}b_{54};$$
$$d_{35} = b_{15}b_{31} + b_{33}b_{35} + b_{34}b_{45} + b_{35}b_{55}; \quad d_{41} = b_{11}b_{41} + b_{31}b_{43} + b_{41}b_{44} + b_{45}b_{51};$$
$$d_{42} = b_{12}b_{41} + b_{45}b_{52}; \quad d_{43} = b_{13}b_{41} + b_{33}b_{43} + b_{43}b_{44} + b_{45}b_{53};$$
$$d_{44} = b_{14}b_{41} + b_{34}b_{43} + b_{44}^2 + b_{45}b_{54}; \quad d_{45} = b_{15}b_{41} + b_{35}b_{43} + b_{44}b_{45} + b_{45}b_{44};$$
$$d_{51} = b_{11}b_{51} + b_{21}b_{52} + b_{31}b_{53} + b_{41}b_{54} + b_{51}b_{55}; \quad d_{52} = b_{12}b_{51} + b_{22}b_{52} + b_{52}b_{55};$$
$$d_{53} = b_{31}b_{51} + b_{33}b_{53} + b_{43}b_{54} + b_{53}b_{55}; \quad d_{54} = b_{14}b_{51} + b_{24}b_{52} + b_{34}b_{53} + b_{44}b_{54} + b_{54}b_{55};$$
$$d_{55} = b_{15}b_{51} + b_{25}b_{52} + b_{35}b_{53} + b_{45}b_{54} + b_{55}^2.$$

References

1. Ruan, W.; Wang, W. Dynamical behavior of an epidemic model with a nonlinear incidence rate. *J. Differ. Equ.* **2003**, *18*, 135–163. [CrossRef]
2. Anderson, R.M.; May, R.M. Population biology of infectious diseases: Part I. *Nature* **1979**, *280*, 361–367. [CrossRef]
3. Wang, W. Global behavior of an seirs epidemic model with time delays. *Appl. Math. Lett.* **2002**, *15*, 423–428. [CrossRef]
4. Meng, X.; Chen, L.; Wu, B. A delay sir epidemic model with pulse vaccination and incubation times. *Nonlinear Anal. Real.* **2010**, *11*, 88–98. [CrossRef]
5. Cai, L.; Xiang, J.; Li, X.; Lashari, A.A. A two-strain epidemic model with mutant strain and vaccination. *Appl. Math. Comput.* **2012**, *40*, 125–142. [CrossRef]
6. Maia, M.; Mimmo, I.; Li, X.Z. Subthreshold coexistence of strains: The impact of vaccination and mutation. *MBE* **2007**, *4*, 287–317.
7. Baba, I.A.; Kaymakmzade, B.; Hincal, E. Two strain epidemic model with two vaccinations. *Solitons Fractals* **2018**, *106*, 342–347. [CrossRef]
8. Bilgen, K.; Evren, H. Two-strain epidemic model with two vaccinations and two time delayed. *Qual. Quant.* **2018**, *52*, 695–709.
9. Øksendal, B. Stochastic Differential Equations: An Introduction with Applications. *J. Am. Stat. Assoc.* **2006**, *51*, 1721–1732.
10. Allen, L.J.S. TAn introduction to stochastic epidemic models, in: Mathematical Epidemiology. *Math. Epidemiol.* **2008**, *10*, 81–130.
11. Beddington, J.R.; May, R.M. Harvesting natural populations in a randomly fluctuating environment. *Science* **1977**, *197*, 463–465. [CrossRef] [PubMed]
12. Liu, W. A SIRS epidemic model incorporating media coverage with random. *Abstr. Appl. Anal.* **2023**, *2013*, 764–787. [CrossRef]
13. Thomas, C.G.; Shelemyahu, Z. Introduction to Stochastic Differential Equations. *J. Am. Stat. Assoc.* **1989**, *84*, 1104.
14. Mao, X.R. *Stochastic Differential Equations and Their Applications*; Horwood: Chichester, UK, 1997.
15. Beretta, E.; Kolmanovskii, V.; Shaikhet, L. Stability of epidemic model with time delays influenced by stochastic perturbations. *Math. Comput. Simul.* **1998**, *45*, 269–277. [CrossRef]
16. Mao, X.R.; Marion, G.; Renshaw, E. Environmental Brownian noise suppresses explosions in population dynamics. *Stoch. Process. Their Appl.* **2002**, *97*, 95–110. [CrossRef]
17. Yu, J.; Jiang, D.; Shi, N. Global stability of two-group SIR model with random perturbation. *J. Math. Anal. Appl.* **2009**, *360*, 235–244. [CrossRef]
18. Britton, T. Stochastic epidemic models: A survey. *Math. Biosci.* **2010**, *225*, 24–35. [CrossRef]
19. Ball, F.; Sirl, D.; Trapman, P. Analysis of a stochastic SIR epidemic on a random network incorporating household structure. *Math. Biosci.* **2010**, *224*, 53–73. [CrossRef]
20. Jiang, D.; Ji, C.; Shi, N.; Yu, J. The long time behavior of DI SIR epidemic model with stochastic perturbation. *J. Math. Anal. Appl.* **2010**, *372*, 162–180. [CrossRef]
21. Jiang, D.; Yu, J.; Ji, C.; Shi, N. Asymptotic behavior of global positive solution to a stochastic SIR model. *Math. Comput. Model.* **2011**, *54*, 221–232. [CrossRef]

22. Gray, A.; Greenhalgh, D.; Hu, L.; Mao, X.R.; Pan, J. A stochastic differential equation SIS epidemic model. *J. Appl. Math.* **2011**, *71*, 876–902. [CrossRef]
23. Cai, Y.; Wang, X.; Wang, W.; Zhao, M. Stochastic dynamics of a SIRS epidemic model with ratio-dependent incidence rate. *Abstr. Appl. Anal.* **2013**, *2013*, 415–425. [CrossRef]
24. Dieu, N.T.; Nguyen, D.H.; Du, N.H.; Yin, G. Classification of asymptotic behavior in a stochastic SIR model. *J. Appl. Dyn. Syst.* **2016**, *15*, 1062–1084. [CrossRef]
25. Du, N.H.; Nhu, N.N. Permanence and extinction for the stochastic SIR epidemic model. *J. Differ. Equ.* **2020**, *269*, 9619–9652. [CrossRef]
26. Liu, W.B.; Zheng, Q.B. A stochastic SIS epidemic model incorporating media coverage in a two patch setting. *Comput. Math. Appl.* **2015**, *262*, 160–168. [CrossRef]
27. Tan, Y.P.; Cai, Y.L.; Wang, X.Q.; Peng, Z.H.; Wang, K.; Yao, R.X.; Wang, W.M. Stochastic dynamics of an SIS epidemiological model with media coverage. *Math. Comput. Simul.* **2023**, *204*, 1–27. [CrossRef]
28. Meyn, D.S.P.; Tweedie, R.L. *Markov Chains and Stochastic Stability*; Springer: London, UK, 1993.
29. Nummelin, E. *General Irreducible Markov Chains and Non-Negative Operations*; Cambridge Press: Cambridge, UK, 1984.
30. Jarner, S.F.; Roberts, G.O. Polynomial convergence rates of Markov chains. *Ann. Appl. Probab.* **2002**, *12*, 224–247. [CrossRef]
31. Kliemann, W. Recurrence and invariant measures for degenerate diffusions. *Ann. Probab.* **1987**, *15*, 690–707. [CrossRef]
32. Higham, D.J. An algorithmic introduction to numerical simulation of stochastic differential equations. *SIAM Rev.* **2001**, *43*, 525–546. [CrossRef]

mathematics

Article

Stability and Bifurcations in a Nutrient–Phytoplankton–Zooplankton Model with Delayed Nutrient Recycling with Gamma Distribution

Mihaela Sterpu [1,*], Carmen Rocşoreanu [2], Raluca Efrem [1] and Sue Ann Campbell [3]

1 Department of Mathematics, University of Craiova, 200585 Craiova, Romania; raluca.efrem@edu.ucv.ro
2 Department of Statistics and Economic Informatics, University of Craiova, 200585 Craiova, Romania; carmen.rocsoreanu@edu.ucv.ro
3 Department of Applied Mathematics, University of Waterloo, Waterloo, ON N2L 3G1, Canada; sacampbell@uwaterloo.ca
* Correspondence: msterpu@inf.ucv.ro; Tel.: +40-744-150-288

Abstract: Two nutrient–phytoplankton–zooplankton (NZP) models for a closed ecosystem that incorporates a delay in nutrient recycling, obtained using the gamma distribution function with one or two degrees of freedom, are analysed. The models are described by systems of ordinary differential equations of four and five dimensions. The purpose of this study is to investigate how the mean delay of the distribution and the total nutrients affect the stability of the equilibrium solutions. Local stability theory and bifurcation theory are used to determine the long-time dynamics of the models. It is found that both models exhibit comparable qualitative dynamics. There are a maximum of three equilibrium points in each of the two models, and at most one of them is locally asymptotically stable. The change of stability from one equilibrium to another takes place through a transcritical bifurcation. In some hypotheses on the functional response, the nutrient–phytoplankton–zooplankton equilibrium loses stability via a supercritical Hopf bifurcation, causing the apparition of a stable limit cycle. The way in which the results are consistent with prior research and how they extend them is discussed. Finally, various application-related consequences of the results of the theoretical study are deduced.

Keywords: plankton; nutrient recycling; delay; gamma distribution; closed ecosystem; dynamics; bifurcation

MSC: 37N25; 35G10; 34D20

Citation: Sterpu, M.; Rocşoreanu, C.; Efrem, R.; Campbell, S.A. Stability and Bifurcations in a Nutrient–Phytoplankton–Zooplankton Model with Delayed Nutrient Recycling with Gamma Distribution. *Mathematics* **2023**, *11*, 2911. https://doi.org/10.3390/math11132911

Academic Editors: Mihaela Neamţu, Eva Kaslik and Anca Rădulescu

Received: 12 June 2023
Revised: 25 June 2023
Accepted: 27 June 2023
Published: 28 June 2023

1. Introduction

Plankton are floating organisms that provide a food source for other organisms ranging from shellfish to whales. As such, they play a crucial role in aquatic foodwebs [1]. Phytoplankton are organisms, such as algae, which carry out photosynthesis and are an important means of carbon storage in the ocean [2]. Zooplankton feed on phytoplankton or other zooplankton and include insect larvae and jellyfish. Due to their fundamental role in aquatic ecosystems and their influence on the global carbon cycle, it is important to understand the temporal dynamics of plankton ecosystems.

A variety of different models have been proposed for plankton ecosystems, emphasizing different aspects of these complex systems [3–11]. Here, we study a model due to Kloosterman et al. [12], which focussed on two aspects. The chemical nutrients in the system are recycled, thus the system is closed—the total amount of nutrient remains constant. This recycling takes time (e.g., due to decomposition of dead organisms) and thus the model should include a time delay. Both are important features of plankton ecosystems that lead to interesting mathematics.

The model of Kloosterman et al. [12] is called an NPZ model as it is a system with three compartments, representing the dissolved nutrient (N), the amount of phytoplankton (P), and the amount of zooplankton (Z). It is described by the following equations:

$$\begin{cases} \frac{dN}{dt}(t) & = & \lambda\int_0^\infty P(t-u)\eta(u)du + \delta\int_0^\infty Z(t-u)\eta(u)du \\ & & +(1-\gamma)g\int_0^\infty Z(t-u)h(P(t-u))\eta(u)du - \mu P(t)f(N(t)) \\ \frac{dP(t)}{dt} & = & \mu P(t)f(N(t)) - gZh(P(t)) - \lambda P(t) \\ \frac{dZ(t)}{dt} & = & \gamma g Z(t)h(P(t)) - \delta Z(t) \end{cases}. \quad (1)$$

Here, $\lambda, \mu, \gamma, \delta$ and g are positive parameters representing biological properties while η is an appropriate distribution representing the time delay in nutrient recycling.

The function f stands for the phytoplankton nutrient uptake as a function of the available nutrient and it has the following properties [4]:

$$f(0) = 0,\ f'(N) > 0,\ f''(N) < 0,\ \lim_{N\to\infty} f(N) = 1. \quad (2)$$

Similarly, the function h stands for the available phytoplankton and it must satisfy conditions [13,14]:

$$h(0) = 0,\ h'(P) > 0,\ \lim_{P\to\infty} h(P) = 1. \quad (3)$$

Kloosterman et al. [12] investigated how this model for a planktonic ecosystem is affected by the quantity of biomass it contains and by the delay distribution. They described the existence of the equilibrium points and gave some stability results for a general distribution function, using methods as in [15]. Other stability results considered particular cases of the distribution function and relied primarily on numerical work.

In this study, we assume that the delay follows a gamma distribution function, with either one or two degrees of freedom, as these numbers of freedom degrees correspond to the biological data. We derive two models, described by systems of ordinary differential equations (ODEs), and analyse how the local stability and local bifurcation of the equilibrium points depend on the amount of total nutrients and on the mean delay of the distribution.

For the numerical simulations we have used a Holling type II functional response for f,

$$f(N) = \frac{N}{N + k_N},$$

with $k_N > 0$. For function h, we used either a Holling Type II functional response

$$h(P) = \frac{P}{P + k_P},$$

or a Holling Type III response

$$h(P) = \frac{P^2}{P^2 + k_P^2},$$

with $k_P > 0$.

Using this delay, we have extended the results obtained in [12].

2. The Models

Consider η the gamma distribution of mean τ, with k degrees of freedom:

$$\eta(u) = \begin{cases} \frac{k^k}{\tau^k(k-1)!}u^{k-1}e^{-\frac{k}{\tau}u},\ u \geq 0 \\ 0,\ u < 0 \end{cases} \quad (4)$$

Starting from system (1) and using the gamma distribution function for the cases $k = 1$ and $k = 2$, and some appropriate new variables, we derive two models, described by systems of ordinary differential equations (ODEs), without explicit delay. This reduction is often called the linear chain trick [16–18].

For the case $k = 1$, we obtain a 4-dimensional system of ODEs, which is then reduced to a three-dimensional one. This will be called the weak model.

For $k = 2$, we obtain a five-dimensional system of ODEs that can be reduced to a four-dimensional system, which will be called the strong model.

2.1. The Weak Model

If $k = 1$, we have $\eta(u) = \frac{1}{\tau}e^{-\frac{u}{\tau}}$, for $u \geq 0$. Denoting

$$Q(t) = \int_0^\infty [\lambda P(t-u) + \delta Z(t-u) + (1-\gamma)gZ(t-u)h(P(t-u))]e^{-\frac{u}{\tau}}du, \tag{5}$$

the equation describing the evolution of the dissolved nutrient N can be written as:

$$\frac{dN}{dt}(t) = \frac{1}{\tau}Q(t) - \mu P(t)f(N(t)).$$

In addition, using the change of variable $t - u = \theta$, we have:

$$\begin{aligned} Q(t) &= -\int_t^{-\infty} [\lambda P(\theta) + \delta Z(\theta) + (1-\gamma)gZ(\theta)h(P(\theta))]e^{-\frac{t-\theta}{\tau}}d\theta \\ &= \int_{-\infty}^{t} [\lambda P(\theta) + \delta Z(\theta) + (1-\gamma)gZ(\theta)h(P(\theta))]e^{-\frac{t-\theta}{\tau}}d\theta. \end{aligned}$$

It follows:

$$\begin{aligned} \frac{dQ}{dt}(t) &= \lambda P(t) + \delta Z(t) + (1-\gamma)gZ(t)h(P(t)) \\ &+ \int_{-\infty}^{t} [\lambda P(\theta) + \delta Z(\theta) + (1-\gamma)gZ(\theta)h(P(\theta))]e^{-\frac{t-\theta}{\tau}}\left(-\frac{1}{\tau}\right)d\theta. \end{aligned}$$

With the change of variable $t - u = \theta$, we have

$$\frac{dQ}{dt}(t) = \lambda P(t) + \delta Z(t) + (1-\gamma)gZ(t)h(P(t)) - \frac{1}{\tau}Q(t)$$

Thus, we obtain a 4D model ($NPZQ$), called "the weak model" in the following, described by

$$\begin{cases} \frac{dN(t)}{dt} = \frac{1}{\tau}Q(t) - \mu P(t)f(N(t)), \\ \frac{dP(t)}{dt} = \mu P(t)f(N(t)) - gZh(P(t)) - \lambda P(t), \\ \frac{dZ(t)}{dt} = \gamma gZ(t)h(P(t)) - \delta Z(t), \\ \frac{dQ(t)}{dt} = \lambda P(t) + \delta Z(t) + (1-\gamma)gZ(t)h(P(t)) - \frac{1}{\tau}Q(t). \end{cases} \tag{6}$$

Since the conservation law $\frac{d}{dt}(N + P + Z + Q) = 0$ is fulfilled, we obtain $N(t) + P(t) + Z(t) + Q(t) = N_T^1 = constant$. The substitution $Q(t) = N_T^1 - N(t) - P(t) - Z(t)$, leads to the following reduced 3D system:

$$\begin{cases} \frac{dN(t)}{dt} = \frac{1}{\tau}(N_T^1 - N(t) - P(t) - Z(t)) - \mu P(t)f(N(t)) \\ \frac{dP(t)}{dt} = \mu P(t)f(N(t)) - gZh(P(t)) - \lambda P(t), \\ \frac{dZ(t)}{dt} = \gamma gZ(t)h(P(t)) - \delta Z(t). \end{cases} \tag{7}$$

with the phase space

$$D_1 = \left\{(N,P,Z), N \geq 0, P \geq 0, Z \geq 0, N+P+Z \leq N_T^1\right\}. \tag{8}$$

2.2. The Strong Model

If the number of freedom degrees is $k = 2$, we have $\eta(u) = \frac{4}{\tau^2}ue^{-\frac{2}{\tau}u}$, for $u \geq 0$. Denoting

$$Q_1(t) = \int_0^{\infty} [\lambda P(t-u) + \delta Z(t-u) + (1-\gamma)gZ(t-u)h(P(t-u))]\frac{2}{\tau}ue^{-\frac{2}{\tau}u}du, \tag{9}$$

the equation describing the evolution of the dissolved phytoplankton nutrient from (1) reads:

$$\frac{dN}{dt}(t) = \frac{2}{\tau}Q_1(t) - \mu P(t)f(N(t)). \tag{10}$$

In addition, using the change of variable $t - u = \theta$, we have

$$\begin{aligned} Q_1(t) &= -\frac{2}{\tau}\int_t^{\infty} [\lambda P(\theta) + \delta Z(\theta) + (1-\gamma)gZ(\theta)h(P(\theta))](t-\theta)e^{-\frac{2}{\tau}(t-\theta)}d\theta \\ &= \frac{2}{\tau}\int_{-\infty}^{t} [\lambda P(\theta) + \delta Z(\theta) + (1-\gamma)gZ(\theta)h(P(\theta))](t-\theta)e^{-\frac{2}{\tau}(t-\theta)}d\theta. \end{aligned}$$

Denoting by

$$Q_2(t) = \int_{-\infty}^{t} [\lambda P(\theta) + \delta Z(\theta) + (1-\gamma)gZ(\theta)h(P(\theta))]e^{-\frac{2}{\tau}(t-\theta)}d\theta, \tag{11}$$

it follows:

$$\frac{dQ_1}{dt}(t) = \frac{2}{\tau}(Q_2(t) - Q_1(t)), \tag{12}$$

$$\begin{aligned} \frac{dQ_2}{dt}(t) &= \lambda P(t) + \delta Z(t) + (1-\gamma)gZ(t)h(P(t)) \\ &\quad + \int_{-\infty}^{t} [\lambda P(\theta) + \delta Z(\theta) + (1-\gamma)gZ(\theta)h(P(\theta))]e^{-\frac{2}{\tau}(t-\theta)}\left(-\frac{2}{\tau}\right)d\theta \\ &= \lambda P(t) + \delta Z(t) + (1-\gamma)gZ(t)h(P(t)) - \frac{2}{\tau}Q_2(t). \end{aligned}$$

Thus, we obtain the following 5D model ($NPZQ_1Q_2$), also called "the strong model":

$$\begin{cases} \frac{dN(t)}{dt} = \frac{2}{\tau}Q_1(t) - \mu P(t)f(N(t)), \\ \frac{dP(t)}{dt} = \mu P(t)f(N(t)) - gZh(P(t)) - \lambda P(t), \\ \frac{dZ(t)}{dt} = \gamma gZ(t)h(P(t)) - \delta Z(t), \\ \frac{dQ_1(t)}{dt} = \frac{2}{\tau}(Q_2(t) - Q_1(t)), \\ \frac{dQ_2}{dt}(t) = \lambda P(t) + \delta Z(t) + (1-\gamma)gZ(t)h(P(t)) - \frac{2}{\tau}Q_2(t). \end{cases} \tag{13}$$

Obviously, the conservation law

$$\frac{d}{dt}(N + P + Z + Q_1 + Q_2) = 0 \tag{14}$$

is fulfilled, so we can substitute $Q_2(t) = N_T^2 - N(t) - P(t) - Z(t) - Q_1(t)$, leading to the following reduced 4D system of ordinary differential equations (ODE):

$$\begin{cases} \frac{dN(t)}{dt} = \frac{2}{\tau}Q_1(t) - \mu P(t)f(N(t)), \\ \frac{dP(t)}{dt} = \mu P(t)f(N(t)) - gZh(P(t)) - \lambda P(t), \\ \frac{dZ(t)}{dt} = \gamma g Z(t)h(P(t)) - \delta Z(t), \\ \frac{dQ_1(t)}{dt} = \frac{2}{\tau}(N_T^2 - N(t) - P(t) - Z(t) - 2Q_1(t)), \end{cases} \quad (15)$$

with the phase space

$$D_2 = \left\{(N, P, Z, Q_1) \in R^4, N \geq 0, P \geq 0, Z \geq 0, Q_1 > 0, N + P + Z + Q_1 \leq N_T^2\right\}. \quad (16)$$

Also, for consistency, the initial conditions of the ODE model must satisfy

$$Q_1(0) = -\frac{2}{\tau}\int_{-\infty}^{0}[\lambda P(\theta) + \delta Z(\theta) + (1-\gamma)gZ(\theta)h(P(\theta))]\theta e^{\frac{2}{\tau}\theta}d\theta$$

2.3. *The Model without Delay*

In the absence of delay, the model (1) is described by the following equations:

$$\begin{cases} \frac{dN(t)}{dt} = \lambda P(t) + \delta Z(t) + (1-\gamma)gZ(t)h(P(t)) - \mu P(t)f(N(t)) \\ \frac{dP(t)}{dt} = \mu P(t)f(N(t)) - gZh(P(t)) - \lambda P(t) \\ \frac{dZ(t)}{dt} = \gamma g Z(t)h(P(t)) - \delta Z(t) \end{cases} . \quad (17)$$

Using conservation law $N_T^0 = N(t) + P(t) + Z(t)$, this system can be reduced to the following 2D system:

$$\begin{cases} \frac{dP}{dt} = \mu P f(N_T^0 - P - Z) - gZh(P) - \lambda P \\ \frac{dZ}{dt} = \gamma g Z h(P) - \delta Z \end{cases}, \quad (18)$$

with the phase space

$$D_0 = \left\{(P, Z) \in \mathbb{R}^2, P \geq 0, Z \geq 0, P + Z \leq N_T^0\right\}. \quad (19)$$

In the following, N_T shall denote the biomass of the model. Thus, when referring to the model without delay $N_T = N_T^0$, for the weak model $N_T = N_T^1$, while for the strong model $N_T = N_T^2$.

3. Equilibrium Solutions

In this section, we determine the stationary solutions of the two reduced systems (7) and (15), for the NPZ model with delayed gamma distribution, with one or two degrees of freedom. These solutions correspond to the equilibrium points of the corresponding dynamical systems.

Each of the three systems has at most three equilibrium points în the region of interest, namely:

- A trivial equilibrium E_1, with no phytoplankton and no zooplankton;
- An equilibrium with phytoplankton and no zooplankton, denoted E_2;
- An equilibrium with both phytoplankton and zooplankton, denoted E_3.

These equilibria may coexist for certain values of the total nutrients. The same property is valid for the reduced 2D system (18) for the NPZ model without delay.

3.1. *Equilibrium Points for the System without Delay*

In [12], it is shown that under the assumptions

$$\lambda < \mu, \qquad \delta < g\gamma \quad (20)$$

system (18) has at most three equilibrium points in D_0, depending on the value of the total nutrient N_T. Denoting as

$$N_{T_1} = f^{-1}\left(\frac{\lambda}{\mu}\right), \quad N_{T_2} = f^{-1}\left(\frac{\lambda}{\mu}\right) + h^{-1}\left(\frac{\delta}{g\gamma}\right), \tag{21}$$

the equilibrium points of system (18) are $E_1 = (0,0)$, for all N_T, $E_2 = (\hat{P},0)$, with $\hat{P} = N_T - N_{T_1}$, for all $N_T \geq N_{T_1}$, and $E_3 = (P^*, Z^*)$, with $P^* = h^{-1}\left(\frac{\delta}{g\gamma}\right)$, and Z^* unique solution of the equation

$$Z^* = \frac{\mu\gamma}{\delta}P^*\left(f(N_T - P^* - Z^*) - \frac{\lambda}{\mu}\right), \tag{22}$$

for all N_T, with $N_T \geq N_{T_2}$.

3.2. *Equilibrium Points for the Reduced Weak System (7)*

The system (7) possesses at most three equilibria with the first three coordinates non-negative, solutions of the system

$$\begin{cases} \frac{1}{\tau}(N_T - N - P - Z) - \mu P f(N) = 0 \\ \mu P f(N) - gZh(P) - \lambda P = 0 \\ \gamma g Z h(P) - \delta Z = 0 \end{cases} \tag{23}$$

It follows that the trivial equilibrium is $E_1 = (N_T, 0, 0)$.

The equilibrium with only phytoplankton is $E_2 = (\hat{N}, \hat{P}, 0)$, with $f(\hat{N}) = \frac{\lambda}{\mu}$. Taking into account the properties of f, if the condition

$$\lambda < \mu \tag{24}$$

is satisfied (that is the growth rate of the plankton must be greater than the death rate), then there exists an unique $\hat{N}$, namely $\hat{N} = f^{-1}\left(\frac{\lambda}{\mu}\right)$, satisfying this condition. From the first equation we obtain

$$\hat{P} = \frac{1}{1+\lambda\tau}(N_T - \hat{N}). \tag{25}$$

while from the conservation law we obtain

$$\hat{Q} = \lambda\tau\hat{P}. \tag{26}$$

This equilibrium is in the domain of interest D_1 if and only if $N_T \geq \hat{N}$. Note that if $N_T = f^{-1}\left(\frac{\lambda}{\mu}\right)$, then $E_1 = E_2$.

The equilibrium with both phyto- and zooplankton is $E_3 = (N^*, P^*, Z^*)$, with $h(P^*) = \frac{\delta}{\gamma g}$ from the third equation in (23). If condition

$$\delta < \gamma g \tag{27}$$

is satisfied, then there exists an unique $P^* > 0$ such that $h(P^*) = \frac{\delta}{\gamma g}$, namely

$$P^* = h^{-1}\left(\frac{\delta}{\gamma g}\right). \tag{28}$$

and

$$Z^* = \frac{\gamma\mu}{\delta}\left(f(N^*) - \frac{\lambda}{\mu}\right)h^{-1}\left(\frac{\delta}{\gamma g}\right). \tag{29}$$

The condition $f(N^*) \geq \frac{\lambda}{\mu}$ must be satisfied in order to have $Z^* \geq 0$. As f is an increasing function, it follows that $N^* \geq f^{-1}(\frac{\lambda}{\mu})$ and using the first equation of system (23) we have

$$\begin{aligned} N_T &= N^* + P^* + Z^* + \tau\mu P^* f(N^*) \\ &\geq f^{-1}\left(\frac{\lambda}{\mu}\right) + (1+\lambda\tau)h^{-1}\left(\frac{\delta}{\gamma g}\right). \end{aligned}$$

To show that there exists an N^* such that

$$N_T = N^* + P^*\left(1 - \frac{\gamma\lambda}{\delta} + \mu\left(\tau + \frac{\gamma}{\delta}\right)f(N^*)\right) \tag{30}$$

is satisfied, consider the function

$$F(N) = N + \left(1 - \frac{\gamma\lambda}{\delta} + \mu\left(\tau + \frac{\gamma}{\delta}\right)f(N)\right)h^{-1}\left(\frac{\delta}{\gamma g}\right) - N_T.$$

It follows that $F\left(f^{-1}\left(\frac{\lambda}{\mu}\right)\right) < 0$ and $\lim_{N\to\infty} F(N) = \infty$. As F is an increasing function, there exists an unique value N^* such that $F(N^*) = 0$.

Denote, as in [12], $N_{T_2}(\tau) = f^{-1}\left(\frac{\lambda}{\mu}\right) + (1+\lambda\tau)h^{-1}\left(\frac{\delta}{\gamma g}\right)$. Remark that $N_{T_2}(0) = N_{T_2}$. As a consequence, the third equilibrium point (N^*, P^*, Z^*) exists in D_1 and is uniquely determined by (30) if the conditions $N_T \geq N_{T_2}(\tau)$ and (20) are satisfied. Note that if $N_T = N_{T_2}(\tau)$, then $E_3 = E_2$. The transitions between the equilibrium points will be discussed further in Section 5.

Finally, we note that if (N_0, P_0, Z_0) is an equilibrium of system (7), then (N_0, P_0, Z_0, Q_0), with $Q_0 = \tau\mu P_0 f(N_0)$ is an equilibrium point for system solution of system (6) and conversely.

In Figure 1, the coordinates N, P, Z, Q of the three equilibrium points are represented as functions of the total nutrient N_T, for a fixed $\tau = 5$. As function h, a type II functional response was considered. The values of the parameters used for simulations are $\mu = 5.9$, $g = 7$, $\lambda = 0.017$, $\gamma = 0.7$, $\delta = 0.17$, $k_N = 1$, $k_P = 1$, as in [12]. For these values of the parameters, the following values where obtained for thresholds: $N_{T_1} = 0.0028$, $N_{T_2}(\tau) = 0.0418$.

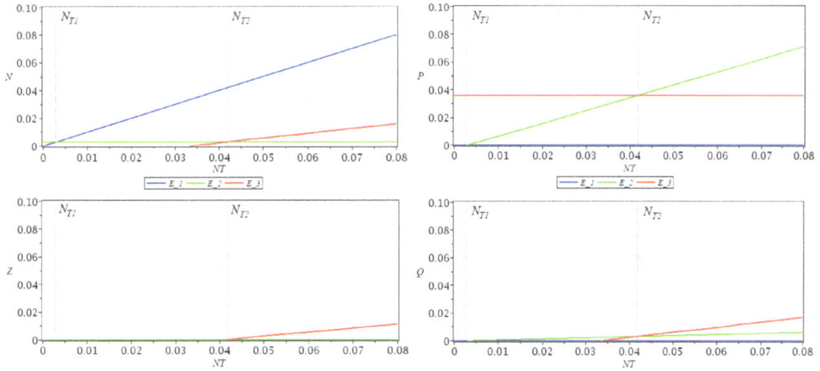

Figure 1. N, P, Z, Q as functions of N_T, for fixed $\tau = 5$, for the equilibrium points E_1 (blue line), E_2 (green line), E_3 (red line), using a type II response.

3.3. Equilibria for the Reduced Strong Model (15)

The equilibria of system (15) correspond to the solutions of the system

$$\begin{cases} \frac{2}{\tau}Q_1 - \mu P f(N) = 0 \\ \mu P f(N) - gZh(P) - \lambda P = 0 \\ \gamma g Z h(P) - \delta Z = 0 \\ \frac{2}{\tau}(N_T - N - P - Z - 2Q_1) = 0 \end{cases} \tag{31}$$

Substituting

$$Q_1 = \frac{\tau}{2}\mu P f(N), \tag{32}$$

from the first equation into the last equation in (31), the remaining three equations coincide with system (23). Consequently, we obtain the same expressions for N, P, and Z as for system (23). Taking into account (32), we obtain the following equilibrium points for system (15):

(1) The trivial equilibrium $E_1 = (N_T, 0, 0, 0)$, for all $N_T \geq 0$;
(2) The equilibrium with no zooplankton $E_2 = (\hat{N}, \hat{P}, 0, \hat{Q}_1)$, with $Q_1 = \frac{\tau\lambda}{2}\hat{P}$, for all N_T, with $N_T \geq N_{T_1}$, if $\lambda < \mu$;
(3) The equilibrium $E_3 = (N^*, P^*, Z^*, Q_1^*)$, with $Q_1^* = \frac{\mu\tau}{2} f(N^*) h^{-1}\left(\frac{\delta}{\gamma g}\right)$, for all N_T, with $N_T \geq N_{T_2}(\tau)$, if $\lambda < \mu$ and $\delta < \gamma g$.

Note that if (N_0, P_0, Z_0, Q_0) is an equilibrium of system (15), then $(N_0, P_0, Z_0, Q_0, Q_0)$ is an equilibrium point for system solution of system (13) and conversely.

In Figure 2, there are represented the coordinates N, P, Z, Q_1 of the three equilibrium points as functions of the total nutrient N_T, for a fixed $\tau = 5$. As function h, a type III functional response was considered. The values of the parameters used for simulations are $\mu = 5.9, g = 7, \lambda = 0.017, \gamma = 0.7, \delta = 0.17, k_N = 1, k_P = 1$, as in [12]. For these values of the parameters, the following values were obtained for stability thresholds: $N_{T_1} = 0.0028$, $N_{T_2(\tau)} = 0.2085$, $N_{T_3(\tau)} = 1.0967$. Remark that $E_1 = E_2$ at $N_T = N_{T_1}$ and $E_2 = E_3$ at $N_T = N_{T_2}(\tau)$.

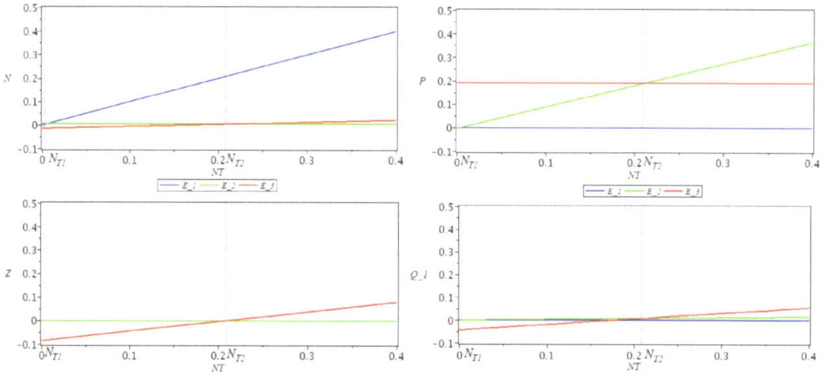

Figure 2. N, P, Z, Q_1 as functions of N_T, for fixed $\tau = 5$, for the equilibrium points E_1 (blue line), E_2 (green line), E_3 (red line), using a type III response.

Comparing the systems with and without delay, we see the following.

- The equilibrium point E_1 is unaffected by the delay.
- For the equilibrium point E_2, the value of P is reduced by the delay.
- For the equilibrium point E_3, the values of N and Z are reduced by the delay.
- The first transition point is unaffected by the delay, $N_{T_1} = N_{T_1}(\tau)$, while the second transition point is increased by the delay, $N_{T_2} < N_{T_2}(\tau)$, if $\tau > 0$.

4. Local Stability

For all three systems (7), (15) and (18), we find that at each value of the total nutrient at most one of the equilibrium points is locally asymptotically stable. More precisely,

- for $N_T < N_{T_1}$, the only equilibrium point is E_1, and it is asymptotically stable,
- for $N_{T_1} < N_T < N_{T_2}(\tau)$ the equilibrium E_2 is asymptotically stable, while E_1 is unstable,
- and, finally, as $N_T > N_{T_2}(\tau)$, the equilibrium E_3 is asymptotically stable either for all $N_T > N_{T_2}(\tau)$ or there exists an $N_{T_3}(\tau)$ such that E_3 is asymptotically stable for $N_{T_2}(\tau) < N_T < N_{T_3}(\tau)$, and unstable for $N_T > N_{T_3}(\tau)$, depending on the response function h, while the other two equilibria are unstable.

Note that for the system without delay (18), N_{T_2} is equal to $N_{T_2}(0)$. Our results for E_1 and E_2 reproduce the results of [12] for the system with general delay (1), while our results for E_3 improve those of [12].

Note that, for the two-dimensional reduced system without delay (18), the local stability of the equilibria on the boundary of the domain can be extended to global stability [12]. Those arguments cannot apply for systems (7) and (15). Results on the global stability could be obtained using Lyapunov functions, if they can be constructed.

4.1. The System without Delay

In [12], it is shown that the equilibrium E_1 is globally asymptotically stable on D_0 if $N_T < N_{T_1}$, the equilibrium E_2 is globally asymptotically stable on D_0, except for the z axis, if $N_{T_1} < N_T < N_{T_2}$, while the stability of the equilibrium point E_3 depends on the sign of the quantity T, denoting the trace of the Jacobi matrix J_0 at (P^*, Z^*),

$$J_0(N_T) = \begin{pmatrix} \frac{\delta Z^*}{\gamma P^*} - \mu P^* a - gZ^* b & -\mu P^* a - \frac{\delta}{\gamma} \\ \gamma g b Z^* & 0 \end{pmatrix}.$$

Here, to simplify the expression, we denoted $a = f'(N_T - P^* - Z^*)$, $b = h'(P^*)$.

They proved that if $h'(P^*) \geq h(P^*)/P^*$, then the equilibrium point E_3 is stable for all $N_T > N_{T_2}$. This is valid for a type III zooplankton grazing response function h. While if $h'(P^*) < h(P^*)/P^*$, then there exists a unique value N_{T_3} of the total nutrient, such that the equilibrium point E_3 is asymptotically stable for all $N_{T_2} < N_T < N_{T_3}$ and unstable if $N_T > N_{T_3}$. The value N_{T_3} is found as the unique solution of the equation $T(N_T) = 0$, with

$$T(N_T) = gZ^* \left(\frac{h(P^*)}{P^*} - h'(P^*) \right) - \mu P^* f'(N_T - P^* - Z^*). \tag{33}$$

For $N_T = N_{T_3}$, the Jacobi matrix J_0 has the purely imaginary eigenvalues $\lambda_{1,2}(N_T) = \pm i\omega_0$, with $\omega_0 > 0$, $\omega_0^2 = \gamma g b Z^* \left(\mu P^* a + \frac{\delta}{\gamma} \right)$. Close to N_{T_3}, we have $\mathrm{Re}\lambda_{1,2}(N_T) = \frac{1}{2} T(N_T)$. Consequently,

$$\frac{d}{dN_T} \mathrm{Re}\lambda_{1,2}(N_T) = \frac{1}{2} \frac{d}{dN_T} T(N_T) > 0, \tag{34}$$

and thus the transversality condition in the Hopf bifurcation theorem is satisfied. A Hopf bifurcation takes place for $N_T = N_{T_3}$ if the Lyapunov coefficient $L_1(N_{T_3})$ is non-zero.

4.2. The Weak Model Case

We analyse here the stability of the equilibrium points for the system (7) corresponding to the gamma distribution delay, with one degree of freedom.

Proposition 1. *For the equilibrium point E_1 of system (7), the following statements hold:*

(i) If $N_T < N_{T_1}$, then E_1 is locally asymptotically stable in D_1;
(ii) If $N_T > N_{T_1}$, then E_1 is a (2,1) type saddle point;
(iii) If $N_T = N_{T_1}$, then E_1 is a fold singularity.

Proof. The Jacobian matrix J_1 associated to system (7) at $E_1 = (N_T, 0, 0)$,

$$J_1 = \begin{pmatrix} -\frac{1}{\tau} & -\frac{1}{\tau} - \mu f(N_T) & -\frac{1}{\tau} \\ 0 & \mu f(N_T) - \lambda & 0 \\ 0 & 0 & -\delta \end{pmatrix}$$

has the eigenvalues

$$\lambda_1^1 = -\frac{1}{\tau} < 0, \lambda_2^1 = \mu\left(f(N_T) - \frac{\lambda}{\mu}\right), \lambda_3^1 = -\delta < 0.$$

As two eigenvalues are negative, the topological type of E_1 is determined by the sign of λ_2^1. Thus, the equilibrium point E_1 is an attractor if $\lambda_2^1 < 0$, i.e., $f(N_T) < \frac{\lambda}{\mu}$. As f is an increasing function, we have $\lambda_2^1 < 0$ if $N_T < f^{-1}\left(\frac{\lambda}{\mu}\right) = N_{T_1}$. □

Proposition 2. *The equilibrium point* $E_2 = (\hat{N}, \hat{P}, 0)$ *of system (7) is locally asymptotically stable in* D_1 *if and only if*

$$N_{T_1} < N_T < N_{T_2}(\tau).$$

In addition,

(i) *if* $N_T = N_{T_1}$ *or* $N_T = N_{T_2}(\tau)$ *then* E_2 *is a fold singularity;*
(ii) *if* $N_T > N_{T_2}(\tau)$ *then* E_2 *is a saddle point of type (2,1);*
(iii) *if* $N_T < N_{T_1}$ *then* E_2 *is not in* D_1.

Proof. For the equilibrium $E_2 = (\hat{N}, \hat{P}, 0)$, we obtain the Jacobi matrix

$$J_2 = \begin{pmatrix} -\frac{1}{\tau} - \mu\hat{P}f'(\hat{N}) & -\frac{1}{\tau} - \lambda & -\frac{1}{\tau} \\ \mu\hat{P}f'(\hat{N}) & 0 & -gh(\hat{P}) \\ 0 & 0 & \gamma gh(\hat{P}) - \delta \end{pmatrix}$$

and the characteristic equation

$$\left(X^2 + p_1 X + p_2\right)(X - \gamma gh(\hat{P}) + \delta) = 0$$

with

$$\begin{aligned} p_1 &= \frac{1}{\tau} + \mu\hat{P}f'(\hat{N}), \\ p_2 &= \frac{\mu(1+\lambda\tau)}{\tau}\hat{P}f'(\hat{N}). \end{aligned}$$

Thus, one eigenvalue is $\lambda_3^2 = \gamma g\left(h(\hat{P}) - \frac{\delta}{\gamma g}\right)$ and we have $\lambda_3^2 < 0$ if $h(\hat{P}) < \frac{\delta}{\gamma g}$ (that is $\hat{P} < P^*$, as h is an increasing function). Consequently, $\lambda_3^2 < 0$ iff

$$N_T < f^{-1}\left(\frac{\lambda}{\mu}\right) + (1+\lambda\tau)h^{-1}\left(\frac{\delta}{\gamma g}\right) = N_{T_2}(\tau)$$

and $\lambda_3^2 = 0$ if $N_T = N_{T_2}(\tau)$.

The other two eigenvalues λ_1^2, λ_2^2, are solutions of the equation $X^2 + p_1 X + p_2 = 0$. Further, if $N_T > N_{T_1}$, it follows that $p_1 > 0, p_2 > 0$, both solutions of this equation have negative real parts. As a consequence, if $N_{T_1} < N_T < N_{T_2}(\tau)$, all eigenvalues have negative real parts, hence the equilibrium point E_2 is an attractor.

Note that if $N_T = N_{T_1}$, then $p_2 = 0$, $p_1 > 0$, thus $\lambda_2^2 = 0$ and $\mathrm{Re}(\lambda_1^2) < 0$. The equilibrium point E_2 is a fold singularity both at $N_T = N_{T_1}$ and $N_T = N_{T_2}(\tau)$. □

For the equilibrium point $E_3 = (N^*, P^*, Z^*)$ of system (7), the Jacobi matrix reads

$$J_3 = \begin{pmatrix} -\frac{1}{\tau} - \mu Pa & -\frac{1}{\tau} - \mu c & -\frac{1}{\tau} \\ \mu Pa & \mu c - gZ^*b - \lambda & -\frac{\delta}{\gamma} \\ 0 & \gamma g Z^* b & 0 \end{pmatrix},$$

where, to simplify computation, we denoted:

$$a = f'(N^*) > 0, b = h'(P^*) > 0, c = f(N^*) > 0, d = h(P^*) > 0, \tag{35}$$

Thus, the characteristic polynomial of J_3 reads

$$X^3 + a_1 X^2 + a_2 X + a_3, \tag{36}$$

with

$$\begin{aligned} a_1 &= \frac{1}{\tau} + \lambda - c\mu + \mu P^* a + Z^* bg \\ a_2 &= \frac{1}{\tau}(\lambda - c\mu + \mu P^* a + Z^* bg) + g\delta Z^* b + \lambda \mu P^* a + g\mu P^* Z^* ab \\ a_3 &= \frac{g}{\tau} Z^* b(\delta + P^* a\gamma\mu + \tau\mu\delta P^* a) \end{aligned} \tag{37}$$

Using the Routh–Hurwitz criterion [19], all the roots of the characteristic polynomial have negative real parts if and only if the following conditions are satisfied:

$$(i) \quad a_1 > 0, (ii) \quad a_3 > 0, (iii) \quad a_1 a_2 - a_3 > 0. \tag{38}$$

Thus, the equilibrium point E_3 is asymptotically stable if all these conditions are fulfilled. In [12], one result on the stability of E_3 with the weak gamma distributed delay was obtained. For completeness and for comparison with the strong gamma distribution case, we repeat that result here with proof.

Proposition 3. *If*

$$P^* h'(P^*) - h(P^*) \geq 0, \tag{39}$$

then the equilibrium E_3 of system (7) is locally asymptotically stable for all $N_T > N_{T_2}(\tau)$.

Proof. The equilibrium point E_3 is stable if all conditions in (38) are fulfilled. To simplify computation, denote

$$A = \mu P^* a > 0, B = \mu c - \lambda > 0, C = \frac{\gamma g b P^*}{\delta} > 0, D = \frac{\delta}{\gamma} > 0, T = A + B(C - 1)$$

Note that, $C - 1 = \frac{\gamma g}{\delta}(P^* h'(P^*) - h(P^*)) > 0$. With these notations, we can write

$$\begin{aligned} a_1 &= T + \frac{1}{\tau}, \\ a_2 &= BCD\gamma + ABC + A\lambda + \frac{1}{\tau} T, \end{aligned}$$

As all parameters are positive, it follow that $a_3 > 0$. As $T > 0$, conditions $a_1 > 0$ and $a_2 > 0$ are satisfied. As

$$a_1 a_2 - a_3 = AT(BC + \lambda) + B^2 CD\gamma(C - 1) + \frac{1 - \gamma}{\tau} ABC + \frac{\lambda}{\tau} A + \frac{1}{\tau^2} T(T\tau + 1) > 0, \tag{40}$$

condition (iii) in (38) is satisfied. Consequently, all eigenvalues have negative real parts, and E_3 is an attractor for all $N_T > N_{T_2}(\tau)$. □

Proposition 4. *If*

$$P^*h'(P^*) - h(P^*) < 0, \tag{41}$$

the following assertions hold for the equilibrium point E_3 of system (7).

(i) *For $N_T > N_{T_2}(\tau)$, close to $N_{T_2}(\tau)$, the equilibrium point E_3 is an attractor.*
(ii) *If $a_1a_2 - a_3 > 0$, then E_3 is locally asymptotically stable.*
(iii) *If $a_1a_2 - a_3 = 0$ then E_3 is a Hopf singularity.*
(iv) *If $a_1a_2 - a_3 < 0$ then E_3 is a (1,2) saddle point. In addition, for each τ there exists a value $N_{T_3}(\tau)$, given by*

$$N_{T_3}(\tau) = \min\{N_T, \quad N_T > N_{T_2}(\tau), \quad a_1a_2 - a_3 = 0\},$$

such that $E_3(N_T)$ is locally asymptotically stable for all $N_{T_2}(\tau) < N_T < N_{T_3}(\tau)$ and unstable for $N_T > N_{T_3}(\tau)$, close to $N_{T_3}(\tau)$.

Proof. (i) The coefficient a_3 is equal to 0 if and only $Z^* = 0$, which occurs when $f(N^*) = \frac{\lambda}{\mu}$. The discussion following (29) then shows that $a_3 = 0$ at $N_T = N_{T_2}(\tau)$, and $a_3 > 0$ for $N_T > N_{T_2}(\tau)$.

For $N_T = N_{T_2}(\tau)$, the other two coefficients of the characteristic equation associated to E_3,

$$\begin{aligned} a_1 &= \frac{1}{\tau} + \mu P^* a > 0, \\ a_2 &= \frac{1}{\tau}\mu P^* a + \lambda\mu P^* a > 0, \end{aligned}$$

have positive values, and also $a_1a_2 - a_3 = a_1a_3 > 0$. As the expressions $a_1, a_2, a_1a_2 - a_3$ are continuous functions of N_T, they remain positive for $N_T > N_{T_2}(\tau)$, in a neighbourhood of $N_{T_2}(\tau)$. Hence (i).

(ii) Considering a_1 as a function of N_T, we obtain

$$\lim_{N_T \to \infty} a_1(N_T) = \frac{1}{\tau} + \lambda + \frac{\gamma}{\delta}(\mu - \lambda)P^* > \frac{1}{\tau} + \lambda > 0.$$

Also,

$$\frac{da_1}{dN_T} = \mu\left(P^* f''(N^*) + f'(N^*)\left(\frac{P^*h'(P^*)}{h(P^*)} - 1\right)\right)\frac{dN^*}{dN_T}$$

Differentiating with respect to N_T in (30), we obtain

$$1 = \frac{dN^*}{dN_T}\left(1 + \frac{\mu(\gamma + \tau\delta}{\delta}P^* f'(N^*)\right),$$

hence $\frac{dN^*}{dN_T} > 0$. As $f'' < 0$ and $\frac{P^*h'(P^*)}{h(P^*)} - 1 < 0$, it follows that $\frac{da_1}{dN_T} < 0$, thus a_1 is a decreasing function of N_T. Consequently, $a_1 > \frac{1}{\tau} + \lambda > 0$. The result follows by applying the Routh–Hurwitz criterion [19].

(iii) The characteristic polynomial (36) has a pair of purely imaginary roots $\lambda_{1,2} = \pm\omega i$ if conditions

$$a_2 = \omega^2 > 0, \; a_1a_2 - a_3 = 0.$$

As $a_1 > 0, a_3 > 0$ for all $N_T > N_{T_2}(\tau)$, if $a_1a_2 - a_3 = 0$ then $a_2 > 0$. Thus, E_3 is a Hopf singularity.

(iv) As $a_1 > 0, a_3 > 0$ for all $N_T > N_{T_2}(\tau)$, and $(a_1a_2 - a_3)(N_{T_2}(\tau)) > 0$, it follows that $N_{T_3}(\tau)$ is the minimum value of $N_T > N_{T_2}(\tau)$ for which condition $a_1a_2 - a_3 > 0$ is not satisfied. □

For the type II response function h, we have

$$Ph'(P) - h(P) = -\frac{P^2}{(P+k_P)^2} < 0, \forall P \geq 0.$$

In this case, Proposition 4 applies for the stability of the equilibrium point E_3. See Figure 3.

For the type III response function h, we obtain

$$Ph'(P) - h(P) = \frac{(k_P^2 - P^2)P^2}{(P^2 + k_P^2)^2}.$$

In this case, if $P^* \leq k_P$ (i.e., $\frac{\delta}{g\gamma} \leq h(k_P)$), then $P^*h'(P^*) - h(P^*) \geq 0$ and the equilibrium point E_3 is stable for all $N_T > N_{T_2}(\tau)$. If $h(k_P) < \frac{\delta}{g\gamma} < 1$, then Proposition 4 applies for the stability of the equilibrium point E_3.

4.3. The Strong Model Case

Proposition 5. *The following assertions hold for the equilibrium point E_1 of system (15).*

(i) If $N_T < N_{T_1}$, then E_1 is locally asymptotically stable in D_2.
(ii) If $N_T > N_{T_1}$, then E_1 is a (3,1) type saddle point.
(iii) If $N_T = N_{T_1}$, then E_1 is a fold singularity.

Proof. For the equilibrium $E_1 = (N_T, 0, 0, 0)$, we obtain the Jacobi matrix

$$J_1 = \begin{pmatrix} 0 & -\mu f(N_T) & 0 & \frac{2}{\tau} \\ 0 & \mu f(N_T) - \lambda & 0 & 0 \\ 0 & 0 & -\delta & 0 \\ -\frac{2}{\tau} & -\frac{2}{\tau} & -\frac{2}{\tau} & -\frac{4}{\tau} \end{pmatrix},$$

and the characteristic polynomial $(X + \frac{2}{\tau})^2(X+\delta)(X+\lambda-\mu f(N_T))$. Thus, J_1 has the eigenvalues

$$\lambda_1^1 = \lambda_2^1 = -\frac{2}{\tau} < 0, \lambda_3^1 = -\delta < 0, \lambda_4^1 = \mu\left(f(N_T) - \frac{\lambda}{\mu}\right).$$

As three eigenvalues are negative, the topological type of E_1 is determined by the sign of λ_4^1. Thus, the equilibrium point E_1 is an attractor if $\lambda_4^1 < 0$, i.e., $f(N_T) < \frac{\lambda}{\mu}$. As f is an increasing function, we obtain $\lambda_4^1 < 0$ if $N_T < f^{-1}\left(\frac{\lambda}{\mu}\right) = N_{T_1}$. □

Proposition 6. *The equilibrium $E_2 = (\hat{N}, \hat{P}, 0, \hat{Q}_1)$ of system (15) is locally asymptotically stable in D_2 if and only if*

$$N_{T_1} < N_T < N_{T_2}(\tau).$$

In addition,

(i) If $N_T = N_{T_1}$ or $N_T = N_{T_2}(\tau)$, then the equilibrium E_2 is a fold singularity;
(ii) If $N_T > N_{T_2}(\tau)$, then the equilibrium E_2 is a saddle point of type (3,1);
(iii) If $N_T < N_{T_1}$, then the equilibrium E_2 is not in D_2.

Proof. For the equilibrium $E_2 = (\hat{N}, \hat{P}, 0, \hat{Q}_1)$, we obtain the Jacobi matrix

$$J_2 = \begin{pmatrix} -\mu\hat{P}f'(\hat{N}) & -\lambda & 0 & \frac{2}{\tau} \\ \mu\hat{P}f'(\hat{N}) & 0 & -gh(\hat{P}) & 0 \\ 0 & 0 & \gamma gh(\hat{P}) - \delta & 0 \\ -\frac{2}{\tau} & -\frac{2}{\tau} & -\frac{2}{\tau} & -\frac{4}{\tau} \end{pmatrix}$$

and the characteristic equation

$$\left(X^3 + p_1 X^2 + p_2 X + p_3\right)(X - \gamma g h(\hat{P}) + \delta) = 0$$

with

$$\begin{aligned} p_1 &= \frac{4}{\tau} + \mu \hat{P} f'(\hat{N}), \\ p_2 &= \frac{4}{\tau^2} + \frac{\mu(4 + \lambda\tau)}{\tau} \hat{P} f'(\hat{N}), \\ p_3 &= \frac{4\mu(1 + \tau\lambda)}{\tau^2} \hat{P} f'(\hat{N}). \end{aligned}$$

Thus, one eigenvalue is $\lambda_4^2 = \gamma g\left(h(\hat{P}) - \frac{\delta}{\gamma g}\right)$ and we have $\lambda_4^2 < 0$ if $h(\hat{P}) < \frac{\delta}{\gamma g}$ (that is $\hat{P} < P^*$, as h is an increasing function). Consequently, $\lambda_4^2 < 0$ if

$$N_T < f^{-1}\left(\frac{\lambda}{\mu}\right) + (1 + \lambda\tau) h^{-1}\left(\frac{\delta}{\gamma g}\right) = N_{T_2}(\tau)$$

and $\lambda_4^2 = 0$ as $N_T = N_{T_2}(\tau)$. The other three eigenvalues $\lambda_1^2, \lambda_2^2, \lambda_3^2$ are solutions of the equation $X^3 + p_1 X^2 + p_2 X + p_3 = 0$. According to the Routh–Hurwitz criterion, all solutions of this equation have negative real parts if conditions

$$p_1 > 0, p_3 > 0, p_1 p_2 > p_3$$

are fulfilled. As all parameters $\mu,\ \lambda,\ \tau$ are positive, if $N_T > N_{T_1}$ the first two conditions $p_1 > 0, p_3 > 0$ are satisfied. A simple computation shows that the third condition is also satisfied if $N_T > N_{T_1}$. As a consequence, if $N_{T_1} < N_T < N_{T_2}(\tau)$ all eigenvalues have negative real part, hence the equilibrium point E_2 is an attractor.

Note that if $N_T = N_{T_1}$, then $p_3 = 0$, $p_1 > 0$, $p_2 > 0$, thus $\lambda_3^2 = 0$ and $\mathrm{Re}(\lambda_{1,2}^2) < 0$. The equilibrium point E_2 is a fold singularity both at $N_T = N_{T_1}$ and $N_T = N_{T_2}(\tau)$. □

For the equilibrium $E_3 = \left(N^*, P^*, Z^*, Q_1^*\right)$ of system (15), the Jacobi matrix reads

$$J_3 = \begin{pmatrix} -\mu P^* f'(N^*) & -\mu f(N^*) & 0 & \frac{2}{\tau} \\ \mu P^* f'(N^*) & \mu f(N^*) - g Z^* h'(P^*) - \lambda & -g h(P^*) & 0 \\ 0 & \gamma g Z^* h'(P^*) & \gamma g h(P^*) - \delta & 0 \\ -\frac{2}{\tau} & -\frac{2}{\tau} & -\frac{2}{\tau} & -\frac{4}{\tau} \end{pmatrix}$$

and the characteristic polynomial is

$$X^4 + b_1 X^3 + b_2 X^2 + b_3 X + b_4, \qquad (42)$$

with

$$\begin{aligned} b_1 &= \frac{4}{\tau} + \mu P^* f'(N^*) + \frac{\gamma g}{\delta}(\mu f(N^*) - \lambda)(P^* h'(P^*) - h(P^*)), \\ b_2 &= \frac{4}{\tau^2} + \frac{4}{\tau}(\lambda - f(N^*)\mu + \mu P^* f'(N^*) + g Z^* h'(P^*)) + g\delta Z^* h'(P^*) + \lambda\mu P^* f'(N^*) + g\mu P^* Z^* f'(N^*) h'(P^*) \\ b_3 &= \frac{4}{\tau}\left(g\delta Z^* h'(P^*) + c\mu^2 P^* f'(N^*) + \mu P^* f'(N^*)(\lambda - c\mu + g Z^* h'(P^*))\right) + \frac{4}{\tau^2}(\lambda - c\mu + \mu P^* f'(N^*) + g Z^* h'(P^*)) \\ &\quad + g\delta Z^* h'(P^*)(\lambda - c\mu + \mu P f'(N^*) + g Z h'(P^*)) - g\delta Z h'(P^*)(\lambda - c\mu + g Z h'(P^*)), \\ b_4 &= \frac{4g}{\tau^2}(\delta + \mu(\gamma + \delta\tau) P^* f'(N^*)) \frac{\mu\gamma}{\delta}\left(f(N^*) - \frac{\lambda}{\mu}\right) P^* h'(P^*). \end{aligned} \qquad (43)$$

Using the Routh–Hurwitz criterion [19], all the roots of the characteristic polynomial have negative real parts if and only if the following conditions are satisfied:

$$(i)\ b_1 > 0, b_2 > 0, b_3 > 0, b_4 > 0, (ii)\ b_5 = b_1 b_2 - b_3 > 0, (iii)\ b_6 = (b_1 b_2 - b_3) b_3 - b_1^2 b_4 > 0. \tag{44}$$

Thus, the equilibrium point E_3 is stable if all these conditions are fulfilled.

Proposition 7. *For the equilibrium point E_3 of system (15), the following assertions hold.*

(i) For $N_T > N_{T_2}(\tau)$, close to $N_{T_2}(\tau)$, the equilibrium point E_3 is an attractor.

(ii) If one of the conditions $b_j > 0,\ j = \overline{1,6}$, in (44) is not satisfied, then E_3 is unstable. In addition, for each τ there exists a value $N_{T_3}(\tau)$, given by

$$N_{T_3}(\tau) = \min\Big\{ N_T \big| N_T > N_{T_2}(\tau),\ \prod_{j=1}^{6} b_j = 0 \Big\},$$

such that E_3 is locally asymptotically stable for all $N_{T_2}(\tau) < N_T < N_{T_3}(\tau)$.

Proof. The coefficient b_4 is equal to 0 if and only $f(N^*) = \frac{\lambda}{\mu}$. Thus, we have $b_4 = 0$ at $N_T = N_{T_2}(\tau)$, and $b_4 > 0$ for $N_T > N_{T_2}(\tau)$.

At $N_T = N_{T_2}(\tau)$, the other three coefficients of the characteristic equation associated with E_3 have the following values:

$$\begin{aligned} b_1 &= \frac{4}{\tau} + \mu P^* a > 0, \\ b_2 &= \frac{4}{\tau^2} + \frac{4}{\tau}\mu P^* a + \mu^2 P^* ac > 0, \\ b_3 &= \frac{4}{\tau}\mu^2 P^* ac + \frac{4}{\tau^2}\mu P^* a > 0. \end{aligned}$$

In addition, we have

$$\begin{aligned} b_5 &= \left(\mu^2 P^* ac + \frac{4}{\tau}\mu P^* a\tau + \frac{16}{\tau^2}\right)\mu P^* a + \frac{16}{\tau^3} > 0, \\ b_6 &= b_3 b_5 > 0. \end{aligned}$$

As the expressions $b_j, j = \overline{1,6}$, are continuous functions of N_T, they remain positive for $N_T > N_{T_2}(\tau)$, in a neighbourhood of $N_{T_2}(\tau)$. Hence (i). Obviously, $N_{T_3}(\tau)$ is the minimum value of $N_T > N_{T_2}(\tau)$ for which one of the conditions (44) is not satisfied. □

Remark 1. *As for $N_T > N_{T_2}(\tau)$, we have $b_4 > 0$, none of the eigenvalues $\lambda_i^3, i = \overline{1,4}$, can be 0. Thus, the topological type of E_3 could change only with the appearance of a pair of purely imaginary eigenvalues. Using the Viète relations, if conditions*

$$b_1 b_3 > 0, (b_1 b_2 - b_3) b_3 - b_1^2 b_4 = 0, \tag{45}$$

are satisfied, then the equilibrium point E_3 is a Hopf singularity. If

$$b_1 = 0, b_2 > 0, b_3 = 0, b_4 > 0, b_2^2 - 4b_4 > 0, \tag{46}$$

then the equilibrium point E_3 has two pairs of purely imaginary eigenvalues and it is a double-Hopf singularity.

Proposition 8. *Assume*

$$P^* h'(P^*) - h(P^*) \geq 0, \tag{47}$$

(i) If $(b_1 b_2 - b_3) b_3 - b_1^2 b_4 > 0$, then the equilibrium E_3 of system (15) is locally asymptotically stable for all $N_T > N_{T_2}(\tau)$.

(ii) *If* $(b_1b_2 - b_3)b_3 - b_1^2b_4 = 0$*, then* E_3 *is a Hopf singularity.*
(iii) *If* $(b_1b_2 - b_3)b_3 - b_1^2b_4 < 0$*, then* E_3 *is unstable. In addition, for each* τ*, there exists a value* $N_{T_3}(\tau)$*, given by*

$$N_{T_3}(\tau) = \min\Big\{N_T | N_T > N_{T_2}(\tau), (b_1b_2 - b_3)b_3 - b_1^2b_4 = 0\Big\},$$

such that E_3 *is locally asymptotically stable for all* $N_{T_2}(\tau) < N_T < N_{T_3}(\tau)$.

Proof. The equilibrium point E_3 is stable if all conditions in (38) are fulfilled. To simplify computation, denote:

$$\begin{aligned} a &= f'(N^*) > 0, b = h'(P^*) > 0, c = f(N^*) > 0, d = h(P^*) > 0, \\ A &= \mu P^* a > 0, B = \mu c - \lambda > 0, C = \frac{\gamma g b P^*}{\delta} > 0, D = \frac{\delta}{\gamma} > 0, T = A + B(C-1) \end{aligned}$$

Note that, $C - 1 = \frac{\gamma g}{\delta}(P^* h'(P^*) - h(P^*)) > 0$. With these notations, we can write:

$$\begin{aligned} b_1 &= T + \frac{4}{\tau}, \\ b_2 &= BCD\gamma + ABC + A\lambda + \frac{4}{\tau}T + \frac{4}{\tau^2}, \\ b_3 &= ABCD\gamma + \frac{4}{\tau}(BCD\gamma + ABC + A\lambda) + \frac{4}{\tau^2}T, \\ b_4 &= \frac{1}{\tau^2}ABC\gamma(AD\tau + A + D) \end{aligned}$$

As all parameters are positive, it follow that $b_4 > 0$. As $T > 0$, conditions $b_1 > 0$, $b_2 > 0$, $b_3 > 0$ are satisfied if the hypothesis (47) is true. As

$$b_1b_2 - b_3 = AT(BC + \lambda) + B^2CD\gamma(C-1) + \frac{4}{\tau^3}(T\tau + 2)^2,$$

condition $b_1b_2 - b_3 > 0$ is satisfied if (47).

Consequently, if $(b_1b_2 - b_3)b_3 - b_1^2b_4 > 0$, then all eigenvalues have negative real parts, thus E_3 is an attractor.

If $(b_1b_2 - b_3)b_3 - b_1^2b_4 < 0$, at least two eigenvalues have negative real parts, thus E_3 is unstable. As for $N_T = N_{T_2}(\tau)$ we have

$$(b_1b_2 - b_3)b_3 - b_1^2b_4 = \left(\mu^2P^*ac + \frac{4}{\tau}\mu P^*a + \frac{24}{\tau^2}\right)\mu P^*a + \frac{16}{\tau^3} > 0,$$

the expression continue to be positive for $N_T > N_{T_2}(\tau)$, close to $N_{T_2}(\tau)$. Obviously, $N_{T_3}(\tau)$ is the minimum value of $N_T > N_{T_2}(\tau)$ for which $(b_1b_2 - b_3)b_3 - b_1^2b_4 = 0$. □

In Figure 3, there are represented the strata in the (τ, N_T) plane that exhibit different behaviours for the three equilibrium points, obtained in the case of a type II response $h(P) = \frac{P}{P+k_P}$. The curve denoted NT_1 (blue line) separates the strata where E_1 changes stability with E_2. The equilibrium E_2 is stable for parameters in the stratum limited by the curves NT_1 (blue line) and NT_2 (green line). The equilibrium E_3 is stable for parameters in region 3, in the stratum limited by the curves NT_2 (green line) and NT_3 (red line), and loses stability in region 4. The other two equilibria are unstable in regions 3 and 4.

The values of the parameters used for simulations are $\mu = 5.9$, $g = 7$, $\lambda = 0.017$, $\gamma = 0.7$, $\delta = 0.17$, $k_N = 1$, $k_P = 1$. The results are consistent with the ones obtained in [12].

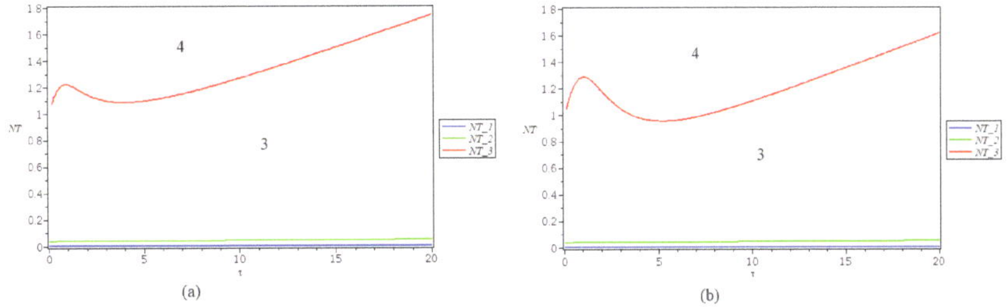

Figure 3. Regions in the (τ, N_T) plane that exhibit different behaviours for the equilibrium E_3, using the Type II response for: (**a**) the weak model; (**b**) the strong model. Region 3 is where the E_3 and is stable, but where E_1, E_2 are unstable. For parameters on the curve separating regions 3 and 4, E_3 is a Hopf singularity, while in region 4, E_3 is unstable. A Hopf bifurcation may take place when parameters cross from region 3 to region 4.

5. Local Bifurcations

In the previous section, we proved that at each value of the total nutrients at most one of the equilibrium points is locally asymptotically stable. In this section, we show that the change of stability is realized either through a transcritical bifurcation or a Hopf bifurcation that may occur at a fold singular point or at a Hopf singularity, respectively.

5.1. Transcritical Bifurcations

Two transcritical bifurcations undergo for both the weak and the strong models, namely:

(i) at $N_T = N_{T_1}$, the equilibrium points E_1 and E_2 collide and interchange stability;
(ii) at $N_T = N_{T_2}(\tau)$, the equilibrium points E_2 and E_3 collide and interchange stability.

We prove these results by using the Sotomayor theorem [20], ([21], p. 338).

5.1.1. Transcritical Bifurcations for the Weak Model

Proposition 9. *A transcritical bifurcation takes place at the equilibrium E_1 of system (7) as $N_T = N_{T_1}$.*

Proof. As $N_T = N_{T_1}$ we have $E_2 = E_1$ and the equilibrium E_1 is a fold singularity. We consider $\varepsilon = \mu f(N_T) - \lambda$ as the bifurcation parameter, and the bifurcation value is $\varepsilon_0 = 0$. It follows $\lambda = \mu f(N_T) - \varepsilon$, and at $\varepsilon = 0$ we have $\lambda = \mu f\left(N_{T_1}\right)$. The normal form on the centre manifold is determined using Sotomayor theorem [20,21]. In order to carry this out, consider first two eigenvectors $v, w \in \mathbb{R}^4$, such that $J_1 v = 0$ and $w^T J_1 = 0$. As for $J_2 = J_1 = \begin{pmatrix} -\frac{1}{\tau} & -\frac{1}{\tau} - \lambda & -\frac{1}{\tau} \\ 0 & 0 & 0 \\ 0 & 0 & -\delta \end{pmatrix}$, we obtain that $w^T = (0,1,0)$ and $v^T = (-(\lambda\tau + 1), 1, 0)$. Then, we compute the quantities A, B, C in Sotomayor theorem, where

$$
\begin{aligned}
A &= \frac{1}{\langle v, w\rangle}\left\langle w, \frac{\partial \Phi}{\partial \varepsilon}(E_2, \varepsilon_0)\right\rangle, B = \frac{1}{\langle v, w\rangle}\sum_{i,j,k=1}^{3} w_i v_j v_k \frac{\partial^2 \Phi_i}{\partial x_j \partial x_k}(E_2, \varepsilon_0), \\
C &= \frac{2}{\langle v, w\rangle}\sum_{i,j=1}^{3} w_i v_j \frac{\partial^2 \Phi_i}{\partial x_j \partial \varepsilon}(E_2, \varepsilon_0),
\end{aligned}
$$

with $\varepsilon_0 = 0$ and $(x_1, x_2, x_3) = (N, P, Z)$, and Φ is the vector field associated with system (7). As $\langle v, w\rangle = 1$ and vector w has only one non-zero component, we need only the second component of the vector field Φ, which can be written as

$$
\Phi_2(N, P, Z) = \mu P(t) f(N(t)) - gZh(P(t)) - (\mu f(N_T) - \varepsilon)P(t).
$$

We obtain

$$\begin{aligned} A &= \frac{\partial \Phi_2}{\partial \varepsilon}(E_2, 0) = 0, \\ B &= \sum_{j,k=1}^{4} v_j v_k \frac{\partial^2 \Phi_2}{\partial x_j \partial x_k}(E_2, 0) = -2(\lambda\tau + 1)\mu f'(N_{T_1}) \neq 0, \end{aligned}$$

and

$$C = 2\sum_{j=1}^{4} v_j \frac{\partial^2 \Phi_2}{\partial x_j \partial \varepsilon}(E_2, 0) = 2v_2 \frac{\partial^2 \Phi_2}{\partial P \partial \varepsilon}(E_2, 0) = -2 \neq 0.$$

Consequently, a transcritical bifurcation takes place as $\varepsilon = 0$, i.e., $f(N_T) = \frac{\lambda}{\mu}$. □

In a similar way we prove that a transcritical bifurcation takes place when the equilibria E_2 and E_3 coincides, as $N_T = N_{T_2}(\tau)$.

Proposition 10. *A transcritical bifurcation takes place at the equilibrium E_2 of system (7) as $N_T = N_{T_2}(\tau)$.*

Proof. As $N_T = N_{T_2}(\tau)$ we have $E_2 = E_3 = (N_0, P_0, Z_0)$, with $N_0 = N_{T_1}$, $P_0 = \frac{1}{1+\lambda\tau}(N_{T_2}(\tau) - N_{T_1})$, $Z_0 = 0$, and the equilibrium is a fold singularity. We consider $\varepsilon = \delta - \gamma g h(\hat{P})$ as the bifurcation parameter, and the bifurcation value is $\varepsilon = 0$. Apply the Sotomayor theorem [21] as above. Consider two eigenvectors $v, w \in \mathbb{R}^4$, such that $J_2 v = 0$ and $w^T J_2 = 0$. As $J_2 = \begin{pmatrix} -\frac{1}{\tau} - \mu P_0 f'(N_0) & -\frac{1}{\tau} - \lambda & -\frac{1}{\tau} \\ \mu P_0 f'(N_0) & 0 & -\frac{\delta}{\gamma} \\ 0 & 0 & 0 \end{pmatrix}$, we obtain that $w^T = (0, 0, 1)$ and $v^T = (v_1, v_2, v_3)$, with $v_1 = \frac{\delta}{\gamma\mu P_0 f'(N_{T_1})}$, $v_2 = -\frac{1}{\lambda\tau+1}\left(\frac{\tau\delta}{\gamma} + 1 + \frac{\delta}{\gamma\mu P_0 f'(N_{T_1})}\right) \neq 0$, $v_3 = 1$. As $\langle v, w \rangle = 1$ and vector w has only one non-zero component, we need only the third component of the vector field Φ, which can be written as

$$\Phi_3(N, P, Z) = \gamma g Z h(P(t)) - \left(\varepsilon + \gamma g h(\hat{P})\right) Z.$$

We obtain

$$\begin{aligned} A &= \frac{\partial \Phi_2}{\partial \varepsilon}(E_2, \varepsilon_0) = 0, \\ B &= \sum_{j,k=1}^{4} v_j v_k \frac{\partial^2 \Phi_3}{\partial x_j \partial x_k}(E_2, \varepsilon_0) = 2v_2 v_3 \frac{\partial^2 \Phi_3}{\partial Z \partial P}(E_2, \varepsilon_0) = 2v_2 \gamma g h'(P_0) \neq 0, \end{aligned}$$

and

$$C = 2\sum_{j=1}^{4} v_j \frac{\partial^2 \Phi_3}{\partial x_j \partial \varepsilon}(E_2, \varepsilon_0) = 2v_3 \frac{\partial^2 \Phi_3}{\partial Z \partial \varepsilon}(E_2, \varepsilon_0) = -2 \neq 0.$$

Consequently, a transcritical bifurcation takes place as $\varepsilon = 0$, i.e., $N_T = N_{T_2}(\tau)$. □

Remark 2. *At the bifurcation, point the two equilibria E_2 and E_3 have the same eigenvalues, $\lambda_j^2 = \lambda_j^3, j = \overline{1,3}$, with $Re\lambda_j^2 < 0$, for $j = 1, 2$, and $\lambda_3^2 = \lambda_3^3 = 0$. As a consequence of the transcritical bifurcation, the eigenvalues these two eigenvalues change signs when passing through the bifurcation values, while the real parts of the other three pairs of eigenvalues remain negative close to the bifurcation value, due to continuity. Thus, the two equilibria exchange stability. Consequently, close to $N_T = N_{T_2}(\tau)$, if $N_T < N_{T_2}(\tau)$ the equilibrium point E_2 is an attractor and E_3 is a saddle of type (2,1), while if $N_T > N_{T_2}(\tau)$ the equilibrium point E_2 is a saddle of type (2,1) and E_3 is an attractor.*

5.1.2. Transcritical Bifurcations for the Strong Model

Proposition 11. *A transcritical bifurcation takes place at the equilibrium E_1 of system (15) as $N_T = N_{T_1}$.*

Proof. As $N_T = N_{T_1}$, we have $E_2 = E_1$ and the equilibrium is a fold singularity. We consider $\varepsilon = \mu f(N_T) - \lambda$ as the bifurcation parameter, and the bifurcation value is $\varepsilon = 0$. It follows $\lambda = \mu f(N_T) - \varepsilon$, and at $\varepsilon = 0$ we have $\lambda = \mu f(N_{T_1})$. Consider two eigenvectors $v, w \in \mathbb{R}^4$, such that $J_2 v = 0$ and $w^T J_2 = 0$. As $J_2 = \begin{pmatrix} 0 & -\lambda & 0 & \frac{2}{\tau} \\ 0 & 0 & 0 & 0 \\ 0 & 0 & -\delta & 0 \\ -\frac{2}{\tau} & -\frac{2}{\tau} & -\frac{2}{\tau} & -\frac{4}{\tau} \end{pmatrix}$, we obtain that $w^T = (0,1,0,0)$ and $v^T = \left(-(\lambda\tau+1), 1, 0, \frac{\lambda\tau}{2}\right)$. Then compute the quantities A, B, C in Sotomayor theorem. As $\langle v, w\rangle = 1$ and vector w has only one non-zero component, we need only the second component of the vector field Φ, associated with system (15), which can be written as

$$\Phi_2(N, P, Z, Q_1) = \mu P(t) f(N(t)) - gZh(P(t)) - (\mu f(N_T) - \varepsilon)P(t).$$

We obtain

$$\begin{aligned} A &= \frac{\partial \Phi_2}{\partial \varepsilon}(E_2, 0) = 0, \\ B &= \sum_{j,k=1}^{4} v_j v_k \frac{\partial^2 \Phi_2}{\partial x_j \partial x_k}(E_2, 0) = -2(\mu f(N_{T_1})\tau + 1)\mu f'(N_{T_1}) \neq 0, \end{aligned}$$

and

$$C = 2\sum_{j=1}^{4} v_j \frac{\partial^2 \Phi_2}{\partial x_j \partial \varepsilon}(E_2, 0) = 2v_2 \frac{\partial^2 \Phi_2}{\partial P \partial \varepsilon}(E_2, 0) = -2 \neq 0.$$

Consequently, a transcritical bifurcation takes place as $\varepsilon = 0$, i.e., $f(N_T) = \frac{\lambda}{\mu}$. □

In a similar way, we prove that a transcritical bifurcation takes place when the equilibria E_2 and E_3 of system (15) coincides, as $N_T = N_{T_2}(\tau)$.

Proposition 12. *A transcritical bifurcation takes place at the equilibrium E_2 of system (15) as $N_T = N_{T_2}(\tau)$.*

Proof. As $N_T = N_{T_2}(\tau)$, we have $E_2 = E_3 = (N_0, P_0, Z_0, Q_{10})$, with $N_0 = N_{T_1}$, $P_0 = \frac{1}{1+\lambda\tau}(N_{T_2}(\tau) - N_{T_1})$, $Z_0 = 0$, $Q_{10} = \frac{\lambda\tau}{2}P_0$, and the equilibrium is a fold singularity. We consider $\varepsilon = \delta - \gamma g h(\hat{P})$ as the bifurcation parameter, and the bifurcation value is $\varepsilon = 0$. Apply the Sotomayor theorem [21] as above. Consider two eigenvectors $v, w \in \mathbb{R}^4$, such that $J_2 v = 0$ and $w^T J_2 = 0$. As $J_2 = \begin{pmatrix} -\mu P a & -\lambda & 0 & \frac{2}{\tau} \\ \mu P a & 0 & -\frac{\delta}{\gamma} & 0 \\ 0 & 0 & 0 & 0 \\ -\frac{2}{\tau} & -\frac{2}{\tau} & -\frac{2}{\tau} & -\frac{4}{\tau} \end{pmatrix}$, we obtain that $w^T = (0,0,1,0)$ and $v^T = (v_1, v_2, v_3, v_4)$, with $v_1 = \frac{\delta}{\gamma\mu P_0 f'(N_{T_1})}$, $v_2 = -\frac{1}{\lambda\tau+1}\left(\frac{\tau\delta}{\gamma} + 1 + \frac{\delta}{\gamma\mu P_0 f'(N_{T_1})}\right) \neq 0$, $v_3 = 1$, $v_4 = \frac{\tau}{2(\lambda\tau+1)}\left(\frac{\delta}{\gamma} - \left(1 + \frac{\delta}{\gamma\mu P_0 f'(N_{T_1})}\right)\right)$. As $\langle v, w\rangle = 1$ and vector w has only one non-zero component, we need only the third component of the vector field Φ, which can be written as

$$\Phi_3(N, P, Z, Q_1) = \gamma g Z h(P(t)) - (\varepsilon + \gamma g h(\hat{P}))Z.$$

We obtain

$$A = \frac{\partial \Phi_3}{\partial \varepsilon}(E_2, \varepsilon_0) = 0,$$

$$B = \sum_{j,k=1}^{4} v_j v_k \frac{\partial^2 \Phi_3}{\partial x_j \partial x_k}(E_2, \varepsilon_0) = 2v_2 v_3 \frac{\partial^2 \Phi_3}{\partial Z \partial P}(E_2, \varepsilon_0) = 2v_2 \gamma g h'(P_0) \neq 0,$$

and

$$C = 2\sum_{j=1}^{4} v_j \frac{\partial^2 \Phi_3}{\partial x_j \partial \varepsilon}(E_2, \varepsilon_0) = 2v_3 \frac{\partial^2 \Phi_3}{\partial Z \partial \delta}(E_2, \varepsilon_0) = -2 \neq 0.$$

Consequently, a transcritical bifurcation takes place as $\varepsilon_0 = 0$, i.e., $N_T = N_{T_2}(\tau)$. □

Remark 3. *At the bifurcation point the two equilibria E_2 and E_3 have the same eigenvalues, $\lambda_j^2 = \lambda_j^3, j = \overline{1,4}$, with $Re\lambda_j^2 < 0$, for $j = 1,2,3$, and $\lambda_4^2 = \lambda_4^3 = 0$. As a consequence of the transcritical bifurcation, the eigenvalues these two eigenvalues change signs when passing through the bifurcation values, while the real parts of the other three pairs of eigenvalues remain negative close to the bifurcation value, due to continuity. Thus, the two equilibria exchange stability. Consequently, close to $N_T = N_{T_2}(\tau)$, if $N_T < N_{T_2}(\tau)$ the equilibrium point E_2 is an attractor and E_3 is a saddle of type (3,1), while if $N_T > N_{T_2}(\tau)$ the equilibrium point E_2 is a saddle of type (3,1) and E_3 is an attractor.*

5.2. Hopf Bifurcations

A Hopf bifurcation may occur at a Hopf singularity. As we proved in Section 4, only the equilibrium point E_3 is a Hopf non-hyperbolic point, in certain conditions (see Propositions 4, 7 and 8). At such a singular point, a Hopf bifurcation takes place if the conditions of the Hopf bifurcation theorem [22] are fulfilled.

5.2.1. Hopf Bifurcations for the Weak Model

As a consequence of Proposition 3, if $P^*h'(P^*) - h(P^*) \geq 0$, then the equilibrium point $E_3 = (N^*, P^*, Z^*)$ of system (7) is locally asymptotically stable for all $N_T > N_{T_2}(\tau)$, so there can be no Hopf bifurcation in this case.

If $P^*h'(P^*) - h(P^*) < 0$, then equilibrium point E_3 is a Hopf sigularity for parameters in the bifurcation stratum defined by the equation

$$a_1 a_2 - a_3 = 0, \tag{48}$$

with a_1, a_2, a_3 given by (37). Consequently, for each $N_T > N_{T_2}(\tau)$ such that (48), a Hopf bifurcation may occur, and a branch of periodic solutions may emerge around E_3.

Note that the eigenvalues of the Jacobi matrix associated with E_3 are $\lambda_{1,2}^1 = \pm i\omega$, $\lambda_3^1 = -a_1$, with $\omega^2 = a_2$. Thus, as $a_1 > 0$, the centre manifold of E_3 is attractive. As a consequence, if the conditions of the Andronov–Hopf bifurcation theorem [22] are satisfied and a supercritical Hopf bifurcation takes place (i.e., the first Lyapunov coefficient is negative), then the stable limit cycle born through this bifurcation on the extended centre manifold is locally asymptotically stable.

For the type II response function h, in the hypotheses of Proposition 4, a Hopf bifurcation may take place for each τ, at the bifurcation value $N_T = N_{T_3}(\tau)$.

The numerical simulations in Figure 4 show the existence of a stable limit cycle for values of $N_T > N_{T_3}(\tau)$. The values of the parameters used for simulations are $\mu = 5.9$, $g = 7$, $\lambda = 0.017$, $\gamma = 0.7$, $\delta = 0.17$, $k_N = 1$, $k_P = 1$. The results are consistent with the ones obtained in [12]. For $\tau = 5$, the approximate value of N_T for the Hopf bifurcation is $N_{T_3}(\tau) = 1.096$. The simulations show time series for an initial point closed to the equilibrium E_3, proving an evolution towards the steady state E_3 for $N_T = 1.05 < N_{T_3}(5)$ and to a limit cycle for $N_T = 1.2 > N_{T_3}(5)$.

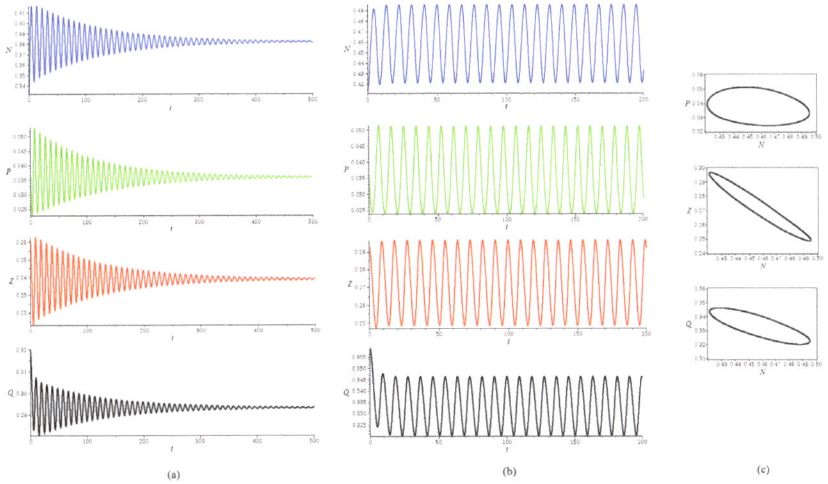

Figure 4. Simulations for the weak model, using a type II response $h(P) = \frac{P}{P+k_P}$: (**a**) $\tau = 5$, $N_T = 1.05$, showing an evolution towards E_3; (**b**) $\tau = 5$, $N_T = 1.2$, showing a periodic behavior; (**c**) projections of the attractor, for $\tau = 5$, $N_T = 1.2$, $t \in [400, 500]$. The stable limit cycle may appear through a supercritical Hopf bifurcation at $N_{T_3}(\tau) = 1.096$.

For the type III response function h, for the values of the parameters considered for simulations we have $\frac{\delta}{g\gamma} \leq h(k_P)$, so there are no Hopf bifurcations at E_3, as $N_T > NT_2(\tau)$.

5.2.2. Hopf Bifurcation for the Strong Model

According to Proposition 8, if $P^*h'(P^*) - h(P^*) \geq 0$ the equilibrium point $E_3 = (N^*, P^*, Z^*, Q_1^*)$ of system (15) is a Hopf singularity if condition

$$(b_1b_2 - b_3)b_3 - b_1^2b_4 = 0, \tag{49}$$

with $b_j, j = \overline{1,4}$ given by (43), is satisfied.

If $P^*h'(P^*) - h(P^*) < 0$, the equilibrium point E_3 is a Hopf singularity for parameters in the bifurcation stratum defined by the conditions (45). Consequently, for each $N_T > N_{T_2}(\tau)$ such that (45), a Hopf bifurcation may occur.

For the type II response function h, Proposition 8 does not apply. For the considered values of the parameters, $\mu = 5.9$, $g = 7$, $\lambda = 0.017$, $\gamma = 0.7$, $\delta = 0.17$, $k_N = 1$, $k_P = 1$, we have found that, for (τ, N_T) on the curve defined by (49) in the (τ, N_T) parameter plane, the equilibrium P^* is a Hopf singularity. This curve separates regions 3 and 4 in Figure 3b, and a Hopf bifurcation may take place when the parameters cross this curve.

For $\tau = 5$, the approximate value of N_T for the Hopf bifurcation is $N_{T_3}(\tau) = 0.955$. The simulations in Figure 5, show the projections of parts of the trajectories for an initial point near the equilibrium E_3, proving an evolution towards a stable limit cycle, for (a) $N_T = 1.05 > N_{T_3}(5)$, (b) $N_T = 1.096 > N_{T_3}(5)$ and (c) $N_T = 1.2 > N_{T_3}(5)$.

The trajectories in Figures 4 and 5 were obtained using the DEtools package in MAPLE 18, applying the fourth-order Runge–Kutta method, with a stepsize 0.01.

Remark 4. *As the parameters vary away from the Hopf bifurcation curve, the limit cycle born through the Hopf bifurcation may disappear, may double the period, etc. Since the dimensions of both the weak and the strong models are greater than three, strange attractors may also exist. Nevertheless, as the domains for each of the two models are bounded, the ω-limit set for each model is also bounded, and so are their attractors.*

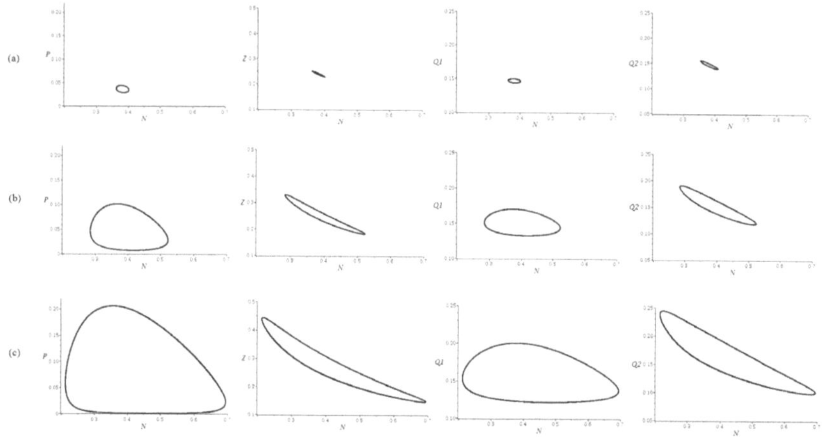

Figure 5. Simulations for the strong model, using a type II response $h(P) = \frac{P}{P+k_P}$. Projections of the attractor for $\tau = 5$ and (**a**) $N_T = 1.05$; (**b**) $N_T = 1.096$; (**c**) $N_T = 1.2$; $t \in [700, 800]$. The stable limit cycle may appear through a supercritical Hopf bifurcation at $N_{T_3}(\tau) = 0.955$.

6. Discussion

In this study, we have analysed two NPZ models for a closed ecosystem with three compartments, dissolved nutrient, phytoplankton and zooplankton, incorporating a delay in nutrient recycling. The models were obtained starting from a NPZ model introduced in [12], by using the gamma distribution function with one or two degrees of freedom. The aim of the paper was to study how the stability and bifurcation of the equilibrium solutions depend on the total amount of nutrient and the delay.

We have shown that each of the two models have at most three equilibrium points in the region of interest, and that at most one of the equilibrium points is locally asymptotically stable at each value of the total nutrients. More precisely,

(1) For $N_T < N_{T_1}$, there is only one equilibrium point with no phytoplankton and no zooplankton (E_1), which is asymptotically stable;
(2) For $N_{T_1} < N_T < N_{T_2}(\tau)$ the equilibrium $E_2$with phytoplankton and no zooplankton is asymptotically stable, while E_1 is unstable;
(3) As $N_T > N_{T_2}(\tau)$, the first two equilibria are unstable, while the equilibrium E_3 with both phytoplankton and zooplankton is asymptotically stable either for all $N_T > N_{T_2}(\tau)$ or there exists an $N_{T_3}(\tau)$ such that E_3 is stable for $N_{T_2}(\tau) < N_T < N_{T_3}(\tau)$, and unstable for $N_T > N_{T_3}(\tau)$, close to $N_{T_3}(\tau)$, depending on the response function h.

Further, we have proven that the changes of stability at N_{T_1} and $N_{T_2}(\tau)$ occur through transcritical bifurcations. Finally, we have shown that the change of stability at N_{T_3} is a Hopf singularity and the associated bifurcation will lead to stable limit cycles if it is supercritical. Numerical simulations show the existence of stable limit cycles for each delay τ, close to the bifurcation value $N_T = N_{T_3}(\tau)$.

Thus, for each of the two considered models, the ω-limit sets contains at most one equilibrium point. In specific hypotheses on the response function h, the ω-limit sets may contain a limit cycle for certain values of the parameters N_T and τ. However, as the dimension of both models is greater than 2, the ω-limit sets may also contain strange attractors.

Our results on the existence of equilibria are consistent with those of [12] for the system with a general distribution (1), who showed the equilibrium values of N, P, Z are only affected by the mean delay and not the form of the distribution. The stability result (1) above reproduces that of [12] for the general distribution case. The stability result (2) is stronger than that of [12] for a general distribution, and thus is likely a consequence of our choice of distributions. In fact, [12] showed that if the system has a discrete delay (Dirac distribution), then the equilibrium E_2 may undergo a Hopf bifurcation; however, we show that it is not possible for the distributions we consider. Our results extend those of [12] by proving the stability result (3) for the two systems studied and by proving the types of bifurcations that occur as the stability of the equilibrium points changes. Further, we showed the possibility of a codimension-two double Hopf bifurcation in the system with the two-degrees of freedom gamma distribution.

To conclude, we discuss the implications of our work for application. The general trend of bifurcations of the equilibrium points as the total amount of nutrients is increased is as follows: first, the phytoplankton only equilibrium point, E_2, appears and then the coexistence equilibrium point, E_3. This is is biologically plausible: as more nutrients are available, the system can support more organisms. Our work highlights the fact that a delay in the recycling can be stabilizing: the amount of nutrients needed for the transcritical bifurcation leading to the emergence of E_3 to occur increases with the size of the mean delay. We also showed, for a given amount of total nutrients, the delay decreases the equilibrium size of at least one of N, P, Z. This is because some of the nutrients are stored in the other compartments of the system, which represent the nutrients that are being recycled. Both these results were identical for the weak and strong models. Where these models differ was in the effect of the delay on the Hopf bifurcation of the E_3 equilibrium point. For both models, as the delay is increased we observe the same qualitative effect: the Hopf bifurcation value N_{T3} increases, then decreases, then increases. However, the variation is larger for the strong model than for the weak model. Thus, the N_{T3} for the weak model is less than that for the strong model for small enough delay, with the reverse for large enough delay.

Author Contributions: M.S., C.R., R.E. and S.A.C. have contributed equally in writing this paper. All authors have read and agreed to the published version of the manuscript.

Funding: This research received no external funding.

Data Availability Statement: Not applicable.

Acknowledgments: This research was supported by Horizon2020-2017-RISE-777911 project. S.A.C. is supported by the Natural Sciences and Engineering Research Council.

Conflicts of Interest: The authors declare no conflict of interest.

References

1. Fenchel, T. Marine plankton food chains. *Ann. Rev. Ecol. Syst.* **1988**, *19*, 19–38. [CrossRef]
2. Basu, S.; Mackey, K.R. Phytoplankton as key mediators of the biological carbon pump: Their responses to a changing climate. *Sustainability* **2018**, *10*, 869. [CrossRef]
3. Edwards, A.M. Adding detritus to a nutrient–phytoplankton–zooplankton model: A dyna mical-systems approach. *J. Plankton Res.* **2001**, *23*, 389–413. [CrossRef]
4. Franks, P.J. NPZ models of plankton dynamics: Their construction, coupling to physics, and application. *J. Oceanogr.* **2002**, *58*, 379–387. [CrossRef]
5. Poulin, F.J.; Franks, P.J. Size-structured planktonic ecosystems: Constraints, controls and assembly instructions. *J. Plankton Res.* **2010**, *32*, fbp145. [CrossRef] [PubMed]
6. Ruan, S. Turing instability and travelling waves in diffusive plankton models with delayed nutrient recycling. *IMA J. Appl. Math.* **1998**, *61*, 15–32. [CrossRef]
7. Ruan, S. Oscillations in plankton models with nutrient recycling. *J. Theor. Biol.* **2001**, *208*, 15–26. [CrossRef] [PubMed]
8. Kmet, T. Material recycling in a closed aquatic ecosystem. II. Bifurcation analysis of a simple food-chain model. *Bull. Math. Biol.* **1996**, *58*, 983–1000. [CrossRef]
9. Jang, S.J.; Baglama, J. Nutrient-plankton models with nutrient recycling. *Comput. Math. Appl.* **2005**, *49*, 375–387. [CrossRef]
10. He, X.Z.; Ruan, S. Global stability in chemostat-type plankton models with delayed nutrient recycling. *J. Math. Biol.* **1998**, *37*, 253–271. [CrossRef]
11. Tao, Y.; Campbell, S.A.; Poulin, F.J. Dynamics of a diffusive nutrient-phytoplankton-zooplankton model with spatio-temporal delay. *SIAM J. Appl. Math.* **2021**, *81*, 2405–2432. [CrossRef]
12. Kloosterman, M.; Campbell, S.A.; Poulin, F.J. A closed NPZ model with delayed nutrient recycling. *J. Math. Biol.* **2014**, *68*, 815–850. [CrossRef] [PubMed]

13. Gentleman, W.; Neuheimer, A. Functional responses and ecosystem dynamics: How clearance rates explain the influence of satiation, food-limitation and acclimation. *J. Plankton Res.* **2008**, *30*, 1215–1231. [CrossRef]
14. Holling, C.S. The functional response of invertebrate predators to prey density. *Mem. Entomol. Soc. Can.* **1966**, *98*, 5–86. [CrossRef]
15. Gu, K.; Kharitonov, V.; Chen, J. *Stability of Time-Delay Systems*; Control Engineering; Birkhäuser: Boston, MA, USA, 2012.
16. Fargue, D. Réducibilité des systèmes héréditaires à des systèmes dynamiques. *CR Acad. Sci. Paris B* **1973**, *277*, 471–473.
17. Kuang, Y. *Delay Differential Equations: With Applications in Population Dynamics*; Academic Press: Cambridge, MA, USA, 1993.
18. Cushing, J.M. *An Introduction to Structured Population Dynamics*; SIAM: Philadelphia, PA, USA, 1998.
19. Hurwitz, A. On the conditions under which an equation has only roots with negative real parts. In *Selected Papers on Mathematical Trends in Control Theory*; Bellman, R., Kalaba, R., Eds.; Dover Publications: Mineola, NY, USA, 1964; pp. 72–82. (In English)
20. Sotomayor, J. Generic bifurcations of dynamical systems. In *Dynamical Systems*; Elsevier: Amsterdam, The Netherlands, 1973; pp. 561–582.
21. Perko, L. *Differential Equations and Dynamical Systems*; Springer Science & Business Media: Berlin/Heidelberg, Germany, 2001; Volume 7.
22. Kuznetsov, Y.A. *Elements of Applied Bifurcation Theory*; Springer: Berlin/Heidelberg, Germany, 2004; Volume 112.

mathematics

MDPI

Article

Semi-Analytical Analysis of Drug Diffusion through a Thin Membrane Using the Differential Quadrature Method

Abdelfattah Mustafa [1], Reda S. Salama [2,*] and Mokhtar Mohamed [2]

[1] Department of Mathematics, Faculty of Science, Islamic University of Madinah, Madinah 42351, Saudi Arabia; aelsayed@iu.edu.sa or amelsayed@mans.edu.eg
[2] Basic Science Department, Faculty of Engineering, Delta University for Science and Technology, Gamasa 11152, Egypt; mokhtar.alsaidi@deltauniv.edu.eg
* Correspondence: reda.salama@deltauniv.edu.eg or prof.dr.reda.salama@gmail.com; Tel.: +20-1061391656

Abstract: The primary goal of this work is to solve the problem of drug diffusion through a thin membrane using a differential quadrature approach with drastically different shape functions, such as Lagrange interpolation and discrete singular convolution (the delta Lagrange kernel and the regularized Shannon kernel). A nonlinear partial differential equation with two time- and space-dependent variables governs the system. To reduce the two independent variables by one, the partial differential equation is transformed into an ordinary differential equation using a one-parameter group transformation. With the aid of the iterative technique, the differential quadrature methods change this equation into an algebraic equation. Then, using a MATLAB program, a code is created that solves this equation for each shape function. To ensure the validity, efficiency, and accuracy of the developed techniques, the computed results are compared to previous numerical and analytical solutions. In addition, the $L\infty$ error is applied. As a consequence of the numerical outcomes, the differential quadrature method, which is primarily based on a discrete singular convolution shape function, is an effective numerical method that can be used to solve the problem of drug diffusion through a thin membrane, guaranteeing a higher accuracy, faster convergence, and greater reliability than other techniques.

Keywords: group theoretic method; drug diffusion; differential quadrature technique; discrete singular convolution; thin membrane; Lagrange interpolation polynomial

MSC: 34A25

Citation: Mustafa, A.; Salama, R.S.; Mohamed, M. Semi-Analytical Analysis of Drug Diffusion through a Thin Membrane Using the Differential Quadrature Method. *Mathematics* **2023**, *11*, 2998. https://doi.org/10.3390/math11132998

Academic Editors: Mihaela Neamțu, Eva Kaslik and Anca Rădulescu

Received: 12 June 2023
Revised: 25 June 2023
Accepted: 30 June 2023
Published: 5 July 2023

1. Introduction

Diffusion through membranes represents a fascinating form of diffusion research that is crucial in the pharmaceutical industry [1–4]. To study the procedure, multiple experiments can be carried out. Testing a drug's non-stationary diffusion across a donor cell through a thin membrane to a recipient cell is one experiment that clearly shows this behavior [2,3]. The problem of drug diffusion through a thin membrane was examined in 2002 utilizing the group theoretical technique, which is considered a special case of the Lie method and yielded limited results. This method was used to determine the drug concentration in the membrane and that in the cells of the donor and receiver [4]. Spoelstra and Van Wyk [5] modeled the process as a pair of cells of identical volume divided by a thin membrane called cells of the donor and the receiver. A high drug concentration dissolves in a saltwater solution in the cell of a donor, while the receiver's cell possesses only a solution of saline. Since both cells are subjected to continual stirring, the drug does not initially diffuse through the membrane. The concentration of the drug starts to rise in the receiver cell and across the membrane. The authors used the finite difference technique to solve the problem numerically, evaluating the results of the model's parameters and determining the concentration in receiving and donor cells. It was demonstrated that diffusion through membranes can be modeled using specific boundary conditions across them at various scales, from macroscopic to microscopic [6]. In this case, the membranes are considered thin in relation to the overall size of the system. The membrane is introduced as a transmission boundary condition on a macroscopic scale, allowing effective modeling of systems involving multiple scales. A numerical lattice Boltzmann scheme with a partial bounce-back condition at the membrane was proposed and analyzed on a microscopic scale [7]. This microscopic approach was shown to provide an accurate approximation of the transmission boundary condition. Moreover, a formula for the permeability of a thin membrane as a function of a microscopic transmission parameter was derived from the analysis of the macroscopic scheme. In a microscopic model, the mean waiting time for a particle to pass through the membrane is proportional to the membrane's permeability [8–10].

The macroscopic transmission conditions were discretized by Aho et al. [11] in order to derive an expression for the mass flux between two discretization points separated by a membrane. The expressions used to solve the diffusion equation were obtained from the finite difference and finite volume methods. The authors proposed a microscopic implementation of the lattice Boltzmann method [12,13], in which the membrane is treated as a partial bounce-back condition between two lattice nodes. They performed a multiple-scale analysis after presenting the discrete scheme and derived an explicit expression for the mass flux at the membrane. Several papers in the literature have presented mathematical models that use the group transformation technique, such as Hansen [14], Gaggioli et al. [15], Boutros et al. [16], and Abd-el-Malek et al. [17], to calculate the diffusion of a drug through a membrane along with that in both donor and receiver cells. Abd-el-Malek et al. [18] recently used the Lie group method to investigate drug diffusion through a biological membrane that typically partially absorbed the drug. The mathematical scheme was defined by a nonlinear partial differential formula which included the process of diffusion along the initial and boundary conditions and afterwards was converted into an ordinary differential equation with its associated conditions by reducing the number of independent variables by one. Fourth- and fifth-order Runge–Kutta methods were used to solve the obtained nonlinear ordinary differential equation.

Finite difference, finite element, finite volume, meshless, and least squares methods have been used to solve such problems. The main disadvantage of these methods is the requirement of a high number of grid points, such that a long performance time is required to obtain the required accuracy. Recently, a differential quadrature method (DQM) has become the most popular method for deriving numerical solutions to boundary value problems. It was developed by Richard Bellman and his associates in the early 1970s [19,20]. The key idea of the DQ application lies in the calculation of the weighting coefficients for the first-order derivative based on the Lagrange polynomial function. This method leads to accurate solutions with fewer grid points compared with finite difference and finite element methods. The convergence and stability of this method depend on the choice of the shape function. Lagrange interpolation polynomials, the cardinal sine function, the delta Lagrange kernel (DLK), and the regularized Shannon kernel (RSK) are some examples of such functions which have led to the development of the polynomial-based differential quadrature method (PDQM) [21], the sinc differential quadrature method (SDQM) [22], and the discrete singular convolution differential quadrature method (DSCDQM), respectively [23]. Thus, the DQ method has emerged as a powerful numerical discretization tool for solving a variety of problems in the engineering and physical sciences [24–30]. Bellman et al. [19] suggested that the nth-order derivative of the function with respect to a grid point can be approximated as a linear summation of the values of the function for all of the sample points in the domain.

In our model, we use a differential quadrature method (DQM) with drastically different shape functions to solve the problem of drug diffusion through a thin membrane. These shape functions are the Lagrange interpolation function [21,31], the Delta Lagrange kernel, and the Regularized Shannon kernel [32–35], and they have been successfully applied to the problem of drug diffusion through a thin membrane. Furthermore, the partial differential equation is transformed into an ordinary differential equation (ODE) using a one-parameter group transformation [4] to reduce the two independent variables by one. To ensure the validity, efficiency, and accuracy of the developed techniques, the computed results are compared to previous numerical and analytical solutions [4,18]. The novelty of this method is to provide a parametric analysis in two cases to explain how time and the membrane section affect the drug concentration and diffusion coefficient for the first time.

2. Formulation of the Problem

Fick's-law-based diffusion mathematical models do not apply to human skin, hair-free rodent skin membranes, or multiple synthetic membranes [5]. Fick's laws of diffusion describe diffusion and were derived by Adolf Fick in 1855. They can be used to calculate the diffusion coefficient. Fick's first law can be used to derive his second law, which in turn is identical to the diffusion equation. Assuming that the rate at which absorption occurs at any place via the membrane corresponds to the drug concentration at that place and that no diffusion occurs through the membrane's edges, the concentration gradient through the membrane is viewed as a function of time and x direction, and the velocity of diffusion in the membrane for each unit area is related to the concentration gradient through the membrane. Consider a unit thickness membrane, wgere "q" is the coefficient that calculates the rate of absorption of the drug in the membrane if "Q" is the partition coefficient. The governing equation of the diffusion process is [4]:

$$\frac{\partial C(x,t)}{\partial t} = \frac{\partial}{\partial x}\left[P(x,t)\frac{\partial C(x,t)}{\partial x}\right] - q\left[\frac{C(x,t)}{t}\right]^2, \; 0 < x < 1, \; 0 < t \tag{1}$$

where C(x,t) is the drug's concentration at an instant of time (t) and at an x-distance from a single side of the membrane. The function utilized to compute the diffusion coefficient is denoted by P(x,t).

Based on the boundary condition (Equations (2) and (3)) and initial conditions (Equation (4)):

$$\begin{cases} C(0,t) = F(t) \\ C(1,t) = G(t) \end{cases} \quad t > 0 \tag{2}$$

$$F(t) = \frac{\alpha Q}{D(t) - \beta}, \quad G(t) = \gamma Q[R(t)]^2 \tag{3}$$

$$C(x,0) = 0 \quad \text{at } 0 \leq x \leq 1 \tag{4}$$

where α, β, and γ are constants. In addition, $D(t)$ and $R(t)$ are the concentrations of drug in the donor and the receiver cells, respectively.

3. Method of Solution

We use a differential quadrature approach with totally different shape functions to solve a nonlinear partial differential equation with two dependent variables, C(x,t) and P(x,t), in both space and time. To begin, we solve the partial differential Equation (1) using a one-parameter group transformation. In this transformation, the two independent variables are minimized by one, and this equation is transformed into an ODE shown in the following:

Assuming the identity function, i.e., $\zeta = x$, according to a similar analysis, the dependent variables "C" and "P" are

$$C(x,t) = \psi(t)U(\zeta) \tag{5}$$

$$P(x,t) = \omega(t)T(\zeta) \tag{6}$$

Thus, using Equations (5) and (6), this is accomplished by substituting "C" and "P" and their partial derivatives as follows:

$$\begin{cases} \frac{\partial C}{\partial t} = U\frac{d\psi}{dt} \\ \frac{\partial C}{\partial x} = \psi\frac{dU}{d\zeta} \\ \frac{\partial^2 C}{\partial x^2} = \psi\frac{d^2U}{d\zeta^2} \\ \frac{\partial P}{\partial x} = \omega\frac{dT}{d\zeta} \end{cases} \tag{7}$$

Then, by substituting Equation (7) into (1):

$$U(\zeta)\frac{d\psi(t)}{dt} = \frac{\partial}{\partial\zeta}\left[\omega(t)T(\zeta)\psi(t)\frac{dU(\zeta)}{d\zeta}\right] - q\left[\frac{\psi(t)U(\zeta)}{t}\right]^2 \tag{8}$$

By simplifying Equation (8)

$$\frac{\partial^2 U}{\partial\zeta^2} + \left[\frac{1}{T}\frac{\partial T}{\partial\zeta}\right]\frac{\partial U}{\partial\zeta} - \left[\frac{1}{\omega\psi T}\frac{\partial\psi}{\partial t}\right]U - q\left[\frac{\psi}{\omega T t^2}\right]U^2 = 0 \tag{9}$$

To reduce Equation (9) to an expression with one independent invariant (ζ), the coefficients must be constants or functions of (ζ) only. Thus,

$$\begin{cases} \frac{1}{T}\frac{\partial T}{\partial\zeta} = E_1(\zeta) \\ \frac{1}{\omega\psi T}\frac{\partial\psi}{\partial t} = E_2(\zeta) \\ \frac{\psi}{\omega T t^2} = E_3(\zeta) \end{cases} \tag{10}$$

3.1. Case 1

Assume $T(\zeta) = exp(-\zeta)$, $\psi(t) = \mu\, t$, and $\omega(t) = \frac{1}{t}$, where μ is a constant, Hence, $E_1 = -1$, $E_2 = exp(\zeta)$, and $E_3 = \mu\, exp(\zeta)$. So, Equation (9) can be written as:

$$\frac{\partial^2 U}{\partial\zeta^2} - \frac{\partial U}{\partial\zeta} - \exp(\zeta)U - q\mu\exp(\zeta)U^2 = 0 \tag{11}$$

with the following boundary conditions:

$$\begin{cases} U(0) = \alpha Q \\ U(1) = Q \end{cases} \tag{12}$$

In addition,

$$\begin{cases} P(x,t) = \frac{\exp(-x)}{t}, \\ D(t) = \frac{1}{\mu t} + \beta, \\ R(t) = \sqrt{\frac{\mu}{\gamma}t}. \end{cases} \tag{13}$$

3.2. Case 2

Assume $T(\zeta) = exp(-\zeta^2)$, $\psi(t) = \mu\, t$, and $\omega(t) = \frac{1}{t}$, where μ is a constant. Hence, $E_1 = -2$, $E_2 = exp(\zeta^2)$, and $E_3 = \mu\, exp(\zeta^2)$. Thus, Equation (9) can be written as:

$$\frac{\partial^2 U}{\partial\zeta^2} - 2\zeta\frac{\partial U}{\partial\zeta} - \exp\left(\zeta^2\right)U - q\mu\exp(\zeta^2)U^2 = 0 \tag{14}$$

with the following boundary conditions:

$$\begin{cases} U(0) = \alpha Q \\ U(1) = Q \end{cases} \tag{15}$$

In addition,

$$P(x,t) = \frac{\exp(-x^2)}{t} \tag{16}$$

Now, for the previous cases, the differential quadrature method (DQM) with various shaped functions is employed to solve nonlinear partial differential equations as follows:

- Shape Function 1: Lagrange Interpolation Polynomial (PDQM);

The functional values associated with any unknown such "U" at a specific number of grid points "N" can be defined by this shape function as [21,31,36]:

$$U(\zeta_i) = \sum_{j=1}^{N} \frac{\prod_{k=1}^{N} (\zeta_i - \zeta_k)}{(\zeta_i - \zeta_j) \prod_{j=1, j \neq k}^{N} (\zeta_j - \zeta_k)} U(\zeta_j),\ (i = 1:N) \tag{17}$$

As a result, the following are the various derivatives of "U":

$$\left.\frac{\partial^n U}{\partial \zeta^n}\right|_{\zeta = \zeta_i} = \sum_{j=1}^{N} \Re_{ij}^{(n)} U(\zeta_j), \quad (i = 1:N) \tag{18}$$

where $\Re_{ij}^{(n)}$ denotes the weighting coefficients for the nth derivative of "U".

As a result, we need the weighting coefficients for the first and second derivatives ($\Re_{ij}^{(1)}$ and $\Re_{ij}^{(2)}$) to solve these cases, which can be discovered by differentiating Equation (17):

$$\Re_{ij}^{(1)} = \begin{cases} \frac{1}{(\zeta_i - \zeta_j)} \prod_{\substack{k=1, \\ k \neq i,j}}^{N} \frac{(\zeta_i - \zeta_k)}{(\zeta_j - \zeta_k)} & i \neq j \\ -\sum_{\substack{j=1, \\ j \neq i}}^{N} \Re_{ij}^{(1)} & i = j \end{cases}, \quad \Re_{ij}^{(2)} = \left[\Re_{ij}^{(1)}\right]\left[\Re_{ij}^{(1)}\right], \tag{19}$$

- Shape Function 2: Discrete Singular Convolution (DSCDQM)

The singular convolution is presented as [34,37–39]:

$$g(\zeta) = (W * \eta)(\zeta) = \int_{-\infty}^{\infty} W(\zeta - s)\, \eta(s)\, ds \tag{20}$$

where $W(\zeta - s)$ denotes a singular kernel and $\eta(\zeta)$ is a function space element for testing.

This shape function is determined by the kernel type. However, because this shape function has many kernels, we will use two of them to describe the functional values of "U" and its derivatives at a given number of grid points "N" as follows:

Kernel (1): Delta Lagrange Kernel (DLK):

The DSC typically uses a weighted linear sum of the function values at 2M+1 points in the direction of the space variable to approximate the derivative of a certain function with regard to a space variable at a discrete point [31,32,40]. The DLK can be applied as a shape function to approximate unknown "U" and its derivatives as the following:

$$U(\zeta_i) = \sum_{j=-M}^{M} \frac{1}{(\zeta_i - \zeta_j)} \times \frac{\prod\limits_{k=-M}^{M} (\zeta_i - \zeta_k)}{\prod\limits_{j=-M,\ k\neq i,j}^{M} (\zeta_j - \zeta_k)} \times U(\zeta_j),\ (i = -N : N),\ M \geq 1 \tag{21}$$

As a result, the following are the various derivatives of "U":

$$\left.\frac{\partial^n U}{\partial \zeta^n}\right|_{\zeta = \zeta_i} = \sum_{j=1}^{N} \Re_{ij}^{(n)} U(\zeta_j), \quad (i = -N : N) \tag{22}$$

As a result, we need the weighting coefficients for the first and second derivatives ($\Re_{ij}^{(1)}$ and $\Re_{ij}^{(2)}$) to solve these cases, which can be discovered by differentiating Equation (21):

$$\begin{aligned} \Re_{ij}^{(1)} &= \begin{cases} \frac{1}{(\zeta_i-\zeta_j)} \prod\limits_{\substack{k=-M,\\ k\neq i,j}}^{M} \frac{(\zeta_i-\zeta_k)}{(\zeta_j-\zeta_k)} & i\neq j \\ -\sum\limits_{\substack{j=-M,\\ j\neq i}}^{M} \Re_{ij}^{(1)} & i=j \end{cases}, \\ \Re_{ij}^{(2)} &= \begin{cases} 2\left(\Re_{ij}^{(1)}\Re_{ii}^{(1)} - \frac{\Re_{ij}^{(1)}}{(\zeta_i-\zeta_j)}\right) & i\neq j \\ -\sum\limits_{\substack{j=-M,\\ j\neq i}}^{M} \Re_{ij}^{(2)} & i=j \end{cases}, \end{aligned} \tag{23}$$

Kernel (2): Regularized Shannon kernel (RSK) [41]:

To make comparisons and demonstrations, the regularized Shannon kernel is used to discuss this problem. In DSCDQM–RSK, it is presumed that the unknown "U" with its derivatives is the estimated weighted linear sum of the nodal values. As a result, the regularized Shannon kernel is discretized by [41]:

$$\begin{gathered} U(\zeta_i) = \sum_{j=-M}^{M} \left\langle \frac{\sin\left[\frac{\pi(\zeta_i-\zeta_j)}{\Delta}\right]}{\frac{\pi(\zeta_i-\zeta_j)}{\Delta}} \exp\left(\frac{-(\zeta_i-\zeta_j)^2}{2\sigma^2}\right) \right\rangle U(\zeta_j) \\ \text{where } (i = -N : N), \sigma = (\tau \times \Delta) > 0 \end{gathered} \tag{24}$$

where $\Delta, \tau,$ and σ are the step size, the computational parameter, and the factor regularized Shannon respectively. The truncation error is very tiny due to the use of the Gaussian regularizer; thus, the above version provided by Equation (24) is feasible and has basically compact numerical interpolation support.

As a result, the following are the various derivatives of "U":

$$\left.\frac{\partial^n U}{\partial \zeta^n}\right|_{\zeta = \zeta_i} = \sum_{j=1}^{N} \Re_{ij}^{(n)} U(\zeta_j) \quad (i = -N : N) \tag{25}$$

As a result, we need the weighting coefficients for the first and second derivatives ($\Re_{ij}^{(1)}$ and $\Re_{ij}^{(2)}$) to solve these cases, which can be discovered by differentiating Equation (24):

$$\Re_{ij}^{(1)} = \begin{cases} \frac{(-1)^{i-j}}{\Delta(i-j)} \exp(-\Delta^2(\frac{(i-j)^2}{2\sigma^2})), & i \neq j \\ 0 & i = j \end{cases},$$
$$\Re_{ij}^{(2)} = \begin{cases} (\frac{2(-1)^{i-j+1}}{\Delta^2(i-j)^2} + \frac{1}{\sigma^2}) \exp\left(-\Delta^2\left(\frac{i-j}{\sqrt{2}\sigma}\right)^2\right), & i \neq j \\ -\frac{1}{\sigma^2} - \frac{\pi^2}{3\Delta^2} & i = j \end{cases} \tag{26}$$

This discussion has revealed that the kernel type, regular grid points (N), and bandwidth (2M+1) play a significant role in achieving convergence and accuracy solutions.

The linear ODE is then obtained using the iterative quadrature method, which is a numerical method used to solve initial value problems (IVPs) for ordinary differential equations (ODEs). This method involves the use of numerical quadrature formulas to approximate a solution of the ODE, and then iteratively improving the approximation until the desired level of accuracy is achieved.

1. Firstly, solving Equations (11) and (13) as a linear system;

Case 1:

$$\sum_{j=1}^{N} \Re_{ij}^{(2)} U_j - \sum_{j=1}^{N} \Re_{ij}^{(1)} U_j - \exp(\zeta) \sum_{j=1}^{N} \delta_{ij} U_j - q\mu \exp(\zeta) \sum_{j=1}^{N} \delta_{ij} U_j = 0 \tag{27}$$

Case 2:

$$\sum_{j=1}^{N} \Re_{ij}^{(2)} U_j - 2\zeta \sum_{j=1}^{N} \Re_{ij}^{(1)} U_j - \exp\left(\zeta^2\right) \sum_{j=1}^{N} \delta_{ij} U_j - q\mu \exp(\zeta^2) \sum_{j=1}^{N} \delta_{ij} U_j = 0 \tag{28}$$

2. Then, we solve the following iterative system until the required convergence is reached [31,40];

$$\left| \frac{U_{s+1}}{U_s} \right| < 1$$

where $s = 0, 1, 2, \ldots$

Case 1:

$$\sum_{j=1}^{N} \Re_{ij}^{(2)} U_{s+1,j} - \sum_{j=1}^{N} \Re_{ij}^{(1)} U_{s+1,j} - \exp(\zeta) \sum_{j=1}^{N} \delta_{ij} U_{s+1,j} - q\mu \exp(\zeta) \times \left[\sum_{j=1}^{N} \delta_{ij} U_{s,j} U_{s+1,j} \right] = 0 \tag{29}$$

Case 2:

$$\sum_{j=1}^{N} \Re_{ij}^{(2)} U_{s+1,j} - 2\zeta \sum_{j=1}^{N} \Re_{ij}^{(1)} U_{s+1,j} - \exp\left(\zeta^2\right) \sum_{j=1}^{N} \delta_{ij} U_{s+1,j} - q\mu \exp(\zeta^2) \times \left[\sum_{j=1}^{N} \delta_{ij} U_{s,j} U_{s+1,j} \right] = 0 \tag{30}$$

So, the key to DQM accuracy is finding the weighting coefficients, which are based on the appropriate selection of a shape function.

4. Numerical Results

In this section, the DQM is examined with totally different shape functions (PDQM [21,31,36], DSCDQM–DLK, and DSCDQM–RSK [34,37–39]) to solve the problem of drug diffusion through a thin membrane. These techniques are introduced after applying a one-parameter group transformation to Equation (1), classified as a partial differential equation with two independent variables, which was reduced by one and transformed into an ordinary differential equation. We accomplished our computations by designing the MATLAB code for each approach. The most important aim of our article is to know the validity, efficiency, and accuracy of the developed techniques by comparing the computed results with earlier numerical and analytical solutions [4,18]. To examine the convergence and accuracy of the developed methods, we compute error as the following:

$$L_\infty\ Error = \max_{1\leq i\leq N} |C_{numerical}(x_i, t_1) - C_{exact}(x_i, t_1)| \tag{31}$$

where $L_\infty Error$ expresses the maximum error norm. max is the maximum value of the absolute difference between the numerical and exact drug concentration results in the interval [1, N].

Now, we begin to demonstrate the obtained results in order to determine the stability, convergence, and validity of DQM based on three different types of shape functions in the following.

Table 1 explains the effect of using uniform and non-uniform grid points (N) on calculating C(x,t) via PDQM for both cases at different times (t), with $x = 0.5, \mu = \frac{10^{-6}}{4}$, $\alpha = 2$, $Q = 81.95$, and $q = 1.16$. For uniform grid points, the results match with previous studies [4,18] at $N \geq 9$ and execution time 0.25 s, and at $N \geq 7$ and execution time 0.013 s for non-uniform grid points. Thus, using non-uniform grid points is the best way to avoid Runge's phenomenon. A non-uniform distribution (Gauss–Chebyshev–Lobatto discretization) is used as the following:

$$\mathrm{x_i} = \frac{1}{2}\left[1 - \cos\left(\frac{\mathrm{i}-1}{\mathrm{N}-1}\pi\right)\right], \ (\mathrm{i} = 1, 2, \ldots \mathrm{N}) \tag{32}$$

Table 1. Computation of $C(x,t)$ via PDQM for cases (1 and 2) at grid points (N) and time (t) for $x = 0.5$, $\mu = \frac{10^{-6}}{4}$, $\alpha = 2$, $Q = 81.95$, and $q = 1.16$.

Uniform (N)	C(x, 25)		C(x, 50)		Non-Uniform (N)	C(x, 25)		C(x, 50)	
	Case 1	Case 2	Case 1	Case 2		Case 1	Case 2	Case 1	Case 2
4	0.00235	0.00241	0.00325	0.00344	4	0.00167	0.00175	0.00259	0.00262
5	0.00201	0.00206	0.00211	0.00235	5	0.00087	0.00088	0.00237	0.00239
6	0.00138	0.00139	0.00198	0.00200	6	0.00071	0.00072	0.00140	0.00145
7	0.00099	0.00105	0.00145	0.00148	7	0.00069	0.00071	0.00138	0.00142
8	0.00072	0.00075	0.00140	0.00141	8	0.00069	0.00071	0.00138	0.00142
9	0.00069	0.00071	0.00138	0.00142	9	0.00069	0.00071	0.00138	0.00142
10	0.00069	0.00071	0.00138	0.00142	10	0.00069	0.00071	0.00138	0.00142
11	0.00069	0.00071	0.00138	0.00142	11	0.00069	0.00071	0.00138	0.00142
Previous Studies [4,18]	0.00069	0.00071	0.00138	0.00142		0.00069	0.00071	0.00138	0.00142
Execution time	0.25 (second)—uniform $N \geq 9$					0.013 (second)—non-uniform $N \geq 7$			

Table 2 compares the PDQM to previous studies [4,18] in terms of calculating the $U(x)$, $C(x,t)$, and L_∞ error norms in [0, 1] for both cases at distances (x) for a non-uniform grid $(N = 7), t = 20$ min, $\mu = \frac{10^{-6}}{4}$, $\alpha = 2$, $Q = 81.95$, and $q = 1.16$. It is noticed that the L_∞ error reaches 10^{-7}, which ensures the validity of the PDQM at t = 20 min and different distances (x). In addition, the results match with previous works [4,18] in both cases with an error of about 10^{-6} and an execution time of 0.013 s for computing $U(x)$ and $C(x,t)$. All of this proves that the PDQM is an efficient and effective method for solving the problem of drug diffusion through membranes.

Table 2. Computation of $U(x), C(x,t)$, and L_∞ error norms in [0, 1] via the PDQM for cases (1 and 2) at distances (x) for a non-uniform grid $(N = 7), t = 20$ min, $\mu = \frac{10^{-6}}{4}, \alpha = 2, Q = 81.95$, and $q = 1.16$.

x	PDQM				Previous Studies [4,18]		L_∞
	$U(x)$		$C(x,20)$		$C(x,20)$		
	Case 1	Case 2	Case 1	Case 2	Case 1	Case 2	
0	163.9000	163.9000	0.0008195	0.0008195	0.000820	0.000820	5.0×10^{-07}
0.1	151.9837	151.5689	0.0007599	0.0007584	0.000760	0.000758	1.0×10^{-07}
0.2	140.5881	140.5502	0.00070294	0.0007028	0.000703	0.000703	1.0×10^{-07}
0.3	129.8072	130.5885	0.000649	0.0006529	0.000650	0.000653	1.0×10^{-06}
0.4	119.7429	121.4970	0.0005987	0.0006075	0.000600	0.000608	1.3×10^{-06}
0.5	110.5066	113.1459	0.0005525	0.0005657	0.000553	0.000566	5.0×10^{-07}
0.6	102.2230	105.4577	0.00051112	0.000528	0.000512	0.000528	8.8×10^{-07}
0.7	95.0357	98.4086	0.00047518	0.000492	0.000476	0.000492	8.2×10^{-07}
0.8	89.11420	92.0381	0.00044447	0.0004602	0.000446	0.000461	1.5×10^{-06}
0.9	84.66554	86.47	0.00042333	0.0004325	0.000424	0.000433	6.7×10^{-07}
1	81.9500	81.9500	0.00040975	0.00040975	0.000410	0.000410	2.5×10^{-07}
CPU (second)				0.013 (second)			

Table 3 investigates the effect of some values on the accuracy of DSCDQM–RSK and DSCDQM–DLK, such as the band width (2M+1), the regularized Shannon factor (σ), the computational parameter (τ), and step size (Δ). Table 3 explains that DSCDQM–RSK is more accurate than DSCDQM–DLK in computing the concentration C(x,t) at t = 20 min compared with earlier solutions [4,18]. In addition, the bandwidth (2M+1 = 5) and $[\sigma = 1.45\Delta]$ are the most suitable choices for numerical results, which achieve more efficient results. It is noticed that the L_∞ error reaches 10^{-7} and 10^{-8}, which ensures the validity of DSCDQM–DLK and DSCDQM–RSK at t = 20 min and different distances (x), respectively. In addition, the results match with the previous literature [4,18] in both cases, with an error of about 10^{-8} and an execution time of 0.0108 s for computing C(x,t). All of this proves that DSCDQM–RSK is an efficient and effective method for analyzing drug diffusion through a thin membrane compared with previous methods, the PDQM, and DSCDQM–DLK.

The relative difference between two cases can be computed as follows:

$$\begin{aligned} \text{R.D.\%} &= \frac{\text{U(x)}_{\text{case2}} - \text{U(x)}_{\text{case1}}}{\text{U(x)}_{\text{case2}}} \times 100\% \\ &= \frac{\text{C(x,t)}_{\text{case2}} - \text{C(x,t)}_{\text{case1}}}{\text{C(x,t)}_{\text{case2}}} \times 100\% \end{aligned} \quad (33)$$

Thus, Table 4 shows the computation of $C(x,t)$ and $R.D.\%$ via DSCDQM–DLK and DSCDQM–RSK with band widths of $[2M + 1 = 5]$ and $[\sigma = 1.45\ \Delta]$ for both cases at distances (x) for $t = 100$ min, $\mu = \frac{10^{-6}}{4}$, $\alpha = 2$, $Q = 81.95$, and $q = 1.16$. The results demonstrated that the DSCDQM–RSK technique is the best; thus, it is used with a band width of $[2M{+}1 = 5]$ and $\sigma[= 1.45\Delta]$ to present a parametric study for a drug diffusion problem through a thin membrane.

Table 3. Computation of $C(x,t)$ and L_∞ error norms in [0, 1] via DSCDQM (DLK and RSK) with different band widths $[2M+1]$ for case (1) at distances (x) for $t = 20$ min, $\mu = \frac{10^{-6}}{4}$, $\alpha = 2$, $Q = 81.95$, and $q = 1.16$.

x	$2M+1$	$C(x,20)$						L_∞	
		DSCDQM–DLK	DSCDQM–RSK				Previous Studies [4,18]		
			$\sigma = 1.2\Delta$	$\sigma = 1.35\Delta$	$\sigma = 1.45\Delta$	$\sigma = 1.5\Delta$		DLK	RSK
0.2	3	0.000813	0.000787	0.000763	0.000752	0.000726	0.000703	1×10^{-7}	1×10^{-8}
	4	0.0007072	0.000729	0.000718	0.000711	0.000701			
	5	0.0007031	0.000718	0.000709	0.000703	0.000698			
	6	0.0007031	0.000718	0.000709	0.000703	0.000698			
0.4	3	0.0006274	0.000641	0.000635	0.000622	0.000629	0.000600	1×10^{-7}	1×10^{-8}
	4	0.0006050	0.000631	0.000618	0.000608	0.000613			
	5	0.0005999	0.000617	0.000608	0.000600	0.000595			
	6	0.0005999	0.000617	0.000608	0.000600	0.000595			
0.6	3	0.0005333	0.000541	0.000532	0.000528	0.000525	0.000512	6×10^{-7}	1×10^{-8}
	4	0.0005222	0.000537	0.000522	0.000517	0.000516			
	5	0.0005114	0.000530	0.000518	0.000512	0.000507			
	6	0.0005114	0.000530	0.000518	0.000512	0.000507			
0.8	3	0.0004529	0.000499	0.000472	0.000458	0.000449	0.000446	3×10^{-7}	1×10^{-8}
	4	0.0004480	0.000480	0.000459	0.000450	0.000445			
	5	0.0004457	0.000471	0.000452	0.000446	0.000441			
	6	0.0004457	0.000471	0.000452	0.000446	0.000441			
CPU (second)		0.0115 (seconds)				0.0108 (seconds)			

Table 4. Computation of $C(x,t)$ and $R.D.\%$ via DSCDQM–DLK and DSCDQM–RSK with a band width of [$2M$+1 = 5] and [$\sigma = 1.45\Delta$] for cases (1 and 2) at distances (x) for $t = 100$ min, $\mu = \frac{10^{-6}}{4}$, $\alpha = 2, Q = 81.95$, and $q = 1.16$.

x	DSCDQM–DLK			DSCDQM–RSK			Previous Studies [4,18]		
	$C(x,100)$		R.D.%	$C(x,100)$		R.D.%	$C(x,100)$		R.D.%
	Case 1	Case 2		Case 1	Case 2		Case 1	Case 2	
0	0.004099	0.004099	0	0.00410	0.00410	0	0.00410	0.00410	0
0.1	0.003801	0.00379	−0.29	0.00380	0.00379	−0.26	0.00380	0.00379	−0.26
0.2	0.003516	0.003515	0	0.00352	0.00352	0	0.00352	0.00352	0
0.3	0.003246	0.003266	0.61	0.00325	0.00327	0.61	0.00325	0.00327	0.61
0.4	0.002994	0.003038	1.44	0.00300	0.00304	1.315	0.00300	0.00304	1.315
0.5	0.002763	0.002829	2.33	0.00276	0.00283	2.33	0.00276	0.00283	2.33
0.6	0.002556	0.002637	3.07	0.00256	0.00264	3.03	0.00256	0.00264	3.03
0.7	0.002376	0.002461	3.45	0.00238	0.00246	3.25	0.00238	0.00246	3.25
0.8	0.002228	0.002302	3.21	0.00223	0.00230	3.18	0.00223	0.00230	3.18
0.9	0.002117	0.002162	2.08	0.00212	0.00216	2.08	0.00212	0.00216	2.08
1	0.002049	0.002049	0	0.00205	0.00205	0	0.00205	0.00205	0

Table 5 shows the results of C(x,t) for two cases at different distances (x) and times (t) using DSCDQM–RSK. The computed results demonstrated that C(x,t) reduces by a small amount with distance and increases with time. Tables 4 and 5 explain the tiny relative differences in C(x,t) for the two cases; therefore, the influence of the coefficient of diffusion in Equation (1) is negligible.

Figure 1 $U(x)$ is inversely proportional to specific sections of membrane (x), and the obtained results with the proposed schemes match with previous studies [4,18], which proves the validity, efficiency, and accuracy of the developed techniques.

At different times, Figures 2 and 3 show the variance of concentration with different sections of membrane (x) using DSCDQM–RSK for two cases. These figures demonstrate that the value of concentration increases with increasing time, but decreases with increasing membrane section (x).

Table 5. Computation of $C(x,t)$ and $R.D.\%$ via DSCDQM–RSK with [2*M*+1 = 5] and [$\sigma = 1.45\Delta$] for cases (1 and 2) at distances (x) and time (t) for $\mu = \frac{10^{-6}}{4}, \alpha = 2, Q = 81.95$, and $q = 1.16$.

x	$C(x,25)$			$C(x,50)$			$C(x,75)$		
	Case 1	**Case 2**	**R.D.%**	**Case 1**	**Case 2**	**R.D.%**	**Case 1**	**Case 2**	**R.D.%**
0	0.00102	0.00102	0	0.00205	0.00205	0	0.00307	0.00307	0
0.1	0.00095	0.00095	0	0.0019	0.0019	0	0.00285	0.00284	−0.35
0.2	0.00088	0.00088	0	0.00176	0.00176	0	0.002637	0.00264	0.11
0.3	0.00081	0.00082	1.22	0.001623	0.00163	0.43	0.002435	0.00245	0.61
0.4	0.00075	0.00076	1.32	0.00150	0.00152	1.32	0.002246	0.00228	1.49
0.5	0.00069	0.00071	2.82	0.00138	0.00142	2.82	0.002073	0.00212	2.22
0.6	0.00064	0.00066	3.03	0.00128	0.00132	3.03	0.001918	0.00198	3.13
0.7	0.00059	0.00062	4.84	0.00119	0.00123	3.25	0.001783	0.00185	3.62
0.8	0.00056	0.00058	3.45	0.00111	0.00115	3.48	0.001672	0.00173	3.35
0.9	0.00053	0.00054	1.85	0.00106	0.00108	1.85	0.001588	0.00162	1.98
1	0.00051	0.00051	0	0.00102	0.00102	0	0.001537	0.001537	0

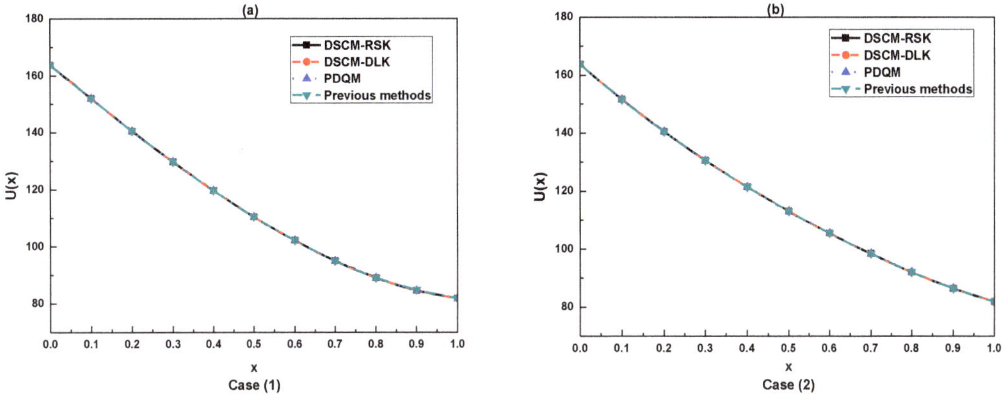

Figure 1. Variance of $U(x)$ with specific sections of membrane (x) via different methods for two cases (**a**) $P(x,t) = \frac{exp(-x)}{t}$ and (**b**) $P(x,t) = \frac{exp(-x^2)}{t}$, where $t = 100$ min, $2M + 1 = 5, \sigma = 1.45\Delta$, $\mu = \frac{10^{-4}}{4}, Q = 81.95$, and $q = 1.16$.

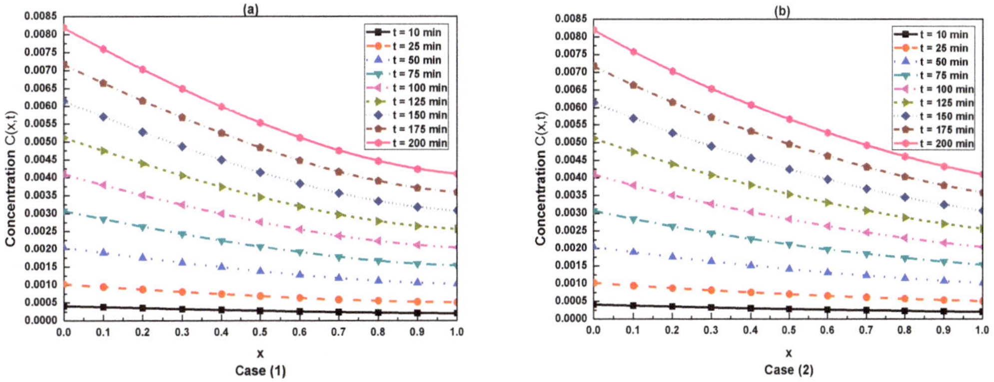

Figure 2. Variance of concentration $C(x,t)$ with specific sections of membrane (x) via DSCDQM–RSK for two cases (**a**) $P(x,t) = \frac{exp(-x)}{t}$ and (**b**) $P(x,t) = \frac{exp(-x^2)}{t}$ at different times (t), where $2M + 1 = 5$, $\sigma = 1.45\Delta$, $\mu = \frac{10^{-4}}{4}, Q = 81.95$, and $q = 1.16$.

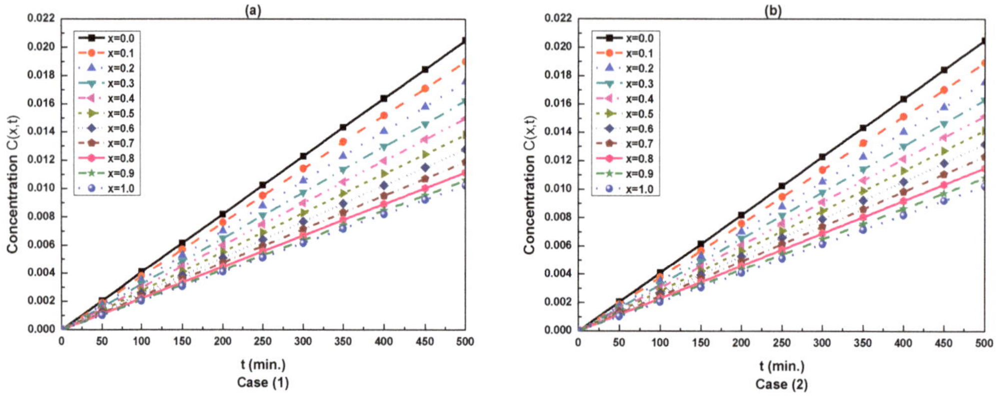

Figure 3. Variance of concentration $C(x,t)$ with time (t) via DSCDQM–RSK for two cases (**a**) $P(x,t) = \frac{exp(-x)}{t}$ and (**b**) $P(x,t) = \frac{exp(-x^2)}{t}$ at different specific sections of membrane (x), where $2M+1=5, \sigma = 1.45\Delta, \mu = \frac{10^{-4}}{4}, Q = 81.95,$ and $q = 1.16$.

Figure 4 shows that the value of R.D.% grows gradually toward x, reaching its highest value at x = 0.7, before decreasing to zero at x = 1.

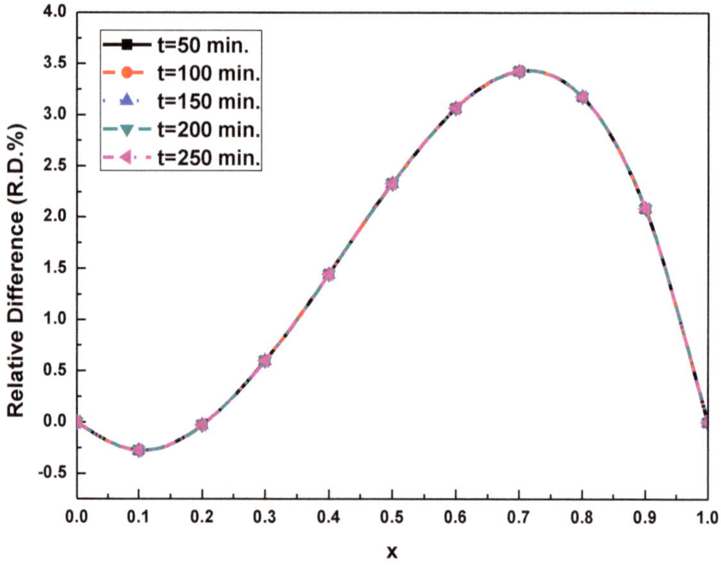

Figure 4. Variance of relative difference $(R.D.\%)$ with specific sections of membrane (x) via DSCDQM–RSK for two cases at different times (t), where $2M+1=5$, $\sigma = 1.45\Delta$, $\mu = \frac{10^{-4}}{4}, Q = 81.95$, and $q = 1.16$.

Figure 5 depicts the variation in donor D(t) and recipient R(t) cell concentrations over time (t). The concentration in the donor cell D(t) decreases with time, while that in the recipient cell R(t) rises, which is consistent with the theoretical model.

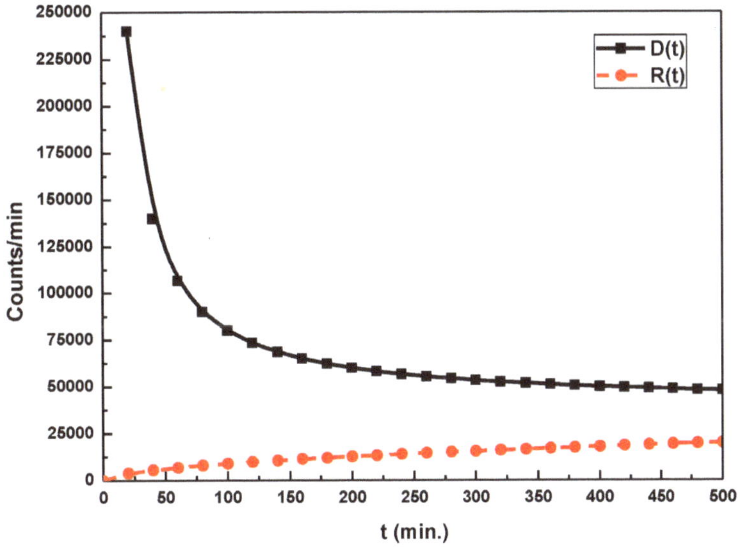

Figure 5. Variance of the donor $D(t)$ and receiver $R(t)$ cells concentrations with time (t) via DSCDQM–RSK, where $2M + 1 = 5, \sigma = 1.45\Delta, \beta = 40,000, \mu = \frac{10^{-4}}{4}$, and $\gamma = 10^{-11}/32$.

5. Conclusions

Here, efficient numerical approaches are applied to solve the problem of drug diffusion through a thin membrane. The proposed technique is based on various shape functions such as Lagrange interpolation polynomials, delta Lagrange, and regularized Shannon kernels for the differential quadrature method (DQM). A nonlinear partial differential equation with two time- and space-dependent variables governs this problem. To decrease the two independent variables by one, a one-parameter group transformation is used and the partial differential equation is converted into an ordinary differential equation. Then, with the aid of the iterative technique, differential quadrature methods change this equation into an algebraic equation. Then, using a MATLAB program, a code that solves this equation for each shape function is created. To ensure the validity, efficiency, and accuracy of the developed techniques, the computed results are compared to previous numerical and analytical solutions.

We solved the problem using the techniques presented, and the numerical confirmation verified the previously established solutions [4,18]. We also confirmed the convergence of the offered techniques by computing L∞ error norms. As a result, our methods produce much more accurate, stable, and efficient results. A comparison between PDQM, DSCDQM–DLK, DSCDQM–RSK, and previous methods [4,18] in both cases at t = 100 min is presented. The results demonstrated that the DSCDQM–RSK technique is the best; thus, it is used to present a parametric study for a drug diffusion problem through a thin membrane. The best values for the parameters controlling our methods are a band width of [2M+1 = 5] and [σ = 1.45Δ], which are obtained with errors of 10^{-7} and 10^{-8} and an execution time = 0.0108 s. The novelty of this method is that it provides a parametric analysis in two cases to explain how the time and membrane section affect the drug concentration and diffusion coefficient for the first time as follows:

- The computed results demonstrated that the concentration reduces slightly with distance and increases with time.
- The tiny relative differences in concentration for the two cases prove that the influence of the coefficient of diffusion is negligible.
- The value of R.D.% grows gradually toward x, reaching its highest value at x = 0.7, before decreasing to zero at x = 1.

- The concentration in the donor cell D(t) decreases with time, while that in the recipient cell R(t) rises, which is consistent with the theoretical model.

Furthermore, it is demonstrated that the proposed techniques have a one-of-a-kind ability to solve such problems with initial and boundary conditions. As a result, we anticipate applying these techniques to other nonlinear partial differential problems in a variety of applied sciences.

Author Contributions: Conceptualization, M.M. and R.S.S.; methodology, M.M.; software, M.M.; validation, A.M. and R.S.S.; formal analysis, investigation, M.M.; resources, A.M.; data curation, writing—original draft preparation, M.M.; writing—review and editing, R.S.S.; visualization, supervision, A.M. All authors have read and agreed to the published version of the manuscript.

Funding: The Deanship of Scientific Research at the Islamic University of Madinah provided support to the Post-Publishing Program (2).

Data Availability Statement: The data presented in this study are available in the article.

Acknowledgments: The researchers wish to extend their sincere gratitude to the Deanship of Scientific Research at the Islamic University of Madinah for the support provided to the Post-Publishing Program (2).

Conflicts of Interest: The authors declare no conflict of interest.

References

1. Hansen, S.; Lehr, C.-M.; Schaefer, U.F. Improved Input Parameters for Diffusion Models of Skin Absorption. *Adv. Drug Deliv. Rev.* **2013**, *65*, 251–264. [CrossRef] [PubMed]
2. Špaček, P.; Kubin, M. Diffusion in Gels. *J. Polym. Sci. Part C Polym. Symp.* **1967**, *16*, 705–714.
3. Hoogervorst, C.J.P.; Van Dijk, J.; Smit, J.A.M. Transient Diffusion through a Membrane Separating Two Unequal Volumes of Well Stirred Solution. CJP Hoogervorst, Non-Stationary Diffusion through Membranes. Ph.D. Thesis, Rijksuniversiteit te Leiden, Leiden, The Netherlands, 1977.
4. Kasem, M.M.M. *Group Theoretic Approach for Solving the Problem of Di# Usion of a Drug through a Thin Membrane*; Elsevier: Amsterdam, The Netherlands, 2002; pp. 1–11.
5. Spoelstra, J.; Van Wyk, D.J. A Method of Solution for a Non-Linear Diffusion Model and for Computing the Parameters in the Model. *J. Comput. Appl. Math.* **1987**, *20*, 379–385. [CrossRef]
6. Hoelz, A.; Debler, E.W.; Blobel, G. The Structure of the Nuclear Pore Complex. *Annu. Rev. Biochem.* **2011**, *80*, 613–643. [CrossRef] [PubMed]
7. Petrotos, K.B.; Lazarides, H.N. Osmotic Concentration of Liquid Foods. *J. Food Eng.* **2001**, *49*, 201–206. [CrossRef]
8. Parisio, G.; Stocchero, M.; Ferrarini, A. Passive Membrane Permeability: Beyond the Standard Solubility-Diffusion Model. *J. Chem. Theory Comput.* **2013**, *9*, 5236–5246. [CrossRef]
9. Nagle, J.F.; Mathai, J.C.; Zeidel, M.L.; Tristram-Nagle, S. Theory of Passive Permeability through Lipid Bilayers. *J. Gen. Physiol.* **2008**, *131*, 77–85. [CrossRef]
10. Li, D.; Wang, H. Recent Developments in Reverse Osmosis Desalination Membranes. *J. Mater. Chem.* **2010**, *20*, 4551–4566. [CrossRef]
11. Aho, V.; Mattila, K.; Kühn, T.; Kekäläinen, P.; Pulkkinen, O.; Minussi, R.B.; Vihinen-Ranta, M.; Timonen, J. Diffusion through Thin Membranes: Modeling across Scales. *Phys. Rev. E* **2016**, *93*, 43309. [CrossRef]
12. Aidun, C.K.; Clausen, J.R. Lattice-Boltzmann Method for Complex Flows. *Annu. Rev. Fluid Mech.* **2010**, *42*, 439–472. [CrossRef]
13. Benzi, R.; Succi, S.; Vergassola, M. The Lattice Boltzmann Equation: Theory and Applications. *Phys. Rep.* **1992**, *222*, 145–197. [CrossRef]
14. Hansen, A.G. *Similarity Analyses of Boundary Value Problems in Engineering*; Prentice-Hall: Hoboken, NJ, USA, 1964.
15. Gaggioli, R.A.; Moran, M.J. *Group Theoretic Techniques for the Similarity Solution of Systems of Partial Differential Equations with Auxiliary Conditions*; Wisconsin Univ Madison Mathematics Research Center: Madison, WI, USA, 1966.
16. Boutros, Y.Z.; Abd-el-Malek, M.B.; Badran, N.A. Group Theoretic Approach for Solving Time-Independent Free-Convective Boundary Layer Flow on a Nonisothermal Vertical Flat Plate. *Arch. Mech. Stosow.* **1990**, *42*, 377–395.
17. Abd-el-Malek, M.B.; El-Mansi, S.M.A. Group Theoretic Methods Applied to Burgers' Equation. *J. Comput. Appl. Math.* **2000**, *115*, 1–12. [CrossRef]
18. Abd-el-Malek, M.B.; Amin, A.M. Lie Group Analysis for Solving the Problem of Diffusion of Drugs across a Biological Membrane. *J. Gen. Lie Theory Appl.* **2015**, *9*, 1–4.
19. Bellman, R.; Kashef, B.G.; Casti, J. Differential Quadrature: A Technique for the Rapid Solution of Nonlinear Partial Differential Equations. *J. Comput. Phys.* **1972**, *10*, 40–52. [CrossRef]
20. Bellman, R.; Casti, J. Differential Quadrature and Long-Term Integration. *J. Math. Anal. Appl.* **1971**, *34*, 235–238. [CrossRef]

21. Shu, C. *Differential Quadrature and Its Application in Engineering*; Springer Science & Business Media: Berlin/Heidelberg, Germany, 2012; ISBN 1447104072.
22. Korkmaz, A.; Dağ, İ. Shock Wave Simulations Using Sinc Differential Quadrature Method. *Eng. Comput.* **2011**, *28*, 654–674. [CrossRef]
23. Wei, G. Vibration Analysis by Discrete Singular Convolution. *J. Sound Vib.* **2001**, *244*, 535–553. [CrossRef]
24. Nassar, M.; Matbuly, M.S.; Ragb, O. Vibration Analysis of Structural Elements Using Differential Quadrature Method. *J. Adv. Res.* **2013**, *4*, 93–102. [CrossRef]
25. Ragb, O.; Matbuly, M.S.; Nassar, M. Analysis of Composite Plates Using Moving Least Squares Differential Quadrature Method. *Appl. Math. Comput.* **2014**, *238*, 225–236. [CrossRef]
26. Salah, M.; Amer, R.M.; Matbuly, M.S. The Differential Quadrature Solution of Reaction-Diffusion Equation Using Explicit and Implicit Numerical Schemes. *Appl. Math.* **2014**, *5*, 42639. [CrossRef]
27. Ragba, O.; Matbulya, M.S.; Nassarb, M. Quadrature Analysis of Functionally Graded Materials. *Int. J. Eng. Technol.* **2014**, *14*, 69–80.
28. Matbuly, M.S.; Ragb, O.; Nassar, M. Natural Frequencies of a Functionally Graded Cracked Beam Using the Differential Quadrature Method. *Appl. Math. Comput.* **2009**, *215*, 2307–2316. [CrossRef]
29. Osman, T.; Matbuly, M.S.; Mohamed, S.A.; Nassar, M. Analysis of Cracked Plates Using Localized Multi-Domain Differential Quadrature Method. *Appl. Comput. Math.* **2013**, *2*, 109–114. [CrossRef]
30. Salah, M.; Amer, R.M.; Matbuly, M.S. Analysis of Reaction Diffusion Problems Using Differential Quadrature Method. *Int. J. Eng. Technol.* **2013**, *13*, 1–6.
31. Ragb, O.; Mohamed, M.; Matbuly, M.S. Vibration Analysis of Magneto-Electro-Thermo NanoBeam Resting on Nonlinear Elastic Foundation Using Sinc and Discrete Singular Convolution Differential Quadrature Method. *Mod. Appl. Sci.* **2019**, *13*, 49. [CrossRef]
32. Civalek, Ö. Free Vibration of Carbon Nanotubes Reinforced (CNTR) and Functionally Graded Shells and Plates Based on FSDT via Discrete Singular Convolution Method. *Compos. Part B Eng.* **2017**, *111*, 45–59. [CrossRef]
33. Civalek, Ö.; Kiracioglu, O. Free Vibration Analysis of Timoshenko Beams by DSC Method. *Int. J. Numer. Methods Biomed. Eng.* **2010**, *26*, 1890–1898. [CrossRef]
34. Wan, D.C.; Zhou, Y.C.; Wei, G.W. Numerical Solution of Incompressible Flows by Discrete Singular Convolution. *Int. J. Numer. Methods Fluids* **2002**, *38*, 789–810. [CrossRef]
35. Zhang, L.; Xiang, Y.; Wei, G.W. Local Adaptive Differential Quadrature for Free Vibration Analysis of Cylindrical Shells with Various Boundary Conditions. *Int. J. Mech. Sci.* **2006**, *48*, 1126–1138. [CrossRef]
36. Tornabene, F.; Fantuzzi, N.; Ubertini, F.; Viola, E. Strong Formulation Finite Element Method Based on Differential Quadrature: A Survey. *Appl. Mech. Rev.* **2015**, *67*, 020801. [CrossRef]
37. Wei, G.W. Discrete Singular Convolution for the Solution of the Fokker–Planck Equation. *J. Chem. Phys.* **1999**, *110*, 8930–8942. [CrossRef]
38. Shao, Z.; Wei, G.W.; Zhao, S. DSC Time-Domain Solution of Maxwell's Equations. *J. Comput. Phys.* **2003**, *189*, 427–453. [CrossRef]
39. Wang, X.; Yuan, Z.; Deng, J. A Review on the Discrete Singular Convolution Algorithm and Its Applications in Structural Mechanics and Engineering. *Arch. Comput. Methods Eng.* **2020**, *27*, 1633–1660. [CrossRef]
40. Ragb, O.; Mohamed, M.; Matbuly, M.S. Free Vibration of a Piezoelectric Nanobeam Resting on Nonlinear Winkler-Pasternak Foundation by Quadrature Methods. *Heliyon* **2019**, *5*, e01856. [CrossRef]
41. Ragb, O.; Mohamed, M.; Matbuly, M.S.; Civalek, O. An Accurate Numerical Approach for Studying Perovskite Solar Cells. *Int. J. Energy Res.* **2021**, *45*, 16456–16477. [CrossRef]

mathematics

MDPI

Article

Stability Analysis in a New Model for Desensitization of Allergic Reactions Induced by Chemotherapy of Chronic Lymphocytic Leukemia

Rawan Abdullah [1,†], Irina Badralexi [2,*,†] and Andrei Halanay [1,*]

1 Department of Mathematics-Informatics, Faculty of Applied Sciences, Politehnica University of Bucharest, 060042 București, Romania
2 Department of Mathematical Methods and Models, Faculty of Applied Sciences, Politehnica University of Bucharest, 060042 București, Romania
* Correspondence: irina.badralexi@gmail.com (I.B.); andrei.halanay@upb.ro (A.H.)
† These authors contributed equally to this work.

Abstract: We introduce a new model that captures the cellular evolution of patients with chronic lymphocytic leukemia who are receiving chemotherapy. As chemotherapy can induce allergic reactions and tumor lysis syndrome, we took into account the process of desensitization and the number of dead leukemic cells in the body. The mathematical model uses delayed-differential equations. Qualitative properties of the solutions are proved, including partial stability with respect to some variables and to the invariant set of positive initial data. Numerical simulations are also used to complete the description of the interplay between the immune system's function, the chemotherapeutic activity and the allergic reactions caused by the therapy.

Keywords: delayed-differential equations; chronic lymphocytic leukemia; drug-induced allergies; desensitization

MSC: 92-10; 34K20; 34K21; 34K60

Citation: Abdullah, R.; Badralexi, I.; Halanay, A. Stability Analysis in a New Model for Desensitization of Allergic Reactions Induced by Chemotherapy of Chronic Lymphocytic Leukemia. *Mathematics* **2023**, *11*, 3225. https://doi.org/10.3390/math11143225

Academic Editor: Mirosław Lachowicz

Received: 15 June 2023
Revised: 17 July 2023
Accepted: 18 July 2023
Published: 22 July 2023

1. Introduction

Scientists from all across the world have been studying cancer for a long time. Mathematical models which capture the cell dynamics in different types of cancer are essential in offering a better understanding of the process. This contributes deeply to the development of new treatment methods or to the improvement of the existing tactics. Any new perspective can be a stepping stone in the process of curing the disease or, at the very least, in improving the patient's quality of life (see [1,2]).

Chronic lymphocytic leukemia (CLL) is a type of leukemia distinguished by uncontrolled proliferation and accumulation of dysfunctional mature B lymphocytes (a group of white blood cells which are supposed to help fight infection).

Recent research studies have shown great promise in refining the administration method of treatment for CLL patients. Although drug administration is necessary in most cases, there some setbacks may appear. The most common problems that can arise are drug toxicity, tumor lysis syndrome (TLS) and drug-induced allergies. Part of the studies which capture these problems represent the basis of our model.

The treatments used in CLL increase the risk for tumor lysis syndrome (TLS). TLS is a condition in which the kidneys are not able to remove the contents of dead cancer cells fast enough. This can happen if a large number of cancer cells break down within a short period of time.

According to [3], many patients with CLL reported cases of TLS, some of them fatal. Furthermore, in [4], venetoclax-based therapy was shown to be related to TLS. Thus, the need for preventing and monitoring TLS is evident.

The authors of [5] examined the cytotoxicity of three chemotherapy drugs, chlorambucil (Chl), melphalan (Mel) and cytarabine (Cyt), against surrogate leukemic cells in vitro. Using the results, they developed a dynamic model that integrates both cancer cell growth and death rates in proportion to drug concentration.

Besides the toxicity-related problems, some patients also suffer from drug-induced allergic reactions. In both [6,7], there are documented cases of hypersensitivity to chlorambucil (which is often used in CLL treatments).

Allergies are an overly exaggerated response of the immune system after coming in contact with an allergen. A brief recount of the most important cells and molecules that are responsible for the appearance and the disappearance of allergic reactions is offered.

Allergic reactions are a result of an abundance of IgE (immunoglobulin E) antibodies.

White blood cells (lymphocytes) play an important part in our body's immune response. Lymphocytes consist of myeloid cells (dendritic cells, macrophages etc.) and lymphoid cells (mainly T cells and B cells). Antigen presenting cells (APCs) are immune cells which help activate T cells. The immune system is regulated by cytokines, which are small proteins. These can boost or restrict the production of immune cells.

Among the different types of T cells, we will be focusing on T helper cells and regulatory T cells. All T cells are producers of cytokines which can inhibit the production of other T cells. For example, type 1 T helper cells (Th1) and type 2 T helper cells (Th2) inhibit each other, while regulatory T cells (Treg cells) suppress both Th1 and Th2 cells. We know [8] that Th2 cells stimulate IgE production. An immunological imbalance between Th1 and Th2 cells towards Th2 cells is often associated with allergies.

Allergen immunotherapy, also known as desensitization, is a process in which the subject is repeatedly exposed to small doses (often incrementally larger) of the allergen. This basically makes the immune system less sensitive to the allergen—it becomes acclimated. Desensitization can be used for drug-induced allergies as well. It is very useful because the patient can receive the first-line treatment for their disease. At a cellular level, a positive result of desensitization may represent a balance shift between Th1 and Th2 cells [9].

The mathematical model we propose describes the immune response and evolution of leukemic cells in case of CLL. The treatment is considered to be chlorambucil. Since, as already mentioned above, there have been reports of allergic reactions to this drug, we will consider variations in the desensitization dose of chemotherapy. Our mathematical model will incorporate the risk of TLS by considering the concentration of dead cancer cells in the system at any given time. Our new model may help determine the optimal drug concentration without any allergic reactions or risk of TLS.

In order to capture the flow of the allergen better, we considered two body compartments: the central compartment and the peripheral compartment (following [10]). The drug—the allergen in our case—is injected in the bloodstream, which is part of the central compartment, and it spreads throughout the compartments.

2. The Mathematical Model

The model contains a set of eleven nonlinear delay-differential equations for which the state variables are:

1. the concentration of $Th1$ cells—T_1;
2. the concentration of $Th2$ cells—T_2;
3. the concentration of T_{reg} cells—T_r;
4. the concentration of naive T helper cells—N;
5. the concentration of naive APC cells—A_1;
6. the concentration of mature APC cells—A_2;
7. the flow of the chemotherapeutic drug—D;
8. the concentration of induced cytokines during chemotherapy—C;
9. the concentration of living leukemic cells—L;
10. the concentration of dead leukemic cells—L_d;
11. the concentration of effector T cells—I.

In the construction of the model, we considered three time delays which are biological relevant:

- τ_1 is the propagation time of allergen from the central compartment to the peripheral compartment [11]:

$$\tau_1 = \frac{arctg(\frac{2\pi}{K_{cp}})t_0}{2\pi},$$

where t_0 is the infusion time interval and K_{cp} is a pharmacokinetic parameter related to the transition between the central and peripheral compartment;
- τ_2 is the cytokines production time (by APCs and T cells);
- τ_3 is the duration of a cell cycle for the division of leukemic cells.

In what follows, we will describe each equation of the model.

The first four equations, which were deduced in [9], but with the consideration of a delay for the action of APCs (as suggested in [10]), describe the CD4+ cells implied in allergic reactions during desensitization for treatment with chlorambucil.

$$\dot{N} = \alpha - \beta_1 N - NA_2(t-\tau_1)\left(\frac{T_1\eta}{1+\mu_2 T_2}\right) - \phi NA_2(t-\tau_1)T_2 - \kappa NA_2(t-\tau_1)T_r \quad (1)$$

$$\dot{T_1} = -\beta_2 T_1 + \frac{vNA_2(t-\tau_1)}{(1+\mu_r T_r)}\left(\frac{T_1}{1+\mu_2 T_2}\right) \quad (2)$$

$$\dot{T_2} = -\beta_3 T_2 + \phi\frac{vNA_2(t-\tau_1)}{(1+\mu_r T_r)}\left(\frac{T_2}{1+\mu_1\frac{T_1}{1+\mu_2 T_2}}\right) \quad (3)$$

$$\dot{T_r} = -\beta_4 T_r + \kappa\, vs.\, NA_2(t-\tau_1)T_r - \eta_r\frac{CT_r}{1+C} \quad (4)$$

Equation (1) represents the variation in the concentration of naive T cells, which are produced at a constant rate α. The second term represents the degradation of naive cells. The last three terms stands for the differentiation of naive cells into $Th1$, $Th2$ and T_{reg}, respectively.

The next three equations are similar in design.

Equation (2) represents the variation in $Th1$ concentration, which is proportional to the concentration of naive cells and the concentration of presented allergen.The first term represents the degradation of $Th1$ cells. The second term represents the differentiation of naive cells into $Th1$, diminished due to suppression by T_{reg} and $Th2$ cells.

Equation (3) represents the variation in $Th2$ concentration, which is proportional to the concentration of naive cells, the concentration of presented allergen and the concentration of their respective cytokines. The first term represents the degradation of $Th2$ cells. The second term represents the differentiation of naive cells into $Th2$ divided by the suppression of T_{reg} and $Th1$ cells.

Equation (4) represents the variation in T_{reg} concentration, which is proportional to the concentration of naive cells, the concentration of the presented allergen and the concentration of their respective cytokines. The first term represents the degradation of T_{reg} cells and the second term represents the differentiation of naive cells into T_{reg}. The last term stands for the inhibition of T_{reg} by the induced cytokines during chemotherapy with inhibition rate η_r.

The parameter v determines how many differentiated T cells arise from a single naive cell. ϕ and κ account for differences in autocrine action between the three subsets.

The suppression strength of $Th1$, $Th2$ and T_{reg} is controlled by the parameters μ_1, μ_2, and μ_r, in that order.

In the fifth and the sixth equations, we consider an activation process for APCs after contact with an allergen, with A_1 being the concentration of naive APC cells and A_2 the concentration of the mature ones.

$$\dot{A_1} = a - \beta_0 D A_1 - \gamma_{11} A_1 \quad (5)$$

$$\dot{A_2} = \beta_0 D A_1 - \gamma_{12} A_2 - \mu_0 A_2 T_r \quad (6)$$

In Equation (5) the first term accounts for the supply rate of naive APCs and the second term represent the APC activation by the antigen during chemotherapy. The third term represents the death rate of nature APCs and the last term represent the reversed activation of mature APCs by regulatory T cells with a rate μ_0.

In Equation (6) the first term accounts for the supply rate of mature APCs due to maturation of the naive ones, the second term represents the death rate of mature APCs and the last term represents the reversed activation of mature APCs by regulatory T cells with a rate μ_0.

The seventh equation represents the flow of the chemotherapeutic drug, denoted by D.

$$\dot{D} = \Lambda - \gamma_D D - \frac{\mu_D L D}{a + D} \quad (7)$$

Equation (7) represents the variation in the dose of chemotherapy, eventually leading to desensitization. The first term is the supply rate of the drug, the second one refers to the washout rate of the chemotherapeutic drug, $\gamma_D = \frac{ln2}{t_{\frac{1}{2}}}$, where $t_{\frac{1}{2}}$ is the drug elimination half-life (about 1.5 h for Chl). The last term illustrates the log-kill hypothesis, where μ_D is the rate of the clearance of drug due to the interaction with cancer cells (see [5]).

The eighth equation represents the concentration of induced cytokines during chemotherapy.

$$\dot{C} = -\gamma_2 C + k_1[A_2(t - \tau_2) + N(t - \tau_2) + T_1(t - \tau_2) + T_2(t - \tau_2) + T_r(t - \tau_2)] \quad (8)$$

For Equation (8), we follow [12] and consider the mature APCs and the mature T cells as the sources of production. The first term accounts for the clearing rate of these cytokines, the second term represents the production of cytokines by mature APCs, naive T cells, $Th1$ cells, $Th2$ cells and T reg cells. The concentration of cytokines is denoted by C for simplicity.

Equations (9) and (10) show the dynamics of living (L) and dead leukemic cells (L_d).

$$\dot{L} = -\gamma_L L - \beta(L)L + 2e^{-\gamma_L \tau_3}\beta(L_{\tau_3})L_{\tau_3} - c_1 I L - \frac{\mu_L L D}{a + D} \quad (9)$$

$$\dot{L_d} = \gamma_L L - d L_d + \frac{\mu_L L D}{a + D} \quad (10)$$

Equation (9) describes the dynamics of living leukemic cells, where we include in the same equation the stem and mature cells. The first term corresponds to the cell death due to apoptosis or necrosis with a rate γ_L. The cells go through division at a rate $\beta(L)$ and, as a result, the number doubles after a delay time τ_3, corresponding to the cell cycle of leukemic cells. The total number is corrected by $e^{-\gamma_L \tau_3}$, which represents the loss during the cell cycle.

The function β is (see [13]):

$$\beta(x) = \beta_L \frac{\theta^2}{\theta^2 + x^2}.$$

The term $-c_1IL$ represents the death of tumor cells due to the action of the immune system. The last term represent the log-kill hypothesis, where μ_L is the death rate resulting from the action of the drug on the cancer cells.

Equation (10) describes the dynamic of dead leukemic cells. The first term is the death of leukemic cells with a rate coefficient of γ_T due to apoptosis or necrosis. The negative term corresponds to the dissolution of dead cells at a rate of d. The last term represents the log-kill hypothesis, with μ_L being the death rate resulting from the action of the drug on the cancer cells.

The eleventh equation represents the concentration of effector T cells of the immune system.

$$\dot{I} = s - mI + \frac{\rho LI}{\gamma + L} - \frac{\delta ID}{c + D} - c_2LI \tag{11}$$

Equation (11) represents the dynamics of the immune cell population when it is activated by the leukemic population at a rate ρ, with γ being the half-saturation constant of the Michaelis–Menten functional response given by $\frac{\rho TI}{\gamma + T}$ (see [14]). There is a natural death rate of immune cells given by m. δ represents the mortality rate of immune cells due to the chemotherapeutic drug. Since some immune cells are inactivated by tumor cells (see [14]), the last term was introduced to account for this.

A list of all the parameters, with a short description and relevant values, can be found in Table A1.

3. Introducing New Notations for State Variables

In order to facilitate the study of the DDE system, we introduce the following notations:

- x_1 = concentration of naive T cells(N).
- x_2 = concentration of Th1 cells;
- x_3 = concentration of Th2 cells;
- x_4 =concentration of T_{reg} cells;
- x_5 = concentration of naive APCs;
- x_6 = concentration of mature APCs;
- x_7 = amount of chlorambucil injected during desensitization;
- x_8 = concentration of cytokines induced during chemotherapy;
- x_9 = population of living leukemic cells;
- x_{10} = population of dead leukemic cells;
- x_{11} = concentration of effector T cells of the immune system.

We also consider the following notation for the delayed variables: $x(t - \tau) = x_\tau$.

The system becomes:

$$
\begin{aligned}
\dot{x}_1 &= \alpha - \beta_1 x_1 - x_1 x_{6\tau_1} \frac{x_2}{1+\mu_2 x_3} - \phi x_1 x_{6\tau_1} x_3 - \kappa x_1 x_{6\tau_1} x_4 \\
\dot{x}_2 &= -\beta_2 x_2 + v \frac{x_1 x_{6\tau_1} x_2}{(1+\mu_r x_4)(1+\mu_2 x_3)} \\
\dot{x}_3 &= -\beta_3 x_3 + \phi v \frac{x_1 x_{6\tau_1} x_3 (1+\mu_2 x_3)}{(1+\mu_r x_4)(1+\mu_1 x_2 + \mu_2 x_3)} \\
\dot{x}_4 &= -\beta_4 x_4 + \kappa\ vs.\ x_1 x_{6\tau_1} x_4 - \eta_r \frac{x_8 x_4}{1+x_8} \\
\dot{x}_5 &= a - \beta_0 x_7 x_5 - \gamma_{11} x_5 \\
\dot{x}_6 &= \beta_0 x_7 x_5 - \gamma_{12} x_6 - \mu_0 x_6 x_4 \\
\dot{x}_7 &= \Lambda - \gamma_D x_7 - \frac{\mu_D x_9 x_7}{a+x_7} \\
\dot{x}_8 &= -\gamma_2 x_8 + k_1 [x_{6\tau_2} + x_{1\tau_2} + x_{2\tau_2} + x_{3\tau_2} + x_{4\tau_2}] \\
\dot{x}_9 &= -\gamma_L x_9 - \beta(x_9) x_9 + 2e^{-\gamma_L \tau_3} \beta(x_{9\tau_3}) x_{9\tau_3} - c_1 x_9 x_{11} - \frac{\mu_L x_9 x_7}{a+x_7} \\
\dot{x}_{10} &= \gamma_L x_9 - d x_{10} + \frac{\mu_L x_9 x_7}{a+x_7} \\
\dot{x}_{11} &= s - m x_{11} + \frac{\rho x_9 x_{11}}{\gamma + x_9} - \frac{\delta x_{11} x_7}{c + x_7} - c_2 x_9 x_{11}
\end{aligned}
\tag{12}
$$

4. Equilibria and Stability Analysis

The following biologically relevant equilibrium points will be studied:

- $E_1 = (x_1^*, 0, 0, 0, x_5^*, x_6^*, x_7^*, x_8^*, 0, 0, x_{11}^*)$,

with $x_1^* = \dfrac{\alpha}{\beta_1}$, $x_5^* = \dfrac{a}{\gamma_{11} + \beta_0 x_7^*}$, $x_6^* = \dfrac{\beta_0 x_7^* x_5^*}{\gamma_{12}}$, $x_7^* = \dfrac{\Lambda}{\gamma_D}$, $x_8^* = \dfrac{k1(x_1^* + x_6^*)}{\gamma_2}$ and $x_{11}^* = \dfrac{s(c + x_7^*)}{mc + x_7^*(m+\delta)}$;

- $E_2 = (x_1^*, x_2^*, 0, 0, x_5^*, x_6^*, x_7^*, x_8^*, 0, 0, x_{11}^*)$,

with $x_2^* = \dfrac{\alpha - \beta_1 x_1^*}{x_1^* x_6^*}$, $x_5^* = \dfrac{a}{\gamma_{11} + \beta_0 x_7^*}$, $x_6^* = \dfrac{\beta_0 x_7^* x_5^*}{\gamma_{12}}$, $x_7^* = \dfrac{\Lambda}{\gamma_D}$, $x_8^* = \dfrac{k_1(x_6^* + x_1^* + x_2^*)}{\gamma_2}$ and $x_{11}^* = \dfrac{s(c + x_7^*)}{mc + x_7^*(m+\delta)}$.

When we substitute x_6^* and then x_8^*, in the second equation of system (12), we get

$$x_1^* = \frac{\beta_2 \gamma_{12} \gamma_D \gamma_{11}}{v \beta_0 \Lambda a}$$

The linearized system around an equilibrium point is written as:

$$\dot{x} = Ax + Bx_{\tau_1} + Cx_{\tau_2} + Dx_{\tau_3} \tag{13}$$

with $f = (\dot{x}_1, \cdots, \dot{x}_{11})$, $x = (x_1, \cdots, x_{11})$, $x_{\tau_i} = (x_{1\tau_i}, \cdots, x_{11\tau_i})$ and $i = 1,2,3$

$$A = \left.\frac{\partial f}{\partial x}\right|_{E_i}, \quad B = \left.\frac{\partial f}{\partial x_{\tau_1}}\right|_{E_i}, \quad C = \left.\frac{\partial f}{\partial x_{\tau_2}}\right|_{E_i}, \quad D = \left.\frac{\partial f}{\partial x_{\tau_3}}\right|_{E_i}, \quad i = 1,2 \tag{14}$$

The characteristic equation corresponding to (13) is :

$$det\left(\lambda I_9 - A - Be^{-\lambda\tau_1} - Ce^{-\lambda\tau_2} - De^{-\lambda\tau_3}\right) = 0 \tag{15}$$

To study the stability of an equilibrium point, we use this characteristic equation. It is known that if all the roots of the characteristic equation have negative real parts, then the equilibrium point is uniformly asymptotically stable. If there exists at least one root with a positive real part then the equilibrium point is unstable.

A complete list of the matrix elements can be found in Appendix A.

4.1. Stability Analysis of E_1

For E_1 the characteristic equation becomes:

$$\begin{aligned} d_1(\lambda) &= det\left(\lambda I_{11} - A - Be^{-\lambda\tau_1} - Ce^{-\lambda\tau_2} - De^{-\lambda\tau_3}\right) = \\ &= (a_{11}-\lambda)(a_{22}-\lambda)(a_{33}-\lambda)(a_{44}-\lambda)(a_{55}-\lambda)(a_{66}-\lambda)(a_{77}-\lambda)\cdot \\ &\cdot (a_{88}-\lambda)(a_{99}+d_{99}e^{-\lambda\tau_3}-\lambda)(a_{10,10}-\lambda)(a_{11,11}-\lambda) = 0 \end{aligned} \tag{16}$$

E_1 is asymptotically stable if all the roots of the characteristic equation have negative real parts. We first verify if $a_{11}, a_{22}, a_{33}, a_{44}, a_{55}, a_{66}, a_{77}, a_{88}, a_{10,10}$ and $a_{11,11}$ are negative and notice that this happens if:

$$\begin{aligned} -\beta_2 + vx_1^* x_6^* &< 0 \\ -\beta_3 + \phi\ vs.\ x_1^* x_6^* &< 0 \\ -\beta_4 + \kappa\ vs.\ x_6^* x_1^* - \frac{\eta_r x_8^*}{1+x_8^*} &< 0. \end{aligned} \tag{17}$$

Next, we study the roots of the equation

$$\lambda - a_{99} - d_{99}e^{-\lambda\tau_3} = 0 \tag{18}$$

According to [15], necessary and sufficient conditions for Equation (16) to have roots with negative real part are given in the following theorem.

Theorem 1 ([15])**.** *The equilibrium point E_1 is stable if and only if the following conditions are met:*

$$a_{99}\tau_3 < 1$$

$$a_{99}\tau_3 < -d_{99}\tau_3 < (\theta^2 + a_{99}^2\tau_3^2)^{\frac{1}{2}},$$

where , since $a_{99} \neq 0$, θ is the unique root of $\theta = a_{99}\tau_3 \tan(\theta)$.

We performed numerical computations using parameter values taken from relevant literature (see Table A1) and noticed that $a_{22} = 1.4045$ and $a_{33} = 0.0702$. Seeing as these real roots of the characteristic equation are positive, we conclude that the equilibrium point E_1 is not stable.

4.2. Stability Analysis of E_2

From the block-diagonal structure of the matrix, the characteristic equation corresponding to E_2 is:

$$\begin{aligned} d_2(\lambda) &= det\left(\lambda I_{11} - A - Be^{-\lambda\tau_1} - Ce^{-\lambda\tau_2} - De^{-\lambda\tau_3}\right) = \\ &= [(\lambda-a_{11})(\lambda-a_{22}) - a_{12}a_{21}](a_{33}-\lambda)(a_{44}-\lambda)(a_{55}-\lambda)(a_{66}-\lambda)\cdot \\ &\cdot (a_{77}-\lambda)(a_{88}-\lambda)(a_{99}+d_{99}e^{-\lambda\tau_3}-\lambda)(a_{10,10}-\lambda)(a_{11,11}-\lambda) = 0 \end{aligned}$$

Equilibrium point E_2 is asymptotically stable if all the roots of the characteristic equation have negative real parts. Using the parameter values found in Table A1, we noticed that solutions of equation

$$(\lambda - a_{11})(\lambda - a_{22}) - a_{12}a_{21} = 0$$

are $0.0150 + 0.0288i$ and $0.0150 - 0.0288i$. These roots have positive real parts. Thus, we conclude that the equilibrium point E_2 is not stable.

5. Partial Stability

There are some cases in which, from a biological point of view, we are only interested in the partial stability of the equilibrium points. Basically, we just need some of the variables to have a stable behavior. The study of partial stability usually needs the proof of some properties of the solutions, like boundedness of some components and global existence, that, in the case of usual stability are deduced from the existence of Lyapunov functions.

Positivity, Boundedness and Global Existence

Define $\tau = max\{\tau_1, \tau_2, \tau_3\}$ and let $PC([-\tau, 0], \mathbb{R}^{11})$ denote the space of piecewise continuous functions defined on $[-\tau, 0]$ with values in $\mathbb{R}^n$. The norm in $PC([-\tau, 0], \mathbb{R}^{11})$ will be defined by

$$||\varphi||_\tau = sup\{||\varphi(t)||_2 | t \in [-\tau, 0]\},$$

with $||\cdot||_2$ the euclidean norm in $\mathbb{R}^n$. For (12) consider the initial data:

$$x(s) = \varphi(s), s \in [-\tau, 0]. \tag{19}$$

Proposition 1. *If the initial data $\varphi \in PC([-\tau, 0], \mathbb{R}^{11})$ satisfies $\varphi_j(s) > 0 \; \forall \; s \in [-\tau, 0], j = \overline{1, 11}$ then the solution of the Cauchy problem (12)+(19) will satisfy $x_j(t) \geq 0, j = \overline{1, 11}$ for all t in the domain of existence.*

Proof. Since $x_j(0) > 0 \; \forall \; j = \overline{1, 11}$, there exists $t_0 > 0$, so that $x_j(t) > 0 \; \forall \; t \in [0, t_0)$, $\forall \; j = \overline{1, 11}$. It follows that $x_1(t) > 0 \; \forall \; t \in [-\tau, t_1), t_1 \geq t_0$.

If $x_1(t_1) = 0$, one has $x_1'(t_1) = \alpha > 0$, so x_1 will increase for $t > t_1$ and, consequently, $x_1(t) > 0 \; \forall \; t$ in the domain of existence, let it be $[-\tau, T)$.

The same reasoning applies to x_5, x_7 and x_{11}.

Then if $x_6(t_6) = 0$ for some $t_6 > t_0$, it follows that $x_6'(t_6) > 0$ and $x_6(t) > 0 \; \forall \; t \in [0, T)$. If $x_9(t) > 0$, $\forall \; t \in [-\tau, t_9), t_9 \geq t_0$ and $x_9(t_9) = 0 \Rightarrow x_9'(t_9) = 2e^{-\gamma_L \tau_3}\beta(x_9(t_9 - \tau_3)x_9(t_9 - \tau_3) > 0 \Rightarrow x_9(t) > 0 \; \forall \; T > t \geq t_0$.

Once again, if $x_{10}(t_{10}) = 0$ for some $t_{10} \geq t_0 \Rightarrow x_{10}'(t_{10}) > 0 \Rightarrow x_{10}(t) > 0 \; \forall \; T > t \geq t_0$.

In the same vein, we see that if $x_8(t_8) = 0 \Rightarrow x_8'(t_8) > 0 \Rightarrow x_8(t) > 0 \; \forall \; t \in [t_0, T), \Rightarrow 1 + x_8(t) > 0 \; \forall \; t \in [0, T)$.

Then, since

$$x_4(t) = x_4(0)e^{-\int_0^t [\beta_4 + kvx_1(s)x_6(s-\tau_1) - \eta_r \frac{x_8(s)}{1+x_8(s)}]ds}$$

one has $x_4(t) > 0 \; \forall \; t \in [0, T)$.

Remark that we have

$$1 + \mu_2 x_3(t) > 0, 1 + \mu_1 x_2(t) + \mu_2 x_3(t) > 0 \; \forall \; t \in [0, t_2) \subset [0, \tau_T), t_2 \geq t_0.$$

Then

$$x_3(t) = x_3(0)e^{\int_0^t [-\beta_3 + \frac{x_1(s)x_7(s-\tau_1)[1+\mu_2 x_3(s)]}{[1+\mu_r x_4(s)][1+\mu_1 x_2(t)+\mu_2 x_3(t)]}]ds} > 0 \; \forall \; t \in [0, t_2).$$

Since $x_3(t_2) = 0$ is clearly impossible, we conclude that $x_3(t) > 0 \; \forall \; t \in [0, T)$.

Similarly,

$$x_2(t) = x_2(0)e^{-\int_0^t [-\beta_2 + v\frac{x_1(s)x_6(s-\tau_1)}{[1+\mu_r x_4(s)][1+\mu_2 x_3(s)]}]ds}$$

we conclude that $x_2(t) > 0 \; \forall \; t \in [0, T)$. □

From now on, the initial data for (12) will be supposed positive.

Proposition 2. *Assume that:*

$$C_1 < \gamma_L, \quad 4\beta_L < \gamma_L. \tag{20}$$

Then, x_1, x_5, x_6, x_7, x_9 *and* x_{10} *are bounded on the whole interval of existence.*

Proof. From (12), it follows that

$$\dot{x_1}(t) = \alpha - \beta_1 x_1(t) - x_1(t)p_1(t)$$

with $p_1(t) \geq 0$ for positive initial data. Then

$$x_1(t) = x_1(0)e^{-\beta_1 t - \int_0^t p_1(s)ds} + \alpha\left(\int_0^t e^{\beta_1 s}e^{\int_0^s p_1(r)dr}ds\right)e^{-\beta_1 t}e^{-\int_0^t p_1(s)ds}$$

and we have the following estimation for the second term

$$\alpha\left(\int_0^t e^{\beta_1 s}e^{\int_0^s p_1(r)dr}ds\right)e^{-\beta_1 t}e^{-\int_0^t p_1(s)ds} \leq$$

$$\leq \alpha\left(\int_0^t e^{\beta_1 s}e^{\int_0^t p_1(r)dr}ds\right)e^{-\beta_1 t}e^{-\int_0^t p_1(s)ds} = \alpha\frac{(1-e^{-\beta_1 t})}{\beta_1} \leq \frac{\alpha}{\beta_1} \; \forall \; t \geq 0$$

It follows that $|x_1(t)| \leq M_1$ for some positive M_1.
For $x_7(t)$ we have that

$$x_7(t) = x_7(0)e^{\int_0^t [-\gamma_D - \mu_D \frac{x_9(s)}{a+x_7(s)}]ds} +$$

$$+\Lambda \int_0^t e^{\gamma_D(s-t)}e^{-\int_s^t \mu_D \frac{x_9(r)}{a+x_7(r)}dr}ds \leq x_7(0) + \frac{\Lambda}{\gamma_D} = M_7 \; \forall \; t \geq 0$$

(for positive initial data, $x_9(t)$ *and* $x_7(t)$ are positive, according to Proposition 1).
For x_5, remark that

$$x_5(t) = x_5(0)e^{-\gamma_{11}t - \beta_0 \int_0^t x_7(s)ds} + a\left(\int_0^t e^{\gamma_{11}s}e^{\beta_0 \int_0^s x_7(r)dr}ds\right)e^{-\gamma_{11}t}e^{-\beta_0 \int_0^t x_4(s)ds} \leq$$

$$\leq x_5(0) + a\left(\int_0^t e^{\gamma_{11}s}ds\right)e^{\beta_0 \int_0^t x_7(r)dr}e^{-\gamma_{11}t}e^{-\beta_0 \int_0^t x_4(s)ds} = x_5(0) + \frac{a}{\gamma_{11}}(1 - e^{-\gamma_{11}t}) \leq$$

$$\leq x_5(0) + \frac{a}{\gamma_{11}} = M_5.$$

With similar arguments one obtains that x_6 is bounded:

$$x_6(t) = x_6(0)e^{-\gamma_{12}t - \mu_0 \int_0^t x_4(s)ds} + \beta_0\left(\int_0^t x_7(s)x_5(s)e^{\gamma_{12}s}e^{\mu_0 \int_0^s x_4(r)dr}ds\right)e^{-\gamma_{12}t}e^{-\mu_0 \int_0^t x_4(s)ds}.$$

Then

$$x_6(t) \le x_6(0) + \beta_0 M_7 M_5 \left(\int_0^t e^{\gamma_{12} s} ds \right) e^{\mu_0 \int_0^t x_4(s) ds} e^{-\gamma_{12} t} e^{-\mu_0 \int_0^t x_4(s) ds} \le$$
$$\le x_6(0) + \frac{\beta_0}{\gamma_{12}} M_7 M_5 = M_6$$

Passing to x_9 denote for convenience $h(t) = \gamma_L + \beta[x_9(t)] + c_1 x_{11}(t) + \mu_L \frac{x_7(t)}{a+x_7(t)} = \gamma_L + h_1(t)$ and $C_1 = 2\beta_L e^{-\gamma_L \tau_3}, C_1' = 2e^{-\gamma_L \tau_3}$. For $t \in [0, \tau_3]$ we have

$$x_9(t) = x_9(0) e^{-\int_0^t h(s) ds} + \left(C_1' \int_0^t \varphi_8(s) \beta[\varphi_8(s)] e^{\int_0^s h(r) dr} ds \right) e^{-\int_0^t h(s) ds} \le$$

$$\le ||\varphi||_\tau e^{-\gamma_L t} + C_1 ||\varphi||_\tau \left(\int_0^t e^{\int_0^s h(r) dr} ds \right) e^{-\int_0^t h(s) ds} =$$

$$= ||\varphi||_\tau \left[1 + C_1 \left(\int_0^t e^{\gamma_L s} e^{\int_0^s h_1(r) dr} ds \right) e^{-\gamma_L t} e^{-\int_0^t h_1(s) ds} \right] = \le$$

$$\le ||\varphi||_\tau \left[1 + C_1 \left(\int_0^t e^{\gamma_L s} e^{\int_0^t h_1(r) dr} ds \right) e^{-\gamma_L t} e^{-\int_0^t h_1(s) ds} \right] \le$$

$$\le ||\varphi||_\tau \left[1 + \frac{C_1}{\gamma_L} (1 - e^{-\gamma_l t}) \right] \le ||\varphi||_\tau \left(1 + \frac{C_1}{\gamma_L} \right) \le 2||\varphi||_\tau$$

if (20) is used. For $t \in [\tau_3, 2\tau_3]$, repeating the previous estimations, one has

$$x_9(t) \le ||\varphi||_\tau e^{-\gamma_L t} + \frac{C_1}{\gamma_L} 2||\varphi||_\tau \le ||\varphi||_\tau e^{-\gamma_L \tau_3} \left(1 + 4\frac{\beta_L}{\gamma_L} \right) \le 2||\varphi||_\tau$$

so the argumentation can be extended to the whole axis and the results show that $|x_9(t)| \le M_9$.

For $x_{10}(t)$ we have:

$$x_{10}(t) = x_{10}(0) e^{-dt} + e^{-dt} \int_0^t e^{ds} \left[\gamma_L x_9(s) + \mu_L \frac{x_9(s) x_7(s)}{a + x_7(s)} \right] ds.$$

It follows that

$$|x_{10}(t)| \le |x_{10}(0)| e^{-dt} + e^{-dt} \int_0^t e^{ds} (\gamma_L + \mu_L) M_9 \le$$
$$\le ||\varphi||_\tau + \frac{1 - e^{-dt}}{d} M_8 (\gamma_L + \mu_L) = M_{10} \ \forall \, t \ge 0$$

□

Proposition 3. *The solution of system (12) exists on $[-\tau, \infty)$.*

Proof. The Proposition will follow from a slight generalization of Theorem 1.2. in [16], remarking that the condition of the theorem needs to hold only for the solutions of (12). So we must show that, with $\varphi = (\varphi_1, \dots, \varphi_{11})$, a solution of (12) and $f = (f_1, \dots, f_{11})$, the right-hand side of (12),

$$|f_j(\varphi)| \le h(||\varphi||_\tau), \int_{r_0}^{\infty} \frac{1}{h(r)} dr = \infty, \forall \, r_0 > 0.$$

We will show that there exist constants K_1, K_2 so that

$|f_j(\varphi)| \leq K_1 + K_2||\varphi||_\tau, j = \overline{1,11}$ and the Proposition will result.

$$|f_1(\varphi)| \leq |\alpha| + \beta_1|\varphi_1(t)| + M_1M_6|\varphi_2(t)| + \phi M_1M_6|\varphi_3(t)| + \kappa M_1M_6|\varphi_4(t)| \leq$$

$$\leq |\alpha| + (\beta_1 + M_1M_6 + \phi M_1M_6 + \kappa M_1M_6)||\varphi||_\tau$$

$$|f_2(\varphi)| \leq (\beta_2 + vM_1M_6)||\varphi||_\tau$$

$$|f_3(\varphi)| \leq (\beta_3 + \phi\ vs.\ M_1M_6)||\varphi||_\tau$$

$$|f_4(\varphi)| \leq (\beta_4 + \kappa\ vs.\ M_1M_6 + \eta_r)||\varphi||_\tau$$

$$|f_5(\varphi)| \leq a + \gamma_{11}M_5 + M_5M_7\beta_0,$$

$$|f_6(\varphi)| \leq M_5M_7\beta_0 + \gamma_{12}M_6 + \mu_0M_6||\varphi||_\tau,$$

$$|f_7(\varphi)| \leq \Lambda + \gamma_LM_7 + \mu_DM_9|f_8(\varphi)| \leq k_1(M_1 + M_5) + (\gamma_2 + 3k_1)||\varphi||_\tau$$

$$|f_9(\varphi)| \leq M_9(\beta_L + \mu_L) + c_1M_9||\varphi||_\tau,$$

$$|f_{10}(\varphi)| \leq (\gamma_L + mu_L)M_9 + dM_{10},$$

$$|f_{11}(\varphi)| \leq s + (m + \rho + \delta + c_2M_9)||\varphi||_\tau$$

□

5.1. Partial Stability of E_1

In this section, we will find delay-independent partial stability conditions for the equilibrium point E_1. The necessary mathematical framework and relevant results can be found in [17–19]. Recall that $E_1 = (x_1^*, 0, 0, 0, x_5^*, x_6^*, x_7^*, x_8^*, 0, 0, x_{11}^*)$.

Proposition 4. *When, besides (20), the following conditions are fulfilled*

$$k\ vs.\ x_1^*x_6^* < \beta_4, \quad \beta_0x_7^* + \beta_0x_5^* < 2\gamma_{12}, \quad \beta_0x_5^* < \gamma_D \tag{21}$$

E_1 is partially stable with respect to variables x_4, x_5, x_6, x_7, x_9 and with respect to the invariant manifold of solutions with positive components.

Proof. We perform a translation of the equilibrium E_1 to zero by $y_i = x_i - x_i^*$, for $i = \overline{1,11}$. We are interested only in Equations (4)–(7) and (9).

$$\begin{aligned}
\dot{y_4} &= -\beta_4y_4 + \kappa\ vs.\ (y_1 + x_1^*)(y_{6\tau_1} + x_7^*)y_4 - \eta_r\frac{(y_8 + x_8^*)y_4}{1 + y_8 + x_8^*} \\
\dot{y_5} &= -(\gamma_{11} + \beta_0x_7^*)y_5 - \beta_0y_7y_5 - \beta_0y_7x_5^* \\
\dot{y_6} &= \beta_0y_5(y_7 + x_7^*) + \beta_0x_5^*y_7 - \gamma_{12}y_6 - \mu_0(y_6 + x_6^*)y_4 \\
\dot{y_7} &= -\gamma_Dy_7 - \frac{\mu_Dy_8(y_7 + x_7^*)}{a + y_7 + x_7^*} \\
\dot{y_9} &= -\gamma_Ly_9 - \beta(y_9)y_9 + 2e^{-\gamma_L\tau_3}\beta(y_{9\tau_3})y_{9\tau_3} - c_1y_9(y_{11} + x_{11}^*) - \frac{\mu_Ly_9(y_7 + x_7^*)}{a + y_7 + x_7^*}
\end{aligned} \tag{22}$$

By the previous result on some components of the solution being bounded, the right-hand sides of system (22) are bounded for bounded $(y_4, y_5, y_6, y_7, y_9)$.

Consider the candidate Lyapunov function

$$V(y_4, y_5, y_6, y_7, y_9) = \alpha_1 \frac{y_4^2}{2} + \alpha_2 \frac{y_5^2}{2} + \alpha_3 \frac{y_6^2}{2} + \alpha_4 \frac{y_7^2}{2} + \alpha_5 \frac{y_9^2}{2} + b_1 \int_{t-\tau_3}^{t} y_9^2(s) ds$$

with $\alpha_1, \alpha_2, \alpha_3, \alpha_4, \alpha_5, b_1 \in (0, \infty)$ subject to further constraints. Remark that one has

$$m||(y_4, y_5, y_6, y_7, y_9)||_2 \leq V(y_4, y_5, y_6, y_7, y_9) \leq M||y||^2, y = (y_1, \ldots, y_{11})$$

for some $M > 0$. The derivative along (22) of V is given by

$$\frac{dV}{dt} = \alpha_1 y_4 \dot{y}_4 + \alpha_2 y_5 \dot{y}_5 + \alpha_2 y_6 \dot{y}_6 + \alpha_4 y_7 \dot{y}_7 + \alpha_5 y_9 \dot{y}_9 + b_1 y_9^2(s) \Big|_{t-\tau_3}^{t}$$

$$\frac{dV}{dt} = -\alpha_1 \beta_4 y_4^2 + \alpha_1 k\ vs.\ y_1 y_4^2 y_{6\tau_1} + \alpha_1 k v y_1 y_4^2 x_6^* + \alpha_1 k v x_1^* y_4^2 y_{6\tau_1} + \alpha_1 k v x_1^* y_4^2 x_6^* - \eta_r \frac{y_4^2(y_8 + x_8^*)}{1 + y_8 + x_8^*)}$$

$$-\alpha_2 \beta_0 y_5^2 y_7 - \alpha_2(\gamma_{11} + \beta_0 x_7^*) y_5^2 - \alpha_2 \beta_0 y_5 y_7 x_5^* + \alpha_3 \beta_0 y_6 y_5 y_7 + \alpha_3 \beta_0 y_6 y_5 x_7^* + \alpha_3 \beta_0 x_5^* y_7 y_6 -$$

$$-\alpha_3 \gamma_{12} y_6^2 - \alpha_3 \mu_0 y_4 y_6^2 - \alpha_3 \mu_0 y_4 y_6 x_6^* - \alpha_4 \gamma_D y_7^2 - \alpha_4 \mu_D \frac{y_9 y_7^2}{a + y_7 + x_7^*} - \alpha_4 \mu_D \frac{y_9 y_7 x_7^*}{a + y_7 + x_7^*} -$$

$$-\alpha_5 \gamma_L y_9^2 - \alpha_5 \beta(y_9) y_9^2 + 2\alpha_5 e^{-\gamma_L \tau_3} \beta(y_{9\tau_3}) y_9 y_{9\tau_3} - \alpha_5 c_1 y_9^2(y_{11} + x_{11}^*) - \alpha_5 \mu_L \frac{y_9^2(y_7 + x_7^*)}{a + y_7 + x_7^*} +$$

$$+b_1 y_9^2 - b_1 y_{9\tau_3}^2$$

If we use the inequality

$$xy \leq \frac{x^2}{2} + \frac{y^2}{2},$$

remark that $\beta(x) \leq \beta_L \ \forall\ x \geq 0$ and neglect some negative terms we get

$$\frac{dV}{dt} \leq y_4^2(-\alpha_1 \beta_4 + \alpha_1 k\ vs.\ x_1^* x_6^*) + y_5^2 \left[-\alpha_2(\gamma_{11} + \beta_0 x_7^*) + \frac{\alpha_3 \beta_0 x_7^*}{2} \right] +$$

$$+y_6^2 \left(-\alpha_3 \gamma_{12} + \frac{\alpha_3 \beta_0 x_7^*}{2} + \frac{\alpha_3 \beta_0 x_5^*}{2} \right) - \left(\frac{\alpha_3 \beta_0 x_5^*}{2} - \alpha_4 \gamma_D \right) y_7^2 +$$

$$+y_9^2(-\alpha_5 \gamma_L - \alpha_5 c_1 x_{11}^* + \alpha_5 \beta_L e^{-\gamma_L \tau_3} + b_1) + y_{9\tau_3}^2(\alpha_5 \beta_L e^{-\gamma_L \tau_3} - b_1) +$$

$$+\alpha_1 k\ vs.\ y_1 y_4^2 y_{6\tau_1} + \alpha_1 k v y_1 y_4^2 x_6^* + \alpha_1 k v x_1^* y_4^2 y_{6\tau_1} + \alpha_3 \beta_0 y_6 y_5 y_7$$

If, besides the conditions (21), we choose $\alpha_2, \alpha_3, \alpha_5, b_1$ so that

$$\alpha_3 \beta_0 x_1^* < 2\alpha_2(\gamma_{11} + \beta_0 x_7^*), \quad \alpha_3 \beta_0 x_5^* < \alpha_4 \gamma_D, \tag{23}$$

$$-\alpha_5 \gamma_L - \alpha_5 c_1 x_{11}^* + \alpha_5 \beta_L e^{-\gamma_L \tau_3} + b_1 < 0, \quad \alpha_5 \beta_L e^{-\gamma_L \tau_3} - b_1 < 0$$

then the quadratic terms in $\frac{dV}{dt}$ give a negative definite quadratic form. Remark that while the first two conditions in (21) involve the specific parameters of the system, the third one in (22), as well as (23), can be achieved by appropriately choosing $\alpha_2, \alpha_3, \alpha_5 b_1$. Introduce $z = (y_4, y_5, y_6, y_7, y_9, y_{9\tau_3})$. Using the boundedness of y_1, y_5, y_6, y_7, y_9 , it follows that:

$$\frac{dV}{dt} \leq -\omega(||z_t||_\tau^2) + G(z_t)$$

where $G(z_t) = \alpha_1 k\ vs.\ y_1 y_4^2 y_{6\tau_1} + \alpha_1 kvy_1 y_4^2 x_6^* + \alpha_1 kvx_1^* y_4^2 y_{6\tau_1} + \alpha_3 \beta_0 y_6 y_5 y_7$, ω is strictly positively defined and $|G(z_t)| \leq M||y_t||_\tau^3$. Then the derivative of V along the shifted system (12) is strictly negatively defined for positive initial data with the norm small enough and uniform asymptotic partial stability is proved (see also [17–22]). □

5.2. Partial Stability of E_2

In this section, we will derive delay-independent partial stability conditions for the equilibrium $E_2 = (x_1^*, x_2^*, 0, 0, x_5^*, x_6^*, x_7^*, x_8^*, 0, 0, x_{11}^*)$ of system (12).

Proposition 5. *Under condition (20) and assuming that*

$$k\ vs.\ x_1^* x_6^* < \beta_4, \quad \beta_0 x_7^* + \beta_0 x_5^* < 2\gamma_{12} \tag{24}$$

E_2 is partially stable with respect to variables $x_1, x_4, x_5, x_6, x_7, x_9$ and with respect to the invariant manifold of solutions with positive components.

Proof. As before, we start by performing a translation of the equilibrium E_2 to zero by $y_i = x_i - x_i^*$, for $i = 1, \ldots, 11$. We are interested only in Equations (1), (4)–(7) and (9).

$$\begin{aligned}
\dot{y}_1 &= -\beta_1 y_1 - \frac{(y_1 + x_1^*)(y_6 + x_6^*) y_2}{1 + \mu_2 y_3} - \frac{y_1 (y_6 + x_6^*) x_2^*}{1 + \mu_2 y_3} - \frac{x_1^* y_{6\tau_1} x_2^*}{1 + \mu_2 y_3} - \phi(y_1 + x_1^*)(y_{6\tau_1} + x_6^*)) y_3 \\
&-\kappa (y_1 + x_1^*)(y_{6\tau_1} + x_6^*) y_4 \\
\dot{y}_4 &= -\beta_4 y_4 + \kappa\ vs.\ (y_1 + x_1^*)(y_{6\tau_1} + x_6^*) y_4 - \eta_r \frac{(y_8 + x_8^*) y_4}{1 + y_8 + x_8^*} \\
\dot{y}_5 &= -(\gamma_{11} + \beta_0 x_7^*) y_5 - \beta_0 y_7 y_5 - \beta_0 y_7 x_5^* \\
\dot{y}_6 &= \beta_0 y_5 (y_7 + x_7^*) + \beta_0 x_5^* y_7 - \gamma_{12} y_6 - \mu_0 (y_6 + x_6^*) y_4 \\
\dot{y}_7 &= -\gamma_D y_7 - \frac{\mu_D y_8 (y_7 + x_7^*)}{a + y_7 + x_7^*} \\
\dot{y}_9 &= -\gamma_L y_9 - \beta(y_9) y_9 + 2e^{-\gamma_L \tau_3} \beta(y_{9\tau_3}) y_{9\tau_3} - c_1 y_9 (y_{11} + x_{11}^*) - \frac{\mu_L y_9 (y_7 + x_7^*)}{a + y_7 + x_7^*}
\end{aligned} \tag{25}$$

Consider the candidate Lyapunov function

$$V(y_1, y_4, y_5, y_6, y_7, y_9) = \alpha_1 \frac{y_1^2}{2} + \alpha_2 \frac{y_4^2}{2} + \alpha_3 \frac{y_5^2}{2} + \alpha_4 \frac{y_6^2}{2} + \alpha_5 \frac{y_7^2}{2} + \alpha_6 \frac{y_9^2}{2} + b_1 \int_{t-\tau_3}^{t} y_9^2(s) ds$$

with $\alpha_1, \alpha_2, \alpha_3, \alpha_4, \alpha_5, \alpha_6, b_1 \in (0, \infty)$ subject to further constraints. Remark that one has

$$m||(y_1, y_4, y_5, y_6, y_7, y_9)||_2 \leq V(y_1, y_4, y_5, y_6, y_7, y_9) \leq M||y||_\tau^2, y = (y_1, \ldots, y_{11})$$

for some $m, M > 0$. The derivative along (25) of V is given by

$$\frac{dV}{dt} = \alpha_1 y_1 \dot{y}_1 + \alpha_2 y_4 \dot{y}_4 + \alpha_3 y_5 \dot{y}_5 + \alpha_4 y_6 \dot{y}_6 + \alpha_5 y_7 \dot{y}_7 + \alpha_6 y_9 \dot{y}_9 + b_1 y_9^2 - b_1 y_{9\tau_3}^2$$

$$\frac{dV}{dt} = -\alpha_1\beta_1 y_1^2 - \frac{\alpha_1 y_1 (y_1 + x_1^*)(y_{6\tau_1} + x_6^*) y_2}{1+\mu_2 y_3} - \frac{\alpha_1 y_1^2 (y_{6\tau_1} + x_6^*) x_2^*}{1+\mu_2 y_3}$$

$$-\frac{\alpha_1 y_1 x_1^* y_{6\tau_1} x_2^*}{1+\mu_2 y_3} - \phi\alpha_1 y_1 (y_1 + x_1^*)(y_{6\tau_1} + x_6^*) y_3$$

$$-\alpha_1 \kappa y_1 (y_1 + x_1^*)(y_{6\tau_1} + x_6^*) y_4 - \alpha_2 \beta_4 y_4^2 + \alpha_2 k\ vs.\ y_1 y_4^2 y_{6\tau_1} + \alpha_2 k v y_1 y_4^2 x_6^* + \alpha_2 k v x_1^* y_4^2 y_{6\tau_1}$$

$$+\alpha_2 k v x_1^* y_4^2 x_6^* - \alpha_2 \eta_r \frac{y_4^2 (y_8 + x_8^*)}{1 + y_8 + x_8^*} - \alpha_3 y_5^2 (\gamma_{11} + \beta_0 x_7^*) - \alpha_3 \beta_0 y_7 y_5^2 - \alpha_3 \beta_0 y_5 y_7 x_5^* +$$

$$+\alpha_4 \beta_0 y_6 y_5 y_7 + \alpha_4 \beta_0 y_6 y_5 x_7^* + \alpha_4 \beta_0 x_5^* y_7 y_6 - \alpha_4 \gamma_{12} y_6^2 - \alpha_4 \mu_0 y_6 y_4 (y_6 + x_6^*) - \alpha_5 \gamma_D y_7^2 -$$

$$-\alpha_5 \frac{\mu_D y_7 y_8 (y_7 + x_7^*)}{a + y_7 + x_7^*} - \alpha_6 \gamma_L y_9^2 - \alpha_6 \beta(y_9) y_9^2 + 2\alpha_6 e^{-\gamma_L \tau_3} \beta(y_{9\tau_3}) y_9 y_{9\tau_3} - \alpha_6 c_1 y_9^2 (y_{11} + x_{11}^*) -$$

$$-\alpha_6 \mu_L \frac{y_9^2 (y_7 + x_7^*)}{a + y_7 + x_7^*} + b_1 y_9^2 - b_1 y_{9\tau_3}^2$$

Similarly as above, neglecting some negative terms and using

$$xy \leq \frac{x^2}{2} + \frac{y^2}{2}$$

one obtains

$$\frac{dV}{dt} \leq -\alpha_1\beta_1 y_1^2 + y_4^2(-\alpha_2\beta_4 + \alpha_2 k\ vs.\ x_1^* x_6^*) + y_5^2\left(\frac{\alpha_4\beta_0 x_7^*}{2} - \alpha_3\gamma_{11} - \alpha_3\beta_0 x_7^*\right) +$$

$$+y_6^2\left(+\frac{\alpha_4\beta_0 x_5^*}{2} + \frac{\alpha_4\beta_0 x_7^*}{2} - \alpha_4\gamma_{12}\right)\left(\frac{\alpha_4\beta_0 x_5^*}{2} - \alpha_5\gamma_D\right) y_7^2 +$$

$$+y_9^2(-\alpha_6\gamma_L - \alpha_6 c_1 x_{11}^* + \alpha_6 \beta_L e^{-\gamma_L \tau_3} + b_1) + y_{9\tau_3}^2(\alpha_6 \beta_L e^{-\gamma_L \tau_3} - b_1) +$$

$$+\alpha_2 k\ vs.\ y_1 y_4^2 y_{6\tau_1} + \alpha_2 k v y_1 y_4^2 x_6^* + \alpha_2 k v x_1^* y_4^2 y_{6\tau_1} + \alpha_4 \beta_0 y_6 y_5 y_7.$$

As in the case of E_1, besides (24) we impose the conditions

$$\alpha_4\beta_0 x_7^* < 2\alpha_3(\gamma_{11} + \beta_0 x_7^*), \quad \alpha_4\beta_0 x_5^* < \alpha_5\gamma_D, \tag{26}$$

$$-\alpha_6\gamma_L - \alpha_6 c_1 x_{11}^* + \alpha_6\beta_L e^{-\gamma_L\tau_3} + b_1 < 0, \quad \alpha_6\beta_L e^{-\gamma_L\tau_3} - b_1 < 0$$

then the quadratic terms in $\frac{dV}{dt}$ give a negative definite quadratic form. Again, the first two conditions involve the specific parameters of the system, but the third one can be achieved by appropriately choosing α_3, α_4. Introduce $z = (y_1, y_4, y_5, y_6, y_7)$. Using also that y_1, y_6, y_7 and y_8 are bounded, it follows that

$$\frac{dV}{dt} \leq -\omega(||z_t||_\tau^2) + G(z_t)$$

where ω is strictly positively defined and $|G(z_t)| \leq M||z_t||_\tau^3$. Then, the derivative of V along the shifted system 12 is strictly negatively defined for small $||z_t||_\tau$ and uniform partial stability is proved (see also [17–22]). □

6. Numerical Simulations

6.1. Numerical Simulations for E_1

E_1 is an equilibrium point showing a successful chemoimmunotherapy without detection of allergic reactions, because the $Th1$ cell population dominates the $Th2$ cell population, as shown in Figure 1. When the stability for E_1 holds we will have successful therapy, and this shows that small quantities of allergens do not harm.

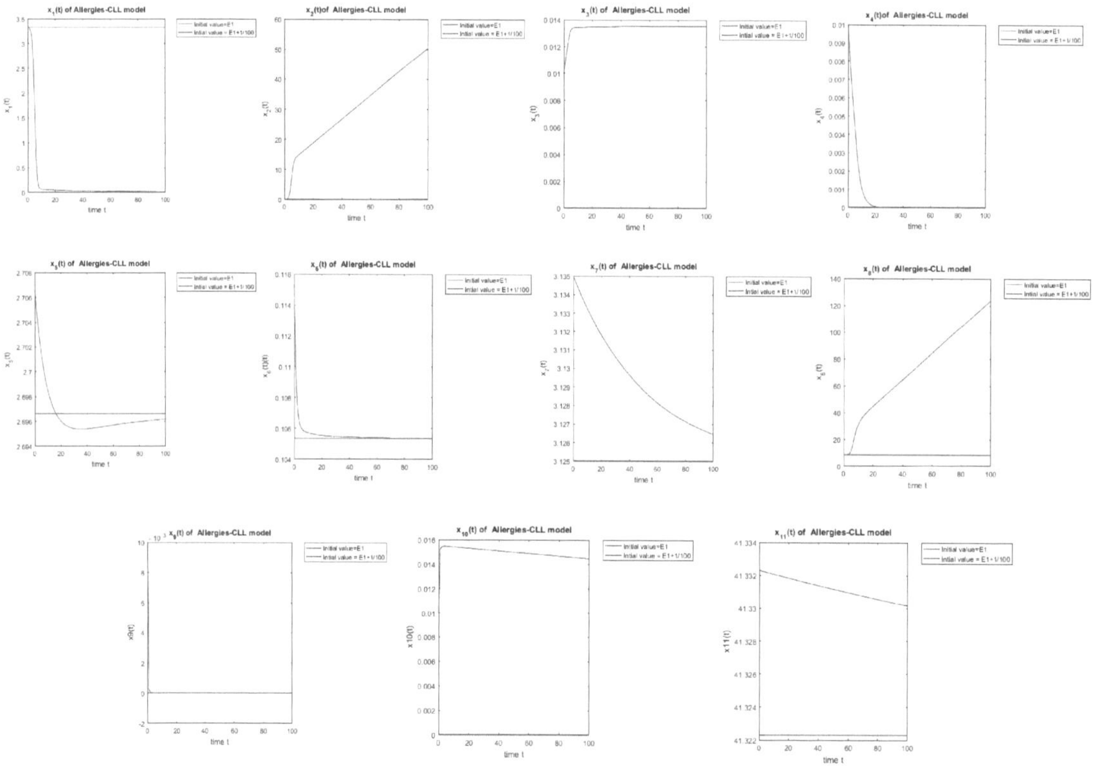

Figure 1. For a small disturbance in initial conditions near E_1, the system exhibits partial stability, where E_1 = (3.3333, 0, 0, 0, 3.4164, 0.0334, 0.7813, 8.4167, 0, 0, 41.3223).

6.2. Numerical Simulations for E_2

According to the simulations shown in Figure 2 starting with a desensitization dose of chemotherapy we will have successful chemoimmunotherapy without the detection of allergies even if we start with small values of $Th1$ cells, because the $Th1$ cell population will dominate the $Th2$ cell population.

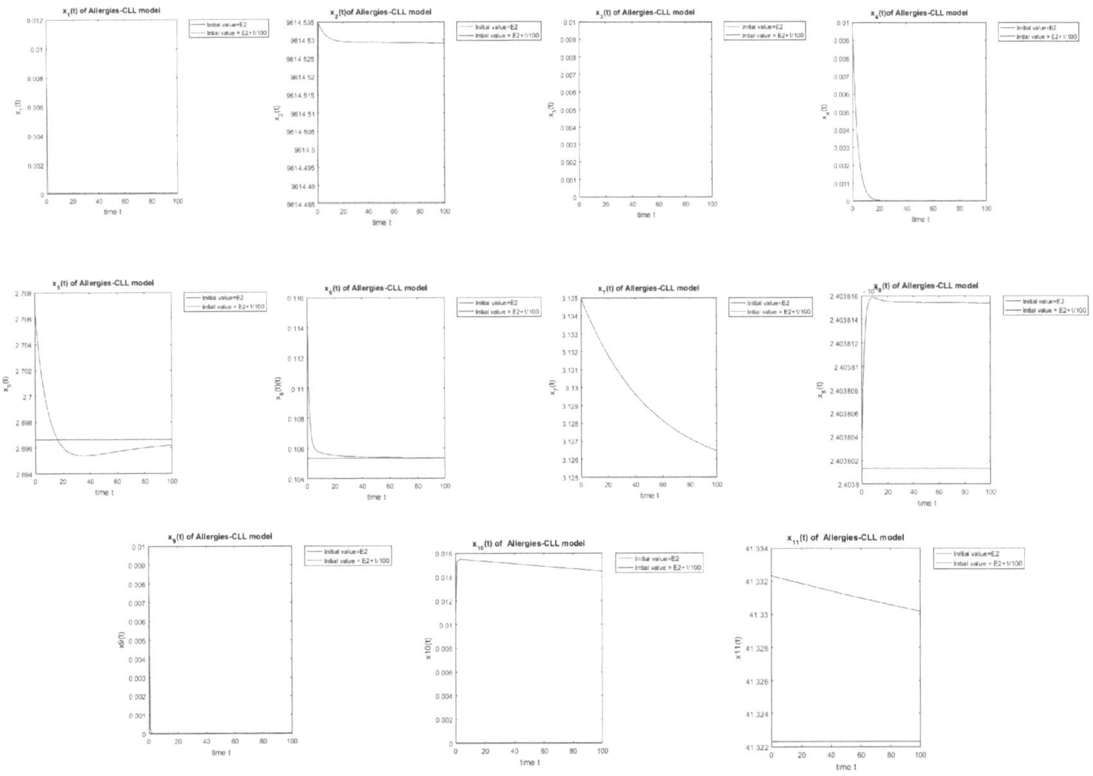

Figure 2. Simulation of a small disturbance in initial conditions near E_2. The equilibrium exhibits partial stability. $E_2 = (3.1172 \times 10^{-4}, 9.6145 \times 10^3, 0, 0, 3.4164, 0.0334, 0.7813, 2.4036 \times 10^4, 0, 0, 41.3223)$.

7. Conclusions

Our paper presents a new model for cellular evolution in the case of chronic lymphocytic leukemia (CLL). We assumed that the treatment is with chlorambucil. As this drug has been proven to cause allergic reactions, we included the effects of desensitization. We also included an equation which captures the number of dead leukemic cells present in the body at any given time. We included this in order to monitor the risk of tumor lysis syndrome (TLS), which is caused by an abundance of leukemic cells dying in a short period of time.

The mathematical model which illustrates the complex interplay between the immune system, the presence of the leukemic cells and the effects of the treatment, consists of 11 delayed-differential equations, the dynamics of which are thoroughly described in the paper.

We have established qualitative properties of the solutions, including partial stability with respect to certain variables and the invariant set of positive initial data. By proving these properties, we have gained insights into the behavior of the system and its response to chemotherapy and allergic reactions.

Furthermore, numerical simulations have been conducted to complement the theoretical analysis. The simulations explore the interplay between the immune system's function, the involvement of chemotherapy in cancer treatment, and the occurrence of allergic reactions due to the therapy. Numerical results obtained from the simulations have been presented.

Based on the provided information, it appears that the theoretical analysis shows that both equilibrium points E_1 and E_2 are not stable. The numerical computations align with this finding, confirming that both E_1 and E_2 are indeed not stable, contrary to the initial expectations. The numerical simulations further validate the theoretical results, reinforcing the conclusion that neither E_1 nor E_2 exhibit stability.

Theoretical results on partial stability have been derived under certain conditions. Specifically, we have shown that E_1 is partially stable with respect to variables x_4, x_5, x_6, x_7 and x_9, as well as with respect to the invariant manifold of solutions with positive components. Similarly, E_2 is partially stable with respect to variables x_1, x_4, x_5, x_6, x_7 and x_9, and with respect to the invariant manifold of solutions with positive components.

Additionally, the numerical simulations of equilibrium points E_1 and E_2 reinforce the theoretical findings on partial stability. The simulations demonstrate that both E_1 and E_2 exhibit partial stability with respect to the same variables that were studied and stated in the theoretical analysis. This consistency between the theoretical and numerical results further supports the validity of the partial stability conclusions for E_1 and E_2.

Furthermore, the numerical simulations of equilibrium points E_1 and E_2 provide valuable biological insights into the behavior of the system. The simulations shed light on the dynamics of chemoimmunotherapy and the occurrence of allergic reactions in patients with chronic lymphocytic leukemia (CLL).

The simulation results for E_1 reveal a scenario of successful chemoimmunotherapy without the detection of allergic reactions. This is attributed to the dominance of the Th1 cell population over the Th2 cell population, as observed in the simulation results. Even when starting with small quantities of allergens, the simulations demonstrate that the therapy remains effective, indicating that small amounts of allergens do not cause harm.

In the case of E_2, the simulations show a different outcome. Starting with a desensitization dose of chemotherapy, the simulations illustrate successful chemoimmunotherapy without the detection of allergies. Importantly, even with initially low levels of $Th1$ cells, the dominance of the $Th1$ cell population over the $Th2$ cell population is achieved, contributing to the positive treatment outcome.

These biological interpretations of the simulation results highlight the intricate interplay between the immune system, chemotherapy and allergic reactions. The simulations provide evidence that appropriate therapeutic strategies, such as desensitization dosing and the regulation of immune cell populations, can lead to successful treatment outcomes in CLL patients undergoing chemoimmunotherapy.

Overall, this study provides valuable insights into the dynamics of CLL patients undergoing chemotherapy and the impact of desensitization for chemotherapy-induced allergies. The combination of theoretical analysis and numerical simulations enhances our understanding of the system, and can potentially guide future clinical decision-making processes.

Author Contributions: Conceptualization, A.H.; methodology, A.H. and R.A.; writing, I.B. and R.A.; writing—review and editing, I.B. and A.H., formal analysis, R.A., I.B. and A.H. All authors have read and agreed to the published version of the manuscript.

Funding: This research received no external funding.

Data Availability Statement: Data is contained within the article.

Conflicts of Interest: The authors declare no conflict of interest.

Appendix A. Linearization Matrices

The matrices used for the linearization of the system are calculated below. The calculations are around a general equilibrium point. The values of the state variables must be replaced by the values corresponding to the equilibrium point under study.

$$A = \frac{\partial f}{\partial x}$$

- $a_{11} = -\beta_1 - x_6 \dfrac{x_2}{1 + \mu_2 x_3} - \phi x_6 x_3 - \kappa x_6 x_4$

- $a_{12} = -\dfrac{x_1 x_6}{1+\mu_2 x_3}$
- $a_{13} = \dfrac{\mu_2 x_1 x_6 x_2}{(1+\mu_2 x_3)^2} - \phi x_1 x_6$
- $a_{14} = -\kappa x_1 x_6$
- $a_{21} = \dfrac{v x_6 x_2}{(1+\mu_r x_4)(1+\mu_2 x_3)}$
- $a_{22} = -\beta_2 + \dfrac{v x_1 x_6}{(1+\mu_r x_4)(1+\mu_2 x_3)}$
- $a_{23} = \dfrac{-v\mu_2 x_6 x_1 x_2}{(1+\mu_r x_4)(1+\mu_2 x_3)^2}$
- $a_{24} = \dfrac{-v\mu_r x_6 x_1 x_2}{(1+\mu_r x_4)^2(1+\mu_2 x_3)}$
- $a_{31} = \dfrac{\phi\ vs.\ x_6 x_3}{(1+\mu_r x_4)(1+\mu_1 \frac{x_2}{1+\mu_2 x_3})}$
- $a_{32} = -\dfrac{\phi\ vs.\ x_1 x_6 x_3 \mu_1}{(1+\mu_r x_4)(1+\mu_2 x_3)(1+\mu_1 \frac{x_2}{1+\mu_2 x_3})^2}$
- $a_{33} = -\beta_3 + \dfrac{\phi\ vs.\ x_1 x_6}{1+\mu_r x_4} \dfrac{1+\mu_2 x_3 + \mu_2^2 x_3^2 + \mu_1 x_2 + 2\mu_1\mu_2 x_2 x_3}{(1+\mu_1 x_2 + \mu_2 x_3)^2}$
- $a_{34} = -\dfrac{\phi\mu_r v x_1 x_6 x_3}{(1+\mu_r x_4)^2(1+\mu_1 \frac{x_2}{1+\mu_2 x_3})}$
- $a_{41} = \kappa\ vs.\ x_6 x_4$
- $a_{44} = -\beta_4 + \kappa\ vs.\ x_6 x_1 - \dfrac{\eta_r x_8}{1+x_8}$
- $a_{48} = -\dfrac{\eta_r x_4}{(1+x_8)^2}$
- $a_{55} = -\beta_0 x_7 - \gamma_{11}$
- $a_{57} = -\beta_0 x_5$
- $a_{64} = -\mu_0 x_6$
- $a_{65} = \beta_0 x_7$
- $a_{66} = -\gamma_{12} - \mu_0 x_4$
- $a_{67} = \beta_0 x_5$
- $a_{77} = -\gamma_D - \dfrac{a\mu_D x_9}{(a+x_7)^2}$
- $a_{79} = \dfrac{-\mu_D x_7}{a+x_7}$
- $a_{88} = -\gamma_2$
- $a_{97} = -\dfrac{a\mu_L x_9}{(a+x_7)^2}$
- $a_{99} = -\gamma_L - \beta'(x_9)x_9 - \beta(x_9) - c_1 x_{11} - \dfrac{\mu_L x_7}{a+x_7}$
  $a_{9,11} = -c_1 x_9$
- $a_{10,7} = \dfrac{a\mu_L x_9}{(a+x_7)^2}$

- $a_{10,9} = \gamma_L + \dfrac{\mu_L x_7}{a + x_7}$
- $a_{10,10} = -d$
- $a_{11,7} = -\dfrac{\delta c x_{11}}{(c + x_7)^2}$
- $a_{11,9} = \dfrac{\rho \gamma x_{11}}{(\gamma + x_9)^2} - c_2 x_{11}$
- $a_{11,11} = -m - c_2 x_9 + \dfrac{\rho x_9}{\gamma + x_9} - \dfrac{\delta x_7}{c + x_7}$

$$B = \frac{\partial f}{\partial x_{\tau_1}}$$

- $b_{16} = -\dfrac{x_1 x_2}{1 + \mu_2 x_3} - \phi x_1 x_3 - \kappa x_1 x_4$
- $b_{26} = \dfrac{v x_1 x_2}{(1 + \mu_r x_4)(1 + \mu_2 x_3)}$
- $b_{36} = \dfrac{\phi\ vs.\ x_1 x_3}{(1 + \mu_r x_4)(1 + \mu_1 \frac{x_2}{1+\mu_2 x_3})}$
- $b_{46} = \kappa\ vs.\ x_1 x_4$

$$C = \frac{\partial f}{\partial x_{\tau_2}}$$

- $c_{81} = k_1$
- $c_{82} = k_1$
- $c_{83} = k_1$
- $c_{84} = k_1$
- $c_{86} = k_1$

$$D = \frac{\partial f}{\partial x_{\tau_3}}$$

- $d_{99} = 2e^{-\gamma_L \tau_3}(\beta'(x_9)x_9 + \beta(x_9))$

  The elements which are not calculated explicitly are zero.

Appendix B. Parameters

Table A1. List of the system parameters and their values.

The production rate of naive CD4+ cells. [23]	α	0.1
The strength of suppression rate of Th1 by Th2 [9]	μ_2	0.1
The strength of suppression of Th2 by Th1 [9]	μ_1	0.2
The strength of suppression rate by Treg [9]	μ_r	0.25
The differences in the autocrine action of the three subsets [9]	ϕ	0.05
The differences in the autocrine action of the three subsets [9]	κ	0.1
The death rate of immature APCs [23]	γ_{11}	0.08
The death rate of mature APCs [23]	γ_{12}	0.8
The death rate of naive T cells [23]	β_1	0.03
The death rate of T_1 cells [24]	β_2	$10^{-3}h^{-1} = 0.0416 \times 10^{-3}$ day^{-1}

Table A1. *Cont.*

The death rate of T_2 cells [24]	β_3	$10^{-3}h^{-1} = 0.0416 \times 10^{-3}$ day^{-1}
The death rate of T_{reg} cells [24]	β_4	$10^{-3}h^{-1} = 0.0416 \times 10^{-3}$ day^{-1}
The proliferation rate of stimulated T cells [9]	v	4
Natural decay of induced cytokine during chemotherapy [25]	γ_4	0.4152
Inhibition rate of Treg cells by the induced cytokines [26]	η_r	0.4
First time delay [10]	τ_1	0.0794
Second time delay [25]	τ_2	0.25
Third time delay [27]	τ_3	2.8
The production of induced cytokines by other cells [11]	k_1	1
The supply rate of naive APCs[23]	a	0.3
Rate of APC activation by the antigen [28]	β_0	0.01
Rate of APC inhibition by regulatory T cells [28]	μ_0	10^{-2}
Chemical deactivation rate of drug [5]	γ_D	0.462 h^{-1} = 0.0192 day^{-1}
Supply rate of drug [29]	Λ	0.06g/L day^{-1}
Deactivation rate of drug due to killing of tumor cells [5]	μ_D	0.18 h^{-1} = 0.00748 day^{-1}
Drug dose that produce 50 % maximum effect [5]	a	2×10^3 mL = 2 in microliter
Tumor cells growth rate [5]	r	0.07 h^{-1} = 0.002912 day^{-1}
Maximal tumor cell population [5]	K	4×10^6 cell/mL = 0.57 cells/ microliter
Death rate of leukemic cells estimated from [13]	γ_L	2 day^{-1}
Death rate resulting from the action of drug of cancer cells estimated from [5]	μ_L	0.74 day^{-1}
Rate of dissolution of dead tumor cells [5]	d	0.017 h^{-1} = 0.000707 day^{-1}
Initial number of immune cells [14]	s	7×10^5 cells day^{-1} = 0.1 cells day^{-1} in microliter
Natural death rate of immune cells [14]	m	10^{-3} day^{-1}
Rate of immune cell population activated by the tumor [14]	ρ	10^{-12} day^{-1}
Rate of immune cell population activated by the tumor [14]	γ	10^2 cells = 0.0000142 cells in microliter
The mortality rate of immune cells due to the chemotherapeutic drug [14]	δ	10^4 day^{-1} =0.00142 cells in microliter
Half-saturation parameter [14]	c	5 kg = 7.14 $\times 10^{-7}$ in microliter
Rate of elimination of tumor cells by immune cells [14]	c_1	5×10^{-11} cells day^{-1}
Rate of immune cells which directly eliminate tumor cells [14]	c_2	10^{-13} cells day^{-1}
Component of the rate of self-renewal [13]	β_L	1.77 day^{-1}
Component of the rate of self-renewal [13]	θ	0.5×10^6 cells = 0.071 cells in microliter

References

1. Michor, F.; Beal, K. Improving Cancer Treatment via Mathematical Modeling: Surmounting the Challenges is Worth the Effort. *Cell* **2015**, *163*, 1059–1063. [CrossRef] [PubMed]
2. Gammon, K. Mathematical modelling: Forecasting cancer. *Nature* **2012**, *491*, S66–S67. [CrossRef] [PubMed]
3. Tambaro, F.P.; Wierda, W.G. Tumour lysis syndrome in patients with chronic lymphocytic leukaemia treated with BCL-2 inhibitors: Risk factors, prophylaxis, and treatment recommendations. *Lancet Haematol.* **2020**, *7*, e168–e176. [CrossRef]
4. Fischer, K.; Al-Sawaf, O.; Hallek, M. Preventing and monitoring for tumor lysis syndrome and other toxicities of venetoclax during treatment of chronic lymphocytic leukemia. *Hematology* **2020**, *2020*, 357–362. [CrossRef] [PubMed]
5. Guzev, E.; Luboshits, G.; Bunimovich-Mendrazitsky, S.; Firer, M.A. Experimental Validation of a Mathematical Model to Describe the Drug Cytotoxicity of Leukemic Cells. *Symmetry* **2021**, *13*, 1760. [CrossRef]
6. Torricelli, R.; Kurer, S.B.; Kroner, T.; Wüthrich, B. Delayed allergic reaction to Chlorambucil (Leukeran). Case report and literature review. *Schweiz. Med. Wochenschr.* **1995**, *125*, 1870–1873.
7. Levin, M.; Libster, D. Allergic reaction to chlorambucil in chronic lymphocytic leukemia presenting with fever and lymphadenopathy. *Leuk. Lymphoma* **2005**, *46*, 1195–1197. [CrossRef]
8. Segel, L.A.; Fishman, M.A. Modeling immunotherapy for allergy. *Bull. Math. Biol.* **1996**, *58*, 1099–1121.

9. Gross, F.; Behn, U. Mathematical modeling of allergy and specific immunotherapy: Th1, Th2 and Treg interactions. *J. Theor. Biol.* **2011**, *269*, 70–78. [CrossRef]
10. Wu, G. Calculation of steady-state distribution delay between central and peripheral compartments in two-compartment models with infusion regimen. *Eur. J. Drug Metab. Pharmacokinet.* **2002**, *27*, 259–264. [CrossRef]
11. Kareva, I.; Berezovskaya, F.; Karev, G. Mathematical model of a cytokine storm. *bioRxiv* 2022, *preprint*. [CrossRef]
12. Gubernatorova, E.O.; Gorshkova, E.A.; Namakanova, O.A.; Zvartsev, R.V.; Hidalgo, J.; Drutskaya, M.S.; Tumanov, A.V.; Nedospasov, S.A. Non-redundant Functions of IL-6 Produced by Macrophages and Dendritic Cells in Allergic Airway Inflammation. *Front. Immunol.* **2018**, *9*, 2718. [CrossRef]
13. Colijn, C.; Mackey, M.C. A mathematical model of hematopoiesis—I. Periodic chronic myelogenous leukemia. *J. Theor. Biol.* **2005**, *237*, 117–132. [CrossRef]
14. Gil, W.F.F.M.; Carvalho, T.; Mancera, P.F.A.; Rodrigues, D.S. A Mathematical Model on the Immune System Role in Achieving Better Outcomes of Cancer Chemotherapy. *TEMA* **2019**, *20*, 343–357. [CrossRef]
15. Cooke, K.; Grossman, Z. Discrete Delay, Distribution Delay and Stability Switches. *J. Math. Anal. Appl.* **1982**, *86*, 592–627. [CrossRef]
16. Kharitonov, V.L. *Time-Delay Systems, Lyapunov Functionals and Matrices*; Springer: Berlin/Heidelberg, Germany, 2013.
17. Rumyantsev, V.; Vorotnikov, V.I. *Foundations of Partial Stability and Control*; Birkhouser: Nijnii Tagil, Russia, 2014. (In Russian)
18. Aleksandrov, A.; Aleksandrova, E.; Zhabko, A.; Chen, Y. Partial stability analysis of some classes of nonlinear systems. *Acta Math. Sci.* **2017**, *37B*, 329–341. [CrossRef]
19. Corduneanu, C. On partial stability for delay systems. *Ann. Pol. Math.* **1975**, *29*, 357–362. [CrossRef]
20. Vorotnikov, V.I. *Partial Stability and Control: The State-of-the-Art and Development Prospects*; Ural State Technical University: Nizhni Tagil, Russia, 2003.
21. Aristide, H. *Differential Equation: Stability, Oscillations, Time-Lags*; Academic Press: New York, NY, USA, 1966.
22. Hatvani, L. On partial asymptotic stability and instability, I (Autonomous systems). *Acta Sci. Math.* **1983**, *45*, 219–231.
23. Kim, P.; Lee, P.; Levy, D. A theory of immunodominance and adaptive regulation. *Bull. Math. Biol.* **2011**, *73*, 1645–1665. [CrossRef]
24. Kogan, Y.; Agur, Z.; Elishmereni, M. A mathematical model for the immunotherapeutic control of the TH1/TH2 imbalance in melanoma. *Discret. Contin. Dyn. Syst. Ser. B* **2013**, *18*, 1017–1030. [CrossRef]
25. Nazari, F.; Pearson, A.T.; Nor, J.E.; Jackson, T.L. A mathematical model for IL-6-mediated, stem cell driven tumor growth and targeted treatment. *PLoS Comput. Biol.* **2018**, *14*, e1005920. . [CrossRef]
26. Hong, T.; Xing, J.; Li, L.; Tyson, J.J. A Mathematical Model for the Reciprocal Differentiation of T Helper 17 Cells and Induced Regulatory T Cells. *PLoS Comput. Biol.* **2011**, *7*, e1002122. [CrossRef] [PubMed]
27. Rădulescu, I.; Cândea, D.; Halanay, A. A study on stability and medical implications for a complex delay model for CML with cell competition and treatment. *J. Theor. Biol.* **2014**, *363*, 30–40. [CrossRef] [PubMed]
28. Fouchet, D.; Regoes, R. A Population Dynamics Analysis of the Interaction between Adaptive Regulatory T Cells and Antigen Presenting Cells. *PLoS ONE* **2008**, *3*, e2306. [CrossRef]
29. Rodrigues, D.; Mancera, P.; Carvalho, T.; Gonçalves, L. A mathematical model for chemoimmunotherapy of chronic lymphocytic leukemia. *Appl. Math. Comput.* **2019**, *349*, 118–133. [CrossRef]

mathematics

MDPI

Article

Mathematical Modeling and Stability Analysis of the Delayed Pine Wilt Disease Model Related to Prevention and Control

Ruilin Dong, Haokun Sui and Yuting Ding *

Department of Mathematics, Northeast Forestry University, Harbin 150040, China; drl2020222500@nefu.edu.cn (R.D.); 2020211102@nefu.edu.cn (H.S.)
* Correspondence: dingyt@nefu.edu.cn

Abstract: Forest pests and diseases have been seriously threatening ecological security. Effective prevention and control of such threats can extend the growth cycle of forest trees and increase the amount of forest carbon sink, which makes a contribution to achieving China's goal of "emission peak and carbon neutrality". In this paper, based on the insect-vector populations (this refers to *Monochamus alternatus*, which is the main vector in Asia) in pine wilt disease, we establish a two-dimensional delay differential equation model to investigate disease control and the impact of time delay on the effectiveness of it. Then, we analyze the existence and stability of the equilibrium of the system and the existence of Hopf bifurcation, derive the normal form of Hopf bifurcation by using a multiple time scales method, and conduct numerical simulations with realistic parameters to verify the correctness of the theoretical analysis. Eventually, according to theoretical analysis and numerical simulations, some specific suggestions are put forward for prevention and control of pine wilt disease.

Keywords: pine wilt disease; time delay; stability; normal form of Hopf bifurcation

MSC: 34K18; 37L10

Citation: Dong, R.; Sui, H.; Ding, Y. Mathematical Modeling and Stability Analysis of the Delayed Pine Wilt Disease Model Related to Prevention and Control. *Mathematics* **2023**, *11*, 3705. https://doi.org/10.3390/math11173705

Academic Editors: Mihaela Neamţu, Eva Kaslik and Anca Rădulescu

Received: 4 June 2023
Revised: 23 August 2023
Accepted: 27 August 2023
Published: 28 August 2023

1. Introduction

The world has long been confronted with hazads of climate change caused by global warming. China is taking pragmatic actions facing the challenges brought by climate change. At the general debate of the 75th Session of the United Nations General Assembly on 22 September 2020, President Xi Jinping announced that China would scale up its NDCs (Nationally Determined Contributions) by adopting more vigorous policies and measures, strive to peak CO_2 emissions before 2030, and achieve carbon neutrality before 2060.

Forests' annual carbon sequestration accounts for about 2/3rd of the whole terrestrial system, which is the main body of the terrestrial ecosystem. According to the China Forest Resources Report, by 2018, China's forest coverage rate was 22.96%, forest area was 220 million hm^2, forest stock volume was 17.56 billion m^3, and total carbon storage was 91.86 billion tons. From 1990 to 2020, China's forest carbon sink capacity witnessed an escalation from 185.5 $GtCO_2$ to 321.4 $GtCO_2$. A vigorous increase of forest carbon sink has become a top priority to achieve the carbon peaking and carbon neutrality goals. Effective control of forest pests and diseases can prolong the growth cycle of trees and increase the forest carbon sink, which is of great significance for the realization of China's "30·60" goal.

Pine wilt disease (PWD) is a devastating forest disease caused by pine wood nematode (PWN). The PWD is a multipartite system involving intimate relationships between the pathogen, PWN, Bursaphelenchus xylophilus (Steiner & Buhrer) Nickle, its vectors, and symbiotic microorganisms [1]. It is mainly transmitted by *Monochamus alternatus* (*M. alternatus*) in Asia [1], which spreads rapidly and kills trees quickly. Through consulting relevant data, PWN is thought to have originated in North America [2], then gradually invaded other countries, such as Japan [3], Korea [4], China [5], Mexico [6], and Spain [7].

How to effectively control the occurrence and spread of PWD has become the focus and frontier topic of researchers. Ecologists have made remarkable progress in many aspects. Kim et al. [8] used recombinant BxPrx as an antigen to generate a novel antibody that can be used to quickly and accurately determine PWD. Ding et al. [9] improved the genome sequence of PWN and explained the interaction between PWD and pine trees. Palomares-Rius et al. [10] determined a gene set affected by genomic variation finding that the level of genomic diversity of PWN was related to its phenotypic variability, including variations in pathogenicity and ecological traits. Presently, global strategies for PWD prevention and control encompass chemical control, physical control, biological control and biomimetic technology, with avermectin (AVM) as a predominant insecticidal agent [11]. Lee et al. [12] conducted comparative analyses on 16 avermectin benzoate formulations against PWD to support disease control. Alvarez et al. [13] engineered diverse trap designs assessing their efficacy in maximizing the attraction and retention of live insects through field experiments and comparative modeling. Mannaa et al. [14] found that treatment with resistance-induced chemical inducers MeSA and ASM significantly reduced the severity of PWD, providing new ideas for its prevention and treatment.

While ecologists have largely concentrated on the biological structure, distribution and control factors of PWN, attention to the dynamic characteristics of PWD transmission system remains scant. In recent years, mathematicians have established various models to predict the occurrence trend of PWD. Shi and Song [15] investigated the dynamical behavior of PWD by incorporating a standard incidence rate and the threshold value of the relative basic reproductive number R_0 which determined the spread of infection has been worked out. Ozair [16] discussed the global stability of PWD by considering the nonlinear incidence rate with the horizontal transmission in the model. Khan et al. [17] introduced a mathematical model that described the dynamics of PWD by presenting the stability analysis of the disease-free and endemic equilibria base on basic reproduction number R_0, and an optimal control strategy was formulated by adding control variables related to time to the model. Subsequent work by Khan et al. [18] continued this line of inquiry by exploring the effect of asymptomatic carriers of PWD and further elaborating on the optimal control strategies in 2020.

As we know from the literature, most of the literature studied the occurrence of PWD in its natural state or the effects of prevention and control on PWD infectivity, with limited examination of time-delay in the control process. Therefore, it is feasible to propose a model that can comprehensively show intensity and time-delay of disease control. Based on the infectious disease model, we divide *M. alternatus* into susceptible *M. alternatus* (not carrying PWN) and infected *M. alternatus* (carrying PWN). After the outbreak of PWD in a forest area, we usually take measures to protect pine trees and kill *M. alternatus*. However, given the extensive adaptability of PWN and the rapid spread of PWD, there is a certain time delay of the control to take effect (that is, the infection rate of *M. alternatus* begins to decline). We use delay differential equations to describe the dynamic changes in the insect-vector populations system more truly and accurately. Delay differential equations are used to describe the development systems that depend on both the current state and the past state and have been widely used in many fields. In the study of the bifurcation phenomenon, it is very important to derive the bifurcation normal form of differential equations. Nayfeh [19] proposed the method of multiple time scales (MTS) to solve the problem of nonlinear vibration and gave the calculation process of Hopf bifurcation normal form of delay differential equations by MTS in 2008 [20]. Later, many scholars studied the stability and bifurcation theory of various differential equations [21–23]. Based on this background, we establish a two-dimensional differential equation model with time delay to discuss the stability and bifurcation phenomenon of PWD infection-control system to predict the occurrence of PWD, and provide theoretical support for the prevention and control of PWD.

The rest of the content is arranged as follows. In Section 2, we first build a differential equation model with time delay based on the epidemic model among the medium insects.

In Section 3, we analyze the existence and stability of equilibrium and the existence of Hopf bifurcation for the model with time delay. In Section 4, we derive the normal form of the Hopf bifurcation by using MTS and analyze the stability of the periodic solution of the Hopf bifurcation. In Section 5, we discuss and analyze the unknown parameters in the model and then present numerical simulations to verify the correctness of the theoretical analysis. Finally, the conclusion is drawn in Section 6.

2. Mathematical Modeling

After the outbreak of PWD in an area, we take control measures (such as nematicide injection and vaccination) to protect pine trees. The transmission of PWN is not reliant upon direct contact between *M. alternatus*, but hinges on the process of infected *M. alternatus* transmitting PWN to healthy pine trees during feeding and oviposition. Newly formed adult *M. alternatus* remain within the pupation chamber prior to emergence, where they become infected by PWN from deceased host tree wood, then they carry PWN to continue to infect other healthy pine trees after emergence. Upon implementation of nematicide injection or vaccination, the quantity of PWN in pine trees diminishes, leading to a concomitant decline in infection rate. Therefore, taking control measures on trees can effectively reduce the infection rate of *M. alternatus*. Moreover, measures such as insecticidal spraying insecticides can kill *M. alternatus*, which also reduces the rate of infection. However, the transmission speed of PWN is very fast when the forest is in the outbreak period of PWD, so in the early stage of control, the transmission efficiency of PWN may be higher than that of control. Consequently, there is a time delay between taking control measures and the beginning of the decline in the infection rate of *M. alternatus*, so there is a certain time delay in the effective of prevention and control. Since not every time infected *M. alternatus* can "feed" PWN, we introduce an infection coefficient. We suppose that the infection coefficient of PWD is reduced to β after adopting control measures. Other influencing factors in the infection-control system are analyzed below.

It is assumed that *M. alternatus* are divided into susceptible *M. alternatus* $S(t)$ which did not carry PWN and infected *M. alternatus* $I(t)$ which did carry PWN at a certain time in a PWD epidemic area. For the input of *M. alternatus*, the born *M. alternatus* and the dead *M. alternatus* are mainly considered. Because the resources are limited, it is more realistic for us to use the logistic function to describe the growth rate of the *M. alternatus*. We assume the natural mortality of susceptible and infected *M. alternatus* as d_1, d_2, respectively. In the process of the spread of PWD, prevention and control can increase the mortality rate of *M. alternatus*, thereby inhibiting the spread of the disease. With the progress of control, the mortality rate of *M. alternatus* will tend to be saturated. Therefore, the number of *M. alternatus* killed by artificial control grows following nonlinear logistic growth, and the mortality rate of *M. alternatus* is related to the intensity of control, with the increase of control efforts, the mortality rate also increases nonlinearly, so we use $k_1\alpha$ to describe its linear part and $k_2\alpha$ to describe its nonlinear part, where $k_1\alpha$ represents control measures efficiency of PWD. Adding the nonlinear part better reflects the saturation effect of artificial prevention and control, which is more consistent with reality. To better study the impact of prevention and control on PWD infection-control system, we present the variable relationships shown in Figure 1.

According to Figure 1, we can construct the following delayed differential equation model:

$$\begin{cases} \dfrac{\mathrm{d}S}{\mathrm{d}t} = B(1 - \dfrac{S(t)}{K})S(t) - d_1 S(t) - \beta S(t)I(t-\tau) - k_1\alpha S(t) + k_2\alpha S^2(t), \\ \dfrac{\mathrm{d}I}{\mathrm{d}t} = \beta S(t)I(t-\tau) - d_2 I(t) - k_1\alpha I(t) + k_2\alpha I^2(t), \end{cases} \tag{1}$$

where $S(t)$ and $I(t)$ are the variables; B, d_1, d_2, k_1, k_2, β, α and K are the positive constants; and τ is the time delay of disease control to take effect. The specific descriptions are given in Table 1.

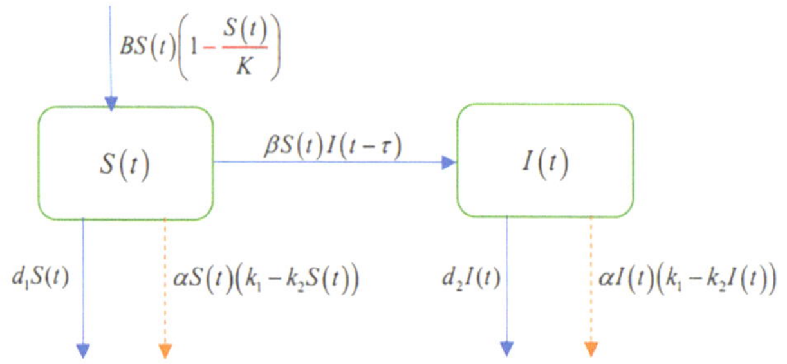

Figure 1. Variable relation of the infection-control system.

Table 1. Descriptions of parameters in the model (1).

Symbol	Description	Unit
S	Amount of susceptible *M. alternatus*	10^4 head
I	Amount of infected *M. alternatus*	10^4 head
B	Natural birth rate of *M. alternatus*	% (year)
d_1	Natural mortality of susceptible *M. alternatus*	% (year)
d_2	Natural mortality of infected *M. alternatus*	% (year)
k_1	Linear coefficient related to mortality caused by control	-
k_2	Nonlinear coefficient related to mortality caused by control	-
β	Infection coefficient	-
α	Intensity of prevention and control against *M. alternatus*	%
K	Environmental capacity	-
τ	Time delay of disease control to take effect	year
t	Time	year

For convenience, we denote that $n_1 = B - d_1 - k_1\alpha$, $n_2 = k_2\alpha - \frac{B}{K}$, $n_3 = d_2 + k_1\alpha$; then, model (1) becomes:

$$\begin{cases} \frac{\mathrm{d}S}{\mathrm{d}t} = n_1S(t) + n_2S^2(t) - \beta S(t)I(t-\tau), \\ \frac{\mathrm{d}I}{\mathrm{d}t} = \beta S(t)I(t-\tau) - n_3I(t) + k_2\alpha I^2(t). \end{cases} \quad (2)$$

Due to the wide distribution and strong concealment of *M. alternatus*, we believe that the number of births of susceptible *M. alternatus* is always greater than the number of deaths, that is, $n_1 > 0$, which is also consistent with the data we found in the later parameter analysis. Moreover, we believe that the intensity of prevention and control against *M. alternatus* will be change within 0~1, that is, the maximum value of α is 100%.

Then, we prove that the solution of system (2) is nonnegative under positive initial conditions.

The initial condition of system (2) is $\varphi = (\varphi_s(\theta), \varphi_I(\theta)) \in C([-\tau,0], R^2_{+0}), \theta \in [-\tau,0]$, where $\varphi_s(\theta) \geq 0$, $\varphi_I(\theta) \geq 0$, $C([-\tau,0], R^2_{+0})$ is a continuous function mapping from $[-\tau,0]$ to R^2_{+0} in Banach space, for system (2), $R^2_{+0} = \{(S(t), I(t)) | S(t) \geq 0, I(t) \geq 0\}$.

Theorem 1. *If $\varphi_s(\theta) \geq 0$, $\varphi_I(\theta) \geq 0$, $\theta \in [-\tau,0]$, then the solution of system* (2) *$S(t)$, $I(t)$ is nonnegative for $t \geq 0$.*

Proof. Assume that the system (2) in the nonnegative initial function $\varphi_s(\theta) \geq 0, \theta \in [-\tau,0]$, the solution $S(t)$ is not nonnegative when $t \geq 0$, then there must be the first time $t_1 > 0$, such that $S(t_1) = 0$, $S'(t_1) < 0$. According to the first equation of system (2), we can obtain $S'(t_1) = 0$, contradicting with $S'(t_1) < 0$ at this time.

Similarly, assuming that the solution of system (2) $I(t)$ is not nonnegative when $t \geq 0$ in the case of nonnegative initial function $\varphi_I(\theta) \geq 0, \theta \in [-\tau, 0]$, then there must be a first time $t_2 > 0$, such that $I(t_2) = 0$, $I(t_2 - \tau) > 0$, $I'(t_2) < 0$, according to the second equation of system (2): $I'(t_2) = \beta S I(t_2 - \tau)$, note the parameter $\beta > 0$, so $I'(t_2) > 0$, contradicting with $I'(t_2) < 0$ at this time.

In summary, when $t \geq 0$, the solutions $S(t)$ and $I(t)$ of system (2) are still nonnegative for nonnegative initial functions. □

3. Stability Analysis of Equilibrium and Existence of Hopf Bifurcation

In this section, we will discuss the stability of equilibria and the existence of Hopf bifurcation for system (2).

3.1. Existence of Equilibrium Point

Firstly, we give the following assumptions:

$$(\mathrm{H1})\ n_2 < 0,$$

$$(\mathrm{H2}) \begin{cases} \dfrac{(d_2 + k_1\alpha)(\beta^2 + k_2\alpha n_2) - k_2\alpha(n_1\beta + n_2 n_3)}{\beta(\beta^2 + k_2\alpha n_2)} > 0, \\ \dfrac{n_1\beta + n_2 n_3}{\beta^2 + k_2\alpha n_2} > 0. \end{cases}$$

System (2) always has a zero equilibrium $E_1 = (S^{(1)}, I^{(1)}) = (0, 0)$ and a boundary equilibrium $E_2 = (S^{(2)}, I^{(2)}) = (0, \frac{n_3}{k_2\alpha})$, since $n_3 > 0, k_2\alpha > 0$. When (H1) holds, system (2) has a disease-free equilibrium:

$$E_3 = (S^{(3)}, I^{(3)}) = (-\frac{n_1}{n_2}, 0).$$

When (H2) holds, system (2) has a positive equilibrium:

$$E_4 = (S^{(4)}, I^{(4)}) = (\frac{d_2 + k_1\alpha - k_2\alpha I^{(4)}}{\beta}, \frac{n_1\beta + n_2 n_3}{\beta^2 + k_2\alpha n_2}).$$

Based on the practical significance, we pay more attention to the existence and stability of disease-free equilibrium E_3 and positive equilibrium E_4.

Remark 1. *If $n_2 = k_2\alpha - \frac{B}{K} < 0$, that is $k_2\alpha < \frac{B}{K}$. When k_2, α, B are fixed, the smaller K is, the greater possibility of the assumption* (H1) *is established. Therefore, when the natural conditions of a forest area are better, that is, the environmental carrying capacity of M. alternatus is large, the assumption* (H1) *may not hold, and thus, the disease-free equilibrium E_3 may not exist. This indicates that when the forest conditions are suitable for the survival of M. alternatus, the infected M. alternatus cannot be completely eliminated, which is consistent with the actual situation.*

Next, we will discuss the existence and stability of equilibrium E_3, E_4.

3.2. Stability and Existence of Hopf Bifurcation for E_3

When (H1) holds, system (2) has a disease-free equilibrium E_3. Transferring the equilibrium E_3 to the origin and linearizing the surrounding system (2), we obtain the characteristic equation of the linearized system as follows:

$$(\lambda + n_1)\left(\lambda + n_3 + \frac{\beta n_1}{n_2} e^{-\lambda\tau}\right) = 0. \tag{3}$$

When $\tau = 0$, Equation (3) becomes:

$$(\lambda + n_1)\left(\lambda + \frac{\beta n_1 + n_2 n_3}{n_2}\right) = 0. \tag{4}$$

Then, We give the following hypothesis:

$$\text{(H3)}\ \beta n_1 + n_2 n_3 < 0.$$

Equation (4) has two characteristic roots $\lambda_1 = -n_1$, $\lambda_2 = -\frac{\beta n_1 + n_2 n_3}{n_2}$. Since $n_2 < 0$, when (H3) holds, $\lambda_1 < 0$ and $\lambda_2 < 0$, then E_3 is locally asymptotically stable; when $\beta n_1 + n_2 n_3 = 0$, $\lambda_2 = 0$, the equilibrium E_3 undergoes a fixed point bifurcation; when $\beta n_1 + n_2 n_3 > 0$, $\lambda_1 < 0$ but $\lambda_2 > 0$, and thus, the equilibrium E_3 is unstable at this time.

When $\tau > 0$, we try to discuss the existence of Hopf bifurcation. We assume that $\lambda = \mathrm{i}\omega (\omega > 0)$ is a pure imaginary root of Equation (3). Substituting it into Equation (3) and separating the real and imaginary parts, we obtain:

$$\begin{cases} \omega^2 - n_1 n_3 = \dfrac{\beta n_1^2}{n_2}\cos(\omega\tau) + \dfrac{\beta n_1 \omega}{n_2}\sin(\omega\tau), \\ (n_1 + n_3)\omega = \dfrac{\beta n_1^2}{n_2}\sin(\omega\tau) - \dfrac{\beta n_1 \omega}{n_2}\cos(\omega\tau). \end{cases} \tag{5}$$

Equation (5) derives the following results:

$$\begin{aligned} \sin(\omega\tau) &= \frac{n_2(\beta n_1 \omega^3 + \beta n_1^3 \omega)}{\beta^2 n_1^4 + \beta^2 n_1^2 \omega^2} \triangleq X_0, \\ \cos(\omega\tau) &= \frac{-n_2(\beta n_1^3 n_3 + \beta n_1 n_3 \omega^2)}{\beta^2 n_1^4 + \beta^2 n_1^2 \omega^2} \triangleq Y_0. \end{aligned} \tag{6}$$

Adding the square of the two equations in Equation (5), letting $\omega^2 = z$, we obtain:

$$h(z) = z^2 + \frac{n_1^2 n_2^2 + n_2^2 n_3^2 - \beta^2 n_1^2}{n_2^2} z + \frac{n_1^2(n_2^2 n_3^2 - \beta^2 n_1^2)}{n_2^2}. \tag{7}$$

When (H3) holds, $\beta^2 n_1^2 < n_2^2 n_3^2$, Equation (7) has no positive root, the equilibrium E_3 is locally asymptotically stable for any $\tau > 0$; when $\beta n_1 + n_2 n_3 = 0$, $\beta^2 n_1^2 = n_2^2 n_3^2$, Equation (7) also only has a zero root and no pair of pure imaginary roots, and thus, the equilibrium E_3 still undergoes a fixed point bifurcation; when $\beta n_1 + n_2 n_3 > 0$, $\beta^2 n_1^2 > n_2^2 n_3^2$, Equation (7) always has one positive root z_0. From Equation (6), we can solve the critical value of time delay:

$$\tau_0^{(j)} = \begin{cases} \dfrac{\arccos Y_0 + 2j\pi}{\omega_0}, X_0 > 0, \\ \dfrac{2\pi - \arccos Y_0 + 2j\pi}{\omega_0}, X_0 \leq 0, j = 0, 1, 2, \cdots, \end{cases} \tag{8}$$

where X_0 and Y_0 are given in Equation (6).

Lemma 1. *If* (H1) *holds and* $\beta n_1 + n_2 n_3 > 0$, *when* $\tau = \tau_0^{(j)} (j = 0, 1, 2, \cdots)$, *then Equation* (3) *has a pair of pure imaginary roots* $\pm \mathrm{i}\omega_0$, *and all the other roots of Equation* (3) *have nonzero real parts.*

Let $\lambda = \lambda(\tau)$ be the root of Equation (3), satisfying $\lambda(\tau_0^{(j)}) = \mathrm{i}\omega_0 (j = 0, 1, 2, \cdots)$. Then, we will calculate transversality condition.

Lemma 2. *If* (H1) *holds and* $\beta n_1 + n_2 n_3 > 0$, *Equation* (7) *has one positive root* z_0 *and* $z_0 = \omega_0^2$, $h'(z_0) > 0$, *where* $h'(z)$ *is the derivative of* $h(z)$ *with respect to* z. *Then, we have the following transversality condition:*

$$\mathrm{Re}\left(\frac{\mathrm{d}\lambda}{\mathrm{d}\tau}\right)^{-1}\Bigg|_{\tau=\tau_0^{(j)}} = \frac{n_2^2 h'(z_0)}{\beta^2 n_1^2 (n_1^2 + z_0)} > 0.$$

Therefore, when (H1) holds and $\beta n_1 + n_2 n_3 > 0$, system (2) undergoes a Hopf bifurcation near equilibrium E_3.

Theorem 2. *If the parameters of system* (2) *meet* (H1), *then:*

(1) *When* (H3) *holds, the equilibrium* E_3 *is locally asymptotically stable for any* $\tau \geq 0$.
(2) *When* (H3) *does not hold, if* $\beta n_1 + n_2 n_3 = 0$, *the equilibrium* E_3 *undergoes a fixed point bifurcation for any* $\tau \geq 0$; *if* $\beta n_1 + n_2 n_3 > 0$, *it is unstable for any* $\tau \geq 0$ *and system* (2) *undergoes a Hopf bifurcation near equilibrium* E_3 *when* $\tau = \tau_0^{(j)}$.

3.3. Stability and Existence of Hopf Bifurcation for E_4

Next, we analyze the stability of system (2) for $E_4 = (S^{(4)}, I^{(4)})$. Similarly, transferring the equilibrium E_4 to the origin and linearizing the system (2) around it, we obtain the characteristic equation of the linearized system as follows:

$$\lambda^2 + \left(a_1 - \beta S^{(4)} \mathrm{e}^{-\lambda\tau}\right)\lambda + a_2 + a_3 \mathrm{e}^{-\lambda\tau} = 0. \tag{9}$$

where

$$\begin{aligned} a_1 &= n_3 - 2k_2\alpha I^{(4)} - n_2 S^{(4)}, \\ a_2 &= 2n_2 k_2 \alpha S^{(4)} I^{(4)} - n_2 n_3 S^{(4)}, \\ a_3 &= n_2 \beta (S^{(4)})^2 + \beta^2 S^{(4)} I^{(4)}. \end{aligned}$$

When $\tau = 0$, Equation (9) becomes:

$$\lambda^2 + \left(a_1 - \beta S^{(4)}\right)\lambda + a_2 + a_3 = 0. \tag{10}$$

We consider the following assumption obtained by Vieta theorem:

$$(\mathrm{H4}) \begin{cases} \beta S^{(4)} - a_1 < 0, \\ a_2 + a_3 > 0. \end{cases}$$

Under the assumption (H4), all the roots of Equation (10) have negative real parts, and the equilibrium $E_4 = (S^{(4)}, I^{(4)})$ is locally asymptotically stable when $\tau = 0$.

When $\tau > 0$, we will discuss the existence of Hopf bifurcation. We assume that $\lambda = \mathrm{i}\omega (\omega > 0)$ is a pure imaginary root of Equation (9). Substituting it into Equation (9) and separating the real and imaginary parts, we obtain:

$$\begin{cases} a_1\omega = a_3 \sin(\omega\tau) + \beta S^{(4)} \omega \cos(\omega\tau), \\ \omega^2 - a_2 = a_3 \cos(\omega\tau) - \beta S^{(4)} \omega \sin(\omega\tau). \end{cases} \tag{11}$$

Equation (11) derives the following results:

$$\begin{aligned} \sin(\omega\tau) &= \frac{a_1 a_3 \omega + \beta S^{(4)} a_2 \omega - \beta S^{(4)} \omega^3}{a_3^2 + \beta^2 (S^{(4)})^2 \omega^2} \triangleq X_1, \\ \cos(\omega\tau) &= \frac{a_3 \omega^2 - a_2 a_3 + \beta S^{(4)} a_1 \omega^2}{a_3^2 + \beta^2 (S^{(4)})^2 \omega^2} \triangleq Y_1. \end{aligned} \tag{12}$$

Adding the square of the two equations in Equation (11), letting $\omega^2 = z$, we obtain:

$$l(z) = z^2 + A_1 z + A_2 = 0, \tag{13}$$

where $A_1 = a_1^2 - 2a_2 - \beta^2 (S^{(4)})^2$ and $A_2 = a_2^2 - a_3^2$. Then, if $A_1 > 0$ and $A_2 > 0$ hold, Equation (13) has no positive root; if $A_2 < 0$ holds, Equation (13) has one positive root z_1; if $A_1 < 0$ and $A_2 > 0$ hold, Equation (13) has two positive roots z_2, z_3. We hypothesize that Equation (13) has positive roots $z_n (n = 1, 2, 3)$, then $\omega_n = \sqrt{z_n} (n = 1, 2, 3)$. From Equation (12), we can solve the critical value of time delay:

$$\tau_n^{(j)} = \begin{cases} \dfrac{\arccos Y_1 + 2j\pi}{\omega_n}, X_1 > 0, \\ \dfrac{2\pi - \arccos Y_1 + 2j\pi}{\omega_n}, X_1 \leq 0, n = 1, 2, 3, j = 0, 1, 2, \cdots, \end{cases} \tag{14}$$

where X_1 and Y_1 are given in Equation (12).

Lemma 3. *When* (H2) *and* (H4) *hold, if $A_2 < 0$ or $A_1 < 0, A_2 > 0$, where A_1 and A_2 are given in Equation* (13)*, when $\tau = \tau_n^{(j)} (n = 1, 2, 3, j = 0, 1, 2, \cdots)$, then Equation* (9) *has a pair of pure imaginary roots $\pm i\omega_n$, and all the other roots of Equation* (9) *have nonzero real parts.*

Let $\lambda = \lambda(\tau)$ be the root of Equation (9), satisfying $\lambda(\tau_n^{(j)}) = i\omega_n (n = 1, 2, 3)$. Then, we will calculate transversality condition.

Lemma 4. *When* (H2) *and* (H4) *hold, if $A_2 < 0$ or $A_1 < 0, A_2 > 0$, where A_1, A_2 are given in Equation* (13)*, and $z_n = \omega_n^2, l'(z_n) \neq 0 (n = 1, 2, 3)$, where $l'(z)$ is the derivative of $l(z)$ with respect to z. Then, we have the following transversality condition:*

$$\mathrm{Re}\left(\frac{d\lambda}{d\tau}\right)^{-1}\Bigg|_{\tau = \tau_n^{(j)}} = \frac{l'(z_n)}{\beta^2 (S^{(4)})^2 z_n + a_3^2} \neq 0.$$

Theorem 3. *When* (H2) *holds, system* (2) *has a positive equilibrium E_4. When* (H4) *holds as well:*

(1) *If $A_1 > 0$, $A_2 > 0$ hold, Equation* (13) *has no positive root, the equilibrium E_4 is locally asymptotically stable for any $\tau \geq 0$;*

(2) *If $A_2 < 0$ holds, Equation* (13) *has one positive roots z_1, then when $\tau \in [0, \tau_1^{(0)})$, the equilibrium E_4 is locally asymptotically stable, and unstable when $\tau > \tau_1^{(0)}$, and it undergoes a Hopf bifurcation when $\tau = \tau_1^{(j)}, j = 0, 1, 2, \cdots$;*

(3) *If $A_1 < 0$, $A_2 > 0$ hold, system* (2) *undergoes a Hopf bifurcation near the equilibrium E_4 when $\tau = \tau_n^{(j)}, n = 2, 3, j = 0, 1, 2, \cdots$. Then, $\exists m \in N$ makes $0 < \tau_3^{(0)} < \tau_2^{(0)} < \tau_3^{(1)} < \tau_2^{(1)} < \cdots < \tau_2^{(m-1)} < \tau_3^{(m)} < \tau_3^{(m+1)}$. When $\tau \in \left[0, \tau_3^{(0)}\right) \cup \bigcup_{l=1}^{m} \left(\tau_2^{(l-1)}, \tau_3^{(l)}\right)$, the equilibrium E_4 of the system* (2) *is locally asymptotically stable, and when $\tau \in \bigcup_{l=0}^{m-1} \left(\tau_3^{(l)}, \tau_2^{(l)}\right) \cup \left(\tau_3^{(m)}, +\infty\right)$, the equilibrium E_4 is unstable.*

4. Normal Form of Hopf Bifurcation

In Section 3, we have shown that when $\beta n_1 + n_2 n_3 < 0$, the equilibrium E_3 is locally asymptotically stable for any $\tau \geq 0$; when $\beta n_1 + n_2 n_3 > 0$, the bifurcating periodic solution near the equilibrium E_3 is unstable by Theorem 2. Thus, we only care about the stability of bifurcating periodic solution near the positive equilibrium E_4. In order to be more realistic, we focus on the delay between taking control measures and the beginning of control to take effect. Therefore, we consider the time-delay τ as a bifurcation parameter and denote the critical value $\tau = \tau_c = \tau_n^{(j)}$, where $\tau_n^{(j)}$ is given in Equation (14). When $\tau = \tau_n^{(j)}$,

Equation (13) has a pair of pure imaginary roots $\lambda = \pm i\omega$. Therefore, system (2) undergoes a Hopf bifurcation near equilibrium E_4. In this section, we derive the normal form of Hopf bifurcation for the system (2) by using the multiple time scales method.

In order to normalize the delay, we first re-scale the time t by using $t \mapsto t/\tau$, then translate the equilibrium $E_4 = (S^{(4)}, I^{(4)}) = (\frac{d_2+k_1\alpha-k_2\alpha I^{(4)}}{\beta}, \frac{n_1\beta+n_2n_3}{\beta^2+k_2\alpha n_2})$ to the origin, so system (2) is transformed into:

$$\begin{cases} \frac{dS}{dt} = \tau[(n_1 + 2n_2S^{(4)} - \beta I^{(4)})S(t) + n_2S^2(t) - \beta(S(t) + S^{(4)})I(t-1)], \\ \frac{dI}{dt} = \tau[(2k_2\alpha I^{(4)} - n_3)I(t) + k_2\alpha I^2(t) + \beta I^{(4)}S(t) + \beta(S(t) + S^{(4)})I(t-1)]. \end{cases} \tag{15}$$

Equation (15) can also be written as:

$$\dot{Z(t)} = \tau N_1 Z(t) + \tau N_2 Z(t-1) + \tau F(Z(t), Z(t-1)), \tag{16}$$

where

$$Z(t) = (S(t), I(t))^T, Z(t-1) = (S(t-1), I(t-1))^T,$$

and

$$N_1 = \begin{pmatrix} n_1 + 2n_2S^{(4)} - \beta I^{(4)} & 0 \\ \beta I^{(4)} & 2k_2\alpha I^{(4)} - n_3 \end{pmatrix}, N_2 = \begin{pmatrix} 0 & -\beta S^{(4)} \\ 0 & \beta S^{(4)} \end{pmatrix},$$
$$F(Z(t), Z(t-1)) = \begin{pmatrix} n_2S^2(t) - \beta S(t)I(t-1) \\ k_2\alpha I^2(t) + \beta S(t)I(t-1) \end{pmatrix}.$$

Let h be eigenvector corresponding to eigenvalue $\lambda = i\omega\tau$ of linearized system of Equation (16), and h^* be the eigenvector corresponding to eigenvalue $\lambda = -i\omega\tau$ of adjoint matrix of linearized system of Equation (16), satisfying:

$$\langle h^*, h \rangle = \overline{h^*}^T h = 1. \tag{17}$$

By calculating, we have:

$$\begin{cases} h = (h_{11}, h_{12})^T = (1, \frac{n_2S^{(4)} - i\omega}{\beta S^{(4)} e^{-i\omega\tau}})^T, \\ h^* = d(h_{21}, h_{22})^T = d(\frac{i\omega - n_3 + 2k_2\alpha I^{(4)} + \beta S^{(4)} e^{i\omega\tau}}{\beta S^{(4)} e^{i\omega\tau}}, 1)^T, \end{cases} \tag{18}$$

where $d = (\overline{h_{11}}h_{21} + \overline{h_{12}}h_{22})^{-1}$.

We suppose the solution of Equation (16) is as follows:

$$Z(t) = Z(T_0, T_1, T_2, \cdots) = \sum_{k=1}^{+\infty} \varepsilon^k Z_k(T_0, T_1, T_2 \cdots), \tag{19}$$

where

$$Z(T_0, T_1, T_2, \cdots) = (S(T_0, T_1, T_2, \cdots), I(T_0, T_1, T_2, \cdots))^T,$$
$$Z_k(T_0, T_1, T_2, \cdots) = (S_k(T_0, T_1, T_2, \cdots), I_k(T_0, T_1, T_2, \cdots))^T.$$

The derivative with respect to t is transformed:

$$\frac{d}{dt} = \frac{\partial}{\partial T_0} + \varepsilon \frac{\partial}{\partial T_1} + \varepsilon^2 \frac{\partial}{\partial T_2} + \cdots = D_0 + \varepsilon D_1 + \varepsilon^2 D_2 + \cdots, \tag{20}$$

where D_i is differential operator, and:

$$D_i = \frac{\partial}{\partial T_i}(i = 0, 1, 2 \cdots).$$

Note that:

$$\begin{aligned} Z_i &= (S_i, I_i)^T = Z_i\left(t, \varepsilon t, \varepsilon^2 t, \cdots\right), \\ Z_{i1} &= (S_i, I_i)^T = Z_i\left(t-1, \varepsilon t, \varepsilon^2 t, \cdots\right), i = 1, 2, \cdots. \end{aligned}$$

Then, we obtain:

$$\dot{Z}(t) = \varepsilon D_0 Z_1 + \varepsilon^2 D_1 Z_1 + \varepsilon^3 D_2 Z_1 + \varepsilon^2 D_0 Z_2 + \varepsilon^3 D_1 Z_2 + \varepsilon^3 D_0 Z_3 + \cdots. \tag{21}$$

Using a Taylor series expansion of $Z(t-1)$, we obtain: that

$$Z(t-1) = \varepsilon Z_{11} + \varepsilon^2(Z_{21} - D_1 Z_{11}) + \varepsilon^3(Z_{31} - D_1 Z_{21} - D_2 Z_{11}) + \cdots, \tag{22}$$

where $Z_{i1} = Z_i(T_0 - 1, T_1, T_2, \cdots), i = 1, 2, 3, \cdots$.

As we stated, τ is the bifurcation parameter, and $\tau = \tau_c + \varepsilon\mu$, where $\tau_c = \tau_n^{(j)}$ $(j = 0, 1, 2, \cdots)$ is the Hopf bifurcation critical value, μ is perturbation parameter, and ε is dimensionless scale parameter. Substituting Equations (19)–(22) into Equation (16) and balancing the coefficients before ε on both sides of the equation, the following expression is obtained:

$$\begin{cases} D_0 S_1 = \tau_c[(n_1 + 2n_2 S^{(4)} - \beta I^{(4)})S_1 - \beta S^{(4)} I_{11}], \\ D_0 I_1 = \tau_c[(2k_2\alpha I^{(4)} - n_3)I_1 + \beta S^{(4)} I_{11}]. \end{cases} \tag{23}$$

Thus, Equation (23) has the following solution form:

$$Z(T_1, T_2, T_3, \cdots) = G(T_1, T_2, T_3, \cdots)e^{i\omega\tau_c T_0}h + \bar{G}(T_1, T_2, T_3, \cdots)e^{-i\omega\tau_c T_0}\bar{h}. \tag{24}$$

The expression of the coefficient before ε^2 is as follows:

$$\begin{cases} D_0 S_2 - \tau_c[(n_1 + 2n_2 S^{(4)} - \beta I^{(4)})S_2 - \beta S^{(4)} I_{21}] \\ = - D_1 S_1 + \tau_c[n_2 S_1^2 - \beta S_1 I_{11} + \beta S^{(4)} D_1 I_{11}] + \mu[(n_1 + 2n_2 S^{(4)} - \beta I^{(4)})S_1 - \beta S^{(4)} I_{11}], \\ D_0 I_2 - \tau_c[(2k_2\alpha I^{(4)} - n_3)I_2 + \beta I^{(4)} S_2 + \beta S^{(4)} I_{21}] \\ = - D_1 I_1 + \tau_c[k_2\alpha I_1^2 + +\beta S_1 I_{11} - \beta S^{(4)} D_1 I_{11}] + \mu[(2k_2\alpha I^{(4)} - n_3)I_1 + \beta S^{(4)} I_{11}]. \end{cases} \tag{25}$$

Substituting Equation (24) into the right-hand side of Equation (25), and the coefficient vector of $e^{i\omega\tau_c T_0}$ is denoted by m_1. According to the solvability condition $\langle h^*, m_1 \rangle = 0$, the expression of $\frac{\partial G}{\partial T_1}$ is obtained as follows:

$$\frac{\partial G}{\partial T_1} = \mu M G, \tag{26}$$

where $M = \frac{\overline{h_{21}}\left[\left(n_1 + 2n_2 S^{(4)} - \beta I^{(4)}\right)h_{11} - \beta S^{(4)} e^{-i\omega\tau_c} h_{12}\right] + \overline{h_{22}}\left[(2k_2\alpha - n_3)h_{12} + \beta S^{(4)} e^{-i\omega\tau_c} h_{12}\right]}{\overline{h_{21}}\left(h_{11} - \beta S^{(4)}\tau_c e^{-i\omega\tau_c} h_{12}\right) + \overline{h_{22}}\left(h_{12} + \beta S^{(4)}\tau_c e^{-i\omega\tau_c} h_{12}\right)}$.

Since μ is a disturbance parameter, we only consider its effect on the linear part. Therefore, we ignore the part containing μ in the higher order. We suppose the solutions of Equation (25) are given as follows:

$$\begin{cases} S_2 = \eta_0 G\bar{G} + \eta_1 e^{2i\omega\tau_c T_0} G^2 + \bar{\eta}_1 e^{-2i\omega\tau_c T_0} \bar{G}^2, \\ I_2 = \xi_0 G\bar{G} + \xi_1 e^{2i\omega\tau_c T_0} G^2 + \bar{\xi}_1 e^{-2i\omega\tau_c T_0} \bar{G}^2, \end{cases} \tag{27}$$

where

$$\begin{aligned}
\begin{pmatrix} \eta_0 \\ \xi_0 \end{pmatrix} &= V_0 \begin{pmatrix} n_3 - 2k_2\alpha I^{(4)} - \beta S^{(4)} & \beta S^{(4)} \\ \beta I^{(4)} & \beta I^{(4)} - n_1 - 2n_2 S^{(4)} \end{pmatrix} \begin{pmatrix} x_0 \\ y_0 \end{pmatrix}, \\
\begin{pmatrix} \eta_1 \\ \xi_1 \end{pmatrix} &= V_1 \begin{pmatrix} 2i\omega - 2k_2\alpha I^{(4)} + n_3 - \beta S^{(4)} \mathrm{e}^{-2\mathrm{i}\omega\tau_c} & \beta S^{(4)} \mathrm{e}^{\mathrm{i}\omega\tau_c} \\ \beta I^{(4)} & 2i\omega - n_1 - 2n_2 S^{(4)} I^{(4)} \mathrm{e}^{\mathrm{i}\omega\tau_c} \end{pmatrix} \begin{pmatrix} x_1 \\ y_1 \end{pmatrix},
\end{aligned} \tag{28}$$

where $h_{11}, h_{12}, h_{21}, h_{22}$ are given in Equation (18) and

$$\begin{aligned}
x_0 &= 2n_2\overline{h_{11}}h_{11} - \beta\overline{h_{12}}h_{11}\mathrm{e}^{\mathrm{i}\omega\tau_c} - \beta\overline{h_{11}}h_{12}\mathrm{e}^{-\mathrm{i}\omega\tau_c}, \\
y_0 &= 2k_2\alpha\overline{h_{12}}h_{12} + \beta\overline{h_{12}}h_{11}\mathrm{e}^{\mathrm{i}\omega\tau_c} + \beta\overline{h_{11}}h_{12}\mathrm{e}^{-\mathrm{i}\omega\tau_c}, \\
x_1 &= n_2 h_{11}^2 - \beta h_{11}h_{12}\mathrm{e}^{-\mathrm{i}\omega\tau_c}, y_1 = k_2\alpha h_{12}^2 + \beta h_{11}h_{12}\mathrm{e}^{-\mathrm{i}\omega\tau_c}, \\
V_0 &= \left[\left(\beta I^{(4)} - n_1 - 2n_2 S^{(4)}\right)\left(n_3 - 2k_2\alpha I^{(4)} - \beta S^{(4)}\right) - \beta^2 S^{(4)} I^{(4)}\right]^{-1}, \\
V_1 &= \left[\left(2\mathrm{i}\omega - n_1 - 2n_2 S^{(4)} I^{(4)} \mathrm{e}^{\mathrm{i}\omega\tau_c}\right)\left(2i\omega - 2k_2\alpha I^{(4)} + n_3 - \beta S^{(4)} \mathrm{e}^{-2\mathrm{i}\omega\tau_c}\right) - \beta^2 S^{(4)} I^{(4)} \mathrm{e}^{\mathrm{i}\omega\tau_c}\right]^{-1}.
\end{aligned}$$

The expression of the coefficient before ε^3 is:

$$\begin{cases}
D_0 S_3 - \tau_c[(n_1 + 2n_2 S^{(4)} - \beta I^{(4)})S_3 - \beta S_3 - \beta S^{(4)} I_{31}] \\
= -D_1 S_2 - D_2 S_1 + \tau_c[2n_2 S_1 S_2 - \beta(S_1 I_{21} + S_2 I_{11} - S^{(4)} D_1 I_{21} - S^{(4)} D_2 I_{11})] \\
+\mu[(n_1 + 2n_2 S^{(4)} - \beta I^{(4)})S_2 + n_2 S_1^2 - \beta S_1 I_{11} - \beta S^{(4)}(I_{21} - D_1 I_{11})], \\
D_0 I_3 - \tau_c[(2k_2\alpha I^{(4)} - n_3)I_3 + \beta I^{(4)} S_3 + \beta S_3 + \beta S^{(4)} I_{31}] \\
= -D_1 I_2 - D_2 I_1 + \tau_c[2k_2\alpha I_1 I_2 + \beta(S_1 I_{21} + S_2 I_{11} - S^{(4)} D_1 I_{21} - S^{(4)} D_2 I_{11})] \\
+\mu[(2k_2\alpha I^{(4)} - n_3)I_2 + k_2\alpha I_1^2 + \beta I^{(4)} S_2 + \beta S_1 I_{11} + \beta S^{(4)}(I_{21} - D_1 I_{11})].
\end{cases} \tag{29}$$

Next, substituting solution (24) and (27) into Equation (29), and with the coefficient vector of $\mathrm{e}^{\mathrm{i}\omega\tau_c T_0}$ noted as m_2, by solvability condition, we have $\langle h^*, m_2\rangle = 0$. Note that μ is a disturbance parameter, and μ^2 has little influence for small unfolding parameter, and thus, we can ignore the $\mu^2 G$, then the expression of $\frac{\partial G}{\partial T_2}$ can be obtained as follows:

$$\frac{\partial G}{\partial T_2} = HG^2\bar{G}, \tag{30}$$

where

$$\begin{aligned}
H &= P\begin{pmatrix} Q - 2\tau_c n_2 \eta_0 h_{11} \\ Q + 2\tau_c k_2\alpha\left(\xi_0 h_{12} + \xi_1\overline{h_{12}}\right) \end{pmatrix}^T \begin{pmatrix} \overline{h_{21}} \\ -\overline{h_{22}} \end{pmatrix}, \\
P &= \left[\overline{h_{21}}\left(2\beta S^{(4)}\tau_c\mathrm{e}^{-\mathrm{i}\omega\tau_c}h_{12} - h_{11}\right) - \overline{h_{22}}\left(2\beta S^{(4)}\tau_c\mathrm{e}^{-\mathrm{i}\omega\tau_c}h_{12} + h_{12}\right)\right]^{-1}, \\
Q &= \beta\tau_c\left(\xi_0 h_{11} + \xi_1\overline{h_{11}}\mathrm{e}^{-2\mathrm{i}\omega\tau_c} + \eta_0 h_{12}\mathrm{e}^{-\mathrm{i}\omega\tau_c} + \eta_1\overline{h_{12}}\mathrm{e}^{\mathrm{i}\omega\tau_c}\right),
\end{aligned}$$

where $h_{11}, h_{12}, h_{21}, h_{22}$ are given in Equation (18), and $\xi_0, \eta_0, \xi_1, \eta_1$ are given in Equation (28).

Let $G \mapsto G/\varepsilon$, then, the deduced third-order normal form of Hopf bifurcation of system (2) is:

$$\dot{G} = \mu MG + HG^2\bar{G}, \tag{31}$$

where M is given in (26) and H is given in (30).

Substituting $G = re^{i\theta}$ into Equation (31), the following normal form of Hopf bifurcation in polar coordinates is obtained:

$$\begin{cases} \dot{r} = \text{Re}(M)\mu r + \text{Re}(H)r^3, \\ \dot{\theta} = \text{Im}(M)\mu + \text{Im}(H)r^2. \end{cases} \tag{32}$$

According to the normal form of Hopf bifurcation in polar coordinates, we only need to consider the first equation in system (32). Thus, the following theorem holds:

Theorem 4. *For the system* (32), *when* $\frac{\text{Re}(M)\mu}{\text{Re}(H)} < 0$, *there is a semitrivial fixed point* $r = \sqrt{-\frac{\text{Re}(M)\mu}{\text{Re}(H)}}$, *and system* (2) *has periodic solution.*

(1) *If* $\text{Re}(M)\mu < 0$, *then the periodic solution reduced on the center manifold is unstable.*
(2) *If* $\text{Re}(M)\mu > 0$, *then the periodic solution reduced on the center manifold is stable.*

5. Numerical Simulations

In this part, we first analyze the reasonable values of the parameters based on the existing practical research and then we give numerical simulation based on the selected parameters by using Matlab software (R2021a). Finally, we draw some conclusions according to the simulation results, providing practical guidance for the prevention and control of PWD.

5.1. Determination of Parameter Values

5.1.1. Parameter Analysis of Mortality d_1, d_2

Firstly, Ref. [24] provides us with the relationship between the longevity of *M. alternatus* and the number of PWN carried, as shown in Table 2.

Table 2. Longevity and the number of PWN carried of *M. alternatus*.

No.	Quantity of PWN Carried/Pieces	Longevity of *M. alternatus*/d
1	131	30
2	425	42
3	4904	39
4	3031	39
5	3633	39
6	206	30
7	13,232	30
8	8324	45
9	2339	45
10	1209	42
11	1860	45
12	884	42
13	1084	42
14	3440	36
15	36	39
16	209	33
17	1759	30
18	30,754	33

Based on the data in Table 2, we remove the maximum and minimum values of the PWN number carried by *M. alternatus*, and then plot the original curve and curve after quadratic fitting by interpolation, as shown in Figure 2.

It can be seen from Figure 2 that PWN has a certain weak negative effect on the longevity of *M. alternatus*. Despite this, findings from the experiments conducted by

Jikumaru et al. [25] reveal that the quantity of nematodes carried by *M. alternatus* seldom exceeds 10,000 per individual. Consequently, the effect on the lifespan of *M. alternatus* attributable to the carriage of nematodes is not considered within this analysis. Therefore, for the mortality of *M. alternatus*, we use data from Ref. [17], which holds that the mortalities of susceptible and infected *M. alternatus* are both 0.01, so we set $d_1 = d_2 = 0.01$.

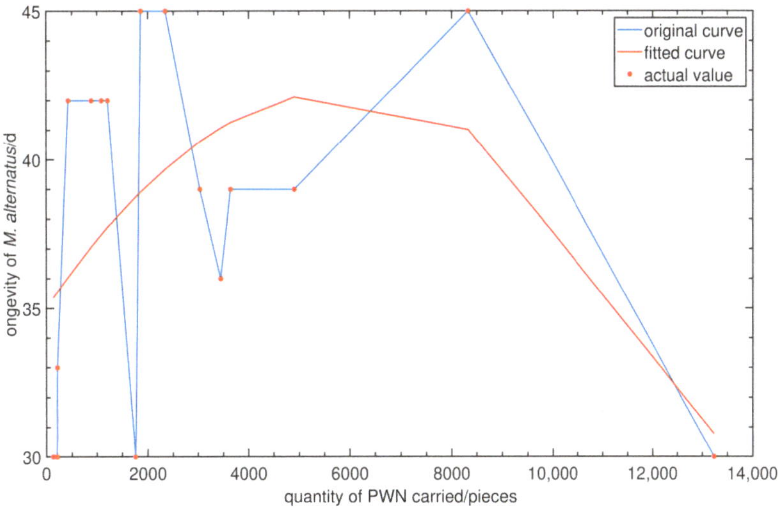

Figure 2. Relationship curve between longevity of *M. alternatus* and amount of PWN carried.

5.1.2. Parameter Analysis of Birth Rate B

The female of *M. alternatus* has strong fecundity, with more than 100 eggs per female [26]. In southern China, the larval stage of *M. alternatus* lasts about 240–330 days. Most larvae overwinter from October to March and begin to hatch in mid-May, and its hatching rate is as high as 90% [27]. We define the birth rate of *M. alternatus* (unit time: year) as follows: $B = \frac{C}{N}, N = C + N_1 - N_2$, where C denotes the number of new born *M. alternatus* (head/year), N denotes the average number of *M. alternatus* (head/year), N_1 denotes the initial number of *M. alternatus* (head/year), and N_2 denotes the number of dead *M. alternatus* (head/year). For a certain forest, regardless of the entry of alien *M. alternatus*, it is considered that the initial *M. alternatus* are formed by the hatching of larvae in the previous year. It can be seen that *M. alternatus* have strong fecundity and low mortality by above analysis and the given mortality rate, and thus $C \gg N_1 - N_2$, that is $N \approx C$. Therefore, the formula of the birth rate can be approximated as $B = \frac{C}{C}$, from which we believe that $B \approx 1$.

5.1.3. Parameter Analysis of Infection Coefficient β

The transmission of PWN by *M. alternatus* occurs through various activities, such as oviposition and feeding on pine trees, so the infection coefficient β was related to the number of infected trees in the epidemic area, the frequency with which *M. alternatus* carry PWN upon emergence from dead trees, and the rate at which *M. alternatus* transmit PWN through oviposition and feeding and so on. Acquiring precise values for the aforementioned rates proves challenging, yet Ref. [28] provided approximate statistical probabilities, specifically 0.00305 and 0.00166, respectively. For the number of infected trees in the epidemic area, although we can take control measures to reduce this value, completely removing diseased trees is a challenging task, and it may require cutting or burning of all the trees immediately after PWD occurs. However, it is unrealistic for most epidemic areas as we cannot guarantee that there are no remnants of diseased trees. According to the data released by the National Forestry and Grassland Administration of China (http://www.forestry.gov.cn/search/364152 (accessed on 10 August 2023)), more than 6 million pine trees died in Chongqing, China in 2022. We assume that the burning and crushing rate of above dead trees can reach 96%, then we can get $\beta \approx 6 \times 10^6 \times (1 - 0.96) \times 0.00305 \times 0.00166 \approx 1.2$.

5.1.4. Analysis of Other Parameters

We use $k_1\alpha$ to represent the control measures efficiency against PWD. Evidently, as the control intensity increases, the efficiency of these measures does not simply increase linearly, yet exhibits an overall positive impact across the forested region. In order to more accurately portray the nuanced characteristics of this, we choose quadratic growth of control efficiency for system (1) expressed as $k_1 = \alpha$.

According to the analysis of the model in Section 1, α changes within 0∼1. When $\alpha = 0$, it means that there is no prevention and control; when $\alpha = 1$, it means that the theoretically infected beetles are completely eliminated, and obviously, this is not possible in reality. Moreover, considering the average level of disease-affected areas, the control measures efficiency is mainly maintained at 30∼50%, and thus, we set $\alpha \in [0, 0.85]$, which is more reasonable. When $\alpha = 0.85$, the effective control rate of PWD was about 70% which is slightly higher; when $\alpha = 0.65$, the effective control rate of PWD was about 40%, which is more consistent with the reality.

In this system, the environmental carrying capacity is affected by disease control, and it decreases as the control intensity increases. Moreover, in order to reflect the difference of the initial environment and highlight the impacts of the control intensity on the system to be consistent with the actual situation, we set $K = 10(1 - \alpha)$ or $K = 50(1 - \alpha)$.

$k_2\alpha$ shows that the mortality rate of *M. alternatus* follows logistic growth, leading to a saturation in the eradication of *M. alternatus*. The saturation rate is tied to control intensity, in that an increase in control intensity results in an accelerated rate of saturation. In reality, however, this change is relatively slow, so we set $k_2 = 0.1$.

Based on the above analysis, we take three groups of parameters as follows:

$$\begin{aligned}
&\textit{group}\ \text{I}: \ B = 1, d_1 = d_2 = 0.01, \beta = 1.2, \alpha = 0.85, K = 10(1-\alpha) = 1.5, k_1 = \alpha = 0.85,\\
&k_2 = 0.1,\\
&\textit{group}\ \text{II}: \ B = 1, d_1 = d_2 = 0.01, \beta = 1.2, \alpha = 0.65, K = 10(1-\alpha) = 3.5, k_1 = \alpha = 0.65,\\
&k_2 = 0.1,\\
&\textit{group}\ \text{III}: \ B = 1, d_1 = d_2 = 0.01, \beta = 1.2, \alpha = 0.65, K = 50(1-\alpha) = 17.5, k_1 = \alpha = 0.65,\\
&k_2 = 0.1.
\end{aligned}$$

5.2. *Simulation Results*

5.2.1. Simulation Results under *Group* I

According to the analysis in Section 5.1, we choose the first group of parameters:

$$B = 1, d_1 = d_2 = 0.01, \beta = 1.2, \alpha = 0.85, K = 1.5, k_1 = 0.85, k_2 = 0.1.$$

It is easy to calculate that (H_1) $n_2 = -0.5817 < 0$ and (H_3) $\beta n_1 + n_2 n_3 = -0.1051 < 0$ hold, and $E_4 = (0.61577, -0.07556)$, so there is only one disease-free equilibrium $E_3 = (S^{(3)}, I^{(3)}) = (0.45989, 0)$ of the system (2). The equilibrium E_3 is locally asymptotically stable for any $\tau \geq 0$ by Theorem 2. We choose $\tau = 0$ for the initial values $[0.48, 0.1]$ and $\tau = 1$ for the initial function $\varphi(\theta) = [0.48, 0.1]^T, \theta \in [-\tau, 0]$ for the simulations. Clearly, the equilibrium E_3 is locally asymptotically stable, as shown in Figure 3.

When $\tau = 0$, as we can see in Figure 3a, the number of infected *M. alternatus* will decrease rapidly in five years, and eventually, the infection would disappear completely. This case shows that when there is no time delay of the control to take effect, PWD will disappear. When $\tau = 1$, the solution is shown in Figure 3b. In this case, there is a time delay of the control to take effect and compared with $\tau = 0$, it takes a bit longer for equilibrium

E_3 to be stable. However, eventually, there will be no infected *M. alternatus*, and PWD will still disappear in this case.

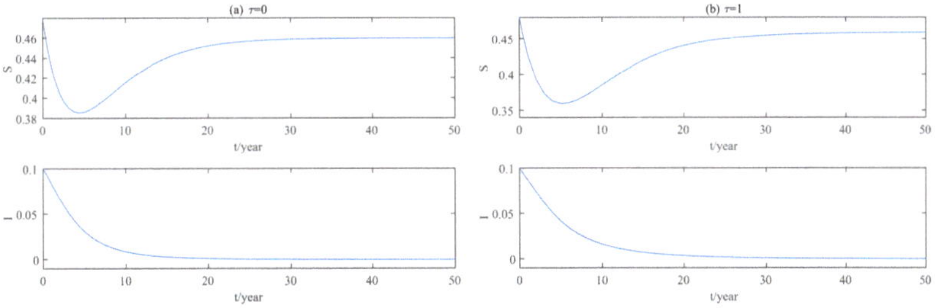

Figure 3. Equilibrium E_3 of system (2) is locally asymptotically stable.

Remark 2. *According to the above parameter analysis, we find that when α is large, the positive equilibrium E_4 does not exist, and for any $\tau \geq 0$, the equilibrium E_3 of the system (2) is locally asymptotically stable, so PWD is completely eliminated, which verifies our theoretical analysis. However, the shorter the time delay is, the faster the equilibrium will stabilize. This suggests that with strong disease control efforts, the disease will eventually disappear regardless of the time delay in the effective of control. However, given the difficulty and cost of disease control, greater control intensity means greater difficulty and investment in the control process, and thus, there is the possibility of a lack of practice in some areas. Therefore, we mainly analyze the stability of the system when $\alpha < 65\%$ for the general situation, and in this way, the control measures efficiency $k_1\alpha$ is about 40% or less, which is more consistent with the reality.*

5.2.2. Simulation Results under *Group* II

We choose the second group of parameters given in Section 5.1:

$$B = 1, d_1 = d_2 = 0.01, \beta = 1.2, \alpha = 0.65, K = 3.5, k_1 = 0.65, k_2 = 0.1,$$

where we find that (H_1) $n_2 = -0.2207 < 0$ and (H3) $\beta n_1 + n_2 n_3 = 0.5855 > 0$, so (H1) holds and (H3) does not hold, while system (2) always has a disease-free equilibrium $E_3 = (2.5712, 0)$, but it is unstable for any $\tau \geq 0$ by Theorem 2. (H2) holds still under these condition, and thus, system (2) always has a positive equilibrium $E_4 = (0.33817, 0.41072)$. When $\tau = 0$, (H_4) holds. As shown in Figure 4, the equilibrium E_4 is always locally asymptotically stable.

When $\tau > 0$, calculated by Equations (13) and (14), $A_2 = -0.0280 < 0, \tau_1^{(0)} = 0.3024$. When $\tau \in [0, 0.3024)$, due to Theorem 3, E_4 is locally asymptotically stable and when $\tau \in (0.3024, +\infty)$, E_4 is unstable; and system (2) undergoes a Hopf bifurcation near E_4 when $\tau = 0.3024$. It can be calculated from Equations (26)–(30) that $\text{Re}(M) > 0, \text{Re}(H) < 0$, and thus, system (2) displays stable and forward Hopf bifurcation periodic solution near equilibrium E_4 by Theorem 3. We choose $\tau = 0.05 \in [0, 0.3024)$, which is about 20 days, and the positive equilibrium E_4 of system (2) is locally asymptotically stable as shown in Figure 5. Then, we choose $\tau = 0.30245 > 0.3024$, which is about 110 days, and a stable and forward Hopf bifurcation periodic solution appears near the positive equilibrium E_4 of system (2), as shown in Figure 6. The numerical simulation results are consistent with the theoretical analysis.

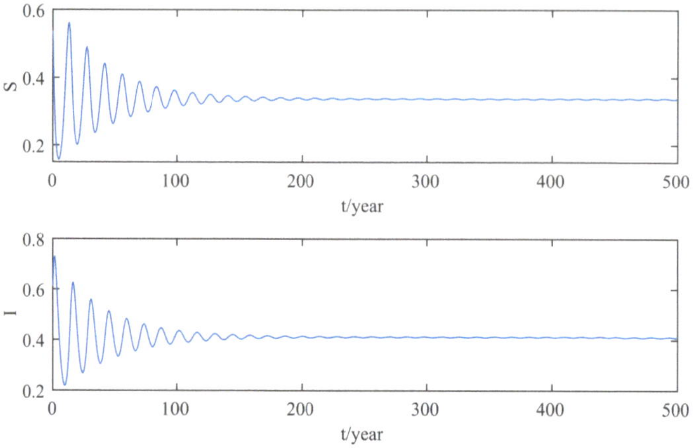

Figure 4. Equilibrium E_4 of system (2) for $\tau = 0$ is locally asymptotically stable.

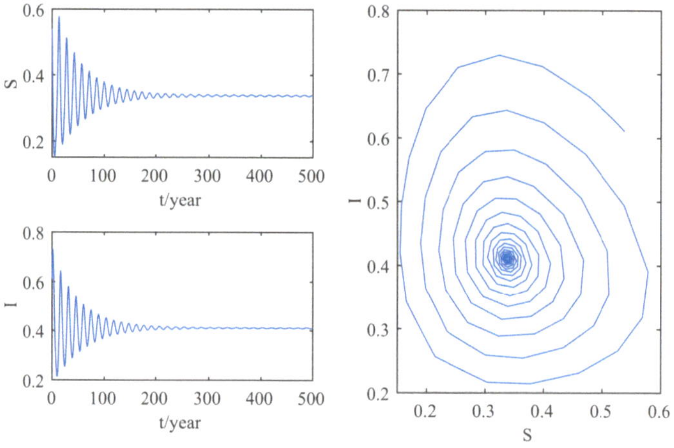

Figure 5. Equilibrium E_4 of system (2) for $\tau = 0.05$ is locally asymptotically stable.

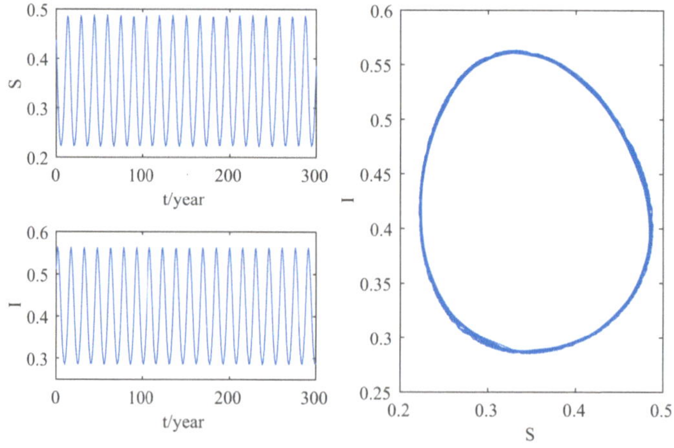

Figure 6. System (2) for $\tau = 0.30245$ occurs stable and forward Hopf bifurcation periodic solution near equilibrium E_4.

Remark 3. *According to Figure 5, it can be seen that when the infection rate of M. alternatus begins to decline after about 20 days (that is, the control begins to take effect in about 20 days), when system* (2) *will reach a stable state, and thus, the spread of PWD is controllable at this moment, and the number of susceptible and infected M. alternatus will tend to be a fixed value; when the infection rate of M. alternatus begins to decline at around 110 days (that is, the control begins to take effect in about 110 days), system* (2) *displays a stable Hopf bifurcation periodic solution, and the disease will have a periodic outbreak. At this time, it is difficult for us to cure the disease, and we need to invest in higher costs to control its spread. According to Figure 6, we find that the period of disease outbreak is about 14 years, and therefore, prevention can be implemented proactively based on outbreak patterns, strengthening the intensity of monitoring for forest areas before the outbreak of PWD, and taking measures such as trunk injection of nematicides or spraying nematicides and insecticides in advance.*

Moreover, when $\alpha < 65\%$ and $B = 1, d_1 = 0.01$, $d_2 = 0.01$, $\beta = 1.2$, $K = 10(1-\alpha)$, $k_1 = \alpha$, $k_2 = 0.1$, it is found that $n_2 < 0$, $\beta n_1 + n_2 n_3 > 0$ in our calculations, and thus, the system has two equilibrium E_3, E_4 and the disease-free equilibrium E_3 is unstable by Theorem 2. We draw the dynamic change curve of equilibrium $E_4 = (S^{(4)}, I^{(4)})$ under different control intensities, as shown in Figure 7. It is easy to find that with the increase of α, $S^{(4)}$ increases and $I^{(4)}$ decreases, which means the bigger the intensity of control, the smaller the number of infected *M. alternatus* that eventually reach stability. When the value of α is more than about 84%, infected *M. alternatus* will disappear, which corresponds with the previous analysis.

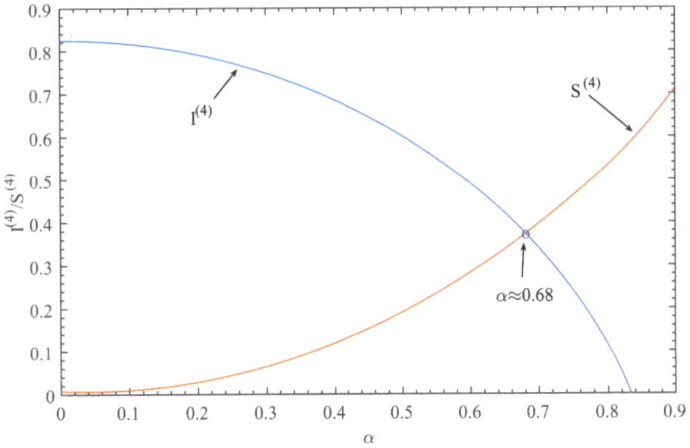

Figure 7. Dynamic curve of the equilibrium E_4 with the intensity of artificial control α.

Remark 4. *According to Figure 7, we find that the number of infected M. alternatus decreases as the control intensity increases. Therefore, it is necessary to increase the value of α on the premise of considering the cost. Considering some real situations in epidemic areas, eliminating all potentially diseased trees immediately at the beginning of the outbreak is the best way to control PWD [29]. However, this is not a method to control or treat PWD before PWN infection. In addition to removing trees, we should also take control measures against M. alternatus. Traditional chemical control is effective, but there are some defects, such as short duration and the destruction of ecological balance. In recent years, physical control, biological control, biomimetic technology, and other control methods have developed rapidly. Physical and biological control are environmentally friendly and have a long duration, but the effect is slow; using attractants to trap M. alternatus is part of biomimetic technology, which is easy to operate and has a low cost compared with other control methods. However, most attractants need to be improved in terms of trapping specificity, which is worthy of further exploration by scholars. Based on the above analysis, on the premise of all potentially diseased trees being removed as soon as possible, we recommend using chemical control in the early stage of disease control to quickly improve the value of α to control the number of infected*

M. alternatus; in the middle and late stages of control, we can prolong the duration combined with other control methods, which can further improve the value of α and has a preventive effect on PWD.

Then, we will compare the convergence speed of S, I. When $\tau = 0$, we choose $\alpha = 0.45$, $\alpha = 0.55$, $\alpha = 0.65$, $\alpha = 0.75$ for comparison based on $B = 1$, $d_1 = 0.01$, $d_2 = 0.01$, $\beta = 1.2$, $K = 10(1-\alpha)$, $k_1 = \alpha$, $k_2 = 0.1$. When $\alpha = 0.45$, $\beta S^{(4)} - a_1 = 0.0078 > 0$, $a_2 + a_3 = 0.1403 > 0$, (H4) does not hold, so E_4 is unstable now by Theorem 3; when $\alpha = 0.55$, $\beta S^{(4)} - a_1 = -0.0097 < 0$, $a_2 + a_3 = 0.1821 > 0$, (H4) holds this moment, so E_4 is locally asymptotically stable by Theorem 3. As we can see in Figure 8, we find that $\alpha = 0.45$, S, I do not converge, which is consistent with theoretical analysis, when $\alpha = 0.55$, S, I converge, but the convergence rate is very slow. Moreover, the convergence speed of S, I increases as α increases from 0.55 to 0.75. When $\tau > 0$, we still choose *group* II to compare the convergence speed of S, I for different time delays τ, as shown in Figure 9. It can be obtained that as the time delay τ increases from 0.05 to 0.15, the time required for the system (2) to reach stability increases accordingly.

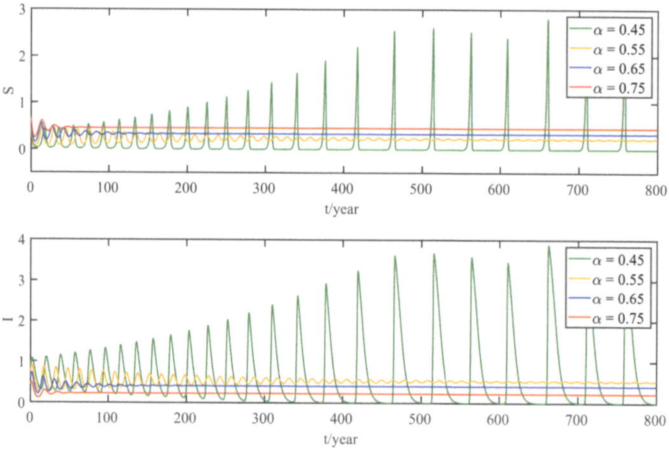

Figure 8. Comparison of convergence speed of S and I for $\tau = 0$ under different α.

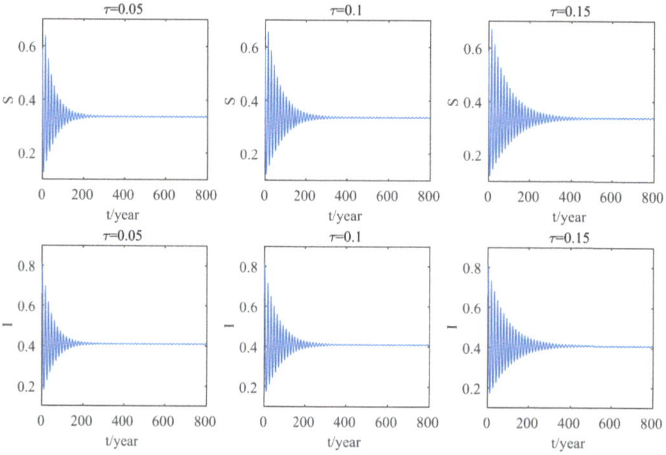

Figure 9. Comparison of convergence speed of S and I for $\alpha = 0.65$ under different τ.

Remark 5. *According to Figure 8, when $\alpha > 0.55$, the system will eventually reach a stable state without time delay. Moreover, with the increase of α, the time needed for the system to reach stability* *decreases correspondingly, so the difficulty of control and investment cost decrease correspondingly. In addition, when $\alpha > 0.55$, it will take a lengthy time although the system finally tends to be stable. During this period, the disease is still unstable and causes damage to the forest. Therefore, in this case, the control measures should get timely adjustment to improve the intensity of control, so as to improve control efficiency to shorten this time. Combining with Figure 7, we can also illustrate the necessity of increasing the value of α. It can be observed from Figure 9 that when the time delay exists, the control will take effect later, and the time required for the system to reach stability will be longer; thus, the loss will be greater. However, $\tau = 0$ means that there is no time delay of the control to take effect. When we take measures to protect trees such as nematicide injection, considering the limitation of detection technology, nematicide injection may not be carried out in time. This will cause a huge hidden danger for the spread of PWN. Therefore, the ideal situation of $\tau = 0$ is difficult to achieve in practice. However, we can shorten this delay in other ways. For example, we can reduce the time delay of control to take effect by expanding the range of trees injected with nematicide, increasing the number of injections and giving them before the emergence of larvae.*

5.2.3. Simulation Results under *Group* III

We choose the third group of parameters given in Section 5.1:

$$B = 1, d_1 = d_2 = 0.01, \beta = 1.2, \alpha = 0.65, K = 17.5, k_1 = 0.65, k_2 = 0.1,$$

under the condition of this group of parameters, $n_2 = 0.0079 > 0$, so the disease-free equilibrium E_3 does not exist at this time. When $\tau = 0$, $\beta S^{(4)} - a_1 = 0.0335 > 0$, $a_2 + a_3 = 0.2291 > 0$, (H4) does not hold, so E_4 is unstable now by Theorem 3, as shown in Figure 10. That is, the equilibrium E_4 is unstable when the environment of PWD epidemic area is suitable for the growth of *M. alternatus*. Moreover, it can be seen from Figure 10 that a large-scale outbreak occurs about every 50 years. We should try our best to avoid this situation, so it is important to reduce the environmental capacity of *M. alternatus*. Releasing competitive or predatory natural enemies of *M. alternatus* can help achieve this to some extent. Although biological control is slow to take effect, it can greatly shorten the environmental carrying capacity of *M. alternatus* and, as an auxiliary measure, it is beneficial to control the spread of PWD when it breaks out.

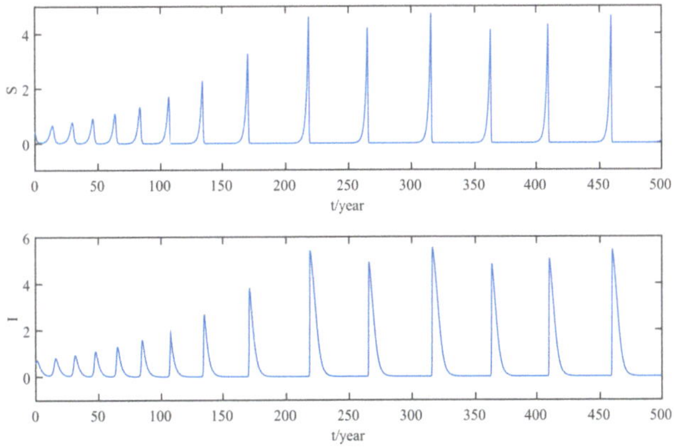

Figure 10. Equilibrium E_4 of system (2) for $\tau = 0$ is unstable.

6. Conclusions

This paper focuses on the dynamics of the insect-vector populations based on SI epidemic model. By dividing *M. alternatus* into susceptible and infected, we have constructed a two-dimensional delay differential equation model considering the control intensity and the time delay for control to take effect. After that, we have analyzed the existence and stability of the equilibrium and the existence of Hopf bifurcation, and derived the normal form of Hopf bifurcation by using a multiple time scales method. Finally, by selecting scientific parameters for numerical simulation, the results of our theoretical analysis have been verified. Numerical analysis shows that when the intensity of control is large (obviously, if the intensity of control is large, then the environmental carrying capacity of *M. alternatus* will decrease accordingly), the disease-free equilibrium E_3 is always stable; when the intensity of control is 55%$\sim$75%, the disease-free equilibrium E_3 is unstable for any $\tau \geq 0$, and oppositely, the positive equilibrium E_4 is stable before the critical time delay $\tau_1^{(0)}$, and the system will occur stable Hopf bifurcation periodic solution near equilibrium E_4. If the environmental carrying capacity of *M. alternatus* is large, the disease-free equilibrium E_3 does not exist and the positive equilibrium E_4 cannot reach stability, which provides a theoretical support for the prevention and control of PWD. However, in fact, there are many difficulties in the disease control. For example, the effect of control is affected by many factors, so it is unrealistic for the intensity of disease control α to remain constant. In the process of modeling, we assume that the parameters are constant; in reality, the parameters are changing over time. However, in general, the stability of our model is consistent with the reality. Based on the stability analysis, more effective measures can be taken to reduce the damage caused by PWD.

In addition, our numerical analysis also shows that the number of infected *M. alternatus* decreases with the control intensity increasing, and the time for the system to reach stability increases with the time delay increasing. Therefore, it is important to increase the control intensity and shorten the time delay of control to take effect. Here, we suggest that in the process of prevention and control, we can choose combined measures to increase control intensity. Meanwhile, we suggest strengthening the monitoring of trees to take measures on trees as soon as possible to shorten the time delay. Moreover, when the the system eventually fails to reach stability, the disease outbreak shows apparent periodicity. In this way, we can better prevent the outbreak of PWD according to some rules, which can prolong the growth cycle of trees and reduce the loss of forest resources, and thus, improve the carbon sink capacity of forests and accelerate the realization of the goal of "emission peak and carbon neutrality", so as to build a modernized country in which humanity and nature coexist in harmony.

Author Contributions: Writing—original draft preparation: R.D. and H.S.; funding acquisition: R.D., H.S. and Y.D.; methodology and supervision: Y.D. All authors have read and agreed to the published version of the manuscript.

Funding: This study was funded by the Fundamental Research Funds for the Central Universities of China (Grant No. 2572022DJ06).

Data Availability Statement: The authors confirm that the data supporting the findings of this study are available within the article.

Conflicts of Interest: The authors declare no conflict of interest.

References

1. Boone, C.K.; Sweeney, J.; Silk, P.; Hughes, C.; Webster, R.P.; Stephen, F.; Maclauchlan, L.; Bentz, B.; Drumont, A.; Zhao, B.; et al. Monochamus species from different continents can be effectively detected with the same trapping protocol. *J. Pest Sci.* **2018**, *92*, 3–11. [CrossRef]
2. Futai, K. Pine Wood Nematode, *Bursaphelenchus xylophilus*. *Annu. Rev. Phytopathol.* **2013**, *51*, 61–83. [CrossRef]
3. Mamiya, Y. History of pine wilt disease in Japan. *J. Nematol.* **1988**, *20*, 26–219.
4. Han, H.; Chung, Y.J.; Shin, S.C. First report of pine wilt disease on *Pinus koraiensis* in Korea. *Plant Dis.* **2008**, *92*, 1251. [CrossRef]
5. Zhao, B.G. Pine wilt disease in China. In *Pine Wilt Disease*; Springer: Tokyo, Japan, 2008; pp. 18–25
6. Dwinell, L.D. First report of pinewood nematode (*Bursaphelenchus xylophilus*) in Mexico. *Plant Dis.* **1993**, *77*, 846. [CrossRef]
7. Abelleira, A.; Picoaga, A.; Mansilla, J.P.; Aguin, O. Detection of *Bursaphelenchus xylophilus*, causal agent of pine wilt disease on Pinus pinaster in Northwestern Spain. *Plant Dis.* **2011**, *95*, 776. [CrossRef]
8. Kim, S.H.; Yun, H.Y.; Jeong, H.J. Generation of a novel antibody against BxPrx, a diagnostic marker of pine wilt disease. *Mol. Biol. Rep.* **2023**, *50*, 4715–4721. [CrossRef] [PubMed]

9. Ding, X.; Ye, J.; Wu, X.; Huang, L.; Zhu, L.; Lin, S. Deep sequencing analyses of pine wood nematode *Bursaphelenchus xylophilus* microRNAs reveal distinct miRNA expression patterns during the pathological process of pine wilt disease. *Gene* **2015**, *555*, 346–356. [CrossRef]
10. Palomares-Rius, J.E.; Tsai, I.J.; Karim, N.; Akiba, M.; Kato, T.; Maruyama, H.; Takeuchi, Y.; Kikuchi, T. Genome-wide variation in the pinewood nematode *Bursaphelenchus xylophilus* and its relationship with pathogenic traits. *BMC Genom.* **2015**, *16*, 1–13. [CrossRef]
11. Wang, G.; Xu, X.; Cheng, Q.; Hu, J.; Xu, X.; Zhang, Y.; Guo, S.; Ji, Y.; Zhou, C.; Gao, F.; et al. Preparation of sustainable release mesoporous silica nano-pesticide for control of *Monochamus alternatus*. *Sustain. Mater. Technol.* **2023**, *35*, e00538. [CrossRef]
12. Lee, J.W.; Mwamula, A.O.; Choi, J.H.; Lee, H.W.; Kim, Y.S.; Kim, J.H.; Choi, Y.H.; Lee, D.W. Comparative bioactivity of emamectin benzoate formulations against the pine wood nematode, *Bursaphelenchus xylophilus*. *Plant Pathol. J.* **2023**, *39*, 75–87. [CrossRef] [PubMed]
13. Alvarez, G.; Etxebeste, I.; Gallego, D.; David, G.; Bonifacio, L.; Jactel, H.; Sousa, E.; Pajares, J.A. Optimization of traps for live trapping of Pine Wood Nematode vector *Monochamus galloprovincialis*. *J. Appl. Entomol.* **2015**, *139*, 618–626. [CrossRef]
14. Mannaa, M.; Han, G.; Jeon, H.W.; Kim, J.; Kim, N.; Park, A.R.; Kim, J.C.; Seo, Y.S. Influence of resistance-inducing chemical elicitors against pine wilt disease on the rhizosphere microbiome. *Microorganisms* **2020**, *8*, 884. [CrossRef]
15. Shi, X.Y.; Song, G.H. Analysis of the mathematical model for the spread of pine wilt disease. *J. Appl. Math.* **2013**, *184054*, 227–261. [CrossRef]
16. Ozair, M. Analysis of pine wilt disease model with nonlinear incidence and horizontal transmission. *J. Appl. Math.* **2014**, 204241, 1–9. [CrossRef]
17. Khan, M.A.; Ali, K.; Bonyah, E.; Okosun, K.O.; Islam, S.; Khan, A. Mathematical modeling and stability analysis of pine wilt disease with optimal control. *Sci. Rep.* **2017**, *7*, 3115. [CrossRef]
18. Khan, M.A.; Ahmed, L.; Mandal, P.K.; Smith, R.; Haque, M. Modelling the dynamics of pine wilt disease with asymptomatic carriers and optimal control. *Sci. Rep.* **2020**, *10*, 11412. [CrossRef] [PubMed]
19. Nayfeh, A.H. *Introduction to Perturbation Techniques*; Wiley-Interscience: New York, NY, USA, 1981.
20. Nayfeh, A.H. Order reduction of retarded nonlinear systems—The method of multiple scales versus center-manifold reduction. *Nonlinear Dyn.* **2008**, *51*, 483–500. [CrossRef]
21. Ding, Y.T.; Zheng, L.Y. Mathematical modeling and dynamics analysis of delayed nonlinear VOC emission system. *Nonlinear Dyn.* **2022**, *109*, 3157–3167. [CrossRef]
22. Shen, H.; Song, Y.L.; Wang, H. Bifurcations in a diffusive resource-consumer model with distributed memory. *J. Differ. Equ.* **2023**, *347*, 170–211. [CrossRef]
23. Liu, M.; Wang, H.B.; Jiang, W.H. Bifurcations and pattern formation in a predator-prey model with memory-based diffusion. *J. Differ. Equ.* **2023**, *350*, 1–40. [CrossRef]
24. Wang, Y.; Chen, J.; Chen, F.; Zhou, Q.; Zhou, L.; Sun, S. Transmission of *Bursaphelenchus xylophilus* (Nematoda: Aphelenchoididae) through feeding activity of Monochamus alternatus (Coleoptera: Cerambycidae). *J. Nanjing For. Univ.* **2019**, *43*, 1–10.
25. Jikumaru, S.; Togashi, K. Temperature Effects on the transmission of *Bursaphelenchus xylophilus* (Nemata: Aphelenchoididae) by *Monochamus alternatus* (Coleoptera: Cerambycidae). *J. Nematol.* **2000**, *32*, 110–116. [PubMed]
26. Koutroumpa, F.A.; Vincent, B.; Roux-Morabito, G.; Martin, C.; Lieutier, F. Fecundity and larval development of *Monochamus galloprovincialis* (Coleoptera Cerambycidae) in experimental breeding. *Ann. For. Sci.* **2008**, *65*, 707. [CrossRef]
27. Li, M.; Dai, Y.; Wang, Y.; Wang, L.; Sun, S.; Chen, F. New insights into the life history of *Monochamus saltuarius* (Cerambycidae: Coleoptera) can enhance surveillance strategies for pine wilt disease. *J. For. Res.* **2021**, *32*, 2699–2707. [CrossRef]
28. Ahmed, E.S.; Rida, S.Z.; Gaber, Y.A. On the stability analysis and solutions of fractional order pine wilt disease model. *Appl. Math. Inf. Sci.* **2020**, *14*, 1137–1146.
29. Zhao, L.; Sun, J. *Pinewood Nematode Bursaphelenchus xylophilus (Steiner and Buhrer) Nickle*; Springer: Singapore, 2017; Volume 13, pp. 3–21.

Σ mathematics

MDPI

Article

Asymptotic Behavior for a Coupled Petrovsky–Petrovsky System with Infinite Memories

Hicham Saber [1], Mohamed Ferhat [2], Amin Benaissa Cherif [2], Tayeb Blouhi [2], Ahmed Himadan [3,*], Tariq Alraqad [1] and Abdelkader Moumen [1]

1 Department of Mathematics, Faculty of Sciences, University of Ha'il, Ha'il 55473, Saudi Arabia; hi.saber@uoh.edu.sa (H.S.); t.alraqad@uoh.edu.sa (T.A.); mo.abdelkader@uoh.edu.sa (A.M.)
2 Department of Mathematics, Faculty of Mathematics and Informatics, University of Science and Technology of Oran Mohamed-Boudiaf (USTOMB), El Mnaouar, BP 1505, Bir El Djir, Oran 31000, Algeria; ferhat22@hotmail.fr (M.F.); amin.benaisacherif@univ-usto.dz (A.B.C.); blouhitayeb1984@gmail.com (T.B.)
3 Department of Mathematics, College of Sciences and Arts, Qassim University, Ar-Rass 51452, Saudi Arabia
* Correspondence: ah.mohamed@qu.edu.sa

Abstract: The main goal of this article is to obtain the existence of solutions for a nonlinear system of a coupled Petrovsky–Petrovsky system in the presence of infinite memories under minimal assumptions on the functions g_1, g_2 and φ_1, φ_2. Here, g_1, g_2 are relaxation functions and φ_1, φ_2 represent the sources. Also, a general decay rate for the associated energy is established. Our work is partly motivated by recent results, with a necessary modification imposed by the nature of our problem. In this work, we limit our results to studying the system in a bounded domain. The case of the entire domain $\mathbb{R}^n$ requires separate consideration. Of course, obtaining such a result will require not only serious technical work but also the use of new techniques and methods. In particular, one of the most significant points in achieving this goal is the use of the perturbed Lyapunov functionals combined with the multiplier method. To the best of our knowledge, there is no result addressing the linked Petrovsky–Petrovsky system in the presence of infinite memory, and we have overcome this lacune.

Keywords: Lyapunov functions; energy decay; infinite memories; source terms; partial differential equation

MSC: 35L05; 35L15; 35L70; 93D15

Citation: Saber, H.; Ferhat, M.; Benaissa Cherif, A.; Blouhi, T.; Himadan, A.; Alraqad, T.; Moumen, A. Asymptotic Behavior for a Coupled Petrovsky–Petrovsky System with Infinite Memories. *Mathematics* **2023**, *11*, 4457. https://doi.org/10.3390/math11214457

Academic Editors: Mihaela Neamțu, Eva Kaslik and Anca Rădulescu

Received: 23 September 2023
Revised: 20 October 2023
Accepted: 26 October 2023
Published: 27 October 2023

1. Introduction

From a mathematical point of view, partial differential equations (in short, PDEs) are a very powerful instrument to describe real phenomena (e.g., explosion, boundedness, and stability) arising from biology, plasma physics, epidemiology, etc. In this context, we mention, for instance, refs. [1–3].

This study is concerned with the following viscoelastic system:

$$\begin{cases} |u_t|^{\ell} u_{tt} - \Delta_x^2 u + \int_0^{\infty} g_1(s)\Delta_x^2 u(x,t-s)ds + \varphi_1(u,v) = 0, & \text{in } \Omega_\infty, \\ |v_t|^{\ell} v_{tt} - \Delta_x^2 v + \int_0^{\infty} g_2(s)\Delta_x^2 v(x,t-s)ds + \varphi_2(u,v) = 0, & \text{in } \Omega_\infty, \\ u(x,t) = v(x,t) = 0 & \text{on } \Gamma_\infty, \\ u(x,-t) = u_0(x,t),\ v(x,-t) = v_0(x,t), & \text{in } \Omega_\infty, \\ u_t(x,t=0) = u_1(x),\ v_t(x,t=0) = v_1(x), & x \in \Omega, \\ u(x,t=0) = u_0(x),\ v(x,t=0) = v_0(x), & x \in \Omega, \end{cases} \quad (1)$$

where $\Omega_\infty = \Omega \times (0,\infty)$; $\Gamma_\infty = \partial\Omega \times (0,\infty)$; Ω is a regular and bounded domain in $\mathbb{R}^n (n \geq 1)$, with a smooth boundary $\partial\Omega$ of class C^4; and ℓ is a real number such that

$$\begin{cases} 0 < \ell \leq \frac{2}{n-2}, & \text{if } n \geq 3, \\ \ell > 0, & \text{if } n \in \{1,2\}. \end{cases}$$

The functions u and v denote the transverse displacements of equations, and φ_1, φ_2 are source terms that define how the two equations interact with one another. The softening functions g_1 and g_2 represent the viscoelastic materials that have the property of keeping past memories. The initial data $(u_0, u_1), (v_0, v_1)$ belong to a suitable space. The interaction of two scalar fields is described in the theory of viscoelasticity by this problem (see [4–8]). For the single viscoelastic wave equation, there are many results concerning global well-posedness and stability; see, for example, [9–13]. To get us started, consider the wave equation presented; the authors of [14] investigated the conventional version of the following coupled system of quasilinear viscoelastic equations:

$$\begin{cases} |u_t|^\rho u_{tt} + \int_0^t g_1(t-s)\Delta_x u(s)ds + \varphi_1(x,u) = \Delta_x u + \gamma_1 \Delta_x u_{tt}, \\ |v_t|^\rho v_{tt} + \int_0^t g_2(t-s)\Delta_x v(s)ds + \varphi_2(x,u) = \Delta_x v + \gamma_2 \Delta_x v_{tt}. \end{cases}$$

Here, Ω is a bounded domain in $\mathbb{R}^n$, with a smooth boundary $\partial\Omega$, $\gamma_i \geq 0, i = 1,2$ are constants, and ρ is a real number, such that

$$\begin{cases} 0 < \rho < \frac{2n}{(n-2)}, & \text{if } n \geq 3 \\ \rho > 0, & \text{if } n \in \{1,2\}, \end{cases}$$

and the initial data are given by the functions u_0, v_0, u_1, and v_1. The relaxation functions g_1 and g_2 are continuous, and the nonlinear terms are represented by $\varphi_1(u,v)$, $\varphi_2(u,v)$. The authors used the perturbed energy approach to demonstrate the energy decay finding.

Many authors thought about the very initial boundary value problem in the following coupled system:

$$\begin{cases} u_{tt} + \int_0^t g_1(t-s)\Delta_x u(s)ds + h_1(u_t) = \varphi_1(x,u) + \Delta_x u, \\ v_{tt} + \int_0^t g_2(t-s)\Delta_x v(s)ds + h_2(v_t) = \varphi_2(x,u) + \Delta_x v. \end{cases} \tag{2}$$

If the viscoelastic terms $g_i = 0, i = 1,2$ are not included in (2), several results concerning the local and global existence in the presence of a weak solution were found by Rammaha and Sakuntasathien [15]. Using the same method as in [16], the authors demonstrated that any weak solution with negative starting energy will blow up in finite time. In case of the presence of the memory, that is, $g_i \neq 0, i = 1,2$, there are various results concerning the asymptotic behavior and blow up of viscoelastic system solutions. For example, Liang and Gao [17] investigated the problem (2), with $h_1(u_t) = -\Delta_x u_t$, $h_2(v_t) = -\Delta_x u_t$. The authors showed that the decay rate of the energy functions is exponential under appropriate conditions on the functions $g_i, i = 1,2$, $\varphi_i, i = 1,2$, and for a specific initial data in the stable set. On the other hand, there are solutions with positive initial energy that blow up in finite time given certain specific initial data in the unstable set. Moreover, $h_1(u_t) = |u_t|^{m-1}u_t$ and $h_2(v_t) = |v_t|^{r-1}v_t$. Han and Wang [18] provided numerous results concerning local existence, global existence, and finite temporal blow-up (the initial energy $E(0) < 0$).

The generic version of the weakly damped viscoelastic wave equations is written as

$$\begin{cases} u_{tt} + \int_0^t g_1(t-s)\Delta_x u(s)ds + h_1(u_t) = \varphi_1(x,u) + \Delta_x u, \\ v_{tt} + \int_0^t g_2(t-s)\Delta_x v(s)ds + h_2(v_t) = \varphi_2(x,u) + \Delta_x v. \end{cases}$$

When the memory is infinite, the more general form of the wave equation can be given by

$$u_{tt} - \int_0^\infty \mu(s)\Delta_x u(t-s)ds + g(u_t) = f + \alpha\Delta_x u.$$

There have been so many results concerning the wave equation with respect to global well-posedness and stability up until now; see, for instance, [19]. For the coupled wave equations with infinite memories, Messaoudi and Al-Gharabli [20] considered the following system:

$$\begin{cases} u_{tt} + \int_0^\infty g(s)\Delta_x u(t-s) + \lambda|u_t|^{m-1}u_t = \varphi_1(u,v) + \Delta_x u, \\ v_{tt} + \int_0^\infty h(s)\Delta_x v(t-s) + \mu|v_t|^{r-1}v_t = \varphi_2(u,v) + \Delta_x v. \end{cases}$$

For coupled Petrovsky–Petrovsky equations, here we mention the work in [21] where the author considered the following coupled system:

$$\begin{cases} u_{tt} + \Delta_x^2 u + au_2 + g_1(u_t) = 0, \\ v_{tt} + \Delta_x^2 v + av_2 + g_2(v_t) = 0, \end{cases}$$

with Ω being a bounded domain in $\mathbb{R}^n$ with a smooth boundary $\partial\Omega$ of class C^4, and $a : \Omega \to \mathbb{R}$, $(g_i)_{i\in\{1,2\}} : \mathbb{R} \to \mathbb{R}$ are some given functions. Under suitable assumptions, he proved that this system is well-posed by using the nonlinear semi-groups theory, and dissipative by exploiting the multiplier method.

Motivated by prior research, the current study investigates the effect of infinite memory and source terms on the solutions to (1). Under suitable assumptions, we establish the decay properties of the solutions of (1). It is noted that our system is different from the one in Bahlil and Feng [1], making the methods used in our work different from theirs. In this research, we are able, essentially and mainly, to link the rate of decrease to the energy functional associated with the solution directly to that of the functions g_1, g_2 with an improvement in the conditions taken on these relaxation functions. We found that the two functions g_1, g_2 are responsible for the decay rate of the energy functional and then that of the existed solution. On the other hand, the functions φ_1, φ_2 obstruct the solution if they can overcome and dominate it.

This paper is structured as follows. In the next section, we provide some preliminaries and useful lemmas used to obtain our results. In the Section 3, we derive the decay properties and separately report the general results obtained for the most important case. The decaying results are obtained without the assumptions (A_1) in Section 4. Finally, in the Section 5 we give some examples on the relaxation functions to illustrate the energy decay rate given by Theorem 2.

2. Assumptions and Supporting Results

This part contains some material required for the statement and proof of our result. Set

$$H_0^1(\Omega) = \Big\{u \in H^1(\Omega) : u_0 = 0\Big\}.$$

Let λ_1 be the first eigenvalue of the spectral Dirichlet problem

$$\begin{cases} \Delta_x^2 u = \lambda_1 u, & \text{in } \Omega, \\ u = \dfrac{\partial u}{\partial \nu} = 0 & \text{in } \partial\Omega, \\ \|\nabla_x u\|_2 \le \frac{1}{\sqrt{\lambda_1}}\|\Delta_x u\|_2. \end{cases}$$

We will employ embedding $H_0^1(\Omega) \hookrightarrow L^q(\Omega)$, for $\frac{2n}{n-2} \ge q \ge 2$, if $0 \le n$ and $2 \le q$, if $n = 1,2$ and $L^r(\Omega) \hookrightarrow L^q(\Omega)$, for $q < r$. Then, for some $c_s > 0$,

$$\|\nu\|_q \le c_s\|\nabla_x \nu\|_2, \quad \|\nu\|_q \le c_s\|\nu\|_r, \quad \text{for } \nu \in H_0^1(\Omega).$$

We will need the following assumptions:

(A_1) The relaxation functions $(g_i)_{i\in\{1,2\}}$ are differentiable functions such that,

$$g_i(s) \geq 0, \qquad \text{for } s \geq 0 \text{ and } i \in \{1,2\},$$

$$1 - \int_0^\infty g_i(s)ds = l_i > 0, \qquad \text{for } i \in \{1,2\},$$

and there are two differentiable positive nonincreasing functions $(\zeta_i)_{i\in\{1,2\}}$, such that

$$g_i'(s) \leq -\zeta_i(s)g_i(s), \quad \text{for } s \geq 0 \text{ and } i \in \{1,2\},$$

and

$$g_i'(s) \leq 0, \quad \text{for } s \geq 0 \text{ and } i \in \{1,2\}.$$

Our assumptions about the functions $g_i, i = 1,2$ are currently the most general. These assumptions are natural for systems arising in the study of time-PDEs.

(A_2) For $i \in \{1,2\}$, the functions $\varphi_i : \mathbb{R}^2 \to \mathbb{R}$ are C^1, such that

$$\begin{cases} \varphi_1(u,v) = a|u+v|^{p-1}(u+v) + b|u|^{\frac{p-3}{2}}|v|^{\frac{p+1}{2}}u, \\ \varphi_2(u,v) = \varphi_1(v,u), \end{cases} \qquad \text{for all } (u,v) \in \mathbb{R}^2,$$

with $a, b > 0$, and a function Φ exists, such that

$$u\varphi_1(u,v) + v\varphi_2(u,v) = (p+1)\Phi(u,v), \text{ for all } (u,v) \in \mathbb{R}^2,$$

where

$$\Phi(u,v) = \frac{1}{(p+1)}(a|u+v|^{p+1} + 2b|uv|^{\frac{p+1}{2}}), \quad \varphi_1(u,v) = \frac{\partial\Phi}{\partial u}, \quad \varphi_2(u,v) = \frac{\partial\Phi}{\partial v}.$$

(A_3) Two constants $c_0, c_1 > 0$ exist, such that

$$c_0(|u|^{p+1} + |v|^{p+1}) \leq \Phi(u,v) \leq c_1(|u|^{p+1} + |v|^{p+1}), \text{ for all } (u,v) \in \mathbb{R}^2,$$

and

$$\left|\frac{\partial\varphi_i}{\partial u}(u,v)\right| + \left|\frac{\partial\varphi_i}{\partial v}(u,v)\right| \leq C(|u|^{p-1} + |v|^{p-1}), \quad \text{for } i \in \{1,2\} \quad \text{where} \quad 1 \leq p < 6.$$

(A_4)

$$\begin{cases} p \geq 3, & \text{if } n = 1,2, \\ p = 3, & \text{if } n = 3. \end{cases}$$

3. Main Result for System

To demonstrate our solution for the problem (1), we follow the approach of Dafermos [22] by taking into account a new auxiliary variable, the relative history of u and v, as follows:

$$\eta_1 = \eta^{1t}(x,s) = u(x,t) - u(x,t-s) \quad \text{in } \Omega_\infty \times (0,\infty),$$

$$\eta_2 = \eta^{2t}(x,s) = v(x,t) - v(x,t-s) \quad \text{in} \quad \Omega_\infty \times (0,\infty),$$

and the weighted L^2-spaces

$$
\begin{aligned}
\mathcal{M}_i &= L^2_{g_i}(\mathbb{R}, H^4(\Omega)) \cap H^2_0(\Omega)) \\
&= \left\{ \zeta_i : \mathbb{R}^+ \to H^4(\Omega) \cap H^2_0(\Omega) : \int_0^\infty g_i(s) \|\Delta_x \zeta_i(s)\|_2^2 ds < \infty \right\}, \quad \text{for } i \in \{1, 2\},
\end{aligned}
$$

which are a Hilbert spaces endowed with inner products and norms

$$
\langle \xi_i, \zeta_i \rangle_{\mathcal{M}_i} = \int_0^\infty g_i(s) \left(\int_\Omega \Delta_x \xi_i(s) \Delta_x \zeta_i(s) dx \right) ds, \quad \text{for } i \in \{1, 2\},
$$

and

$$
\|\xi_i\|^2_{\mathcal{M}_i} = \int_0^\infty g_i(s) \|\Delta_x \xi_i(s)\|_2^2 ds, \quad \text{for } i \in \{1, 2\}.
$$

Our analysis is given in phase space

$$
\widetilde{\mathcal{H}} = H^2_0(\Omega) \cap H^4(\Omega) \times H^2_0(\Omega) \cap H^4(\Omega) \times H^2_0(\Omega) \times H^2_0(\Omega) \times \mathcal{M}_1 \times \mathcal{M}_2.
$$

Therefore, problem (1) is equivalent to

$$
\begin{cases}
|u_t|^\ell u_{tt} - l_1 \Delta_x^2 u - \Delta_x u_{tt} - \int_0^\infty g_1(s) \Delta_x^2 \eta^{1t}(x, s) ds + \varphi_1(u, v) = 0 & \text{in } \Omega_\infty, \\
|v_t|^\ell v_{tt} - l_2 \Delta_x^2 v - \Delta_x v_{tt} - \int_0^\infty g_2(s) \Delta_x^2 \eta^{2t}(x, s) ds + \varphi_2(u, v) = 0 & \text{in } \Omega_\infty, \\
\eta_t^{1t}(x, t) + \eta_s^{1t}(x, s) = u_t(x, t) & \text{in } \Omega_\infty \times (0, \infty), \\
\eta_t^{2t}(x, t) + \eta_s^{2t}(x, s) = v_t(x, t) & \text{in } \Omega_\infty \times (0, \infty), \\
\eta^{10}(x, s) = \eta_{10}(x, s) & \text{in } \Omega_\infty, \\
\eta^{20}(x, s) = \eta_{20}(x, s) & \text{in } \Omega_\infty, \\
u(x, t) = v(x, t) = \eta^{1t}(x, t = 0) = \eta^{2t}(x, t = 0) = 0 & \text{on } \Gamma_\infty, \\
u(x, -t) = u_0(x, t), \ v(x, -t) = v_0(x, t), & \text{in } \Omega_\infty, \\
u_t(x, t = 0) = u_1(x), v_t(x, t = 0) = v_1(x), & x \in \Omega, \\
u(x, t = 0) = u_0(x), v(x, t = 0) = v_0(x), & x \in \Omega.
\end{cases}
\tag{3}
$$

We define the energy function associated with the problem (3) by

$$
\begin{aligned}
E(t) \ : &= \frac{1}{\ell + 2} \|u_t(t)\|_{\ell+2}^{\ell+2} + \frac{1}{\ell + 2} \|v_t(t)\|_{\ell+2}^{\ell+2} + \frac{1}{2} \|\nabla_x u_t(t)\|_2^2 + \frac{1}{2} \|\nabla_x v_t(t)\|_2^2 + \\
& \frac{l_1}{2} \|\Delta_x u(t)\|_2^2 + \frac{l_2}{2} \|\Delta_x v(t)\|_2^2 + \int_0^\infty g_1(s) \|\Delta_x \eta^1(s)\|_2^2 ds \\
& + \int_0^\infty g_2(s) \|\Delta_x \eta^2(s)\|_2^2 ds + \int_\Omega \Phi(u(t), v(t) dx.
\end{aligned}
$$

The following result can be proven by the Faedo–Galerkin procedure.

Theorem 1. *Suppose that (A_1)–(A_4) holds, and assume that $(u_0, v_0, u_1, v_1, \eta_{10}, \eta_{20}) \in \widetilde{\mathcal{H}}$. Then, a unique weak solution exists*

$$
(u, v, u_t, v_t, \eta^1, \eta^2) \in C([0, \infty) : \widetilde{\mathcal{H}}),
$$

of (3) *satisfying*

$$
u, v \in L^\infty([0, \infty) : H^4(\Omega) \cap H^2_0(\Omega)), \quad \eta^i \in L^\infty([0, \infty) : \mathcal{M}_i), \quad \textit{for } i \in \{1, 2\},
$$

$$
u_t, v_t \in L^\infty([0, \infty) : H^2_0(\Omega)).
$$

Proof. To generate an approximation solution, we employ the conventional Faedo–Galerkin approach. Let $\{w_j\}_{j=1}^\infty$ be the eigenfunctions of the operator $A = -\Delta_x$ with the zero Dirichlet boundary condition and $D(A) = H^4(\Omega) \cap H^2_0(\Omega)$. It is known that $\{w_j\}_{j=1}^\infty$ forms an orthonormal basis for $L^2(\Omega)$, $H^2_0(\Omega)$ and $H^4(\Omega) \cap H^2_0(\Omega)$. We consider two smooth orthonormal bases $\{\xi_j^1(x,s)\}_{j=1}^{\infty}$ and $\{\xi_j^2(x,s)\}_{j=1}^{\infty}$ for $\mathcal{M}_1$ and $\mathcal{M}_2$, respectively. For any integer $n \in \mathbb{N}$, we consider the finite-dimensional subspaces

$$W_n = \text{Span}\{\omega_1, \ldots, \omega_n\} \subset V_2, \quad Q_1n = \text{Span}\{\xi_1^1, \ldots, \xi_n^1\} \subset \mathcal{M}_1,$$
$$Q_2n = \text{Span}\{\xi_1^2, \ldots, \xi_n^2\} \subset \mathcal{M}_2.$$

We will find an approximate solution in the following form:

$$u^n(t) = \sum_{j=1}^{j=n} a_{nj}(t)\omega_j(x) \ , \ \eta^{1,n}(s) = \sum_{j=1}^{j=n} b_{nj}(t)\xi_j^1(x,s),$$

$$v^n(t) = \sum_{j=1}^{j=n} d_{nj}(t)\omega_j(x) \ , \ \eta^{2,n}(s) = \sum_{j=1}^{j=n} h_{nj}(t)\xi_j^2(x,s),$$

satisfying the approximate problem:

$$\begin{aligned}\langle |u_t|^{\ell} u_{tt}^n, \omega_j\rangle_\Omega \quad &+ \quad \ell_1\langle \Delta_x u^n, \Delta_x \omega_j\rangle_\Omega + \langle \nabla_x u_{tt}^n, \nabla_x \omega_j\rangle_\Omega - \left\langle \int_0^\infty g_1(s)\Delta_x \eta^{1,n}(s)ds, \Delta_x\omega_j \right\rangle_\Omega \\ &+\langle \varphi_1(u^n, v^n), \omega_j\rangle_\Omega = 0,\end{aligned}$$

$$\begin{aligned}\langle |v_t|^{\ell} v_{tt}^n, \omega_j\rangle_\Omega \quad &+ \quad \ell_2\langle +\Delta_x v^n, \Delta_x \omega_j\rangle_\Omega + \langle \nabla_x u_{tt}^n, \nabla_x \omega_j\rangle_\Omega - \left\langle \int_0^\infty g_2(s)\Delta_x \eta^{2,n}(s)ds, \Delta_x\omega_j \right\rangle_\Omega \\ &+\langle \varphi_2(u^n, v^n), \omega_j\rangle_\Omega = 0,\end{aligned}$$

$$\begin{aligned}\left\langle \partial_t \eta^{1,n}, \xi_j^1 \right\rangle_{\mathcal{M}_1} &= -\left\langle \partial_s \eta^{1,n}, \xi_j^1 \right\rangle_{\mathcal{M}_1} + \left\langle u_t^n(t), \xi_j^1 \right\rangle_{\mathcal{M}_1}, \\ \left\langle \partial_t \eta^{2,n}, \xi_j^2 \right\rangle_{\mathcal{M}_2} &= -\left\langle \partial_s \eta^{2,n}, \xi_j^2 \right\rangle_{\mathcal{M}_2} + \left\langle v_t^n(t), \xi_j^2 \right\rangle_{\mathcal{M}_2}.\end{aligned}$$

□

Lemma 1. *The energy function satisfies the following inequality:*

$$E'(t) \leq \frac{1}{2}\int_0^\infty g_1'(s)\|\Delta_x \eta^1(s)\|^2 ds + \frac{1}{2}\int_0^\infty g_2'(s)\|\Delta_x \eta^2(s)\|^2 ds.$$

Proof. Multiply the first equation in (3) by $u_t(t)$ and the second one by $v_t(t)$; then, integrate the result over Ω to obtain

$$\begin{aligned}&\frac{d}{dt}\left[\frac{1}{\ell+2}\|u_t(t)\|_{\ell+2}^{\ell+2} + \frac{1}{\ell+2}\|v_t(t)\|_{\ell+2}^{\ell+2} + \tfrac{1}{2}\|\nabla_x u_t(t)\|_2^2 + \right. \\ &\left.\frac{1}{2}\|\nabla_x v_t(t)\|_2^2 + \ell_1\|\Delta_x u(t)\|_2^2 + l_2\|\Delta_x v(t)\|_2^2\right] + \\ &\frac{d}{dt}\int_\Omega \Phi(u(t), v(t))dx - \int_0^\infty g_1(s)\int_\Omega \Delta_x\eta^1(s)\Delta_x u_t(t)dxds - \\ &\int_0^\infty g_2(s)\int_\Omega \Delta_x\eta^2(s)\Delta_x v_t(t)dxds = 0.\end{aligned} \tag{4}$$

Since

$$\begin{cases} u_t(x,t) = \eta_t^1(x,s) + \eta_s^1(x,s), \\ v_t(x,t) = \eta_t^2(x,s) + \eta_s^2(x,s), \end{cases} \quad \text{for } (x,s,t) \in \Omega \times \mathbb{R}^+ \times \mathbb{R}^+,$$

we have

$$\begin{aligned}
&\int_0^\infty g_1(s) \int_\Omega \Delta_x\eta^1(s)\Delta_x u_t(t)dxds \\
= &\int_0^\infty g_1(s) \int_\Omega \Delta_x\eta^1(s)\Delta_x\eta_t^1(t)dxds \\
&+\int_0^\infty g_1(s) \int_\Omega \Delta_x\eta^1(s)\Delta_x\eta_s^1(t)dxds \\
= &\frac{1}{2}\int_0^\infty g_1(s)\frac{d}{dt}\|\Delta_x\eta^1(s)\|_2^2 ds - \frac{1}{2}\int_0^\infty \left\|g_1'^1(s)\right\|_2^2 ds,
\end{aligned} \tag{5}$$

and

$$\int_0^\infty g_2(s) \int_\Omega \Delta_x\eta^2(s)\Delta_x v_t(t)dxds = \frac{1}{2}\int_0^\infty g_2(s)\frac{d}{dt}\|\Delta_x\eta^2(s)\|_2^2 ds - \frac{1}{2}\int_0^\infty \left\|g_2'^2(s)\right\|_2^2 ds. \tag{6}$$

By substituting (5) and (6) into (4), we obtain

$$\begin{aligned}
&\frac{d}{dt}\left[\frac{1}{\ell+2}\|u_t(t)\|_{\ell+2}^{\ell+2} + \frac{1}{\ell+2}\|v_t(t)\|_{\ell+2}^{\ell+2} + \frac{1}{2}\|\nabla_x u_t(t)\|_2^2 + \frac{1}{2}\|\nabla_x v_t(t)\|_2^2\right. \\
&+\frac{l_1}{2}\|\Delta_x u(t)\|_2^2 + \frac{l_2}{2}\|\Delta_x v(t)\|_2^2 \\
&+\int_\Omega \Phi(u(t),v(t))dx + \frac{1}{2}\frac{d}{dt}\int_0^\infty g_1(s)\|\nabla_x\eta^1(s)\|_2^2 ds - \frac{1}{2}\int_0^\infty g_1'^1(s)\|_2^2 ds \\
&+\frac{1}{2}\frac{d}{dt}\int_0^\infty g_2(s)\|\nabla_x\eta^2(s)\|_2^2 ds - \frac{1}{2}\int_0^\infty \|g_2'^2(s)\|_2^2 ds = 0.
\end{aligned} \tag{7}$$

Integrating (7) over $(0,t)$ yields

$$E(t) - \frac{1}{2}\int_0^t\int_0^\infty \left\|g_1'^1(s)\right\|_2^2 ds - \frac{1}{2}\int_0^t\int_0^\infty \left\|g_2'^2(s)\right\|_2^2 ds = E(0).$$

□

Lemma 2. *Under the assumptions of Theorem 1, the functional $\phi(t)$ defined by*

$$\phi(t) = \frac{1}{\ell+1}\int_\Omega |u_t|^\ell u_t u dx + \int_\Omega |v_t|^\ell v_t v dx + \int_\Omega \nabla_x u_t \nabla_x u dx + \int_\Omega \nabla_x v_t \nabla_x v dx,$$

satisfies, for some positive constants c', c'', c_1, c_2 and for any $t \geq 0$,

$$\begin{aligned}
\phi'(t) \leq\ &\frac{1}{\ell+1}\|u_t(t)\|_{\ell+2}^{\ell+2} + \frac{1}{\ell+1}\|v_t(t)\|_{\ell+2}^{\ell+2} - c'\|\Delta_x u(t)\|_2^2 - c''\|\Delta_x v(t)\|_2^2 \\
&+c_1\int_0^\infty g_1(s)\|\Delta_x\eta^1(s)\|_2^2 ds + c_2\int_0^\infty g_2(s)\|\Delta_x\eta^2(s)\|_2^2 ds + \\
&+\|\nabla_x u_t\|_2^2 + \|\nabla_x v_t\|_2^2 - (p+1)\int_\Omega \Phi(u,v)dx.
\end{aligned} \tag{8}$$

Proof. Differentiating $\phi(t)$ with respect to t and using (3) gives

$$\begin{aligned}
\phi'(t) =\ &\|u_t\|_{\ell+2}^{\ell+2} + \|v_t(t)\|_{\ell+2}^{\ell+2} + \int_\Omega u(t)\left(l_1\Delta_x^2 u + \int_0^\infty g_1(s)\Delta_x^2\eta^1(s)ds - \varphi_1(u,v)\right)dx \\
&+\int_\Omega v(t)\left(l_2\Delta_x^2 v + \int_0^\infty g_2(s)\Delta_x^2\eta^2(s)ds - \varphi_2(u,v)\right)dx \\
&+\|\nabla_x u_t\|_2^2 + \|\nabla_x v_t\|_2^2.
\end{aligned}$$

By using Young and Hölder's inequality, we can obtain for any $\delta > 0$,

$$\begin{aligned} -\int_\Omega \Delta_x u \int_0^\infty g_1(s)\Delta_x\eta^1(s)dsdx &\leq \delta\|\Delta_x u\|_2^2 + \frac{1}{4\delta}\int_\Omega\left(\int_0^\infty g_1(s)\Delta_x\eta^1(s)ds\right)^2 dx \\ &\leq \delta\|\Delta_x u\|^2 + \frac{1-l_1}{4\delta}\int_0^\infty g_1(s)\|\Delta_x\eta^1(s)\|_2^2 ds, \end{aligned} \tag{9}$$

$$-\int_\Omega \Delta_x v \int_0^\infty g_2(s)\Delta_x\eta^2(s)dsdx \leq \delta\|\Delta_x v\|_2^2 + \frac{1-l_2}{4\delta}\int_0^\infty g_2(s)\|\Delta_x\eta^2(s)\|_2^2 ds. \tag{10}$$

It follows from the assumptions on φ_1 and φ_2 that

$$-\int_\Omega(\varphi_1(u,v)u + \varphi_2(u,v)v)dx = -(p+1)\int_\Omega \Phi(u,v)dx. \tag{11}$$

By summing up (9)–(11), we obtain that for any $\delta > 0$,

$$\begin{aligned} \phi'(t) \leq\ & \frac{1}{\ell+1}\|u_t(t)\|_{\ell+2}^{\ell+2} + \frac{1}{\ell+1}\|v_t(t)\|_{\ell+2}^{\ell+2} - (l_1-\delta)\|\Delta_x u(t)\|_2^2 - (l_2-\delta)\|\Delta_x v(t)\|_2^2 \\ & + c_1\int_0^\infty g_1(s)\|\Delta_x\eta^1(s)\|_2^2 ds + c_2\int_0^\infty g_2(s)\|\Delta_x\eta^2(s)\|_2^2 ds \\ & + \|\nabla_x u_t\|_2^2 + \|\nabla_x v_t\|_2^2 - (p+1)\int_\Omega \Phi(u,v)dx. \end{aligned} \tag{12}$$

Now, by taking $\delta > 0$ so small so that

$$l_1 - \delta > \frac{l_1}{2}, \qquad l_2 - \delta > \frac{\ell_2}{2},$$

we can obtain (8) from (12), and hence the proof is completed. □

Lemma 3. *Under the assumptions of Theorem 1, some positive constants c_3, δ_1 exist such that, along the solution of system (3), the function $\psi_1(t)$ defined by*

$$\psi_1(t) = \int_\Omega\left(\Delta_x u_t(t) - \frac{1}{1+\ell}|u_t|^\ell u_t\right)\int_0^\infty g_1(s)\eta^1(s)dsdx,$$

satisfies

$$\begin{aligned} \psi_1'(t) \leq\ & \left(\frac{\delta_1 c}{\lambda_1}\left(\frac{2(\ell+2)}{\ell+1}E(0)\right)^{2\ell+1} + \delta_1\right)\|\Delta_x u\|_2^2 + \\ & + (1-l_1)\left(\frac{l_1^2}{4\delta_1} + 1 + \frac{c_s^2}{4\delta_1\lambda_1}\right)\int_0^\infty g_1(s)\Delta_x\eta^1(s)ds \\ & + \frac{\delta_1 c}{\lambda_1}\left(\frac{2(\ell+2)}{\ell+1}E(0)\right)^{\ell+1}\|\Delta_x v\|_2^2 + \frac{3(1-\ell_1)}{4}\|\Delta_x u_t\|_2^2 + \frac{3(1-l_1)}{4}\|u_t\|_{\ell+2}^{\ell+2} \\ & - \frac{2g_1(0)}{\lambda_1(1-l_1)}\int_0^\infty g_1'(s)\|\Delta_x\eta^1(s)\|_2^2 ds. \end{aligned} \tag{13}$$

Proof. From (3), we obtain

$$\begin{aligned}
\psi_1'(t) &= \int_\Omega \left(-l_1\Delta_x^2 u - \int_0^\infty g_1(s)\Delta_x^2\eta^1(s)ds + \varphi_1(u,v)\right)\left(\int_0^\infty g_1(s)\eta^1(s)ds\right)dx \\
&\quad - \int_\Omega \left(\Delta_x u_t(t) - \frac{1}{1+\ell}|u_t|^\ell u_t\right)\int_0^\infty g_1(s)\eta_t^1(s)dsdx \\
&= \underbrace{l_1\int_\Omega \Delta_x u(t)\int_0^\infty g_1(s)\Delta_x\eta^1(s)dsdx}_{=I_1} + \underbrace{\int_\Omega\left(\int_0^\infty g_1(s)\Delta_x\eta^1(s)ds\right)^2dx}_{=I_2} \\
&\quad + \underbrace{\int_\Omega \varphi_1(u,v)\int_0^\infty g_1(s)\eta^1(s)dsdx}_{=I_3} + \underbrace{\int_\Omega \nabla_x u_t\int_0^\infty g_1(s)\nabla_x\eta_t^1(s)dsdx}_{=I_4} \qquad (14) \\
&\quad + \underbrace{\int_\Omega |u_t|^\ell u_t\int_0^\infty g_1(s)\eta_t^1(s)dsdx}_{=I_5}.
\end{aligned}$$

By using Young and Hölder's inequality, we conclude that for any $\delta_1 > 0$,

$$I_1 \le \delta_1\|\Delta_x u\|^2 + \frac{l_1^2(1-\ell_1)}{4\delta_1}\|\eta^1\|_{\mathcal{M}_1}^2, \qquad (15)$$

$$I_2 \le (1-l_1)\|\eta^1\|_{\mathcal{M}_1}^2, \qquad (16)$$

and

$$\begin{aligned}
I_3 &\le \delta_1\int_\Omega|\varphi_1(u,v)|^2dx + \frac{1}{4\delta_1}\int_\Omega\left(\int_0^\infty g_1(s)\eta^1(s)ds\right)^2dx \qquad (17) \\
&\le C\delta_1(\|\nabla_x u\|^2 + \|\nabla_x v\|^2)^{2\ell+3} + \frac{(1-l_1)c_s^2}{4\delta_1}\int_0^\infty g_1(s)\|\nabla_x\eta^1(s)\|^2ds \\
&\le C\delta_1\left(\frac{2(\ell+2)}{\ell+1}E(0)\right)^{2\ell+1}(\|\nabla_x u\|^2 + \|\nabla_x v\|^2) + \frac{(1-\ell_1)c_s^2}{4\delta_1}\int_0^\infty g_1(s)\|\nabla_x\eta^1(s)\|^2ds \\
&\le \frac{\delta_1}{\lambda_1}C\left(\frac{2(\ell+2)}{\ell+1}E(0)\right)^{2\ell+1}(\|\Delta_x u\|_2^2 + \delta_1\|\Delta_x v\|_2^2) + \frac{(1-l_1)c_s^2}{4\delta_1\lambda_1}\int_0^\infty g_1(s)\|\Delta_x\eta^1(s)\|^2ds,
\end{aligned}$$

where we used the fact

$$\int_\Omega|\varphi_1(u,v)|^2dx \le C(\|\nabla_x u\|^2 + \|\nabla_x v\|^2)^{2p+3}.$$

Noting that

$$\begin{aligned}
\int_0^\infty g_1(s)\eta_t^1(s)ds &= -\int_0^\infty g_1(s)\eta_s^1(s)ds + \int_0^\infty u_t(t)g_1(s)ds \\
&= \int_0^\infty g_1'(s)\eta^1(s)ds + (1-l_1)u_t, \qquad (18)
\end{aligned}$$

I_4 can be estimated as follows:

$$\begin{aligned} I_4 &= (1-l_1)\|\nabla_x u_t\|_2^2 + \int_\Omega \nabla_x u_t \int_0^\infty g_1'(s)\eta^1(s)dsdx \\ &\leq \frac{3(1-l_1)}{4}\|\nabla_x u_t\|_2^2 + \frac{1}{1-l_1}\int_\Omega \left(\int_0^\infty -g_1'(s)ds\right)\left(\int_0^\infty -g_1'(s)\nabla_x\eta^1(s)ds\right)dx \\ &\leq \frac{3(1-l_1)}{4}\|\nabla_x u_t\|_2^2 - \frac{g_1(0)}{1-l_1}\int_0^\infty g_1'(s)\|\nabla_x\eta^1(s)\|_2^2 ds \\ &\leq \frac{3(1-l_1)}{4}\|\nabla_x u_t\|_2^2 - \frac{g_1(0)}{\lambda_1(1-l_1)}\int_0^\infty g_1'(s)\|\Delta_x\eta^1(s)\|_2^2 ds, \end{aligned} \tag{19}$$

by using (18), we obtain

$$\begin{aligned} I_5 &= (1-l_1)\|u_t\|_{\ell+2}^{\ell+2} + \int_\Omega |u_t|^\ell u_t \int_0^\infty g_1'(s)\eta^1(s)dsdx \\ &\leq \frac{3(1-l_1)}{4}\|u_t\|_{\ell+2}^{\ell+2} + \frac{1}{1-l_1}\int_\Omega \left(\int_0^\infty -g_1'(s)ds\right)\left(\int_0^\infty -g_1'(s)\eta^1(s)ds\right)dx \\ &\leq \frac{3(1-l_1)}{4}\|u_t\|_{\ell+2}^{\ell+2} - \frac{g_1(0)c_s^2}{1-l_1}\int_0^\infty g_1'(s)\|\nabla_x\eta^1(s)\|_2^2 ds \\ &\leq \frac{3(1-l_1)}{4}\|u_t\|_{\ell+2}^{\ell+2} - \frac{g_1(0)c_s^2}{\lambda_1(1-l_1)}\int_0^\infty g_1'(s)\|\Delta_x\eta^1(s)\|_2^2 ds. \end{aligned} \tag{20}$$

Inserting (15), (16), (17), (19), and (20) into (14), we obtain (13). This completes the proof. □

We have the following lemma using the same argument as Lemma 3.

Lemma 4. *According to the assumptions of Theorem 1, the functional ψ_2 defined by*

$$\psi_2(t) = \int_\Omega \left(\Delta_x v_t(t) - \frac{1}{1+\ell}|v_t|^\ell v_t\right)\int_0^\infty g_2(s)\eta^2(s)dsdx,$$

satisfies, along the solution of system (3) *for some positive constant c_3, δ_1,*

$$\begin{aligned} \psi_2'(t) &\leq \delta_1\left[\frac{c}{\lambda_1}\left(\frac{2(\ell+2)}{\ell+1}E(0)\right)^{2\ell+1} + 1\right]\|\Delta_x v\|_2^2 \\ &+ (1-l_2)\left[\frac{l_2^2}{4\delta_1} + 1 + \frac{c_s^2}{4\delta_1\lambda_1}\right]\int_0^\infty g_2(s)\Delta_x\eta^2(s)ds \\ &+\frac{\delta_1 c}{\lambda_1}\left(\frac{2(\ell+2)}{\ell+1}E(0)\right)^{\ell+1}\|\Delta_x u\|_2^2 + \frac{3(1-l_2)}{4}\|\Delta_x v_t\|_2^2 + \frac{3(1-l_1)}{4}\|v_t\|_{\ell+2}^{\ell+2} \\ &-\frac{2g_2(0)}{\lambda_1(1-l_2)}\int_0^\infty g_2'(s)\|\Delta_x\eta^2(s)\|_2^2 ds. \end{aligned}$$

In the sequel, we shall define the functional $\mathcal{L}(t)$ by

$$\mathcal{L}(t) = E(t) + \varepsilon_1\phi(t) + \varepsilon_2(\psi_1(t) + \psi_2(t)),$$

where ε_1 and ε_2 are positive constants that will be determined later.

Lemma 5. *For small enough $\varepsilon_1 > 0$ and $\varepsilon_2 > 0$,we can obtain for any $t \geq 0$,*

$$\frac{1}{2}E(t) \leq \mathcal{L}(t) \leq \frac{3}{2}E(t). \tag{21}$$

Proof. It is not difficult to see that a positive constant $\varepsilon > 0$ exists, such that

$$
\begin{aligned}
|\mathcal{L}(t) - E(t)| &\leq \frac{\varepsilon_1 + \varepsilon_2}{2}(\|u_t\|_{\ell+2}^{\ell+2} + \|v_t\|_{\ell+2}^{\ell+2} + \|\nabla_x u_t\|_2^2 + \|\nabla_x v_t\|_2^2) \\
&\quad + \varepsilon_1 \|\Delta_x u\|^2 + \varepsilon_2 \|\Delta_x v\|^2 + C\varepsilon_2 \int_0^\infty g_1(s) \|\Delta_x \eta^1(s)\|^2 ds \\
&\quad + C\varepsilon_2 \int_0^\infty g_2(s) \|\Delta_x \eta^2(s)\|^2 ds + \varepsilon_1 \int_\Omega \Phi(u,v) dx \\
&\leq \varepsilon E(t).
\end{aligned}
$$

This implies that

$$
(1-\varepsilon)E(t) \leq \mathcal{L}(t) \leq (1+\varepsilon)E(t).
$$

Noting that $\varepsilon > 0$ is small enough if $\varepsilon_1 > 0$ and $\varepsilon_2 > 0$ are small. Hence, we can obtain (21) if we choose small enough $\varepsilon_1 > 0$ and $\varepsilon_2 > 0$.

This completes the proof. □

Lemma 6. *Two positive constants, k_0 and k_1, exist such that for any $t \geq 0$,*

$$
\mathcal{L}'(t) \leq -k_0 E(t) + k_1 \left(\int_0^\infty g_1(s) \|\Delta_x \eta^1(s)\|_2^2 ds + \int_0^\infty g_2(s) \|\Delta_x \eta^2(s)\|_2^2 ds \right). \tag{22}
$$

Proof. It follows from Lemmata 1–4, that for any $t \geq 0$,

$$
\begin{aligned}
\mathcal{L}'(t) \leq\ & -\left(\varepsilon_1 - \frac{3(1-l_1)}{4}\varepsilon_2\right)\|u_t\|_{\ell+2}^{\ell+2} - \left(\varepsilon_1 - \frac{3(1-l_2)}{4}\varepsilon_2\right)\|v_t\|_{\ell+2}^{\ell+2} \\
& - \left[\varepsilon_1 c' - \varepsilon_2 \left\{ \frac{2\delta_1 c}{\lambda_1} \left(\frac{2(\ell+2)}{(\ell+1)} E(0) \right)^{2\ell+1} \right\}\right] \|\Delta_x u\|_2^2 \\
& - \left[\varepsilon_1 c'' - \varepsilon_2 \left\{ \frac{2\delta_1 c}{\lambda_1} \left(\frac{2(\ell+2)}{(\ell+1)} E(0) \right)^{2\ell+1} \right\}\right] \|\Delta_x v\|_2^2 \\
& - \left[\varepsilon_1 \left[1 - \delta_1 c_s^2 \frac{\ell+2}{\ell+1} \left(\frac{2(\ell+2)}{(\ell+1)} E(0) \right)^{\ell+1}\right] - \varepsilon_2 \frac{3(1-l_1)}{4}\right] \|\Delta_x u_t\|_2^2 \\
& - \left[\varepsilon_1 \left[1 - \delta_1 c_s^2 \frac{\ell+2}{\ell+1} \left(\frac{2(\ell+2)}{(\ell+1)} E(0) \right)^{\ell+1}\right] - \varepsilon_2 \frac{3(1-l_2)}{4}\right] \|\Delta_x v_t\|_2^2 \\
& + \left[\varepsilon_1 \left[\frac{(1-l_1)l_1^2}{4\delta_1} + 1 + \frac{c_s^2}{4\delta_1 \lambda_1} + c_1\right]\right] \int_0^\infty g_1(s) \|\Delta_x \eta^1(s)\|_2^2 ds \\
& + \left[\varepsilon_1 \left(\frac{(1-l_1)l_2^2}{4\delta_1} + 1 + \frac{c_s^2}{4\delta_1 \lambda_1} + c_1\right)\right] \int_0^\infty g_2(s) \|\Delta_x \eta^2(s)\|_2^2 ds \\
& + \left(\frac{1}{2} - \frac{2\varepsilon_2 g_1(0)}{\lambda_1(1-\ell_1)}\right) \int_0^\infty g_1'^1(s)\|_2^2 ds \\
& + \left[\frac{1}{2} - \frac{2\varepsilon_2 g_2(0)}{\lambda_1(1-\ell_2)}\right] \int_0^\infty g_2'^2(s)\|_2^2 ds - (p+1)\varepsilon_1 \int_\Omega \Phi(u,v) dx.
\end{aligned}
$$

First, we take δ_1 satisfying

$$
\delta_1 < \frac{1}{c_s^2 \frac{(\ell+2)}{(\ell+1)} \left(\frac{2(\ell+2)}{(\ell+1)} E(0) \right)^{\ell+1}}.
$$

Now, choose small enough $\varepsilon_2 > 0$ so that

$$\varepsilon_1\left[1-\delta_1 c_s^2\frac{\ell+2}{\ell+1}\left(\frac{2(\ell+2)}{(\ell+1)}E(0)\right)^{\ell+1}\right]-\varepsilon_2\frac{3(1-l_1)}{4}>0,$$

$$\varepsilon_1\left[1-\delta_1 c_s^2\frac{\ell+2}{\ell+1}\left(\frac{2(\ell+2)}{(\ell+1)}E(0)\right)^{\ell+1}\right]-\varepsilon_2\frac{3(1-l_2)}{4}>0,$$

$$\varepsilon_1-\frac{3(1-l_1)}{4}\varepsilon_2>0,\quad \varepsilon_1-\frac{3(1-l_2)}{4}\varepsilon_2>0.$$

In light of the above estimates, we can obtain (22). The proof is completed. □

Theorem 2. *Assume that (A_1)–(A_4) hold. Let $(u_0, v_0, u_1, v_1, \eta^{10}, \eta^{20}) \in \widetilde{\mathcal{H}}$. Then, two constants $\mu \in (0,1)$ and $\delta_1 > 0$ exist such that for any $\delta_0 \in (0, \mu]$,*

$$E(t) \le \delta_1\left(1+\int_0^t h^{1-\delta_0}(s)\right)exp\left(-\delta_0\int_0^t \zeta(s)ds\right)+\delta_1\int_t^\infty h(s)ds, \tag{23}$$

where $\zeta(t) = \min\{\zeta_1(t), \zeta_2(t)\}$ and $h(t) = \max\{g_1(t), g_2(t)\}$.

In order to prove this theorem, the following lemma from [20] is needed.

Lemma 7 ([20]). *Under the assumptions of Theorem 2, two constants $\beta_1 > 0$ and $\beta_2 > 0$ exist such that for any $t \ge 0$,*

$$\zeta(t)\mathcal{L}'(t)+\beta_1 E'(t) \le -k_0\zeta(t)E(t)+\beta_2\zeta(t)\int_t^\infty h(s)ds,$$

where $\zeta(t) = \min\{\zeta_1(t), \zeta_2(t)\}$ and $h(t) = \max\{g_1(t), g_2(t)\}$.

Proof of Theorem 2. Define the functional $\mathcal{E}(t)$ by

$$\mathcal{E}(t) = \zeta(t)\ell(t) + \beta_1 E(t). \tag{24}$$

It is not difficult to verify that $\mathcal{E}(t) \sim E(t)$. Let

$$R(t) = \zeta(t)\int_0^\infty h(s)ds.$$

Using (24) and the fact that $\zeta(t) > 0$ and $\zeta'(t) \le 0$ a.e. $t \ge 0$, we deduce that for some $\gamma_0 > 0$,

$$\mathcal{E}'(t) \le -\gamma_0\zeta(t)\mathcal{E}(t) + \beta_2 R(t), \qquad a.e.\ t \ge 0.$$

In addition, the following inequality holds for any $\delta_0 \in (0, \gamma_0]$,

$$\mathcal{E}'(t) \le -\delta_0\zeta(t)\mathcal{E}(t) + \beta_2 R(t), \qquad \text{a.e. } t \ge 0. \tag{25}$$

Integrating (25) over $[0, T]$ leads to

$$\mathcal{E}(T) \le e^{-\delta_0\int_0^T\zeta(s)ds}\left(\mathcal{E}(0)+\beta_2\int_0^T e^{\delta_0\int_0^T\zeta(s)ds}R(t)dt\right),$$

which, together with the fact $\mathcal{E}(t) \sim E(t)$, yields

$$E(T) \le \frac{1}{\beta_1}e^{-\delta_0\int_0^T\zeta(s)ds}\left(\mathcal{E}(0)+\beta_2\int_0^T e^{\delta_0\int_0^T\zeta(s)ds}R(t)dt\right). \tag{26}$$

It follows that

$$\begin{aligned}\int_0^T e^{\delta_0 \int_0^T \zeta(s)ds} R(t)dt &= \frac{1}{\delta_0}\int_0^T \left(\int_0^\infty h(s)ds\right)\frac{d}{dt}\left(e^{\delta_0 \int_0^T \zeta(s)ds}\right)dt \\ &= \frac{1}{\delta_0}(e^{\delta_0 \int_0^t \zeta(s)ds}\int_T^\infty h(s)ds - \int_0^\infty h(s)ds \\ &+ \int_0^T e^{\delta_0 \int_0^t \zeta(s)ds} h(t)dt).\end{aligned} \tag{27}$$

Inserting (27) into (26) gives

$$E(T) \le \frac{1}{\beta_1}\left(\mathcal{E}(0) + \frac{\beta_2}{\delta_0}\int_0^T e^{\delta_0 \int_0^t \zeta(s)ds} h(t)dt\right)e^{-\delta_0 \int_0^T \zeta(s)ds} + \frac{\beta_2}{\beta_1\delta_0}\int_T^\infty h(s)ds. \tag{28}$$

By using (A_1), we infer that for any $t \ge 0$,

$$\begin{aligned}&\frac{d}{dt}\left(e^{\int_0^t \zeta(s)ds}(g_1(t)+g_2(t))\right) \\ =\ & (g_1'(t)+g_2'(t))e^{\int_0^t \zeta(s)ds} + (g_1(t)+g_2(t))\zeta(t)e^{\int_0^t \zeta(s)ds} \\ \le\ & [-\zeta_1(t)g_1(t) - \zeta_2(t)g_2(t)]e^{\int_0^t \zeta(s)ds} + \zeta(t)(g_1(t)+g_2(t))e^{\int_0^t \zeta(s)ds} \\ \le\ & [(\zeta(t)-\zeta_1(t))g_1(t) + (\zeta(t)-\zeta_2(t))g_2(t)]e^{\int_0^t \zeta(s)ds} \le 0.\end{aligned} \tag{29}$$

It follows from (29) that

$$e^{\int_0^t \zeta(s)ds} h(t) \le e^{\int_0^t \zeta(s)ds}(g_1(t)+g_2(t)) \le g_1(0)+g_2(0) \le 2h(0),$$

and

$$\int_0^T e^{\delta_0 \int_0^t \zeta(s)ds} h(t)dt \le (2h(0))^{\delta_0}\int_0^T h^{1-\delta_0}(t)dt.$$

Therefore, (23) follows from (28) and (29), and thus demonstrating Theorem 2. □

Remark 1. *If* $\varepsilon_0 \in (0,1)$ *exists, for which*

$$\int_0^{+\infty} (h(s))^{1-\varepsilon_0} ds < +\infty, \tag{30}$$

then we can choose $0 < \delta_0 \le \gamma_1$, $\gamma_1 = \min\{\varepsilon_0, \gamma_0\}$, *such that* $\int_0^{+\infty}(h(s))^{1-\delta_0}ds < +\infty$, *and, consequently,* (23) *takes the form*

$$E(t) \le \delta_2\left(exp\left(-\delta_0\int_0^t \zeta(s)ds\right) + \int_t^\infty h(s)ds\right), \quad \delta_2 > 0. \tag{31}$$

4. Kernels with Exponential Decay

In this section, we investigate the cases of exponentially decaying kernels, and the results will be obtained without (A_1).

Theorem 3. *Assume that* (A_2)*–*(A_4) *hold true. Let* $(u_0, v_0, u_1, v_1, \eta^{10}, \eta^{20}) \in \widetilde{\mathcal{H}}$, *such that*

$$g_i'(t) \le -\xi_i g_i(t), \quad \text{for } t \ge 0,\ i \in \{1,2\}.$$

Then, there are two constants $\mu > 0$ *and* $\delta_1 > 0$*; we have*

$$E(t) \le \delta_1 e^{-\mu t}. \tag{32}$$

Proof. We multiply (23) by $\xi = \min\{\xi_1, \xi_2\}$ and use Lemma 1 to obtain

$$\xi \mathcal{L}'(t) \leq -k_0 \xi E(t) + k_1 \xi \bigg(\int_0^\infty g_1(s) \|\Delta_x \eta^1(s)\|^2 ds + \int_0^\infty g_2(s) \|\Delta_x \eta^2(s)\|^2 ds \bigg). \quad (33)$$

Now, using the fact that

$$\begin{aligned} k_1 \bigg(\int_0^\infty g_1(s) \|\Delta_x \eta^1(s)\|^2 ds + \int_0^\infty g_2(s) \|\Delta_x \eta^2(s)\|^2 ds \bigg) &\leq -\frac{k_1}{\xi} \int_0^\infty g_1(s)'^1(s)\|^2 ds \\ &\quad -\frac{k_1}{\xi} \int_0^\infty g_2(s)'^2(s)\|^2 ds \\ &\leq -cE'(t). \end{aligned} \quad (34)$$

implies that

$$\xi \mathcal{L}'(t) \leq -k_0 \xi E(t) - cE'(t).$$

The functional $\Phi = \xi \mathcal{L}(t) + cE(t)$ satisfies $\Phi \sim E$; we easily obtain

$$E(t) \leq \delta_1 e^{-\mu t}.$$

□

Remark 2. *It is worth mentioning here that our stability result was obtained without imposing the condition (A_4), which was imposed in [20].*

5. Examples

We illustrate the energy decay rate given by Theorem 2 throughout the following examples, which are introduced in [9].

Example 1. *Let $g_i(t) = a_i e^{-b_i(1+t)}$, with $b_i > 0$ and $a_i > 0$, for $i \in \{1,2\}$ small enough so that (A_1), with $(\zeta_i)_{i\in\{1,2\}} = (b_i)_{i\in\{1,2\}}$, holds. In this case, $\zeta(t) = \min\{b_1, b_2\} = b_0$ and $h(t) = A_0 e^{-b_0(1+t)}$, where $A_0 = \max\{a_1, a_2\}$. Then, (30) is satisfied and, consequently, (31) gives, for two positive constants c_1, c_2,*

$$E(t) \leq c_1 e^{-c_2(1+t)}, \quad \text{for all } t \in \mathbb{R}^+.$$

Example 2. *Let $g_i(t) = \frac{a_i}{(1+t)^{b_i}}$, with $b_i > 1$ and $a_i > 0$, for $i \in \{1,2\}$ small enough so that (A_1) with $(\zeta_i)_{i\in\{1,2\}} = \left(\frac{b_i}{1+t}\right)_{i\in\{1,2\}}$ holds. In this case, $\zeta(t) = \frac{b_0}{1+t}$ and $h(t) = \frac{A_0}{(1+t)^{b_0}}$, where $A_0 = \max\{a_1, a_2\}$ and $b_0 = \min\{b_1, b_2\}$. Then, (30) is satisfied, and, hence, (31) yields*

$$E(t) \leq c_1 e^{-c_2 \ln(1+t)} = c_1 (1+t)^{-c_2}, \quad \text{for all } t \in \mathbb{R}^+,$$

where $\zeta(t) = \min\{\zeta_1(t), \zeta_2(t)\}$, $\quad h(t) = \max\{g_1(t), g_2(t)\}$.

6. Concluding Remarks

The main purpose of this paper was to establish the solution of nonlinear systems in coupling Petrovsky–Petrovsky systems with infinite memory under minimum assumptions on the functions g_1, g_2 and φ_1, φ_2. Moreover, the general decay rate of the relevant energy is also established. The results are limited on the bounded domain Ω of $\mathbb{R}^n$. To conclude, we should mention that the original contributions in the present paper are:

1. We used classical methods to solve a non-trivial problem with useful new results to rival state-of-the-art work in Thorems 1–3.
2. It is shown that we are able to link the rate of decrease to the energy functional associated with the solution directly to that of the functions g_1, g_2, with an improvement in the conditions taken on these relaxation functions in (23).

3. We found that the two functions g_1, g_2 are responsible for the decay rate of the energy functional and then that of the existed solution. On the other hand, the functions φ_1, φ_2 obstruct the solution if they can overcome and dominate [23].
4. We give more cases to the kernel functions to discuss their impact on the decay rate.

Author Contributions: Writing—original draft preparation, M.F., A.B.C. and T.B.; writing—review and editing, H.S., A.M. and T.A.; supervision, A.H. All authors have read and agreed to the published version of the manuscript.

Funding: This research received no external funding.

Data Availability Statement: Not applicable.

Acknowledgments: The researchers would like to thank the Deanship of Scientific Research, Qassim University for their continuous support.

Conflicts of Interest: The authors declare no conflict of interest.

References

1. Bahlil, M.; Feng, B. Global existence and energy decay of solutions to a coupled wave and Petrovsky system with nonlinear dissipations and source terms. *Mediterr. J. Math.* **2020**, *17*, 27. [CrossRef]
2. Rashidinia, J.; Mohammadi, R. Tension spline approach for the numerical solution of nonlinear Klein–Gordon equation. *Comput. Phys. Commun.* **2010**, *181*, 78–91. [CrossRef]
3. Nikan, O.; Avazzadeh, Z.; Rasoulizadeh, M.N. Soliton wave solutions of nonlinear mathematical models in elastic rods and bistable surfaces. *Eng. Anal. Bound. Elem.* **2022**, *143*, 14–27. [CrossRef]
4. Segal, I.E. The global Cauchy problem for a relativistic scalar field with power interaction. *Bull. Soc. Math. France* **1963**, *91*, 129–135. [CrossRef]
5. Choucha, A.; Ouchenane, D.; Zennir, K. Exponential growth of solution with Lp-norm for class of non-linear viscoelastic wave equation with distributed delay term for large initial data. *Open J. Math. Anal.* **2020**, *3*, 76–83. [CrossRef]
6. Choucha, A.; Ouchenane, D.; Zennir, K. General Decay of Solutions in One-Dimensional Porous-Elastic with Memory and Distributed Delay Term. *Tamkang J. Math.* **2021**, *52*, 1–17. [CrossRef]
7. Moumen, A.; Beniani, A.; Alraqad, T.; Saber, H.; Ali, E.E.; Bouhali, K.; Zennir, K. Energy decay of solution for nonlinear delayed transmission problem. *AIMS Math.* **2023**, *8*, 13815–13829. [CrossRef]
8. Doud, N.; Boulaaras, S. Global existence combined with general decay of solutions for coupled Kirchhoff system with a distributed delay term. *Rev. Real Acad. Cienc. Exactas Fís. Nat. Ser. A Mat.* **2020**, *114*, 1–31. [CrossRef]
9. Wu, S.T. On decay and blow-up of solutions for a system of nonlinear wave equations. *J. Math. Anal. Appl.* **2012**, *394*, 360–377. [CrossRef]
10. Zennir, K. Stabilization for Solutions of Plate Equation with Time-Varying Delay and Weak-Viscoelasticity in $\mathbb{R}^n$. *Russ. Math.* **2020**, *64*, 21–33. [CrossRef]
11. Bahri, N.; Abdelli, M.; Beniani, A.; Zennir, K. Well-posedness and general energy decay of solution for transmission problem with weakly nonlinear dissipative. *J. Integral Equ. Appl.* **2021**, *33*, 155–170. [CrossRef]
12. Laouar, L.K.; Zennir, K.; Boulaaras, S. The sharp decay rate of thermoelastic transmission system with infinite memories. *Rend. Circ. Mat. Palermo II Ser.* **2020**, *69*, 403–423. [CrossRef]
13. Laouar, L.K.; Zennir, K.; Boulaaras, S. General decay of nonlinear viscoelastic Kirchhoff equation with Balakrishnan-Taylor damping and logarithmic nonlinearity. *Math. Meth. Appl. Sci.* **2019**, *42*, 4795–4814.
14. Liu, W. Uniform decay of solutions for a quasilinear system of viscoelastic equations. *Nonlinear Anal.* **2009**, *71*, 2257–2267. [CrossRef]
15. Rammaha, M.A. Sakuntasathien, Sawanya. Global existence and blow up of solutions to systems of nonlinear wave equations with degenerate damping and source terms. *Nonlinear Anal.* **2010**, *72*, 2658–2683. [CrossRef]
16. Ono, K. Global existence, decay, and blowup of solutions for some mildly degenerate nonlinear Kirchhoff strings. *J. Diff. Equ.* **1997**, *137*, 273–301. [CrossRef]
17. Liang, F.; Gao, H. Exponential energy decay and blow-up of solutions for a system of nonlinear viscoelastic wave equations with strong damping. *Bound. Value Probl.* **2011**, *2011*, 19. [CrossRef]
18. Han, X.; Wang, M. Global existence and blow-up of solutions for a system of nonlinear viscoelastic wave equations with damping and source. *Nonlinear Anal.* **2009**, *71*, 5427–5450. [CrossRef]
19. Pata, V. Stability and exponential stability in linear viscoelasticity. *Milan J. Math.* **2009**, *77*, 333–360. [CrossRef]
20. Messaoudi, S.A.; Al-Gharabli, M. A general decay result of a nonlinear system of wave equations with infinite memories. *Appl. Math. Comput.* **2015**, *259*, 540–551. [CrossRef]
21. Guesmia, A. Energy decay for a damped nonlinear coupled system. *J. Math. Anal. Appl.* **1999**, *239*, 38–48. [CrossRef]

22. Dafermos, C.M. Asymptotic stability in viscoelasticity. *Arch. Rational Mech. Anal.* **1970**, *37*, 297–308. [CrossRef]
23. Appleby, J.A.D.; Fabrizio, M.; Lazzari, B.; Reynolds, D.W. On exponential asymptotic stability in linear viscoelasticity. *Math. Meth. Appl. Sci.* **2006**, *16*, 1677–1694. [CrossRef]

mathematics

MDPI

Article

Algorithmic Approach for a Unique Definition of the Next-Generation Matrix

Florin Avram [1,*,†], Rim Adenane [2,†], Lasko Basnarkov [3,†] and Matthew D. Johnston [4,†]

1 Laboratoire de Mathématiques Appliquées, Université de Pau, 64000 Pau, France
2 Laboratoire des Equations aux Dérivées Partielles, Algébre et Géométrie Spectrales, Département des Mathématiques, Université Ibn-Tofail, Kenitra 14000, Morocco; rim.adenane@uit.ac.ma
3 Faculty of Computer Science and Engineering, Ss. Cyril and Methodius University in Skopje, 1000 Skopje, North Macedonia; lasko.basnarkov@finki.ukim.mk
4 Department of Mathematics, Computer Science Lawrence Technological University, 21000 W 10 Mile Rd., Southfield, MI 48075, USA; mjohnsto1@ltu.edu
* Correspondence: avramf3@gmail.com
† These authors contributed equally to this work.

Abstract: The basic reproduction number R_0 is a concept which originated in population dynamics, mathematical epidemiology, and ecology and is closely related to the mean number of children in branching processes (reflecting the fact that the phenomena of interest are well approximated via branching processes, at their inception). Despite the very extensive literature around R_0 for deterministic epidemic models, we believe there are still aspects which are not fully understood. Foremost is the fact that R_0 is not a function of the original ODE model, unless we also include in it a certain (F, V) gradient decomposition, which is not unique. This is related to the specification of the "infected compartments", which is also not unique. A second interesting question is whether the extinction probabilities of the natural continuous time Markovian chain approximation of an ODE model around boundary points (disease-free equilibrium and invasion points) are also related to the (F, V) gradient decomposition. We offer below several new contributions to the literature: (1) A universal algorithmic definition of a (F, V) gradient decomposition (and hence of the resulting R_0). (2) A fixed point equation for the extinction probabilities of a stochastic model associated to a deterministic ODE model, which may be expressed in terms of the (F, V) decomposition. Last but not least, we offer Mathematica scripts and implement them for a large variety of examples, which illustrate that our recipe offers always reasonable results, but that sometimes other reasonable (F, V) decompositions are available as well.

Keywords: deterministic epidemic model; disease-free equilibrium; stability threshold; basic reproduction number; (F, V) gradient decomposition; next-generation matrix; Jacobian approach; CTMC stochastic model associated to a deterministic epidemic model; probability of extinction; rational univariate representation

MSC: 34D20; 65L07; 37N30

Citation: Avram, F.; Adenane, R.; Basnarkov, L.; Johnston, M.D. Algorithmic Approach for a Unique Definition of the Next-Generation Matrix. *Mathematics* **2024**, *12*, 27. https://doi.org/10.3390/math12010027

Academic Editor: Mihaela Neamţu, Eva Kaslik, Anca Rădulescu

Received: 16 November 2023
Revised: 12 December 2023
Accepted: 13 December 2023
Published: 21 December 2023

1. Introduction

Motivation. Mathematical epidemiology had started by proposing simple models for specific epidemics and computing explicitly certain important characteristics like the basic reproduction number and the final size; for example, the SIR model was introduced, among other concepts, in the celebrated "A contribution to the mathematical theory of epidemics" [1]. The most fundamental, and actually the only general result of the field due to Diekmann, Heesterbeek, Van den Driesche and Watmough, expresses the disease-free equilibrium stability domain in terms of R_0, which is defined as the Perron–Frobenius eigenvalue of a certain (F, V) gradient decomposition (this is presented in detail in Section 2.2).

But, since the (F, V) decomposition is not unique, it seems to us that the question of what R_0 is still deserves further discussion.

On the other hand, one may note that nowadays, mathematical epidemiologists typically either restrict themselves to low-dimensional models, resolved symbolically, even by hand, or consider very complicated models which are resolved only numerically, for particular values gleaned from the medical literature. Missing from here are moderately complex models, which may be solved partly symbolically for any values of the parameters, but in a way where the use of computer algebra systems (CAS) is either indispensable or greatly facilitating. Even in the case of papers belonging to this level—see, for example [2], that the role of the CAS is deemphasized. Our paper is also an attempt to cast the CAS as one of the main heroes of our story.

Our main result . We provide below, for the first time, a universal recipe for choosing a natural (F, V) gradient decomposition, which only requires specifying the disease compartments (a subset of those which are zero for the boundary point under consideration) (informally, these are not far conceptually from the so-called fast components of singular perturbation theory). This decomposition is useful both for determining R_0 and for computing the extinction probabilities of an associated stochastic model. We identify also examples in which the (F, V) decomposition is not unique and in which choosing another decomposition with F of a lower rank may be beneficial for simplifying the R_0 formula.

First restriction (among others to follow). In this paper, we will restrict to mathematical epidemiology models for which there exist at least two possible special fixed states. The first, the disease-free equilibrium (DFE), corresponds to the elimination of all possible compartments involving sickness and will be assumed to be unique. Typically, this point is locally stable only for certain values of the parameters. Outside of this domain, it is typically replaced by another fixed point, which will be called "endemic" if all its components are positive, and "resident boundary point" otherwise.

Importantly, the stability of the DFE may be related to the historically famous **basic reproduction number** and **net reproduction rate**—see (1). These pillar concepts in population dynamics, mathematical epidemiology, virology, ecology, etc., were already introduced by the father of mathematical demography Lotka—see [3,4]—and also the introduction of the book [5], and in [6], the authors described the stability of the solution of differential systems.

A bit of history of the net reproduction rate $\mathcal{R}$, and its evolution into the mathematical concept of basic reproduction number/stability threshold R_0. Loosely speaking, in the case of only one infectious class, the net reproduction rate $\mathcal{R}$ describes the expected number of secondary cases which **one infected case** would produce in a homogeneous, completely susceptible population during the lifetime of the infection. This description is especially relevant at the start of an epidemic, when the dynamics is well approximated by that of a branching process (a fact which goes back to Bartlett and Kendall—see for example [7,8]). The main characteristic of a branching process is the "fertility", i.e., the expected number of descendants one individual produces in the next generation. As a consequence, in epidemiology, the branching result insuring extinction when the fertility is less than one translates into local stability results of the disease-free equilibrium involving $\mathcal{R}$.

The reproduction number $\mathcal{R}$ intervened already, in a particular case, in the foundational paper "A contribution to the mathematical theory of epidemics" [1], which showed that:

1. The condition

$$R_0 < 1, \quad \text{where } R_0 = \mathsf{s}_{dfe}\mathcal{R}, \tag{1}$$

implies local stability of the DFE. Here $\mathcal{R}$ is the net reproduction rate (number of secondary infections produced by one infectious individual), and s_{dfe} is the fraction of susceptibles at the DFE.

2. The condition

$$R_0 > 1$$

implies instability of the DFE.

With more infectious classes, one deals, at the inception of an epidemic, with approximate multi-class branching processes, whose stability is determined via a "**next-generation matrix** " (NGM)—see Section 2.2.

The "Jacobian approach" for computing R_0. For big size problems, this approach is doomed to fail symbolically, since it is equivalent to the Routh–Hurwitz conditions (RH), which rarely succeed symbolically beyond dimension 4 (also, RH is irrelevant numerically, since the eigenvalues themselves are just as easy to compute). Therefore, we studied below a variant, the "Jacobian factorization approach", which focuses on an approximation, which we show to yield always upper or lower bounds of the NGM R_0, depending on whether $R_0 \leq 1$ or not—see Theorem 1. Several questions around this bound are scattered below in Sections 6.3, 8.1, and 8.2.

Note, as mentioned in [9], that an example where the Jacobian method does not yield R_0 is offered in [10] (Exe 5.43) and that of [11] suggesting that when threshold parameters determined from the Jacobian do not have the biological interpretation of the dominant eigenvalue of the next-generation matrix, then they should not be called basic reproductive ratios nor denoted as R_0 (we follow their suggestion and use the notation R_J in this case).

The dilemma of the several different methods for computing R_0 has been discussed in many papers, see for example [9,12]. But, this is a direct consequence of the non-uniqueness of the (F, V) decomposition.

Deterministic or stochastic models? Most of the mathematical epidemiology papers belong exclusively to one of these two paradigms. However, any deterministic model may also be viewed as a stochastic continuous time Markov field (CTMC) evolving on the integers. One interesting CTMC, which seems not to have been discussed before, is presented in Section 2.4.

Contents. Our paper is structured as follows. Section 2 recalls the definition of the DFE and provides our algorithmic definition of the (F,V) decomposition, in the form of a Mathematica script, as well as a discussion—see Remark 6—of why other decompositions might turn out useful. This section also provides a new Equation (8) for computing extinction probabilities for associated continuous time Markov chain models in terms of the (F, V) decomposition, showing that the Jacobian factorization approach yields upper bounds and lower bounds for NGM R_0's in Appendix A.

We turn then to a series of examples, chosen to help investigate what may be the major open problem in the field nowadays, which, in our opinion, relates on one hand to R_0, and on the other hand, to the extinction probabilities—see below—and duration of minor epidemics [13–17], which is not further touched on here.

Let us now briefly explain why so many examples were included in the paper.

Section 4 is dedicated to a host-only model, with a single susceptible class and an F matrix of rank one, where the formula of R_0 may be "guessed by inspection" of the flow chart. These kinds of examples have kept alive the hope of "interpretable R_0 formulas", as illustrated in other recent papers—see for example [18,19]. But in fact, as far as we know, no interpretable R_0 formula has emerged outside the rank one case, which is already fully studied in [20]. The papers [18,19] start by presenting simple rank one cases, then proposing algorithms for more complex cases based on the graph structure of the flow chart, which, in our opinion, are not sufficiently detailed or documented. While it may well be that tools like Petri nets, as proposed in the second paper, will one day succeed for resolving flow charts with certain structures, this does not seem to have happened yet. Also, for models with a next-generation matrix of high rank, the lack of simple formulas for R_0 and of "simple biological interpretations" is naturally to be expected; simple formulas for the spectral radius can only be a consequence of a simple graph structure which has not been pinpointed yet.

Sections 5.1 and 7.1 offer two examples in which several R_0 formulas were offered in the literature, but we are at a loss of how to choose among them. In the first case (a virus–tumor model), the recipe R_0 is simpler than its competitor, but in the second case (a vector–host model), it is more complicated.

Section 6.2 shows that the boundary equilibria and the (invasion) reproduction numbers may be easily computed with our scripts; to illustrate this, we use a two-strain host-only model from [21] (Ch.8), where our recipe NGM yields the same answer as that given by the Jacobian factorization.

Section 6.3 offers another two-strain host-only example, this time including also vaccination, in which our recipe NGM yields again the same answer as that given by the Jacobian factorization.

Section 7.2 offers an example from the textbook of [21] in which the square relation stops holding.

Sections 8.1 and 8.2 offer yet more examples, this time in the two-strain vector–host context, in which our recipe NGM yields an R_0 formula which is precisely the square root of that given by the Jacobian approach. Note that here, the first of the three elegant relations concerning the invasion numbers from Section 6.3—see Remark 22—holds, but the other two seem to break down.

The last subsection provides, for the invasion numbers, a second example where another choice of R_0 may be more reasonable, on the grounds of leading to a simpler answer (but the admissibility requirement forces then extra assumptions on the parameters).

2. A Bird's Eye View of Mathematical Epidemiology: The Disease-Free Equilibrium, the Next-Generation Matrix, and an Algorithmic Definition of a Stability Threshold Associated to the Basic Reproduction Number R_0

2.1. The Disease-Free Equilibrium (DFE)

The DFE may be defined as a "maximal boundary state" and may be found by identifying a maximal sub-system of the ODE epidemic model which factors

$$i' = Mi, \tag{2}$$

where the prime denotes the derivative with respect to time, and M is a matrix that may depend on $\boldsymbol{i}$, but also may not explode in the domain of interest, which we will take for the sake of simplicity to be $\mathbb{R}^n_+$.

Remark 1. *One fixed point of this system is* $\boldsymbol{i} = 0$*. This motivates us to call the components* $\boldsymbol{i}$ *disease or infectious states. The set of all its indices will be denoted by* $\mathcal{I}$*. Note that specifying '*$\mathcal{I}$ *induces a partition of both the coordinates and the equations of our original system into infection (eliminable) and "non-infection" (the others) components.*

The eventual other fixed points may be found by solving $M = 0$ *together with the other non-infection equations under the condition* $\boldsymbol{i} = 0$*.*

In this paper, we will assume the uniqueness of the DFE, at least after excluding biologically irrelevant fixed points, like an unreachable origin.

We end this section with the very elementary script that implements this. Note that any ODE model "mod" (like SIR, etc...) is a pair mod = (dyn,X) consisting of a vector field "dyn" and a list of variables "X", and that to find any boundary fixed point, it suffices to know the set of indices "inf" where it is 0, so that we solve the system "dyn==0" under the condition "X[[inf]]->0". But, since sometimes only numeric solutions are possible, our DFE Mathematica script below also has an optional numerical condition parameter "cn", which is taken by default as the empty set.

```
DFE[mod_,inf_,cn_:{}]:=Module[{dyn,X},
 dyn=mod[[1]]/.cn;X=mod[[2]];
 Solve[Thread[dyn==0]/.Thread[X[[inf]]->0],X]];
```

For the non-Mathematica users, only the Solve command is relevant, with the others being just Mathematica implementation details.

2.2. (F, V) Gradient Decompositions, the Next-Generation Matrix, R_0, and a Simple Recipe for Computing Them

From now on, the infection Equation (2) will be rewritten as

$$i' = \mathcal{F} - \mathcal{V} = (F - V)\boldsymbol{i}. \tag{3}$$

Of course, such a decomposition is not unique, but we will also ask, following [7,22,23], that F, the gradient of $\mathcal{F}$, is a matrix with non-negative elements, and $-V$, the gradient of $-\mathcal{V}$, is a Markovian generating matrix (i.e., a matrix with non-negative off-diagonal elements and non-positive row sums). Conceptually, F models input to the disease compartments from outside ("new infections"), and $-V$ models transfer between the disease compartments. Still, a priori, the decomposition (3) is not unique.

Example 1. *Let us illustrate this via an SIR example with superinfection parameter ξ, in which the classes S and R play symmetric roles inspired by the works of [24–26]*

$$\begin{cases} \mathsf{s}'(t) &= \Lambda_s - \mathsf{s}(t)[\beta_s \mathsf{i}(t)(1+\xi\mathsf{i}(t)) + d_s] + i_s\mathsf{i}(t) + \gamma_r\mathsf{r}(t) \\ \mathsf{i}'(t) &= \mathsf{i}(t)\Big[[\beta_s\mathsf{s}(t) + \beta_r\mathsf{r}(t)](1+\xi\mathsf{i}(t))\Big] - d_i\mathsf{i}(t), d_i = i_r + i_s + \Lambda_s + \Lambda_r + \delta. \\ \mathsf{r}'(t) &= \Lambda_r - \mathsf{r}(t)[\beta_r\mathsf{i}(t)(1+\xi\mathsf{i}(t)) + d_r] + i_r\mathsf{i}(t) + \gamma_s\mathsf{s}(t) \end{cases}$$

When $\xi = 0$, this reduces to the symmetric SIR model introduced for mathematical purposes by [25,26], in which births may also directly enter the R class, with parameter Λ_r, and may also infect, with parameter β_r. Furthermore, there are linear flows from i to both s and r, where the former does not make epidemiologic sense.

Here, the only infection equation, the second, is already written in a decomposed form $\mathcal{F} - \mathcal{V}, \mathcal{V} = d_i\mathsf{i}(t)$, and $F = \Big[[\beta_s\mathsf{s}(t) + \beta_r\mathsf{r}(t)](1+\xi\mathsf{i}(t))\Big] + \xi\mathsf{i}(t)[\beta_s\mathsf{s}(t) + \beta_r\mathsf{r}(t)]$.

Note that for the application of the next-generation matrix method, we must finally plug $\mathsf{i} = 0$; therefore, the second term in F, due to "superinfection", is irrelevant for this purpose.

Remark 2. *The possible non-uniqueness of the decomposition brings us to a delicate point in mathematical epidemiology. Anticipating a bit, since R_0 is the Perron–Frobenius eigenvalue of FV^{-1}, strictly speaking, R_0 is not determined just by an ODE epidemical model, but also by the (F, V) gradient decomposition. If we want an ODE epidemical model to uniquely determine an R_0, we must include, in the definition of the ODE epidemical model, the (F, V) gradient decomposition we also adopt.*

Remark 3. *For us, an ODE epidemic model is an ODE dynamical model in which a certain subset of equations, usually called "disease/infection" equations, referred from now on as a* **zeroable set***, admits at least one admissible decomposition* (3), *with $(\mathcal{F}, \mathcal{V})$ satisfying the conditions (A1–A5) of [23].*

Remark 4. *Note that* (3) *is the most common model used in population dynamics. This makes it natural to informally define ODE epidemic models as population dynamics models* (3), *with extra equations modeling interactions with the non-disease compartments, which admits at least one admissible decomposition.*

Remark 5. *The definition of ODE epidemic models above is imprecise, since it does not list all the requirements we must put on an ODE model. Some reasonable restrictions are*

1. *Essentially non-negative processes have a non-empty set of disease classes, so we deal with an epidemic (note, however, that we define disease classes in the sense of classes which satisfy* (2), *which excludes, for example, importation models).*
2. *Processes with a unique DFE, at least after excluding biologically irrelevant fixed points, like an unreachable origin.*
3. *The local stability domain of the DFE is non-empty and not the full set.*

4. *The dynamical system has polynomial coefficients to be able to take advantage of the remarkable symbolic computation tools available for this class.*

We make these assumptions because they are satisfied by most mathematical models which have already been used for modeling real-life biological phenomena. However, these assumptions might not be enough and further ones might be necessary for obtaining the currently missing precise definition of "real life ODE mathematical epidemiology models".

Remark 6. *Admissible decompositions need not be unique. A priori, one may "move terms from F to V", to lower its rank and simplify the formula for R_0, and also "move off-diagonal terms from V to F", which enlarges the domain of parameters which ensure that V^{-1} has positive terms. There is a tradeoff between these two possible moves, since the simplicity of R_0 comes at the cost of extra assumptions on the parameters. Our universal decomposition seems to strike a balance between the two directions.*

Remark 7. *It was emphasized from the outstart—see for example [12,27–29]—that an ODE mathematical epidemiology model might have several "admissible decompositions", which might yield distinct next-generation matrices and distinct R_0's.*

For any admissible decomposition, Diekmann, Heesterbeek, Van den Driesche, and Watmough established the following celebrated DFE stability theorem:

Proposition 1. *For any admissible decomposition (F, V), let*

$$R_0 = \rho(FV^{-1})$$

denote the Perron–Frobenius eigenvalue of the **next-generation matrix.** *Then, the DFE is unstable on $R_0 > 1$, and locally stable on $R_0 < 1$ [7,10,22,23].*

For a recent historical overview of R_0, next-generation matrices, and their calculation in many examples, we refer the reader to the delightful paper [30].

Unfortunately, the standard definition of a next-generation matrix (and hence of R_0) involves concepts like "new infections", which were defined in the original papers based on epidemiological considerations and therefore require the intervention of a human expert. This had created the impression that this method cannot be encapsulated into a computer program. However, we offer and implement below a simple algorithmic definition, based only on the structure of the system and of the "infectious/disease equations".

Our proposal is to use a special F-V decomposition, with F constructed as the positive part of all the interactions in the disease equations which involve both disease compartments and input/susceptible ones. The latter are defined as the complement of the disease compartments, after the possible removal of output compartments, which may be specified as deterministic functions of the other compartments (i.e., may be computed, once the other compartments are known). Note now that the concept of the "positive part of the interactions" may be hard to pinpoint mathematically, but useful enough to have been implemented in CAS's (Mathematica, Maple, Sage, etc.); this made us adopt the following definition:

Remark 8. *For a given zeroable set, an admissible (F, V) gradient decomposition* (3) *is one where F, the gradient of $\mathcal{F}$, does not contain, in its expanded form, syntactic minuses in its CAS representation, and also where V, the gradient of $\mathcal{V}$, is such that $-V$ is a "sub-generating matrix" under the assumption of non-negativity of all the model parameters.*

The problem of whether the R_0 of the decomposition provided satisfies, under certain conditions, the stability theorem of Van den Driessche and Watmough is still open; therefore, it should be viewed for now just as a recipe that works well in simple cases.

After lots of experimenting, we have found only few cases—see for example Section 8.2, where the recipe NGM has a serious competitor; it is for computing the invasion reproduction number for a two-strain vector–host model, with altered infectivity for co-infected vectors, and with ADE (antibody-dependent enhancement).

2.3. An Algorithmic $F - V$ Decomposition

We complement now the famous $\mathcal{F} - \mathcal{V}$ "equations decomposition" and the next-generation matrix method of [7,22,23] using a algorithmic $F - V$ decomposition.

1. The user supplies the model "mod" (a pair containing the RHS of the dynamical system and its variables) and the indices "inf" of the disease (or infectious) variables; the indices of the other compartments are denoted by "infc".
2. Subsequently, the Jacobian of the infectious equations M with respect to the corresponding variables is computed.
3. Define the interaction terms as terms in M which contain variables $s \in$ infc, and which, if positive, must end up in F. Their complement, denoted by $V1$, will form part of V.
4. As a first guess for F, $F1$ is constructed as the complement of $V1$. It contains all the interaction terms (which involve both disease and susceptible compartments).
5. F is obtained by retaining only the positive part of the matrix $F1$, i.e., the terms which do not contain syntactic minuses (we use the simplest algebraic representation of the equations and do not study the effect which algebraic manipulations introducing minuses might have). Finally, $V1$ is increased to V, which is the complement of F.
6. The script outputs $\{M, V1, F1, F, V, K\}$.

```
NGM[mod_,inf_]:=Module[{dyn,X,infc,M,V,F,F1,V1,K},
   dyn=mod[[1]];X=mod[[2]];
   infc=Complement[Range[Length[X]],inf];
   M=Grad[dyn[[inf]],X[[inf]]]
   (*The jacobian of the infectious equations*);
   V1=-M/.Thread[X[[infc]]->0]
   (*V1 is a first guess for V, retains all gradient terms which
   disappear when the non infectious components are null*);
   F1=M+V1
   (*F1 is a first guess for F, containing all other gradient terms*);
   F=Replace[F1, _. _?Negative -> 0, {2}];
   (*all terms in F1 containing minuses are set to 0*);
   V=F-M;
   K=(F . Inverse[V])/.Thread[X[[inf]]->0]//FullSimplify;
{M,V1,F1,F,V,K}]
```

Note that our NGM script requires a minimal input from the user, which is just the specification of the disease compartments; there is no need to specify "new infections".

The results of this decomposition seem to yield correct results in all the examples from the literature we checked. We would like to add that for dynamical systems satisfying the four conditions in Remark 5, this decomposition yields "admissible gradient decompositions" in the sense that V^{-1} will contain only non-negative terms, and that it is furthermore obtainable from an equations' decomposition, which is admissible in the sense of [23] and therefore yields the correct stability domain.

Remark 9. *Note that the "Replace" command in the script uses the powerful Mathematica capability of applying a "rule" to parts of an "expression", specified by "levelspec", and that it was furnished to us by the user Michael E2 in*

`https://mathematica.stackexchange.com/questions/286500/how-to-set-to-0-all-terms-in-a-matrix-which-contain-a-minus/287406?noredirect=1#comment715559_287406`

Finally, let us discuss an alternative possible implementation. We could just provide NGM with the right-hand side of the differential equations, compute the steady states, specify one of them, and then define the infected classes as the components with zeros.

However, this would be impractical, since for the majority of the models with explicit DFE, the other fixed points are either not explicit or require very long execution times. It is therefore much simpler to have the user help the AI by providing it with $\mathcal{I}$, which leads immediately to the matrix M. Essentially, we jump directly to the factorization (2) of the infected equations, postponing the solving of the non-infection variables to later.

2.4. A Multi-Dimensional Birth-and-Death CTMC Process Associated to a (F, V) Decomposition, Its Branching Process Approximation, and the Bacaer Equation for the Probability of Extinction

The works of Kendall and Bartlett suggest that ODE epidemic models may be associated to corresponding birth-and-death CTMC processes and then approximated further via branching process.

Citing [31] :"It has been noted by Bartlett (1955), p. 129, that for an epidemic in a large population, the number of susceptibles may, at least in the early stages of an outbreak, be regarded as approximately constant at its initial value and that this approximation will continue to hold throughout the course of an epidemic, provided that the final epidemic size is small relative to the total susceptible population. Thus the general epidemic process may be approximated by a simple birth-and-death process".

To make this more precise, a (F, V) decomposition (3) determines a naturally associated multi-dimensional birth-and-death CTMC process by fixing the values of the non-disease variables, so that the matrices (F, V) depend only on $\boldsymbol{i}$, and interpreting the transition rates between compartments as rates of BD transitions.If the CTMC has rates which are linear in the disease variables, one may associate it to a branching process and take advantage of the well-known equation for extinction probabilities. This procedure has been detailed in previous works like [13–17] and used to approximate extinction and invasion probabilities, as well as the duration of minor epidemics. If the CTMC has rates which are super linear in the disease variables, a further approximation of ignoring the higher power terms in $\boldsymbol{i}$ is necessary. At the end, this results in assuming that the matrices (F, V) are constant (they do not depend on $\boldsymbol{i}$).

Let us illustrate this philosophy on the famous SIR example. However, in line with our interest in this paper and also getting a bit ahead of ourselves, we will only look at a "disease process" of the infected, with the other components fixed. The state space of the process will thus be $\mathbb{N}$. We note this is similar in spirit with the "slow-fast/singular perturbation" technique of considering only variables whose lifetime is short and fixing the other variables whose lifetime is longer, which in fact is the idea behind the famous next-generation matrix approach.

Example 2. *The "SIR" disease process (i.e., defined on the disease compartments) is $i' = (\beta s - \gamma)i$. The natural* **SIR/linear CT birth-and-death** *disease stochastic process (DSP) is a Markov process $X_t \in \mathbb{N}$ with a generating operator on the set of functions $f : \mathbb{N}- > \mathbb{N}$ defined by*

$$\mathcal{G}f(i) = \beta si(f(i+1) - f(i)) + \gamma i(f(i-1) - f(i)) = Af(i), \tag{4}$$

and corresponding to a semi-infinite generator matrix

$$A = \begin{pmatrix} -\beta & \beta & 0 & \cdots & 0 \\ \gamma & -\beta-\gamma & \beta & \cdots & 0 \\ 0 & \gamma & -\beta-\gamma & \beta & \ddots \\ \vdots & \ddots & \ddots & \ddots & \beta \\ 0 & 0 & \cdots & \gamma & -\beta-\gamma \end{pmatrix}. \tag{5}$$

Remark 10. *We recall, for the benefit of readers who have not been exposed to the (immense) literature on Markov processes, that the behavior of expectations of this class of stochastic processes always involves one deterministic operator A, the generator of the Markovian semigroup, which acts on a space of "appropriate functions" on the state space* (4) *and where "appropriate" may be skipped in simple cases like ours* (5)*. The essential thing to note here is that our Markov generator operator A is completely defined by the rates, just like its "mean-field" deterministic ODE. Thus, from the practical point of view of estimating rates, we have added nothing to the parameters of the ODE model (as would be the case with other stochastic processes involving Brownian motion, etc.). We have only modified the state space and the operator; however, this way, phenomena which are invisible in the continuous mean-field limit become relevant.*

Finally, for readers puzzled by the question of where the randomness hidden in the deterministic operator (4) *is , we mention that this arrives via two Poisson processes describing the times when the process jumps up and down, respectively, and we refer to the literature for more details.*

This process converges to ∞ *(i.e., is non-recurrent) or to a stationary distribution if* $R_0 := \frac{\beta s}{\gamma}$ *is strictly bigger than 1, or strictly smaller than 1, respectively. The probability of "extinction/absorbtion into 0", when starting the process with j infected, are*

$$p(j) = q^j, \quad q = \begin{cases} 1 & R_0 < 1 \\ \frac{\gamma}{\beta s} = \frac{1}{R_0} & R_0 \geq 1 \end{cases}. \tag{6}$$

This result may be found for example in the textbook [32] (it is, up to technical difficulties caused by the non-compact state space, the simplest illustration of the fact that solutions of "Dirichlet problems" of the form $p(j) = E_{X_0=j}[g(X_\tau)]$*, where* τ *is the exit time from a domain S, must solve* $\mathcal{G}p = 0$ *and* $p = g$ *on the boundary of S).*

The expected time to extinction when starting the process, with j infected and when $R_0 < 1$ *may be found using the fact that solutions of "Poisson problems" of the form* $T(j) = E_{X_0=j}[\int_0^\tau h(X(s)ds]$*, must solve*

$$\begin{cases} \mathcal{G}T + h = 0 \\ T = 0 \text{ on the boundary of } S \end{cases}.$$

Another interesting quantity is the expected time to extinction when $R_0 > 1$*, in the case that extinction occurs. This "Dirichlet-Poisson problem" may be written as*

$$T(j) = E_{X_0=j}[g(X_\tau) \int_0^\tau h(X(s)ds],$$

where $h = 1$*, and g is the indicator of extinction occurring. Such expectations must solve*

$$\begin{cases} \mathcal{G}T + hp = 0 \\ T = 0 \text{ on the boundary of } S \end{cases},$$

where p is the solution of the Dirichlet problem with boundary value g.

For SIR, we must solve, respectively,

$$\begin{cases} \beta s x(T(x+1) - T(x)) + \gamma x(T(x-1) - T(x)) + 1 = 0, T(0) = 0, T(K) = 0, K- > \infty, & \text{when } R_0 < 1 \\ \beta s x(T(x+1) - T(x)) + \gamma x(T(x-1) - T(x)) + q^x = 0, T(0) = 0, T(K) = 0, K- > \infty, & \text{when } R_0 \geq 1 \end{cases}. \tag{7}$$

These two equations may be solved explicitly. The limits are quite challenging even with Mathematica, as shown in Appendix A.1. We are able to recover and generalize the results of [33] (see also ([16] eq(10))) when $j \geq 1$ *for the first problem, but not for the second one).*

The Bacaer equation. One missing aspect in the previous works, however, characterizes the extinction probabilities via one final equation, without going through the discretization procedure employed in [13–17], solving each example individually. Interestingly, such an equation in terms of (F, V) decompositions was provided by Griffiths in [31], except that this paper considers only BD's with no transfers.

We review now the work of [34] (who were motivated by analyzing the case of periodic steady solutions), but on the way also spelled out the simple Equation (8) below. To each fixed value for the disease variables, one may associate to a (F, V) decomposition $\boldsymbol{i}' = (F - V)\boldsymbol{i}$ a "multi-dimensional birth and death process" (BD), with birth rates given by F, and with transfer and death rates given by $-V$. ($\boldsymbol{i}' = (F - V)\boldsymbol{i}$ are precisely the mean-field equation for the multi-dimensional birth-and-death process; this is precisely ([31] eq(6)), under the extra condition that we assume that the immigration vector into the disease compartments is 0. In fact, the $-V$ matrix by itself generates an absorbing CTMC (and the F matrix models' rough inputs to be fed into this absorbing CTMC). This observation explains that an ODE mathematical epidemiology model has associated it to both a birth-and-death process, as well as a "death and transfer only" absorption CTMC—see Remark 24 for an example. Furthermore, if (F, V) are independent of $\boldsymbol{i}$, we are dealing with a branching process (approximation).

A useful fact to recall is that the probabilities of extinction of a multi-variate discrete time-branching process are of the form

$$\mathbb{P}_0 = q_1^{j_1} q_2^{j_2} ...,$$

where $q = (q_j, j = 1, ..., J)$, J is the number of disease compartments, andq_j satisfies the "Bacaer equation"

$$(q^t \circ F) * q + (1 - q) \circ V - q * f = 0 \Leftrightarrow q_j = \frac{\sum_{k=1}^{J} (1 - q_k) V_{kj}}{f_j - \sum_{k=1}^{J} q_k F_{kj}}, \tag{8}$$

where $*$ denotes the coordinate-wise product, the dot product is denoted by $\circ$, and $f_j = \sum_k F_{k,j}$. This equation is new, but it may be inferred from ([31] eq(9)) and refs. ([34] eq(11)) and ([35] eq(5.3)) (after some changes in the variables).

For the SIR process for example, (8) becomes

$$(q - 1)\beta s q + (1 - q)\gamma = (q - 1)(\beta s q - \gamma) = 0,$$

with the two roots $q = 1$ and $q = \frac{\gamma}{\beta s} = \frac{1}{R_0}$, recovering Whittle's result (the two roots yield the correct result when R_0 is strictly smaller than 1 and strictly bigger than 1, respectively).

We will check below that (8) also recovers other explicit particular cases offered in the literature, like SEIR [13], ([14] (Section 4)), SIV [36], etc.

2.5. The Jacobian Factorization Bound

Note first the following elementary fact:

Lemma 1. *A sufficient (but not necessary) condition for a polynomial with real coefficients and a* **positive leading term** *to admit a positive root is that $c_0 < 0$, where c_0 is the constant term of the polynomial.*

For polynomials of degree 1, this condition is also necessary. This converse result may be strengthened to "Descartes type polynomials".

Definition 1. *We will say that a parametric polynomial with real coefficients, whose constant coefficient may change signs, but whose all other coefficients are "sign definite" and of the same sign (which w.l.o.g. could be supposed as +), is of Descartes type.*

As an immediate consequence of Descartes's rule of signs, it follows that

Lemma 2. *A sufficient and necessary condition for a Descartes polynomial with a* **positive leading term** *to admit a positive root is that* $c_0 < 0$*, where* c_0 *is the constant term of the polynomial.*

Remark 11. *Note the immense simplification with respect to the Routh–Hurwitz conditions, when we need to establish the existence of a positive root for a Descartes type polynomial .*

We believe that "the mystery of the success of the Jacobian factorization approach" comes from the fact that "simple epidemic models" often feature Descartes type polynomials. However, this leaves us with many further questions, like when does this happen and what to do when it does not.

The Jacobian factorization approach consists in:

1. Putting all the rational factors of the characteristic polynomial of the Jacobian in a form normalized to have positive leading term, assuming they are sign definite (if this is not the case, this approach does not work but may be generalized).
2. Removing all linear factors with eigenvalues which are negative.
3. For all remaining factors F_i for which $c_0^{(i)} < 0$ may hold for certain parameter values, rewrite this inequality into the form
$$c_0^{(i)} = c_+ - c_- = c_+(1 - R_J^{(i)}) < 0 \Leftrightarrow R_J^{(i)} := \frac{c_-}{c_+} > 1,$$
where c_+, c_- are the positive and negative parts of the expanded form of $c_0^{(i)}$.
4. Define the "Jacobian factorization R_0"
$$R_J = \max_i [R_J^{(i)}]. \tag{9}$$

Theorem 1. *(A) In the instability domain,* R_J *is a lower bound for* $\inf_{F\ admissible} R_F$*.*

(B) In the stability domain, R_J *is an upper bound for* $\sup_{F\ admissible} R_F$*.*

Proof. (A) Fix any admissible F and let R_F be its associated NGM R_0. Then
$$R_J > 1 \Leftrightarrow \exists i : R_J^{(i)} > 1 \Leftrightarrow \exists i : c_0^{(i)} < 0 \Longrightarrow \text{ DFE instability } \Leftrightarrow R_F > 1.$$
Thus
$$R_J > 1 \Longrightarrow R_F > 1 \Leftrightarrow R_J \le R_F, \tag{10}$$
and the result follows.

(B) Similar proof.

Conjecture: We conjecture that if all the factors F_i are Descartes polynomials, then $R_J = R_F$ for any admissible decomposition (F, V) will denote the resulting object by R_0.

Open question 1: Under what conditions do our NGM R_0 and our Jacobian R_J coincide?

The implementation of the Jacobian factorization approach is provided in Appendix A. □

2.6. The "Rational Univariate Representation" (RUR) and the Reduced Order Quasi-Stationary Approximation

Hundreds of mathematical epidemiology papers have already employed the idea of reducing the fixed point system to one scalar equation in one of the disease variables via rational substitutions for the other variables. We note that this is a particular case of the so-called "rational univariate representation" (RUR), but for Mathematica users, this is irrelevant, since RUR is not implemented currently and we had to write our own script, included below, in which the user chooses a variable in a system that they want to restrict to.

The current code for this reduction to one equation algorithm is

```
RUR[mod_, ind_, cn_ : {}] := Module[{dyn, X, par, eq, elim},
      dyn = mod[[1]]; X = mod[[2]]; par = mod[[3]];
```

```
    elim = Complement[Range[Length[X]],ind];
    eq = Thread[dyn == 0];
    ratsub = Solve[Drop[eq, ind], X[[elim]]][[1]];
    pol =
     Collect[GroebnerBasis[Numerator[Together[dyn /. cn]],
       Join[par, X[[ind]]], X[[elim]]], X[[ind]]];
        {ratsub, pol}
]
```

Remark 12. *The command which does the essential work is "GroebnerBasis". When "ind" is a set with just one component, this reduces the system to a polynomial in this variable. Alternatively, this could be achieved by plugging the results of "ratsub" into the system.*

The script above works directly for models with demographics but must be modified for "conservation systems", where the fixed points are only determined by adding the total mass conservation equation to the fixed point equations.

This script may also be used for order reduction, both in the spirit of the (quasi-steady-state assumption) QSSA method in biochemistry and of the recent epidemiology paper [37]. We illustrate this for the simplest SIR example.

Example 3. *For the SIR process* $(S(t), I(t), R(t), t \geq 0)$ *with linear birth rates* b_s, b_r *for the susceptible and the recovered, the system for the fractions* $\mathsf{s}(t) = \frac{S(t)}{N}, \mathsf{i}(t) = \frac{I(t)}{N}, \mathsf{r}(t) = \frac{R(t)}{N}$, $N = S + I + R$ *is:*

$$\begin{cases} \mathsf{s}'(t) = b_s - \beta \mathsf{s}(t)\mathsf{i}(t) + \gamma_r \mathsf{r}(t) - d_s \mathsf{s}(t), & d_s = \gamma_s + \mu \\ \mathsf{i}'(t) = \beta \mathsf{s}(t)\mathsf{i}(t) - d_i \mathsf{i}(t), & d_i = \gamma_i + \mu + \delta. \\ \mathsf{r}'(t) = b_r + \gamma_i \mathsf{i}(t) + \gamma_s \mathsf{s}(t) - d_r \mathsf{r}(t), & d_r = \gamma_r + \mu \end{cases} \tag{11}$$

The DFE is: $\left(\frac{b_r\gamma_r + b_s(\mu+\gamma_r)}{\mu(\mu+\gamma_r+\gamma_s)}, 0, \frac{b_r(\mu+\gamma_s)+b_s\gamma_s}{\mu(\mu+\gamma_r+\gamma_s)}\right)$.

The rational substitution with respect to i obtained via RUR is:

$$\left(s \to \frac{\gamma_r(b_r + b_s + i\gamma_i) + \mu b_s}{\beta i(\mu + \gamma_r) + \mu(\mu + \gamma_r + \gamma_s)}, r \to \frac{b_r(\beta i + \mu + \gamma_s) + b_s\gamma_s + i\gamma_i(\beta i + \mu + \gamma_s)}{\beta i(\mu + \gamma_r) + \mu(\mu + \gamma_r + \gamma_s)}\right).$$

Note that this reduces to the DFE when $i = 0$.

The reduced approximate model obtained via RUR is:

$$\begin{aligned} &i' = i[a_0 - a_1 i], a_1 = \beta(\mu\gamma_i + (\delta + \mu)(\mu + \gamma_r)), \\ &a_0 = \beta(b_r\gamma_r + b_s(\mu + \gamma_r)) - \mu(\mu + \gamma_r + \gamma_s)(\delta + \gamma_i + \mu) \\ &= \mu(\mu + \gamma_r + \gamma_s)(\delta + \gamma_i + \mu)\left(\mathsf{s}_{dfe}\mathcal{R} - 1\right) = \mu(\mu + \gamma_r + \gamma_s)(\delta + \gamma_i + \mu)(R_0 - 1). \end{aligned}$$

This has an explicit (rather formidable) analytic solution, provided in the Mathematica file.

One may notice that for the chosen numerical illustration, the plots of i and its approximation converge towards the same value but differ sharply for the chosen numeric values as far as shape is concerned; see Figure 1.

We mention finally the possibility to develop yet another possible algorithm for computing a "bifurcation R_0", suggested by the example above, which is based on the known fact that this parameter is expected to produce bifurcations at $R_0 = 1$.

The steps are:

1. Factor out the variable in the scalar polynomial of the reduced model (always possible if this is a disease variable).

2. Write the free coefficient of the divided polynomial as $F(R_0) = G(R_0)(R_0 - 1)$, where $F(R)$ is rational (always possible due to the known bifurcation at $R_0 = 1$).
3. Identify a factor which is linear in susceptible variables like s_{dfe}, etc., and write it as a difference of positive and negative terms. Upon normalizing one of them to one, the other will be R_0, or $1/R_0$.

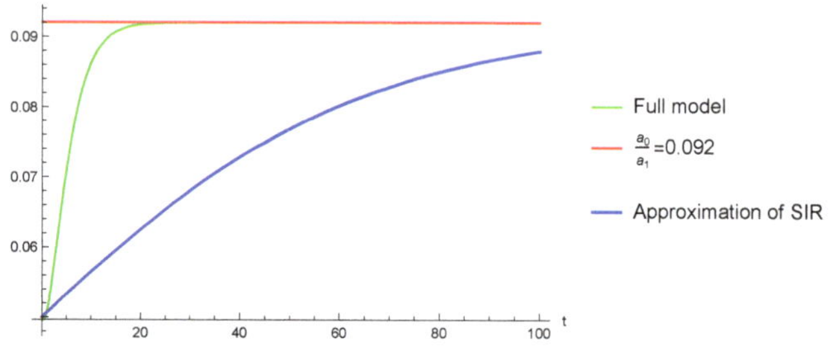

Figure 1. Illustration of the asymptotic convergence of $i(t)$ towards the endemic value $\frac{a_0}{a_1} = 0.092$, both for the full SIR model and its approximation.

3. R_0 and Extinction Probabilities for the SEIR Epidemic Model

The SEIR process $(S(t), E(t), I(t), R(t), t \geq 0)$ adds to the SIR model the class E(exposed). The model for the fractions $s(t) = \frac{S(t)}{N}$, $e(t) = \frac{E(t)}{N}$, $i(t) = \frac{I(t)}{N}$, $r(t) = \frac{R(t)}{N}$, $N = S + E + I + R$ is:

$$\begin{cases} s'(t) = b_s - \beta s(t)i(t) + \gamma_r r(t) - d_s s(t), & d_s = \gamma_s + \mu \\ e'(t) = \beta s(t)i(t) - \gamma_e e(t) - d_e e(t), & d_e = \gamma_e + \mu \\ i'(t) = \gamma_e e(t) - d_i i(t), & d_i = \gamma_i + \mu + \delta \\ r'(t) = b_r + \gamma_i i(t) + \gamma_s s(t) - d_r r(t), & d_r = \gamma_r + \mu \end{cases}.$$

This is both a textbook model and one for which answers to many open questions (concerning, for example, the emergence of chaos under stochastic and periodic perturbations) are still awaited—see for example [38–40].

The DFE of (14) is $(\frac{b_r\gamma_r + b_s(\mu+\gamma_r)}{\mu(\mu+\gamma_r+\gamma_s)}, 0, 0, \frac{b_r(\mu+\gamma_s)+b_s\gamma_s}{\mu(\mu+\gamma_r+\gamma_s)})$. The decomposition matrices and basic reproduction number are:

$$F = \begin{pmatrix} 0 & \beta s \\ 0 & 0 \end{pmatrix}, V = \begin{pmatrix} \gamma_e + \mu & 0 \\ -\gamma_e & \delta + \gamma_i + \mu \end{pmatrix}, R_0 = \frac{\beta s \gamma_e}{(\gamma_e + \mu)(\delta + \gamma_i + \mu)}.$$

The associated disease stochastic process $X = (e, i) \in \mathbb{N}^2$ has a generating operator

$$\mathcal{G} = \beta si(f(x+e_1) - f(x)) + \gamma_e e(f(x+tr) - f(x)) + d_e e(f(x+e_3) - f(x)) + d_i i(f(x+e_2) - f(x)),$$

where $x = (e, i), e_1 = (1, 0) = -e_3, tr = (-1, 1), e_2 = (0, -1)$.

The extinction probabilities obtained by solving (8) are

$$\begin{cases} q_i = 1, q_e = 1 & \text{when } R_0 < 1 \\ q_i = \frac{1}{R_0}, q_e = \frac{\mu}{d_e} + \frac{\gamma_e}{d_e}\frac{1}{R_0} & \text{when } R_0 \geq 1 \end{cases}.$$

This checks with the particular case in [13], where $s_{dfe} = 1$.

Remark 13. *It is not clear intuitively why separating the transition rates into those of F (which increase the norm of x) and those of V (which do not increase the norm of x) should matter for determining the extinction probabilities, as happens in* (8). *This seems to be an interesting question.*

4. Rank One Host-Only Models with Pathogen and R_0 Readable from the Flow-Chart

The SEIARW Model with "Catalyzing Pathogen" of [18] Has Rank One Next-Generation Matrix and $R_0 = R_J$

Ref. [18] attempted to offer a "**definition-based method**" for "computing R_0 of dynamic models of single host species, which is mutually coherent with the next-generation method (NGM)" (and somewhat unclear for "computing R_0 for a population with multi-group models"). Unfortunately, these authors do not seem aware of the fact that all the single host species they examined have a next-generation matrix of rank one, and that in this case, there exists a simple general formula [20,41,42], which is also related to the definition-based method of [43].

We review now the SEIAR model (susceptibles, exposed, infected, asymptomatic, and recovered), to which [18] add also a pathogen compartment W, resulting in the SEIARW model. See also Figure 2.

$$\begin{cases} \begin{cases} e' = s(a\beta_a + i\beta_i + w\beta_w) - ed_e, & d_e = e_i + e_a + \mu \\ i' = ee_i - id_i, & d_i = \gamma_i + \mu + \delta, \\ a' = ee_a - ad_a, & d_a = \gamma_a + \mu, \\ w' = a\epsilon_a + i\epsilon_i - wd_w \\ r' = a\gamma_a + \gamma_i i - \mu r \end{cases} \\ s' = \Lambda - s(a\beta_a + i\beta_i + w\beta_w + \mu). \end{cases} \tag{12}$$

In matrix form, the disease equations are:

$$\begin{pmatrix} e' \\ i' \\ a' \\ w' \\ r' \end{pmatrix} = \begin{pmatrix} -d_e & s\beta_i & s\beta_a & s\beta_w & 0 \\ e_i & -d_i & 0 & 0 & 0 \\ e_a & 0 & -d_a & 0 & 0 \\ 0 & \epsilon_i & \epsilon_a & -d_w & 0 \\ 0 & \gamma_i & \gamma_a & 0 & -\mu \end{pmatrix} \begin{pmatrix} e \\ i \\ a \\ w \\ r \end{pmatrix}.$$

In the absence of a pathogen, SEIAR is a rank one "generalized stage-structured infectious disease model" as revealed by its $F = \begin{pmatrix} 0 & s\beta_i & s\beta_a \\ 0 & 0 & 0 \\ 0 & 0 & 0 \end{pmatrix}$ and by its $V = \begin{pmatrix} d_e & 0 & 0 \\ -e_i & d_i & 0 \\ -e_a & 0 & d_a \end{pmatrix}$ matrix, which is triangular (compare to ([14] (Section 3))).

The R_0 has a very intuitive and easily explainable form:

$$R_0 = \frac{s_{dfe}}{d_e}\left[\beta_i \frac{e_i}{d_i} + \beta_a \frac{d_a}{e_a}\right] \tag{13}$$

(compare to ([14] (Section 3)) to see the general pattern for more stages).

Remark 14. *Note that this result may be obtained with* $\mathcal{I} = \{e, i, a, r\}$ *and also with* $\mathcal{I} = \{e, i, a\}$, *which raises the question of defining the concept of a minimal or "sufficient disease" set in such a way that it allows for deriving both* R_0 *and the extinction probabilities.*

After the addition of the catalyzing pathogen, the SEIARW is still a rank one "generalized stage-structured infectious disease model", but the R_0 is less intuitive

$$R_0 = \frac{s_{dfe}}{d_e}\left[\beta_i \frac{e_i}{d_i} + \beta_a \frac{d_a}{e_a} + \frac{\beta_w}{d_w}\left(\epsilon_i \frac{e_i}{d_i} + \epsilon_a \frac{e_a}{d_a}\right)\right]; \tag{14}$$

still, it may be read out of the flow chart "almost by inspection" (see also [18] for an algorithm computing this).

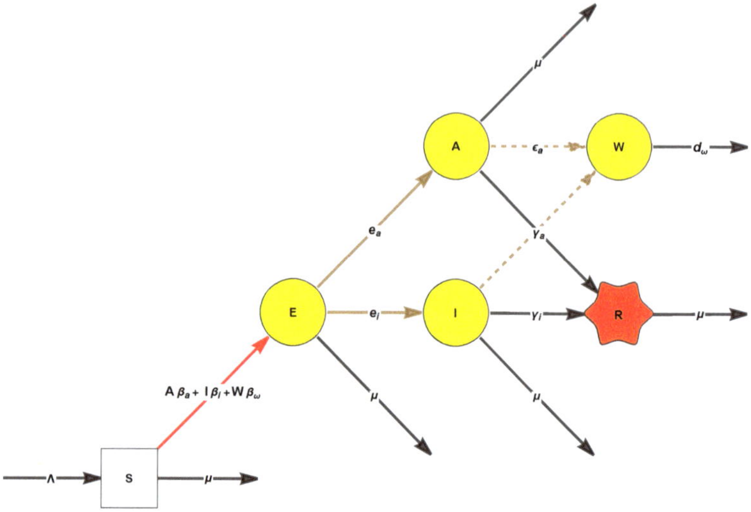

Figure 2. Flow chart corresponding to the SEIARW model (14).

Despite the fact that the characteristic polynomial is not of the Descartes type, all our three R_0 recipes yield the above result. We provide now details for the NGM method. After removing the compartment r (since it does not appear in the other equations), the calls "inf=Range[4];DFE[SEIARW,inf]; NGM[SEIARW,inf]" of our scripts yield that the DFE is

$$\left\{s \to \frac{\Lambda}{\mu}, e \to 0, i \to 0, a \to 0, w \to 0\right\}$$

and

$$F = s\begin{pmatrix} 0 & \beta_i & \beta_a & \beta_w \\ 0 & 0 & 0 & 0 \\ 0 & 0 & 0 & 0 \\ 0 & 0 & 0 & 0 \end{pmatrix} = s\begin{pmatrix} 1 \\ 0 \\ 0 \\ 0 \end{pmatrix}\begin{pmatrix} 0 & \beta_i & \beta_a & \beta_w \end{pmatrix}, V = \begin{pmatrix} d_e & 0 & 0 & 0 \\ -e_i & d_i & 0 & 0 \\ -e_a & 0 & d_a & 0 \\ 0 & -\epsilon_i & -\epsilon_a & d_w \end{pmatrix}. \tag{15}$$

Here the dominant eigenvalue of $K = FV^{-1}$, that of the transpose

$$K^t = s\begin{pmatrix} \frac{\beta_i d_w e_i d_a + \beta_a e_a d_w d_i + \beta_w (e_i \epsilon_i d_a + e_a \epsilon_a d_i)}{d_e d_i d_a d_w} & \frac{\beta_i d_w + \epsilon_i \beta_w}{d_w d_i} & \frac{\beta_a d_w + \epsilon_a \beta_w}{d_w d_a} & \frac{\beta_w}{d_w} \\ 0 & 0 & 0 & 0 \\ 0 & 0 & 0 & 0 \\ 0 & 0 & 0 & 0 \end{pmatrix},$$

the rank 1 formula of [20,41,42]

$$(1,0,0,0).(V^t)^{-1}.(0, \beta_i, \beta_a, \beta_w)^t,$$

as well as the Jacobian factorization confirm all the results (16) of [18].

5. Target-Infection-Virus Models

5.1. *Two Admissible (F, V) Decompositions and R_0's for the Three Dimensional Model of [44]*

The three dimensional model of ([44] eq(1)) is:

$$\begin{cases} x' = \Lambda(x) - \beta x v - \beta_{xy} x y, \quad \Lambda(x) = \mu_x (x_{dfe} - x) \\ \begin{pmatrix} y' \\ v' \end{pmatrix} = \begin{pmatrix} \beta x v + \beta_{xy} x y \\ 0 \end{pmatrix} - \begin{pmatrix} \mu_y y \\ \mu_v v + \beta_{xv} x v + \beta_{yv} y v - b \mu_y y \end{pmatrix}, \end{cases} \tag{16}$$

where we represented already the infectious equations as a difference of "new (positive) infection" terms and "transfers". The DFE is $x = x_{dfe}, y = 0, v = 0$.

This reduces to the case with zero delays in ([45] eq(5.1)), when the rate of viruses moving into a healthy cell β_{xv} and the rate of viruses moving into an infected cell β_{yv} are both 0, and to the case in [46], when $\beta_{yv} = 0 = \beta_{xy}$ (the latter is the cell-to-cell infection rate) and $\beta_{xv} = \beta$.

The gradient of the infectious equations is

$$M = \begin{pmatrix} x\beta_{xy} - \mu_y & \beta x \\ b\mu_y - v\beta_{yv} & -\mu_v - x\beta_{xv} - y\beta_{yv} \end{pmatrix}. \tag{17}$$

Calling our NGM script with "inf = {2,3}" yields [44]'s result: namely,

$$F = x_{dfe}\begin{pmatrix} \beta_{xy} & \beta \\ 0 & 0 \end{pmatrix}, -V = \begin{pmatrix} -\mu_y & 0 \\ b\mu_y & -\mu_v - x_{dfe}\beta_{xv} \end{pmatrix},$$

the next-generation matrix (NGM) of the infectious coordinates at the DFE

$$K = \begin{pmatrix} \frac{\beta bx}{\mu_v + x\beta_{xv}} + \frac{x\beta_{xy}}{\mu_y} & \frac{\beta x}{\mu_v + x\beta_{xv}} \\ 0 & 0 \end{pmatrix},$$

and that the DFE is Lyapunov–Malkin stable when R_0 defined in

$$R_0 = \frac{x_{dfe}}{x_c} + \beta b\frac{x_{dfe}}{\mu_v + x_{dfe}\beta_{xv}}, \quad x_c := \frac{\mu_y}{\beta_{xy}}, \tag{18}$$

is smaller than 1 and unstable when $R_0 > 1$.

The Jacobian factorization provides the same formula, despite the fact that the characteristic polynomial is of the Descartes type only conditionally, when $\beta_{xv} \geq \beta_{xy}$.

Remark 15. *Interestingly, another admissible decomposition* $\mathcal{F} = \begin{pmatrix} \beta xv + \beta_{xy}xy \\ beta\mu_y y \end{pmatrix}$*, appears in an earlier version of [44] at https://people.clas.ufl.edu/pilyugin/files/cosner60-dcdsB.pdf (accessed on 1 November 2023):*

$$F = \begin{pmatrix} x\beta_{xy} & \beta x \\ b\mu_y & 0 \end{pmatrix}, \quad V = \begin{pmatrix} \mu_y & 0 \\ 0 & \mu_v + \beta_{xv}x_{dfe} \end{pmatrix}, K = \begin{pmatrix} \frac{x_{dfe}}{x_c} & \frac{\beta x_{dfe}}{\mu_v + \beta_{xv}x_{dfe}} \\ b & 0 \end{pmatrix} \tag{19}$$

This second decomposition yields a different R_0*:*

$$R_0 = \frac{x_{dfe}}{2x_c}\left(1 + \sqrt{1 + \frac{4\beta b x_c^2}{x_{dfe}(x_{dfe}\beta_{xv} + \mu_v)}}\right). \tag{20}$$

Furthermore, this early version also shows that the two decompositions have the same stability domain for the DFE, which may be reexpressed as

$$R_0 = K_{1,1} + K_{1,2}K_{2,1} = \frac{x_{dfe}}{x_c} + b\beta\frac{x_{dfe}}{\mu_v + \beta_{xv}x_{dfe}} < 1. \tag{21}$$

We note that this equivalence also follows by applying the first criterion in [47] (when the characteristic polynomial, given here by $\lambda^n - a_1\lambda^{n-1} - a_2\lambda^{n-1} - \ldots$ *has all coefficients as non-negative, then* $\sum_i a_i$ *may be used as the threshold parameter instead of* R_0*), with* $n = 3, a_1 = K_{1,1}, a_2 = K_{1,2}K_{2,1}$*,* $a_3 = 0$*.*

Remark 16. *Note the second decomposition has one more non-zero term in F, which does not appear in ours, since we view it as a transfer and not as an interaction. We see here an excellent* *example of non-uniqueness, where one must choose between an answer with F of a lower rank and a simpler R_0 formula, but which is valid only under certain conditions (that the non-diagonal term $b\mu_y$ in V is small enough), and an answer with a simpler V, which requires less assumptions on the parameters but yields a more complicated R_0.*

Remark 17. The domain of stability, in terms of the parameters. *As an aside, it is easy to show that (23) is equivalent to*

$$x_{dfe} < x_c, b < b_0 := \frac{\mu_v + \beta_{xv} x_{dfe}}{\beta x_{dfe}} \left(1 - \frac{x_{dfe}}{x_c}\right), \tag{22}$$

where b_0 is the solution of equation $R_0(b) = 1$. Thus, the stability of the DFE is equivalent to both x_{dfe} and the "burst parameter" b being small enough.

We offer now a third gradient decomposition, which turns out to be inadmissible sometimes, but it again yields our recipe's R_0. Taking $F = \begin{pmatrix} x_{dfe}\beta_{xy} & 0 \\ b\mu_y & 0 \end{pmatrix}$ yields

$$V = F - M = \begin{pmatrix} \mu_y & -\beta x_{dfe} \\ 0 & \mu_v + x_{dfe}\beta_{xv} \end{pmatrix}, V^{-1} = \begin{pmatrix} \frac{1}{\mu_y} & \frac{\beta x_{dfe}}{\mu_y(\mu_v + x_{dfe}\beta_{xv})} \\ 0 & \frac{1}{\mu_v + x_{dfe}\beta_{xv}} \end{pmatrix}.$$

Note that V is a sub-generating matrix only if $x_{dfe} \leq \frac{\mu_y}{\beta}$.

However $K = \begin{pmatrix} \frac{x_{dfe}\beta_{xy}}{\mu_y} & \frac{\beta x_{dfe}^2 \beta_{xy}}{\mu_v\mu_y + x_{dfe}\beta_{xv}\mu_y} \\ b & \frac{\beta b x_{dfe}}{\mu_v + x_{dfe}\beta_{xv}} \end{pmatrix}$ yields the correct

$$R_0 = \max\left(0, \frac{\beta b x_{dfe}}{\mu_v + x_{dfe}\beta_{xv}} + \frac{x_{dfe}\beta_{xy}}{\mu_y}\right).$$

In the current example, the RUR algorithm works as well. The difference of the two positive terms is

$$\beta b x_{dfe}\mu_y + x_{dfe}\beta_{xy}(\mu_v + x_{dfe}\beta_{xv}) - \mu_y(\mu_v + x_{dfe}\beta_{xv}) = \mu_y(\mu_v + x_{dfe}\beta_{xv})(R_0 - 1),$$

for both choices y and v as scalar variables, and the appropriate cosmetics recover the recipe NGM R_0.

This example illustrates the fact that sometimes several admissible and even conditionally non-admissible decompositions, as well as other approaches, may lead to the same R_0.

5.2. Two Distinct Approximate Extinction Probabilities, One for Each Admissible (F, V) Decomposition for the Model of [44]

The extinction probabilities of the stochastic model are of course unique. We may use the result of Bacaer's formula as approximations. In this interesting example, we find out that both (F, V) decompositions yield reasonable results. This suggests that we have not one, but two deterministic epidemiologic approximations for a single stochastic model. This strengthens our point of view that a deterministic epidemiologic model must include a specification of the (F, V) decomposition.

The respective results we obtained are:

1. For the first decomposition, the extinction probabilities obtained by solving (8) are

$$\begin{cases} q_y = 1, q_z = 1, \text{when } R_0 \leq 1, \\ q_y = \frac{\pm\sqrt{x^2\left(\left(\beta_{xy}(\mu_v + x(\beta + \beta_{xv})) + \beta\mu_y\right)^2 - 4\beta\beta_{xy}\mu_y(x(\beta - b\beta + \beta_{xv}) + \mu_v)\right)} + x\left(\mu_v\beta_{xy} + \beta\mu_y\right) + x^2(\beta + \beta_{xv})\beta_{xy}}{2\beta x^2 \beta_{xy}}, \text{when } R_0 > 1 \\ q_z = \frac{(\mu_v + x\beta_{xv})\left(\pm\sqrt{x^2\left(\left(\beta_{xy}(\mu_v + x(\beta + \beta_{xv})) + \beta\mu_y\right)^2 - 4\beta\beta_{xy}\mu_y(x(\beta - b\beta + \beta_{xv}) + \mu_v)\right)} - x\mu_v\beta_{xy} + x^2(\beta + \beta_{xv})(-\beta_{xy}) + \beta x\mu_y\right)}{2\beta^2 b x^2 \mu_y}. \end{cases}$$

2. For the second decomposition, the extinction probabilities obtained by solving (8) are:

$$\begin{cases} q_y = 1, q_z = 1, \text{when } R_0 \le 1, \\ q_y = \frac{\pm\sqrt{x^2\left(\left(\beta(b+1)\mu_y+\beta_{xy}(\mu_v+x(\beta+\beta_{xv}))\right)^2-4\beta\beta_{xy}\mu_y(\mu_v+x(\beta+\beta_{xv}))\right)}+\beta(b+1)x\mu_y+x\mu_v\beta_{xy}+x^2(\beta+\beta_{xv})\beta_{xy}}{2\beta x^2\beta_{xy}}, \text{when } R_0 > 1, \\ q_z = \frac{(\mu_v+x\beta_{xv})\left(\pm\sqrt{x^2\left(\left(\beta(b+1)\mu_y+\beta_{xy}(\mu_v+x(\beta+\beta_{xv}))\right)^2-4\beta\beta_{xy}\mu_y(\mu_v+x(\beta+\beta_{xv}))\right)}+\beta(b+1)x\mu_y-x\mu_v\beta_{xy}+x^2(\beta+\beta_{xv})(-\beta_{xy})\right)}{2\beta b x\mu_y(\mu_v+x(\beta+\beta_{xv}))}. \end{cases}$$

In a numeric instance, we found the two results reasonably close to each other.

6. Multi-Strain Host-Only Models

Multi-strain diseases are diseases that consist of several strains, or serotypes. One interesting thing about multi-strain models is that, besides the DFE, we have new boundary points which are relevant epidemiologically, in which one subset of strains A is present ("resident"). We have then a natural coexistence of several "$\mathcal{R}$ thresholds":

1. R_A is the bifurcation threshold at which the DFE stops being stable, when the only compartments present are those of A.
2. $\mathcal{R}_A$ is the bifurcation threshold at which the boundary point E_A starts existing (in the presence of the A^c compartments).
3. $R_{A^c,A}$ is the bifurcation threshold at which the boundary point E_A stops being stable, i.e., when the A^c compartments invade the A compartments.

Note that for two strains already, we have at least two new thresholds, R_{21}, R_{12}, which, together with R_0 and the thresholds R_1, R_2 of the individual strains, divide the line into six regions with different stability properties. Studying the relations between the various thresholds in the parameter space is quite a challenging topic. However, their calculation is a priori of the same level of difficulty as for the DFE.

6.1. The Two-Strain SIS Tuberculosis Model of ([22] (Section 4.4))

The model presented here is a limiting case of that presented in the next section, obtained when the transition rates γ_1, γ_2 converge to ∞. It also generalizes the two-strain SIS tuberculosis model of ([22] (Section 4.4)) by allowing for cross infections in both directions

$$\begin{cases} i_1' = i_1(i_2(\nu_2-\nu_1)+\beta_1 s-\sigma_1-b) = i_1(i_2(\nu_2-\nu_1)+\beta_1 s-d_1), \\ i_2' = i_2(i_1(\nu_1-\nu_2)+\beta_2 s-\sigma_2-b) = i_2(i_1(\nu_1-\nu_2)+\beta_2 s-d_2), \\ s' = b-s(\beta_1 i_1+\beta_2 i_2+b)+i_1\sigma_1+i_2\sigma_2, \end{cases}$$

where we put $d_1 = \sigma_1 - b, d_2 = \sigma_2 - b$ in the first two equations to simplify their notation (the last equation may be removed, since $s = 1 - i_1 - i_2$).

Noting that the first two equations' factor yields the following three boundary steady states, where $\mathbf{x} = (i_1, i_2, s)$:

$$\mathbf{x}_0 = (0,0,1),$$
$$\mathbf{x}_1 = \left(1-\mathcal{R}_1^{-1}, 0, \mathcal{R}_1^{-1}\right),$$
$$\mathbf{x}_2 = \left(0, 1-\mathcal{R}_2^{-1}, \mathcal{R}_2^{-1}\right),$$

where we put

$$\mathcal{R}_1 = \frac{\beta_1}{b+\sigma_1}, \mathcal{R}_2 = \frac{\beta_2}{b+\sigma_2}.$$

The *disease-free steady state* $\mathbf{x}_0$ exists for all parameter values, while the *original strain-only steady state* $\mathbf{x}_1$ is physically relevant if and only if $\mathcal{R}_1 > 1$, and the *emerging strain-only steady state* $\mathbf{x}_2$ is physically relevant if and only if $\mathcal{R}_2 > 1$.

There may also be a fourth non-negative coexistence equilibrium (COE), given by

$$\begin{cases} i_1 = \frac{\beta_1 d_2 - \beta_2 d_1 - (\nu_1 - \nu_2)(\beta_2 - d_2)}{(\nu_1 - \nu_2)(\beta_1 - \beta_2 + \nu_1 - \nu_2)} \\ i_2 = \frac{d_1(\beta_2 - \nu_1 + \nu_2) - \beta_1(d_2 - \nu_1 + \nu_2)}{(\nu_1 - \nu_2)(\beta_1 - \beta_2 + \nu_1 - \nu_2)} \\ s = 1 - i_1 - i_2 \end{cases}. \tag{23}$$

Note that this depends only on $\nu_1 - \nu_2$, which shows that the case $\nu_1 = 0$ considered in ([22] (Section 4.4)) is not that restrictive (However, the appearance of $\nu_1 - \nu_2$ in the denominator suggests limiting the diffusion phenomena, which may be worth studying in their own right.) In this case, the COE point simplifies to:

$$\begin{cases} i_1 = \frac{d_2(d_1(\mathcal{R}_1 - \mathcal{R}_2) + \nu(\mathcal{R}_2 - 1))}{\nu(-d_1\mathcal{R}_1 + d_2\mathcal{R}_2 + \nu)} \\ i_2 = \frac{d_1(d_2(\mathcal{R}_2 - \mathcal{R}_1) + \nu(1 - \mathcal{R}_1))}{\nu(-d_1\mathcal{R}_1 + d_2\mathcal{R}_2 + \nu)} \\ s = 1 - i_1 - i_2 \end{cases}, \tag{24}$$

which is positive if $\mathcal{R}_2 > 1$ and the following conditions hold

$$\begin{cases} \mathcal{R}_1 > \frac{\nu + \mathcal{R}_2 d_2}{\nu + d_2}, \; 0 < \nu < \frac{d_1(\mathcal{R}_2 - \mathcal{R}_1)}{\mathcal{R}_2 - 1}, \text{ or}, \\ \mathcal{R}_1 < \frac{\nu + \mathcal{R}_2 d_2}{\nu + d_2}, \left(0 < d_1 < \nu(1 - \frac{1}{\mathcal{R}_2}) \text{ or } d_1 > \nu(1 - \frac{1}{\mathcal{R}_2}), \nu < \frac{d_1(\mathcal{R}_2 - \mathcal{R}_1)}{1 - \mathcal{R}_2}\right). \end{cases} \tag{25}$$

We give now some details of the NGM implementation for the three boundary points. Recall that the idea is to project the ODE at each boundary point on the 0 coordinates (or some subset), while fixing the other coordinates. We must therefore compute new (F, V) pairs at each boundary point, since the respective zero coordinates are different.

1. At the DFE, the zero coordinates are $\{i_1, i_2\}$, and so $\mathcal{I} = \{1, 2\}$.
   Our script yields the expected result

$$R_0 = Max\left[\frac{\beta_2 s_{dfe}}{\sigma_2 + b}, \frac{\beta_1 s_{dfe}}{\sigma_1 + b}\right] = Max[R_1, R_2], R_i = s_{dfe}\mathcal{R}_i = \mathcal{R}_i, i = 1, 2.$$

2. At $\mathbf{x}_2$, $\mathcal{I} = \{1\}$, and

$$R_{12} = \frac{\mathcal{R}_1}{\mathcal{R}_2} + \frac{(\nu_2 - \nu_1)\left(1 - \mathcal{R}_2^{-1}\right)}{b + \sigma_1}.$$

   When $\nu_1 = 0, \nu_2 = \nu$, we recover the result ([22] (18)) $R_{12} = \frac{\mathcal{R}_1}{\mathcal{R}_2} + \frac{\nu}{b+\sigma_1}\left(1 - \mathcal{R}_2^{-1}\right)$. This implies that the stability holds if $\mathcal{R}_2 > 1$ and $\mathcal{R}_1$ are not too big, more precisely:

$$R_{12} < 1 \Leftrightarrow \mathcal{R}_1 < \mathcal{R}_2 + \frac{\nu(1 - \mathcal{R}_2)}{b + \sigma_1}. \tag{26}$$

   For a sanity check, we will derive the stability condition of the point $\mathbf{x}_2$ also by the direct Jacobian approach. The Jacobian at $\mathbf{x}_2$ is

$$\begin{pmatrix} \frac{-\beta_2(b + \nu_1 - \nu_2 + \sigma_1) + \beta_1(b + \sigma_2) + (\nu_1 - \nu_2)(b + \sigma_2)}{\beta_2} & 0 & 0 \\ -\frac{(\nu_1 - \nu_2)(b - \beta_2 + \sigma_2)}{\beta_2} & 0 & -b + \beta_2 - \sigma_2 \\ \sigma_1 - \frac{\beta_1(b + \sigma_2)}{\beta_2} & -b & \sigma_2 - \beta_2 \end{pmatrix}.$$

   In the case of [22], the eigenvalues are

$$\left\{-b, -((\mathcal{R}_2 - 1)(b + \sigma_2)), \frac{(b + \sigma_1)(\mathcal{R}_1 - \mathcal{R}_2) + \nu(\mathcal{R}_2 - 1)}{\mathcal{R}_1}\right\}.$$

The second eigenvalue is negative if $\mathcal{R}_2 > 1$, and the third eigenvalue is negative when

$$(\mathcal{R}_1 - \mathcal{R}_2) + \frac{\nu}{b + \sigma_1}(\mathcal{R}_2 - 1) < 0 \Leftrightarrow R_{12} < 1 \text{ see (30).}$$

3. An analog result holds via symmetry at $\mathbf{x}_1$, where $\mathcal{I} = \{2\}$, and

$$\mathcal{R}_{21} = \frac{(\nu_1 - \nu_2)(\mathcal{R}_1 - 1)}{d_2 \mathcal{R}_1} + \frac{\mathcal{R}_2}{\mathcal{R}_1}.$$

We illustrate now in Figure 3 via an i_1 bifurcation diagram that, as natural, when β_1 is small enough, the x_2 fixed point is stable enough to be replaced as an attractor, first by the COE, and finally by the x_1 fixed point, when β_1 increases. Figure 4 illustrate time and phase plots at the critical point $\beta_{1c} = 2$.

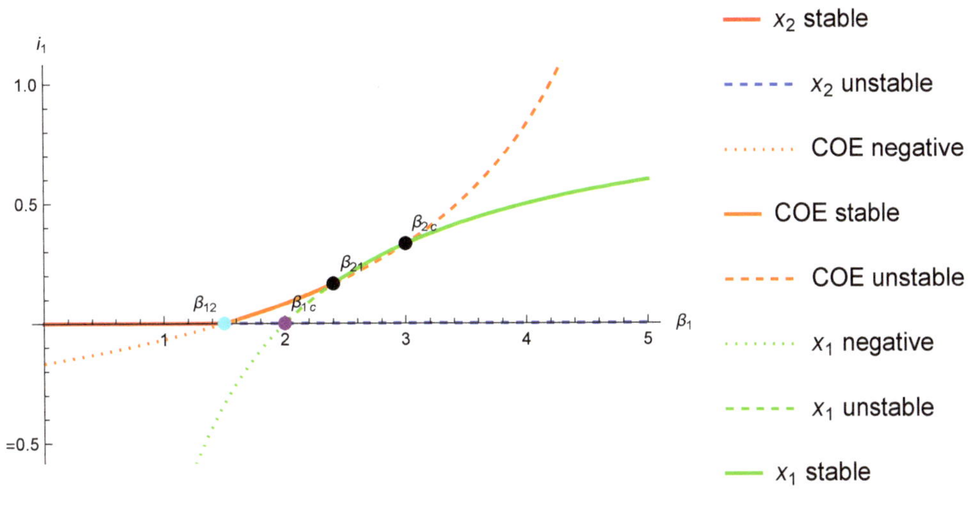

Figure 3. i_1 bifurcation diagram when β_1 varies and $\nu_1 = 0, \nu_2 = \nu = 3 = \beta_2 = 3, b = \sigma_1 = \sigma_2 = 1$, $R_1 = \frac{\beta_1}{2}, R_2 = \frac{3}{2}$, so that x_2 is always positive. Since $R_0 \geq R_2 > 1$, the DFE is never stable. Observe the following three regimes: (a) until $\beta_{12} = 1.5$ is defined by equality in $R_{12} := \frac{\nu(\mathcal{R}_2 - 1)}{d_1 \mathcal{R}_2} + \frac{\mathcal{R}_1}{\mathcal{R}_2} \leq 1$ $\Leftrightarrow \beta_{12} \leq \frac{\beta_2(b - \nu + \sigma_1)}{b + \sigma_2} + \nu$, where the only stable solution is x_2. (b) At $\beta_{12} = 1.5$, x_2 becomes unstable and the coexistence solution becomes non-negative and stable, until β_{21} is defined by $\mathcal{R}_{21} = \frac{\mathcal{R}_2}{\mathcal{R}_1} - \frac{\nu(\mathcal{R}_1 - 1)}{d_2 \mathcal{R}_1} = 1 \Leftrightarrow \beta_{21} = \frac{(b + \sigma_1)(\beta_2 + \nu)}{b + \nu + \sigma_2} = 2.4$. This is also the first intersection point of the COE and x_1. For a numerical check, at $\beta_{1c} = 2$, defined by $\mathcal{R}_1 = 1 \Leftrightarrow \beta_{1c} = b + \sigma_1$, where the x_1 solution emerges and is initially unstable, the eigenvalues for the COE are $(-1, -0.333333 \pm 0.235702 \text{ Im})$. (c) After $\beta_1 = \beta_{21} \Leftrightarrow \mathcal{R}_{21} < 1$, the x_1 solution becomes stable and the COE loses its stability (the latter was checked numerically). Note that at $\beta_{2c} = 3 \Leftrightarrow \mathcal{R}_1 = R_{12} \Leftrightarrow \beta_1 = \nu$, there is no stability change: the COE and x_1 continue to be unstable and stable, respectively.

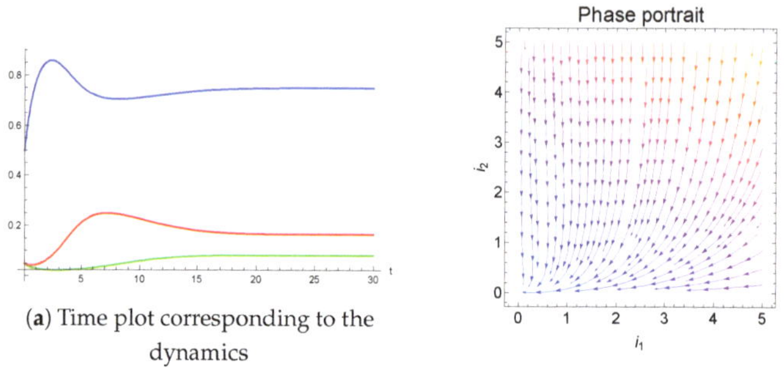

(**a**) Time plot corresponding to the dynamics

(**b**) Phase plot at $\beta_{1c} = 2$

Figure 4. Time and phase plot at the point $\beta_{1c} = 2$ illustrating convergence towards COE = $(i_1 \to 0.0833333, i_2 \to 0.166667, s \to 0.75)$. (**a**) (i_1, i_2, s)-time plot at the point $\beta_{1c} = 2$ reveals convergence towards the COE. (**b**) (i_1, i_2)−stream plot.

6.2. The Minimal Disease Set of the Multi-Strain Host-Only Dengue Model with Antibody-Dependent Enhancement (ADE) [48]

The ADE (antibody-dependent enhancement) effect, believed to occur for dengue and Zika, means that infection with a single serotype is asymptomatic, but infection with a second serotype may lead to serious illness accompanied by greater infectivity. It was first studied mathematically by [49,50], who showed that for sufficiently small ADE, the numbers of infectives of each serotype synchronize, with outbreaks occurring in phase, but when the ADE increases past a threshold, the system becomes chaotic, and infectives of each serotype desynchronize (however, certain groupings of the primary and secondary infectives remain synchronized even in the chaotic regime). Subsequently, Ref. [51] examined the effects of single-strain vaccine campaigns on the dynamics of an epidemic multi-strain dengue model. We cite now the eloquent dengue description given by these authors:

"What makes modeling the dengue virus so interesting is that it has developed a sophisticated spreading process. Dengue is known to exhibit as many as four coexisting serotypes (strains) in a region. Once a person is infected and recovered from one serotype, they confer life-long immunity from that serotype. However, the antibodies that the body develops for the first serotype will not counteract a second infection by a different serotype. In fact, due to the nature of the disease, the antibodies developed from the first infection form complexes with the second serotype so that the virus can enter more cells, increasing viral production. The increased transmission rate in subsequent infections is known as antibody-dependent enhancement (ADE). ADE is an alarming evolutionary development in multistrain viruses with respect to vaccines. An optimal vaccination would need to cover all strains of the disease at once, or the vaccinations could increase transmission of the strains not covered. This is particularly dangerous for people who have dengue because the infections are more severe in individuals who already have dengue antibodies".

A multi-strain model which adds further compartments allowing for temporary cross-immunity has been developed in the works of Aguiar, Stollenwerk, and Kooi [48,52–55].

In this section, we consider a ten-compartmentasymmetric version of the model of [48], whose variables, denoted by capital letters, represent

1. S as individuals susceptible to both strains;
2. I_i, for $i, j = 1, 2$, as individuals infected with strain i and with temporary cross-immunity to strain $j \neq i$;
3. R_i as individuals who have recovered from strain i, but are not yet susceptible to the other strain j;
4. S_i as individuals who have recovered from strain i, and have become susceptible to the other strain j;
5. $Y_j = I_{ij}$ as individuals previously infected with strain i and are now immune to it, but became reinfected with strain $j, i, j = 1, 2, i \neq j$;

6. R, omitted in (31) since they do not feed back to the other components, as the recovered individuals immune to all the strains.

After denoting by small letters the corresponding proportions, we arrive at:

$$\begin{cases} s' = \mu - s(\beta_1 i_1 + \beta_2 i_2 + \mu + \beta_1 y_1 \phi_1 + \beta_2 y_2 \phi_2), \\ i_1' = \beta_1 s(i_1 + y_1 \phi_1) - i_1(\gamma_1 + \mu), \\ r_1' = \gamma_1 i_1 - r_1(\theta_1 + \mu), \\ s_1' = \theta_1 r_1 - s_1(\beta_2 \alpha_2 (i_2 + y_2 \phi_2) + \mu), \\ y_2' = \beta_2 \alpha_2 s_1 (i_2 + y_2 \phi_2) - y_2(\gamma_2 + \mu), \\ i_2' = \beta_2 s(i_2 + y_2 \phi_2) - i_2(\gamma_2 + \mu), \\ r_2' = \gamma_2 i_2 - r_2(\theta_2 + \mu), \\ s_2' = \theta_2 r_2 - s_2(\beta_1 \alpha_1 (i_1 + y_1 \phi_1) + \mu), \\ y_1' = \beta_1 \alpha_1 s_2 (i_1 + y_1 \phi_1) - y_1(\gamma_1 + \mu). \end{cases} \tag{27}$$

In addition to the DFE where $s = 1$ and all the other compartments are 0, this system also has two other boundary points. With $\mathcal{R}_i = \frac{\beta_i}{\gamma_i + \mu}$, these are:

1. one with $i_2 = r_2 = s_2 = y_1 = y_2 = 0$, given by

$$E_1 = \left(\frac{\mu}{\beta_1}(\mathcal{R}_1 - 1), \frac{\mu \gamma_1}{\beta_1(\alpha_1 + \mu)}(\mathcal{R}_1 - 1), \frac{\alpha_1 \gamma_1}{\beta_1(\alpha_1 + \mu)}(\mathcal{R}_1 - 1), 0, 0, 0, 0, 0, \frac{1}{\mathcal{R}_1} \right),$$

2. and one with $i_1 = r_1 = s_1 = y_1 = y_2 = 0$, given by

$$E_2 = \left(0, 0, 0, 0, \frac{\mu}{\beta_2}(\mathcal{R}_2 - 1), \frac{\mu \gamma_2}{\beta_2(\alpha_2 + \mu)}(\mathcal{R}_2 - 1), \frac{\alpha_2 \gamma_2}{\beta_2(\alpha_2 + \mu)}(\mathcal{R}_2 - 1), 0, \frac{1}{\mathcal{R}_2} \right).$$

Thus, $\mathcal{R}_i, i = 1, 2$ are the bifurcation values at which these two boundary points appear.

The maximal disease set contains $I_i, R_i, S_i, Y_i, i = 1, 2$. The DFE may be determined already using the disease set $I_i, Y_i, i = 1, 2$, which has the advantage of possessing a simple characteristic polynomial with two factors $R_1(X), R_2(X)$, which yields:

$$R_J = \max[R_1(X), R_2(X)], R_1(X) = \frac{\beta_2(\alpha_2 s_1 \phi_2 + s)}{\gamma_2 + \mu}, R_2(X) = \frac{\beta_1(\alpha_1 s_2 \phi_1 + s)}{\gamma_1 + \mu}.$$

Also, our scripts find that

$$R_{ji} = s_{dfe}\, \mathcal{R}_j, j \neq i, i = 1, 2. \tag{28}$$

Finally, applying the NGM script to $E_i, i = 1, 2$ yields the elegant relation

$$R_0 = s_{dfe} \max[\mathcal{R}_1, \mathcal{R}_2] = \max[R_{21}, R_{12}]. \tag{29}$$

Remark 18. *Note the notations $R_1(X), R_2(X)$, suggesting that we want to view these as polynomials in the variables of the model, rather than as values evaluated at one of the fixed points.*

We end this section by drawing the attention to the object which allowed for computing the key polynomials $R_1(X), R_2(X)$.

Definition 2. *(A) A minimal disease set $\mathcal{I}$ is a minimal set which still allows the computation of the DFE, after being set to 0.*

(B) The model factors are the factors which may admit positive roots in the characteristic polynomial of the Jacobian with all variables in $\mathcal{I}$ set to 0.

Remark 19. *Assume w.l.o.g.* $\mathcal{R}_1 < \mathcal{R}_2$. *Two situations may arise:*

$$\begin{cases} s_{dfe}\mathcal{R}_1 < \mathcal{R}_1 < s_{dfe}\mathcal{R}_2 < \mathcal{R}_2 \\ s_{dfe}\mathcal{R}_1 < s_{dfe}\mathcal{R}_2 < \mathcal{R}_1 < \mathcal{R}_2, \end{cases}$$

and in each of them, 1 may lie in any of the partition intervals. This gives raise to six disjoint cases:

$$\begin{cases} \mathcal{R}_1 < \mathcal{R}_2 \leq 1 & \text{the DFE is the only boundary equilibrium} \\ s_{dfe}\mathcal{R}_1 < s_{dfe}\mathcal{R}_2 < 1 < \mathcal{R}_1 < \mathcal{R}_2 & \text{both } E_1, E_2 \text{ exist and are unstable} \\ s_{dfe}\mathcal{R}_1 < 1 < \min[\mathcal{R}_1, s_{dfe}\mathcal{R}_2] < \mathcal{R}_2 & E_1 \text{ unstable, } E_2 \text{ stable} \\ s_{dfe}\mathcal{R}_1 < \mathcal{R}_1 < 1 < s_{dfe}\mathcal{R}_2 < \mathcal{R}_2 & \text{only } E_2 \text{ exists and is stable} \\ s_{dfe}\max[\mathcal{R}_1, s_{dfe}\mathcal{R}_2] < 1 < \mathcal{R}_2 & \text{only } E_2 \text{ exists and is unstable} \\ 1 < s_{dfe}\mathcal{R}_1 < s_{dfe}\mathcal{R}_2 & \text{competition between the two stable dominants} \\ & \text{strains } E_1, E_2. \end{cases} \tag{30}$$

All these cases have been investigated in detail; for a more general model, see [56], which reviewed in the next section. Thus, it turns out that the results are fully determined by the model factors.

Before proceeding, let us give a name to the very interesting structure we have started to investigate.

Definition 3. *A Descartes multi-strain model of order M is an epidemic model for which the characteristic polynomial of the Jacobian factors are completely over the rationals as a product of terms, where precisely M of which are "Descartes polynomials". For such models, the Jacobian factorization threshold is defined as*

$$R_J(X) := \max_{1 \leq m \leq M} R_m(X).$$

One may check that

Lemma 3. *For Descartes multi-strain models of order K, the local stability set is a subset of*

$$R_J(X) \leq 1.$$

Remark 20. *The example of this section is a Descartes two-strain model (since the characteristic polynomial has only linear factors, precisely two of which have constant coefficients which may change signs).*

6.3. *Effects of Single-Strain Vaccination on the Dynamics of a Multi-Strain Host-Only Dengue Model with ADE*

In this section, we will show that the mysterious Formula (34) continues to hold under the considerably more complicated two-strains model of [56], with vaccination applied to one strain only. The model studied in [56] is depicted in Figure 5.

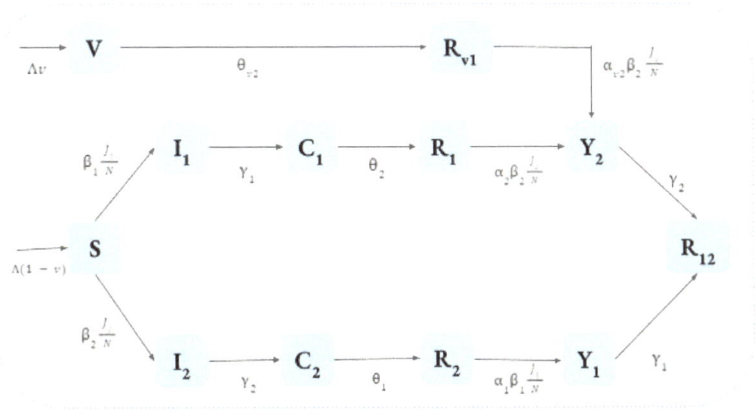

Figure 5. Schematic representation of the infection status due to the concomitant transmission of viruses 1 and 2, considering that the population is vaccinated against virus 1.

This model involves twelve compartments, two of which capture the vaccination against strain 1.

1. $S = S_0$ are individuals susceptible to both strains;
2. I_i, for $i, j = 1, 2$ are individuals infected with strain i, with temporary cross-immunity to strain $j \neq i$;
3. C_i (R_i in the original model of [52]) are individuals recovered from strain i, and hence, are permanently immune to it, with temporary cross-immunity to strain $j \neq i$;
4. R_i (S_i in the original model of [52]) are unvaccinated individuals who have recovered from strain i, but have now become susceptible to the other strain j;
5. Y_j (I_{ij} in the original model of [52]) are individuals previously infected with strain i and are immune to it, but have become reinfected with strain $j, i, j = 1, 2, i \neq j$;
6. $R = R_{12}$ are individuals immune to all the strains;
7. Finally, there are individuals V who are vaccinated against strain 1 and are still susceptible to strain 2, and individuals $R_{v1} = S_v = Z$ who have been vaccinated against strain 1 and have subsequently become infected by strain 2.

Denote by $N(t) = S(t) + V(t) + I_1(t) + I_2(t) + C_1(t) + C_2(t) + R_1(t) + R_2(t) + Y_1(t) + Y_2(t) + S_v(t) + R_{12}(t)$ the total population, put $J_i = I_i + Y_i, \quad i = 1, 2$, and assume that the two forces of infection acting on S are:

$$F_i = \beta_i \frac{J_i}{N},$$

and that the forces of infection acting on $Y_i = S_i, i = 1, 2$ are:

$$\alpha_1\beta_1\frac{J_1}{N}, \alpha_2\beta_2\frac{J_2}{N}, \alpha_v\beta_2\frac{J_2}{N},$$

where $\alpha_1, \alpha_2, \alpha_v$ denote the decreases or increases in the susceptibility to secondary infections ($\alpha_i > 1$ implying an ADE effect).

The following equations, with appropriate initial conditions, represent the disease dynamics model:

$$\begin{aligned}
\frac{dS}{dt} &= (1-\xi)\mu - \beta_1 J_1 \frac{S}{N} - \beta_2 J_2 \frac{S}{N} - \mu S \\
\frac{dI_1}{dt} &= \beta_1 J_1 \frac{S}{N} - (\gamma_1 + \mu) I_1 \\
\frac{dC_1}{dt} &= \gamma_1 I_1 - (\theta_1 + \mu) C_1 \\
\frac{dR_1}{dt} &= \theta_2 C_1 - \alpha_2 \beta_2 J_2 \frac{R_1}{N} - \mu R_1 \\
\frac{dY_2}{dt} &= \alpha_2 \beta_2 J_2 \frac{R_1}{N} + \alpha_v \beta_2 J_2 \frac{S_v}{N} - (\gamma_2 + \mu) Y_2 \\
\frac{dI_2}{dt} &= \beta_2 J_2 \frac{S}{N} - (\gamma_2 + \mu) I_2 \\
\frac{dC_2}{dt} &= \gamma_2 I_2 - (\theta_2 + \mu) C_2 \\
\frac{dR_2}{dt} &= \theta_1 C_2 - \alpha_1 \beta_1 J_1 \frac{R_2}{N} - \mu R_2 \\
\frac{dY_1}{dt} &= \alpha_1 \beta_1 J_1 \frac{R_2}{N} - (\gamma_1 + \mu) Y_1 \\
\frac{dV}{dt} &= \xi\mu - (\theta_v + \mu) V \\
\frac{dS_v}{dt} &= \theta_v V - \alpha_v \beta_2 J_2 \frac{S_v}{N} - \mu S_v \\
\frac{dR_{12}}{dt} &= \gamma_1 Y_1 + \gamma_2 Y_2 - \mu R_{12}
\end{aligned} \tag{31}$$

Table 1 summarizes the parameters and compartments of the model.

Table 1. Parameters and compartments of the model.

Parameter	Description (for $i, j = 1, 2$)
μ	Birth rate
μ	Per capita death rate
β_i	Transmission rate of virus i
γ_i	Per capita recovery rate of infected people with virus i
θ_i	Per capita loss rate of cross-immunity to virus i after previous infection with virus j
θ_v	Per capita loss rate of cross-immunity to virus 2 obtained via vaccination
α_i	ADE factor that can alter the susceptibility of unvaccinated individuals to the virus i
α_v	ADE factor that can alter the susceptibility of vaccinated individuals to virus 2
ξ	Per capita vaccination rate
Compartments	**Description**
S	Susceptible individuals to both viruses
V	Vaccinated individuals against the virus 1
I_i	Individuals with primary infection by the virus i
C_i	Individuals recovered from infection with virus i and have cross-immunity to virus j
R_i	Unvaccinated individuals immune to virus i and susceptible to virus j
$Z = S_v$	Individuals vaccinated for virus 1, and susceptible to virus 2
Y_1	Individuals infected by virus 1 and recovered and hence, immune to virus 2
Y_2	Individuals infected by virus 2 and immune to virus 1 either due to recovery or vaccination
R_{12}	Individuals immune to both virus

This system does not have negative cross effects; therefore, it leaves the non-negative quadrant invariant [57]. It follows from the equations that

$$\frac{dN(t)}{dt} = \mu(1 - N(t)).$$

Therefore,

$$\lim_{t\to+\infty} N(t) = 1.$$

Assuming $N(0) = 1$ implies that $N(t) = 1$, for $t \geq 0$. Using this, we may assume w.l.o.g. that $N = 1$, working with the proportions, is to be denoted by the corresponding lowercase letters.

The only non-zero compartments in the DFE, to be denoted by E_0, are easily found to be

$$s_0 = 1 - \xi, z_0 = \xi \frac{\theta_v}{\mu + \theta_v}, v_0 = \xi \frac{\mu}{\mu + \theta_v};$$

in fact, the last value holds at any fixed point. As known from [56], there are also two endemic points on the boundary, whose rather complicated formulas will be given later.

Remark 21. *From a modeling point of view, this system has crucial parameters like α_v (note that $\alpha_v = 0$ means perfect vaccination, and $\alpha_v = 1$, which means that infection by the second strain is equally likely for vaccinated people).*

Due to conservation, the system evolves in a compact domain, and so we may eliminate one compartment, for example, V, from the analysis. Finally, the last compartment does not send input to the others and therefore may also be disregarded in the analysis.

6.3.1. The Jacobian $R_J(X)$ is the Max of Two Polynomials, Obtained Using a Minimal Disease Set

We may tackle this example via the Jacobian factorization approach, choosing the **minimal disease set** $\mathcal{I} = (i_1, i_2, y_1, y_2)$, just like in the previous section. Again, the characteristic polynomial of the Jacobian with the variables in $\mathcal{I}$ are set to 0 factors completely as a product of the linear terms

$$(\mu + u)^5(\gamma_1 + \mu + u)(\gamma_2 + \mu + u)(\theta_1 + \mu + u)(\theta_2 + \mu + u)(\mu + u + \theta_v)\times$$

$$(\gamma_1 + \mu - \alpha_1\beta_1 r_2 - \beta_1 s + u)(\gamma_2 + \mu - \alpha_2\beta_2 r_1 - \beta_2 s - \beta_2 z\alpha_v + u),$$

only two of which (the seventh and eighth factors) may yield positive eigenvalues. Both are of the Descartes type, and instability may occur if

$$R_J(X) := \max[R_1(X), R_2(X)] = \max[\frac{\beta_1(\alpha_1 r_2 + s)}{\gamma_1 + \mu}, \frac{\beta_2(\alpha_2 r_1 + z\alpha_v + s)}{\gamma_2 + \mu}] > 1. \quad (32)$$

At the DFE, $r_1 = r_2 = 0$, and this yields

$$R_J := R_J(E_0) = R_N = \max[s_0\frac{\beta_1}{d_1}, s_0\frac{\beta_2}{d_2} + z_0\frac{\beta_2\alpha_v}{d_2}], \quad d_1 = \gamma_1 + \mu, d_2 = \gamma_2 + \mu. \quad (33)$$

This expression reveals a pattern similar to (16), with the difference that the existence of two strains are reflected in the max and that the second strain is alimented by two classes of susceptibles, one of which is the people vaccinated against the first strain.

In addition to the disease-free equilibrium, there might exist two more equilibriums on the boundary: the endemic equilibrium where there are only infections by strain 1, E_1, and the endemic equilibrium where there are only infections by strain 2, E_2; this will be reviewed in the next section.

6.3.2. The Endemic Boundary Equilibrium E_i Exist If $R_i(E_0) > 1$

At the equilibrium E_1, the values of I_2, C_2, R_2, Y_1, Y_2 and R_{12} are zero. The coordinates are easily found using the "Solve" command. Those of V, Z are the same as at the DFE, and the others are:

$$s_1 = \frac{\gamma_1 + \mu}{\beta_1}, \; i_1 = \frac{\mu}{\beta_1}\left[\frac{1-\xi}{s_1} - 1\right] := \frac{\mu}{\beta_1}(\mathcal{R}_1 - 1), \; c_1 = \frac{\gamma_1}{\theta_1 + \mu} i_1, \; r_1 = \frac{\theta_1}{\mu} c_1 \quad (34)$$

where

$$\mathcal{R}_1 = (1-\xi)\frac{\beta_1}{\gamma_1+\mu} = R_1(E_0) \tag{35}$$

(the endemic equilibrium E_1 exists if and only if $\mathcal{R}_1 > 1$).

At the equilibrium E_2, the values of I_1, C_1, R_1 and Y_1 are zero, and that of V is the same as at the DFE.

The solutions of the E_2 system involve all complicated square roots. In such a case, it is more convenient to replace the "Solve" command by our RUR algorithm, which requires the user to input a variable to reduce 2. The normal choice is i_2 (which transitions to positive at the bifurcation value), but here we will use s, to check the results of [56], who find, using as a reduction scalar $x = \beta_2 j_2$, that

$$\begin{aligned}
s_2 &= \frac{(1-\xi)\mu}{x+\mu}, \quad i_2 = \frac{(1-\xi)x\mu}{(x+\mu)(\gamma_2+\mu)}, \quad c_2 = \frac{(1-\xi)x\gamma_2\mu}{(x+\mu)(\gamma_2+\mu)(\theta_1+\mu)}, \\
r_2 &= \frac{(1-\xi)x\gamma_2\theta_1}{(x+\mu)(\gamma_2+\mu)(\theta_1+\mu)}, \quad z_2 = \frac{v\theta_v\mu}{(\theta_v+\mu)(\alpha_v x+\mu)}, \\
y_2 &= \frac{v\alpha_v x\theta_v\mu}{(\alpha_v x+\mu)(\theta_v+\mu)(\gamma_2+\mu)},
\end{aligned} \tag{36}$$

and that x is the solution of the quadratic equation

$$ax^2+bx+c=0, \quad \begin{cases} a &= \alpha_v \\ b &= \mu\alpha_v\left[1-\frac{\beta_2(1-\xi)}{\gamma_2+\mu}\right]+\mu\left[1-\frac{\beta_2\alpha_v\theta_v v}{(\gamma_2+\mu)(\theta_v+\mu)}\right]. \\ c &= \mu^2(1-\mathcal{R}_2) \end{cases}$$

The equilibrium E_2 exists if $\mathcal{R}_2 > 1$, where

$$\mathcal{R}_2 = \frac{\beta_2}{\gamma_2+\mu}\left[1-\xi+\xi\frac{\alpha_v\theta_v}{\theta_v+\mu}\right] = \frac{\beta_2}{\gamma_2+\mu}[s_0+\alpha_v z_0] = R_2(E_0). \tag{37}$$

If $\mathcal{R}_2 \le 1$, the fractions in the expression of b must be smaller than one or equal to one, and it is not possible for both to be one. Therefore, $b > 0$. We also have $c \ge 0$. Since that $a > 0$, Equation (42) does not have roots with positive real parts. This implies that there is no endemic equilibrium like E_2. Thus, in this case, $c < 0$. Since the coefficient a is positive, Equation (42) has two real roots and only one of them is positive. To resume, if $\mathcal{R}_2 > 1$, there is a unique endemic equilibrium where there are infections only by strain 2.

6.3.3. The Recipe next-generation matrix R_0 and the Jacobian Factorization One Coincide

This section shows that the polynomials $R_1(X), R_2(X)$ in this example may also be obtained via the next-generation matrix approach as eigenvalues of the K matrix via a judicious choice of infectious classes.

One may choose, as the infectious subset, the nine compartments that are 0 in the limit, but a luckier choice here is the smaller subset $\mathcal{I} = \{I_1, I_2, Y_2, Y_1\}$, which precisely has, as eigenvalues, the expressions $R_1(X), R_2(X)$ in (37).

The decomposition matrices are

$$V = \begin{pmatrix} \gamma_1+\mu & 0 & 0 & 0 \\ 0 & \gamma_2+\mu & 0 & 0 \\ 0 & 0 & \gamma_1+\mu & 0 \\ 0 & 0 & 0 & \gamma_2+\mu \end{pmatrix}, F = \begin{pmatrix} \beta_1 s & 0 & 0 & \beta_1 s \\ 0 & \beta_2 s & \beta_2 s & 0 \\ 0 & \beta_2 z\alpha_v & \beta_2\zeta\alpha_v & 0 \\ 0 & 0 & 0 & 0 \end{pmatrix} = sB_0 + zB_v,$$

where B_0, B_v are:

$$B_0 = \begin{pmatrix} \beta_1 & 0 & 0 & \beta_1 \\ 0 & \beta_2 & \beta_2 & 0 \\ 0 & 0 & 0 & 0 \\ 0 & 0 & 0 & 0 \end{pmatrix}, \; B_v = \begin{pmatrix} 0 & 0 & 0 & 0 \\ 0 & 0 & 0 & 0 \\ 0 & \beta_2\alpha_v & \beta_2\alpha_v & 0 \\ 0 & 0 & 0 & 0 \end{pmatrix}.$$

The explicit non-zero eigenvalues of the next-generation matrix $(sB_0 + zB_v)V^{-1}$ are

$$\left(\frac{\beta_1 s}{\gamma_1 + \mu}, \frac{\beta_2(z\alpha_v + s)}{\gamma_2 + \mu}\right), \tag{38}$$

confirming the result of the Jacobian method.

Let us note finally that (37), as well as the result of this section, imply the relation

$$R_0 = \max[\mathcal{R}_1, \mathcal{R}_2], \tag{39}$$

where $\mathcal{R}_i, i = 1,2$ denote the bifurcation parameters at which the boundary points E_i start to exist.

Remark 22. *Interestingly, $R_0 = \max[\mathcal{R}_1, \mathcal{R}_2]$ is the max of two quantities which satisfy that $\mathcal{R}_i > 1, i = 1,2$ are precisely the domains where endemic points E_i containing exactly one of the strains appear—see* (44). *This formula, natural in cases where the next-generation matrix has a block structure, seems to be a general feature of multi-strain models, even when the block structure is not apparent.*

In the case of this section, there seems to be a more specific structure: the Jacobian factorization approach allows for introducing two "Descartes type" (see Definition 1) factors $R_i(X), i = 1,2$ of the characteristic polynomial, which are that

1. *The existence conditions for E_i may be expressed as $\mathcal{R}_i := R_i(DFE) > 1$—see* (40), (42), *and* (46).
2. *The invasion reproduction numbers may be obtained simply by substituting the coordinates of the dominance boundary equilibria into the corresponding factor. More precisely, the invasion number of the fixed point E_i for strain i is given by $R_{ji} = R_j(E_i)$.*

Open question 2: Does the relation $R_0 = \max_1^K \mathcal{R}_k$ hold for all Descartes multi-strain models of order K? (recall Definition 3 and Lemma 3).

6.3.4. The Invasion Reproduction Number of E_i is Given by $R_j(E_i)$

The invasion reproduction numbers (see for example [58]) may, just as the basic reproduction number, be calculated using the next-generation matrix.

Our script yields quickly that

$$\mathcal{R}_{ji} = R_j(E_i), i = 1,2, j \neq i. \tag{40}$$

Open question 3: Do the formulas connecting (44) and (45) to the Jacobian factorization

$$\begin{cases} \mathcal{R}_i = R_i(E_0), R_0 = \max[\mathcal{R}_1, \mathcal{R}_2], \\ \mathcal{R}_{ji} = R_j(E_i), \text{ where } R_i \text{ denote polynomials obtained via} \\ \text{the Jacobian factorization approach,} \end{cases} \tag{41}$$

hold for some general class of epidemic models?

(C) For "two strain epidemic models", what conditions must be satisfied to ensure the inequalities $\mathcal{R}_{ji} < \mathcal{R}_j, i = 1,2, j \neq i$?

To resolve these questions, it might be useful to study the three and four strain generalizations of this problem and to investigate "non-simple" multi-strain models (in which the characteristic polynomial contains non-Descartes type polynomials).

7. Vector–Host Models

7.1. The Jacobian R_0 is the Square of the Recipe NGM R_0 for the Dengue Vector–Host Model without Demography of [30]

Ref. ([30] eq(28)) considers a "no demography/conservation" model with six compartments, three of which represent hosts, while the rest represent the vector. Note that such models with no demography do not have a finite set of fixed points. The DFE is not unique, it coincides with the initial conditions. However, our algorithm works just fine. The model, after removing two "R" classes which do not affect the rest, is:

$$\begin{cases} S_1' = -\frac{\beta_{21} I_2 S_1}{N_1} \\ S_2' = -\frac{\beta_{12} I_1 S_2}{N_2} \\ \begin{pmatrix} I_1' \\ I_2' \end{pmatrix} = \begin{pmatrix} -\gamma_1 & \frac{\beta_{21} S_1}{N_1} \\ \frac{\beta_{12} S_2}{N_2} & -\gamma_2 \end{pmatrix} \begin{pmatrix} I_1 \\ I_2 \end{pmatrix} \end{cases} . \tag{42}$$

The call "inf $= \{1,2\}; NGM[Brouwer22, \text{inf}]$" of our script yields that the decomposition matrices are

$$F = \begin{pmatrix} 0 & \frac{\beta_{21} S_1}{N_1} \\ \frac{\beta_{12} S_2}{N_2} & 0 \end{pmatrix}, \quad V = \begin{pmatrix} \gamma_1 & 0 \\ 0 & \gamma_2 \end{pmatrix},$$

$$K = \begin{pmatrix} 0 & \frac{\beta_{21} S_1}{\gamma_2 N_1} \\ \frac{\beta_{12} S_2}{\gamma_1 N_2} & 0 \end{pmatrix},$$

and

$$R_F = \sqrt{\frac{S_1 S_2 \beta_{12} \beta_{21}}{N_1 N_2 \gamma_1 \gamma_2}}. \tag{43}$$

After using the fact that the DFE is determined by the initial conditions $S_1 = N_1$, and $S_2 = N_2$, we obtain the basic reproduction number

$$R_F = \sqrt{\frac{\beta_{12} \beta_{21}}{\gamma_1 \gamma_2}} \tag{44}$$

of ([30] eq(40)).

Here the characteristic polynomial is of the Descartes type and the Jacobian method, as well as the RUR method, yielding for both the square of the (modified) formula (48) $R_J = \frac{\beta_{12}\beta_{21}}{\gamma_1\gamma_2}$.

Remark 23. *Note that ([30] eq(35)) offers yet another admissible decomposition, based on a different biological interpretation, with $R_F = R_J$, and raises the question of which of the answers is more relevant for a given epidemic. Deciding this from the ODE model only seems impossible.*

7.2. The Two Groups Model in ([21] eq(5.8)) Does not Obey a Square Relation

The two groups model in ([21] eq(5.8)) defined by

$$\begin{cases} S_1' = -\frac{\beta_{11} I_1 S_1}{N_1} - \frac{\beta_{21} I_2 S_1}{N_1} + \lambda_1 - \mu_1 S_1 \\ S_2' = -\frac{\beta_{12} I_1 S_2}{N_2} - \frac{\beta_{22} I_2 S_2}{N_2} + \lambda_2 - \mu_2 S_2 \\ \begin{pmatrix} I_1' \\ I_2' \end{pmatrix} = \begin{pmatrix} -\gamma_1 - \mu_1 - \delta_1 + \frac{\beta_{11} S_1}{N_1} & \frac{\beta_{21} S_1}{N_1} \\ \frac{\beta_{12} S_2}{N_2} & \frac{\beta_{22} S_2}{N_2} - \gamma_2 - \mu_2 - \delta_2 \end{pmatrix} \begin{pmatrix} I_1 \\ I_2 \end{pmatrix} \end{cases}$$

is not a vector–host model anymore, due to the addition of the "intra-group contact infection rates" β_{11}, β_{22}.

The DFE is $\left\{0, 0, \frac{\lambda_1}{\mu_1}, \frac{\lambda_2}{\mu_2}\right\}$, and the R_N is quite complicated:

$$\frac{\sqrt{(\beta_{22}N_1S_2(\gamma_1+\delta_1+\mu_1)+\beta_{11}N_2S_1(\gamma_2+\delta_2+\mu_2))^2+4(\beta_{12}\beta_{21}-\beta_{11}\beta_{22})N_1N_2S_1S_2(\gamma_1+\delta_1+\mu_1)(\gamma_2+\delta_2+\mu_2)}}{2N_1N_2(\gamma_1+\delta_1+\mu_1)(\gamma_2+\delta_2+\mu_2)}$$
$$+\frac{\beta_{22}\gamma_1N_1S_2+\beta_{11}\gamma_2N_2S_1+\beta_{22}\delta_1N_1S_2+\beta_{11}\delta_2N_2S_1+\beta_{22}\mu_1N_1S_2+\beta_{11}\mu_2N_2S_1}{2N_1N_2(\gamma_1+\delta_1+\mu_1)(\gamma_2+\delta_2+\mu_2)}.$$

The Jacobian factorization method yields a different answer for a characteristic polynomial which is not of the Descartes type, precisely because of the addition of β_{11}, β_{22}.

$$R_J = \frac{\beta_{22}N_1S_2(\gamma_1+\delta_1+\mu_1)+\beta_{11}\gamma_2N_2S_1+\beta_{11}\delta_2N_2S_1+\beta_{11}\mu_2N_2S_1+\beta_{12}\beta_{21}S_1S_2}{N_1N_2(\gamma_1+\delta_1+\mu_1)(\gamma_2+\delta_2+\mu_2)+\beta_{11}\beta_{22}S_1S_2}.$$

8. Multi-Strain Vector–Host Models

8.1. A Two-Strain Vector–Host Model of Feng and Velasco-Hernández [59], Where the Square Relation Holds for the Basic Reproduction Number

Ref. [59] considered a human population settled in a region where a mosquito population of the genus Aedes is present and is a carrier of two strains of the dengue virus. Let $V_i, I_i, Y_i, i = 1,2$ denote the infected mosquitoes, individuals infected by one strain, and individuals having suffered a secondary infection, respectively, let $N = S + R + \sum_{i=1}^{2} I_i + Y_i$ denote the total human population, and let $B_1 = \frac{\beta_1 V_1(t)}{c+w_h N}, B_2 = \frac{\beta_2 V_2(t)}{c+w_h N}$ denote the rates of infections in human hosts produced by the two strains. The model is defined as follows:

$$\begin{cases} S'(t) = h - S(t)(B_1+B_2) - \mu S(t), \\ I_1'(t) = B_1S(t) - \sigma_2 B_2 I_1(t) - \mu I_1(t), \\ I_2'(t) = B_2S(t) - \sigma_1 B_1 I_2(t) - \mu I_2(t), \\ Y_1'(t) = \sigma_1 B_1 I_2(t) - (e_1+\mu+r)Y_1(t), \\ Y_2'(t) = \sigma_2 B_2 I_1(t) - (e_2+\mu+r)Y_2(t), \\ R'(t) = r(Y_1(t)+Y_2(t)) - \mu R(t), \\ \\ V_1'(t) = \alpha_1 \frac{I_1(t)+Y_1(t)}{c+w_v N} M(t) - \delta V_1(t), \\ V_2'(t) = \alpha_2 \frac{I_2(t)+Y_2(t)}{c+w_v N} M(t) - \delta V_2(t) \\ M'(t) = q - M(t)\left(\alpha_1 \frac{I_1(t)+Y_1(t)}{c+w_v N} + \alpha_2 \frac{I_2(t)+Y_2(t)}{c+w_v N}\right) - \delta M(t). \end{cases}$$

The DFE is given by $E_0 = (h/\mu, 0, 0, 0, 0, 0, 0, 0, q/\delta)$. For the infectious set $I_1, I_2, Y_1, Y_2, V_1, V_2$, the F and V matrices used in the next-generation approach are given by

$$F = \begin{pmatrix} 0 & 0 & 0 & 0 & \beta_1 s_{dfe} & 0 \\ 0 & 0 & 0 & 0 & 0 & \beta_2 s_{dfe} \\ 0 & 0 & 0 & 0 & 0 & 0 \\ 0 & 0 & 0 & 0 & 0 & 0 \\ \alpha_1 M_{dfe} & 0 & \alpha_1 M_{dfe} & 0 & 0 & 0 \\ 0 & \alpha_2 M_{dfe} & 0 & \alpha_2 M_{dfe} & 0 & 0 \end{pmatrix},$$

$$V = \begin{pmatrix} \mu & 0 & 0 & 0 & 0 & 0 \\ 0 & \mu & 0 & 0 & 0 & 0 \\ 0 & 0 & e_1+r+\mu & 0 & 0 & 0 \\ 0 & 0 & 0 & e_2+r+\mu & 0 & 0 \\ 0 & 0 & 0 & 0 & \delta & 0 \\ 0 & 0 & 0 & 0 & 0 & \delta \end{pmatrix}$$

with $M_{dfe} = q/\delta$. Then,

$$FV^{-1} = \begin{pmatrix} 0 & 0 & 0 & 0 & \frac{\beta_1 s_{dfe}}{\delta} & 0 \\ 0 & 0 & 0 & 0 & 0 & \frac{\beta_2 s_{dfe}}{\delta} \\ 0 & 0 & 0 & 0 & 0 & 0 \\ 0 & 0 & 0 & 0 & 0 & 0 \\ \frac{\alpha_1 M_{dfe}}{\mu} & 0 & \frac{\alpha_1 M_{dfe}}{e_1+\mu+\xi} & 0 & 0 & 0 \\ 0 & \frac{\alpha_2 M_{dfe}}{\mu} & 0 & \frac{\alpha_2 M_{dfe}}{e_2+\mu+\xi} & 0 & 0 \end{pmatrix}$$

We obtain a basic reproduction number, which is a max

$$\mathcal{R} = max\left(\sqrt{\mathcal{R}_1}, \sqrt{\mathcal{R}_2}\right), \mathcal{R}_i := s_0 m_0 \frac{\alpha_i \beta_i}{\delta \mu}, \quad (45)$$

just like (44), but also contains the extra square roots typical of vector–host models.

Furthermore, it may be checked that this is precisely the square root of the answer given by the Jacobian factorization method, which decomposes the characteristic polynomial of the Jacobian as the product of five linear factors with negative roots and two quadratic Descartes type polynomials.

There also two boundary (dominance) equilibria where only one strain survives. The non-zero coordinates at the first one, E_1, are given by

$$\alpha_1 i_1 = \delta \frac{\mathcal{R}_1 - 1}{m_0 \beta_1/(\mu) + 1}, \beta_1 v_1 = \mu \frac{\mathcal{R}_1 - 1}{s_0 \alpha_1(\delta) + 1}, s = \mu \frac{\alpha_1 s_0 + \delta}{\alpha_1 \beta_1 m_0 + \alpha_1 \mu},$$

with similar formulas holding for the other boundary point E_2, using symmetry. Thus, these points become positive precisely when the corresponding factor of the DFE becomes bigger than 1, causing instability.

Since we had trouble with computing the invasion reproduction numbers, we switched to the "simplified model" of [59], in which M is eliminated by noting that the equation for the total vector population $T = M + V_1 + V_2$ is $T' = q - \delta T$, and also by assuming that $T_0 = \lim_{t \to \infty} T(t) = q/\delta$, M can be removed from the system by substituting

$$M = q/\delta - V_1 - V_2. \quad (46)$$

As a first consequence of using (54), the R_N becomes equal to R_J.

However, the recipe R_0 at E_1 for the natural choice of "inf" is very complicated, and [59] provides here a laborious local stability analysis, with a complicated result, via the third-order Routh–Hurwitz conditions.

We note finally that the characteristic polynomial for $jac(E_1)$ has two factors of degree 3, one of which is the Descartes type, and one which is not. The Descartes type factor yields a polynomial $R_1(X)$. Putting this together with its symmetric $R_2(X)$ allows us to finally define

$$R_J(X) = max_j[R_1(X), R_2(X)] = max_j[\frac{\alpha_j \beta_j q s/\delta}{(\beta_j v_j + \mu)(\alpha_j i_j + \delta) + \beta_j v_j \alpha_j s}].$$

Invasion Numbers of [59]

The two-strain vector–host model in [59] admits two boundary equilibria beside the DFE in which

$S_1^*, S_2^*, I_1^*, I_2^*, V_1^*, V_2^*$ are the invasion infection classes. In this case, we consider the subset $\text{in}_1 = (I_2, Y_1, Y_2, V_2)$ corresponding to the invasion infection class of E_1, then

$$F = \begin{pmatrix} 0 & 0 & 0 & b_2 S \\ b_1\sigma_1 v_1 & 0 & 0 & 0 \\ 0 & 0 & 0 & b_2 i_1 \sigma_2 \\ a_2(\frac{q}{\delta} - v_1) & 0 & a_2(\frac{q}{\delta} - V_1) & 0 \end{pmatrix},$$

$$V = \begin{pmatrix} b_1\sigma_1 V_1 + \mu & 0 & 0 & 0 \\ 0 & e_1 + \mu + \xi & 0 & 0 \\ 0 & 0 & e_2 + \mu + \xi & 0 \\ a_2(\frac{q}{\delta} - V_1) - a_2(\frac{q}{\delta} - V_1 - V_2) & 0 & a_2(\frac{q}{\delta} - V_1) - a_2(\frac{q}{\delta} - V_1 - V_2) & a_2(I_2 + Y_2) + \delta \end{pmatrix},$$

$$K = \begin{pmatrix} 0 & 0 & 0 & \frac{b_2 S}{\delta} \\ \frac{b_1\sigma_1 V_1}{b_1\sigma_1 V_1 + \mu} & 0 & 0 & 0 \\ 0 & 0 & 0 & \frac{b_2 I_1 \sigma_2}{\delta} \\ \frac{a_2(\frac{q}{\delta} - V_1)}{b_1\sigma_1 V_1 + \mu} & 0 & \frac{a_2(\frac{q}{\delta} - V_1)}{e_2 + \mu + \xi} & 0 \end{pmatrix}$$

then the IRN of strain 1 at E_1 is

$$R_1 = \frac{\sqrt{a_2}\sqrt{b_2}\sqrt{q}\sqrt{S(e_2 + \mu + \xi)}}{\delta\sqrt{\mu}\sqrt{e_2 + \mu + \xi}}.$$

Similarly, we chose the other subset $\text{in}_1 = (I_1, Y_1, Y_2, V_1)$ corresponding to the invasion infection class at E_2, where we obtain

$$F = \begin{pmatrix} 0 & 0 & 0 & b_1 S \\ 0 & 0 & 0 & b_1 I_2 \sigma_1 \\ b_2\sigma_2 V_2 & 0 & 0 & 0 \\ a_1(\frac{q}{\delta} - V_2) & a_1(\frac{q}{\delta} - V_2) & 0 & 0 \end{pmatrix},$$

$$V = \begin{pmatrix} b_2\sigma_2 V_2 + \mu & 0 & 0 & 0 \\ 0 & e_1 + \mu + \xi & 0 & 0 \\ 0 & 0 & e_2 + \mu + \xi & 0 \\ a_1(\frac{q}{\delta} - V_2) - a_1(\frac{q}{\delta} - V_1 - V_2) & a_1(\frac{q}{\delta} - V_2) - a_1(\frac{q}{\delta} - V_1 - V_2) & 0 & a_1(I_1 + Y_1) + \delta \end{pmatrix},$$

$$K = \begin{pmatrix} 0 & 0 & 0 & \frac{b_1 S}{\delta} \\ 0 & 0 & 0 & \frac{b_1 I_2 \sigma_1}{\delta} \\ \frac{b_2\sigma_2 V_2}{b_2\sigma_2 V_2 + \mu} & 0 & 0 & 0 \\ \frac{a_1(\frac{q}{\delta} - V_2)}{b_2\sigma_2 V_2 + \mu} & \frac{a_1(\frac{q}{\delta} - V_2)}{e_1 + \mu + \xi} & 0 & 0 \end{pmatrix}$$

then the maximum eigenvalue of K yields the IRN at E_2 which is

$$R_2 = \frac{\sqrt{a_1}\sqrt{b_1}\sqrt{q - \delta v_2}\sqrt{I_2\sigma_1(b_2\sigma_2 V_2 + \mu) + e_1 S + S(\mu + \xi)}}{\delta\sqrt{e_1 + \mu + \xi}\sqrt{b_2\sigma_2 V_2 + \mu}}.$$

8.2. The dengue–Zika Model with Coinfection and ADE [2]

The model studied in this paper continues previous papers like Isea and Lonngren 2016 [60] and Okuneye et al. 2017 [61], most notably by taking into account the possibility of coinfection and of direct transmission of Zika via sex (which entails two forces of infection for Zika transmissions in their flowchart, hence leading to an asymmetry in the results).

Introduce the following forces of infection:

$$\begin{cases} F_{vd} = \beta_{hd} T_{vd}, T_{vd} = I_{vd} + I_{vc} \nu_d, & \text{dengue vector force} \\ F_{vz} = \beta_{hz} T_{vz}, T_{vz} = I_{vz} + I_{vc} \nu_z, & \text{zika vector force} \\ F_{hz} = \beta_{vz} T_{hz}, T_{hz} = I_z + I_c + J_z k_z, & \text{zika human force} \\ F_{hd} = \beta_{vd} T_{hd}, T_{hd} = I_d + I_c + J_d k_d, & \text{dengue human force} \\ F_s = \beta_s T_{hz} & \text{zika human-to-human force.} \end{cases} \tag{47}$$

Note that ν_d, ν_z and k_d, k_z are, respectively, the parameters of altered infectivity for co-infected vectors and of ADE, and note that even when $\nu_d = \nu_z = 1$, the co-infection model is more accurate than previous works like [59], since it takes into account the existence of doubly infected vectors I_{vc} which influence both chains of infection.

We will consider the model :

$$\begin{cases} S_h' = (N_h - S_h)\mu - S_h(F_{vd} + F_{vz} + F_s), \\ I_d' = S_h F_{vd} - \rho I_d(F_{vz} + F_s) - I_d(\gamma_d + \mu), \\ I_z' = S_h(F_{vz} + F_s) - \rho I_z F_{vd} - I_z(\gamma_d + \mu), \\ I_c' = \rho[I_d(F_{vz} + F_s) + I_z F_{vd} - I_c(\gamma_d + \gamma_c)] - \mu I_c, \\ R_d' = I_d \gamma_d - R_d(F_{vz} + F_s + \mu), \\ R_z' = I_z \gamma_d - R_z(F_{vd} + \mu), \\ J_d' = \rho \gamma_z I_c + R_z(F_{vd} - \gamma_d - \mu), \\ J_z' = \rho \gamma_d I_c + R_d(F_{vz} + F_s - \gamma_z - \mu), \\ R' = J_d \gamma_d + J_z \gamma_z - \mu R, \\ S_v' = (N_v - S_v)\mu_v - S_v(F_{hd} + T_{hz}), \\ I_{vd}' = F_{hd} S_v - \rho F_{hz} I_{vd} - I_{vd} \mu_v, \\ I_{vz}' = F_{hz} S_v - \rho F_{hd} I_{vz} - I_{vz} \mu_v, \\ I_{vc}' = \rho(F_{hz} I_{vd} + F_{hd} I_{vz}) - I_{vc} \mu_v, \end{cases} \tag{48}$$

which generalizes a bit [2] by introducing the parameter ρ, whose purpose is to allow for simplifying the model to remove the I_c, I_{vc} classes, by setting $\rho = 0$.

Note that humans are born fully susceptible to dengue and Zika at a rate of μN_h, where μ is the natural birth/death rate for humans and N_h is the total human population. Susceptible individuals can become infected with dengue from either a dengue-infected (I_{vd}) or coinfected female mosquito (I_{vc}). The mosquito-to-human dengue infection rate is given by β_{hd}. This rate is modified by a factor of ν_d to indicate the altered infectivity of coinfected mosquitoes. Once infected with dengue, humans can recover or become co-infected with Zika (by a Zika-infected (I_{vz}) or a coinfected female mosquito (I_{vc}), or via sexual transmission from a Zika-infected (I_z) or coinfected (I_c) human) and transition into the Rd or Ic class, respectively. In a similar manner, fully susceptible humans become infected with Zika from a mosquito in the I_{vz} or I_{vc} compartment.

The DFE has only non-zero components $S_v = N_v, S_h = N_h$. Choosing, as the infectious set, all the compartments except S_v, S_h yields

$$R_0 = \max[\sqrt{\frac{\beta_{hd} N_v \beta_{vd}}{N_h \mu_v (\gamma_d + \mu)}}, \frac{\beta_s + \sqrt{\beta_s^2 + \frac{4 N_v \beta_{hz} \beta_{vz} (\mu + \gamma_z)}{N_h \mu_v}}}{2(\mu + \gamma_z)}] := \max[\mathcal{R}_d, \mathcal{R}_z], \tag{49}$$

confirming ([2] (Section 4)) and also the multi-strain structure we already met in (44) and (53). Furthermore, one may show that $\mathcal{R}_d > 1, \mathcal{R}_z > 1$ are necessary and sufficient conditions for the existence of the dengue-only and Zika-only fixed points—see subsequent sections.

We end this section by reporting on the Jacobian factorizations at E_0, when choosing as the infectious set

$$\mathcal{I} = \{I_d, I_z, I_c, J_d, J_z, I_{vd}, I_{vz}, I_{vc}\}.$$

Now the characteristic polynomial has two second-order factors:

1. One of the Descartes type which yields the polynomial $R_1(X) = \frac{\beta_{hd} S_v \beta_{vd}(k_d R_z + S_h)}{N_h^2 \mu_v(\gamma_d+\mu)}$, which generalizes $\mathcal{R}_d$, in the sense that $R_1(E_0) = \mathcal{R}_d^2$; this raises the question of whether this is related to the Zika IRN.
2. One not of the Descartes type, which raises the question of how to exploit non-Descartes type second-order factors.

8.2.1. The Dengue-Only Resident Fixed Point E_d

Even though the coordinates of the dengue-only resident fixed point E_d are pretty simple, obtaining them is not. We have an a priori choice of zeroable set $in_{1'} = \{I_z, R_z, J_z, I_{zv}\}$ which turns out to lead to about 2.5 h for "Solve" (due to the existence of four extra fixed points which are non-positive for the numeric values of [2]. After performing the computation, it turns out that the full zeroable set is $in_1 = \{I_z, I_c, R_z, J_d, J_z, R, I_{vz}, I_{vc}\}$. The remaining set of equations:

$$\begin{pmatrix} -\gamma_d I_d - \mu I_d + \frac{I_{vd} S_h \beta_{hd}}{N_h} & = 0 \\ \gamma_d I_d - \mu R_d & = 0 \\ \frac{I_d S_v \beta_{vd}}{N_h} - I_{vd}\mu_v & = 0 \\ \mu(N_h - S_h) - \frac{I_{vd} S_h \beta_{hd}}{N_h} & = 0 \\ -\frac{I_d S_v \beta_{vd}}{N_h} + N_v \mu_v - S_v \mu_v & = 0 \end{pmatrix}$$

may be easily solved. In addition to the DFE, it has one extra fixed point:

$$\begin{aligned} R_d &= \frac{\gamma_d I_d}{\mu}, S_v = \frac{\mu_v N_h N_v}{\mu_v N_h + \beta_{vd} I_d} = \frac{\mu_v(\gamma_d + \mu)(\mu N_h + \beta_{hd} N_v)}{\beta_{hd}[\mu_v(\gamma_d + \mu) + \mu\beta_{vd}]}, \\ S_h &= \frac{N_h^2(\mu_v(\gamma_d + \mu) + \mu\beta_{vd})}{\beta_{vd}(\mu N_h + \beta_{hd} N_v)}, I_d = \frac{\mu N_h^2 \mu_v}{\beta_{vd}(\mu N_h + \beta_{hd} N_v)}\left(\frac{N_v \beta_{hd}\beta_{vd}}{N_h \mu_v(\gamma_d + \mu)} - 1\right), \\ I_{dv} &= \beta_{vd} I_d \frac{S_v}{\mu_v N_h} = \frac{I_d N_v \beta_{vd}}{I_d \beta_{vd} + N_h \mu_v}, I_{vz} = 0, I_{vc} = 0. \end{aligned}$$

The bifurcation value for E_d is thus

$$\frac{N_v \beta_{hd} \beta_{vd}}{N_h \mu_v(\gamma_d + \mu)} := \mathcal{R}_d^2,$$

confirming ([2] Lemma 1).

The Jacobian factorizations when choosing, as the infectious set, the complement of $I_d, R_d, I_{vd}, S_v, S_h$, has a characteristic polynomial with one non-Descartes type, third-order factor.

8.2.2. The Zika Only Resident Fixed Point E_z

Using the full zeroable set given in [2] $in_2 = \{I_d, I_c, R_d, J_d, J_z, R, I_{dv}, I_{vc}\}$, yields the set of equations:

$$\begin{pmatrix} S_h\left(\frac{\beta_{hz} I_{vz}}{N_h} + \frac{I_z \beta_s}{N_h}\right) - I_z\gamma_z - \mu I_z & = 0 \\ I_z \gamma_z - \mu R_z & = 0 \\ \frac{I_z S_v \beta_{vz}}{N_h} - I_{vz}\mu_v & = 0 \\ \mu(N_h - S_h) - S_h\left(\frac{\beta_{hz} I_{vz}}{N_h} + \frac{I_z\beta_s}{N_h}\right) & = 0 \\ -\frac{I_z S_v \beta_{vz}}{N_h} + N_v\mu_v - S_v\mu_v & = 0 \end{pmatrix}.$$

The Zika-only resident fixed point E_z satisfies

$$R_z = \frac{\gamma_z I_z}{\mu}, S_v = \frac{\mu_v N_h N_v}{\mu_v N_h + \beta_{vz} I_z}, I_{dv} = \beta_{vz} I_z \frac{S_v}{\mu_v N_h} = \frac{I_z \beta_{vz} N_v}{\mu_v N_h + \beta_{vz} I_z}, I_{vz} = 0, I_{vc} = 0,$$
$$S_h = \frac{\mu N_h^2 (N_h \mu_v + I_z \beta_{vz})}{I_z \beta_{vz}(\mu N_h + \beta_{hz} N_v + I_z \beta_s) + N_h \mu_v (\mu N_h + I_z \beta_s)} = \frac{N_h^2(\mu_v(\gamma_d + \mu) + \mu \beta_{vd})}{\beta_{vd}(\mu N_h + \beta_{hd} N_v)},$$

where I_z is a positive root of the quadratic equation $a I_z^2 + b I_z + c = 0$, with coefficients:

$$\begin{cases} c = \mu N_h (N_h \mu_v (\mu - \beta_s + \gamma_z) - \beta_{hz} N_v \beta_{vz}), \\ b = N_h \beta_s \mu_v (\mu + \gamma_z) + \mu N_h \beta_{vz} (\mu - \beta_s + \gamma_z) + \beta_{hz} N_v \beta_{vz} (\mu + \gamma_z), \\ a = \beta_s \beta_{vz} (\mu + \gamma_z) \end{cases}$$

Assume first that β_s is small enough so that $b > 0$; then, this equation has a unique positive root if $c < 0$, which may be written also as

$$\frac{N_h \beta_s \mu_v + \beta_{hz} N_v \beta_{vz}}{N_h \mu_v (\mu + \gamma_z)} > 1. \tag{50}$$

It is shown in ([2] Theorem 1) that this is equivalent to $R_z > 1$ (both conditions determine the correct stability domain and both reduce when $\beta_s = 0$ to the same answer $\frac{\beta_{hz} N_v \beta_{vz}}{N_h \mu_v (\mu + \gamma_z)}$).

The model of [2] contains several interesting particular cases, to which we turn next.

8.2.3. The Dengue Invasion Reproduction Number (IRN) and Two Possible (F, V) Decompositions

The dengue fixed point has non-zero values $S_h, S_v, I_d, R_d, I_{dv}$. Computing the IRN's requires specifying the "invasion infection classes". Ref. [2] works with a subset of

$$in_{2'} = \{I_d, I_c, R_d, J_d, J_z, I_{dv}, I_{cv}, R_c\},$$

given by $in_2 = \{I_d, I_c, J_d, I_{dv}, I_{cv}\}$.

The resulting recipe V matrix is diagonal, and the recipe F matrix, after denoting proportions by minuscule letters, is:

$$F = \begin{pmatrix} 0 & 0 & 0 & s_h \beta_{hd} & v_d s_h \beta_{hd} \\ \rho(\beta_{hz} i_{zv} + i_z \beta_s) & 0 & 0 & \rho \beta_{hd} i_z & \rho v_d \beta_{hd} i_z \\ 0 & 0 & 0 & \beta_{hd} r_z & v_d \beta_{hd} r_z \\ s_v \beta_{vd} & s_v \beta_{vd} & k_d s_v \beta_{vd} & 0 & 0 \\ i_{zv} \beta_{vd} & i_{zv} \beta_{vd} & k_d i_{zv} \beta_{vd} & i_z \beta_{vz} & 0 \end{pmatrix} \tag{51}$$

and the spectral radius of the resulting recipe K matrix satisfies a polynomial equation of degree 4.

Now ([2] Section 5.1) move two of the F terms in the V matrix, yielding

$$F = \begin{pmatrix} 0 & 0 & 0 & s_h \beta_{hd} & v_d s_h \beta_{hd} \\ 0 & 0 & 0 & \rho \beta_{hd} i_z & \rho v_d \beta_{hd} i_z \\ 0 & 0 & 0 & \beta_{hd} r_z & v_d \beta_{hd} r_z \\ s_v \beta_{vd} & s_v \beta_{vd} & k_d s_v \beta_{vd} & 0 & 0 \\ i_{zv} \beta_{vd} & i_{zv} \beta_{vd} & k_d i_{zv} \beta_{vd} & 0 & 0 \end{pmatrix}, \tag{52}$$

with the $-V$ matrix being:

$$\begin{pmatrix} -\gamma_d - \mu - \rho(\beta_{hz} i_{zv} + i_z \beta_s) & \rho(\beta_{hz} i_{zv} + i_z \beta_s) & 0 & 0 & 0 \\ 0 & -\rho(\gamma_d + \gamma_z) - \mu & \rho\gamma_z & 0 & 0 \\ 0 & 0 & -\gamma_d - \mu & 0 & 0 \\ 0 & 0 & 0 & -i_z\beta_{vz} - \mu_v & i_z\beta_{vz} \\ 0 & 0 & 0 & 0 & -\mu_v \end{pmatrix}. \quad (53)$$

They thus reduce the rank of K to 2 and obtain a simpler R_0. On the other hand, their decomposition is admissible only under extra conditions of the parameters which ensure the non-positivity of the row sums of $-V$, which they omit to mention.

Remark 24. *The associated CTMC is the union of two disjoint generalized Erlangs, on the host and vector, respectively. These are employed in the probabilistic/epidemic interpretations in [2].*

The probabilistic/epidemic significance of F is better understood after decomposing this matrix as a sum of matrices of rank 1 *as follows:*

$$F = \begin{pmatrix} \beta_{hd} s_h \\ \rho\beta_{hd} i_z \\ \beta_{hd} k_d r_z \\ 0 \\ 0 \end{pmatrix} \begin{pmatrix} 0 & 0 & 0 & 1 & v_d \end{pmatrix} + \begin{pmatrix} 0 \\ 0 \\ 0 \\ \beta_{vd} s_v \\ \beta_{vd} i_{zv} \end{pmatrix} \begin{pmatrix} 1 & 1 & 1 & 0 & 0 \end{pmatrix}. \quad (54)$$

The column vector are total infectivity rates for the resident compartments, the row vectors are distribution vectors, and this decomposition yields immediately both the Diekmann kernel and R_0*—see [41,42].*

9. Conclusions

The possible non-uniqueness of the NGM matrix has not been sufficiently studied in the literature. Sometimes, like in the example of the last section, one simplifying choice is justified a posteriori on the grounds of some interpretability of the results, ignoring the fact that other choices might lead to even simpler answers, and there is the fact that a priori, there is no reason to expect simple answers.

To this classic dilemma, we answer by showing, via numerous examples, that the first "recipe NGM" to come to mind leads quickly to most of the results found in the literature. The question of whether our recipe may always be associated to admissible equation decompositions remains open.

We have also examined a variant of the Jacobian approach, a "factorization Jacobian approach", which draws the attention to certain polynomials with interesting properties (46) and raises interesting questions—see especially Open Question 3. Notably, the relation (44) holds in all the three "multi-strain" examples we examined and raises the additional question of how to define multi-strain models in terms of the dynamical system, to ensure that this always holds for this class.

Author Contributions: Writing—review & editing, F.A., R.A., L.B. and M.D.J. All authors have read and agreed to the published version of the manuscript.

Funding: This research received no external funding.

Data Availability Statement: No new data were created or analyzed in this study. Data sharing is not applicable to this article.

Acknowledgments: We thank Andrew Brouwer, Corey Shanbrom, Matija Vidmar, and James Watmough for useful exchanges.

Conflicts of Interest: The authors declare no conflict of interest.

Appendix A. The Implementation of the Jacobian Factorization Approach

First, we use a utility which, for a given model, infectious set, and dummy variable (taken always as u, to avoid confusions) outputs the Jacobian at the DFE, the trace and determinant (for other purposes), the characteristic polynomial in u, the NGM matrix, and R_F.

```
JR0[mod_,inf_,u_,cn_:{}]:=
  Module[{dyn,X,par,cinf,cp,cX,jac,tr,det,chp,ngm,K,R0},
    dyn=mod[[1]];X=mod[[2]];par=mod[[3]];
    Print['' dyn='',dyn//FullSimplify//MatrixForm,X,par];
    cinf=Thread[X[[inf]]->0];
    cp=Thread[par>0];cX=Thread[X>0];
    cdfe=Join[DFE[mod,inf],cinf];
    jac=Grad[dyn,X]/.cinf/.cn;
    tr=Tr[jac];
    det=Det[jac];
    chp=CharacteristicPolynomial[jac,u];
    ngm=NGM[mod,inf];
    K=ngm[[6]];
   Print[''K='',K//MatrixForm];
   R0=Assuming[Join[cp,cX],Max[Eigenvalues[K]]];
  {chp,R0,K,jac,tr,det}];
```

Most of the work is performed after calling this utility by another one, JR02. This splitting of JR0 in two parts is necessary since the detection of the non-sign definite factors, which must be analyzed, is easier to perform by eye than by using a program. The JR02 script is:

```
JR02[pol_,u_]:=Module[{co,co1,cop,con,R_J},co=CoefficientList[pol,u];
  Print[''the  factor '',pol,'' has degree '',Length[co]-1];
  co1=Expand[co[[1]]* co[[Length[co]]]];
  Print[''its leading * constant coefficient product is '',co1];
  cop=Replace[co1, _. _?Negative -> 0, {1}](*level 1 here ?*);
  con=cop-co1;
  Print[''R_J is''];
  R_J=con/cop//FullSimplify;
{R_J,co}
]
```

For a specific "mod", both R_0's may be obtained by typing:

```
jr = JR0[mod, inf, u];
chp = jr[[1]] // Factor
Print[''factor is '', pol = chp[[5]]]
pc = JR02[pol,
   u];(*the script JR02 determines R_J, using the index,
   for example 5, determined by \eye inspection in the previous command*)
Print[''R_J is '', R_J = pc[[1]] // FullSimplify]
Print[''R_N is '', R_N = jr[[2]] // FullSimplify]
```

Appendix A.1. Proof of [33]'s Result via Mathematica

1. The solution of the first recurrence equation in (7) for the expected time to extinction of a linear birth-and-death process with arrival rate A and death rate qA (relevant when $R_0 < 1$) via Mathematica is:

$$\frac{q\left(H_K\left(1-q^j\right)+H_j\left(q^K-1\right)+\log\left(\frac{q-1}{q}\right)\left(q^K-q^j\right)\right)-\left(\left(q^j-1\right)\Phi\left(\frac{1}{q},1,K+1\right)\right)+\left(q^K-1\right)\Phi\left(\frac{1}{q},1,j+1\right)}{A(q-1)q\left(q^K-1\right)},$$

where H denotes the Harmonic function.

Since Mathematica cannot compute the limit when K converges to infinity directly, we break the limit into its three parts and end up with the following generalization: Making now $j = 1$ yields [33]'s result, which is

$$\frac{\log(q) - \log(q-1)}{A}.$$

2. When $R_0 > 1$, we cannot obtain the limit for general j. When $j = 1$, similarly with the previous case, the limit is divided into four parts:

$$\begin{cases} a_1 = \text{Limit}\left[\dfrac{\frac{q\left(q^K\left(q\left(-\left(-\frac{\log(1-q)}{q}-1\right)\right)\right)\right)}{q} - q^K(H_K + \log(1-q))}{A(q-1)\left(q^K-1\right)}, K \to \infty, \text{Assumptions} \to \{A > 0, 0 < q < 1\}\right], \\ a_2 = \text{Limit}\left[\dfrac{q\left((H_K-1)q^K + \log(1-q) - \frac{\log(1-q)}{q}\right)}{A(q-1)\left(q^K-1\right)}, K \to \infty, \text{Assumptions} \to \{A > 0, 0 < q < 1\}\right], \\ a_3 = \text{Limit}\left[-\dfrac{qq^K\Phi(q,1,K+1)}{A(q-1)\left(q^K-1\right)}, K \to \infty, \text{Assumptions} \to \{A > 0, 0 < q < 1\}\right], \\ a_4 = \text{Limit}\left[\dfrac{q\left(q^K(q\Phi(q,1,K+1))\right)}{A(q-1)\left(q^K-1\right)}, K \to \infty, \text{Assumptions} \to \{A > 0, 0 < q < 1\}\right] \end{cases}$$

Here Mathematica yields that $a_1 = 0$, $a_2 = -\frac{\log(1-q)}{A}$, the second being precisely Whittle's result, but we were unable to confirm with Mathematica that $a_3 = a_4 = 0$.

References

1. Kermack, W.O.; McKendrick, A.G. A contribution to the mathematical theory of epidemics. *Proc. R. Soc. Lond. Ser. A Contain. Pap. A Math. Phys. Character* **1927**, *115*, 700–721.
2. Olawoyin, O.; Kribs, C. Coinfection, altered vector infectivity, and Antibody-Dependent enhancement: The dengue–zika interplay. *Bull. Math. Biol.* **2020**, *82*, 1–20. [CrossRef]
3. Lotka, A.J. *Analyse Démographique avec Application Particulière à L'espèce Humaine*; Actualités Scientifiques et Industrielle: Hermann, MO, USA, 1939.
4. Dietz, K. The estimation of the basic reproduction number for infectious diseases. *Stat. Methods Med. Res.* **1993**, *2*, 23–41. [CrossRef] [PubMed]
5. Bacaër, N. *Mathématiques et Épidémies*; Cassini: Paris, France, 2021.
6. Li, P.; Peng, X.; Xu, C.; Han, L.; Shi, S. Novel extended mixed controller design for bifurcation control of fractional-order Myc/E2F/miR-17-92 network model concerning delay. *Math. Methods Appl. Sci.* **2023**, *46*, 18878–18898. [CrossRef]
7. Diekmann, O.; Heesterbeek, J.A.P.; Metz, J.A. On the definition and the computation of the basic reproduction ratio R0 in models for infectious diseases in heterogeneous populations. *J. Math. Biol.* **1990**, *28*, 365–382. [CrossRef] [PubMed]
8. Kendall, D.G. Deterministic and stochastic epidemics in closed populations. In *Contributions to Biology and Problems of Health*; University of California Press: Berkeley, CA, USA, 2020; pp. 149–166.
9. Heffernan, J.M.; Smith, R.J.; Wahl, L.M. Perspectives on the basic reproductive ratio. *J. R. Soc. Interface* **2005**, *2*, 281–293. [CrossRef] [PubMed]
10. Diekmann, O.; Heesterbeek, J.A.P. *Mathematical Epidemiology of Infectious Diseases: Model Building, Analysis and Interpretation*; John Wiley & Sons: Hoboken, NJ, USA, 2000; Volume 5.
11. Roberts, M.G.; Heesterbeek, J.A.P. A new method for estimating the effort required to control an infectious disease. *Proc. R. Soc. Lond. Ser. B Biol. Sci.* **2003**, *270*, 1359–1364. [CrossRef]
12. Li, J.; Blakeley, D. The failure of R0. *Comput. Math. Methods Med.* **2011**, *2011*, 527610. [CrossRef]
13. Allen, L.J.; Lahodny Jr, G.E. Extinction thresholds in deterministic and stochastic epidemic models. *J. Biol. Dyn.* **2012**, *6*, 590–611. [CrossRef]
14. Allen, L.J.; van den Driessche, P. Relations between deterministic and stochastic thresholds for disease extinction in continuous- and discrete-time infectious disease models. *Math. Biosci.* **2013**, *243*, 99–108. [CrossRef]
15. Xue, L.; Scoglio, C. The network-level reproduction number and extinction threshold for vector-borne diseases. *arXiv* **2013**, arXiv:1308.0718.
16. Tritch, W.; Allen, L.J. Duration of a minor epidemic. *Infect. Dis. Model.* **2018**, *3*, 60–73. [CrossRef] [PubMed]
17. Nandi, A.; Allen, L.J. Stochastic multigroup epidemic models: Duration and final size. *Model. Stoch. Control Optim. Appl.* **2019**, 164, 483–507.
18. Guo, X.; Guo, Y.; Zhao, Z.; Yang, S.; Su, Y.; Zhao, B.; Chen, T. Computing R0 of dynamic models by a definition-based method. *Infect. Dis. Model.* **2022**, *7*, 196–210. [CrossRef]
19. Segovia, C. Petri nets in epidemiology. *arXiv* **2022**, arXiv:2206.03269.

20. Arino, J.; Brauer, F.; van den Driessche, P.; Watmough, J.; Wu, J. A final size relation for epidemic models. *Math. Biosci. Eng.* **2007**, *4*, 159.
21. Martcheva, M. *An Introduction to Mathematical Epidemiology*; Springer: Berlin/Heidelberg, Germany, 2015; Volume 61.
22. Van den Driessche, P.; Watmough, J. Reproduction numbers and sub-threshold endemic equilibria for compartmental models of disease transmission. *Math. Biosci.* **2002**, *180*, 29–48. [CrossRef]
23. Van den Driessche, P.; Watmough, J. Further notes on the basic reproduction number. In *Mathematical Epidemiology*; Springer: Berlin/Heidelberg, Germany, 2008; pp. 159–178.
24. Alexander, M.; Moghadas, S. Periodicity in an epidemic model with a generalized non-linear incidence. *Math. Biosci.* **2004**, *189*, 75–96. [CrossRef]
25. Jin, Y.; Wang, W.; Xiao, S. An SIRS model with a nonlinear incidence rate. *Chaos Solitons Fractals* **2007**, *34*, 1482–1497. [CrossRef]
26. Nill, F. Symmetries and normalization in 3-compartment epidemic models I: The replacement number dynamics. *arXiv* **2022**, arXiv:2301.00159.
27. Diekmann, O.; Heesterbeek, J.; Roberts, M.G. The construction of next-generation matrices for compartmental epidemic models. *J. R. Soc. Interface* **2010**, *7*, 873–885. [CrossRef] [PubMed]
28. Cushing, J.M.; Diekmann, O. The many guises of R0 (a didactic note). *J. Theor. Biol.* **2016**, *404*, 295–302. [CrossRef] [PubMed]
29. Van den Driessche, P. Reproduction numbers of infectious disease models. *Infect. Dis. Model.* **2017**, *2*, 288–303. [CrossRef] [PubMed]
30. Brouwer, A.F. Why the Spectral Radius? An intuition-building introduction to the basic reproduction number. *Bull. Math. Biol.* **2022**, *84*, 96. [CrossRef] [PubMed]
31. Griffiths, D. Multivariate birth-and-death processes as approximations to epidemic processes. *J. Appl. Probab.* **1973**, *10*, 15–26. [CrossRef]
32. Dawson, D.A. Introductory lectures on stochastic population systems. *arXiv* **2017**, arXiv:1705.03781.
33. Whittle, P. The outcome of a stochastic epidemic—A note on Bailey's paper. *Biometrika* **1955**, *42*, 116–122.
34. Bacaër, N.; Ait Dads, E.H. On the probability of extinction in a periodic environment. *J. Math. Biol.* **2014**, *68*, 533–548. [CrossRef]
35. Bacaër, N.; Maxin, D.; Munteanu, F.; Avram, F.; Georgescu, P.; Stoleriu, I.; Halanay, A. *Matematica si Epidemii*; Cassini: Paris, France, 2021.
36. Milliken, E.; Pilyugin, S.S. A model of infectious salmon anemia virus with viral diffusion between wild and farmed patches. *Discret. Cont. Dyn. Sys. B* **2016**, *21*, 1869–1893. [CrossRef]
37. Johnston, M.D.; Pell, B.; Rubel, D.A. A two-strain model of infectious disease spread with asymmetric temporary immunity periods and partial cross-immunity. *arXiv* **2023**, arXiv:2306.15011.
38. Dietz, K. The incidence of infectious diseases under the influence of seasonal fluctuations. In *Mathematical Models in Medicine: Workshop, Mainz, March 1976*; Springer: Berlin/Heidelberg, Germany, 1976; pp. 1–15.
39. Schwartz, I.B.; Smith, H.L. Infinite subharmonic bifurcation in an SEIR epidemic model. *J. Math. Biol.* **1983**, *18*, 233–253. [CrossRef] [PubMed]
40. Forgoston, E.; Billings, L.; Schwartz, I.B. Accurate noise projection for reduced stochastic epidemic models. *Chaos Interdiscip. J. Nonlinear Sci.* **2009**, *19*, 043110. [CrossRef] [PubMed]
41. Avram, F.; Adenane, R.; Basnarkov, L.; Bianchin, G.; Goreac, D.; Halanay, A. An Age of Infection Kernel, an *R* Formula, and Further Results for Arino–Brauer A, B Matrix Epidemic Models with Varying Populations, Waning Immunity, and Disease and Vaccination Fatalities. *Mathematics* **2023**, *11*, 1307. [CrossRef]
42. Avram, F.; Adenane, R.; Goreac, D.; Halanay, A. Explicit mathematical epidemiology results on age renewal kernels and R0 formulas are often consequences of the rank one property of the next generation matrix. *arXiv* **2023**, arXiv:2307.04774.
43. de Camino-Beck, T.; Lewis, M.A.; van den Driessche, P. A graph-theoretic method for the basic reproduction number in continuous time epidemiological models. *J. Math. Biol.* **2009**, *59*, 503–516. [CrossRef] [PubMed]
44. Pourbashash, H.; Pilyugin, S.S.; De Leenheer, P.; McCluskey, C. Global analysis of within host virus models with cell-to-cell viral transmission. *Discret. Contin. Dyn. Syst. Ser. B* **2014**, *19*, 3341–3357. [CrossRef]
45. Yang, Y.; Zou, L.; Ruan, S. Global dynamics of a delayed within-host viral infection model with both virus-to-cell and cell-to-cell transmissions. *Math. Biosci.* **2015**, *270*, 183–191. [CrossRef]
46. Adenane, R.; Avila-Vales, E.; Avram, F.; Halanay, A.; Pérez, A.G. On a three-dimensional and two four-dimensional oncolytic viro-therapy models. *Boletín Soc. Matemática Mex.* **2023**, *29*, 63. [CrossRef]
47. Yang, H.M.; Greenhalgh, D. Proof of conjecture in: The basic reproduction number obtained from Jacobian and next generation matrices—A case study of dengue transmission modelling. *Appl. Math. Comput.* **2015**, *265*, 103–107. [CrossRef]
48. Aguiar, M.; Kooi, B.; Stollenwerk, N. Epidemiology of dengue fever: A model with temporary cross-immunity and possible secondary infection shows bifurcations and chaotic behaviour in wide parameter regions. *Math. Model. Nat. Phenom.* **2008**, *3*, 48–70. [CrossRef]
49. Ferguson, N.; Anderson, R.; Gupta, S. The effect of antibody-dependent enhancement on the transmission dynamics and persistence of multiple-strain pathogens. *Proc. Natl. Acad. Sci. USA* **1999**, *96*, 790–794. [CrossRef] [PubMed]
50. Schwartz, I.B.; Shaw, L.B.; Cummings, D.A.; Billings, L.; McCrary, M.; Burke, D.S. Chaotic desynchronization of multistrain diseases. *Phys. Rev. E* **2005**, *72*, 066201. [CrossRef] [PubMed]

51. Billings, L.; Fiorillo, A.; Schwartz, I.B. Vaccinations in disease models with antibody-dependent enhancement. *Math. Biosci.* **2008**, *211*, 265–281. [CrossRef] [PubMed]
52. Aguiar, M.; Stollenwerk, N. A new chaotic attractor in a basic multi-strain epidemiological model with temporary cross-immunity. *arXiv* **2007**, arXiv:0704.3174.
53. Aguiar, M.; Stollenwerk, N.; Kooi, B.W. Torus bifurcations, isolas and chaotic attractors in a simple dengue fever model with ADE and temporary cross immunity. *Int. J. Comput. Math.* **2009**, *86*, 1867–1877. [CrossRef]
54. Stollenwerk, N.; Sommer, P.F.; Kooi, B.; Mateus, L.; Ghaffari, P.; Aguiar, M. Hopf and torus bifurcations, torus destruction and chaos in population biology. *Ecol. Complex.* **2017**, *30*, 91–99. [CrossRef]
55. Aguiar, M.; Anam, V.; Blyuss, K.B.; Estadilla, C.D.S.; Guerrero, B.V.; Knopoff, D.; Kooi, B.W.; Srivastav, A.K.; Steindorf, V.; Stollenwerk, N. Mathematical models for dengue fever epidemiology: A 10-year systematic review. *Phys. Life Rev.* **2022**, *40*, 65–92. [CrossRef] [PubMed]
56. Bulhosa, L.C.; Oliveira, J.F. Vaccination in a two-strain model with cross-immunity and antibody-dependent enhancement. *arXiv* **2023**, arXiv:2302.02263.
57. Hárs, V.; Tóth, J. On the inverse problem of reaction kinetics. *Qual. Theory Differ. Equ.* **1981**, *30*, 363–379.
58. Feng, Z.; Qiu, Z.; Sang, Z.; Lorenzo, C.; Glasser, J. Modeling the synergy between HSV-2 and HIV and potential impact of HSV-2 therapy. *Math. Biosci.* **2013**, *245*, 171–187. [CrossRef]
59. Feng, Z.; Velasco-Hernández, J.X. Competitive exclusion in a vector-host model for the dengue fever. *J. Math. Biol.* **1997**, *35*, 523–544. [CrossRef] [PubMed]
60. Isea, R.; Lonngren, K.E. A preliminary mathematical model for the dynamic transmission of dengue, chikungunya and zika. *arXiv* **2016**, arXiv:1606.08233.
61. Okuneye, K.O.; Velasco-Hernandez, J.X.; Gumel, A.B. The "unholy" chikungunya–dengue–Zika trinity: A theoretical analysis. *J. Biol. Syst.* **2017**, *25*, 545–585. [CrossRef]

mathematics

MDPI

Article

On the Analytical Solution of the SIRV-Model for the Temporal Evolution of Epidemics for General Time-Dependent Recovery, Infection and Vaccination Rates

Martin Kröger [1,*] and Reinhard Schlickeiser [2,3,*]

1 Magnetism and Interface Physics & Computational Polymer Physics, Department of Materials, ETH Zurich, Leopold-Ruzicka-Weg 4, CH-8093 Zurich, Switzerland
2 Institut für Theoretische Physik, Lehrstuhl IV: Weltraum- und Astrophysik, Ruhr-Universität Bochum, D-44780 Bochum, Germany
3 Institut für Theoretische Physik und Astrophysik, Christian-Albrechts-Universität zu Kiel, Leibnizstr. 15, D-24118 Kiel, Germany
* Correspondence: mk@mat.ethz.ch (M.K.); rsch@tp4.rub.de (R.S.)

Abstract: The susceptible–infected–recovered/removed–vaccinated (SIRV) epidemic model is an important generalization of the SIR epidemic model, as it accounts quantitatively for the effects of vaccination campaigns on the temporal evolution of epidemic outbreaks. Additional to the time-dependent infection ($a(t)$) and recovery ($\mu(t)$) rates, regulating the transitions between the compartments $S \to I$ and $I \to R$, respectively, the time-dependent vaccination rate $v(t)$ accounts for the transition between the compartments $S \to V$ of susceptible to vaccinated fractions. An accurate analytical approximation is derived for arbitrary and different temporal dependencies of the rates, which is valid for all times after the start of the epidemics for which the cumulative fraction of new infections $J(t) \ll 1$. As vaccination campaigns automatically reduce the rate of new infections by transferring persons from susceptible to vaccinated, the limit $J(t) \ll 1$ is even better fulfilled than in the SIR-epidemic model. The comparison of the analytical approximation for the temporal dependence of the rate of new infections $\mathring{J}(t) = a(t)S(t)I(t)$, the corresponding cumulative fraction $J(t)$, and $V(t)$, respectively, with the exact numerical solution of the SIRV-equations for different illustrative examples proves the accuracy of our approach. The considered illustrative examples include the cases of stationary ratios with a delayed start of vaccinations, and an oscillating ratio of recovery to infection rate with a delayed vaccination at constant rate. The proposed analytical approximation is self-regulating as the final analytical expression for the cumulative fraction J_∞ after infinite time allows us to check the validity of the original assumption $J(t) \leq J_\infty \ll 1$.

Keywords: nonlinear differential equations; analytic solution; vaccination; pandemic spreading; infinite sums

MSC: 34A34; 34A45

Citation: Kröger, M.; Schlickeiser, R. On the Analytical Solution of the SIRV-Model for the Temporal Evolution of Epidemics for General Time-Dependent Recovery, Infection and Vaccination Rates. *Mathematics* **2024**, *12*, 326. https://doi.org/10.3390/math12020326

Academic Editors: Mihaela Neamţu, Eva Kaslik and Anca Rădulescu

Received: 2 January 2024
Revised: 12 January 2024
Accepted: 18 January 2024
Published: 19 January 2024

1. Introduction

Vaccination campaigns on a considered population, subject to pandemic and epidemic outbursts, have a profound influence on the temporal evolution of the rate of infected persons. The necessity to calculate quantitatively this influence has prompted the development of the susceptible–infected–recovered/removed–vaccinated (SIRV) epidemic model [1–22]. The compartmental SIRV model generalizes the simpler susceptible–infected–recovered/removed (SIR) epidemic model [23–26]. Three time-dependent rates, namely the infection ($a(t)$), recovery ($\mu(t)$) and vaccination ($v(t)$) rates, regulate the transitions between the compartments $S \to I$, $I \to R$ and $S \to V$, respectively. The ratios $k(t) = \mu(t)/a(t)$ of the recovery to infection rate and $b(t) = v(t)/a(t)$ of the vaccination to infection rate are the important key parameters of the SIRV pandemic model. Existing analytical solutions to the SIRV equations available in the literature [1,2] have adopted originally stationary values of the ratios $k(t) = k_0$ and $b(t) = b_0$, allowing for arbitrary time-dependent infection rates $a(t)$ so that the recovery and vaccination rates have the same time dependence as the infection rate.

Here, we apply the recently developed analytical approach towards the solution of the compartmental SIR model [27] to the SIRV-epidemic model. For all times after the start of the epidemic, for which the cumulative fraction of infected persons $J(t) \ll 1$ is much less then unity, an accurate analytical approximate solution of the SIRV equations is possible for general and arbitrary time dependencies of the infection $(a(t))$, recovery $(\mu(t))$ and vaccination $(v(t))$ rates. As vaccination campaigns automatically reduce the rate of new infections by transferring susceptible persons directly to vaccinated persons, who then no longer can get infected, the limit $J \ll 1$ is even better fulfilled than in the SIR-epidemic model.

A number of numerical studies to quantify the effect of vaccination campaigns are available in the literature [28–32] using generalized SIRV-model equations with additional compartments. In these works, the time dependence of individual compartment quantities such as $I(t)$ and $R(t)$ have been derived, but these quantities are not regularly observed and monitored during pandemic waves. Of higher interest, especially from the medical and public health care points of view, are the rate of new infections $\mathring{J}(t)$ and its corresponding cumulative number $J(t)$, defined by

$$\mathring{J}(t) = a(t)S(t)I(t), \qquad J(t) = J(t_0) + \int_{t_0}^{t} d\xi \, \mathring{J}(\xi), \tag{1}$$

respectively, after the start of the pandemic outburst at time t_0, as the hospitalization and death rates are directly proportional to $\mathring{J}(t)$. Forecasts of the hospitalization and death rates are essential in order to prepare a community for an upcoming pandemic outburst by introducing non-pharmaceutical interventions and/or vaccination campaigns at an optimized time.

The organization of the manuscript is as follows. In Section 2, we introduce the starting SIRV-model equations both in terms of the real time t and the reduced time $\tau = \int_{t_0}^{t} d\xi a(\xi)$. It is beneficial for the analysis to express the SIRV-equations in a form directly involving the observable quantities, such as rate of new infections $j(\tau) = S(\tau)I(\tau)$, the cumulative fraction of infections $J(\tau) = J(0) + \int_0^\tau dx\, j(x) = \eta + \int_0^\tau dx\, j(x) = 1 - S(\tau) - V(\tau) = R(\tau) + I(\tau)$, and the cumulative fraction of vaccinated persons $V(\tau)$. As shown in Section 3 the SIRV-equations in this form allow an approximate analytical solution in the limit of small cumulative fractions $J \ll 1$. The approximate solution can be written both as function of the real and the reduced time. In Section 4, the approximate solutions are compared with the earlier obtained analytical results for the special case of stationary ratios between the recovery to infection rate and the vaccination to infection rate, respectively. In Sections 5 and 6, we investigate two applications which were inaccessible to analytical treatment before. The considered applications include the cases of stationary ratios with a delayed start of vaccinations (Section 5), and an oscillating ratio of recovery to infection rate with a delayed vaccination at constant rate (Section 6). Here, the analytical approximations are compared with the exact numerical solution of the SIRV-equations for these two applications in order to test the accuracy of the analytical approach. A summary and conclusion (Section 7) completes the manuscript.

2. SIRV Model

The original SIRV-equations read [1]:

$$\begin{aligned}\frac{dS}{dt} &= -a(t)SI - v(t)S, && (2)\\ \frac{dI}{dt} &= a(t)SI - \mu(t)I, && (3)\\ \frac{dR}{dt} &= \mu(t)I, && (4)\\ \frac{dV}{dt} &= v(t)S, && (5)\end{aligned}$$

obeying the sum constraint

$$S(t) + I(t) + R(t) + V(t) = 1 \quad (6)$$

at all times $t \geq t_0$ after the start of the wave at time t_0 with the initial conditions

$$I(t_0) = \eta, \quad S(t_0) = 1 - \eta, \quad R(t_0) = 0, \quad V(t_0) = 0, \quad (7)$$

where η is positive and usually very small, $\eta \ll 1$. We refer to this case as the semi-time case [25].

Recently, it has been demonstrated [33] that the SIRV Equations (2)–(5) can be expressed as

$$\begin{aligned}b(\tau) &= \frac{\frac{dV}{d\tau}}{1 - V(\tau) - J(\tau)}, && (8)\\ I(\tau) &= \frac{j(\tau)}{1 - V(\tau) - J(\tau)}, && (9)\end{aligned}$$

and

$$k(\tau) = 1 - V(\tau) - J(\tau) - \frac{d}{d\tau}\ln\left[\frac{j(\tau)}{1 - V(\tau) - J(\tau)}\right] \quad (10)$$

in terms of the reduced time

$$\tau = \int_{t_0}^{t} d\xi\, a(\xi), \quad (11)$$

and the ratios

$$k(\tau) = \frac{\mu(\tau(t))}{a(\tau(t))}, \qquad b(\tau) = \frac{v(\tau(t))}{a(\tau(t))}. \quad (12)$$

The great advantage of the SIRV equations written in the form (8)–(10) is the direct involvement of observable and monitored quantities, such as the rate of new infections $j(\tau) = S(\tau)I(\tau)$, the cumulative fraction of new infections $J(t) = J(\tau) = J(0) + \int_0^\tau dx j(x) = \eta + \int_0^\tau dx j(x) = 1 - S(\tau) - V(\tau) = R(\tau) + I(\tau)$, and the cumulative fraction of vaccinated persons $V(t) = V(\tau)$. This has enabled the determination [33] of the time variation of the ratios $k(t)$ and $b(t)$ from past COVID-19 mutant waves. For completeness, we note the SIRV Equations (2)–(6) in terms of the reduced time (11)

$$\begin{aligned}\frac{dS}{d\tau} &= -SI - b(\tau)S, && (13)\\ \frac{dI}{d\tau} &= SI - k(\tau)I, && (14)\\ \frac{dR}{d\tau} &= k(\tau)I, && (15)\\ \frac{dV}{d\tau} &= b(\tau)S, && (16)\\ 1 &= S(\tau) + I(\tau) + R(\tau) + V(\tau). && (17)\end{aligned}$$

In the following, we will derive approximate analytical solutions of the four nonlinear differential Equations (13)–(16) in the limit of small $J(\tau) \ll 1$ and prove its accuracy by comparing with the exact numerical solutions of these equations for a number of illustrative examples of the reduced time dependence of the ratios $k(\tau)$ and $b(\tau)$. As will be demonstrated, the proposed analytical approximation is self-regulating as the final analytical expression for the cumulative fraction $J_\infty = \lim_{t\to\infty} J(t)$ after infinite time allows us to check the validity of the original assumption $J(t) = J(\tau) \leq J_\infty \ll 1$.

3. Approximate Analytical Solutions

$J(t) = J(\tau)$ denotes the cumulative fraction of new infections. In the semi-time case considered here, this fraction starts with very small values $J(t_0) = \eta \simeq \mathcal{O}(10^{-5})$ at the start for all pandemic outbreaks and approaches J_∞ after infinite time. In Table 1 we have collected the monitored values for the COVID-19 outbreaks in different countries. As can be seen, these are smaller than 0.62 and, in many countries, smaller than 0.1. Especially for the countries with values $J_\infty < 0.2$, the assumption $J \ll 1$ is well justified.

Table 1. Reported data as of 12 Jan 2024 for final values J_∞ and D_∞ for several countries with more than $P = 10^7$ inhabitants. Here, P denotes the total population size, PJ_∞ and PD_∞ the reported total number of infections and fatalities, and J_∞ and D_∞ the population fractions at the declared end of the pandemics. The table is sorted by ascending J_∞. The data were collected from the following github repository: https://pomber.github.io/covid19/timeseries.json (accessed on 20 December 2023).

Country	$P/10^6$	$PJ_\infty/10^6$	J_∞	$PD_\infty/10^6$	D_∞
France	64.88	39.867	0.6145	0.166	0.0026
Korea South	51.63	30.616	0.5930	0.034	0.0007
Portugal	10.33	5.570	0.5395	0.026	0.0025
Greece	10.75	5.548	0.5163	0.035	0.0032
Netherlands	17.02	8.713	0.5120	0.024	0.0014
Australia	24.13	11.399	0.4725	0.020	0.0008
Germany	84.08	38.249	0.4549	0.169	0.0020
Czechia	10.56	4.618	0.4373	0.042	0.0040
Italy	60.60	25.604	0.4225	0.188	0.0031
Belgium	11.35	4.739	0.4176	0.034	0.0030
United Kingdom	65.64	24.659	0.3757	0.221	0.0034
United States	323.13	103.803	0.3212	1.124	0.0035
Spain	46.44	13.770	0.2965	0.119	0.0026
Chile	17.91	5.192	0.2899	0.064	0.0036
Japan	126.99	33.320	0.2624	0.073	0.0006
Argentina	43.85	10.045	0.2291	0.130	0.0030
Turkey	79.51	17.043	0.2143	0.101	0.0013
Brazil	207.65	37.076	0.1785	0.699	0.0034
Romania	19.71	3.346	0.1698	0.068	0.0034
Poland	37.95	6.445	0.1698	0.119	0.0031
Malaysia	31.18	5.045	0.1618	0.037	0.0012
Russia	144.34	22.076	0.1529	0.388	0.0027
Peru	31.77	4.488	0.1412	0.220	0.0069
Colombia	48.65	6.359	0.1307	0.142	0.0029
Canada	36.28	4.617	0.1272	0.052	0.0014
Ukraine	45.01	5.712	0.1269	0.119	0.0027
Vietnam	92.70	11.527	0.1243	0.043	0.0005
Bolivia	10.89	1.194	0.1097	0.022	0.0021
Cuba	11.48	1.113	0.0970	0.009	0.0007
Iran	80.27	7.572	0.0943	0.145	0.0018
Guatemala	16.58	1.238	0.0747	0.020	0.0012
South Africa	55.91	4.067	0.0727	0.103	0.0018
Thailand	68.86	4.728	0.0687	0.034	0.0005
Iraq	37.20	2.466	0.0663	0.025	0.0007

Table 1. *Cont.*

Country	$P/10^6$	$PJ_\infty/10^6$	J_∞	$PD_\infty/10^6$	D_∞
Ecuador	16.38	1.057	0.0645	0.036	0.0022
Dominican Republic	10.65	0.661	0.0621	0.004	0.0004
Mexico	127.54	7.483	0.0587	0.333	0.0026
Philippines	103.32	4.077	0.0395	0.066	0.0006
Morocco	35.27	1.272	0.0361	0.016	0.0005
India	1420.00	44.691	0.0315	0.531	0.0004
Indonesia	261.12	6.738	0.0258	0.161	0.0006
Saudi Arabia	32.28	0.830	0.0257	0.010	0.0003
Venezuela	31.57	0.552	0.0175	0.006	0.0002
Algeria	40.61	0.271	0.0067	0.007	0.0002
Senegal	15.41	0.089	0.0058	0.002	0.0001
Egypt	95.69	0.516	0.0054	0.025	0.0003
China	1410.00	4.904	0.0035	0.101	0.0001

3.1. Solution in the Limit of Small $J \ll 1$

Initially at reduced time $\tau = 0$, the cumulative number of new infections is extremely small. In the limit $J(\tau) \leq J_\infty \ll 1$, where $J_\infty = J(\tau = \infty)$, and also at later times, we use the approximations $1 - J(\tau) \simeq 1 - J_\infty$ to obtain for Equation (8)

$$b(\tau) \simeq \frac{\frac{dV}{d\tau}}{1 - J_\infty - V(\tau)} = \frac{d}{d\tau}\ln[1 - J_\infty - V(\tau)]^{-1}. \tag{18}$$

With the initial condition $V(0) = 0$ for arbitrary but given dependencies $b(\tau)$, Equation (18) immediately integrates to

$$V(\tau) \simeq (1 - J_\infty)[1 - e^{-\int_0^\tau dx\, b(x)}], \tag{19}$$

which approaches $V_\infty = V(\infty) = 1 - J_\infty$ after infinite time. Likewise, in the same limit $J \leq J_\infty \ll 1$, Equation (10) becomes

$$\begin{aligned} k(\tau) &\simeq 1 - J_\infty - V(\tau) - \frac{d}{d\tau}\ln\left[\frac{j(\tau)}{1 - J_\infty - V(\tau)}\right] \\ &= (1 - J_\infty)e^{-\int_0^\tau dx\, b(x)} - \frac{d}{d\tau}\ln\left[\frac{j(\tau)e^{\int_0^\tau dx\, b(x)}}{1 - J_\infty}\right], \end{aligned} \tag{20}$$

where we inserted Equation (19). With the initial condition $j(0) = \eta(1 - \eta)$ Equation (20) integrates to

$$j(\tau) \simeq \eta(1 - \eta)\exp\int_0^\tau dx\left[(1 - J_\infty)e^{-\int_0^x dy\, b(y)} - k(x) - b(x)\right]. \tag{21}$$

Because of the adopted smallness $J_\infty \ll 1$, we simplify the approximative solution (21) in the following as

$$j(\tau) \simeq \eta(1 - \eta)\exp\int_0^\tau dx\left[e^{-\int_0^x dy\, b(y)} - k(x) - b(x)\right]. \tag{22}$$

but we keep the J_∞ in the solution (19) in order not to violate the restriction $J(\tau) + V(\tau) \leq J_\infty + V_\infty \leq 1$. In terms of the real time the approximative solutions, (19) and (22) read

$$V(t) \simeq (1 - J_\infty)[1 - e^{-\int_{t_0}^t d\xi\, v(\xi)}], \tag{23}$$

and

$$\mathring{J}(t) \simeq a(t)\eta(1-\eta)\exp\left[\int_{t_0}^{t} d\xi[a(\xi)e^{-\int_{t_0}^{\xi} dyv(y)} - \mu(\xi) - v(\xi)]\right], \tag{24}$$

respectively.

3.2. Comparison with the SIR Model Limit

The SIR model corresponds to the limit of no vaccinations $v = b = 0$, corresponding to $V = 0$. In this limit, the solutions (22) and (24) reduce to

$$j_{\rm SIR}(\tau) \simeq \eta(1-\eta)e^{\int_0^\tau dx\,[1-k(x)]} \tag{25}$$

and

$$\mathring{J}_{\rm SIR}(t) \simeq a(t)\eta(1-\eta)e^{\int_{t_0}^{t} d\xi[a(\xi)-\mu(\xi]}, \tag{26}$$

respectively, in perfect agreement with the earlier derived Equations (12) and (15) of ref. [27].

3.3. Properties of the Approximate Solution (22)

The approximate solution (22) is predominantly determined by the reduced time variation of the ratios $k(\tau)$ and $b(\tau)$. For the first and second time derivatives of the solution (22) we obtain

$$\begin{aligned}
\frac{dj}{d\tau} &= \eta(1-\eta)\left[e^{-\int_0^\tau dyb(y)} - k(\tau) - b(\tau)\right]\exp\int_0^\tau dx\left[e^{-\int_0^x dy\,b(y)} - k(x) - b(x)\right], \quad (27)\\
\frac{d^2j}{d\tau^2} &= \eta(1-\eta)\left([e^{-\int_0^\tau dyb(y)} - k(\tau) - b(\tau)]^2 - \frac{dk}{d\tau} - \frac{db}{d\tau} - b(\tau)e^{-\int_0^\tau dyb(y)}\right)\times\\
&\quad \exp\int_0^\tau dx\left[e^{-\int_0^x dy\,b(y)} - k(x) - b(x)\right]. \quad (28)
\end{aligned}$$

Consequently, extrema of the rate of new infections occur at reduced times τ_E determined by

$$k(\tau_E) + b(\tau_E) = e^{-\int_0^{\tau_E} dy\,b(y)}. \tag{29}$$

As the right-hand side of this Equation is smaller than or equal to unity, no extrema of infections occur for a sum of variations

$$k(\tau) + b(\tau) > 1 \tag{30}$$

greater than unity at all times. As both rates are semi-positive the condition (30) for no extrema in the rate of new infections is fulfilled if either the vaccination rate $v(t) > a(t)$ is greater than the infection rate and/or the recovery rate $\mu(t) > a(t)$ is greater than the infection rate. For large enough values of k and b, so that $k(\tau) + b(\tau) > 1$, we have thus shown in Equation (27) that no extrema of the rate of new infections $j(\tau)$ occur at any reduced time $\tau \geq 0$. According to Equation (27), then, this rate continually decreases from its original positive initial value $j(\tau = 0) = \eta(1-\eta)$ to even smaller values at later times. As $j(\tau) = S(\tau)I(\tau)$ and $S(\tau)$, as well as $I(\tau)$, are originally positive for $\tau = 0$, they will remain positive. With $I(\tau)$ and $S(\tau)$ positive, it is clear from Equations (15) and (16) that $R(\tau)$ and $V(\tau)$ are also positively valued at all times.

In the case of reduced time intervals, where

$$k(\tau) + b(\tau) < 1, \tag{31}$$

we obtain

$$\begin{aligned}
[\frac{d^2j}{d\tau^2}]_{\tau_E} &= -\eta(1-\eta)\left([\frac{dk}{d\tau}]_{\tau_E} + [\frac{db}{d\tau}]_{\tau_E} + b^2(\tau_E) + b(\tau_E)k(\tau_E)\right)\times\\
&\quad \exp\left[\int_0^{\tau_E} dx\left(e^{-\int_0^x dy\,b(y)} - k(x) - b(x)\right)\right], \quad (32)
\end{aligned}$$

so that the extrema are maxima if

$$[\frac{dk}{d\tau}]_{\tau_E} + [\frac{db}{d\tau}]_{\tau_E} + b^2(\tau_E) + b(\tau_E)k(\tau_E) > 0 \tag{33}$$

is positive. Alternatively, the extrema are minima if

$$[\frac{dk}{d\tau}]_{\tau_E} + [\frac{db}{d\tau}]_{\tau_E} + b^2(\tau_E) + b(\tau_E)k(\tau_E) < 0 \tag{34}$$

is negative. Note that there can be multiple minima and maxima depending on the reduced time variation of the ratios $k(\tau)$ and $b(\tau)$. The extreme values of the rate of new infections are given by

$$j_E(\tau_E) = \eta(1-\eta)e^{\int_0^{\tau_E} dx\, \left[e^{-\int_0^x dy\, b(y)} - k(x) - b(x)\right]}. \tag{35}$$

3.4. Cumulative Fraction

Integrating the rate of new infections (22) provides us with the corresponding cumulative fraction

$$J(\tau) = \eta + \eta(1-\eta)\int_0^{\tau} dz\, \exp\left[\int_0^z dx\,(e^{-\int_0^x dy\, b(y)} - k(x) - b(x))\right]. \tag{36}$$

For general reduced time variations $k(\tau)$ and $b(\tau)$, the integral in Equation (36) can be reasonably well approximated and evaluated using the method of steepest descent [34,35] by expanding the argument in the exponential function in Equation (36) to second order in z around its (possible multiple) minimum values τ_m

$$h(z) = -\int_0^z dx\,(e^{-\int_0^x dy\, b(y)} - k(x) - b(x)) \simeq h(\tau_m) + \frac{(z-\tau_m)^2 h''_m}{2}, \tag{37}$$

where

$$h''_m = [\frac{d^2h(z)}{dz^2}]_{\tau_m}. \tag{38}$$

With this expansion, we obtain for the cumulative fraction (36)

$$J(\tau) \simeq \eta + \eta(1-\eta)\sum_m \sqrt{\frac{\pi}{2h''_m}}e^{-h(\tau_m)}\left[\operatorname{erf}\left(\sqrt{\frac{h''_m}{2}}(\tau-\tau_m)\right) + \operatorname{erf}\left(\sqrt{\frac{h''_m}{2}}\tau_m\right)\right], \tag{39}$$

where the sum of m accounts for possible multiple minima and

$$\begin{aligned} h(\tau_m) &= \int_0^{\tau_m} dx\,\left[k(x) + b(x) - e^{-\int_0^x dy\, b(y)}\right], \\ h''_m &= [\frac{dk}{d\tau}]_{\tau_m} + [\frac{db}{d\tau}]_{\tau_m} + b^2(\tau_m) + b(\tau_m)k(\tau_m). \end{aligned} \tag{40}$$

For a minimum, the second derivative $h''_m > 0$ has to be positive. The minima occur at times given by

$$k(\tau_m) + b(\tau_m) = e^{-\int_0^{\tau_m} dy\, b(y)}, \tag{41}$$

and, as discussed before (see Equations (29)–(31)), only for reduced time intervals where the sum $k(\tau) + b(\tau) < 1$ is less than unity.

4. Special Case: Stationary Ratios

We first consider the approximative solutions (19) and (22) in the special case of stationary ratios

$$\begin{aligned} k(\tau) &= k_0, \\ b(\tau) &= b_0, \end{aligned} \tag{42}$$

considered before [1]. We readily obtain

$$V(\tau) = (1 - J_\infty)[1 - e^{-b_0\tau}], \tag{43}$$

and

$$j(\tau) = \eta(1-\eta)\exp\left[\frac{1-e^{-b_0\tau}}{b_0} - (k_0+b_0)\tau\right]. \tag{44}$$

Provided $k_0 + b_0 < 1$, the rate of new infections (44) attains its maximum value at the reduced time

$$\tau_m = -\frac{\ln(k_0+b_0)}{b_0}. \tag{45}$$

The maximum rate of new infections, then, is

$$j_{\max} = j(\tau_m) = \eta(1-\eta)(k_0+b_0)^{\frac{k_0+b_0}{b_0}} e^{\frac{1-(k_0+b_0)}{b_0}}. \tag{46}$$

Equations (45) and (46) agree exactly with Equations (98) and (100) derived before [1].

4.1. Cumulative Fraction

Integrating Equation (44) yields for the cumulative fraction

$$J(\tau) = \eta + \eta(1-\eta)H(\tau), \tag{47}$$

with the integral

$$H(\tau) = \int_0^\tau dx\, \exp\left[\frac{1-e^{-b_0x}}{b_0} - (k_0+b_0)x\right] = b_0^{\frac{k_0}{b_0}} e^{\frac{1}{b_0}} \int_{\frac{e^{-b_0\tau}}{b_0}}^{\frac{1}{b_0}} dy\, y^{\frac{k_0}{b_0}} e^{-y}, \tag{48}$$

where we substituted $y = e^{-b_0x}/b_0$. The integral (48) can be expressed as the difference of two lower incomplete gamma functions

$$\gamma(s,x) = \int_0^x t^{s-1}e^{-t}dt = \Gamma(s) - \Gamma(s,x), \tag{49}$$

yielding

$$H(\tau) = b_0^{\frac{k_0}{b_0}} e^{\frac{1}{b_0}} \left[\gamma\left(1+\frac{k_0}{b_0}, \frac{1}{b_0}\right) - \gamma\left(1+\frac{k_0}{b_0}, \frac{e^{-b_0\tau}}{b_0}\right)\right], \tag{50}$$

so that the cumulative fraction (47) is given by

$$J(\tau) = \eta + \eta(1-\eta)b_0^{\frac{k_0}{b_0}} e^{\frac{1}{b_0}} \left[\gamma\left(1+\frac{k_0}{b_0}, \frac{1}{b_0}\right) - \gamma\left(1+\frac{k_0}{b_0}, \frac{e^{-b_0\tau}}{b_0}\right)\right]. \tag{51}$$

For infinitely large times, the fraction (51) approaches the final value

$$J_\infty = J(\tau=\infty) = \eta + \eta(1-\eta)b_0^{\frac{k_0}{b_0}} e^{\frac{1}{b_0}} \gamma\left(1+\frac{k_0}{b_0}, \frac{1}{b_0}\right). \tag{52}$$

Equations (51) and (52) agree exactly with the earlier derived Equations (A10) and (102) of ref. [1], using a different approach.

Because the analytical approximations were derived in the limit $J \leq J_\infty \ll 1$, for consistency, we have to require $J_\infty < 1$ for the values of k_0 and b_0 for which our approximation holds. In Figure 1, we calculate the required values of k_0 and b_0 fulfilling $J_\infty < 1$ using Equation (52). The required values depend on the initial condition encoded by η, and are located above the line shown in this figure. For sufficiently large k_0, $J_\infty < 1$, for any ratio b_0, while at low recovery to infection ratios k_0, the vaccination to infection rate must be significant to ensure $J_\infty < 1$. The regime of b_0 close to zero is numerically difficult to evaluate using Equation (52).

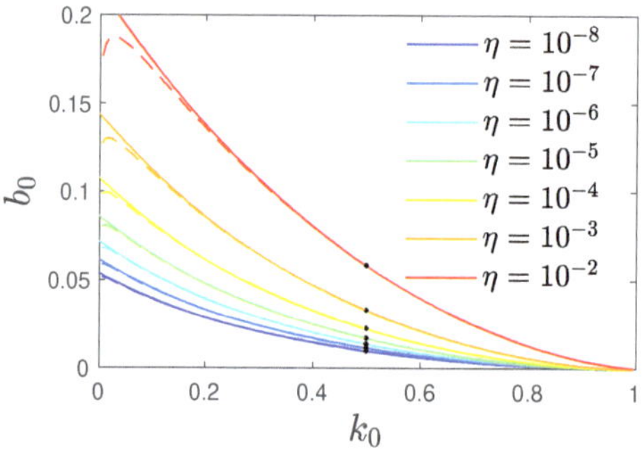

Figure 1. Required lower limiting values of b_0 versus k_0, fulfilling $J_\infty \leq 1$ using Equation (52), for various initial η (solid lines). Within the (k_0, b_0) region above a certain solid line, $J_\infty < 1$, while the exact numerical solution features $J_\infty \leq 1$ for any choice of k_0 and b_0. The regime $b_0 \ll 1$ is numerically difficult to evaluate using Equation (52); beyond $k_0 > 1/2$ (marked by black dots), we use the explicit Equation (58). For $k_0 < 1/2$, Equation (58) is shown as dashed line, highlighting the region of k_0 where Equation (58) cannot be used.

4.2. Limit $b_0 \ll 1$

In the limit of small $b_0 \ll 1$, we use relation (49) and the asymptotic expansion (Equation 6.5.32 in [36]) of the upper incomplete gamma function for large arguments $x \gg 1$

$$\Gamma(s, x \gg 1) \simeq x^{s-1} e^{-x} \left[1 + \frac{s-1}{x} + \frac{(s-1)(s-2)}{x^2} + \ldots \right], \tag{53}$$

to obtain for

$$\gamma\left(1 + \frac{k_0}{b_0}, \frac{1}{b_0}\right) \simeq \Gamma\left(1 + \frac{k_0}{b_0}\right) - b_0^{\frac{k_0}{b_0}} e^{-\frac{1}{b_0}} [1 + k_0 + k_0(k_0 - 1) + \ldots]; \tag{54}$$

the fraction (52) then becomes

$$J_\infty(b_0 \ll 1) \simeq \eta + \eta(1-\eta) \left[\Gamma\left(1 + \frac{k_0}{b_0}\right) b_0^{\frac{k_0}{b_0}} e^{\frac{1}{b_0}} - [1 + k_0 + k_0(k_0 - 1) + \ldots] \right]. \tag{55}$$

Using Stirling's formula (Equation 6.1.37 in [36]) for the gamma function $\Gamma(x+1) \sim \sqrt{2\pi x}(x/e)^x [1 + (12x)^{-1}]$ for large x, Equation (55) becomes,

$$J_\infty(b_0 \ll 1) \simeq \eta + \eta(1-\eta) \left[\sqrt{\frac{2\pi k_0}{b_0}}\, k_0^{\frac{k_0}{b_0}} e^{\frac{1-k_0}{b_0}} \left(1 + \frac{b_0}{12k_0}\right) - [1 + k_0 + k_0(k_0 - 1) + \ldots] \right]. \tag{56}$$

For values of $b_0 < k_0 < 1$, the fraction (56) to leading orders is given by

$$J_\infty(b_0 \ll 1) \simeq \eta + \eta(1-\eta)\left[\sqrt{2\pi k_0/b_0}\, e^{(1-k_0)/b_0} k_0^{k_0/b_0} - 1\right]. \tag{57}$$

Because one has to require $J_\infty \leq 1$, or equivalently, $\ln(J_\infty) \leq 0$, Equation (57) turns into an inequality for b_0, which can be written in terms of the principal branch W_0 of Lambert's W-function, because $(x/b_0) - \ln b_0 = \ln y$ is solved for any $x \geq 0$ and y by $x/W_0(xy)$, leading to

$$b_0 \geq \frac{2(1-k_0+k_0\ln k_0)}{W_0\left(\frac{(1+\eta)^2[1-k_0+k_0\ln(k_0)]}{\pi k_0 \eta^2}\right)}. \tag{58}$$

This inequality (58) ensures $J_\infty \leq 1$. Along with the information contained in Equation (52), it is visualized in Figure 1.

5. Stationary Ratios with Delayed Start of Vaccinations

As first new application of our results, we discuss the case of stationary ratio $k(\tau) = k_0$ for all reduced times and the influence of a stationary ratio $b(\tau)$ starting at the delayed reduced time $\tau_v > 0$, i.e.,

$$\begin{aligned} k(\tau) &= k_0, \\ b(\tau) &= b_0\Theta(\tau - \tau_v) \end{aligned} \tag{59}$$

where $\Theta(x < 0) = 0$ and $\Theta(x \geq 0) = 1$ denotes the step function. We then obtain for Equation (19), i.e., in the limit $J \ll 1$, $V = 0$ for $\tau < \tau_V$ and

$$V(\tau \geq \tau_v) = (1 - J_\infty)[1 - e^{-b_0(\tau - \tau_v)}]. \tag{60}$$

Likewise, the rate (22) becomes the SIR-rate [27]

$$j(0 \leq \tau < \tau_v) = \eta(1-\eta)e^{(1-k_0)\tau} \tag{61}$$

at times without vaccination, and

$$j(\tau \geq \tau_v) = \eta(1-\eta)\exp\left[(1-k_0)\tau_v + \frac{1 - e^{-b_0(\tau-\tau_v)}}{b_0} - (k_0+b_0)(\tau - \tau_v)\right] \tag{62}$$

at later times. While the SIR-rate (61) is exponentially increasing in reduced time, the rate (62) has a maximum value

$$\begin{aligned} j_{\max} = j(\tau_m) &= \eta(1-\eta)\exp\left[(1-k_0)\tau_v + \frac{1 - e^{-b_0(\tau_m-\tau_v)}}{b_0} - (k_0+b_0)(\tau_m - \tau_v)\right] \\ &= \eta(1-\eta)(k_0+b_0)^{\frac{k_0+b_0}{b_0}} \exp\left[(1-k_0)\tau_v + \frac{1-(k_0+b_0)}{b_0}\right], \end{aligned} \tag{63}$$

provided $k_0 + b_0 < 1$, the rate of new infections attains its maximum at the reduced time

$$\tau_m = \tau_v - \frac{\ln(k_0 + b_0)}{b_0}. \tag{64}$$

We first note that for $\tau_v = 0$, the rates (62) and (63) correctly reproduce the earlier results (44) and (46). We emphasize that the delayed start of the vaccinations increases both the maximum time of the rate of infections and the maximum rate of new infections.

Compared to the case of no delay in the start of vaccinations ($\tau_v = 0$), we introduce the enhancement factor for the maximum rate

$$E(\tau_v) = \frac{j_{\max}(\tau_v)}{j_{\max}(\tau_v = 0)} = e^{(1-k_0)\tau_v}, \tag{65}$$

shown in Figure 2, which is independent of the vaccination rate and determined by the values of k_0 and τ_v. Apparently, this exponential enhancement solely results from the new infections before the vaccinations start. While the enhancement factor increases exponentially over a wide range of $k_0\tau_v$, in accord with Equation (65), it numerically reaches a plateau as $k_0\tau_v$ approaches infinity, whose height increases with decreasing η. This is a clear indication that for large values of the enhancement factor, a regime is reached where $J(\tau_m)$ is no longer much smaller than unity, so that the analytical approximation no longer holds. This explanation is supported by the cumulative fraction at large times (68) (see below) being directly proportional to the enhancement factor (65).

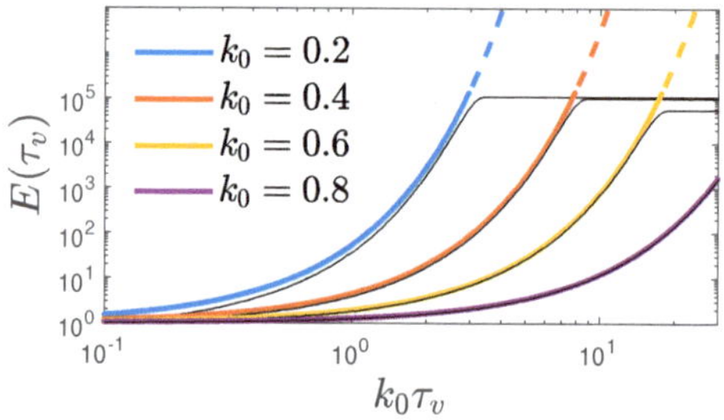

Figure 2. The enhancement factor $E(\tau_v)$ as function of $k_0\tau_v$ for various k_0. Analytical result (65) (colored) compared with the numerical result (black) for $b_0 = 0.5$ and $\eta = 10^{-5}$. Note the double-logarithmic representation. The dashed parts of the analytic results highlight the regimes for which Equation (65) cannot be used anymore, as J_∞ (68) exceeds unity.

Integrating the rates of new injections (61) and (63) yields for the cumulative fraction

$$J(0 \le \tau < \tau_v) = \eta + \frac{\eta(1-\eta)}{1-k_0}[e^{(1-k_0)\tau} - 1], \tag{66}$$

and

$$\begin{aligned} J(\tau \ge \tau_v) &= \eta + \frac{\eta(1-\eta)}{1-k_0}\left[e^{(1-k_0)\tau_v} - 1\right] + \eta(1-\eta) b_0^{\frac{k_0}{b_0}} e^{(1-k_0)\tau_v + \frac{1}{b_0}} \times \\ &\quad \left[\gamma\left(1 + \frac{k_0}{b_0}, \frac{1}{b_0}\right) - \gamma\left(1 + \frac{k_0}{b_0}, \frac{e^{-b_0(\tau-\tau_v)}}{b_0}\right)\right]. \end{aligned} \tag{67}$$

For infinitely large times, the fraction (67) approaches the final value $J_\infty = J(\tau = \infty)$ with

$$\begin{aligned} J_\infty &= \eta + \frac{\eta(1-\eta)}{1-k_0}\left[e^{(1-k_0)\tau_v} - 1\right] + \eta(1-\eta) b_0^{\frac{k_0}{b_0}} e^{(1-k_0)\tau_v + \frac{1}{b_0}} \gamma\left(1 + \frac{k_0}{b_0}, \frac{1}{b_0}\right) \\ &= \frac{\eta(1-\eta)}{1-k_0} E(\tau_v)\left[1 + (1-k_0) b_0^{\frac{k_0}{b_0}} e^{\frac{1}{b_0}} \gamma\left(1 + \frac{k_0}{b_0}, \frac{1}{b_0}\right)\right] + \frac{\eta(\eta - k_0)}{1-k_0}. \end{aligned} \tag{68}$$

An example showing all quantities calculated analytically in this section, along with the numerical solution for a case with $J_\infty \ll 1$, is given in Figure 3.

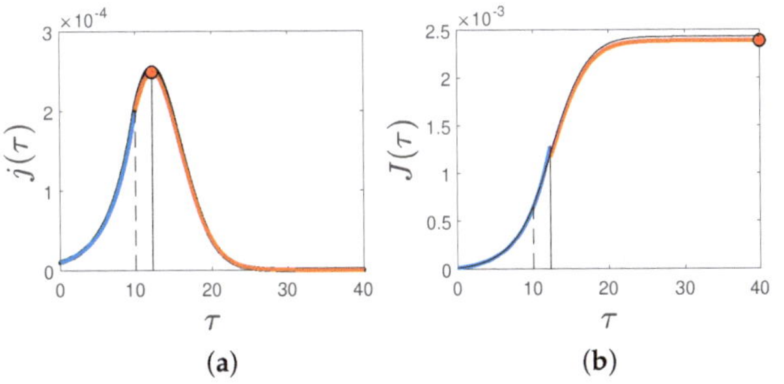

Figure 3. Example for Section 5 using $k_0 = 0.7$, $b_0 = 0.1$, $\tau_v = 10$, and $\eta = 10^{-5}$. Numerical solution (solid black curve) for (**a**) $j(\tau)$ and (**b**) $J(\tau)$. In (**a**), the analytical expressions (61) (blue) and (62) (red) had been added. The vertical lines are at $\tau = \tau_v$ (dashed) and $\tau = \tau_m$ (solid), according to Equation (64). The filled red circle corresponds to Equation (63). In (**b**), the analytical expressions are taken from Equations (66) (blue) and (67) (red), while the red circle marks the analytical expression for J_∞ according to Equation (68).

6. Oscillating Ratio k with Delayed Vaccinations at Constant Rate b_0

As a second application, we investigate the influence of delayed vaccinations with constant rate on the earlier discussed SIR-application [27] with an oscillating k ratio and delayed vaccination ratio b,

$$k(\tau) = 1 + \alpha \sin(\beta\tau), \tag{69}$$

$$b(t) = b_0 \Theta(\tau - \tau_v), \tag{70}$$

with constant values α and β. As noted before [27] the oscillating ratio (69) represents a series of repeating pandemic outbursts with equal amplitudes in the rate of new infections. We then obtain for Equation (19) $V = 0$ for $\tau < \tau_V$ and

$$V(\tau \geq \tau_v) = 1 - e^{-b_0(\tau - \tau_v)}. \tag{71}$$

Likewise, the rate (22) becomes the SIR-rate [27]

$$j(0 \leq \tau \leq \tau_v) = \eta(1-\eta)e^{\frac{\alpha}{\beta}[\cos(\beta\tau)-1]} \tag{72}$$

at times without vaccination, and

$$j(\tau \geq \tau_v) = \eta(1-\eta)\exp\left\{\frac{\alpha}{\beta}[\cos(\beta\tau) - 1] + \frac{1 - e^{-b_0(\tau-\tau_v)}}{b_0} - (1 + b_0)(\tau - \tau_v)\right\} \tag{73}$$

at later times. In Figure 4a, we show the rate of new infections (72)–(73) in the case $\alpha = 0.8$ and $\beta = 0.5$ for several values of the starting time of vaccinations τ_v and the vaccination rate $b_0 = 0.2$. We also compare, in each case, the analytical approximations with the exact rates of new infections from solving the SIRV equations numerically.

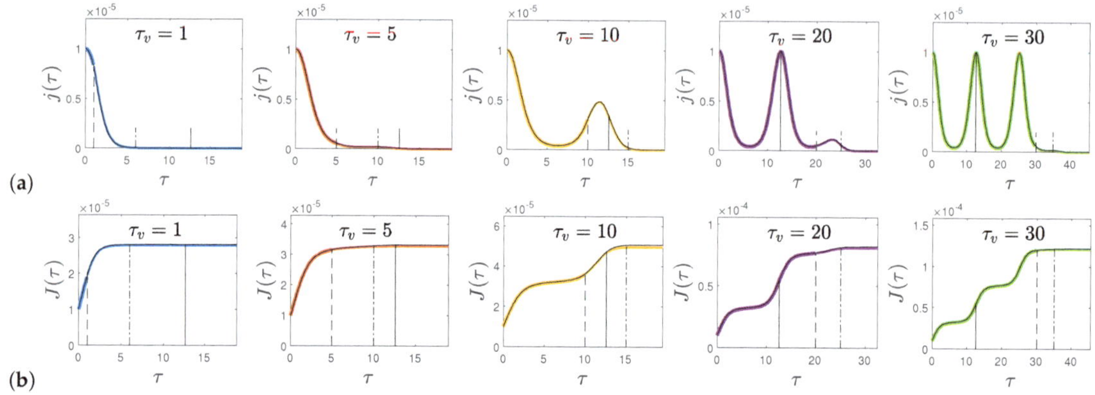

Figure 4. (**a**) Perfect agreement between the analytical solutions (72) and (73) (colored) with the numerical solutions (black) for different values of $\tau_v = 1, 5, 10, 20, 30$ (see figure legends) at $\alpha = 0.8$, $\beta = 0.5$, $b_0 = 0.2$, and $\eta = 10^{-5}$. For times $\tau < \tau_v$, the analytical solution is insensitive to τ_v, and branches from this curve at $\tau = \tau_v$. The vertical black lines are at $\tau = \tau_v$ (dashed) and $\tau = 2\pi/\beta$ (solid), and $\tau = \tau_v + b_0^{-1}$ (dot-dashed). (**b**) Corresponding cumulative $J(\tau)$. Numerical solution (black) together with the analytical Equations (74) and (89)–(90) (colored).

For the corresponding cumulative fractions, one finds [27]

$$J(\tau \le \tau_v) = \eta + \eta(1-\eta)e^{-\frac{\alpha}{\beta}}\left[\tau I_0\left(\frac{\alpha}{\beta}\right) + 2\sum_{n=1}^{\infty}\frac{I_n(\frac{\alpha}{\beta})}{n\beta}\sin(n\beta\tau)\right] \tag{74}$$

in terms of an infinite series of the modified Bessel function of the first kind $I_n(z)$, and

$$J(\tau \ge \tau_v) = \eta + \eta(1-\eta)e^{-\frac{\alpha}{\beta}}\Big\{M(\tau) + \tau_v I_0(\frac{\alpha}{\beta}) + 2\sum_{n=1}^{\infty}\frac{I_n(\frac{\alpha}{\beta})}{n\beta}\sin(n\beta\tau_v)\Big\}, \tag{75}$$

with the integral

$$M(\tau) = \int_{\tau_v}^{\tau} dx\, e^{\frac{\alpha}{\beta}\cos(\beta x) - (1+b_0)(x-\tau_v) + \frac{1-e^{-b_0(x-\tau_v)}}{b_0}} = \int_0^{\tau-\tau_v} dy\, e^{\frac{\alpha}{\beta}\cos[\beta(y+\tau_v)] + g(y)}, \tag{76}$$

where we substituted $y = x - \tau$ and introduced the function

$$g(y) = \frac{1-e^{-b_0 y}}{b_0} - (1+b_0)y. \tag{77}$$

This function (77) has the following asymptotic behaviors for small and large values of $b_0 y$, i.e.,

$$g(y) \simeq \begin{cases} -b_0 y(1+\frac{y}{2}), & \text{for } y \ll b_0^{-1}, \\ \frac{1}{b_0} - (1+b_0)y, & \text{for } y \gg b_0^{-1}. \end{cases} \tag{78}$$

In the following, we therefore approximate the function (77) as $g(y) \simeq g_A(y)$ with

$$g_A(y) = -b_0 y\left(1+\frac{y}{2}\right)\Theta\left[b_0^{-1} - y\right] + \left[\frac{1}{2b_0} - (1+b_0)y\right]\Theta\left[y - b_0^{-1}\right]. \tag{79}$$

With this approximation, we calculate the integral (76). For values of $\tau \leq \tau_v + b_0^{-1}$ we obtain

$$
\begin{aligned}
M(\tau - \tau_v \leq b_0^{-1}) &\simeq \int_0^{\tau-\tau_v} dy e^{\frac{\alpha}{\beta}\cos[\beta(y+\tau_v)] - b_0 y(1+\frac{y}{2})} \\
&= \int_0^{\tau-\tau_v} dy \left[I_0\left(\frac{\alpha}{\beta}\right) + 2\sum_{n=1}^{\infty} I_n\left(\frac{\alpha}{\beta}\right)\cos[n\beta(y+\tau_v)] \right] e^{-b_0 y(1+\frac{y}{2})} \\
&= \sqrt{\frac{\pi}{2b_0}} e^{\frac{b_0}{2}} \left\{ I_0\left(\frac{\alpha}{\beta}\right)\left[\operatorname{erf}\left(\sqrt{\frac{b_0}{2}}(\tau-\tau_v+1)\right) - \operatorname{erf}\sqrt{\frac{b_0}{2}} \right] \right. \\
&\left. + 2\sum_{n=1}^{\infty} I_n\left(\frac{\alpha}{\beta}\right) e^{-\frac{n^2\beta^2}{2b_0}} W_n(\tau) \right\},
\end{aligned} \tag{80}
$$

with

$$
\begin{aligned}
W_n(\tau) &= \sqrt{\frac{2b_0}{\pi}} e^{-b_0/2} e^{\frac{n^2\beta^2}{2b_0}} \int_0^{\tau-\tau_v} dy \cos[n\beta(y+\tau_v)] e^{-b_0 y(1+\frac{y}{2})} \\
&= \Re\left[e^{\imath n\beta(\tau_v - 1)} \left[\operatorname{erf}\left(\sqrt{\frac{b_0}{2}}(\tau-\tau_v+1) - \frac{\imath n\beta}{\sqrt{2b_0}}\right) - \operatorname{erf}\left(\sqrt{\frac{b_0}{2}} - \frac{\imath n\beta}{\sqrt{2b_0}}\right) \right] \right]
\end{aligned} \tag{81}
$$

in terms of error functions with complex arguments. The real part in Equation (81) is calculated in detail in Appendix A, providing

$$
\begin{aligned}
W_n(\tau) &= \cos[n\beta(\tau_v - 1)] \left[\operatorname{erf}\left(\sqrt{\frac{b_0}{2}}(\tau - \tau_v + 1)\right) - \operatorname{erf}\sqrt{\frac{b_0}{2}} \right] \\
&+ \frac{e^{-\frac{b_0}{2}(\tau-\tau_v+1)^2}}{\pi\sqrt{2b_0}(\tau - \tau_v + 1)} \{\cos[n\beta(\tau_v - 1)] - \cos n\beta\tau\} \\
&- \frac{e^{-\frac{b_0}{2}}}{\pi\sqrt{2b_0}} \{\cos[n\beta(\tau_v - 1)] - \cos n\beta\tau_v\} \\
&+ \frac{2e^{-\frac{b_0}{2}(\tau-\tau_v+1)^2}}{\pi} \sum_{m=1}^{\infty} \frac{e^{-\frac{m^2}{4}} A_{n,m}(\tau)}{m^2 + 2b_0(\tau - \tau_v + 1)^2} \\
&- \frac{2e^{-\frac{b_0}{2}}}{\pi} \sum_{m=1}^{\infty} \frac{e^{-\frac{m^2}{4}} B_{n,m}(\tau)}{m^2 + 2b_0}
\end{aligned} \tag{82}
$$

with

$$
\begin{aligned}
A_{n,m}(\tau) &= \sqrt{2b_0}(\tau - \tau_v + 1) \left[\cos[n\beta(\tau_v - 1)] - \cosh\left(\frac{mn\beta}{\sqrt{2b_0}}\right) \cos n\beta\tau \right], \\
&+ m \sinh\left(\frac{mn\beta}{\sqrt{2b_0}}\right) \sin n\beta\tau,
\end{aligned} \tag{83}
$$

$$
\begin{aligned}
B_{n,m}(\tau) &= \sqrt{2b_0} \left[\cos[n\beta(\tau_v - 1)] - \cosh\left(\frac{mn\beta}{\sqrt{2b_0}}\right) \cos n\beta\tau_v \right] \\
&+ m \sinh\left(\frac{mn\beta}{\sqrt{2b_0}}\right) \sin n\beta\tau_v.
\end{aligned} \tag{84}
$$

Likewise, in the alternative case $\tau \geq \tau_v + b_0^{-1}$, we find

$$\begin{aligned} M(\tau-\tau_v \geq b_0^{-1}) \;\simeq\;& \int_0^{b_0^{-1}} dy\, e^{\frac{\alpha}{\beta}\cos[\beta(y+\tau_v)]-b_0 y(1+\frac{y}{2})} \\ &+e^{\frac{1}{2b_0}} \int_{b_0^{-1}}^{\tau-\tau_v} dy\, e^{\frac{\alpha}{\beta}\cos[\beta(y+\tau_v)]-(1+b_0)y} \\ =\;& e^{\frac{1}{2b_0}} \int_{b_0^{-1}}^{\tau-\tau_v} dy \left[I_0\left(\frac{\alpha}{\beta}\right) + 2\sum_{n=1}^{\infty} I_n\left(\frac{\alpha}{\beta}\right) \Re e^{\imath n\beta(y+\tau_v)} \right] e^{-(1+b_0)y} \\ &+\sqrt{\frac{\pi}{2b_0}} e^{\frac{b_0}{2}} \left\{ I_0\left(\frac{\alpha}{\beta}\right) \left[\operatorname{erf}\left(\sqrt{\frac{b_0}{2}}(1+b_0^{-1}) \right) - \operatorname{erf}\sqrt{\frac{b_0}{2}} \right] \right. \\ &\left. +2\sum_{n=1}^{\infty} I_n\left(\frac{\alpha}{\beta}\right) e^{-\frac{n^2\beta^2}{2b_0}} W_n\left(\tau_v + b_0^{-1}\right) \right\}. \end{aligned} \tag{85}$$

The remaining integrals can be evaluated with the help of

$$\int_{b_0^{-1}}^{\tau-\tau_v} dy e^{-(1+b_0)y} = \frac{e^{-\frac{1+b_0}{b_0}} - e^{-(1+b_0)(\tau-\tau_v)}}{1+b_0}, \tag{86}$$

and

$$\begin{aligned} \Re \int_{b_0^{-1}}^{\tau-\tau_v} dy\, e^{\imath n\beta(y+\tau_v)-(1+b_0)y} \;=\;& \\ & \frac{1}{n^2\beta^2+(1+b_0)^2} \Big[\big(n\beta\sin n\beta\tau - (1+b_0)\cos n\beta\tau\big) e^{-(1+b_0)(\tau-\tau_v)} \\ & - \Big(n\beta\sin n\beta(\tau_v+b_0^{-1}) - (1+b_0)\cos n\beta(\tau_v+b_0^{-1})\Big) e^{-\frac{1+b_0}{b_0}} \Big]. \end{aligned} \tag{87}$$

Consequently, Equation (85) becomes

$$\begin{aligned} M(\tau-\tau_v \geq b_0^{-1}) \simeq\;& \sqrt{\frac{\pi}{2b_0}} e^{\frac{b_0}{2}} \left\{ I_0\left(\frac{\alpha}{\beta}\right) \left[\operatorname{erf}\left(\sqrt{\frac{b_0}{2}}(\frac{1}{b_0}+1) \right) - \operatorname{erf}\sqrt{\frac{b_0}{2}} \right] \right. \\ &\left. +2\sum_{n=1}^{\infty} I_n\left(\frac{\alpha}{\beta}\right) e^{-\frac{n^2\beta^2}{2b_0}} W_n(\tau_v+b_0^{-1}) \right\} \\ &+e^{\frac{1}{2b_0}} I_0\left(\frac{\alpha}{\beta}\right) \frac{e^{-\frac{1+b_0}{b_0}} - e^{-(1+b_0)(\tau-\tau_v)}}{1+b_0} + 2e^{\frac{1}{2b_0}} \sum_{n=1}^{\infty} \frac{I_n(\frac{\alpha}{\beta})}{n^2\beta^2+(1+b_0)^2} \times \\ & \Big[\big(n\beta\sin n\beta\tau - (1+b_0)\cos n\beta\tau\big) e^{-(1+b_0)(\tau-\tau_v)} \\ & - (n\beta\sin[n\beta(\tau_v+b_0^{-1})] - (1+b_0)\cos[n\beta(\tau_v+b_0^{-1})]) e^{-\frac{1+b_0}{b_0}} \Big]. \end{aligned} \tag{88}$$

For the cumulative fraction (75), we obtain

$$\begin{aligned} J(\tau_v \leq \tau \leq \tau_v + b_0^{-1}) \;=\;& \eta + \eta(1-\eta) e^{-\frac{\alpha}{\beta}} \times \\ & \left[\tau_v I_0\left(\frac{\alpha}{\beta}\right) + M(\tau-\tau_v \leq b_0^{-1}) + 2\sum_{n=1}^{\infty} \frac{I_n(\frac{\alpha}{\beta})}{n\beta} \sin(n\beta\tau_v) \right], \end{aligned} \tag{89}$$

and

$$\begin{aligned} J(\tau \geq \tau_v + b_0^{-1}) \;=\;& \eta + \eta(1-\eta) e^{-\frac{\alpha}{\beta}} \times \\ & \left[\tau_v I_0\left(\frac{\alpha}{\beta}\right) + M(\tau-\tau_v \geq b_0^{-1}) + 2\sum_{n=1}^{\infty} \frac{I_n(\frac{\alpha}{\beta})}{n\beta} \sin(n\beta\tau_v) \right], \end{aligned} \tag{90}$$

by inserting Equation (85) and (88), respectively. Hence, the cumulative fraction after infinite time is given by

$$
\begin{aligned}
J_\infty \quad = \quad & \eta + \eta(1-\eta)e^{-\frac{\alpha}{\beta}}\left\{\tau_v I_0\left(\frac{\alpha}{\beta}\right) + 2\sum_{n=1}^{\infty}\frac{I_n(\frac{\alpha}{\beta})}{n\beta}\sin(n\beta\tau_v)\right. \\
& + \sqrt{\frac{\pi}{2b_0}}e^{\frac{b_0}{2}}\left[I_0\left(\frac{\alpha}{\beta}\right)\left[\operatorname{erf}\left(\sqrt{\frac{b_0}{2}}(1+b_0^{-1})\right) - \operatorname{erf}\sqrt{\frac{b_0}{2}}\right]\right. \\
& \left. + 2\sum_{n=1}^{\infty} I_n\left(\frac{\alpha}{\beta}\right)e^{-\frac{n^2\beta^2}{2b_0}}W_n(\tau_v + b_0^{-1})\right] \\
& + e^{\frac{1}{2b_0}}I_0\left(\frac{\alpha}{\beta}\right)\frac{e^{-\frac{1+b_0}{b_0}}}{1+b_0} + 2e^{-\frac{1+2b_0}{2b_0}}\sum_{n=1}^{\infty}\frac{I_n(\frac{\alpha}{\beta})}{n^2\beta^2 + (1+b_0)^2}\times \\
& \left.\left[(1+b_0)\cos[n\beta(\tau_v + b_0^{-1})] - n\beta\sin[n\beta(\tau_v + b_0^{-1})]\right]\right\}, \qquad (91)
\end{aligned}
$$

which is compared in Figure 5 with the numerical values. It is sufficient to evaluate the sums up to $n = m = 50$; with this setting, the calculation of a J_∞ value lasts only a fraction of a second.

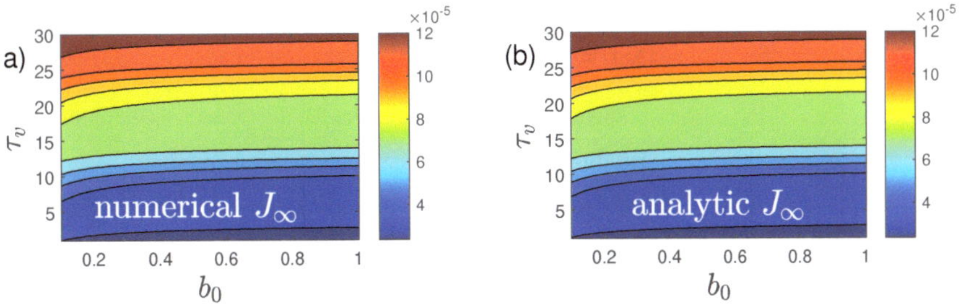

Figure 5. J_∞ as function of b_0 and τ_v. Remaining parameters as in Figure 4, i.e., $\alpha = 0.8$, $\beta = 0.5$, and $\eta = 10^{-5}$. (**a**) The numerical result, (**b**) the analytic result using Equation (91).

7. Summary and Conclusions

The dynamical equations of the susceptible–infected–recovered/removed–vaccinated (SIRV) epidemic model play an important role in predicting and/or analyzing the temporal evolution of epidemic outbreaks accounting quantitatively for the influence of vaccination campaigns. Additional to the time-dependent infection ($a(t)$) and recovery ($\mu(t)$) rates, regulating the transitions between the compartments $S \to I$ and $I \to R$, respectively, the time-dependent vaccination ($v(t)$ accounts for the transition between the compartments $S \to V$ of susceptible to vaccinated fractions. Here, apparently for the first time a new approximate analytical solution is derived for arbitrary and different but given temporal dependencies of the infection, recovery and vaccination rates, which is valid for all times after the start of the epidemic for which the cumulative fraction of new infections $J(t) \ll 1$ is much less than unity. As vaccination campaigns automatically reduce the rate of new infections by transferring susceptible persons to vaccinated persons, who then no longer can get infected, the limit $J \ll 1$ is even better fulfilled than in the SIR-epidemic model, which does not account for vaccinations. The proposed analytical approximation is self-regulating, as the final analytical expression for the cumulative fraction J_∞ after infinite time allows us to check the validity of the original assumption $J(t) \leq J_\infty \ll 1$, thus indicating the allowed range of parameter values describing the temporal dependence of the ratios $k(t) = \mu(t)/a(t)$ and $b(t) = v(t)/a(t)$.

The comparison of the analytical approximation for the temporal dependence of the rate of new infections $\mathring{J}(t) = a(t)S(t)I(t)$, the corresponding cumulative fraction of new infections $J(t) = J(t_0) + \int_{t_0}^{t} d\xi\, \mathring{J}(\xi)$, and the fraction of vaccinated persons $V(t)$, respectively, with the exact numerical solution of the SIRV-equations for two different and interesting applications proves the accuracy of the analytical approach. These two applications were not accessible to analytical treatment before. The considered applications include the cases of stationary ratios with a delayed start of vaccinations, and an oscillating ratio of recovery to infection rate with a delayed vaccination at constant rate. The excellent agreement of the analytical approximations with the exact numerical solution of the SIRV-equations for these two applications proves the accuracy of the analytical approach. In the first case, the effect of a delayed start of vaccinations on the maximum rate of new infections and on the final cumulative fraction of infected persons is quantitatively calculated, demonstrating the importance of an early start of vaccinations during a new epidemic outburst. Moreover, the new analytical approximation agrees favorably well with the earlier obtained analytical approximation [1] for the case of stationary ratios between the recovery to infection rate and the vaccination to infection rate, respectively, implying that the time dependence of the three rates $a(t)$, $\mu(t)$, and $v(t)$ is the same.

This work has calculated approximately the temporal dependence of the rate of new infections and its corresponding cumulative fraction for a given population size using the SIRV-epidemic model equations for spatially integrated quantities. No attempt has been made to include any spatial spread by diffusion. Future work will be concerned with finding analytical approximations for the more complex set of equations including spatial diffusion [19,37–43].

Author Contributions: Conceptualization, R.S.; Methodology, R.S. and M.K.; Formal analysis, M.K. and R.S.; Writing—original draft, R.S.; Writing—review & editing, M.K.; Visualization, M.K. All authors have read and agreed to the published version of the manuscript.

Funding: This research received no external funding.

Data Availability Statement: All data are enclosed with this publication.

Conflicts of Interest: The authors declare no conflicts of interest.

Appendix A. Reduction of the Function $W_n(\tau)$

In order to reduce the function $W_n(\tau)$ introduced in Equation (81), we use their infinite series representation (Equation 7.1.29 in [36]) for the error function with a complex argument

$$\begin{aligned} \mathrm{erf}\,(X+\imath Y) &= \mathrm{erf}\,(X) + \frac{e^{-X^2}}{2\pi X}[1-\cos(2XY)+\imath\sin(2XY)] \\ &\quad + \frac{2}{\pi}e^{-X^2}\sum_{m=1}^{\infty}\frac{[f_m(X,Y)+\imath g_m(X,Y)]e^{-\frac{m^2}{4}}}{m^2+4X^2}, \end{aligned} \tag{A1}$$

with

$$\begin{aligned} f_m(X,Y) &= 2X - 2X\cosh(mY)\cos(2XY) + m\sinh(mY)\sin(2XY), \\ g_m(X,Y) &= 2X\cosh(mY)\sin(2XY) + m\sinh(mY)\cos(2XY) \end{aligned} \tag{A2}$$

and the properties $f_m(X,-Y) = f_m(X,Y)$ and $g_m(X,-Y) = -g_m(X,Y)$. After straightforward but tedious algebra, one obtains for general real values of A, B and C for

$$\begin{aligned}
&\Re\left[e^{\imath A}\mathrm{erf}\,(C-\imath B)\right] \\
=\;& \cos(A)\,\mathrm{erf}\,(C)+\frac{e^{-C^2}}{2\pi C}[(1-\cos(2BC))\cos A+\sin(2BC)\sin A] \\
&+\frac{2e^{-C^2}}{\pi}\sum_{m=1}^{\infty}\frac{e^{-\frac{m^2}{4}}}{m^2+4C^2}[f_m(C,B)\cos A+g_m(C,B)\sin A] \\
=\;& \cos(A)\,\mathrm{erf}\,(C)+\frac{e^{-C^2}}{2\pi C}[\cos(A)-\cos(A+2BC)] \\
&+\frac{2e^{-C^2}}{\pi}\sum_{m=1}^{\infty}\frac{e^{-\frac{m^2}{4}}}{m^2+4C^2}\{2C[\cos(A)-\cosh(mB)\cos(A+2BC)] \\
&+m\sinh(mB)\sin(A+2BC)\}.
\end{aligned} \tag{A3}$$

Applying Equation (A3) to the two error functions in Equation (81) then yields Equation (82). For A, B, C equally distributed in the range $[0, 10]$, the first term $\cos(A)\mathrm{erf}(C)$ in Equation (A3) contributes on average about 97% to the full expression. This feature can be used to write down a simplified expression for $W_n(\tau)$.

References

1. Schlickeiser, R.; Kröger, M. Analytical modeling of the temporal evolution of epidemics outbreaks accounting for vaccinations. *Physics* **2021**, *3*, 386–426. [CrossRef]
2. Babaei, N.A.; Özer, T. On exact integrability of a COVID-19 model: SIRV. *Math. Meth. Appl. Sci.* **2023**, *1*, 1–18.
3. Rifhat, R.; Teng, Z.; Wang, C. Extinction and persistence of a stochastic SIRV epidemic model with nonlinear incidence rate. *Adv. Diff. Eqs.* **2021**, *2021*, 200. [CrossRef] [PubMed]
4. Ameen, I.; Baleanu, D.; Ali, H.M. An efficient algorithm for solving the fractional optimal control of SIRV epidemic model with a combination of vaccination and treatment. *Chaos Solit. Fract.* **2020**, *137*, 109892. [CrossRef]
5. Oke, M.; Ogunmiloro, O.M.; Akinwumi, C.T.; Raji, R.A. Mathematical Modeling and Stability Analysis of a SIRV Epidemic Model with Non-linear Force of Infection and Treatment. *Commun. Math. Appl.* **2019**, *10*, 717–731. [CrossRef]
6. Liu, X.D.; Wang, W.; Yang, Y.; Hou, B.H.; Olasehinde, T.S.; Feng, N.; Dong, X.P. Nesting the SIRV model with NAR, LSTM and statistical methods to fit and predict COVID-19 epidemic trend in Africa. *BMC Public Health* **2023**, *23*, 138. [CrossRef]
7. Mahayana, D. Lyapunov Stability Analysis of COVID-19 SIRV Model. In Proceedings of the 2022 IEEE 18th International Colloquium on Signal Processing & Applications (CSPA 2022), Selangor, Malaysia, 12 May 2022; pp. 287–292. [CrossRef]
8. Petrakova, V.S.; Shaydurov, V.V. SIRV-D Optimal Control Model for COVID-19 Propagation Scenarios. *J. Siber. Fed. Univ. Math. Phys.* **2023**, *16*, 87–97.
9. Zhao, Z.; Li, X.; Liu, F.; Jin, R.; Ma, C.; Huang, B.; Wu, A.; Nie, X. Stringent Nonpharmaceutical Interventions Are Crucial for Curbing COVID-19 Transmission in the Course of Vaccination: A Case Study of South and Southeast Asian Countries. *Healthcare* **2021**, *9*, 1292. [CrossRef]
10. Smith, D.K.; Lauro, K.; Kelly, D.; Fish, J.; Lintelman, E.; McEwen, D.; Smith, C.; Stecz, M.; Ambagaspitiya, T.D.; Chen, J. Teaching Undergraduate Physical Chemistry Lab with Kinetic Analysis of COVID-19 in the United States. *J. Chem. Educ.* **2022**, *99*, 3471–3477. [CrossRef]
11. Huntingford, C.; Rawson, T.; Bonsall, M.B. Optimal COVID-19 Vaccine Sharing Between Two Nations That Also Have Extensive Travel Exchanges. *Front. Public Health* **2021**, *9*, 633144. [CrossRef]
12. Marinov, T.T.; Marinova, R.S. Adaptive SIR model with vaccination: Simultaneous identification of rates and functions illustrated with COVID-19. *Sci. Rep.* **2022**, *12*, 15688. [CrossRef] [PubMed]
13. Beenstock, M.; Felsenstein, D.; Gdaliahu, M. The joint determination of morbidity and vaccination in the spatiotemporal epidemiology of COVID-19. *Spat. Spat.-Tempor. Epidem.* **2023**, *47*, 100621. [CrossRef] [PubMed]
14. Haas, F.; Kröger, M.; Schlickeiser, R. Multi-Hamiltonian structure of the epidemics model accounting for vaccinations and a suitable test for the accuracy of its numerical solvers. *J. Phys. A* **2022**, *55*, 225206. [CrossRef]
15. Li, X.; Li, X.; Zhang, Q. Time to extinction and stationary distribution of a stochastic susceptible-infected-recovered-susceptible model with vaccination under Markov switching. *Math. Popul. Stud.* **2020**, *27*, 259–274. [CrossRef]
16. Cai, C.R.; Wu, Z.X.; Guan, J.Y. Behavior of susceptible-vaccinated-infected-recovered epidemics with diversity in the infection rate of individuals. *Phys. Rev. E* **2013**, *88*, 062805. [CrossRef] [PubMed]
17. Widyaningsih, P.; Nugroho, A.A.; Saputro, D.R.S. Susceptible Infected Recovered Model with Vaccination, Immunity Loss, and Relapse to Study Tuberculosis Transmission in Indonesia. *AIP Conf. Proc.* **2018**, *2014*, 020121. [CrossRef]

18. Chapman, J.D.; Evans, N.D. The structural identifiability of susceptible-infective-recovered type epidemic models with incomplete immunity and birth targeted vaccination. *Biomed. Signal Process. Control* **2009**, *4*, 278–284. [CrossRef]
19. Wang, J.; Zhang, R.; Kuniya, T. A reaction-diffusion Susceptible-Vaccinated-Infected-Recovered model in a spatially heterogeneous environment with Dirichlet boundary condition. *Math. Comp. Simul.* **2021**, *190*, 848–865. [CrossRef]
20. Khader, M.M.; Adel, M. Numerical Treatment of the Fractional Modeling on Susceptible-Infected-Recovered Equations with a Constant Vaccination Rate by Using GEM. *Int. J. Nonlin. Sci. Numer. Simul.* **2019**, *20*, 69–75. [CrossRef]
21. Dai, Y.; Zhou, B.; Jiang, D.; Hayat, T. Stationary distribution and density function analysis of stochastic susceptible-vaccinated-infected-recovered (SVIR) epidemic model with vaccination of newborns. *Math. Meth. Appl. Sci.* **2022**, *45*, 3401–3416. [CrossRef]
22. Kiouach, D.; El-idrissi, S.E.A.; Sabbar, Y. The impact of Levy noise on the threshold dynamics of a stochastic susceptible-vaccinated-infected-recovered epidemic model with general incidence functions. *Math. Meth. Appl. Sci.* **2023**, *47*, 297–317. [CrossRef]
23. Kermack, W.O.; McKendrick, A.G. A contribution to the mathematical theory of epidemics. *Proc. R. Soc. A* **1927**, *115*, 700. [CrossRef]
24. Kendall, D.G. Deterministic and stochastic epidemics in closed populations. In *Proceedings of the Third Berkeley Symposium on Mathematical Statistics and Probability*; University of California Press: Berkeley, CA, USA, 1956; Volume 4, p. 149. [CrossRef]
25. Schlickeiser, R.; Kröger, M. Analytical solution of the SIR-model for the temporal evolution of epidemics: Part B. Semi-time case. *J. Phys. A* **2021**, *54*, 175601. [CrossRef]
26. Albidah, A.B. A proposed analytical and numerical treatment for the nonlinear SIR model via a hybrid approach. *Mathematics* **2023**, *11*, 2749. [CrossRef]
27. Schlickeiser, R.; Kröger, M. Analytical solution of the SIR-model for the not too late temporal evolution of epidemics for general time-dependent recovery and infection rates. *COVID* **2023**, *3*, 1781–1796. [CrossRef]
28. Al-Shbeil, I.; Djenina, N.; Jaradat, A.; Al-Husban, A.; Ouannas, A.; Grassi, G. A New COVID-19 Pandemic Model including the Compartment of Vaccinated Individuals: Global Stability of the Disease-Free Fixed Point. *Mathematics* **2023**, *11*, 576. [CrossRef]
29. Sepulveda, G.; Arenas, A.J.; Gonzalez-Parra, G. Mathematical Modeling of COVID-19 Dynamics under Two Vaccination Doses and Delay Effects. *Mathematics* **2023**, *11*, 369. [CrossRef]
30. Ul Haq, I.; Ullah, N.; Ali, N.; Nisar, K.S. A New Mathematical Model of COVID-19 with Quarantine and Vaccination. *Mathematics* **2023**, *11*, 142. [CrossRef]
31. Liu, X.; Ding, Y. Stability and Numerical Simulations of a New SVIR Model with Two Delays on COVID-19 Booster Vaccination. *Mathematics* **2022**, *10*, 1772. [CrossRef]
32. Olivares, A.; Staffetti, E. Optimal control applied to vaccination and testing Ppolicies for COVID-19. *Mathematics* **2021**, *9*, 3100. [CrossRef]
33. Schlickeiser, R.; Kröger, M. Key epidemic parameters of the SIRV model determined from past COVID-19 mutant waves. *COVID* **2023**, *3*, 592–600. [CrossRef]
34. Morse, P.M.; Feshbach, H. *Methods of Theoretical Physics, Part I*; McGraw-Hill: New York, NY, USA, 1953.
35. Mathews, J.; Walker, R.L. *Mathematical Methods in Physics*, 2nd ed.; Benjamin: Menlo Park, CA, USA, 1970.
36. Abramowitz, M.; Stegun, I.A. *Handbook of Mathematical Functions*; Dover Publications: New York, NY, USA, 1970.
37. Bärwolff, G. A Local and Time Resolution of the COVID-19 Propagation—A Two-Dimensional Approach for Germany Including Diffusion Phenomena to Describe the Spatial Spread of the COVID-19 Pandemic. *Physics* **2021**, *3*, 536–548. [CrossRef]
38. Baazeem, A.S.; Nawaz, Y.; Arif, M.S.; Abodayeh, K. Modelling infectious disease dynamics: A robust computational approach for stochastic SIRS with partial immunity and an incidence rate. *Mathematics* **2023**, *11*, 4794. [CrossRef]
39. Gribaudo, M.; Iacono, M.; Manini, D. COVID-19 spatial diffusion: A Markovian agent-based model. *Mathematics* **2021**, *9*, 485. [CrossRef]
40. Wu, K.; Zhou, K. Traveling waves in a nonlocal dispersal SIR model with standard incidence rate and nonlocal delayed transmission. *Mathematics* **2019**, *7*, 641. [CrossRef]
41. Wang, Z.; Guo, Q.; Sun, S.; Xia, C. The impact of awareness diffusion on SIR-like epidemics in multiplex networks. *Appl. Math. Comput.* **2019**, *349*, 134–147. [CrossRef]
42. Pastor-Satorras, R.; Castellano, C.; Van Mieghem, P.; Vespignani, A. Epidemic processes in complex networks. *Rev. Mod. Phys.* **2015**, *87*, 925–979. [CrossRef]
43. Yang, J.; Liang, S.; Zhang, Y. Travelling waves of a delayed SIR epidemic model with nonlinear incidence rate and spatial diffusion. *PLoS ONE* **2011**, *6*, e21128. [CrossRef] [PubMed]

mathematics

Article

Dynamic Cooperative Oligopolies

Ferenc Szidarovszky [1,*] and Akio Matsumoto [2]

1 Department of Mathematics, Corvinus University, Fővám tér 8, 1093 Budapest, Hungary
2 Department of Economics, Chuo University, 742-1, Higashi-Nakano, Hachioji 192-0393, Japan; akiom@tamacc.chuo-u.ac.jp
* Correspondence: ferenc.szidarovszky@uni-corvinus.hu

Abstract: An n-person cooperative oligopoly is considered without product differentiation. It is assumed that the firms know the unit price function but have no access to the cost functions of the competitors. From market data, they have information about the industry output. The firms want to find the output levels that guarantee maximum industry profit. First, the existence of a unique maximizer is proven, which the firms cannot determine directly because of the lack of the knowledge of the cost functions. Instead, a dynamic model is constructed, which is asymptotically stable under realistic conditions, and the state trajectories converge to the optimum output levels of the firms. Three models are constructed: first, no time delay is assumed; second, information delay is considered for the firms on the industry output; and third, in addition, information delay is also assumed about the firms' own output levels. The stability of the resulting no-delay, one-delay, and two-delay dynamics is examined.

Keywords: cooperative game; oligopolies; asymptotic stability; time delays; Hopf bifurcation; stability switching curve

MSC: 91A12; 91A20

1. Introduction

Based on the pioneering work of Cournot A. [1], an intensive study on his oligopoly model started, which continues until today. Most studies consider this model as a multi-player non-cooperative game. First, the existence and uniqueness of the Nash equilibrium were the main research subjects [2,3]. Several versions of oligopolies were introduced and studied, including models with product differentiation, multi-product, labor-managed oligopolies, oligopsonies, and group equilibrium problems, among others [4]. In dynamic extensions, first linear models were studied since local and global asymptotic stability are equivalent [5,6]. Based on the mathematical development of nonlinear dynamics, oligopolies with nonlinear payoff functions have become the main focus [7–9]. In recent years, oligopolies with time delays have been receiving increasing attention, since data collection in order to determine the best decisions and their implementations need time. If the delay is due to contractual or institutional circumstances, then fixed delays are considered. If the delays are uncertain due to the large number of firms, or the firms want to react to an average of past information rather than to sudden market changes, then continuously distributed delays are assumed. In the first case, differential–difference equations model the situation [10], whereas in the second case, integro-differential equations model the situation [11]. In the past, oligopoly studies of mainly non-cooperative models were considered, and the Nash equilibrium in static games or the steady states of the dynamic models were the focus. In the case of cooperative games, the players want to obtain maximum overall profit, which is then distributed among them based on certain fairness principles [12]. Several concepts and methods were developed [13], among which the Shapley values are the most popular [14].

Citation: Szidarovszky, F.; Matsumoto, A. Dynamic Cooperative Oligopolies. *Mathematics* **2024**, *12*, 891. https://doi.org/10.3390/math12060891

Academic Editors: Mihaela Neamțu, Eva Kaslik and Anca Rădulescu

Received: 13 February 2024
Revised: 5 March 2024
Accepted: 8 March 2024
Published: 18 March 2024

Many applications of non-cooperative games are known from the literature, which can be found in many text books, like [15]. The applications of cooperative games also cover a huge and diverse field in applied sciences, including natural resource management [16,17], power systems [18], waste management [19], transportation [20,21], insurance industry [22], social network analysis [23], communication network [24], manufacturing systems [25], pattern clustering [26], and business and economics [27], among others. In this paper, n-person oligopolies without product differentiation will be considered and examined under the assumption that the firms know the unit price function and are able to obtain information about the industry output; however, they do not know the cost functions of the others since no technology information is shared among the players. Therefore, they cannot determine their total industry profit maximizing output levels. Hence, an asymptotically stable dynamic process is assumed in which the steady state gives the optimal output levels.

The paper is developed as follows. In Section 2, the basic model is outlined, and in Section 3, its dynamic extension is examined without time delays. Two-delay models are introduced and analyzed in Section 4. In the first case, data on the industry output are assumed to be delayed, and in the second case, in addition, data on the firms' own output levels are also considered delayed. The model without delay is asymptotically stable under realistic conditions. In the single delay case, it is asymptotically stable if the length of the delay is smaller than a threshold value, where stability is lost by Hopf bifurcation. In the two-delay case, the stability switching curve is determined in the delays' space. Section 5 offers concluding remarks and outlines further research directions.

2. The Basic Model

In a cooperative oligopoly, the firms want to maximize their overall profit:

$$\varphi(x_1, x_2, \dots, x_n) = sp(s) - \sum_{k=1}^{n} C_k(x_k). \tag{1}$$

Here, x_k is the output of firm k with $0 \le x_k \le L_k$, where L_k is the capacity limit of this firm. Furthermore, $s = \sum_{k=1}^{n} x_k$, $p(s)$ is the price function and $C_k(x_k)$ is the cost function of firm k. Assume that functions p and all C_k values are twice continuously differentiable; then

(A) $p'(s) < 0$ for $0 \le s \le \sum_{k=1}^{n} L_k$,

(B) $p'(s) + sp''(s) \le 0$ for $0 \le s \le \sum_{k=1}^{n} L_k$,

(C) $C_k'(x_k) > 0,\ C_k''(x_k) > 0$ for $0 \le x_k \le L_k$ and all k.

Notice that

$$\frac{\partial \varphi}{\partial x_k} = sp'(s) + p(s) - C_k'(x_k), \tag{2}$$

$$\frac{\partial^2 \varphi}{\partial x_k^2} = sp''(s) + 2p'(s) - C_k''(x_k)$$

and for $k \neq \ell$,

$$\frac{\partial^2 \varphi}{\partial x_k \partial x_\ell} = sp''(s) + 2p'(s).$$

Introduce matrices

$$\boldsymbol{A} = \begin{pmatrix} 1 & 1 & \cdots & 1 \\ 1 & 1 & \cdots & 1 \\ \cdot & \cdot & \cdots & \cdot \\ 1 & 1 & \cdots & 1 \end{pmatrix} \text{ and } \boldsymbol{B} = \begin{pmatrix} -C_1''(x_1) & 0 & \cdots & 0 \\ 0 & -C_2''(x_2) & \cdots & 0 \\ \cdot & \cdot & \cdots & \cdot \\ 0 & 0 & \cdots & -C_n''(x_n) \end{pmatrix},$$

then, the Hessian matrix of φ can be written as

$$\boldsymbol{H} = \big(sp''(s) + 2p'(s)\big)\boldsymbol{A} + \boldsymbol{B}. \tag{3}$$

Here, $\boldsymbol{B}$ is a negative definite, and eigenvalues of $\boldsymbol{A}$ are 0 and n; furthermore,

$$sp''(s) + 2p'(s) = p'(s) + sp''(s) + p'(s) < 0.$$

Therefore, $\boldsymbol{H}$ is negative definite, implying that φ is strictly concave as an n-variable function.

Since $sp''(s) + 2p'(s)$ is the derivative of $sp'(s) + p(s)$, this function is strictly decreasing in s. With given $s \geq 0$, the best choice of firm k is given as continuous function:

$$R_k(s) = \begin{cases} 0 \text{ if } sp'(s) + p(s) - C_k'(0) \leq 0, \\ L_k \text{ if } sp'(s) + p(s) - C_k'(L_k) \geq 0, \\ x_k^* \text{ otherwise,} \end{cases} \tag{4}$$

where x_k^* solves the equation

$$h(x_k) = sp'(s) + p(s) - C_k'(x_k) = 0. \tag{5}$$

In the third case of (4), $h(x_k)$ strictly decreases in x_k, $h(0) > 0$ and $h(L_k) < 0$. Therefore, there is a unique solution of Equation (5). It is easy to show that $R_k(s)$ is a non-increasing continuous function of s.

Consider finally the following equation:

$$g(s) = \sum_{k=1}^{n} R_k(s) - s = 0. \tag{6}$$

The left hand-side strictly decreases:

$$g(0) \geq 0 \text{ and } g\left(\sum_{k=1}^{n} L_k\right) \leq 0.$$

Therefore, there is a unique solution $s^* > 0$ of (6) and then the optimal choices of the firms are given by (4) as

$$x_k^* = R_k(s^*).$$

3. Dynamic Extension

Using gradient adjustments, the output adjustments are generally driven by the differential equations:

$$\begin{aligned} \dot{x}_k(t) &= K_k\big[s(t)p'(s(t)) + p(s(t)) - C_k'(x_k(t))\big] \\ &= K_k\big[(\textstyle\sum_{\ell=1}^{n} x_\ell(t))p'(\sum_{\ell=1}^{n} x_\ell(t)) + p(\sum_{\ell=1}^{n} x_\ell(t)) - C_k'(x_k(t))\big]. \end{aligned} \tag{7}$$

The right hand-side is a constant multiple of the marginal profit with $K_k > 0$. Notice that

$$\begin{aligned} \frac{\partial \dot{x}_k(t)}{\partial x_k} &= K_k\big\{2p'(\textstyle\sum_{\ell=1}^{n} x_\ell(t)) + (\sum_{\ell=1}^{n} x_\ell(t))p''(\sum_{\ell=1}^{n} x_\ell(t)) - C_k''(x_k(t))\big\} \\ &= K_k\big[2p'(s(t)) + s(t)p''(s(t)) - C_k''(x_k(t))\big] \end{aligned} \tag{8}$$

and for $\ell \neq k$,

$$\frac{\partial \dot{x}_k(t)}{\partial x_\ell} = K_k(2p'(s(t)) + s(t)p''(s(t))). \tag{9}$$

The Jacobian of this system is clearly

$$\boldsymbol{J} = \boldsymbol{K}\boldsymbol{H}$$

with

$$\mathbf{K} = diag(K_1, K_2, \ldots, K_n).$$

It is well known that all eigenvalues of $\boldsymbol{J}$ have negative real parts (see Theorem 4.9 of Szidarovszky and Bahill [28], implying the local asymptotical stability of the optimal solution without delays).

Theorem 1. *The steady state of system (7) is always locally asymptotically stable.*

4. Dynamic Extension with Time Delay

Assume next that the firms have delayed information about the industry output. If τ_k is the delay for firm k, then Equation (7) is modified as follows:

$$\dot{x}_k(t) = K_k\left[s_k p'(s_k) + p(s_k) - C_k'(x_k(t))\right] \tag{10}$$

with

$$s_k = \sum_{\ell=1}^{n} x_\ell(t - \tau_k)$$

Notice that

$$\frac{\partial \dot{x}_k(t)}{\partial s_k} = K_k\left[s_k p''(s_k) + 2p'(s_k)\right]$$

and

$$\frac{\partial \dot{x}_k(t)}{\partial x_k} = -K_k C_k''(x_k(t)).$$

Let s^* and x_k^* denote the values of s and x_k at the optimal solution. Clearly

$$s^* = \sum_{k=1}^{n} x_k^*.$$

Introduce the notation

$$A = s^* p''(s^*) + 2p'(s^*)$$

and

$$B_k = -C_k''(x_k^*),$$

then, the linearized homogenous equation is as follows:

$$\dot{x}_k(t) = K_k A \sum_{\ell=1}^{n} x_\ell(t - \tau_k) + K_k B_k x_k(t). \tag{11}$$

Upon examining the stability of the equilibrium of this system, we will use the methodology offered by Bellman and Cooke [10].

Notice that A and all B_k values are negative. Assume exponential solutions results in $x_k(t) = e^{\lambda t} u_k$ to have

$$\lambda u_k = K_k A \sum_{\ell=1}^{n} e^{-\lambda \tau_k} u_\ell + K_k B_k u_k \text{ for } k = 1, 2, \ldots, n$$

showing that the characteristic equation becomes

$$\det\begin{pmatrix} \lambda - K_1 A e^{-\lambda\tau_1} - K_1 B_1 & -K_1 A e^{-\lambda\tau_1} & \cdots & -K_1 A e^{-\lambda\tau_1} \\ -K_2 A e^{-\lambda\tau_2} & \lambda - K_2 A e^{-\lambda\tau_2} - K_2 B_2 & \cdots & -K_2 A e^{-\lambda\tau_2} \\ \cdot & \cdot & \cdots & \cdot \\ -K_n A e^{-\lambda\tau_n} & -K_n A e^{-\lambda\tau_n} & \cdots & \lambda - K_n A e^{-\lambda\tau_n} - K_n B_n \end{pmatrix} = 0. \tag{12}$$

It can be represented in closed form based on the result given in Appendix E of Bischi et al.'s work [29]. Introduce

$$a = \begin{pmatrix} -K_1 A e^{-\lambda\tau_1} \\ -K_2 A e^{-\lambda\tau_2} \\ \cdot \\ -K_n A e^{-\lambda\tau_n} \end{pmatrix}, \; \mathbf{1}^T = (1, 1, \ldots, 1)$$

and

$$D = diag(\lambda - K_1 B_1, \lambda - K_2 B_2, \ldots, \lambda - K_n B_n)$$

to have (12) in the following form:

$$\begin{aligned} \det\left(D + a\mathbf{1}^T\right) &= \det(D) \det\left(I + D^{-1} a \mathbf{1}^T\right) \\ &= \det(D) \det\left[1 + \mathbf{1}^T D^{-1} a\right] \\ &= \Pi_{k=1}^{n} (\lambda - K_k B_k) \left[1 - \Sigma_{k=1}^{n} \frac{K_k A e^{-\lambda\tau_k}}{\lambda - K_k B_k}\right] = 0. \end{aligned}$$

From the first factor,

$$\lambda = K_k B_k < 0,$$

which does not disturb stability. The expression inside the brackets is very difficult to deal with in general, so we make the following simplifying assumption:

$$(D)\; K_1 = K_2 = \ldots = K_n = K,\; B_1 = B_2 = \ldots = B_n = B \text{ and } \tau_1 = \tau_2 = \ldots = \tau_n = \tau.$$

In this special case, we have to examine the following equation

$$1 - \sum_{k=1}^{n} \frac{K A e^{-\lambda\tau}}{\lambda - KB} = 0$$

or

$$\lambda - KB - nKAe^{-\lambda\tau} = 0. \tag{13}$$

Without delay, $\tau = 0$ and $\lambda = KB + nKA < 0$. Stability switch might occur if $\lambda = i\omega$ $(\omega > 0)$, which is now substituted into Equation (13) to have

$$i\omega - KB - nKA(\cos\omega\tau - i\sin\omega\tau) = 0.$$

Separating the real and imaginary parts gives

$$nKA\cos\omega\tau = -KB \tag{14}$$

and

$$nKA\sin\omega\tau = -\omega. \tag{15}$$

Adding the squares of these equations, we have

$$\omega^2 = K^2\left(n^2A^2 - B^2\right).$$

Theorem 2. *If $n^2A^2 \leq B^2$, then no stability switch occurs, and optimal solution is locally asymptotically stable for all $\tau \geq 0$.*

Assume next that $n^2A^2 > B^2$, then

$$\omega^* = K\sqrt{n^2A^2 - B^2}.$$

From (14) and (15), we see that $\cos\omega\tau < 0$ and $\sin\omega\tau > 0$, implying that

$$\tau_m = \frac{1}{\omega^*}\left(\pi - \sin^{-1}\left(\frac{-\omega^*}{nKA}\right) + 2m\pi\right) \quad m = 0, 1, 2, \ldots \tag{16}$$

The directions of the stability switches are obtained by Hopf bifurcation. Select τ as the bifurcation parameter and assume $\lambda = \lambda(\tau)$. Implicitly differentiating Equation (13) with respect to τ, we have

$$\lambda' - nKAe^{-\lambda\tau}(-\lambda'\tau - \lambda) = 0$$

so

$$\lambda' = \frac{-nKAe^{-\lambda\tau}\lambda}{1 + nKAe^{-\lambda\tau}\tau} = \frac{-(\lambda - KB)\lambda}{1 + (\lambda - KB)\tau}.$$

With $\lambda = i\omega$, the real part is

$$\begin{aligned} \mathrm{Re}\left[\lambda'|_{\lambda=i\omega}\right] &= \mathrm{Re}\left[\frac{\omega^2 + iKB\omega}{1 - KB\tau + i\omega\tau}\right] \\ &= \frac{\omega^2}{(1 - KB\tau)^2 + (\omega\tau)^2} > 0. \end{aligned}$$

Theorem 3. *If $n^2A^2 > B^2$, then the optimal solution is locally asymptotically stable for $\tau < \tau_0$, stability is lost at $\tau = \tau_0$ with Hopf bifurcation, and stability cannot be regained with larger values of τ.*

In addition to Assumption (D), assume that the firms have an identical delay τ_1 in the industry output and an identical delay τ_2 in their own output values. Then, Model (10) is modified as follows:

$$\dot{x}_k(t) = K\left[sp'(s) + p(s) - C_k'(x_k(t - \tau_2))\right] \tag{17}$$

with

$$s = \sum_{\ell=1}^{n} x_\ell(t - \tau_1).$$

This is a system of two-delay equations. The stability of its equilibrium will be examined by the method offered by Matsumoto and Szidarovszky [30] based on Gu et al. [31].

The linearized equation is now the following:

$$\dot{x}_k(t) = KA\sum_{\ell=1}^{n} x_\ell(t - \tau_1) + KBx_k(t - \tau_2). \tag{18}$$

Assuming exponential solutions $x_\ell(t) = e^{\lambda t}u_\ell$, we then obtain by substitution

$$\left(\lambda - KBe^{-\lambda\tau_2}\right)u_k - KA\sum_{\ell=1}^{n} e^{-\lambda\tau_1}u_\ell = 0,$$

implying that the characteristic equation has the form

$$\det\begin{pmatrix} \lambda - KAe^{-\lambda\tau_1} - KBe^{-\lambda\tau_2} & -KAe^{-\lambda\tau_1} & \cdots & -KAe^{-\lambda\tau_1} \\ -KAe^{-\lambda\tau_1} & \lambda - KAe^{-\lambda\tau_1} - KBe^{-\lambda\tau_2} & \cdots & -KAe^{-\lambda\tau_1} \\ \cdot & \cdot & \cdots & \cdot \\ -KAe^{-\lambda\tau_1} & -KAe^{-\lambda\tau_1} & \cdot & \lambda - KAe^{-\lambda\tau_1} - KBe^{-\lambda\tau_2} \end{pmatrix} = 0. \tag{19}$$

Let **1** be again the n-element vector with all unity elements, and $\boldsymbol{I}$ be the $n \times n$ identity matrix. Then, (19) can be rewritten as

$$\begin{aligned}\det\left(\boldsymbol{D} + \boldsymbol{a}\mathbf{1}^T\right) &= \det(\boldsymbol{D}) \det\left(\boldsymbol{I} + \boldsymbol{D}^{-1}\boldsymbol{a}\mathbf{1}^T\right) \\ &= \det(\boldsymbol{D}) \det\left[1 + \mathbf{1}^T\boldsymbol{D}^{-1}\boldsymbol{a}\right] \\ &= \left(\lambda - KBe^{-\lambda\tau_2}\right)^n \left[1 - \Sigma_{k=1}^{n} \frac{KAe^{-\lambda\tau_1}}{\lambda - KBe^{-\lambda\tau_2}}\right] = 0,\end{aligned} \tag{20}$$

where

$$\boldsymbol{a} = -KAe^{-\lambda\tau_1}\mathbf{1} \text{ and } \boldsymbol{D} = \left(\lambda - KBe^{-\lambda\tau_2}\right)\boldsymbol{I}.$$

Thus, we have two-delay equations:

$$\lambda - KBe^{-\lambda\tau_2} = 0 \tag{21}$$

and

$$\lambda - K\left(nAe^{-\lambda\tau_1} + Be^{-\lambda\tau_2}\right) = 0. \tag{22}$$

Notice that (21) is a single-delay equation, and at $\tau_2 = 0$, the eigenvalue is $\lambda = KB < 0$. The sign of the real part of the eigenvalue might change at $\lambda = i\omega$. Then

$$i\omega - KB(\cos\omega\tau_2 - i\sin\omega\tau_2) = 0.$$

Separation of the real and imaginary parts shows that

$$KB\cos\omega\tau_2 = 0 \tag{23}$$

and

$$KB\sin\omega\tau_2 = -\omega, \tag{24}$$

implying that

$$\cos\omega\tau_2 = 0 \text{ and } \sin\omega\tau_2 = 1,$$

and the critical values of τ_2 are

$$\tau_{2n} = -\frac{1}{KB}\left(\frac{\pi}{2} + 2n\pi\right) \text{ for } n = 0, 1, 2, \ldots$$

since, from (24), $\omega = -KB$. The directions of stability switches are determined by Hopf bifurcation, when τ_2 is selected as the bifurcation parameter and let $\lambda = \lambda(\tau_2)$. Implicit differentiation of Equation (21) with respect to τ_2 shows that

$$\lambda' - KBe^{-\lambda\tau_2}\left(-\lambda'\tau_2 - \lambda\right) = 0,$$

implying that

$$\lambda' = \frac{-\lambda^2}{1 + \lambda\tau_2},$$

where we use $KBe^{-\lambda\tau_2} = \lambda$. At $\lambda = i\omega$, the real part of λ' is positive:

$$\begin{aligned} \mathrm{Re}[\lambda'] &= \mathrm{Re}\left[\frac{\omega^2}{1+i\omega\tau_2}\right], \\ &= \mathrm{Re}\left[\frac{\omega^2(1-i\omega\tau_2)}{1+(\omega\tau_2)^2}\right], \\ &= \frac{\omega^2}{1+(\omega\tau_2)^2} > 0. \end{aligned}$$

Therefore, the eigenvalues of Equation (21) have negative real parts for $\tau < \tau_{20}$, and at all critical values τ_{2n} $(n = 0, 1, 2, \ldots)$, at least one pair of eigenvalues changes the sign of its real part from negative to positive.

We now turn to Equation (22), which can be written as

$$1 + a_1(\lambda)e^{-\lambda\tau_1} + a_2(\lambda)e^{-\lambda\tau_2} = 0$$

with

$$a_1(\lambda) = -\frac{nKA}{\lambda} \text{ and } a_2(\lambda) = -\frac{KB}{\lambda}.$$

Notice first that without delays, $\lambda = nKA + KB < 0$, and with increasing values of the delays, stability may be lost when $\lambda = i\omega$. Then, we have

$$1 + a_1(i\omega)e^{-i\omega\tau_1} + a_2(i\omega)e^{-i\omega\tau_2} = 0$$

where

$$a_1(i\omega) = i\frac{nKA}{\omega},\ a_2(i\omega) = i\frac{KB}{\omega},$$

$$|a_1(i\omega)| = -\frac{nKA}{\omega} \text{ and } |a_2(i\omega)| = -\frac{KB}{\omega},$$

and

$$\arg[a_1(i\omega)] = \arg[a_2(i\omega)] = \frac{3\pi}{2}.$$

If we place vectors, 1, $a_1(i\omega)e^{-i\omega\tau_1}$ and $a_2(i\omega)e^{-i\omega\tau_2}$ head to tail, then they form a triangle. The sufficient and necessary conditions for the existence of a triangle are

$$\begin{aligned} |a_1(i\omega)| + |a_2(i\omega)| &\geq 1, \\ -1 \leq |a_1(i\omega)| - |a_2(i\omega)| &\leq 1. \end{aligned}$$

In our case,

$$\begin{aligned} -nKA - KB &\geq \omega, \\ -\omega \leq -nKA + KB &\leq \omega \end{aligned}$$

which can be summarized as

$$|-nKA + KB| \leq \omega \leq -nKA - KB. \tag{25}$$

The triangle is illustrated in Figure 1, when the interior angles are θ_1, θ_2, and $\pi - (\theta_1 + \theta_2)$.

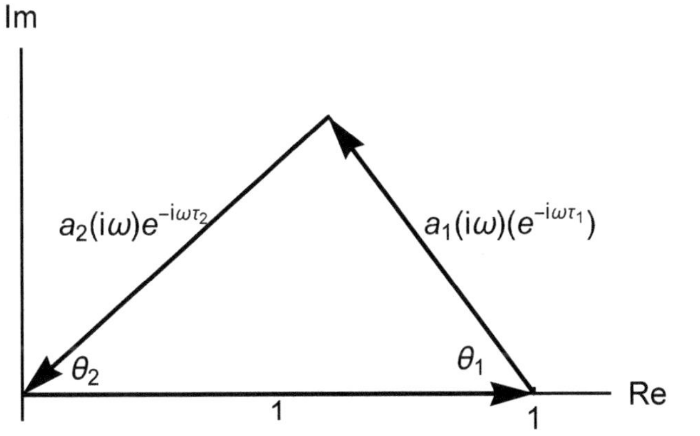

Figure 1. Triangle contitions.

The rule of cosine shows that

$$\theta_1 = \cos^{-1}\left(\frac{1 + |a_1(i\omega)|^2 - |a_2(i\omega)|^2}{2|a_1(i\omega)|}\right) = \cos^{-1}\left(\frac{\omega^2 + (nKA)^2 - (KB)^2}{-2nKA\omega}\right) \tag{26}$$

and

$$\theta_2 = \cos^{-1}\left(\frac{1 + |a_2(i\omega)|^2 - |a_1(i\omega)|^2}{2|a_2(i\omega)|}\right) = \cos^{-1}\left(\frac{\omega^2 + (KB)^2 - (nKA)^2}{-2KB\omega}\right). \tag{27}$$

The arguments of the three sides of the triangle are

$$0,\ \arg[a_1(i\omega)] - \omega\tau_1 \text{ and } \arg[a_2(i\omega)] - \omega\tau_2$$

and the angle balance equations at the end points of the horizontal side show that

$$\tau_1^{k\pm}(\omega) = \frac{1}{\omega}[\arg(a_1(i\omega)) + (2k-1)\pi \pm \theta_1] \text{ for } k = 0,1,2,\ldots$$

and

$$\tau_2^{\ell\mp}(\omega) = \frac{1}{\omega}[\arg(a_2(i\omega)) + (2\ell-1)\pi \mp \theta_2] \text{ for } \ell = 0,1,2,\ldots$$

since the triangle can be located above and under the horizontal axis. Hence,

$$\tau_1^{k\pm}(\omega) = \frac{1}{\omega}\left[\frac{3\pi}{2} + (2k-1)\pi \pm \theta_1\right] \text{ for } k = 0,1,2,\ldots \tag{28}$$

and

$$\tau_2^{\ell\mp}(\omega) = \frac{1}{\omega}\left[\frac{3\pi}{2} + (2\ell-1)\pi \mp \theta_2\right] \text{ for } \ell = 0,1,2,\ldots, \tag{29}$$

implying that the stability switching curves are formed as

$$T_{k,\ell}^{\pm} = \left\{ \left(\tau_1^{k\pm}(\omega), \tau_2^{\ell\mp}(\omega)\right) \,\middle|\, |-nKA + KB| \le \omega \le -nKA - KB \right\} \tag{30}$$

with $k = 0,1,2,\ldots$ and $\ell = 0,1,2,\ldots$ From (28) and (29), we see that increasing the value of k shifts the curves to the right and increasing the value of ℓ shifts the curves up in the delays space.

At each point (τ_1, τ_2) of the stability switching curves, the direction of stability switches can be assessed by computing the stability index. First, we determine the real and imaginary parts of expressions:

$$a_1(i\omega)e^{-i\omega\tau_1} = i\frac{nKA}{\omega}(\cos\omega\tau_1 - i\sin\omega\tau_1)$$

and

$$a_2(i\omega)e^{-i\omega\tau_2} = i\frac{KB}{\omega}(\cos\omega\tau_2 - i\sin\omega\tau_2)$$

to have

$$R_1 = \frac{nKA\sin\omega\tau_1}{\omega},\ I_1 = \frac{nKA\cos\omega\tau_1}{\omega}$$

and

$$R_2 = \frac{KB\sin\omega\tau_2}{\omega},\ I_2 = \frac{KB\cos\omega\tau_2}{\omega}.$$

And then, the stability index is given as follows:

$$\begin{aligned} S &= R_2 I_1 - R_1 I_2 \\ &= \frac{nK^2AB}{\omega^2}(\sin\omega\tau_2\cos\omega\tau_1 - \sin\omega\tau_1\cos\omega\tau_2) \end{aligned}$$

which has the same sign as $\sin[\omega(\tau_2 - \tau_1)]$.

Theorem 4. *In the two-delay model, the stability switching curves are $T^+_{k,\ell}$ and $T^-_{k,\ell}$ $(k = 0, 1, 2, \ldots$ and $\ell = 0, 1, 2, \ldots)$ and $\{\tau_2 = \tau_{20}\}$.*

Theorem 5. *(A) Let (τ_1, τ_{20}) be any point on the line $\tau_2 = \tau_{20}$. When a point crosses the line from below, then at least one pair of eigenvalues changes the sign of the real part from negative to positive. (B) Let (τ_1, τ_2) be a point on curve $T^+_{k,\ell}$ or $T^-_{k,\ell}$ with a simple pure complex eigenvalue. Assume we look on the curve in increasing value of ω. Then, as a point moves from the right to the left of the corresponding curve, a pair of eigenvalues changes the sign of its real part from negative to positive if $S > 0$. If $S < 0$, then the sign change is in the opposite direction.*

Note: Equation (22) reduces to (13) as $\tau = \tau_1$ and $\tau_2 = 0$. If $\tau_2 = 0$, then from (29),

$$\theta_2 = \pm\left[\frac{3\pi}{2} + (2\ell - 1)\pi\right],$$

and with $\cos\theta_2 = 0$ and from (27),

$$\omega^2 + (KB)^2 - (nKA)^2 = 0,$$

implying $\omega^2 = (nKA)^2 - (KB)^2$. The same result was obtained as in the single-delay system.

5. Conclusions

In this paper, n-person single-product oligopolies were considered without product differentiation and with incomplete information. It was assumed that the firms knew the price function, and from market data, they also had access to the industry output. However, each firm knew its own cost function but had no information about those of the others. In a cooperative setting, the firms' usual objective was to find the output levels maximizing the industry profit. Since the cost functions were unknown, they used a dynamic process where the components of the steady state presented the optimal output levels. A model without time delay and two models with one and two delays were analyzed. In the stability analysis, the findings of the paper can be summarized as follows:

1. Under realistic conditions, the steady state in the no-delay case was always asymptotically stable, meaning that the components of the state trajectory converged to the industry profit maximizing output levels.
2. In the one-delay symmetric case, the steady state was always asymptotically stable if the number of firms was small; otherwise, asymptotic stability occurred if the length of the delay was smaller than a given threshold value, at which stability was lost via Hopf bifurcation.
3. In the two-delay case, the stability switching curves were determined in the two-dimensional delay space. The stability region contained the origin and was under or left of these curves.

The study presented in this paper can be extended in several directions. Non-differentiable price and/or cost functions can be assumed, like hyperbolic price and/or piecewise linear cost functions, making the analysis more complicated. The same difficulty is encountered in the nonsymmetric case as well. It is also an interesting problem to work out the details of the solutions based on different cooperative solution concepts.

Author Contributions: Conceptualization, F.S.; methodology, F.S.; software, A.M.; validation, A.M.; formal analysis, F.S.; writing—original draft, F.S. All authors have read and agreed to the published version of the manuscript.

Funding: This research was funded by the Japan Society for the Promotion of Science (Grant-in-Aid for Scientific Research (C), 20K01566, 23K01386).

Data Availability Statement: Data are contained within the article.

Acknowledgments: The authors appreciate three anonymous reviewers for constructive comments that improved the paper's presentation.

Conflicts of Interest: The authors declare no conflicts of interest.

References

1. Cournot, A. *Recherches sur les Principes Mathé matiques de la Théorie des Richessess*; Hachette: Paris, France, 1838; English Translation *Researches into the Mathematical Principles of the Theory of Wealth*; Kelley: New York, NY, USA, 1960.
2. Burger, E. *Einfuhrung in die Theorie der Spiele*; De Gruyter: Berlin, Germany, 1959.
3. Friedman, J. *Oligopoly and the Theory of Games*; North Holland Publishing Company: Amsterdam, The Netherland, 1977.
4. Okuguchi, K. *Expectations and Stability in Oligopoly Models*; Springer: Berlin, Germany, 1976.
5. Hahn, F. The stability of the Cournot oligopoly solution. *Rev. Econ. Stud.* **1962**, *29*, 329–331. [CrossRef]
6. Theocharis, R. On the stability of the Cournot solution on the oligopoly problem. *Rev. Econ. Stud.* **1959**, *27*, 133–134. [CrossRef]
7. Furth, D. Stability and instability in oligopoly. *J. Econ. Theory* **1986**, *40*, 197–228. [CrossRef]
8. Agiza, H.; Elsadany, A. Nonlinear dynamics in the Cournot duopoly game with heterogeneous players. *Phys. A* **2003**, *320*, 512–524. [CrossRef]
9. Puu, T. *Attractors, Bifurcations, and Chaos: Nonlinear Phenomena in Economics*, 2nd ed.; Springer: Berlin, Germany, 2003.
10. Bellman, R.; Cooke, K.-L. *Differential-Difference Equations*; Academic Press: New York, NY, USA, 1963.
11. Cushing, J. *Integro-Difference Equations and Delay Models in Population Dynamics*; Springer: Berlin, Germany, 1977.
12. Driessen, T. *Cooperative Games, Solutions and Applications*; Kluwer Academic Publishers: Dordrecht, The Netherlands, 1988.
13. Szép, J.; Forgó, F. *Introduction to the Theory of Games*; Akadémai Kiadó: Budapest, Hungary, 1985.
14. Shapley, L. A Value for n-Person Games. In *Contributions to the Theory of Games II*; Kuhn, H., Tucker, A., Eds.; Princeton University Press: Princeton, NJ, USA, 1953; pp. 307–317.
15. Petrosyan, L.; Mazalov, V. *Recent Advances in Game Theory and Applications*; Birkhäuser: Basel, Switzerland, 2016.
16. Dinar, A.; Ratner, A.; Yaron, D. Evaluating cooperative game theory in water resources. *Theory Decis.* **1992**, *32*, 1–20. [CrossRef]
17. McKinney, D.; Teasley, R. Cooperative game theory for transboundary river basins: The Syr Darya Basin. In Proceedings of the World Environmental and Water Resources Congress 2007, Restoring Our Natural Habitat, Tampa, FL, USA, 15–19 May 2007; pp. 1–10.
18. Churkin, A.; Bialek, J.; Pozo, D.; Sauma, E.; Korgin, N. Review of cooperative game theory applications in power system expansion planning. *Renew. Sustain. Energy Rev.* **2021**, *145*, 111056. [CrossRef]
19. Eryganov, T.; Šomplàr, K.; Nevrly, V. Application of cooperative game theory in waste manamement. *Chem. Eng. Trans.* **2020**, *81*, 877–882.
20. Song, D.; Panayides, P. A conceptual application of cooperative game theory to liner shipping strategic alliances. *Marit. Policy Manag.* **2002**, *29*, 285–301. [CrossRef]

21. Saeed, N.; Larsen, O. An application of cooperative game among container terminals of one port. *Eur. J. Oper. Res.* **2010**, *203*, 393–403. [CrossRef]
22. Lemaire, J. Cooperative game theory and its insurance applications. *ASTIN Bull. J. IAA* **1991**, *21*, 17–40. [CrossRef]
23. Molinero, X.; Riquelme, F. Influence of decision models: From cooperative game theory to social netwark analysis. *Comput. Sci. Rev.* **2021**, *39*, 100343. [CrossRef]
24. Saad, W.; Han, Z.; Debbah, M.; Hjorungness, A.; Başar, T. Coalition game theory for communication networks. *IEEE Signal Process. Mag.* **2009**, *26*, 77–97. [CrossRef]
25. Tavanayi, M.; Hafezalkotob, A.; Valizadeh, J. Cooperative cellural manufaturing system: A cooperative game theory approach. *Sci. Iran.* **2021**, *28*, 2769–2788.
26. Dhamal, S.; Bhat, S.; Anoop, K.; Embar, V. Pattern clustering using cooperative game theory. *arXiv* **2012**, arXiv1201.0461.
27. Stuart, H., Jr. Cooperative Games and Business Strategy. In *Game Theory and Business Applications, Kluwer's International Series*; Chatteree, K., Samuelson, W.F., Eds.; Springer : Boston, MA, USA, 2001; pp. 189–211.
28. Szidarovszky, F.; Bahill, T. *Linear Systems Theory*, 2nd ed.; CRC Press: Boca Raton, FL, USA; London, UK; New York, NY, USA, 1998.
29. Bischi, G.-I.; Chiarella, C.; Kopel, M.; Szidarovszky, F. *Nonlinear Oligopolies: Stability and Bifurcations*; Springer: Berlin, Germany, 2010.
30. Matsumoto, A.; Szidarovszky, F. *Dynamic Oligopolies with Time Delays*; Springer Nature: Singapore, 2018.
31. Gu, K.; Nicolescue, S.-I.; Chen, J. On stability switching curves for general systems with two delays. *J. Math. Ann. Appl.* **2005**, *311*, 231–253. [CrossRef]

mathematics

MDPI

Article

On a Family of Hamilton–Poisson Jerk Systems

Cristian Lăzureanu [1,2,*,†] and Jinyoung Cho [1,2,†]

1 Department of Mathematics, Politehnica University Timişoara, P-ta Victoriei 2, 300006 Timişoara, Romania; jinyoung.cho@student.upt.ro
2 Department of Mathematics, Faculty of Mathematics and Computer Science, West University of Timşoara, Parvan Blv. 4, 300223 Timişoara, Romania
* Correspondence: cristian.lazureanu@upt.ro
† These authors contributed equally to this work.

Abstract: In this paper, we construct a family of Hamilton–Poisson jerk systems. We show that such a system has infinitely many Hamilton–Poisson realizations. In addition, we discuss the stability and we prove the existence of periodic orbits around nonlinearly stable equilibrium points. Particularly, we deduce conditions for the existence of homoclinic and heteroclinic orbits. We apply the obtained results to a family of anharmonic oscillators.

Keywords: jerk systems; Hamilton–Poisson systems; stability; periodic orbits; homoclinic and heteroclinic orbits

MSC: 70K20; 70K42; 34C37; 37J46

Citation: Lăzureanu, C.; Cho, J. On a Family of Hamilton–Poisson Jerk Systems. *Mathematics* **2024**, *12*, 1260. https://doi.org/10.3390/math12081260

Academic Editors: Mihaela Neamţu, Eva Kaslik and Anca Rădulescu

Received: 30 March 2024
Revised: 16 April 2024
Accepted: 20 April 2024
Published: 22 April 2024

1. Introduction

Jerk is the rate of change of acceleration, the third derivative of position with respect to time [1]. A jerk equation $\dddot{x} = j(x, \dot{x}, \ddot{x})$ and the corresponding jerk system, which is a three-dimensional system given by

$$\begin{cases} \dot{x} = y \\ \dot{y} = z \\ \dot{z} = j(x, y, z) \end{cases}, \tag{1}$$

can model processes characterized by changes in acceleration. Despite their simple form, jerk systems provide examples of chaotic behavior (see, e.g., [2–4]). Bifurcations in the dynamics of jerk systems are also analyzed (see, e.g., [5–8]).

In this paper, we study how Hamilton–Poisson jerk systems can be constructed. Roughly speaking, a three-dimensional system is a Hamilton–Poisson system if it has two independent constants of motion (for details on Hamilton–Poisson mechanics, see e.g., [9]). Using such functions, we obtain a family of Hamilton–Poisson jerk systems, given by $\dddot{x} + f'(x)\dot{x} = 0$, which are in fact jerk versions of the system with one degree of freedom $\ddot{x} + f(x) = 0$ [10]. For instance, the equations of the harmonic oscillator, the mathematical pendulum, the Duffing oscillator, and other anharmonic oscillators are of this form.

Oscillatory systems, characterized by repetitive patterns or cycles, are found in various biological phenomena such as circadian rhythms (see, e.g., [11]), neuronal activity (see, e.g., [12]), and even in cellular processes like metabolic oscillations (see, e.g., [13]). Population dynamics in predator–prey relationships often display cyclic behavior, where changes in predator and prey populations exhibit periodic patterns (see, e.g., [14]). Modeling changes in population sizes or ecological systems often involves sudden shifts or rapid changes in growth rates, which can be compared analogously to jerk-like behavior in dynamic systems. Moreover, in neural systems, sudden changes in firing rates or neuronal activities might indirectly relate to rapid changes in behavior akin to jerk-like dynamics.

The paper is organized as follows: in Section 2, we recall some notions regarding Hamilton–Poisson systems and then we give some conditions for which system (1) is of this type. Using the integrable deformation method (see [15] and references therein), we construct a family of Hamilton–Poisson jerk systems. Also, we give Hamilton–Poisson realizations of such a system. In Section 3, we analyze some dynamical properties of the obtained system, namely, the stability of the equilibrium points, the existence of the periodic orbits around some nonlinearly stable equilibria, and the existence of homoclinic or heteroclinic orbits. In Section 4, we apply these results to a family of anharmonic oscillators [16].

2. A Family of Hamilton–Poisson Jerk Systems

In this section, we construct a family of jerk systems that have Hamilton–Poisson realizations.

Recall that the three-dimensional dynamical system

$$(\dot{x}, \dot{y}, \dot{z}) = (f_1(x, y, x), f_2(x, y, z), f_3(x, y, z))$$

is a Hamilton–Poisson system on $\mathbb{R}^3$ if there are the smooth functions ν, H, C such that

$$(f_1, f_2, f_3)^T = \nu \nabla H \times \nabla C$$

on $\mathbb{R}^3$ (see, e.g., [17,18]). The function ν is called the rescaling function. In addition, the Hamiltonian function H and the Casimir function C are constants of motion of the above system. In fact, a Hamilton–Poisson system on $\mathbb{R}^3$ is a triple $(\mathbb{R}^3, \Pi, H)$, where Π is a Poisson structure, and in this case it is given by the matrix

$$\Pi = \nu \begin{bmatrix} 0 & C_z & -C_y \\ -C_z & 0 & C_x \\ C_y & -C_x & 0 \end{bmatrix}, \tag{2}$$

where we have denoted $C_x = \frac{\partial C}{\partial x}$. Such a system writes $(\dot{x}, \dot{y}, \dot{z})^t = \Pi \cdot \nabla H$. Details on Hamiltonian mechanics can be found, for example, in [19].

In the following, we consider $\nu = 1$. One of our goals is to obtain jerk systems that can be written in the form $(\dot{x}, \dot{y}, \dot{z})^T = \nabla H \times \nabla C$, that is, to determine functions H, C such that

$$\begin{aligned} H_y C_z - H_z C_y &= y \\ H_z C_x - H_x C_z &= z \\ H_x C_y - H_y C_x &= j(x, y, z), \end{aligned}$$

and which are constants of motion of system (1), that is,

$$\begin{aligned} y H_x + z H_y + j(x, y, z) H_z &= 0 \\ y C_x + z C_y + j(x, y, z) C_z &= 0. \end{aligned}$$

We note that achieving this goal appears to be complicated for a general jerk function j. However, the next result holds.

Theorem 1. *If $j_z \neq 0$, then jerk system* (1) *cannot have a Hamilton–Poisson formulation $(\dot{x}, \dot{y}, \dot{z})^T = \nabla H \times \nabla C$.*

Proof. On the one hand, the divergence of system (1) is $div(y, z, j(x, y, z)) = j_z$. On the other hand, $div(\nabla H \times \nabla C) = \nabla \cdot (\nabla H \times \nabla C) = 0$; thus, $j_z = 0$, which finishes the proof. □

Instead of starting with a function j and checking for the existence of the functions H and C, we can construct Hamilton–Poisson jerk systems using integrable deformation method [15].

Consider the jerk equation

$$\dddot{x} = 0$$

and the corresponding jerk system

$$\begin{cases} \dot{x} = y \\ \dot{y} = z \\ \dot{z} = 0 \end{cases}. \quad (3)$$

It is easy to see that the functions

$$H(x,y,z) = \frac{1}{2}y^2 - xz, C(x,y,z) = z$$

are constants of motion for system (3). Moreover, system (3) writes $(\dot{x}, \dot{y}, \dot{z})^T = \nabla H \times \nabla C$; thus, it has the Hamilton–Poisson realization $(\mathbb{R}^3, \Pi, H)$ with the Hamiltonian H and the Poisson structure given by the matrix

$$\Pi = \begin{bmatrix} 0 & 1 & 0 \\ -1 & 0 & 0 \\ 0 & 0 & 0 \end{bmatrix}.$$

Now, we alter the above Hamiltonian and Casimir functions, that is, we consider the functions

$$\tilde{H}(x,y,z) = H(x,y,z) + g_1\alpha(x,y,z) = \frac{1}{2}y^2 - xz + g_1\alpha(x,y,z), \quad (4)$$

$$\tilde{C}(x,y,z) = C(x,y,z) + g_2\beta(x,y,z) = z + g_2\beta(x,y,z), \quad (5)$$

where α and β are smooth, and g_1, g_2 are real parameters. Then, an integrable deformation of system (3) is given by

$$(\dot{x}, \dot{y}, \dot{z})^T = \nabla\tilde{H} \times \nabla\tilde{C}, \quad (6)$$

that is

$$\begin{cases} \dot{x} = y + g_2(y\beta_z + x\beta_y) + g_1\alpha_y + g_1g_2(\alpha_y\beta_z - \alpha_z\beta_y) \\ \dot{y} = z + g_2(z\beta_z - x\beta_x) - g_1\alpha_x + g_1g_2(-\alpha_x\beta_z + \alpha_z\beta_x) \\ \dot{z} = g_2(-z\beta_y - y\beta_x) + g_1g_2(\alpha_x\beta_y - \alpha_y\beta_x) \end{cases}. \quad (7)$$

System (7) is jerk only if

$$\begin{cases} g_2(y\beta_z + x\beta_y) + g_1\alpha_y + g_1g_2(\alpha_y\beta_z - \alpha_z\beta_y) = 0 \\ g_2(z\beta_z - x\beta_x) - g_1\alpha_x + g_1g_2(-\alpha_x\beta_z + \alpha_z\beta_x) = 0 \end{cases}. \quad (8)$$

Now, we choose

$$\alpha(x,y,z) = \alpha(x,y), \beta(x,y,z) = \beta(x,y),$$

and (8) turns into

$$\begin{cases} g_1\alpha_y = -g_2x\beta_y \\ g_1\alpha_x = -g_2x\beta_x \end{cases}.$$

Then,

$$\begin{cases} g_1\alpha_{xy} = -g_2(\beta_y + x\beta_{xy}) \\ g_1\alpha_{xy} = -g_2x\beta_{xy} \end{cases},$$

thus, $\beta_y = 0$ and, consequently, $\alpha_y = 0$. Therefore,

$$\alpha(x,y,z) = \alpha(x), \beta(x,y,z) = \beta(x).$$

Consequently, if the functions $\alpha = \alpha(x)$ and $\beta = \beta(x)$ satisfy the relation

$$g_1\alpha'(x) = -g_2x\beta'(x), \quad (9)$$

then we constructed the following family of Hamilton–Poisson jerk systems

$$\begin{cases} \dot{x} = y \\ \dot{y} = z \\ \dot{z} = -g_2 y \beta'(x) \end{cases} . \tag{10}$$

The corresponding jerk equation is given by

$$\dddot{x} + g_2 \beta'(x) \dot{x} = 0. \tag{11}$$

The jerk versions of the most known oscillators (the harmonic oscillator $\ddot{x} + x = 0$, the mathematical pendulum $\ddot{x} + \sin x = 0$, and the Duffing oscillator $\ddot{x} + x^3 - x = 0$) belong to the above family of jerk equations.

In the following, we give Hamilton–Poisson realizations of system (10). For this purpose, using (2), the functions

$$C(x,y,z) = z + g_2\beta(x) \text{ and } H(x,y,z) = \frac{1}{2}y^2 - xz + g_1\alpha(x) \tag{12}$$

give the matrices

$$\Pi_{1,0} = \begin{bmatrix} 0 & 1 & 0 \\ -1 & 0 & g_2\beta'(x) \\ 0 & -g_2\beta'(x) & 0 \end{bmatrix} \tag{13}$$

and

$$\Pi_{0,1} = \begin{bmatrix} 0 & -x & -y \\ x & 0 & -z + g_1\alpha'(x) \\ y & z - g_1\alpha'(x) & 0 \end{bmatrix}, \tag{14}$$

respectively.

Theorem 2. *Let α, β be smooth functions such that $g_1\alpha'(x) = -g_2 x\beta'(x)$, where $g_1, g_2 \in \mathbb{R}$. Then, system* (10) *has the Hamilton–Poisson realizations*

$$\left(\mathbb{R}^3, \Pi_{1,0}, H\right) \text{ and } \left(\mathbb{R}^3, \Pi_{0,1}, -C\right).$$

Moreover, (10) *is a bi-Hamiltonian system.*

Proof. Using (12)–(14), it is easy to see that system (10) writes $(\dot{x}, \dot{y}, \dot{z})^T = \nabla H \times \nabla C = \nabla(-C) \times \nabla H$. In addition, $\Pi_{0,1} \cdot \nabla H = \Pi_{1,0} \cdot \nabla(-C) = \mathbf{0}$ and $\Pi_{1,0} \cdot \nabla H = \Pi_{0,1} \nabla(-C) = (\dot{x}, \dot{y}, \dot{z})^T$.

The sum of the matrices Π_1 and Π_2 is a Poisson structure. Therefore, Π_1 and Π_2 are compatible Poisson structures, and (10) is a bi-Hamiltonian system. □

As a consequence, we obtain the next result.

Theorem 3. *Let $a, b, c, d \in \mathbb{R}$ such that $ad - bc = 1$. Then, system* (10) *admits infinitely many Hamilton–Poisson realizations $\left(\mathbb{R}^3, \Pi_{a,b}, H_{c,d}\right)$, where the Hamiltonian $H_{c,d}$ is given by*

$$H_{c,d} = cC + dH = c(z + g_2\beta(x)) + d\left(\frac{y^2}{2} - xz + g_1\alpha(x)\right),$$

the Poisson structure is defined by

$$\Pi_{a,b} = a\Pi_{1,0} + b\Pi_{0,1} = \begin{bmatrix} 0 & a - bx & -by \\ -a + bx & 0 & ag_2\beta'(x) + bg_1\alpha'(x) - bz \\ by & -ag_2\beta'(x) - bg_1\alpha'(x) + bz & 0 \end{bmatrix},$$

and a Casimir of the Poisson structure is

$$C_{a,b} = aC + bH = a(z + g_2\beta(x)) + b\left(\frac{y^2}{2} - xz + g_1\alpha(x)\right).$$

Since $\nabla C(x,y,z) = (g_2\beta'(x), 0, 1) \neq (0,0,0)$, for all $(x,y,z) \in \mathbb{R}^3$, every level set of the Casimir function C is a regular surface. We denote such a level set by

$$\mathcal{O}_c = C^{-1}(c) = \{(x,y,z) \in \mathbb{R}^3 | z + g_2\beta(x) = c\}.$$

The regular symplectic leaves associated with the Poisson structure $\Pi_{1,0}$ are given by the connected components corresponding to pre-images of regular values of the Casimir function C. Therefore, $\mathcal{O}_c$ is the regular symplectic leaf of the Poisson structure $\Pi_{1,0}$ corresponding to the regular value $c \in \mathbb{R}$ of C. In addition, the dynamics of the Hamilton–Poisson system $(\mathbb{R}^3, \Pi_{1,0}, H)$ are foliated by these symplectic leaves. Moreover, the restriction of system (10) to a regular leaf $\mathcal{O}_c$ is the following completely integrable Hamiltonian system $(\mathcal{O}_c, \omega = dp \wedge dq, H|_{\mathcal{O}_c})$, where the Hamiltonian $H|_{\mathcal{O}_c} = H(p,q)$ is given by

$$H(p,q) = \frac{1}{2}p^2 + g_1\alpha(q) + g_2 q\beta(q) - cq, \tag{15}$$

The reduced equations are

$$\begin{cases} \dot{q} = H_p = p \\ \dot{p} = -H_q = c - g_2\beta(q) \end{cases}, \tag{16}$$

or equivalent

$$\ddot{q} = W'(q), \tag{17}$$

where $W'(q) = c - g_2\beta(q)$.

Thus, on each level set $\mathcal{O}_c$ the dynamics of system (10) are given by system (16) or Equation (17), representing a nonlinear oscillator with the kinetic energy $T = \frac{1}{2}p^2$ and the potential energy $V(q) = -W(q) = g_1\alpha(q) + g_2 q\beta(q) - cq$ (for details about the system $\ddot{x} = f(x)$, see, e.g., [10,20]).

3. Some Dynamical Properties

In this section, we study the stability of system (10) and we prove the existence of some periodic orbits. Also, we obtain sufficient conditions for the existence of heteroclinic and homoclinic orbits.

The equilibrium points of system (10) are given by the family $\mathcal{E} = \{(M,0,0) | M \in \mathbb{R}\}$. Now, we discuss their stability.

Theorem 4. *Let α, β be smooth functions such that $g_1\alpha'(x) = -g_2 x\beta'(x)$, where $g_1, g_2 \in \mathbb{R}$. Denote $e_M = (M,0,0) \in \mathcal{E}$, $M \in \mathbb{R}$ as an arbitrary equilibrium point of system* (10). *Also consider the function*

$$F(x) = g_1(\alpha(M) - \alpha(x)) + g_2 x(\beta(M) - \beta(x)). \tag{18}$$

(i) *If $g_2\beta'(M) < 0$ or $g_2 = 0$, then the equilibrium point e_M is unstable.*
(ii) *If $g_2\beta'(M) > 0$, then the equilibrium point e_M is nonlineary stable.*
(iii) *If $\beta'(M) = 0$ and there is a neighborhood $V \subset \mathbb{R}$ of M such that $F(x) < 0$, for all $x \in V \setminus \{M\}$, then the equilibrium point e_M is nonlineary stable.*

(iv) If $\beta'(M) = 0$ and there is a neighborhood $V = (a, b) \subset \mathbb{R}$ of M such that $F(x) > 0$, for all $x \in (a, M)$ or $x \in (M, b)$, then the equilibrium point e_M is unstable.

Proof. The Jacobian matrix of system (10) at e_M is

$$J(M,0,0) = \begin{bmatrix} 0 & 1 & 0 \\ 0 & 0 & 1 \\ 0 & -g_2\beta'(M) & 0 \end{bmatrix}, \tag{19}$$

with the characteristic polynomial

$$P_M(\lambda) = -\lambda(\lambda^2 + g_2\beta'(M)) \tag{20}$$

and eigenvalues

$$\lambda_1 = 0\,,\;\; \lambda_{2,3} = \pm\sqrt{-g_2\beta'(M)}. \tag{21}$$

(i) Let $g_2\beta'(M) < 0$. From (21), it results that one of the eigenvalues is a positive number. Therfore, e_M is an unstable equilibrium point.

If $g_2 = 0$, system (10) becomes (3), and it has the solution

$$x(t) = \frac{C_1}{2}t^2 + C_2 t + C_3, y(t) = C_1 t + C_2, z(t) = C_1$$

where $C_1, C_2, C_3 \in \mathbb{R}$. Thus, e_M is an unstable equilibrium point.

(ii) Let $g_2\beta'(M) > 0$. In this case, we use the Arnold stability test (see, e.g., [21]). We consider the function

$$F_\lambda = H(x,y,z) + \lambda C(x,y,z) = \frac{1}{2}y^2 - xz + g_1\alpha(x) + \lambda(z + g_2\beta(x)),$$

where λ is a real parameter. We obtain:

1. $dF_\lambda(M,0,0) = 0$ if and only if $\lambda = M$.
2. $W = \ker dC(M,0,0) = \mathrm{span}_{\mathbb{R}}\{(1,0,-g_2\beta'(M)),(0,1,0)\}$.
3. $d^2F_\lambda(M,0,0)|_{W\times W} = g_2\beta'(M)dx^2 + dy^2$, which is positive definte.

From the Arnold stability test, it results that the equilibrium point e_M is nonlineary stable for $g_2\beta'(M) > 0$.

(iii) Let $U \subset \mathbb{R}^3$ be a neighborhood of $(M,0,0)$ such that $\{x|(x,0,0) \in U\} = V$. We consider the function $L \in C^\infty(U,\mathbb{R})$,

$$L(x,y,z) = \left(\frac{y^2}{2} - xz + g_1\alpha(x) - g_1\alpha(M)\right)^2 + (z + g_2\beta(x) - g_2\beta(M))^2, \tag{22}$$

and we prove that it is a Lyapunov function.

By the condition $L(x,y,z) = 0$, we obtain

$$\frac{y^2}{2} - xz + g_1\alpha(x) = g_1\alpha(M)\,,\; z + g_2\beta(x) = g_2\beta(M), \tag{23}$$

and

$$\frac{1}{2}y^2 = g_1(\alpha(M) - \alpha(x)) + g_2 x(\beta(M) - \beta(x)) = F(x). \tag{24}$$

Then, using the hypothesis, we deduce that $x = M$ and $y = 0$. Therefore, $L(x,y,z) = 0$ on U if and only if $x = M$, $y = z = 0$, that is, L given by (22) is a positive definite function on U. Moreover, by (10) we obtain $\dot{L} = \nabla L \cdot (\dot{x}, \dot{y}, \dot{z}) = 0$; thus, L is a Lyapunov function. Therefore, the equilibrium point $(M,0,0)$ is nonlineary stable.

(iv) Consider, for example, $F(x) > 0$, for all $x \in (M, b)$. From (24), let us take $y = \sqrt{2F(x)}$ for $x \in (M, b)$ and $z = g_2(\beta(M) - \beta(x))$ (23). Then, system (10) reduces to the equation $\dot{x} = \sqrt{2F(x)}$. Considering the initial condition $x(0) \in (M, b)$, near M, we obtain a solution $x = x(t)$ that is increasing and moving away from M, and the conclusion follows. □

Remark 1. *If $g_2\beta$ is an increasing function such that $\beta'(M) = 0$, then the function F fulfills the hypothesis given in Theorem 4 (iii); thus, the equilibrium point $(M, 0, 0)$ is nonlinearly stable.*

The next result shows the existence of a family of periodic orbits around some nonlinearly stable equilibrium points.

Theorem 5. *Let α, β be smooth functions such that $g_1\alpha'(x) = -g_2 x\beta'(x)$, where $g_1, g_2 \in \mathbb{R}$. Let $e_M = (M, 0, 0)$ be a nonlineary stable equilibrium point of system (10) in the case $g_2\beta'(M) > 0$. Then, for each sufficiently small $\epsilon \in \mathbb{R}_+^*$, any integral surface*

$$\Sigma_\epsilon^{e_M} : \frac{1}{2}y^2 + (M - x)z + g_1(\alpha(x) - \alpha(M)) + g_2 M(\beta(x) - \beta(M)) = \epsilon^2$$

contains at least one periodic orbit $\gamma_\epsilon^{e_M}$ of system (10) whose period is close to $\frac{2\pi}{\omega}$, where $\omega = \sqrt{g_2\beta'(M)}$.

Proof. The characteristic polynomial associated with the linearization of system (10) at e_M has the eigenvalues $\lambda_1 = 0$ and $\lambda_{2,3} = \pm i\sqrt{g_2\beta'(M)}$. The eigenspace corresponding to the eigenvalue zero, which is $\text{span}_{\mathbb{R}}\{(1, 0, 0)\}$, has dimension 1.

We consider the constant of motion of system (10) given by

$$I(x, y, z) = \frac{y^2}{2} - xz + g_1\alpha(x) + M(z + g_2\beta(x)).$$

It follows that:

1. $dI(M, 0, 0) = 0$.
2. $d^2 I_\lambda(M, 0, 0)|_{W \times W} = g_2\beta'(M)dx^2 + dy^2 > 0$ is positive definte for $g_2\beta'(M) > 0$, where $W = \ker dC(M, 0, 0) = \text{span}_{\mathbb{R}}\{(1, 0, -g_2\beta'(M)), (0, 1, 0)\}$.

and the conclusion follows via a version of the Moser theorem in the case of zero eigenvalue [22]. □

In the following, we study the existence of homoclinic and heteroclinic orbits of system (10).

Let us consider an arbitrary unstable equilibrium point $(M, 0, 0)$, $M \in \mathbb{R}$ of system (10), which is a saddle, that is, $g_2\beta'(M) < 0$. A homoclinic or heteroclinic orbit is given by the intersection of the level sets $C(x, y, z) = C(M, 0, 0)$ and $H(x, y, z) = H(M, 0, 0)$, provided it exists. In this case, we can reduce system (10) to

$$\begin{cases} \dot{x} = \pm\sqrt{2F(x)} \\ y = \pm\sqrt{2F(x)} \\ z = F'(x) \end{cases}, \tag{25}$$

where the smooth function F is given by (18). We have $F'(x) = g_2(\beta(M) - \beta(x))$ and $F''(x) = -g_2\beta'(x)$. Moreover, $F(M) = 0, F'(M) = 0, F''(M) > 0$.

Considering only the level set $C(x, y, z) = C(M, 0, 0)$, system (10) reduces to

$$\begin{cases} \dot{x} = y \\ \dot{y} = F'(x) \end{cases}, \tag{26}$$

for which an equilibrium point is $(q^*, 0)$, if $F'(q^*) = 0$. The above system writes $\ddot{x} = F'(x)$, and it is given by the Hamiltonian $H = \frac{1}{2}y^2 + V(x)$, where $V(x) = -F(x)$ is the potential energy. Therefore, for a given function F, "a look at the graph of the potential energy is enough for a qualitative analysis of such an equation" [10]. In addition, "if there are two saddle points with the same energy level, corresponding to two maxima of $V(x)$, with no higher maximum between them, then they must be connected by heteroclinic orbits" [20].

The motion of the particle is confined to the region $F(x) \geq 0$, and the points with the property $F(x) = 0$ determine the bounds for the motion. Because heteroclinic and homoclinic orbits are bounded, we assume there is $b > M$ such that $F(b) = 0$ and $F(x) > 0$ for all $x \in (M, b)$. Since $F(M) = 0$, we obtain that F has at least a local maximum $N \in (M, b)$; hence, $(N, 0, 0)$ is an equilibrium point. Moreover, F is concave in a neighborhood of N; thus, $(N, 0, 0)$ is a nonlinearly stable equilibrium point (via Theorem 4 (ii); note that $F''(x)$ is the same for all equilibrium points). Then, we obtain the next result.

Theorem 6. *Let α, β be smooth functions such that $g_1\alpha'(x) = -g_2x\beta'(x)$, where $g_1, g_2 \in \mathbb{R}$ and $(M, 0, 0)$, $M \in \mathbb{R}$ represent an arbitrary unstable equilibrium point of system* (10) *such that $g_2\beta'(M) < 0$. We consider the function F defined in* (18)*, that is, $F(x) = g_1(\alpha(M) - \alpha(x)) + g_2x(\beta(M) - \beta(x))$.*

Assume there is $b > M$ such that $F(b) = 0$, $F(x) > 0$ for all $x \in (M, b)$, and the function F does not have local minima on (M, b).

(i) If $F'(b) = 0$ and $g_2\beta'(b) < 0$, then a heteroclinic orbit $\mathcal{HE}(t) = (x(t), y(t), z(t))$ given by (25) *exists, which connects the unstable equilibrium points $(M, 0, 0)$ and $(b, 0, 0)$.*

(ii) If $F'(b) \neq 0$, then a homoclinic orbit $\mathcal{H}(t) = (x(t), y(t), z(t))$ given by (25) *exists, which connects the unstable equilibrium point $(M, 0, 0)$ with itself.*

Remark 2. *The above theorem also holds for $b < M$.*

4. The Anharmonic Oscillator

In this section, we apply the obtained results to the jerk version of the anharmonic oscillator given by the equation $\ddot{x} + \delta x^n = 0$, where $\delta \neq 0$ and $n > 1$ integer.

We have

$$\dddot{x} + n\delta x^{n-1}\dot{x} = 0,\ n > 1, \delta \neq 0, \tag{27}$$

or equivalent

$$\begin{cases} \dot{x} = y \\ \dot{y} = z \\ \dot{z} = -n\delta x^{n-1}y \end{cases}. \tag{28}$$

Therefore, system (28) belongs to the considered family of Hamilton–Poisson jerk systems (10) if

$$g_1 = -\frac{n\delta}{n+1},\ g_2 = \delta,\ \alpha(x) = x^{n+1},\ \beta(x) = x^n.$$

The constants of motion are given by

$$H(x, y, z) = \frac{y^2}{2} - xz - \frac{n\delta x^{n+1}}{n+1},\ C(x, y, z) = z + \delta x^n. \tag{29}$$

The stability of the equilibrium points follows by Theorem 4.

Proposition 1. *Let $e_M = (M, 0, 0)$, $M \in \mathbb{R}$ be an arbitrary equilibrium point of system* (28)*, $n \in \mathbb{N}, n > 1$, and $\delta \neq 0$.*

(i) If $\delta M^{n-1} < 0$, then the equilibrium point e_M is unstable.

(ii) If $\delta M^{n-1} > 0$, then the equilibrium point e_M is nonlinearly stable.

(iii) If $\delta > 0$ and n is odd, then the equilibrium point $(0, 0, 0)$ is nonlineary stable; otherwise, it is unstable.

Around some nonlinearly stable equilibrium points, there is a family of periodic orbits of the considered system. More precisely, by Theorem 5 we deduce the next result.

Proposition 2. *Let* $e_M = (M, 0, 0)$ *be a nonlineary stable equilibrium point of system* (28) *in the case* $\delta M^{n-1} > 0$. *Then, for each sufficiently small* $\epsilon \in \mathbb{R}_+^*$, *any integral surface*

$$\Sigma_\epsilon^{e_M} : \frac{1}{2}y^2 + (M - x)z - \frac{n\delta}{n+1}(x^{n+1} - M^{n+1}) + \delta M(x^n - M^n) = \epsilon^2$$

contains at least one periodic orbit $\gamma_\epsilon^{e_M}$ *of system* (28) *whose period is close to* $\frac{2\pi}{\omega}$, *where* $\omega = \sqrt{n\delta M^{n-1}}$.

As we have seen in Theorem 6, some homoclinic or heteroclinic orbits can exist in the considered dynamics.

Proposition 3. *Let* $e_M = (M, 0, 0)$ *be an unstable equilibrium point of system* (28). *If* n *is even and* $\delta M < 0$, *then a homoclinic orbit* $\mathcal{H}$ *exists that connects the unstable equilibrium point* $(M, 0, 0)$ *with itself. Moreover, the heteroclinic orbits cannot exist in this case.*

Proof. Let $n\delta M^{n-1} < 0$. We consider the function F defined in (18), namely,

$$F(x) = \frac{-\delta}{n+1}\left[x^{n+1} - (n+1)M^n x + nM^{n+1}\right]. \tag{30}$$

Using $F''(x)$ and $F'(x)$, we deduce the following:

(a) Let $\delta < 0$ and $M > 0$. Then, there is an unique $b \in \mathbb{R} \setminus \{M\}$ such that $F(b) = 0$ ($b < -M$). In fact, $F(b) = F(M) = 0$, $F(x) > 0$ for all $x \in (b, M)$, and $F(x) < 0$ otherwise. Using Theorem 6, a homoclinic orbit $\mathcal{H}$ exists that connects the unstable equilibrium point $(M, 0, 0)$ with itself. Moreover, the heteroclinic orbits cannot exist.

(b) If $\delta > 0$ and $M < 0$, then we obtain the same result on (M, b), which finishes the proof.

□

Remark 3. *If* n *is odd, then* $(M, 0, 0), M \neq 0$ *is an unstable equilibrium point for* $\delta < 0$. *In this case, the above-mentioned function* F *has the property* $F(M) = 0$ *and* $F(x) > 0$ *otherwise. Thus, the motion of system* (28) *is unbounded.*

As a particular case, we consider $n = 2$, that is,

$$\begin{cases} \dot{x} = y \\ \dot{y} = z \\ \dot{z} = -2\delta xy \end{cases}. \tag{31}$$

Let $\delta > 0$. Thus, the equilibrium point $e_M = (M, 0, 0), M > 0$ is nonlinearly stable, and a family of periodic orbits of the above system surrounds it (white curves in Figure 1). Choosing initial conditions farther and farther from e_M, these periodic orbits approach the unstable equilibrium point e_{-M}, that is, they tend towards the homoclinic orbit that connects the unstable equilibrium point e_{-M} with itself (the pink curve in Figure 1). After that, the unbounded curves appear in the dynamics of system (31) (yellow curves in Figure 1).

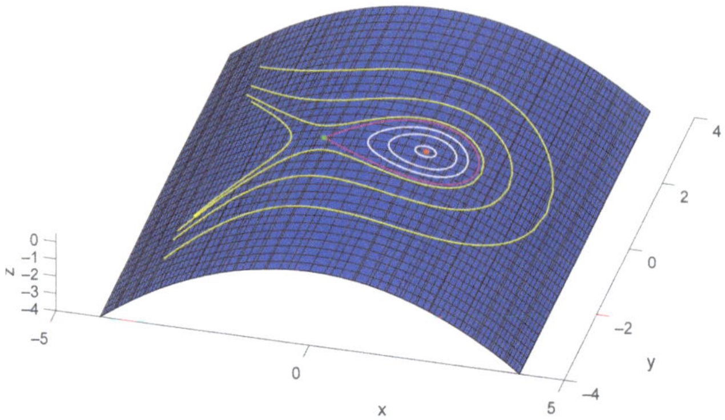

Figure 1. The dynamics of system (31) on the level set $C(x,y,z) = C(M,0,0)$ ($\delta = 0.25; M = 1$): periodic orbits (white) around the stable equilibrium point $(M,0,0)$, $M > 0$ (red), a homoclinic orbit (pink) that connects the unstable equilibrium point $(-M,0,0)$ (green) with itself, and unbounded curves (yellow).

Below, we deduce the parametric representation of the homoclinic orbit of system (31) in the case $\delta > 0$ and $M < 0$. Using (25) and (30), system (31) reduces to the equation

$$\dot{x} = \pm\sqrt{\frac{2\delta}{3}(x-M)^2(-2M-x)}.$$

By integration and (25), (31), we obtain the homoclinic orbit

$$\mathcal{H}_M^- : \mathbb{R} \to \mathbb{R}^3,\ \mathcal{H}_M^-(t) = (x(t), y(t), z(t)),$$

where

$$\begin{aligned}
x(t) &= \frac{432M^3}{\left(e^{(t-t_0)\sqrt{-2\delta M}} - 6M\right)^2} + \frac{72M^2}{e^{(t-t_0)\sqrt{-2\delta M}} - 6M} + M, \\
y(t) &= -\frac{72\sqrt{-2\delta M}\left(M^2 e^{(t-t_0)\sqrt{-2\delta M}}\left(e^{(t-t_0)\sqrt{-2\delta M}} + 6M\right)\right)}{\left(e^{(t-t_0)\sqrt{-2\delta M}} - 6M\right)^3}, \\
z(t) &= -\delta M^2\left[\frac{\left(60Me^{(t-t_0)\sqrt{-2\delta M}} + e^{2(t-t_0)\sqrt{-2\delta M}} + 36M^2\right)^2}{\left(e^{(t-t_0)\sqrt{-2\delta M}} - 6M\right)^4} - 1\right],
\end{aligned}$$

where t_0 is an arbitrary constant.

A similar result is obtained in the case $\delta < 0$ ($M > 0$), namely, the homoclinic orbit

$$\mathcal{H}_M^+ : \mathbb{R} \to \mathbb{R}^3,\ \mathcal{H}_M^+(t) = (x(t), y(t), z(t)),$$

where

$$x(t) = \frac{432M^3}{\left(e^{(t-t_0)\sqrt{-2\delta M}} + 6M\right)^2} - \frac{72M^2}{e^{(t-t_0)\sqrt{-2\delta M}} + 6M} + M,$$

$$y(t) = \frac{72\sqrt{-2\delta M}\left(M^2 e^{(t-t_0)\sqrt{-2\delta M}}\left(e^{(t-t_0)\sqrt{-2\delta M}} - 6M\right)\right)}{\left(e^{(t-t_0)\sqrt{-2\delta M}} + 6M\right)^3},$$

$$z(t) = \frac{144\delta M^3 e^{(t-t_0)\sqrt{-2\delta M}}\left(-24Me^{(t-t_0)\sqrt{-2\delta M}} + e^{2(t-t_0)\sqrt{-2\delta M}} + 36M^2\right)}{\left(e^{(t-t_0)\sqrt{-2\delta M}} + 6M\right)^4}.$$

5. Conclusions

In this paper, we constructed a family of Hamilton–Poisson jerk systems and we studied some dynamical properties.

The dynamics of a three-dimensional Hamilton–Poisson system take place at the intersection of the level sets given by the two constants of motion. Thus, for particular constants of motion, the orbits of the system can be depicted. In general, we studied the stability of the equilibrium points, and we proved the existence of periodic orbits around nonlinearly stable equilibrium points. Also, we established conditions for the existence of homoclinic and heteroclinic orbits. Particularly, we applied the results to a family of anharmonic oscillators.

We noticed that jerk versions of some nonlinear oscillators belong to this family, particularly the harmonic oscillator and some anharmonic oscillators. In quantum field theory (QFT), while the harmonic oscillator is a fundamental concept, there are other general potentials, including anharmonic potentials. Consequently, we expect some connections between our work and QFT, particularly solitons.

Author Contributions: Conceptualization, C.L. and J.C.; methodology, C.L.; formal analysis, C.L. and J.C.; writing—original draft preparation, C.L. and J.C.; writing—review and editing, C.L.; visualization, C.L. and J.C.; and supervision, C.L. All authors have read and agreed to the published version of the manuscript.

Funding: This research received no external funding.

Data Availability Statement: Data are contained within the article.

Acknowledgments: We would like to thank the referees very much for their valuable comments and suggestions.

Conflicts of Interest: The authors declare no conflicts of interest.

References

1. Schot, S.H. Jerk: The time rate of change of acceleration. *Am. J. Phys.* **1978**, *46*, 1090–1094. [CrossRef]
2. Sprott, J.C. Some simple chaotic jerk functions. *Am. J. Phys.* **1997**, *65*, 537–543. [CrossRef]
3. Wei, Z.; Sprott, J.C.; Chen, H. Elementary quadratic chaotic flows with a single non-hyperbolic equilibrium. *Phys. Lett. A* **2015**, *379*, 2184–2187. [CrossRef]
4. Vaidyanathan, S.; Kammogne, A.S.T.; Tlelo-Cuautle, E.; Talonang, C.N.; Abd-El-Atty, B.; Abd El-Latif, A.A.; Kengne, E.M.; Mawamba, V.F.; Sambas, A.; Darwin, P.; et al. A Novel 3-D Jerk System, Its Bifurcation Analysis, Electronic Circuit Design and a Cryptographic Application. *Electronics* **2023**, *12*, 2818. [CrossRef]
5. Sang, B.; Huang, B. Zero-Hopf Bifurcations of 3D Quadratic Jerk System. *Mathematics* **2020**, *8*, 1454. [CrossRef]
6. Braun, F.; Mereu, A.C. Zero-Hopf bifurcation in a 3D jerk system. *Nonlinear Anal. Real World Appl.* **2021**, *59*, 103245. [CrossRef]
7. Lăzureanu, C. On the Double-Zero Bifurcation of Jerk Systems. *Mathematics* **2023**, *11*, 4468. [CrossRef]
8. Lăzureanu, C.; Cho, J. On Hopf and fold bifurcations of jerk systems. *Mathematics* **2023**, *11*, 4295. [CrossRef]
9. Marsden, J.;Raţiu, T.S. *Introduction to Mechanics and Symmetry*, 2nd ed.; Text and Appl. Math. 17; Springer: Berlin, Germany, 1999.
10. Arnold, V.I. *Mathematical Methods of Classical Mechanics*, 2nd ed.; Graduate Texts in Mathematics, 60; Springer: New York, NY, USA, 1989.

11. Walker, W.H.; Walton, J.C.; DeVries, A.C.; Nelson, R.J. Circadian rhythm disruption and mental health. *Transl. Psychiatry* **2020**, *10*, 28. [CrossRef] [PubMed]
12. Goldental, A.; Vardi, R.; Sardi, S.; Sabo, P.; Kanter, I. Broadband macroscopic cortical oscillations emerge from intrinsic neuronal response failures. *Front. Neural Circuits* **2015**, *9*, 65. [CrossRef] [PubMed]
13. Iotti, S.; Borsari, M.; Bendahan, D. Oscillations in energy metabolism. *Biochim. Biophys. Acta BBA-Bioenerg.* **2010**, *1797*, 1353–1361. [CrossRef] [PubMed]
14. Hainzl, J. Stability and Hopf Bifurcation in a predator–prey System with Several Parameters. *SIAM J Appl. Math.* **1988**, *48*, 170–190. [CrossRef]
15. Lăzureanu, C. Integrable Deformations of Three-Dimensional Chaotic Systems. *Int. J. Bifurcat. Chaos* **2018**, *28*, 1850066. [CrossRef]
16. Giné, J.; Sinelshchikov, D.I. On the geometric and analytical properties of the anharmonic oscillator. *Commun. Nonlinear Sci.* **2024**, *131*, 107875. [CrossRef]
17. Gürses, M.; Guseinov, G.S.; Zheltukhin, K. Dynamical systems and Poisson structures. *J. Math. Phys.* **2009**, *50*, 112703. [CrossRef]
18. Tudoran, R.M. A normal form of completely integrable systems. *J. Geom. Phys.* **2012**, *62*, 1167–1174. [CrossRef]
19. Puta, M. *Hamiltonian Mechanical System and Geometric Quantization*; Kluwer Academic Publishers: Dordrecht, The Netherlands, 1993.
20. Guckenheimer, J.; Holmes, P. *Nonlinear Oscillations, Dynamical Systems, and Bifurcations of Vector Fields, Applied Mathematical Sciences*; Springer: Berlin/Heidelberg, Germany, 1983.
21. Arnold, V. Conditions for nonlinear stability of stationary plane curvilinear flows on an ideal fluid. *Dokl. Akad. Nauk. SSSR* **1965**, *162*, 773–777.
22. Birtea, P.; Puta, M.; Tudoran, R.M. Periodic orbits in the case of zero eigenvalue. *C.R. Acad. Sci. Paris Ser. I* **2007**, *344*, 779–784. [CrossRef]

mathematics

MDPI

Article

Global Dynamics of a Social Hierarchy-Stratified Malaria Model: Insight from Fractional Calculus

Sulaimon F. Abimbade [1], Furaha M. Chuma [2], Sunday O. Sangoniyi [3], Ramoshweu S. Lebelo [4], Kazeem O. Okosun [5] and Samson Olaniyi [1,*]

1 Department of Pure and Applied Mathematics, Ladoke Akintola University of Technology, Ogbomoso 212102, Nigeria; sfabimbade81@lautech.edu.ng
2 Department of Physics, Mathematics and Informatics, Dar es Salaam University College of Education, Dar es Salaam 2329, Tanzania; furaha.chuma@udsm.ac.tz
3 Department of Mathematics and Computing Science Education, Emmanuel Alayande University of Education, Oyo 211172, Nigeria; sangoniyiso@eauedoyo.edu.ng
4 Department of Education, Vaal University of Technology, Vanderbijilpark 1911, South Africa; sollyl@vut.ac.za
5 Department of Mathematics, University of Kansas, Lawrence, KS 66045, USA
* Correspondence: solaniyi@lautech.edu.ng

Abstract: In this study, a mathematical model for the transmission dynamics of malaria among different socioeconomic groups in the human population interacting with a susceptible-infectious vector population is presented and analysed using a fractional-order derivative of the Caputo type. The total human population is stratified into two distinguished classes of lower and higher income individuals, with each class further subdivided into susceptible, infectious, and recovered populations. The socio hierachy-structured fractional-order malaria model is analyzed through the application of different dynamical system tools. The theory of positivity and boundedness based on the generalized mean value theorem is employed to investigate the basic properties of solutions of the model, while the Banach fixed point theory approach is used to prove the existence and uniqueness of the solution. Furthermore, unlike the existing related studies, comprehensive global asymptotic dynamics of the fractional-order malaria model around both disease-free and endemic equilibria are explored by generalizing the usual classical methods for establishing global asymptotic stability of the steady states. The asymptotic behavior of the trajectories of the system are graphically illustrated at different values of the fractional (noninteger) order.

Keywords: fractional-order system; social hierarchy model; malaria dynamics; Banach fixed point theory; global stability

MSC: 37N25; 34D23; 34A08; 92D25

Citation: Abimbade, S.F.; Chuma, F.M.; Sangoniyi, S.O.; Lebelo, R.S.; Okosun, K.O.; Olaniyi, S. Global Dynamics of a Social Hierarchy-Stratified Malaria Model: Insight from Fractional Calculus. *Mathematics* **2024**, *12*, 1593. https://doi.org/10.3390/math12101593

Academic Editors: Mihaela Neamţu, Eva Kaslik and Anca Rădulescu

Received: 27 March 2024
Revised: 3 May 2024
Accepted: 16 May 2024
Published: 20 May 2024

1. Introduction

The evolution of infectious diseases has been a regular threat to humanity and a bone of contention for policymakers [1]. Several dangerous infectious diseases such as Ebola, malaria, measles, Zika, Acquired Immune Deficiency Syndrome (AIDS), tuberculosis, chickenpox, chikungunya virus (CHIKV) and COVID-19 have posed an intensifying threat to humanity due to their emergence and re-emergence in the population [2,3]. To date, malaria, which is caused by a single-celled parasite of the genus *Plasmodium* has maintained its stance as one of the vector-borne diseases with an overwhelming adverse effect on the human population [2]. The transmission mode requires the parasitic interaction between a human (host) and a vector (mosquito).

The malaria parasite is typically transmitted to humans through the bite of an infected female *Anopheles* mosquito, which is the main carrier of the parasite. Malaria parasites may also be transmitted to humans through the transfusion of infected blood, organ transplant, or the sharing of contaminated needles or syringes, as well as from a mother to her unborn infant before or during delivery (congenital malaria) [4]. In 2020, the World Health Organization (WHO) stated in their 2021 malaria global report that there were around 241 million cases of malaria globally and 627,000 deaths due to the whip of the disease [2]. Malaria symptoms may include fever, headache, sweats, muscle aches, chills, tiredness, nausea, vomiting, and diarrhea, among others [2]. If promptly detected, the disease is preventable and curable, but symptoms may go out of hand if not detected early and properly treated [5,6].

Mathematical modeling has become an inestimable tool for finding solutions to the complexities encountered in the transmission of infectious diseases. In particular, several recent mathematical models have been devoted to the study of malaria dynamics in the literature; see for instance [5–18] and some of the cited references in the recent scoping review presented in Anwar et al. [19]. Specifically, Abimbade et al. [5] designed a mathematical model for the evolution of recurrent malaria in the human population. The authors considered all categories of recurrent malaria, including recrudescence, relapse, and reinfection. In a similar development, Tasman et al. [6] developed and analyzed a deterministic model to study the transmission dynamics of recurrent malaria with relapse, reinfection, and recrudescence, thus taking into account the inadequacy of hospital beds. Bakare [8] formulated and analyzed a nonautonomous malaria model that took into account five optimal control measures representing the use of insecticide-treated bed nets, educational campaigns, indoor residual sprayings, the clearance of mosquito breeding sites, and treatment control in mitigating the dynamical spread of malaria in the population. Traore [9] designed a temperature-dependent malaria model where the mosquito population was structured into stages. In [10], the authors presented an optimal framework for the transmission dynamics of malaria that incorporated mosquito seasonal factors, and the impacts of insecticide, prevention, and treatment controls on the malaria model were examined. Furthermore, Keno [14] applied optimal control theory and economic analysis to a deterministic mathematical model with atmospheric variation.

In another development, the authors in [15] presented and rigorously analyzed a malaria model incorporating a direct atmospheric-mediated transmission mode. In [16], the authors formulated and analyzed a malaria model incorporating relapse and unenlightened infected individuals. Furthermore, Olaniyi and coworkers [17] presented an optimal control framework for the transmission dynamics of malaria through the transfusion of infected blood and the indirect horizontal transmission (human vector) route with saturated treatment function. The authors in [20] presented an optimal control framework for recurrent malaria dynamics with a view to providing effective optimal control strategies to be implemented in setting the recurrence of malaria in the human population to extinction. In addition, Olaniyi et al. [21] stressed on the efficiency and economic analyses of a recurrent malaria model. Their focus was centered on identifying the most efficient and most cost-effective strategy that best averts the highest number of recurrent malaria infection in the population.

At this point, it is worth noting that all the aforementioned studies did not consider the stratification of the human population into social classes. However, the authors in [22] developed a mathematical model for the transmission dynamics of malaria by categorizing the human population into two main socioeconomic divisions, namely low-income and high-income individuals. The formulated model was analyzed via optimal control theory and extended to include efficiency and economic analyses to procure the most efficient and effective control strategy for mitigating the spread of malaria among social classes in the population. Modeling infectious disease using a fractional-order derivative operator allows for a more accurate description of the disease transmission than the classical modeling approach. The nonlocal nature of the fractional-order system makes it more suitable to model disease dynamics where prior history of the disease governs its future evolution (see, [23,24]). Thus, modeling malaria spread in a social hierarchy-structured population with fractional-order derivative operator will create a history such that the current behavior of the disease will depend on the previous outbreaks. This explains the capacity of fractional-order models in capturing memory effects in the transmission dynamics of disease. Hence, it is of essence to improve on the existing knowledge of malaria transmission dynamics by studying the effect of memory on the evolution of malaria within social classes in the population. This can be achieved by generalizing the model developed in [22] in the framework of fractional calculus.

It is worthy of note that Atangana–Baleanu and piecewise Caputo–Fabrizio fractional versions of the model have been analyzed in Bonyah [25] and Aldwoah et al. [26], respectively. Both studies in [25,26] focused on establishing the existence and uniqueness of the solution of the model, thereby exploring the crossover effects associated with malaria dynamics. However, the comprehensive global stability dynamics of the social hierarchy-structured malaria model with either a classical or fractional derivative operator remains unexplored thus far. As a result of this, the fractional-order of the Caputo type is employed in this present study, with specific focus on gaining insights into the global asymptotic dynamics of social hierarchy-structured malaria transmission with memory using a more generalized approach for establishing the global asymptotic stability of the steady states of the fractional-order model. In other words, this study examines the influence of memory on the global dynamics of malaria among social classes by extending the usual classical methods for investigating the global asymptotic stabilities of both disease-free and endemic equilibrium points to a more general approach using fractional calculus with a Caputo derivative operator. The remaining aspects of the study are organized as follows: In Section 2, the noninteger-order social hierarchy-stratified model is presented with its qualitative analysis for the existence and uniqueness of solutions. Section 3 presents the global asymptotic dynamics of the fractional-order model with simulations and discussion. Section 4 deals with the concluding remarks of the study.

2. Fractional-Order Social Hierarchy-Stratified Model

The mathematical model presented in this study is a fractionalized version of the classical-order nonlinear malaria model developed in Olaniyi et al. [22]. It has been established by a plethora of researchers that fractional-order derivatives define real-life situations better than the usual classical-order derivatives. This is due to the fact that fractional-order derivatives possess distinctive properties such as memory and heredity, which enable adequate and effective comprehension of real-life phenomena [27–33]. It is on this note that this study is focused on the application of fractional calculus to the epidemiology of malaria with a view to gaining further insights into how the consequences of memory affect the transmission dynamics of the disease in a social heirarchy-structured human population. To start with, it is of essence to state some basic concepts and analytic results in fractional calculus following [3,34,35].

Definition 1. *A Riemann–Liouville fractional integral of order α of relation $h : \mathbb{R}_+ \to \mathbb{R}$, designated by $I_t^\alpha h(t)$, is defined as*

$$I_t^\alpha h(t) = \frac{1}{\Gamma(\alpha)} \int_0^t \frac{h(\xi)}{(t-\xi)^{1-\alpha}} d\xi, \tag{1}$$

where $\alpha \in \mathbb{R}_+$ such that $\alpha \in (0,1)$ and $t > 0$. The gamma function, $\Gamma(\alpha)$, is given by

$$\Gamma(\alpha) = \int_0^\infty x^{\alpha-1} e^{-x} dx. \tag{2}$$

Definition 2. *A fractional derivative of order α of $h : \mathbb{R}_+ \to \mathbb{R}$ of the Caputo type, denoted by ${}^C D_t^{\alpha} h(t)$, is defined as*

$$ {}^C D_t^{\alpha} h(t) = \begin{cases} \dfrac{1}{\Gamma(1-\alpha)} \displaystyle\int_0^t \frac{h'(\varrho)}{(t-\varrho)^{\alpha}} d\varrho, \\ \dfrac{d^{\alpha}}{dt^{\alpha}} h(t), \ \ 0 < \alpha \leq 1. \end{cases} \tag{3} $$

Lemma 1 (Generalized Mean Value Theorem). *Let $g(t) \in C[0, t^*]$ and ${}^C D_t^{\alpha} g(t) \in C[0, t^*]$ for $0 < \alpha \leq 1$; then,*

$$ g(t) = g(0) + \frac{{}^C D_t^{\alpha} g(\varphi) t^{\alpha}}{\Gamma(\alpha)}, \quad \varphi \in [0, t], \ \forall \, t \in (0, t^*]. $$

(i) If ${}^C D_t^{\alpha} g(t) \geq 0 \ \forall \, t \in [0, t^*]$, then $g(t)$ is nondecreasing for each $t \in (0, t^*)$.
(ii) If ${}^C D_t^{\alpha} g(t) \leq 0 \ \forall \, t \in [0, t^*]$, then $g(t)$ is nonincreasing for each $t \in (0, t^*)$.

Lemma 2. *Let $\chi(t) \in C([0, \infty))$ satisfy*

$$ {}^C D_t^{\alpha} \chi(t) + a_1 \chi(t) \leq a_2, \ \chi(0) = \chi_0, $$

where $\alpha \in (0, 1]$ and $a_1, a_2 \in \mathbb{R}$, with $a_1 \neq 0$; then,

$$ \chi(t) \leq \left(\chi_0 - \frac{a_2}{a_1} \right) E_{\alpha,1}(-a_1 t^{\alpha}) + \frac{a_2}{a_1}, $$

where $E_{\alpha,1}(\cdot)$ is a Mittag–Leffler function with one parameter α given by

$$ E_{\alpha,1}(x) = \sum_{n=0}^{\infty} \frac{x^n}{\Gamma(\alpha n + 1)}. $$

Lemma 3. *$\chi(t) = \chi(0) E_{\alpha,1}(k t^{\alpha})$ solves the fractional-order differential equation of the form ${}^C D_t^{\alpha} \chi(t) = k \chi(t)$.*

Consequently, the nonlinear fractional-order differential equations of the Caputo type describing the evolution of the social hierarchy-structured malaria model are given by

$$ \begin{aligned} {}^C D_t^{\alpha} S_L(t) &= (1-r)\Lambda_H - \beta_1 S_L(t) I_V(t) + \omega R_L(t) + \sigma_H S_H(t) - (\mu_H + \sigma_L) S_L(t) \\ {}^C D_t^{\alpha} S_H(t) &= r\Lambda_H - b\beta_1 S_H(t) I_V(t) + \epsilon R_H(t) + \sigma_L S_L(t) - (\mu_H + \sigma_H) S_H(t) \\ {}^C D_t^{\alpha} I_L(t) &= \beta_1 S_L(t) I_V(t) - (\mu_H + \gamma + \delta) I_L(t) \\ {}^C D_t^{\alpha} I_H(t) &= b\beta_1 S_H(t) I_V(t) - (\mu_H + \alpha + \phi) I_H(t) \\ {}^C D_t^{\alpha} R_L(t) &= \gamma I_L(t) - (\omega + \mu_H) R_L(t) \\ {}^C D_t^{\alpha} R_H(t) &= \alpha I_H(t) - (\epsilon + \mu_H) R_H(t) \\ {}^C D_t^{\alpha} S_V(t) &= \Lambda_V - \beta_2 (I_L + \theta I_H) S_V(t) - \mu_V S_V(t) \\ {}^C D_t^{\alpha} I_V(t) &= \beta_2 (I_L + \theta I_H) S_V(t) - \mu_V I_V(t). \end{aligned} \tag{4} $$

with initial conditions

$$\begin{aligned} &S_L(0) = S_{L0},\ S_H(0) = S_{H0},\ I_L(0) = I_{L0},\ I_H(0) = I_{H0}, \\ &R_L(0) = R_{L0},\ R_H(0) = R_{H0},\ S_V(0) = S_{V0},\ I_V(0) = I_{V0}. \end{aligned} \tag{5}$$

Malaria transmission dynamics involve the interaction between human and vector populations. The total human population, $N_H(t)$, is socially structured into six mutually exclusive compartments, namely a low social class susceptible population denoted by $S_L(t)$, a high social class susceptible population denoted by $S_H(t)$, a low social class infectious population denoted by $I_L(t)$, a high social class infectious population denoted by $I_H(t)$, a low social class recovered population denoted by $R_L(t)$, and a high social class recovered population denoted by $R_H(t)$. The vector population is stratified into a susceptible population designated by $S_V(t)$ and an infectious population denoted by $I_V(t)$. Then, the total human population, $N_H(t)$ at time t is given by

$$N_H(t) = S_L(t) + S_H(t) + I_L(t) + I_H(t) + R_L(t) + R_H(t), \tag{6}$$

and the total vector population is given by

$$N_V(t) = S_V(t) + I_V(t). \tag{7}$$

The lower social class human population is a set of lower income individuals, given by $\{S_L(t), I_L(t), R_L(t)\}$, who have little or no accessibility to medical treatment and other resources for sustainance in the population unlike the higher social class population set $\{S_H(t), I_H(t), R_H(t)\}$. The population of lower social class is generated by the fraction of recruitment of individuals into the population assumed susceptible at a rate of $(1-r)\Lambda_H$, while the remaining fraction $r\Lambda_H$ goes to the higher social class population. The susceptible individuals in the lower and higher social groups are infected following effective contact with infectious mosquitoes at incidence rates of $\beta_1 S_L I_V$ and $b\beta_1 S_H I_V$, where β_1 is the transmission probability of infection, and b is the modification parameter responsible for the degree of infection within higher social group individuals.

The susceptible lower and higher social class individuals are further increased by the rate at which recovered humans $R_L(t)$ and $R_H(t)$ loss their immunity at rates ω and ϵ, respectively. The infectious individuals in lower and higher income classes recover from the disease at rates γ and α, respectively. The populations of infectious individuals in both social classes are downsized by the disease-induced death at their respective rates δ and ϕ, while the total human population is dwindled by the natural mortality rate μ_H. Furthermore, the population of susceptible mosquitoes is increased by the recruitment of mosquitoes at a rate Λ_V and become infected due to the contact with both infectious lower and higher social class individuals at incidence rate $\beta_2(I_L + \theta I_H)$, with β_2 being the effective contact rate and θ being the modification parameter responsible for the reduction of infection among the higher social class individuals. The total mosquito population is diminished by the natural mortality rate μ_V. The Caputo fractional derivative operator is chosen to formulate system (4) because of its suitability for initial conditions in a classical sense unlike the Riemann–Liouville derivative operator. In addition, the Caputo derivative of a constant function always yields zero, thus satisfying the fundamental principle of calculus, unlike some other fractional-order derivative operators [27,28]. It should be emphasized that the full description and assumptions governing the model formulation can be found in the classical version presented in [22], but it is pertinent to mention that all the parameters of the model governed by the system (4) are measured per fractional-order time, $t^{-\alpha}$ (see, e.g., [28,32,35]), unlike the classical model in [22], where parameters were measured per unit time t^{-1}.

2.1. Basic Properties of the Fractional Model

Herein, the basic properties of solutions of the fractional-order malaria model (4) are investigated using the theory of positivity and boundedness.

2.1.1. Positivity and Boundedness of Solution

Theorem 1. *The solutions* $\{S_L(t), S_H(t), I_L(t), I_H(t), R_L(t), R_H(t), S_V(t)$, *and* $I_V(t)\}$ *of the fractional-order social hierarchy-structured model* (4) *remain non-negative for all* $t > 0$ *if the associated initial conditions* (5) *are non-negative.*

Proof. It is straightforward from system (4) that

$$\begin{aligned}
{}^C D_t^\alpha (S_L)(t)|_{S_L=0} &= (1-r)\Lambda_H + \omega R_L(t) + \sigma_H S_H(t) > 0,\\
{}^C D_t^\alpha (S_H)(t)|_{S_H=0} &= r\Lambda_H + \epsilon R_H(t) + \sigma_L S_L(t) > 0,\\
{}^C D_t^\alpha (I_L)(t)|_{I_L=0} &= \beta_1 S_L(t) I_V(t) \geq 0,\\
{}^C D_t^\alpha (I_H)(t)|_{I_H=0} &= b\beta_1 S_H(t) I_V(t) \geq 0,\\
{}^C D_t^\alpha (R_L)(t)|_{R_L=0} &= \gamma I_L(t) \geq 0,\\
{}^C D_t^\alpha (R_H)(t)|_{R_H=0} &= \alpha I_H(t) \geq 0,\\
{}^C D_t^\alpha (S_V)(t)|_{S_V=0} &= \Lambda_V > 0,\\
{}^C D_t^\alpha (I_V)(t)|_{I_V=0} &= \beta_2 (I_L + \theta I_H) S_V(t) \geq 0.
\end{aligned} \tag{8}$$

Following the fact that the Caputo derivatives in (8) are non-negative on the bounding planes $\mathbb{R}^8_+$ with the non-negative initial conditions, then by using the generalized mean value theorem (see, Lemma 1), it follows that the solutions $S_L(t)$, $S_H(t)$, $I_L(t)$, $I_H(t)$, $R_L(t)$, $R_H(t)$, $S_V(t)$, and $I_V(t)$ are non-decreasing for all time $t > 0$. Hence, we have the proof. □

Theorem 2. *A region* $\mathfrak{D}$ *of the fractional-order social hierarchy-structured malaria model* (4), *which is defined by* $\mathfrak{D} = \mathfrak{D}_H \times \mathfrak{D}_V \subset \mathbb{R}^6_+ \times \mathbb{R}^2_+$, *where*

$$\mathfrak{D}_H = \left\{ (S_L(t), S_H(t), I_L(t), I_H(t), R_L(t), R_H(t)) \in \mathbb{R}^6_+ : N_H(t) \leq \frac{\Lambda_H}{\mu_H} \right\},$$

$$\mathfrak{D}_V = \left\{ (S_V(t), I_V(t)) \in \mathbb{R}^2_+ : N_V(t) \leq \frac{\Lambda_V}{\mu_V} \right\},$$

is positively invariant.

Proof. Given that $N_H(t) = S_L(t) + S_H(t) + I_L(t) + I_H(t) + R_L(t) + R_H(t)$ and $N_V(t) = S_V(t) + I_V(t)$, it then follows that the Caputo derivatives of $N_H(t)$ and $N_V(t)$ are given by

$$\begin{aligned}
{}^C D_t^\alpha N_H(t) &= {}^C D_t^\alpha S_L(t) + {}^C D_t^\alpha S_H(t) + {}^C D_t^\alpha I_L(t) + {}^C D_t^\alpha I_H(t) + {}^C D_t^\alpha R_L(t) + {}^C D_t^\alpha R_H(t)\\
&= \Lambda_H - \mu_H N_H - \delta I_L - \phi I_H,\\
&\leq \Lambda_H - \mu_H N_H.
\end{aligned} \tag{9}$$

Similarly,

$${}^C D_t^\alpha N_V(t) + \mu_V N_V \leq \Lambda_V. \tag{10}$$

Now, invoking Lemma 2 on (9) and (10) yields

$$N_H(t) \leq \left(N_H(0) - \frac{\Lambda_H}{\mu_H} \right) E_{\alpha,1}(-\mu_H t^\alpha) + \frac{\Lambda_H}{\mu_H}, \tag{11}$$

and
$$N_V(t) \leq \left(N_V(0) - \frac{\Lambda_V}{\mu_V}\right) E_{\alpha,1}(-\mu_V t^\alpha) + \frac{\Lambda_V}{\mu_V}. \tag{12}$$

Then, taking the lim sup as $t \to \infty$ implies that $N_H(t) \leq \Lambda_H/\mu_H$ and $N_V(t) \leq \Lambda_V/\mu_V$. Accordingly, the solution path of the system (4) is bounded in $\mathfrak{D}$, thus showing that the region $\mathfrak{D}$ is positively invariant. □

2.1.2. Existence and Uniqueness of Solution

This subsection is dedicated to the investigation of the existence and uniqueness of the solution of the social hierarchy-structured fractional-order malaria model (4) using the Banach's fixed point theory approach [3,33,36,37]. Suppose the noninteger-order malaria model (4) is rewritten in a compact form:
$$\begin{aligned} {}^{C}D_t^\alpha(\mathcal{G}(t)) &= \mathcal{H}(t, \mathcal{G}(t)), \quad 0 \leq t \leq \Phi, \\ \mathcal{G}(0) &= \mathcal{G}_0, \end{aligned} \tag{13}$$

where $\mathcal{G}(t) = (S_L(t), S_H(t), I_L(t), I_H(t), R_L(t), R_H(t), S_V(t), I_V(t))^\intercal$, and $\mathcal{H}(t, \mathcal{G}(t)) : [0, \Phi] \times \mathbb{R}^8_+ \to \mathbb{R}$ are defined by
$$\mathcal{H}(t, \mathcal{G}(t)) = (\mathcal{H}_i(t, S_L(t), S_H(t), I_L(t), I_H(t), R_L(t), R_H(t), S_V(t), I_V(t))^\intercal,$$

for $i = 1, 2, ..., 8$ so that
$$\begin{aligned}
\mathcal{H}_1(t, \mathcal{G}(t)) &= (1 - r)\Lambda_H - \beta_1 S_L(t) I_V(t) + \omega R_L(t) + \sigma_H S_H(t) - (\mu_H + \sigma_L) S_L(t), \\
\mathcal{H}_2(t, \mathcal{G}(t)) &= r\Lambda_H - b\beta_1 S_H(t) I_V(t) + \epsilon R_H(t) + \sigma_L S_L(t) - (\mu_H + \sigma_H) S_H(t), \\
\mathcal{H}_3(t, \mathcal{G}(t)) &= \beta_1 S_L(t) I_V(t) - (\mu_H + \gamma + \delta) I_L(t), \\
\mathcal{H}_4(t, \mathcal{G}(t)) &= b\beta_1 S_H(t) I_V(t) - (\mu_H + \alpha + \phi) I_H(t), \\
\mathcal{H}_5(t, \mathcal{G}(t)) &= \gamma I_L(t) - (\omega + \mu_H) R_L(t), \\
\mathcal{H}_6(t, \mathcal{G}(t)) &= \alpha I_H(t) - (\epsilon + \mu_H) R_H(t), \\
\mathcal{H}_7(t, \mathcal{G}(t)) &= \Lambda_V - \beta_2 (I_L + \theta I_H) S_V(t) - \mu_V S_V(t), \\
\mathcal{H}_8(t, \mathcal{G}(t)) &= \beta_2 (I_L + \theta I_H) S_V(t) - \mu_V I_V(t),
\end{aligned} \tag{14}$$
where $\mathcal{G}_0 = (S_{L0}, S_{H0}, I_{L0}, I_{H0}, R_{L0}, R_{H0}, S_{V0}, I_{V0},)^\intercal$.

Now, following Definition 1 by integrating (13) fractionally gives
$$\mathcal{G}(t) = \mathcal{G}_0 + \frac{1}{\Gamma(\alpha)} \int_0^t (t - \Psi)^{\alpha - 1} \mathcal{H}(\Psi, \mathcal{G}(\Psi)) d\Psi. \tag{15}$$

Assume that $\mathbf{M} = (C[0, \Phi], \| \cdot \|)$ is a Banach space for all real-valued continuous functions with the supremum norm governed by
$$\|\mathcal{G}(t)\| = \sup\{|\mathcal{G}(t)| : t \in [0, \Phi]\},$$

with
$$\sup |\mathcal{G}(t)| = \sup(|S_L(t)| + |S_H(t)| + |I_L(t)| + |I_H(t)| + |R_L(t)| + |R_H(t)| + |S_V(t)| + |I_V(t)|).$$

At this juncture, it is important to establish that $\mathcal{H}(t, \mathcal{G}(t))$ is Lipschitz continuous, and this is investigated as presented in the next result.

Theorem 3. *The vector function $\mathcal{H}(t, \mathcal{G}(t))$ is Lipschitzian in $\mathcal{G}(t)$ on $C([0, \Phi] \times \mathbb{R}^8_+, \mathbb{R})$ if there exists a constant $\mathcal{P} > 0$ such that*

$$\|\mathcal{H}(t, \mathcal{G}_1(t)) - \mathcal{H}(t, \mathcal{G}_2(t))\| \leq \mathcal{P}\|\mathcal{G}_1(t) - \mathcal{G}_2(t)\|. \tag{16}$$

Proof. Since the states of the fractional-order social hierarchy-structured malaria model (4) are bounded by Λ_H/μ_H for the human population and Λ_V/μ_V for the vector population in a positively invariant region $\mathfrak{D}$, then considering $\mathcal{H}_1(t, S_L(t))$, and for $S_{L1}(t)$ and $S_{L2}(t)$, it follows that

$$\|\mathcal{H}_1(t, S_{L1}(t)) - \mathcal{H}_1(t, S_{L2}(t))\| \leq \|(\beta_1 I_V + \mu_H + \sigma_L)\|\|S_{L1} - S_{L2}\|. \tag{17}$$

Since $I_V \leq \Lambda_V/\mu_V$ in $\mathfrak{D}$, then the inequality (17) becomes

$$\|\mathcal{H}_1(t, S_{L1}(t)) - \mathcal{H}_1(t, S_{L2}(t))\| \leq \mathcal{P}_1\|S_{L1} - S_{L2}\|, \tag{18}$$

where $\mathcal{P}_1 = \left(\frac{\beta_1\Lambda_V}{\mu_V} + (\mu_H + \sigma_L)\right) > 0$.

In a similar manner, for any $S_{H1}(t)$ and $S_{H2}(t)$,

$$\|\mathcal{H}_2(t, S_{H1}) - \mathcal{H}_2(t, S_{H2})\| \leq \mathcal{P}_2\|S_{H1} - S_{H2}\|, \tag{19}$$

where $\mathcal{P}_2 = \left(\frac{b\beta_1\Lambda_V}{\mu_V} + (\mu_H + \sigma_H)\right) > 0$, since $I_V \leq \Lambda_V/\mu_V$. For any $I_{L1}(t)$ and $I_{L2}(t)$,

$$\|\mathcal{H}_3(t, I_{L1}) - \mathcal{H}_3(t, I_{L2})\| \leq \mathcal{P}_3\|I_{L1} - I_{L2}\|, \tag{20}$$

where $\mathcal{P}_3 = (\gamma + \delta + \mu_H) > 0$. For any $I_{H1}(t)$ and $I_{H2}(t)$,

$$\|\mathcal{H}_4(t, I_{H1}) - \mathcal{H}_4(t, I_{H2})\| \leq \mathcal{P}_4\|I_{H1} - I_{H2}\|, \tag{21}$$

where $\mathcal{P}_4 = (\alpha + \phi + \mu_H) > 0$. For any $R_{L1}(t)$ and $R_{L2}(t)$,

$$\|\mathcal{H}_5(t, R_{L1}) - \mathcal{H}_5(t, R_{L2})\| \leq \mathcal{P}_5\|R_{L1} - R_{L2}\|, \tag{22}$$

where $\mathcal{P}_5 = (\omega + \mu_H) > 0$. For any $R_{H1}(t)$ and $R_{H2}(t)$,

$$\|\mathcal{H}_6(t, R_{H1}) - \mathcal{H}_6(t, R_{H2})\| \leq \mathcal{P}_6\|R_{H1} - R_{H2}\|, \tag{23}$$

where $\mathcal{P}_6 = (\epsilon + \mu_H) > 0$. Furthermore, considering $\mathcal{H}_7(t, S_V(t))$, and for any $S_{V1}(t)$ and $S_{V2}(t)$, following a similar procedure yields

$$\|\mathcal{H}_7(t, S_{V1}(t)) - \mathcal{H}_7(t, S_{V2}(t))\| \leq \|\beta_2(I_L + \theta I_H)\|\|S_{V1} - S_{V2}\|. \tag{24}$$

Since I_L and I_H are bounded above by Λ_H/μ_H in the invariant region $\mathcal{D}$, it then follows that the inequality (24) becomes

$$\|\mathcal{H}_7(t, S_{V1}(t)) - \mathcal{H}_7(t, S_{V2}(t))\| \leq \mathcal{P}_7\|S_{V1} - S_{V2}\|, \tag{25}$$

where $\mathcal{P}_7 = \left(\frac{\beta_2\Lambda_H}{\mu_H}(1 + \theta) + \mu_V\right) > 0$. Also, for any $I_{V1}(t)$ and $I_{V2}(t)$,

$$\|\mathcal{H}_8(t, I_{V1}(t)) - \mathcal{H}_8(t, I_{V2}(t))\| \leq \mathcal{P}_8\|I_{V1} - I_{V2}\|, \tag{26}$$

where $\mathcal{P}_8 = \mu_V > 0$.

In view of the foregoing, it is clear that the noninteger-order social hierarchy-structured malaria model (4) is Lipschitz continuous, thus satisfying the condition 16, where the Lipschitz constant $\mathcal{P} = \max\{\mathcal{P}_i\}$, and $i = 1, 2, ..., 8$. □

Now, we define a fixed point of an operator $\mathcal{Q} : \mathbf{M} \to \mathbf{M}$ by $\mathcal{Q}(\mathcal{G}(t)) = \mathcal{G}(t)$ so that

$$\mathcal{Q}(\mathcal{G}(t)) = \mathcal{G}_0 + \frac{1}{\Gamma(\alpha)} \int_0^t (t - \Psi)^{\alpha-1} \mathcal{H}(\Psi, \mathcal{G}(\Psi)) d\Psi. \tag{27}$$

Theorem 4. *The fractional-order system* (4) *has a unique solution* $\mathcal{G}(t) \in \mathbf{M}$ *provided that* $\Phi^{\alpha}\mathcal{P} < \Gamma(\alpha + 1)$.

Proof. The main interest in proving this result is to show that $\mathcal{Q}$ is a contraction. Since $\mathcal{H}(t, \mathcal{G}(t))$ is Lipschitz continuous, as theorized in Equation (16), it follows that for any $\mathcal{G}_1(t), \mathcal{G}_2(t) \in \mathbf{M}$ and since $0 \leq t \leq \Phi$,

$$\begin{aligned} \|\mathcal{Q}(\mathcal{G}_1(t)) - \mathcal{Q}(\mathcal{G}_2(t))\| &= \left\| \frac{1}{\Gamma(\alpha)} \int_0^t (t - \Psi)^{\alpha-1} [\mathcal{H}(\Psi, \mathcal{G}_1(\Psi)) - \mathcal{H}(\Psi, \mathcal{G}_2(\Psi))] d\Psi \right\| \\ &\leq \frac{1}{\Gamma(\alpha)} \int_0^t (t - \Psi)^{\alpha-1} \|\mathcal{H}(\Psi, \mathcal{G}_1(\Psi)) - \mathcal{H}(\Psi, \mathcal{G}_2(\Psi))\| d\Psi \\ &\leq \frac{\mathcal{P}}{\Gamma(\alpha)} \|\mathcal{G}_1(t) - \mathcal{G}_2(t)\| \int_0^t (t - \Psi)^{\alpha-1} d\Psi \\ &\leq \mathcal{P}^* \|\mathcal{G}_1(t) - \mathcal{G}_2(t)\|, \end{aligned}$$

where $\mathcal{P}^* = \Phi^{\alpha}\mathcal{P}/(\alpha\Gamma(\alpha))$, thus implying that $\mathcal{Q}$ is a contraction, since $\mathcal{P}^* < 1$. Hence, there exists a unique solution for the fractional-order social hierarchy-structured malaria model (4). □

2.2. Basic Reproduction Number

The malaria-free (disease-free) equilibrium of the fractional-order malaria model (4) is obtained as

$$\varepsilon_0 = (S_L^0, S_H^0, 0, 0, 0, 0, S_V^0, 0), \tag{28}$$

where

$$S_L^0 = \frac{\Lambda_H(\mu_H(1 - r) + \sigma_H)}{\mu_H(\mu_H + \sigma_H + \sigma_L)},$$

$$S_H^0 = \frac{\Lambda_H(\mu_H r + \sigma_L)}{\mu_H(\mu_H + \sigma_H + \sigma_L)},$$

and

$$S_V^0 = \frac{\Lambda_V}{\mu_V}.$$

In what follows, the basic reproduction number of the model is as obtained in [22], and it is given by

$$\mathcal{R}_0 = \sqrt{\frac{\Lambda_H \beta_1 \beta_2 \Lambda_V (\theta b m_1 (r\mu_H + \sigma_L) + m_2(\mu_H(1 - r) + \sigma_H))}{\mu_H \mu_V^2 m_1 m_2 (\mu_H + \sigma_H + \sigma_L)}}, \tag{29}$$

where $m_1 = \mu_H + \gamma + \delta$ and $m_2 = \mu_H + \alpha + \phi$. The basic reproduction number, $\mathcal{R}_0$, is the key epidemiological threshold that determines the average number of secondary cases of malaria infection produced by an infectious individual during its period of infectiousness in a wholly susceptible population [38].

3. Global Asymptotic Dynamics of the Model

This section explores the global asymptotic stability of the fractional-order social hierarchy-structured malaria model (4), since stability analysis has been proven to be an essential performance metric for any dynamical system [29].

3.1. Global Asymptotic Stability of DFE

Since fractional calculus is a generalization of the standard theory of calculus, the global asymptotic stability of the model around the disease-free equilibrium (DFE) of the model (28) is analyzed by extending the classical method that has been x-rayed in [39–42] to a fractional-order derivative operator. To do this, let the fractional-order system (4) be rewritten in a vector form given by

$$\begin{aligned} {}^{C}D_t^{\alpha}\mathbb{X}(t) &= F(\mathbb{X},\mathbb{Z}), \\ {}^{C}D_t^{\alpha}\mathbb{Z}(t) &= G(\mathbb{X},\mathbb{Z}),\ G(\mathbb{X},0) = 0, \end{aligned} \tag{30}$$

of which $\mathbb{X} \in \mathbb{R}^5_+$ and $\mathbb{Z} \in \mathbb{R}^3_+$, where $\mathbb{X}$ represents the uninfected compartments, and $\mathbb{Z}$ represents the population of infected individuals. In essence, $\mathbb{X} = (S_L, S_H, R_L, R_H, S_V)$, and $\mathbb{Z} = (I_L, I_H, I_V)$. Furthermore, let the disease-free equilibrium of the malaria model (4) be represented by $\varepsilon_0 = (\mathbb{X}^*, 0)$; then, the global asymptotic stability of the social hierarchy-structured malaria model can be established if the following conditions are obeyed:

(N_1): For ${}^{C}D_t^{\alpha}\mathbb{X}(t) = F(\mathbb{X},0)$, $\mathbb{X}^*$ is globally asymptotically stable;
(N_2): $G(\mathbb{X},\mathbb{Z}) = A\mathbb{Z} - \hat{G}(\mathbb{X},\mathbb{Z})$, $\hat{G}(\mathbb{X},\mathbb{Z}) \geq 0$, for $(\mathbb{X},\mathbb{Z}) \in \mathfrak{D}$.

where $A = \partial G/\partial \mathbb{Z}$ is an M matrix evaluated at $(\mathbb{X}^*, 0)$ with non-negative off-diagonal elements.

Theorem 5. *The disease-free equilibrium $\varepsilon_0 = (\mathbb{X}^*, 0)$ of the fractional-order social hierarchy-structured malaria model* (4) *is globally asymptotically stable if conditions (N_1) and (N_2) are satisfied.*

Proof. $F(\mathbb{X},\mathbb{Z})$ and $G(\mathbb{X},\mathbb{Z})$ are obtained from (4) as follows:

$$F(\mathbb{X},\mathbb{Z}) = \begin{pmatrix} (1-r)\Lambda_H - \beta_1 S_L I_V + \omega R_L + \sigma_H S_H - (\mu_H + \sigma_L) S_L \\ r\Lambda_H - b\beta_1 S_H I_V + \epsilon R_H + \sigma_L S_L - (\mu_H + \sigma_L) S_H \\ \gamma I_L - (\omega + \mu_H) R_L \\ \alpha I_H - (\epsilon + \mu_H) R_H \\ \Lambda_V - \beta_2 (I_L + \theta I_H) S_V - \mu_V S_V \end{pmatrix} \tag{31}$$

and

$$G(\mathbb{X},\mathbb{Z}) = \begin{pmatrix} \beta_1 S_L I_V - (\mu_H + \gamma + \delta) I_L \\ b\beta_1 S_H I_V - (\mu_H + \alpha + \phi) I_H \\ \beta_2 (I_L + \theta I_H) S_V - \mu_V S_V \end{pmatrix}. \tag{32}$$

Since

$$F(\mathbb{X},0)=\begin{pmatrix}(1-r)\Lambda_H+\omega R_L+\sigma_H S_H-(\mu_H+\sigma_L)S_L\\ r\Lambda_H+\epsilon R_H+\sigma_L S_L-(\mu_H+\sigma_L)S_H\\ -(\omega+\mu_H)R_L\\ -(\epsilon+\mu_H)R_H\\ \Lambda_V-\mu_V S_V\end{pmatrix},\tag{33}$$

then ${}^{C}D_t^{\alpha}\mathbb{X}(t)=F(\mathbb{X},0)$ implies that

$$\begin{aligned}
{}^{C}D_t^{\alpha}S_L&=(1-r)\Lambda_H+\omega R_L+\sigma_H S_H-(\mu_H+\sigma_L)S_L,\\
{}^{C}D_t^{\alpha}S_H&=r\Lambda_H+\epsilon R_H+\sigma_L S_L-(\mu_H+\sigma_L)S_H,\\
{}^{C}D_t^{\alpha}R_L&=-(\omega+\mu_H)R_L,\\
{}^{C}D_t^{\alpha}R_H&=-(\epsilon+\mu_H)R_H,\\
{}^{C}D_t^{\alpha}S_V&=\Lambda_V-\mu_V S_V.
\end{aligned}\tag{34}$$

Using Lemma 3 and solving system (34) simultaneously gives

$$\begin{aligned}
S_L(t)&=\left(\tfrac{(1-r)\Lambda_H}{(\sigma_H+\sigma_L+\mu_H)}+\tfrac{\sigma_H\Lambda_H}{\mu_H(\sigma_H+\sigma_L+\mu_H)}\right)(1-E_{\alpha,1}(-(\sigma_H+\sigma_L+\mu_H)t^{\alpha}))\\
&\quad+\left(\tfrac{\sigma_H}{\sigma_H+\sigma_L}(L(0)+R_L(0)+R_H(0))-\tfrac{\sigma_H\Lambda_H}{\mu_H(\sigma_H+\sigma_L)}\right)\\
&\quad\times(E_{\alpha,1}(-\mu_H t^{\alpha})-E_{\alpha,1}(-(\sigma_H+\sigma_L+\mu_H)t^{\alpha}))+\tfrac{(\omega-\sigma_H)R_L(0)}{\sigma_H+\sigma_L-\omega}\\
&\quad\times(E_{\alpha,1}(-(\omega+\mu_H)t^{\alpha})-E_{\alpha,1}(-(\sigma_H+\sigma_L+\mu_H)t^{\alpha}))+S_L(0)\\
&\quad\times E_{\alpha,1}(-(\sigma_H+\sigma_L+\mu_H)t^{\alpha})+\tfrac{(\sigma_H)R_H(0)}{\sigma_H+\sigma_L-\omega}\\
&\quad\times(E_{\alpha,1}(-(\sigma_H+\sigma_L+\mu_H)t^{\alpha})-E_{\alpha,1}(-(\epsilon+\mu_H)t^{\alpha})),\\
S_H(t)&=\frac{\Lambda_H}{\mu_H}(1-E_{\alpha,1}(-\mu_H t^{\alpha}))+R_L(0)(E_{\alpha,1}(-\mu_H t^{\alpha})-E_{\alpha,1}(-(\omega+\mu_H)t^{\alpha}))\\
&\quad+R_H(0)(E_{\alpha,1}(-\mu_H t^{\alpha})-E_{\alpha,1}(-(\epsilon+\mu_H)t^{\alpha}))\\
&\quad+L(0)E_{\alpha,1}(-\mu_H t^{\alpha})-S_L(t),\\
R_L(t)&=R_L(0)E_{\alpha,1}(-(\omega+\mu_H)t^{\alpha}),
\end{aligned}\tag{35}$$

$$\begin{aligned}
R_H(t)&=R_H(0)E_{\alpha,1}(-(\epsilon+\mu_H)t^{\alpha}),\\
S_V(t)&=\frac{\Lambda_V}{\mu_V}+\left(S_V(0)-\frac{\Lambda_V}{\mu_V}\right)E_{\alpha,1}(-\mu_V t^{\alpha}).
\end{aligned}\tag{36}$$

Consequently, as $t\to\infty$ in (35) and (36), regardless of the initial conditions $S_L(0)$, $S_H(0)$, $R_L(0)$, $R_H(0)$, and $S_V(0)$, then $S_L(t)\to S_L^0, S_H(t)\to S_H^0, R_L(t)\to 0, R_H(t)\to 0$ and $S_V(t)\to S_V^0$. As a consequence, the condition (N_1) is satisfied, thus implying that $\mathbb{X}^*$ is globally asymptotically stable.

Further, to establish (N_2), an M matrix with non-negative off-diagonal entries is given by

$$A = \frac{\partial G}{\partial \mathbb{Z}}|_{(\mathbb{X}^*,0)} = \begin{pmatrix} -(\mu_H+\gamma+\delta) & 0 & \beta_1 S_L^0 \\ 0 & -(\mu_H+\alpha+\phi) & b\beta_1 S_H^0 \\ \beta_2 S_V^0 & \theta\beta_2 S_V^0 & -\mu_V \end{pmatrix}. \quad (37)$$

Simplifying $\hat{G}(\mathbb{X},\mathbb{Z}) = A\mathbb{Z} - G(\mathbb{X},\mathbb{Z})$ gives

$$\hat{G}(\mathbb{X},\mathbb{Z}) = \begin{pmatrix} \beta_1 I_V(S_L^0 - S_L) \\ b\beta_1 I_V(S_H^0 - S_H) \\ \beta_2(I_L+\theta I_H)(S_V^0 - S_V) \end{pmatrix}. \quad (38)$$

It is clear that $\hat{G}(X,Z) \geq 0$, since $0 \leq S_L \leq S_L^0$, $0 \leq S_H \leq S_H^0$, and $0 \leq S_V \leq S_V^0$. Hence, property (N_2) is satisfied. Accordingly, the disease-free equilibrium of the fractional-order malaria model (4) is globally asymptotically stable. This ends the proof. □

3.2. Global Asymptotic Stability of EE

Let the endemic equilibrium point of the fractional-order social hierarchy-structured model (4) be represented by ε^{**} so that

$$\varepsilon^{**} = (S_L^{**}, S_H^{**}, I_L^{**}, I_H^{**}, R_L^{**}, R_H^{**}, S_V^{**}, I_V^{**}).$$

It is important to mention that the explicit form of ε^{**} is omitted due to the complexity of the model. However, if it is assumed that the endemic equilibrium point exists, then it is pertinent to establish the asymptotic behavior of the fractional-order social hierarchy-structured model (4) around the endemic equilibrium. To do this, the following result is considered necessary as a consequence of the idea in [29].

Lemma 4. *If $\mathcal{G}^{**}$ is an equilibrium point of the Caputo fractional-order system* (13)*, and $\mathcal{V}(\mathcal{G}(t))$ is a Lyapunov functional defined by*

$$\mathcal{V}(\mathcal{G}(t)) = \sum_{i=1}^{8} \frac{b_i}{2}(\mathcal{G}_i - \mathcal{G}_i^{**})^2, \ \forall\, b_i > 0,$$

then

$$^{C}D_t^{\alpha}\mathcal{V}(\mathcal{G}(t)) \leq \sum_{i=1}^{8}[b_i(\mathcal{G}_i - \mathcal{G}_i^{**})]\, ^{C}D_t^{\alpha}\mathcal{G}_i(t).$$

Theorem 6. *The endemic equilibrium point, ε^{**}, of the social hierarchy-structured malaria model* (4) *is globally asymptotically stable if the associated threshold quantity, $\mathcal{R}_0$, is greater than unity.*

Proof. Consider a quadratic Lyapunov function $\mathcal{L} : \mathfrak{D} \to \mathbb{R}$ defined by (see, e.g., [43,44])

$$\begin{aligned}\mathcal{L}(\mathcal{G}(t)) = \ & \tfrac{1}{2}[(S_L - S_L^{**}) + (S_H - S_H^{**}) + (I_L - I_L^{**}) + (I_H - I_H^{**}) + (R_L - R_L^{**}) \\ & +(R_H - R_H^{**})]^2 + \tfrac{1}{2}[(S_V - S_V^{**}) + (I_V - I_V^{**})]^2.\end{aligned} \quad (39)$$

With Lemma 4 in mind, the Caputo fractional time derivative of $\mathcal{L}$, along the solution path of the fractional-order system (4), gives

$$
\begin{aligned}
{}^{C}D_t^{\alpha}\mathcal{L} &\leq [(S_L - S_L^{**}) + (S_H - S_H^{**}) + (I_L - I_L^{**}) + (I_H - I_H^{**}) + (R_L - R_L^{**}) \\
&\quad + (R_H - R_H^{**})]\left[{}^{C}D_t^{\alpha}(S_L + S_H + I_L + I_H + R_L + R_H)\right] \\
&\quad + \left[(S_V - S_V^{**}) + (I_V - I_V^{**})\right]\left[{}^{C}D_t^{\alpha}(S_V + I_V)\right] \\
&= [(S_L - S_L^{**}) + (S_H - S_H^{**}) + (I_L - I_L^{**}) + (I_H - I_H^{**}) + (R_L - R_L^{**}) \\
&\quad + (R_H - R_H^{**})][\Lambda_H - \mu_H(S_L + S_H + I_L + I_H + R_L + R_H) - \delta I_L - \phi I_H] \\
&\quad + \left[(S_V - S_V^{**}) + (I_V - I_V^{**})\right](\Lambda_V - \mu_V(S_V + I_V)) \\
&\leq -\mu_H[(S_L - S_L^{**}) + (S_H - S_H^{**}) + (I_L - I_L^{**}) + (I_H - I_H^{**}) + (R_L - R_L^{**}) \\
&\quad + (R_H - R_H^{**})]\left((S_L + S_H + I_L + I_H + R_L + R_H) - \tfrac{\Lambda_H}{\mu_H}\right) \\
&\quad - \mu_V\left[(S_V - S_V^{**}) + (I_V - I_V^{**})\right]\left((S_V + I_V) - \tfrac{\Lambda_V}{\mu_V}\right) \\
&\leq -\mu_H[(S_L - S_L^{**}) + (S_H - S_H^{**}) + (I_L - I_L^{**}) + (I_H - I_H^{**}) + (R_L - R_L^{**}) \\
&\quad + (R_H - R_H^{**})]^2 - \mu_V\left[(S_V - S_V^{**}) + (I_V - I_V^{**})\right]^2.
\end{aligned}
$$

Hence, the Caputo fractional time derivative ${}^{C}D_t^{\alpha}\mathcal{L}(\mathcal{G}(t))$ is negative semidefinite, that is, ${}^{C}D_t^{\alpha}\mathcal{L} \leq 0$ with equality if and only if $S_L = S_L^{**}$, $S_H = S_H^{**}$, $I_L = I_L^{**}$, $I_H = I_H^{**}$, $R_L = R_L^{**}$, $R_H = R_H^{**}$, $S_V = S_V^{**}$, and $I_V = I_V^{**}$. This implies that the largest invariant set in $\{\mathcal{G}(t) \in \mathfrak{D} \mid {}^{C}D_t^{\alpha}\mathcal{L}(\mathcal{G}(t)) = 0\}$ is the singleton $\{\varepsilon^{**}\}$. It follows by LaSalle's invariance principle [45] that the endemic equilibrium point ε^{**} is globally asymptotically stable. □

3.3. Simulations and Discussion

To visualize the overall behavior of the fractional-order system (4), the generalized Euler's method discussed in [46,47] was used. Specifically, in Figure 1, the values of the fractional order parameter α were allowed to vary in the interval $0 < \alpha \leq 1$ at the basic reproduction number $\mathcal{R}_0 = 0.7266$. It can be observed that as the memory increased, the size of the high social class infectious human population reduced and converged to the malaria-free equilibrium rapidly. In other words, a lower value of the fractional-order parameter α makes the convergence to the disease-free equilibrium faster when compared with a higer value of the fractional-order α. Similar behavior can be observed for the infectious vector population. In Figure 2, when the basic reproduction number was greater than unity, that is $\mathcal{R}_0 = 2.2978$, it can be observed that the decrease in the value of the fractional order parameter α increased the convergence of the high social class infectious human population to the endemic equilibrium, thus implying that the presence of the memory enabled the fractional-order social hierarchy-structured system to stabilize more quickly when compared to a memoryless system where $\alpha = 1$. Similar behavior can be observed in Figure 2b for the infectious vector population when $\mathcal{R}_0 > 1$.

In another development, Figure 3 shows the global asymptotic behavior of the fractional-order system (4) for $\alpha = 0.85$ at different values of initial data. In particular, when $\mathcal{R}_0 = 0.7266 < 1$, it is shown that every trajectory of the infectious vector population, regardless of the initial conditions, tended to the disease-free equilibrium. This corroborates the theoretical result established in Theorem 5 for the global asymptotic stability of the disease-free equilibrium. Conversely, in the same Figure 3, when $\mathcal{R}_0 = 2.2978 > 1$, it can be seen that every solution originating at different sizes of the infectious vector population converged asymptotically to the endemic equilibrium point. This is in support of Theorem 6.

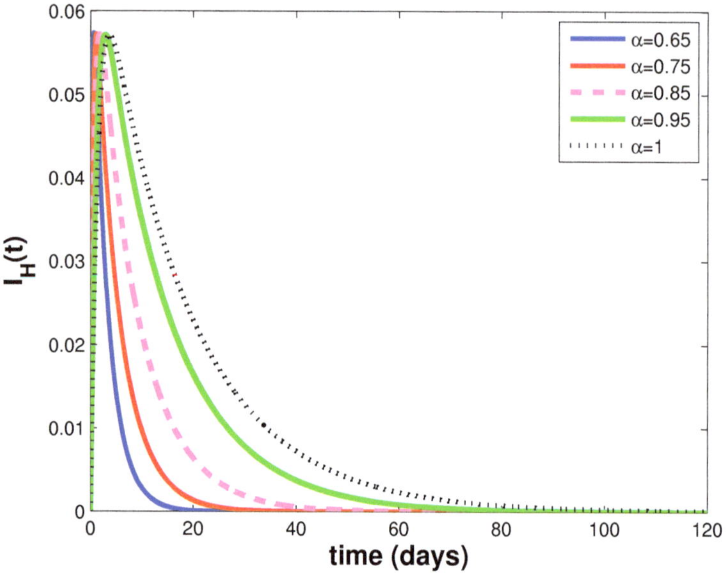

(**a**)

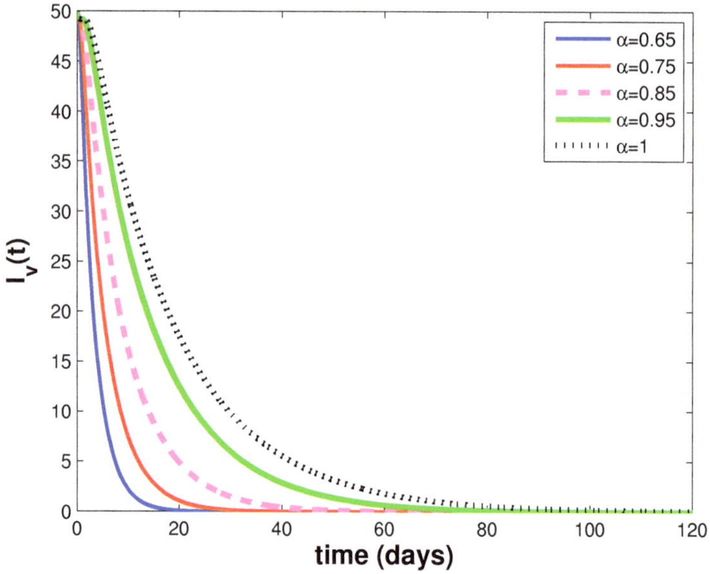

(**b**)

Figure 1. (**a**) Varying effects of the fractional-order parameter α on the high social class infectious human population. (**b**) Varying effects of the fractional-order parameter α on the infectious vector population. In both cases, $r = 0.2$, $\Lambda_H = 0.11$, $\beta_1 = 0.001$, $\beta_2 = 0.002$, $\Lambda_V = 100$, $b = 0.003$, $\theta = 0.65$, $\mu_H = 0.0000548$, $\gamma = 0.82$, $\delta = 0.7$, $\sigma_L = 0.95$, $\alpha = 0.88$, $\phi = 0.5$, $\sigma_H = 0.0065$, and $\mu_V = 0.067$ so that $\mathcal{R}_0 = 0.7266 < 1$.

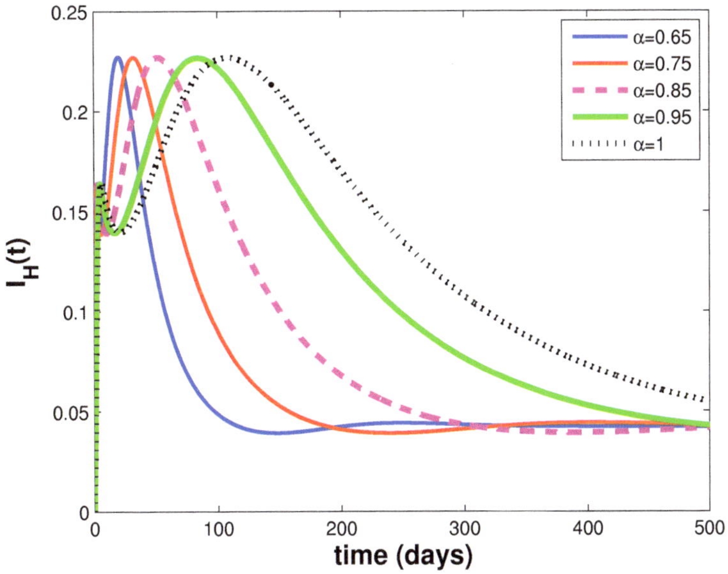

(**a**)

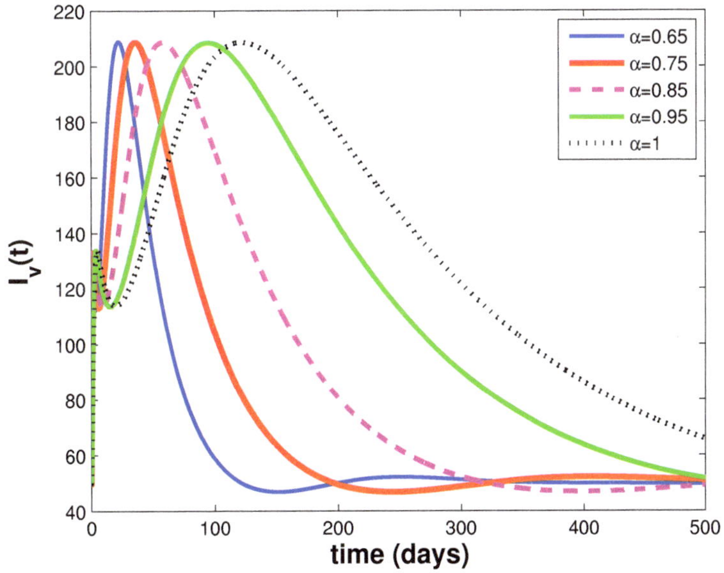

(**b**)

Figure 2. (**a**) Varying effects of the fractional-order parameter α on the high social class infectious human population. (**b**) Varying effects of the fractional-order parameter α on the infectious vector population. Using the same parameter values as in Figure 1, except for $\beta_2 = 0.02$, so that $\mathcal{R}_0 = 2.2978 > 1$.

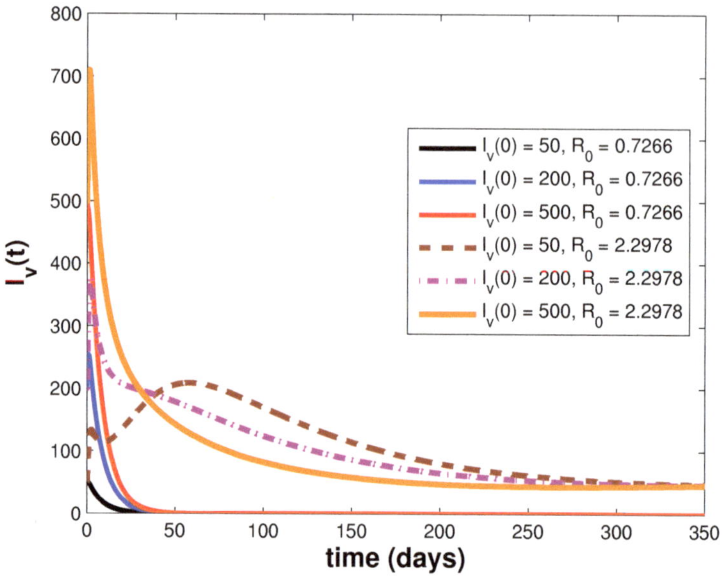

Figure 3. Global asymptotic stability of the fractional-order social hierarchy-structured malaria model (4), at $\alpha = 0.85$, around the disease-free equilirium and endemic equilirium when $\mathcal{R}_0 = 0.7266$ and $\mathcal{R}_0 = 2.2978$, respectively.

4. Conclusions

In this work, fractional calculus has been applied to describe the transmission dynamics of malaria in a social hierarchy-structured population with memory effects. The formulated fractional-order model is a system of differential equations with a Caputo derivative operator. The well-posed nature of the model was established via the generalized mean value theorem for the positivity of bounded solutions, and the Banach fixed point theory was employed for the existence and uniquesness of solutions. The global asymptotic stabilities of both disease-free and endemic equilibria of the fractional-order model were investigated by extending the methods in the classical calculus to the Caputo fractional calculus, and the theoretical results were graphically illustrtated. Consequently, it was proved that at $\mathcal{R}_0 < 1$, the fractional-order social hierarchy-structured malaria model has a globally asymptotically stable disease-free equilibrium where solutions at different initial values converge to. It was also proved that every solution of the model initiating at various values tends to the endemic equilibrium asymptotically when $\mathcal{R}_0 > 1$.

In addition, the effects of various values of the fractional order $0 < \alpha \leq 1$ were tested on the behavior of the fractional-order social hierarchy-structured malaria model. It was revealed that an increase in the fractional order α results in slow convergence of the state solutions of the system to both the disease-free and endemic equilibria. Hence, it was established that solutions of the fractional-order system with values of $\alpha < 1$ stabilize more rapidly than a memoryless system with $\alpha = 1$. Therefore, it can be stated that the presence of memory in a dynamical system operates as a control parameter, which enhances the convergence of the solutions. This underscores the importance of fractional calculus in modeling dynamical systems with memory.

In the presence of real data, fractional-order models can have more degree of freedom for exploring disease dynamics than the classical models. This is so because the fractional order can be employed as a fit parameter to improve the agreement with the real data. Thus, for a more realistic approach and accurate prediction of malaria disease spread in the population, it is worth considering the robust data-driven analysis of the fractional-order model for malaria dynamics. Also worthy of consideration is modeling malaria dynamics via a reaction–diffusion system in order to describe how the disease spreads through contact between host–vector interactions and spatial movement in a heterogeneous environment. These are the limitations of the present work, which can be explored as future considerations.

Author Contributions: Conceptualization, K.O.O. and S.O.; methodology, S.F.A. and S.O.; software, S.O.; validation, S.F.A., F.M.C., S.O.S., R.S.L. and K.O.O.; formal analysis, S.F.A. and S.O.; investigation, S.F.A., F.M.C., S.O.S., R.S.L. and K.O.O.; resources, F.M.C., S.O.S., R.S.L. and K.O.O.; writing—original draft preparation, S.F.A. and S.O.; writing—review and editing, S.F.A., F.M.C., S.O.S., R.S.L., K.O.O. and S.O.; visualization, S.O. All authors have read and agreed to the published version of the manuscript.

Funding: This research received no external funding.

Data Availability Statement: All data are enclosed with this publication.

Conflicts of Interest: The authors declare no conflicts of interest.

References

1. Johnson, N.P.; Muella, J. Updating the accounts: Global mortality of the 1918–1920 "Spanish" influenza pandemic. *Bull. Hist. Med.* **2002**, *76*, 105–115. [CrossRef] [PubMed]
2. World Health Organization (WHO). *World Malaria Report*; WHO: Geneva, Switzerland, 2021. Available online: https://www.who.int/teams/global-malaria-programme/ (accessed on 27 February 2024).
3. Olaniyi, S.; Alade, T.O.; Chuma, F.M.; Ogunsola, A.W.; Aderele, O.R.; Abimbade, S.F. A fractional-order nonlinear model for a within-host chikungunya virus dynamics with adaptive immunity using Caputo derivative operator. *Healthc. Anal.* **2023**, *4*, 100205. [CrossRef]
4. Centres for Diseases Control and Prevention (CDC). Malaria. Available online: http://www.cdc.gov/malaria/ (accessed on 27 February 2024).
5. Abimbade, S.F.; Olaniyi, S.; Ajala, O.A. Recurrent malaria dynamics: Insight from mathematical modelling. *Eur. Phys. J. Plus* **2022**, *137*, 292. [CrossRef]
6. Tasman, H.; Aldila, D.; Dumbela, P.A.; Ndii, M.Z.; Fatmawati; Herdicho, F.F.; Chukwu, C.W. Assessing the impact of relapse, reinfection and recrudescence on malaria eradication policy: A bifurcation and optimal control analysis. *Trop. Med. Infect. Dis.* **2022**, *7*, 263. [CrossRef] [PubMed]
7. Keno, T.D.; Obsu, L.L.; Makinde, O.D. Modeling and Optimal analysis of malaria epidemic in the presence of temperature variability. *Asian-Eur. J. Math.* **2022**, *15*, 2250005. [CrossRef]
8. Bakare, E.A.; Hoskova-Mayerova, S. Numerical treatment of optimal control theory applied to malaria transmission dynamic model. *Qual. Quant.* **2023**, *57*, 409–431. [CrossRef]
9. Traore, B.; Barro, M.; Sangare, B.; Traore, S. A temperature-dependent mathematical model of malaria transmission with stage-structured mosquito population dynamics. *Nonauton. Dyn. Syst.* **2021**, *8*, 267–296. [CrossRef]
10. Fatmawati; Herdicho, F.F.; Windarto; Chukwu, W.; Tasman, H. An optimal control of malaria transmission model with mosquito seasonal factor. *Results Phys.* **2021**, *25*, 104238. [CrossRef]
11. Olaniyi, S.; Okosun, K.O.; Adesanya, S.O.; Lebelo, R.S. Modelling malaria dynamics with partial immunity and protected travellers: Optimal control and cost-effectiveness analysis. *J. Biol. Dynam.* **2020**, *14*, 90–115. [CrossRef]
12. Layaka, A.M.; Abbo, B.; Haggar, D.M.S.; Youssouf, P. Optimal control analysis of intra-host dynamics of malaria with immune response. *Adv. Dyn. Syst. Appl.* **2021**, *16*, 1097–1115.
13. Ndii, M.Z.; Adi, Y.A. Understanding the effects of individual awareness and vector controls on malaria transmission dynamics using multiple optimal control. *Chaos Solitons Fractals* **2021**, *153*, 111476. [CrossRef]
14. Keno, T.D.; Dano, L.B.; Ganati, G.A. Optimal control and cost-effectiveness strategies of malaria transmission with impact of climate variability. *J. Math.* **2022**, 5924549. [CrossRef]
15. Ukawuba, I.; Shaman, J. Inference and dynamic simulation of malaria using a simple climate-driven entomological model of malaria transmission. *PLoS Comput. Biol.* **2022**, *18*, e1010161. [CrossRef] [PubMed]
16. Mangongo, T.T.; Bukweli, J.K.; Kampempe, J.D.B.; Mabela, R.M.; Munganga, J.M.W. Stability and global sensitivity analysis of the transmission dynamics of malaria with relapse and ignorant infected humans. *Phys. Scr.* **2022**, *97*, 024002. [CrossRef]
17. Olaniyi, S.; Falowo, O.D.; Okosun, K.O.; Mukamuri, M.; Obabiyi, O.S. Effect of saturated treatment on malaria spread with optimal intervention. *Alex. Eng. J.* **2023**, *6*, 443–459. [CrossRef]
18. Kuddus, M.A.; Rahman, A. Modelling and analysis of human-mosquito malaria transmission dynamics in Bangladesh. *Math. Comput. Simul.* **2022**, *193*, 123–138. [CrossRef]

19. Anwar, M.N.; Smith, L.; Devine, A.; Mehra, S.; Walker, C.R.; Ivory, E.; Conway, E.; Mueller, I.; McCaw, J.M.; Flegg, J.A.; et al. Mathematical models of Plasmodium vivax transmission: A scoping review. *PLoS Comput. Biol.* **2024**, *20*, e1011931. [CrossRef]
20. Olaniyi, S.; Ajala, O.A.; Abimbade, S.F. Optimal control analysis of a mathematical model for recurrent malaria dynamics. *Oper. Res. Forum.* **2023**, *4*, 14. [CrossRef]
21. Olaniyi, S.; Abimbade, S.F.; Ajala, O.A.; Chuma, F.M. Efficiency and economic analysis of intervention strategies for recurrent malaria transmission. *Qual. Quanty* **2024**, *58*, 627–645. [CrossRef]
22. Olaniyi, S.; Mukamuri, M.; Okosun, K.O.; Adepoju, O.A. Mathematical analysis of a social hierarchy-structured model for malaria transmission dynamics. *Results Phys.* **2022**, *34*, 104991. [CrossRef]
23. Vellappandi, M.; Kumar, P.; Govindaraj, V. Role of fractional derivatives in the mathematical modeling of the transmission of Chlamydia in the United States from 1989 to 2019. *Nonlinear Dyn.* **2023**, *111*, 4915–4929. [CrossRef] [PubMed]
24. Nisar, K.S.; Farman, M.; Abdel-Aty, M.; Cao, J. A review on epidemic models in sight of fractional calculus. *Alex. Eng. J.* **2023**, *75*, 81–113. [CrossRef]
25. Bonyah, E. A malaria status model: The perspective of Mittag-Leffler function with stochastic component. *Commun. Biomath. Sci.* **2022**, *5*, 40–62. [CrossRef]
26. Aldwoah, K.A.; Almalahi, M.A.; Abdulwasaa, M.A.; Shah, K.; Kawale, S.V.; Awadalla, M.; Alahmadi, J. Mathematical analysis and numerical simulations of the piecewise dynamics model of malaria transmission: A case study in Yemen. *AIMS Math.* **2024**, *9*, 4376–4408. [CrossRef]
27. Diethelm, K.; Garrapa, R.; Giusti, A.; Stynes, M. Why fractional derivatives with nonsingular kernels should not be used. *Fract. Calc. Appl. Anal.* **2020**, *23*, 610–634. [CrossRef]
28. Atangana, A.; Qureshi, S. Mathematical modeling of an autonomous nonlinear dynamical system for malaria transmission using Caputo derivative. In *Fractional Order Analysis: Theory, Methods and Applications*; Dutta, H., Akdemir, A.O., Atangana, A., Eds.; John Wiley & Sons: Hoboken, NJ, USA, 2020.
29. Boukhouima, A.; Hattaf, K.; Lotfi, E.M.; Mahrouf, M.; Torres, D.F.M.; Yousfi, N. Lyapunov functions for fractional-order systems in biology: Methods and applications. *Chaos Soliton Fractals* **2020**, *140*, 110224. [CrossRef]
30. Omame, A.; Okuonghae, D.; Nwajeri, U.K.; Onyenegecha, C.P. A fractional-order multi-vaccination model for COVID-19 with non-singular kernel. *Alex. Eng. J.* **2022**, *61*, 6089–6104. [CrossRef]
31. Paul, A.K.; Basak, N.; Kuddus, M.A. A mathematical model for simulating the transmission dynamics of COVID-19 using the Caputo-Fabrizio fractional-order derivative with nonsingular kernel. *Inf. Med. Unlocked* **2023**, *43*, 101416. [CrossRef]
32. Olaniyi, S.; Abimbade, S.F.; Chuma, F.M.; Adepoju, O.A.; Falowo, O.D. A fractional-order tuberculosis model with efficient and cost-effective optimal control interventions. *Decis. Anal. J.* **2023**, *8*, 100324. [CrossRef]
33. Abidemi, A.; Owolabi, K.M. Unravelling the dynamics of Lassa Fever transmission with nosocomial infections via non-fractional and fractional mathematical models. *Eur. Phys. J. Plus* **2024**, *139*, 108. [CrossRef]
34. Boukhouima, A.; Lotfi, E.M.; Mahrouf, M.; Rosa, S.; Torres, D.F.M.; Yousfi, N. Stability analysis and optimal control of a fractional HIV-AIDS epidemic model with memory and general incidence rate. *Eur. Phys. J. Plus* **2021**, *136*, 103. [CrossRef]
35. Ghosh, U.; Thirthar, A.A.; Mondal, B.; Majumdar, P. Effect of fear, treatment, and hunting cooperation on an eco-epidemiological model: Memory effect in terms of fractional derivative. *Iran. J. Sci. Technol. Trans. Electr. Eng.* **2022**, *46*, 1541–1554. [CrossRef] [PubMed]
36. Asamoah, J.K.K.; Addai, E.; Arthur, Y.D.; Okyere, E. A fractional mathematical model for listeriosis infection using two kernels. *Decis. Anal. J.* **2023**, *6*, 100191. [CrossRef]
37. Owolabi, K.; Pindza, E. A nonlinear epidemic model for tuberculosis with Caputo operator and fixed point theory. *Healthcare Anal.* **2022**, *2*, 100111. [CrossRef]
38. van den Driessche, P.; Watmough, J. Reproduction numbers and sub-threshold endemic equilibria for compartmental models of disease transmission. *Math. Biosci.* **2002**, *180*, 29–48. [CrossRef]
39. Castillo-Chavez, C.; Blower, P.; Driessche, P.V.D.; Kirschner, W.; Yakubu, A. *Mathematical Approaches for Emerging and Re-Emerging Infectious Diseases: Models, Methods and Theory*; Springer: New York, NY, USA, 2002.
40. Sulayman, F.; Abdullah, F.A. Dynamical behaviour of a modified tuberculosis model with impact of public health eductaion and hospital treatment. *Axioms* **2022**, *11*, 723. [CrossRef]
41. Wangari, I.M.; Olaniyi, S.; Lebelo, R.S.; Okosun, K.O. Transmission of COVID-19 in the presence of single-dose and double-dose vaccines with hesitancy: Mathematical modeling ad optimal control analysis. *Front. Appl. Math. Stat.* **2023**, *9*, 1292443. [CrossRef]
42. Olaniyi, S.; Kareem, G.G.; Abimbade, S.F.; Chuma, F.M.; Sangoniyi, S.O. Mathematical modelling and analysis of autonomous HIV/AIDS dynamics with vertical transmission and nonlinear treatment. *Iran J. Sci.* **2024**, *48*, 181–192. [CrossRef]
43. Vargas-De-León, C. Constructions of Lyapunov functions for classic SIS, SIR and SIRS epidemic models with variable population size. *Foro-Red-Mat Rev. Electr. Cont. Mat.* **2009**, *26*.
44. Goswami, N.K.; Olaniyi, S.; Abimbade, S.F.; Chuma, F.M. A mathematical model for investigating the effect of media awareness programs on the spread of COVID-19 with optimal control. *Healthc. Anal.* **2024**, *5*, 100300. [CrossRef]
45. Lasalle, J.P. *The Stability of Dynamical Systems*; SIAM: Philadelphia, PA, USA, 1976.

46. Odibat, Z.M.; Momami, S. An algorithm for the numerical solution of differential equations of fractional order. *J. Appl. Math. Inform.* **2008**, *26*, 15–27.
47. Ahmed, N.; Macías-Díaz, J.E.; Raza, A.; Baleanu, D.; Rafiq, M.; Iqbal, Z.; Ahmad, M.O. Design, analysis and comparison of a nonstandard computational method for the solution of a general stochastic fractional epidemic model. *Axioms* **2022**, *11*, 10. [CrossRef]

mathematics

Article

Solving Linear and Nonlinear Delayed Differential Equations Using the Lambert *W* Function for Economic and Biological Problems

Tomas Ruzgas [1,*,†], Irma Jankauskienė [1,†], Audrius Zajančkauskas [1], Mantas Lukauskas [1], Matas Bazilevičius [1], Rugilė Kaluževičiūtė [1] and Jurgita Arnastauskaitė [2]

1 Department of Applied Mathematics, Kaunas University of Technology, Studentų g. 50, LT-44239 Kaunas, Lithuania; irma.jankauskiene@ktu.lt (I.J.); audrius.zajanckauskas@ktu.lt (A.Z.); mantas.lukauskas@ktu.lt (M.L.); matas.bazilevicius@ktu.edu (M.B.); rugile.kaluzeviciute@ktu.edu (R.K.)
2 Department of Computer Sciences, Kaunas University of Technology, Studentų g. 50, LT-44239 Kaunas, Lithuania; jurgita.arnastauskaite@ktu.lt
* Correspondence: tomas.ruzgas@ktu.lt
† These authors contributed equally to this work.

Abstract: Studies of the dynamics of linear and nonlinear differential equations with delays described by mathematical models play a crucial role in various scientific domains, including economics and biology. In this article, the Lambert function method, which is applied in the research of control systems with delays, is proposed to be newly applied to the study of price stability by describing it as a differential equation with a delay. Unlike the previous work of Jankauskienė and Miliūnas "Analysis of market price stability using the Lambert function method" in 2020 which focuses on the study of the characteristic equation in a complex space for stability, this study extends the application of this method by presenting a new solution for the study of price dynamics of linear and nonlinear differential equation with delay used in economic and biological research. When examining the dynamics of market prices, it is necessary to take into account the fact that goods or services are usually supplied with a delay. The authors propose to perform the analysis using the Lambert *W* function method because it is close to exact mathematical methods. In addition, the article presents examples illustrating the applied theory, including the results of the study of the dynamics of the nonlinear Kalecki's business cycle model, which was not addressed in the previous work, when the linearized Kalecki's business cycle model is studied as a nonhomogeneous differential equation with a delay.

Keywords: differential delay equations; delayed arguments; Lambert *W* function; market price; nonlinear differential delay equations; Kalecki's business cycle model

MSC: 37c20; 34K05

Citation: Ruzgas, T.; Jankauskienė, I.; Zajančkauskas, A.; Lukauskas M.; Bazilevičius M.; Kaluževičiūtė R.; Arnastauskaitė J. Solving Linear and Nonlinear Delayed Differential Equations Using the Lambert *W* Function for Economic and Biological Problems. *Mathematics* **2024**, *12*, 2760. https://doi.org/10.3390/math12172760

Academic Editors: Davide Valenti and Jonathan Blackledge

Received: 25 June 2024
Revised: 20 August 2024
Accepted: 4 September 2024
Published: 6 September 2024

1. Introduction

The dynamics of market price are extremely useful and this is shown by a number of published articles [1–5]. Market prices for different products are a concern for both consumers and producers, as falling prices can cause many problems for suppliers and rising prices reduce consumers' purchasing power. This can lead to a loss of profit for product manufacturers. Food prices are by their very nature more volatile than prices for industrial goods. Such fluctuations in food prices are particularly problematic for people on low incomes. In countries where this happens, sudden price increases can have both short- and long-term consequences for people's incomes. For this reason, the study of market price stability is crucial in assessing the parameters that lead to sudden price spikes and, if properly modeled, can provide information that can help stabilize market dynamics. The existence of various delays in markets, for example between supply and demand, must be taken into account. Delays are common to many economic phenomena and can therefore be described by a differential equation with the delay argument [1,2,5–7]. To obtain the solutions of the differential equation with the delay argument, the method of Lambert function can be applied.

Price stability in markets is clearly a key economic issue. Research [8] on how to stabilize chaotic dynamic systems, which depend on initial conditions, using the technique of asymptotic stability analysis is presented in the literature. This technique allows the control of chaotic speculative price fluctuations in a model. Another study analyzes the behavior of a stock market model by identifying traders who optimistically trade in rising markets and pessimistically trade in falling markets, which risks undermining the stability of stock markets [9]. The impact of COVID-19 on financial markets has been widely studied [10,11]. The studies [10] focus on the evolution of market efficiency using two efficiency indicators: the Hurst exponent and the memory parameter of a fractional Levy stable motion. The results [11] show the impact of oil prices on the stability of financial systems, implying that oil price fluctuations can make financial markets unstable, especially during the period of the COVID-19 pandemic. The study shows that business cycle uncertainty has amplified the effects of oil price shocks, thereby increasing their impact on financial system stability. This shows the relevance of price stability studies in financial markets.

The modified method of the Lambert *W* function proposed in the article provides an opportunity to obtain quick solutions for market stability analysis by changing the parameters. After obtaining the market price through supply and demand, it is very relevant to study the effect of elasticity of demand and the argument of lag between supply and demand. The increase in the supply price, due to oil price fluctuations and the impact of COVID-19, increased the need to study as accurately as possible how buyers will react to the price change; for this purpose, the demand elasticity coefficient was used in the research.

A study in the literature [12] analyzes a two-market cobweb model that includes delays in agricultural production and delays in price information between markets. The cobweb model includes two markets because of the interdependence observed between agricultural markets. The model highlights several delays, as each commodity has a different production time (delay) depending on the nature of the product, and the dependence on the two markets creates delays in the information on the different markets. First, the paper confirms that the dynamics of two markets are similar to the dynamics of a single market if the interdependence is one-sided. Second, it is shown that production delays have a destabilizing effect and information delays have a stabilizing effect. In the context of financial market modeling [13], structural stability implies that certain "no-arbitrage" properties have a low impact on the disturbances in the model dynamics, leading to the formulation of a "no-arbitrage" requirement, which is referred to as the "uncertainty principle". The paper shows that structural stability is essential for a correct approximation of the model (which is used in the numerical approach to price calculation). Most of the articles use numerical methods for the analysis of market price dynamics. When conducting experiments with such models, it is important to use exact or near-exact methods. Such methods are the Consequent integration method, which is exact, and the Lambert *W* function method, which is near-exact [14–18].

How can economic entities act to manage an unstable situation in the face of crises and in what ways can these challenges be dealt with? Potential solutions are offered using innovative tools created using artificial intelligence and modern mathematical methods, such as the Lambert function method. Using artificial intelligence methods, such as deep learning and recurrent neural networks, as well as the innovative method of the Lambert *W* function, the information system for analyzing and forecasting market price stability would enable market entities to shape their behavior to obtain the greatest economic benefits. By simulating various scenarios and analyzing the market situation, it is possible to make political decisions that help manage the situation, by regulating the prices of essential products and raising interest rates.

The Lambert *W* function is a function with an infinite number of roots. This function is frequently used in mathematics, physics, and other fields [19–24]. One of the uses of the function in mathematics is to find the roots of differential equations with a delay argument. This application is of great interest because differential equations with a delay argument can be used to mathematically describe real-world models such as various control systems [15–17,24–26]. The problem with such equations is that they are more complex than ordinary differential equations and methods that are suitable for ordinary differential equations are not suitable for delay differential equations, so differential equations with a delay are usually solved by numerical methods, which can limit the accuracy of the solutions. For these reasons, the Lambert function can be used to find exact solutions. The Lambert function can have either scalar or matrix expressions [18,27]. The advantage of the Lambert function method is that as the number of branches of the function N changes, an increasingly accurate result is obtained, and as it approaches infinity, an exact solution is obtained. This method makes it possible to solve various types of differential equations with a delay argument, without changing the expression of the solution, only by changing the values of the constants.

From a systemic point of view, markets are related to information feedback in the form of price signals and, like all feedback systems, can be stable or unstable. Therefore, in this paper, we will study market price stability based on the Lambert function approach, widely used in control theory. We will write the market price as a differential equation with a time delay argument, via the supply and demand equations, assuming that supply has a real-time delay compared to demand. By applying the Lambert function to the resulting mathematical model, we obtain a solution-finding methodology adapted to the study of market price stability. Our research began with finding and representing the transcendental equation in a complex plane. Based on this study and presentation of the results, we published an article titled Analysis of market price stability using the Lambert function method in the journal *Lietuvos matematikos rinkinys* [28]. In this paper, we continue the work we started in the mentioned paper [28] by extending the study to obtain a solution of the differential equation with a delay argument for the study of price dynamics, also including nonhomogeneous and homogeneous cases.

Section 2.1 presents the finding of a solution to a mathematical model of market prices, a homogeneous differential equation with a delayed argument, obtained via the supply and demand equations using the Lambert function. Section 2.2 presents the solution when the mathematical model, a differential equation with a delayed argument, is nonhomogeneous. Section 2.3 presents the nonlinear delayed differential equation used in biological systems. It is proposed to analyze such an equation using the Lambert *W* function. The results section presents two examples related to the study of the dynamics of market price when the mathematical model is a homogeneous differential equation with a delay argument using the Lambert *W* function method and one example of the study of the dynamics of the Kalecki's stationary business cycle model when the model is written with a nonhomogeneous differential equation with a delay argument and the Lambert *W* function method is used for the study and the numerical dde23 method described in the Matlab is used for comparison. This article deals with an example where we have a nonlinear system. Example 4 shows the advantage of the Lambert *W* function method over the numerical method dde23.

This newly proposed method has already been applied in the study of agricultural real market prices and its use is planned to be extended.

2. Modified Lambert *W* Method

In this section, we will present the use of the Lambert function method to study market prices. This method is widely used in studies of control systems with delays, so we will modify this method in such a way that we can apply it in the study of market price stability.

The developed modified method of Lambert's functions is applied only to mathematical models for the study of market price dynamics. This is a novel application of Lambert functions to this type of model. This method was chosen due to its accuracy (Table 1 shows this) and invariance, resulting in a general solution for studies of price dynamics of various products (in Equations (14), (23) and (30)). In the obtained solutions of market price models, the differential equation with a delay argument, it is very easy to model various situations and obtain research results. For example, it is possible to study the influence of various delays between supply and demand on the price to observe the behavior of the price dynamics. It is also possible to analyze the elasticity coefficient, which shows the consumer's behavior in relation to the price. The main Lambert function method used for the three cases with a differential equation with a delay argument is homogeneous, and nonhomogeneous and when we have a nonlinear equation.

Table 1. Comparison results between free methods.

τ	**LAMBERT W**				**DDE32**
	N				
	5	**50**	**100**	**1000**	
1	0.0148	0.0015	0.00075	0.000075	0.7120
computational time, s	0.008841	0.294708	1.110586	103.209791	0.001228
0.1	0.00121	0.0001	0.000065	0.000008	0.08120
computational time, s	0.094167	0.413030	1.129259	104.467406	0.072151

2.1. Homogenous Case

In this article, we will analyze the balance of the market price when the equation is described by a mathematical model—a differential equation with a delay argument. Usually, market price is described by the difference between demand and supply [4,29]:

$$p'(t) = D(p(t)) - S(p(t)), \tag{1}$$

where $D(p(t))$—demand; $S(p(t))$—supply; and variable $p(t)$ is price dependent on time argument t.

The differential equation with a delay argument is as follows:

$$p'(t) = \gamma(D(p(t)) - S(p(t-\tau))), \tag{2}$$

where τ is the delay argument and γ is the coefficient of elasticity of demand. This model was chosen because the supply of goods is only available for the customers once they have been manufactured or transported; therefore, a delay occurs. The Equation (2) of demand and supply can be written as follows [4]:

$$\begin{gathered} D(p(t)) = \alpha + \beta p(t), \qquad \beta < 0, \\ S(p(t-\tau)) = \lambda + \delta p(t-\tau), \qquad \delta > 0. \end{gathered} \tag{3}$$

where α and β are the coefficients of the demand equation and λ and δ are the coefficients of the supply equation.

Then, the market price model can be written as

$$p'(t) = \gamma(\alpha + \beta p(t) - \lambda - \delta p(t-\tau)). \tag{4}$$

We denote variables $v = \gamma\delta$ and $r = -\gamma\beta$. After multiplying and dividing variable $\gamma(\alpha - \lambda)$ by $(\delta - \beta)$ we obtain the following:

$$p'(t) = \gamma(\alpha - \lambda)\frac{(\delta - \beta)}{(\delta - \beta)} - rp(t) - vp(t - \tau) \quad (5)$$

Let us denote market balance price $p(e) = \frac{(\alpha-\lambda)}{(\delta-\beta)}$ and use it in (5):

$$p'(t) + r(p(t) - p(e)) + v(p(t - \tau) - p(e)) = 0. \quad (6)$$

Denoting $z(t) = p(t) - p(e)$ and using (6) we obtain a differential equation with a delay argument:

$$z'(t) + rz(t) + vz(t - \tau) = 0. \quad (7)$$

To solve the delay differential equation, we will use the Lambert W function method [17,25,30]. Then, $z(t) = Ce^{st}$:

$$sCe^{st} + rCe^{st} + vCe^{s(t-\tau)} = 0. \quad (8)$$

Dividing both sides by $Ce^{st} \neq 0$ and moving $ve^{-\tau s}$ to the right-hand side yields the following:

$$s + r = -ve^{-\tau s}. \quad (9)$$

Multiplying both sides of the Equation (9) by $\tau e^{\tau s + r\tau}$ yields the following:

$$(s + r)\tau e^{(s+r)\tau} = -v\tau e^{\tau r}. \quad (10)$$

Using Lambert W function $\psi(w) = we^{w}$ yields the following:

$$(s + r)\tau = W(-v\tau e^{\tau r}). \quad (11)$$

We obtain the following solution:

$$s_k = \frac{1}{\tau}W_k(-v\tau e^{\tau r}) - r. \quad (12)$$

The solution of the transcendental equation of the differential equation with delay argument (4) using $v = \gamma\delta$ and $r = -\gamma\beta$ is obtained:

$$s_k = \frac{1}{\tau}W_k(-\gamma\delta\, \tau e^{-\gamma\beta\tau}) + \gamma\beta. \quad (13)$$

The obtained solution can be used to study the stability of market prices, obtaining results in the complex plane. By changing the variables of the differential equation, it is possible to find out when the price becomes unstable and there is a risk that it will increase; this is presented in more detail in this article [28].

The solution of the mathematical model, described by Equation (4), when $p(t) = z(t) + p(e)$ and $z(t) = \sum_{k=-\infty}^{\infty} e^{s_k t}C_k$, can be written as follows:

$$p(t) = \sum_{k=-\infty}^{\infty} e^{s_k t}C_k + p(e) = \lim_{N\to\infty} \sum_{i=-N}^{N} e^{s_i t}C_k + p(e), \ \ t \in (\tau, +\infty), \quad (14)$$

where C_k is the coefficient of the homogeneous part, which is a vector of complex numbers. The order of the vector depends on the number of branches of the Lambert function k. The coefficient is found $C_k = \lim_{N\to\infty}(\eta^{-1}(\tau, N)\Phi((\tau, N))_k$; here, the number N determines how many parts the studied interval will be divided into (N is equal to the number of k branches of the Lambert W function). $\Phi((\tau, N))_k$ is the initial function and η^{-1} is the pseudo-inverse matrix, which we obtain from the Equation (13): $\eta^{-1}(\tau, N) = e^{s_k(\tau,N)}$.

Computation of this coefficient is described in detail in [31]); N is a sufficiently large natural number. The obtained solution will be used in the analysis of market price dynamics. With the supply and demand models, we will study the dynamics of the market price under different parameters, evaluating the delay argument as well. Using this new method will allow us to obtain accurate results.

2.2. Nonhomogenous Case

When $p(e)$ is equal to the function but not the number, then we cannot solve the differential equations with a delay argument in the homogenous case. In this case, we can use the nonhomogenous case and solve this equation. This happens when α and λ in Equation (3) are the functions. The researched model for the market price is a first-order nonhomogenous differential equation with a delay argument, which can be described as follows:

$$p'(t) + rp(t) + vp(t-\tau) = u(t) \qquad \tau > 0$$
$$p(t) = \varphi(t) \qquad t \in [-\tau, 0], \tag{15}$$

where $u(t) = (r+v)p(e)$. We can write a solution for Equation (15) [25]:

$$p(t) = \int_0^t \Psi(t,\zeta)u(\zeta)d\zeta, \tag{16}$$

where $\Psi(t,\zeta)$ meets the following conditions [31]:

$$\frac{\partial}{\partial\zeta}\Psi(t,\zeta) = -r\Psi(t,\zeta), \qquad t-\tau \le \zeta < t$$
$$\text{(a)}$$
$$\frac{\partial}{\partial\zeta}\Psi(t,\zeta) = -r\Psi(t,\zeta) + v\Psi(t,\zeta+\tau), \qquad \zeta < \tau - t \tag{17}$$
$$\Psi(t,t) = 1 \qquad \text{(b)}$$
$$\Psi(t,\zeta) = 0 \qquad \zeta > t. \qquad \text{(c)}$$

Using the Lambert W function and conditions mentioned above, we can rewrite Equation (17a) as follows:

$$\Psi(t,\zeta) = e^{-r(t-\zeta)}, \qquad t-\tau \le \zeta < t. \tag{18}$$

A second Equation (17b) can be written using the Lambert W function:

$$\Psi(t,\zeta)_k = e^{(\frac{1}{\tau}W_k(-v\tau e^{r\tau})-r)(t-\zeta)}, \tag{19}$$

where $k = -\infty \ldots \infty$. The Lambert W function has an infinite number of solutions; therefore, a solution can be written as a sum:

$$\Psi(t,\zeta)_k = \sum_{k=-\infty}^{\infty} C'_k e^{(\frac{1}{\tau}W_k(-v\tau e^{r\tau})-r)(t-\zeta)}, \tag{20}$$

where C'_k is the coefficient of the nonhomogeneous part, which is a square matrix of complex numbers. The order of the matrix depends on the number of branches of the Lambert function k. The coefficient is found $C'_k = \lim_{N\to\infty}(\eta^{-1}(\tau,N)\Gamma((\tau,N))_k$, where the number N determines how many parts the studied interval will be divided into (N is equal to the number of k branches of the Lambert W function). From the expression

$\Gamma(\tau, N) = e^{v(\tau,N)}$ we find $\Gamma(\tau, N)$ and η^{-1}, which is the pseudo-inverse matrix we obtain from the Equation (13): $\eta^{-1}(\tau, N) = e^{s_k(\tau,N)}$.

The solution of the nonhomogenous scalar differential equation can be described as follows: When $t \leq \tau$

$$p(t) = \int_0^t \Psi(t,\zeta)vu(\zeta)d\zeta = \int_0^t e^{-r(t-\zeta)}vu(\zeta)d\zeta. \quad (21)$$

When $t > \tau$

$$p(t) = \int_0^{t-\tau} \sum_{k=-\infty}^{\infty} C_k' e^{(\frac{1}{\tau}W_k(-v\tau e^{r\tau})-r)(t-\zeta)}vu(\zeta)d\zeta + \quad (22)$$
$$+ \int_{t-\tau}^{t} e^{-r(t-\zeta)}vu(\zeta)d\zeta.$$

The solution of the nonhomogenous differential equation with a delay argument can be written as an equation, where the coefficient C_k is found using functions $p(t) = \varphi(t)$, $t \in [0, \tau]$. Calculation of C_k and C_k' is given in the following equation [25]:

$$p(t) = \sum_{k=-\infty}^{\infty} C_k e^{S_k t} + \int_0^t \sum_{k=-\infty}^{\infty} C_k' e^{S_k(t-\zeta)}bu(\zeta)d\zeta. \quad (23)$$

The obtained solution of the differential equation with a delay, using the modified Lambert function method, provides an opportunity to study mathematical models of the market price in the nonhomogeneous case.

When calculating the coefficients, it is very important to calculate the pseudo-inverse matrix, rather than the simple inverse, since the determinant is close to zero.

2.3. Nonlinear Case

In this subsection, we apply the method of Lambert functions to a nonlinear delay differential equation of the form

$$x'(t) + \alpha x(t) + \beta f(x(t-\tau)) = 0, \quad (24)$$

where α, β, and τ are positive constants and f satisfies the conditions in [32]:

$$f \in C(\mathbf{R}, \mathbf{R}) \quad \text{and} \quad uf(u) > 0, \quad x \neq 0 \quad (25)$$

and

$$\lim_{u \to 0} \frac{f(u)}{u} = 1. \quad (26)$$

where $f(u) = e^u - 1$. According to the Theorem 1 and Remark 1 described in the article [32], there is an oscillation if and only if the characteristic equation

$$F(s) = s + \alpha + \beta e^{-s\tau} = 0 \quad (27)$$

has no real roots.

Theorem 1. *Consider the following equation:*

$$y'(t) + \sum_{j=1}^{n} q_j f(y(t-\tau_j)) = 0, \qquad t \geq \tau \quad (28)$$

with $q_j = x * \beta_j$*, subject to conditions (25), (26), and*

$$f(u) \leq u, \qquad u \geq 0. \quad (29)$$

Then, every solution of Equation (28) oscillates if and only if the characteristic equation

$$\lambda + \sum_{j=1}^{n} q_j e^{-\lambda \tau_j} = 0 \tag{30}$$

of the corresponding linearized variational problem has no real roots.

Remark 1. *It is interesting to note that all of the nonlinear functions in the Equations*

$$y'(t) + \beta \frac{y(t-\tau)}{1+|y(t-\tau)|^r} = 0,$$

$$y'(t) + \alpha y(t) + \beta f(y(t-\tau)) = 0, \tag{31}$$

$$y'(t) + \alpha y(t) + \beta[1 - e^{-y(t-\tau)}] = 0$$

where α, r, β, and τ are positive constants. These equations satisfy conditions (25), (26), and (29) of Theorem 1. Furthermore, our results can be extended to more general equations of the form of Equation (28), which involve different functions f_j, each of which satisfies conditions (25), (26), and (29).

To study the resulting characteristic equation, we propose to apply the Lambert W function

$$s + \alpha = -\beta e^{-s\tau}. \tag{32}$$

Multiplying both sides of the equation by $\tau e^{\tau s + \alpha\tau}$ and using the Lambert W function $\psi(w) = we^{w}$ yields the following:

$$(s+\alpha)\tau = W(-\beta\tau e^{\tau\alpha}). \tag{33}$$

We obtain the solution of characteristic Equation (33):

$$s_k = \frac{1}{\tau} W_k(-\beta\tau e^{\tau\alpha}) - \alpha. \tag{34}$$

Using the Lambert function, we can investigate the parameters used to describe the oscillations of systems described by a nonlinear differential equation under certain conditions. The conditions described are typical of various studies in mathematical biology.

In nonlinear mathematical models of differential equations of biological oscillators, the evaluation of parameters is a difficult task. These models describe the dynamics of biological systems, and an assessment of their parameters is necessary to predict certain processes.

3. Results

Using the Matlab (R2024a) mathematical package, in this section we will present the results obtained by applying the modified Lambert function method to several cases. In the first example, the results are obtained when the differential equation with the delay argument is homogeneous, in the second, when we have the nonhomogeneous case. The third problem is solved and the modified method of Lambert functions is applied when we have a nonlinear case and we straighten it, and the fourth problem is chosen to show the advantage of the method by solving it with three methods: the method of Consequent integration (exact), the numerical method (described in the Matlab package), and the modified Lambert function method.

3.1. Example 1

It is well known in economics that there is a lag between supply and demand, so the estimation of the delay parameter is very important. We will analyze a mathematical model where the market price of a commodity is described by a homogeneous differential equation obtained through supply and demand:

$$p'(t) = \gamma(8 + 2 - 0.4p(t) - 0.6p(t - \tau))$$
$$\phi(t) = 8t - 2 \qquad t \in [-\tau; 0] \tag{35}$$

We are going to research the dynamics of market price. With an initial function that is written in Equation (35), the delay argument $\tau = 0.5$, and the coefficient of elasticity of demand $\gamma = 3$, we observe that the solution slightly oscillates in the interval from 0 to 4 and then equilibrates out at EUR 10. We chose a small delay, considering that automated processes allow us to reach the user faster. The coefficient of elasticity of demand describes the change in the quantity demanded of a good when the price of the good changes. If the demand ratio is greater than 1, buyers will be highly responsive to a change in price, if equal to 1, total revenue will not change when the price is increased or decreased, if it is less than 1, buyers will be unresponsive to a change in the price of the product. We selected parameters that can cause price instability in the longer term. When the coefficient of elasticity of demand increases to $\gamma = 7$ and $\gamma = 9$, the interval of price oscillation increases, and a longer period of time is required in order to reach equilibrium (Figure 1b,c).

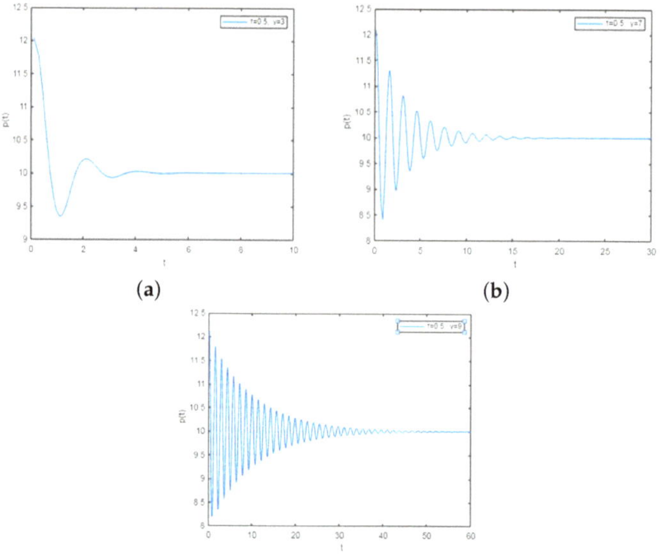

Figure 1. Dynamics of market price with different intensities. (**a**) Shows that the price will oscillate less with an elasticity coefficient equal to 3. (**b**) Shows that the price will fluctuate more with an elasticity coefficient equal to 7. (**c**) Shows that the price is stable when the elasticity of demand is 7, but more oscillating.

3.2. Example 2

The economic example was chosen from the article [5] in hopes of demonstrating the application of the Lambert *W* function method for the analysis of real-life market price dynamics. The subject of our experiment is the market price of poultry meat, which is described by a mathematical model:

$$
\begin{aligned}
p'(t) &= \gamma(375.2 - 166 - 0.78p(t) - 1.78p(t-\tau)) \\
\phi(t) &= 0.181t^2 + 3.4t + 67 \qquad t \in [-\tau; 0].
\end{aligned} \tag{36}
$$

Since, in the article, the delay argument was equal to 0.5, in this article, we conducted an experiment with a delay equal to 0.9.

When the coefficient of elasticity of demand is equal to 0.9, we have a small fluctuation (Figure 2a) because the demand is inelastic (buyers will not react much to the change in the price of the product). As the coefficient values increase, the oscillation interval also increases (Figure 2b). The third graph (Figure 2c) shows a pattern with a demand elasticity coefficient of 1.9, a coefficient in this case indicating that demand is flexible (i.e, buyers will be very responsive to a change in price). In this case, the system is asymptotically unstable and we cannot analyze when the market price will reach the equilibrium point. All presented results were calculated using the Lambert *W* function method and compared with the numerical method dde23 from the Matlab package.

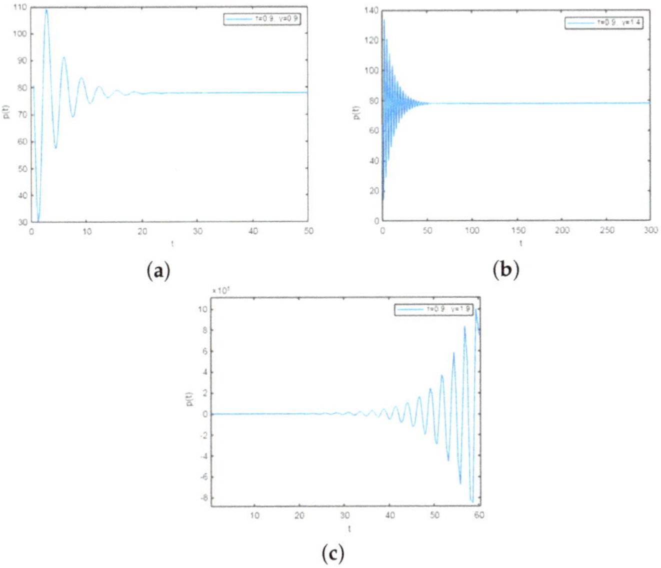

Figure 2. Dynamics of real-life market price with different intensities. (**a**) Shows that the price will fluctuate less with an elasticity coefficient equal to 0.9 and (**b**) shows that the price will fluctuate more with an elasticity coefficient equal to 1.4. (**c**) Shows that the price is unstable when the elasticity of demand is 1.9.

A number of branches of the Lambert *W* function equal to 80 was used during the experiment. The larger the number of branches of the Lambert function that is chosen, the more accurate the result is. To be more accurate than the numerical method dde23, it is enough to select 80 branches (the chosen number of branches is based on the analysis performed in the article [15,26]). The Lambert *W* function method is close to the exact Consequent integration method and is therefore superior to the dde23 method (a more detailed comparative analysis of the methods can be found in articles [15,26]).

3.3. Example 3

In economical theory, Kalecki's stationary business cycle model (in the paper [33] it is denoted KS) has the following form:

$$J'(t) = \frac{m}{\tau}(J(t) - J(t-\tau)) - nJ(t-\tau), \qquad \tau > 0, \tag{37}$$

where $m = a/s$ and $n = b$ are the symbols taken from paper [33]; τ—time delay; $J = k(t) - k_0$, $k(t)$—the capital stock at time t. In the paper [33], Kalecki's model is adapted to growth and is denoted KG. For this purpose, we will investigate linearized KG around the equilibrium point $[k(t), k(t-\tau) = (k_0, k_0) = (1,1)]$, in which it is of the same form as KS [33]:

$$k'(t) = a(k(t) - 1) - b(k(t-\tau) - 1), \qquad \tau > 0, \tag{38}$$

where $a = \frac{m}{\tau}$ and $b = \frac{m}{\tau} + n$. We are going to analyze Kalecki's stationary business cycle model, when $\tau = 0.6, m = 0.95, n = 0.121$. With parameters $a = \frac{0.95}{0.6} = \frac{19}{12}, b = (\frac{19}{12} + 0.121)$ used in the nonhomogenous differential equation, we obtain the following:

$$k'(t) - \frac{19}{12}k(t) + (\frac{19}{12} + 0.121)k(t - 0.6) = 0.121$$
$$k(t) = 1 \qquad t \in [-0.6, 0]$$

We will compare the price dynamics with different delay arguments. In Figure 3, we can see transition function of the system when the delay argument is 0.61 and in Figure 3b, when the delay argument is 0.6, the system becomes asymptotically unstable and capital stock can not be modeled for the future time steps. The method of Lambert functions allows us to estimate the stability limits of Kalecki's model by changing the delay argument. This modified method of Lambert functions allows investors to accurately determine the directions of capital stock dynamics. Using the Lambert *W* function method, we can test the behavior of the system with different values of parameters n, m, and the delay argument τ. In order to ensure the validity of the results, they were compared with the results of the (dde23) numerical method from the Matlab package. The proposed method is superior to numerical methods because it is accurate and responsive to parameter changes, and more sensitive because it provides an accurate solution. It is possible to determine more precisely at which parameter values the system becomes stable. Example 3 results were obtained using the same number of Lambert *W* function branches as in Examples 1 and 2 (more description in articles [15,26]).

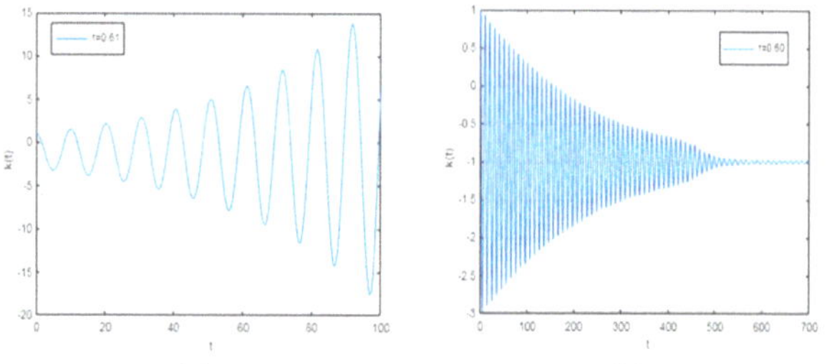

(a) (b)

Figure 3. Dynamics of Kalecki's stationary business cycle model with different delay arguments. Figure (**a**) shows the unstable behavior of stocks. Figure (**b**) shows when Kalecki's model becomes stable up to $\tau = 0.6$.

3.4. Example 4

To demonstrate the advantage of the Lambert *W* function method, we will present an example that we will solve using Laplace transforms, that is, using the Consequent integration method, the numerical dde23 method, and the proposed Lambert *W* function method.

Laplace transforms are used to transform differential equations with a delayed argument into simpler algebraic equations and to solve them using elementary algebraic methods. The method of Consequent integration is accurate, but it is difficult to apply to the solution of different equations with a delay, as a different expression of the solution is obtained for different equations, while in the Lambert *W* function method, only constants are changed, and the method itself is close to exact, and when we have an infinite number of branches of the Lambert *W* function, the method becomes accurate. Numerical methods that provide approximate results are widely used in the literature; one of the most commonly used is dde23, described in the Matlab package. We will present an example that illustrates the superiority of the Lambert *W* function method compared to the numerical method dde23, using the exact method of Consequent integration. We will solve a differential equation with a delayed argument:

$$y'(t) = -y(t-\tau), \text{ when } y(0) = 1. \tag{39}$$

Using the inverse Laplace transform, we will write down the solution ($\tau = 1$) for step response for dynamics of the model:

$$y'(t) = \sum_{n=0}^{\lfloor t \rfloor} \frac{(t-n)^n}{n!} \tag{40}$$

In Figure 4, the dashed line represents the result obtained by the numerical method dde23, which deviates from the Lambert *W* function and the exact method result, which shows that the Lambert *W* function is more accurate than the numerical one. The accuracy of the Lambert *W* function method depends on the numbers of branches. The table shows the relative error at different numbers of branches of the Lambert *W* function and the exact calculation of the method. The numerical method is also compared with the exact one. All results are obtained by choosing one of the freely assigned t = 5. It can be seen from the graph that the relative error between the exact and the numerical method is larger in the interval $t \in [0;5]$. We can conclude that by choosing only five branches, we obtain a more accurate result than in the case of the numerical method.

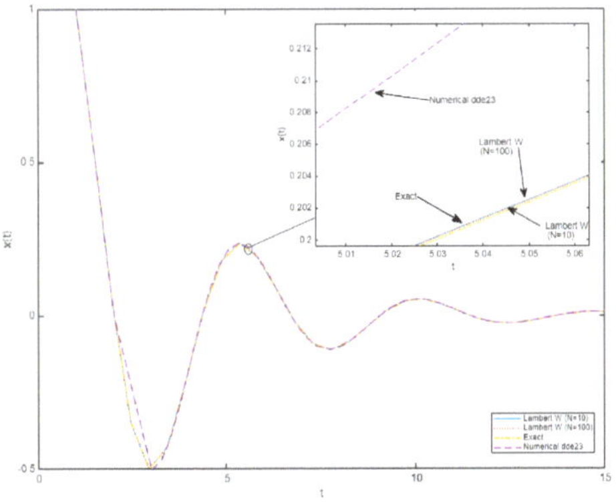

Figure 4. Comparison results between free methods.

In Table 1, we have given computational times to the different number of branches of the Lambert *W* function. We can see that the numerical method is faster, but it is less accurate. When we have a lower delay, the method gives more accurate results, but the computation time is longer.

4. Conclusions and Futures

This paper presents a new application of the Lambert *W* function method to the solution of an economic model described by a differential equation with a delay. The use of the Lambert *W* function method, when we solve delay differential equations, is widely known only in the application of control systems with delays.

This method is close to an exact mathematical method and is proposed in economics as a substitute for numerical solution methods.

The proposed modified method can be used not only for the study of price stability but also for the analytical study of other market models described by a linear delayed differential equation.

It is proposed to apply to a nonlinear Kaleicki's stationary business cycle model a linear first-order nonhomogeneous differential equation with a delay argument and to solve the Lambert *W* function.

It is proposed to apply the Lambert *W* function to the nonlinear differential equation to find the solution of the characteristic equation.

The results are almost exact, which makes the solution suitable for analyzing models with different parameter values. The proposed Lambert *W* function method shows that it is more accurate than the numerical method dde23 described in the Matlab package and compared to the exact Consequent integration method it is superior because there are no complicated expressions. The numerical method outperforms the modified Lambert *W* function only in terms of time.

The study of differential equations and dynamical systems provides valuable insights into the behavior of complex systems, whether in economics, biology, or other scientific disciplines.

In order to strengthen the reliability and applicability of our theoretical model, future research should focus on empirical validation. After integrating case studies and real data, we will more accurately assess the model's ability to predict market stability. This empirical study will not only help to present concrete facts that support our theoretical claims, but will also allow a practical comparison of the performance of the model under various market conditions.

Author Contributions: Conceptualization, T.R.; Methodology, I.J.; Software, A.Z.; Validation, M.L.; Formal analysis, J.A.; Resources, R.K.; Data curation, M.B. All authors have read and agreed to the published version of the manuscript.

Funding: This research received no external funding.

Data Availability Statement: Data is contained within the article.

Conflicts of Interest: The authors declare no conflicts of interest.

Notations

This manuscript uses the following notations: Consequent integration method—exact method using Laplace transforms; dde23—numerical method described in the Matlab package for calculating differential equations with delays; Homogenous—a type of delay differential equation; k—Lambert *W* function branches; KG—indicate that here Kalecki's model is adapted to growth; KS—The Kalecki's stationary business cycle model; Lambert *W*—Lambert *W* function method; Matlab—mathematical package; N—branches of Lambert *W* functions used to calculate coefficients; Nonhomogenous—a type of delay differential equation.

References

1. Anokye, M.; Amankwah, H.; Essel, E.K.; Amponsah, I.K. Dynamics of Equilibrium Prices With Differential and Delay Differential Equations Using Characteristic Equation Techniques. *J. Math. Res.* **2019**, *11*, 1–8. [CrossRef]
2. Das, S.S.; Dalai, D.K.; Nayak, P.C. Delay Differential Equations Using Market Equilibrium. *IOSR J. Math.* **2017**, *13*, 562–576.
3. Grzelak, A.; Kułyk, P. Is Michał Kalecki's theory of investment applicable today? The case study of agricultural holdings in the EU countries. *Agric. Econ.-Czech* **2020**, *66*, 317–324. [CrossRef]

4. Li, Y.C.; Yang, H. A Mathematical Model of Demand-Supply Dynamics with Collectability and Saturation Factors. *Int. J. Bifurc. Chaos* **2017**, *27*, 1750016. [CrossRef]
5. Martina, B.; Veronika, N. The Use of Functional Differential Equations in the Model of the Meat Market with Supply Delay. *Procedia-Soc. Behav. Sci.* **2015**, *213*, 74–79. [CrossRef]
6. Heffernan, J.; Corless, R. Solving some delay differential equations with computer algebra. *Math. Sci.* **2006**, *31*, 21–34.
7. Michiels, W.; Niculescu, S.-I. *Stability, Control, and Computation for Time-Delay Systems: An Eigenvalue-Based Approach*; SIAM: Philadelphia, PA, USA, 2014.
8. Saha, L.M.; Das, M.K.; Bhardwaj, R. Asymptotic stability analysis applied to price dynamics. *Indian J. Ind. Appl. Math.* **2018**, *9*, 186–195. [CrossRef]
9. Gardini, L.; Radi, D.; Schmitt, N.; Sushko, I.; Westerhoff, F. Causes of fragile stock market stability. *J. Econ. Behav. Organ.* **2022**, *200*, 483–498. [CrossRef]
10. Ammy-Driss, A.; Garcin, M. Efficiency of the financial markets during the COVID-19 crisis: Time-varying parameters of fractional stable dynamics. *Phys. A Stat. Mech. Its Appl.* **2023**, *609*, 128335. [CrossRef]
11. Chang, C. Financial stability nexus with oil prices shocks and business cycle uncertainty during COVID-19: Empirical trends of ASEAN economies. *Environ. Sci. Pollut. Res.* **2023**, *30*, 95590–95605. [CrossRef]
12. Matsumoto, A.; Szidarovszky, F. Asymptotic Dynamics in a Multi-market Delayed Cobweb Model. *Comput. Econ.* **2024**, 1–36. [CrossRef]
13. Smirnov, S.N. Structural Stability of the Financial Market Model: Continuity of Superhedging Price and Model Approximation. *J. Oper. Res. Soc. China* **2024**, *12*, 215–241 . [CrossRef]
14. Bin, F.; Fuming, P. Some results of finding the roots of time-delay systems by Lambert *W* function. In Proceedings of the 2021 IEEE International Conference on Power Electronics, Computer Applications (ICPECA), Shenyang, China, 22–24 January 2021; pp. 199–204. [CrossRef]
15. Ivanoviene, I.; Rimas, J. The use of the Lambert *W* function method for analysis of a control system with delays. *Inf. Technol. Control* **2013**, *42*, 325–332.
16. Ivanoviene, I.; Rimas, J. Complement to method of analysis of time delay systems via Lambert *W* function. *Automatica* **2015**, *54*, 25–28. ISSN 0005-1098. [CrossRef]
17. Ivanoviene, I.; Rimas, J. Analysis of control system with delay using the Lambert function. In *Proceedings of the Information and Software Technologies: 19th International Conference, ICIST 2013, Kaunas, Lithuania, 10–11 October 2013*; Skersys, T., Butleris, R., Butkiene, R., Eds.; Springer: Berlin/Heidelberg, Germany, 2013; pp. 1–10.
18. Ulsoy, G.A.; Gitik, R. On the Convergence of the Matrix Lambert *W* Approach to Solution of Systems of Delay Differential Equations. *ASME J. Dyn. Sys. Meas. Control* **2020**, *142*, 024501. [CrossRef]
19. Li, J.; Qin, C.; Yang, C.; Ai, B.; Zhou, Y. Extraction of Single Diode Model Parameters of Solar Cells and PV Modules by Combining an Intelligent Optimization Algorithm with Simplified Explicit Equation Based on Lambert *W* Function. *Energies* **2023**, *16*, 5425. [CrossRef]
20. Mainardi, F.; Masina, E.; González-Santander, J.L. A Note on the Lambert *W* Function: Bernstein and Stieltjes Properties for a Creep Model in Linear Viscoelasticity. *Symmetry* **2023**, *15*, 1654. [CrossRef]
21. Rathie, P.N.; Ozelim, L.C.S.M. On the Relation between Lambert W-Function and Generalized Hypergeometric Functions. *Stats* **2022**, *5*, 1212–1220. [CrossRef]
22. Rawa, M.; Calasan, M.; Abusorrah, A.; Alhussainy, A.A.; Al-Turki, Y.; Ali, Z.M.; Sindi, H.; Mekhilef, S.; Aleem, S.H.E.A.; Bassi, H. Single Diode Solar Cells—Improved Model and Exact Current–Voltage Analytical Solution Based on Lambert's *W* Function. *Sensors* **2022**, *22*, 4173. [CrossRef]
23. Xie, T.; Li, M. Finite-Time Stability of Impulsive Fractional Differential Equations with Pure Delays. *Axioms* **2023**, *12*, 1129. [CrossRef]
24. Ivanoviene, I.; Rimas, J. Investigation of the multidimensional automatic control system, having strucrure of the chain, applying Lambert *W* function. In *Electrical and Control Technologies: Proceedings of the 7th International Conference on Electrical and Control Technologies ECT 2012, Kaunas, Lithuania, 3–4 May 2012*; Kaunas University of Technology, IFAC Committee of National Lithuanian Organisation, Lithuanian Electricity Association; Technologija: Kaunas, Lithuania, 2012; pp. 82–86.
25. Sun, Y.; Nelson, P.W.; Ulsoy, A.G. *Time-Delay Systems: Analysis and Control Using the Lambert W Function*; World Scientific: Singapore, 2010.
26. Jankauskiene, I.; Rimas, J. A Note on the Use of Step Responses Matrix and Lambert *W* Function in the Dynamics Analysis of Time Delay Systems. *Inf. Technol. Control* **2017**, *46*, 228–234. [CrossRef]
27. Ivanoviene, I.; Rimas, J. Analysis of a multidimensional control system with delays. In *Proceedings of the Electrical and Control Technologies: Proceedings of the 6th International Conference on Electrical and Control Technologies ECT 2011, Kaunas, Lithuania, 5–6 May 2011*; Kaunas University of Technology, IFAC Committee of National Lithuanian Organisation, Lithuanian Electricity Association; Technologija: Kaunas, Lithuania, 2011; pp. 124–129.
28. Jankauskiene, I.; Miliūnas, T. The stability analysis of the market price using Lambert function method. *Liet. Mat. Rink.* **2020**, *61*, 13–17. [CrossRef]
29. Liz, E.; Gergely, R. Global dynamics in a commodity market model. *J. Math. Anal. Appl.* **2013**, *398*, 707–714. ISSN 0022-247X. [CrossRef]

30. Corless, R.M.; Gonnet, G.H.D.; Hare, E.G.; Jeffrey, D.J.; Knuth, D.E. On the LambertW function. *Adv. Comput. Math.* **1996**, *5*, 329–359. [CrossRef]
31. Malek-Zavarei, M.; Jasmshidi, M. *Time Delays System*; Elsevier: North Holland, NY, USA, 1987.
32. Kulenović, M.; Ladas, G.; Meimaridou, A. On oscillation of nonlinear delay differential equations. *Q. Appl. Math.* **1987**, *45*, 155–164. [CrossRef]
33. Franke, R. Reviving Kalecki's business cycle model in a growth context. *J. Econ. Dyn. Control* **2018**, *91*, 157–171. [CrossRef]

mathematics
MDPI

Review

Combining Differential Equations with Stochastic for Economic Growth Models in Indonesia: A Comprehensive Literature Review

Muhamad Deni Johansyah [1,*], Endang Rusyaman [1], Bob Foster [2], Khoirunnisa Rohadatul Aisy Muslihin [1] and Asep K. Supriatna [1]

[1] Department of Mathematics, Faculty of Mathematics and Natural Sciences, Universitas Padjadjaran, Jalan Raya Bandung-Sumedang, Km. 21, Jatinangor, Sumedang 45363, Jawa Barat, Indonesia; rusyaman@unpad.ac.id (E.R.); khoirunnisa17002@mail.unpad.ac.id (K.R.A.M.); a.k.supriatna@unpad.ac.id (A.K.S.)
[2] Faculty of Economics and Business, Universitas Informatika dan Bisnis Indonesia, Jalan Soekarno-Hatta No. 643, Bandung 40285, Jawa Barat, Indonesia; bobriset@unibi.ac.id
* Correspondence: muhamad.deni@unpad.ac.id

Abstract: Economic growth modeling is one of the methods a government can use to formulate appropriate economic policies to improve the prosperity of its people. Differential equations and stochastic models play a major role in studying economic growth. This article aims to conduct a literature review on the use of differential equations in relation to stochastics to model economic growth. In addition, this article also discusses the use of differential and stochastic equations in economic growth models in Indonesia. This study involves searching for and selecting articles to obtain a collection of research works relevant to the application of differential and stochastic equations to economic growth models, supported by bibliometric analysis. The results of this literature review show that there is still little research discussing economic growth models using differential equations combined with stochastic models, especially those applied in Indonesia. While the application of these models remains relatively limited, their potential to offer deeper insights into the complex dynamics of economic growth is undeniable. By further developing and refining these models, we can gain a more comprehensive understanding of the factors driving growth and the potential implications of various economic policies. This will ultimately equip policy-makers with a more powerful analytical tool for making informed decisions.

Keywords: economic growth; differential equations; Indonesia; stochastic; systematic literature review

MSC: 34A08; 60H10; 91B02

Citation: Johansyah, M.D.; Rusyaman, E.; Foster, B.; Muslihin, K.R.A.; Supriatna, A.K. Combining Differential Equations with Stochastic for Economic Growth Models in Indonesia: A Comprehensive Literature Review. *Mathematics* **2024**, *12*, 3219. https://doi.org/10.3390/math12203219

Academic Editors: Leonid Piterbarg and Luigi Rodino

Received: 5 September 2024
Revised: 3 October 2024
Accepted: 10 October 2024
Published: 14 October 2024

1. Introduction

Economic growth is one of the most important factors determining the welfare of a country's people. Economic growth essentially refers to the increase in the production of goods and services in a country within a certain period of time [1]. The impact of economic growth can spread to various sectors, ranging from employment and income to people's standard of living [2]. Economic growth is influenced by several factors, including production factors in the form of labor, capital, and natural resources [1,3]. The quality of production factors, technological progress, and education can determine the level of output and productivity of a country, which ultimately determines the rate of its economic growth. The use of information and communication technology and quality education can increase business efficiency, increase productivity, and expand market reach [4,5]. Political stability and government policies also have an impact on a country's economic growth [6].

The importance of economic growth is also reflected in its ability to increase investment. When a country experiences positive economic growth, investors tend to see better opportunities to allocate their capital in investment projects [7]. High economic growth in a country can increase a company's revenue and profit. This allows the company to have greater internal funds to make investments [1]. However, high economic growth can have negative impacts such as increasing interest rates and increasing investment risk. High economic growth can cause inflation. To control inflation, central banks usually raise interest rates. This can make investment more expensive and reduce investor interest. Therefore, the analysis and modeling of economic growth play an important role in examining the complexity of this phenomenon and helping to formulate the right strategy.

One approach that can be used to analyze economic growth is using a differential equation model. A differential equation model is a mathematical model used to describe changes in a variable over time. In the context of economic growth, a differential equation model can be used to describe changes in a country's output (production) over time by visualizing trends and patterns of economic growth, as well as predicting possible future scenarios [4]. This differential equation model can be used to analyze factors that influence economic growth, such as investment levels, savings rates, and population growth rates [6]. By providing an understanding of the factors that play a role in economic growth, differential equation models can help policy-makers to formulate effective policies to encourage growth and achieve national development goals [8].

In finance, stochastic models are commonly used because they incorporate uncertainty and provide a more realistic representation of economic dynamics. For example, these models are used to describe changes in asset values, with one component representing deterministic factors and the other component representing stochastic factors such as stock prices [9]. Furthermore, stochastic models can explain the diverse growth trajectories of developing countries by incorporating technological diffusion and improvements in social infrastructure, thus accounting for conditional and absolute convergence in economic growth [10].

The combined method of using differential and stochastic equations, namely stochastic differential equations, leverages the power of deterministic and probabilistic approaches to solve complex problems, especially in high-dimensional diffusion and anomalous scenarios [11]. These stochastic differential equations combine differential equations, probability theory, and stochastic processes to capture random dynamic phenomena in various domains [12]. These models are used in economics and finance to model the unpredictable behavior of continuous systems [13].

This approach incorporates randomness into financial modeling, which is essential for capturing the unpredictable nature of markets and the dynamics of stock prices and interest rates [14]. The Black–Scholes model utilizes stochastic differential equations to price options, considering market uncertainty [15]. The analytical solutions of these equations enable us to calculate the expected value and variance of option prices, which are key metrics in risk assessment. Moreover, numerical solutions offer greater flexibility in handling various types of stochastic differential equations, allowing us to achieve high accuracy and gain deeper insights into stochastic systems [16]. Therefore, the use of stochastic differential equations to model economic growth can be a novelty for further research.

In this article, we perform a systematic literature review (SLR) regarding the use of mathematical models involving differential equations in modeling economic growth problems. Furthermore, this article discusses economic growth models that combine differential and stochastic equations. This SLR is used to identify and analyze previous studies that are relevant to the topic being studied [17]. In addition, this article also employs bibliometric analysis to study research trends and help to find gaps in existing studies.

To support the objectives of this research, we compiled the following research questions (RQs):

1. What is the state of research on economic growth models using differential equations combined with stochastics?
2. What is the state of research on economic growth models in Indonesia?
3. What are the gaps in existing economic growth research?

This article is structured as follows: Section 2 presents the methods used in compiling this SLR, particularly for how to collect articles for analysis. Section 3 presents the results of the bibliometric analysis and literature review related to the topic discussed. Section 4 contains a discussion of the research results. Finally, conclusions are presented in Section 5.

2. Methods

As part of our method, we referred to the Preferred Reporting Items for Systematic Reviews and Meta-Analyses (PRISMA) [18]. PRISMA provides a standard checklist that guides authors in systematic reporting, ensuring that important aspects of the review process are not understated [19]. Then, a bibliometric analysis was carried out on the data obtained from the PRISMA process with the help of R version 4.4.0 software.

2.1. Article Collection

In this study, article data were obtained through searching international databases, namely Scopus, Science Direct, and Dimensions, using certain keywords. Searches in the Scopus and Science Direct databases were limited to the "title, abstract, and keywords" sections, while in the Dimensions database, they were applied to the "title and abstract" sections, because Dimensions cannot search through the "keywords". Article searches were limited by year of publication, namely to articles published from 2018 to 2024. In this study, we considered articles published in open access journals.

The keywords used in the article search are presented in Table 1. The combinations of keywords presented in Table 2 were established based on the proposed topic, namely differential equations and economic growth. Combinations B, C, and D were established to obtain a more specific search for the type of differential equation used. In addition, keyword E was used to search for articles that combine differential equations and stochastic models. F represented a combination of A with "Indonesia", and was intended to observe the development of this topic specifically in Indonesia. The results of this search are given in Table 2.

Table 1. Keyword combinations in article searches.

Code	Keyword Combination
A	"differential equation" AND "economic growth"
B	"ordinary differential equation" AND "economic growth"
C	"partial differential equation" AND "economic growth"
D	("fractional differential" OR "fractional calculus") AND "economic growth"
E	"differential equation" AND "stochastic" AND "economic growth"
F	"differential equation" AND "economic growth" AND "Indonesia"

Table 2. Number of publications with six keyword combinations.

Code	Scopus	Science Direct	Dimensions	Total
A	42	4	52	98
B	6	1	7	14
C	7	1	9	17
D	13	4	13	30
E	2	1	1	4
F	0	0	0	0
Total	70	11	82	163

2.2. Selection Method

The selection method used in this study was divided into several stages, as shown in Figure 1. The first stage was the identification stage, containing the data search process explained in the previous sub-section. At this stage, 163 articles were obtained from three databases and using six keyword combinations. These articles were then examined during the second stage, namely the screening stage.

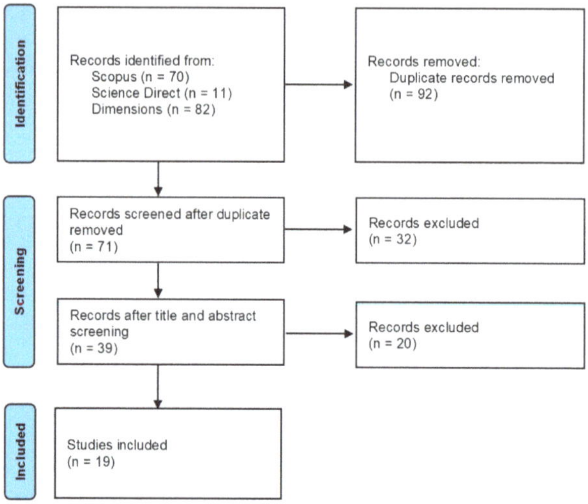

Figure 1. Data selection process diagram.

The screening stage consisted of two checks, the first of which was the duplication check. At this stage, the articles were checked for duplication—that is, checking whether there were articles contained in two or more databases with the same title and author. Duplication checks were carried out with the help of the Jabref reference manager. Through this check, 92 duplicate articles were identified and removed, and the other articles went to the next check, namely the title and abstract checks. At this stage, all articles were checked for their suitability to the research topic based on their titles and abstracts. From this check, 39 articles were obtained which were declared relevant to the research topic. The articles selected at this stage are hereinafter referred to as Dataset 1 and were used in the bibliometric analysis.

The next stage was the eligibility selection. At this stage, the articles in Dataset 1 were thoroughly examined by reading the full text to further evaluate the relevance of each article. From this selection process, 19 articles were obtained that met the criteria. The articles that went through this stage are referred to as Dataset 2 and were analyzed further. The results of the selection process are shown in Table 3.

Table 3. Results of the article selection process.

Code	Total	Duplication		Abstract and Title		Full Text	
		Excluded	Included	Excluded	Included	Excluded	Included
A	98	61	37	17	20	11	9
B	14	11	3	1	2	2	0
C	17	2	15	7	8	4	4
D	30	17	13	7	6	2	4
E	4	1	3	0	3	1	2
F	0	0	0	0	0	0	0
Total	163	92	71	32	39 [1]	20	19 [2]

[1] Dataset 1 used for bibliometric analysis; [2] Dataset 2 used for literature review.

2.3. Bibliometric Analysis

In this article, bibliometric analysis for Dataset 1 was first performed using the R-bibliometrix program. Bibliometrix is a bibliometric analysis package written in the R language and is open-source software [20]. The R-bibliometrix package is equipped with the "biblioshiny" command, which allows for the combination of bibliometrix's functionalities in a web-based interface [21]. This command is used to obtain scientific data mapping and perform a comprehensive analysis of the bibliographic information available from Dataset 1.

3. Results

3.1. Results of Bibliometric Analysis

This section presents the results of the bibliometric analysis based on Dataset 1. The analysis was performed using R version 4.4.0 with bibliometrix package. Dataset 1 consists of 39 articles selected according to the title and abstract, published from 2018 to 2024 and written by 87 authors from 23 countries.

3.1.1. Co-Occurrence Network

The most important result of the bibliometric analysis is the co-occurrence network. We present the co-occurrence network using Keyword Plus, representing words or phrases that frequently appear in the titles of article references and not necessarily in the article title or authors' keywords [22]. The use of Keyword Plus allows us to cover broader terms that are not included in the authors' keywords [23]. The co-occurrence network for Dataset 1 is given in Figure 2.

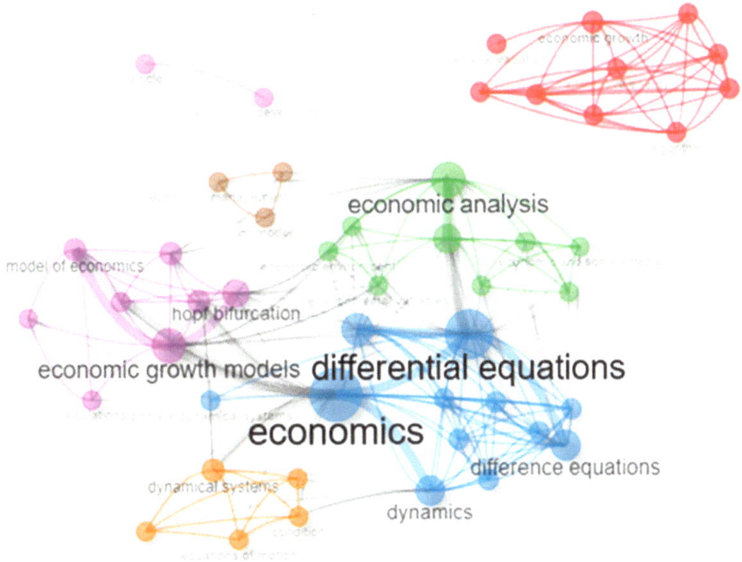

Figure 2. Co-occurrence network of Dataset 1.

The size of the circle of each term indicates how important the term is in the context of the retrieved articles. The presence of a line connecting each term to another indicates that there is a relationship between the terms—in this case, the existence of articles discussing both terms. Based on Figure 2, "differential equations" and "economics" have the largest circles, so both are the most relevant terms in all articles in Dataset 1. In addition, the relationship between the two terms indicates that both are often studied together as a research topic. The presence of the terms "dynamical systems" and "dynamics" indicates an interest in the dynamics of economic systems, i.e., how economic variables change over time.

Furthermore, the terms from Figure 2 are displayed in Figure 3 via the Wordcloud feature of R-bibliometrix. This feature can be used to display keyword data in a visual form that is easy to read and understand, so that it is easier to find the most important or frequently appearing words in the articles being analyzed.

Figure 3. Wordcloud of Dataset 1.

In Figure 3, we can see the terms "ordinary differential equation", "fractional differential equation", "fractional calculus", and "fractional derivative". This shows the complexity of research that examines economic growth models. However, in Figures 2 and 3, the term "partial differential equation" is not found. This shows that the topic of partial differential equations in economic growth modeling has not been the focus of research. In addition, the terms "stochastic" or "stochastic differential equation" do not appear directly in Figures 2 and 3. This also implies that most of the research represented by Dataset 1 focuses more on deterministic models, where the variables that affect the system are clearly defined and do not contain significant elements of chance or uncertainty.

3.1.2. Thematic Mapping

Another form of analysis that can be carried out using R-bibliometrix is thematic mapping, which groups terms based on their level of development and relevance. In this form of mapping, terms derived from bibliometric data are grouped into groups of words, each of which represents a frequently discussed theme. These groups of words are arranged into four quadrants. The first quadrant is the Motor Theme quadrant. In this quadrant, groups show high centrality and density, indicating a strong connection between terms and their relevance to other groups. The second quadrant is the Niche Theme quadrant, characterized by high density but low centrality. Groups in this quadrant have strong internal cohesion but limited connection to other groups. Furthermore, the third quadrant is the Emerging or Declining Theme quadrant. Groups in this quadrant show low density and centrality, indicating the development of new topics or topics that are declining. The fourth quadrant, Basic Theme, displays a strong connection to other groups while having weak internal cohesion.

As shown in Figure 4, Dataset 1 produces three clusters of words in thematic mapping. Cluster 1 is represented by "economics", "economic growth models", and "delay differential equation", while Cluster 2 is represented by "differential equations", "economic analysis", and "difference equations". Both clusters are in the Motor Themes group, where centrality and density are high. Each term included in Cluster 1 and 2 has a high affinity with other terms and with other clusters. Meanwhile, Cluster 3, represented by "dynamical systems" and "dynamics", is in the Emerging or Declining Themes group. This means that this cluster has a tendency to have low development and relevance.

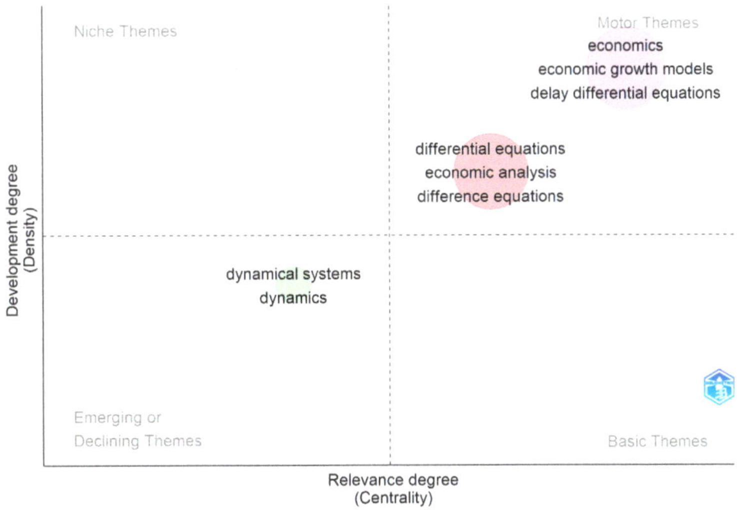

Figure 4. Thematic mapping of Dataset 1.

3.2. Results of the Systematic Literature Review

This section provides the results of the analysis based on the development of research on economic growth models that use differential equations. We identify the purpose of the study, the models used, and check whether the article involves a stochastic process. In addition, we also identify the applications of the model in real-life problems from the articles in Dataset 2. The results of this study are given in Tables 4–6.

Table 4. Objectives and relevant topics of the articles in Dataset 2 that involve a stochastic process but do not include applications.

Author(s)	Research Objectives	Model
[24]	Developing a complete numerical approach to estimate parameters and level weights for the OU Superposed model	Superposed Ornstein–Uhlenbeck model
[25]	Extending the classical Lagrangian approach to solving continuous-time stochastic optimal control problems	Continuous stochastic optimal control model

Table 5. Objectives and relevant topics of the articles in Dataset 2 that do not involve a stochastic process and do not include applications.

Author(s)	Research Objectives	Model
[26]	Finding non-negative classical solutions of partial differential equations describing the dynamics of the capital stock.	Spatial AK growth model
[27]	Developing quadratic nonlinear cost functions in economic growth models and analyzing appropriate solutions.	Riccati fractional differential equation
[28]	Investigating nonlinear RFDE solutions with constant coefficients in economic growth models.	Riccati fractional differential equation
[29]	Measuring the dynamics of uncertainty in an economy by restructuring the Cobb–Douglas paradigm of the Solow–Swan model.	Cobb–Douglas paradigm of the Solow–Swan model
[30]	Building a Lie group-based approach to analyze optimal control problems in economic growth models.	Nonlinear fractional order single-valued triangular neutrosophic fuzzy differential equations

Table 5. *Cont.*

Author(s)	Research Objectives	Model
[31]	Analyzing the Ramsey dynamic model with a Hamiltonian optimal control problem in neoclassical growth models by utilizing Lie group theory.	Ramsey dynamical model with Hamiltonian
[32]	Building a mathematical model of economic growth influenced by memory and lag.	Fractional differential equation of a Keynesian model with memory and lag
[33]	Studying the influence of memory effects on economic growth rates.	Solow model of long-run growth with memory and Solow–Lucas model of a closed economy with memory
[34]	Revisiting the Ramsey economic model with fractional order.	Ramsey model represented by the fractional Caputo–Liouville derivative
[35]	Studying the relationship between growth and inflation using Taylor's rule.	Solow–Tobin Model with Taylor rule
[36]	Investigating the dynamic interaction between supply and demand, with a focus on aggregation, through the introduction of a new mathematical model using the Caputo operator.	Demand–Supply Dynamic with a collectability factor using delay differential equations

Table 6. Objectives and relevant topics of the articles in Dataset 2 with their applications.

Author(s)	Research Objectives	Model	Application
[37]	Construct a general differential equation that describes long-run economic growth in terms of cyclical and trend components.	Continuous RBC (real business cycles) model based on the nonlinear acceleration of induced investment model	Predictions of the dynamics of the United States economy.
[38]	Establish sharp global stability conditions to achieve positive equilibrium of the well-known economic growth model when production function delays are considered.	Solow–Swan model with variable delay	Constant saving ratio and no pollution effect; variable saving ratio and no pollution effect; constant saving ratio and pollution effect.
[39]	Describe a multidecadal pattern of per capita gross domestic product (GDP) growth that increases and then decreases as a region becomes richer.	Nonlinear differential equation model (DEM)	Calculate the IMF's projected GDP and population growth rates, and calculate the projected GDP per capita growth rate.
[40]	Build an approach model for the diffusion of physical capital across national borders that explains the impact of smuggling on the economic growth of Venezuela or other countries facing similar conditions.	Spatial Solow Model	Economic growth of Venezuela.
[41]	Apply Caputo derivatives to simulate China's gross domestic product (GDP) growth.	Integer Order Model (IOM) and Caputo Fractional Order Model (CFOM)	Forecasting China's GDP.
[42]	Build an economic model for the Group of Twenty (G20) countries in the period of 1970–2018.	Keynesian models of the dynamics of economies	Economic growth model for the Group of Twenty (G20) countries.

4. Discussion

4.1. Development

Based on Tables 4–6, the research in Dataset 1 can be identified based on its research objectives. Several articles aim to build economic growth models, including [29,32,33,36,42]. Other articles aim to build models which are accompanied by their applications to real-life problems, including Burges et al. [39], who used nonlinear differential equations to build economic growth models which were then used to calculate the IMF's growth rate in GDP and population. González-Parra et al. [40] built an economic growth model in Venezuela based on the Spatial Solow Model that considers smuggling. Tejado et al. [42] discussed the Keynesian model of the dynamics of the economy applied to countries in the Group of Twenty (G20). Akaev [37] implemented the RBC model to predict the dynamics of the US economy for 2018–2050. The model obtained is a nonlinear differential equation model with the form

$$\frac{d^2Y}{dt^2} + \left\{\lambda + -\lambda v\left[1 - \chi\frac{4}{3}\left(v\frac{dY}{dt}\right)^2\right]\right\}\frac{dY}{dt} - \lambda(1-s)\frac{dY^e}{dt} + \lambda Y \\ -\lambda(1-s)Y^e = \lambda\frac{dA}{dt} + \lambda A, \tag{1}$$

where $Y = C + I + A, C$ represents the level of consumption, I is the actual induced investment, and A is the total output. λ states the rate of the supply reaction, and χ is equal to 0 or 1.

Furthermore, Ming et al. [41] discussed an economic growth model for China using fractional differential equations. This model has the following variables:

- x_1: land area $\left(\text{km}^2\right)$;
- x_2: cultivation area $\left(\text{km}^2\right)$;
- x_3: population (millions of people);
- x_4 : total capital formation (billion);
- x_5: exports of goods and services (billion);
- x_6: general government final consumer spending (billions);
- y: GDP (billion).

The fractional calculus model is given by

$$y(t) = \sum_{k=1}^{7} c_k\left(D_{t_0,t}^{\alpha_k}x_k\right)(t), \tag{2}$$

where t_0 and α_k represent the initial year and the derived order, respectively. In addition, the Caputo derivative $D_{t_0,t}^{\alpha_k}x_k$ for x_k defined as

$$D_{t_0,t}^{\alpha_k}x_k(t) = \frac{1}{\Gamma(1-\alpha_k)}\int_{t_0}^{t}\frac{\frac{dx_k(s)}{ds}}{(t-s)^{\alpha_k}}ds, t > t_0, 0 < \alpha_k < 1. \tag{3}$$

Furthermore, Tejado et al. [42] discussed the fractional differential equation model applied to countries in the Group of Twenty (G20). Of the nine variables identified, the final model used five variables and was generalized using fractional derivatives to obtain

$$y(t) = \sum_{k=1,2} C_k x_k(t) + \sum_{k=3,4,5} C_k D^{\alpha_k} x_k(t), \tag{4}$$

with

- $y(t)$: GDP in 2010 in USD;
- C_k: weight, constant over time, for each input variable x_k;
- x_1: land area, measuring available natural resources;
- x_2: population, measuring available human resources;
- x_3: gross capital formation (GCF) in 2010 in USD, which measures the resources produced (this model takes into account the accumulation of resources produced);
- x_4: exports of goods and services in 2010 in USD, which measures the external impact on the economy;
- x_5: general government final consumption expenditure in 2010 in USD, which measures the impact of the budget on the economy.

Ming et al. [41] and Tejado et al. [42] used the average absolute deviation (MAD) and coefficient of determination $\left(\text{R}^2\right)$ to evaluate the economic growth model with the following formula:

$$MAD = \frac{\sum_{i=1}^{n} |y_i - \hat{y}_i|}{n}, \tag{5}$$

$$R^2 = 1 - \frac{\sum_{i=1}^{n} (y_i - \hat{y}_i)^2}{\sum_{i=1}^{n} (y_i - \hat{y})^2}. \tag{6}$$

Tejado et al. [42] using the Akaike Information Criterion (AIC) to select variables in the model with the following formula:

$$\text{AIC} = N\log \frac{\sum_{j=1}^{N} (y_j - \hat{y}_j)^2}{N} + 2K + \frac{2K(K+1)}{N-K-1}, \tag{7}$$

$$w_i = \frac{\exp\left(-\frac{\text{AIC}_i - \underset{M}{\min} AIC}{2}\right)}{\sum_{j=1}^{M} \exp\left(-\frac{\text{AIC}_j - \underset{M}{\min}\text{AIC}}{2}\right)}. \tag{8}$$

Meanwhile, Ming et al. [41] used the Bayesian Information Criterion (BIC) for variable selection with the following formula:

$$\text{BIC} = \log\left(\frac{1}{n}\sum_{j=1}^{n} (y_j - \hat{y}_j)^2\right) + \frac{p\log n}{n}, \tag{9}$$

$$w_j = \frac{\exp\left(-\frac{\text{BIC}_i - \text{BIC}_{\min}}{2}\right)}{\sum_{j=1}^{p} \exp\left(-\frac{\text{BIC}_j - \text{BIC}_{\min}}{2}\right)}. \tag{10}$$

Several articles focus their research on model analysis, such as that of Buedo-Fernández and Liz [38], who conducted an analysis of the global stability condition for a positive equilibrium of the Solow–Swan economic growth model with variable delay. This study also considers applications to several possible conditions, such as a constant saving ratio and no pollution effects, a variable saving ratio and no pollution effects, and a constant saving ratio and pollution effects. Hu [26] discussed finding non-negative classical solutions of the spatial AK growth model. Johansyah et al. [27,28] investigated the existence and uniqueness of solutions to nonlinear fractional Riccati differential equations with constant coefficients, and then found their numerical solutions using the Adomian Decomposition Method (ADM) and Kamal's Integral Transform (KIT) as well as the Combined Theorem of Adomian Decomposition Methods and Kashuri–Fundo Transformation Methods. Moreover, Polat and Özer [30,31] presented the optimal control problem in economic growth models with differential equations used as constraint functions. Model analysis was conducted by utilizing Lie group theory. Zhang [35] explained the relationship between economic growth and inflation using the Taylor rule. Chen et al. [24] introduced a new mathematical model using the Caputo operator to analyze the dynamic interaction between supply and demand, focusing on accumulation in economic growth.

Most of the models used are nonlinear models that utilize numerical simulations. The differential equations involved are dominated by fractional PD forms, as seen in [27–30,32–34,36,41,42]. In addition, only two articles involve partial differential equations, namely González-Parra et al. [40] and Hu [26]. Both studies use spatial economic growth models, namely the Spatial Solow Model and the spatial AK growth model. Spatial economic growth models can be associated with partial differential equations because they often involve spatial elements that can be described using mathematical equations. Partial differential equations used in spatial economic growth models can detail how various economic variables change over time and space [43]. In addition, Buedo-Fernández and Liz [38] and Chen et al. [36] used a delay differential equation model, where there is a delay in the system's response to changes. This means that the rate of change in a variable at a particular time can depend on its value at a previous time.

Furthermore, stochastic differential equations were used by Mariani et al. [24] and Ewald and Nolan [25]. Mariani et al. [24] discussed a numerical approach to estimate the parameters and level weights of the Ornstein–Uhlenbeck (OU) model. In this model, the Gaussian OU process is defined as the solution of the stochastic differential equation:

$$dX_t = \lambda(m - X_t)dt + \alpha dB_t, t > 0, \tag{11}$$

where λ, m, and α are real constants and B_t is the standard Brownian motion on $\mathbb{R}$. Initial value X_0 is a random variable that is independent of $(B_t)_{t\geq 0}$.

Meanwhile, in the article by Ewald and Nolan [25], stochastic differential equations are used to model the dynamics of a system with uncertainty in optimal control problems. The optimal control model used is stochastic optimal control, which involves stochastic differential equations in the problem constraints, namely

$$\max_{(\alpha_t)\in\mathcal{A}} \mathbb{E}\left(\int_0^T f(t, X_t, \alpha_t)dt + g(X_t)\right), \text{s.t. } dX_t = b(t, X_t, \alpha_t)dt + \sigma(t, X_t, \alpha_t)dW_t, \tag{12}$$

assuming that the state variables (X_t) and Brownian motion (W_t) are one-dimensional but can be adapted to the multidimensional case using vector–matrix notation. The admissible control set $\mathcal{A}$ is the set of progressively measurable stochastic processes that take values in the set A. In addition, the functions $f, b, \sigma : [0, T] \times \mathbb{R} \times A \to \mathbb{R}$ and $g : \mathbb{R} \to \mathbb{R}$ are continuously differentiable with bounded derivatives.

4.2. Economic Growth Modeling in Indonesia

As shown in Table 6, differential equations are used to model the economic growth of several locations around the world, such as the US [24], Venezuela [40], China [41], and the countries in the Group of Twenty [42]. However, differential equation models have not been used to model economic growth in Indonesia.

Articles discussing economic growth models in Indonesia mostly use stochastic models, especially time series models, including vector autoregressive (VAR) models [44–47], autoregressive distributed lag (ARDL) [48–53], error correction models (ECMs) [54–58], and vector error correction models (VECMs) [59–63]. Time series models are usually chosen because economic data include observations of variables at certain time intervals. In addition, economic variables often depend on previous values. Through time series models, this dependency can be easily expressed in the concept of autoregression and can be used to analyze the economic fluctuation cycle that occurs periodically [64,65].

Other models that are widely used are panel data models, such as the fixed effect model (FEM), common effect model (CEM), and random effect model [65–70]. Panel data models provide more accurate estimates of the effects of independent variables on economic growth [71]. In addition, panel data analysis can capture both long-term and short-term relationships between macroeconomic variables and economic development, thus providing insight into the dynamics of economic growth [72]. Panel data analysis also allows for the examination of cross-sectional and time series data, thus allowing for a more comprehensive understanding of the determinants of economic growth [73].

Several studies also use a combination of time series models with panel data models, namely the Panel Vector Error Correction Model (PVECM) [74] and Panel Vector Autoregression (PVAR) [75]. These models allow researchers to use information from both cross-sectional and time series dimensions, thereby increasing the efficiency of parameter estimation compared to traditional time series and panel data models. This framework allows the interactions of different time series behaviors to coexist, making it useful for estimating shifts in the predictability of non-stationary variables and testing the periodic validity of economic theories [76].

4.3. Research Gaps and Future Work

In addition to being used directly to model economic growth, differential equations can also be used in dynamic system modeling or control theory. The topic of dynamic systems appears in the results of the bibliometric analysis (see Figures 2 and 3). Dynamic systems describe changes in variables over time. Differential equations play a role in describing these changes mathematically and predicting future system behavior. Models that have been used previously include the Solow–Swan model [38,39], the Ramsey model [34], and the Keynesian model [42]. Differential equations also play a role in control theory, such as in the research of Polat and Özer [30,31] and Ewald and Nolan [25], who present an optimal control theory model with differential equations used as constraint functions.

From the results of the bibliometric analysis in Figures 2 and 3, there are no terms regarding "partial differential equation" and "stochastic differential equation". This shows that both topics are still rarely studied in relation to economic growth. In addition, our literature review also shows that there are only two articles that use partial differential equation models and two articles that use stochastic differential equations.

Although the use of stochastic differential equations in economic growth studies is still rare, the potential of this method to offer deeper insights should not be overlooked. Incorporating uncertainty and variation in economic variables allows stochastic differential equations to present a more authentic and dynamic framework. Thus, it is imperative for future studies to further investigate the application of stochastic differential equations in economic growth modeling. This effort will not only enhance the current body of literature but also provide a more powerful analytical instrument for economic decision makers.

Furthermore, although differential equation models have been used to model economic growth in several other countries, such as the US, Venezuela, China, and the G20 countries, these models have not been used in Indonesia. This highlights the opportunity for new research to develop a model of Indonesian economic growth using differential equations. In addition, the use of stochastic models combined with differential equation models is still rare. Stochastic differential equation models can also be used to obtain more accurate and comprehensive results in modeling economic growth in Indonesia. Therefore, differential equations can also be utilized in modeling economic growth to study the effects of economic policies on economic growth in Indonesia.

5. Conclusions

This paper presents a comprehensive overview of the literature on the subject of modeling economic growth with differential equations, supplemented by bibliometric analysis. The results of this study indicate that differential equations have been used to determine models and calculate economic growth values. Current research on growth models has used differential equation models of both integer and fractional orders. The lack of research using stochastic differential equations also represents an opportunity for further study.

Several studies have discussed economic growth models and applied them to real-world problems, such as in the US, Venezuela, China, and the G20 countries. In Indonesia, the models used to calculate economic growth values are still predominantly stochastic models, such as time series and panel data models. The use of ordinary and partial differential equation models with a fractional order and combining them with stochastic models can be a novelty method in determining models and calculating economic growth values in a country. Thus, this review article has the potential to help contribute to the work of policy-makers in formulating a better economic direction with a more accurate economic growth model using a combination of differential and stochastic equations, especially for Indonesia.

Although this study offers valuable insights, it is important to acknowledge some of its limitations. The data used in this study were obtained through searches of international databases, namely Scopus, Science Direct, and Dimensions, using specific keywords. Limited access to paid journals is a challenge in obtaining comprehensive data. For more complete and in-depth results, further researchers can use more specific keywords in article searches and utilize access to a wider range of journals.

Author Contributions: Conceptualization, M.D.J.; methodology, E.R.; software, K.R.A.M.; validation, B.F. and A.K.S.; writing—original draft preparation, M.D.J.; writing—review and editing, K.R.A.M.; supervision, E.R., B.F. and A.K.S.; funding acquisition, M.D.J. All authors have read and agreed to the published version of the manuscript.

Funding: This research was funded by the Ministry of Education, Culture, Research and Technology of the Republic of Indonesia through Fundamental Research with the contract number 3953/UN6.3.1/PT.00/2024. The author also thanks the Chancellor of Universitas Padjadjaran and the Director of the Directorate Research and Community Service at Universitas Padjadjaran who provided funds for outreach. The authors of this study received the Universitas Padjadjaran Academic Leadership Grant (ALG) with the contract number 1446/UN6.3.1/PT.00/2024.

Data Availability Statement: No new data were created or analyzed in this study.

Conflicts of Interest: The authors declare no conflict of interest.

References

1. Mankiw, N.G. *Principles of Microeconomics*; Cengage Learning: Boston, MA, USA, 2020.
2. Todaro, M.P.; Smith, S.C. *Economic Development*; Pearson: Harlow, UK, 2020.
3. Barro, R.; Sala-i-Martin, X. *Economic Growth*, 2nd ed.; The MIT Press: Cambridge, MA, UK, 2024.
4. Acemoglu, D. *Introduction to Modern Economic Growth*; Princeton University Press: Princeton, NJ, USA, 2008.
5. Romer, P.M. *Advanced Macroeconomics*; Worth Publishers: Belper, UK, 2018.
6. Solow, R.M. A contribution to the theory of economic growth. *Q. J. Econ.* **1956**, *70*, 65–94. [CrossRef]
7. Wan, X. A literature review on the relationship between foreign direct investment and economic growth. *Int. Bus. Res.* **2010**, *3*, 52. [CrossRef]
8. Johnston, L.D. Lectures on Economic Growth. By Robert E. Lucas Jr. Cambridge, MA: Harvard University Press, 2002. pp. xi, 204. $49.95. *J. Econ. Hist.* **2022**, *62*, 915–916. [CrossRef]
9. Yang, X.; Liu, Y.; Park, G.K. Parameter estimation of uncertain differential equation with application to financial market. *Chaos Solitons Fractals* **2020**, *139*, 110026. [CrossRef]
10. Sng, H.Y.; Rahman, S.; Chia, W.M. Economic Growth and Transition: A Stochastic Technological Diffusion Model. *J. Econ. Dev.* **2009**, *34*, 1. [CrossRef]
11. Craigmile, P.; Herbei, R.; Liu, G.; Schneider, G. Statistical inference for stochastic differential equations. *Wiley Interdiscip. Rev. Comput. Stat.* **2023**, *15*, e1585. [CrossRef]
12. Breda, D.; Canci, J.K.; D'Ambrosio, R. An Invitation to Stochastic Differential Equations in Healthcare. In *Quantitative Models in Life Science Business: From Value Creation to Business Processes*; Springer International Publishing: Cham, Switzerland, 2022; pp. 97–110.
13. Hagenimana, E.; Uwiliniyimana, C.; Umuraza, C. A study on7 stochastic differential equation using fractional power of operator in the semigroup theory. *J. Appl. Math. Phys.* **2023**, *11*, 1634–1655. [CrossRef]
14. Merton, R.C. Theory of rational option pricing. *Bell J. Econ. Manag. Sci.* **1973**, *4*, 141–183. [CrossRef]
15. Black, F.; Scholes, M. The pricing of options and corporate liabilities. *J. Political Econ.* **1973**, *81*, 637–654. [CrossRef]
16. Kloeden, P.E.; Platen, E. *Numerical Solution of Stochastic Differential Equations*; Springer: Berlin/Heidelberg, Germany, 1992.
17. Tranfield, D.; Denyer, D.; Smart, P. Towards a methodology for developing evidence-informed management knowledge by means of systematic review. *Br. J. Manag.* **2003**, *14*, 207–222. [CrossRef]
18. Page, M.J.; Moher, D.; McKenzie, J.E. Introduction to PRISMA 2020 and implications for research synthesis methodologists. *Res. Synth. Methods* **2022**, *13*, 156–163. [CrossRef] [PubMed]
19. Rethlefsen, M.L.; Kirtley, S.; Waffenschmidt, S.; Ayala, A.P.; Moher, D.; Page, M.J.; Koffel, J.B. PRISMA-S: An extension to the PRISMA statement for reporting literature searches in systematic reviews. *Syst. Rev.* **2021**, *10*, 39. [CrossRef] [PubMed]
20. Derviş, H. Bibliometric analysis using bibliometrix an R package. *J. Scientometr. Res.* **2019**, *8*, 156–160. [CrossRef]
21. Rusliana, N.; Komaludin, A.; Firmansyah, M.F. A scientometric analysis of urban economic development: R bibliometrix biblioshiny application. *J. Ekon. Pembang.* **2022**, *11*, 80–94. [CrossRef]
22. Garfield, E.; Sher, I.H. Brief Communication Keywords PlusAlgorithmic Derivative Indexing. *J. Am. Soc. Inf. Sci.* **1993**, *44*, 298. [CrossRef]
23. Zhang, J.; Yu, Q.; Zheng, F.; Long, C.; Lu, Z.; Duan, Z. Comparing keywords plus of WOS and author keywords: A case study of patient adherence research. *J. Assoc. Inf. Sci. Technol.* **2016**, *67*, 967–972. [CrossRef]
24. Mariani, M.C.; Asante, P.K.; Tweneboah, O.K.; Kubin, W. A 3-component superposed Ornstein-Uhlenbeck model applied to financial stock markets. *Res. Math.* **2022**, *9*, 2024339. [CrossRef]
25. Ewald, C.O.; Nolan, C. On the adaptation of the Lagrange formalism to continuous time stochastic optimal control: A Lagrange-Chow redux. *J. Econ. Dyn. Control* **2024**, *162*, 104855. [CrossRef]
26. Hu, H. Asymptotic Behaviors Analysis of the Spatial AK Model with Trade Costs. *Theor. Econ. Lett.* **2021**, *11*, 603–614. [CrossRef]

27. Johansyah, M.D.; Supriatna, A.K.; Rusyaman, E.; Saputra, J. Solving the economic growth acceleration model with memory effects: An application of combined theorem of Adomian decomposition methods and Kashuri–Fundo transformation methods. *Symmetry* **2022**, *14*, 192. [CrossRef]
28. Johansyah, M.D.; Supriatna, A.K.; Rusyaman, E.; Saputra, J. The Existence and Uniqueness of Riccati Fractional Differential Equation Solution and Its Approximation Applied to an Economic Growth Model. *Mathematics* **2022**, *10*, 3029. [CrossRef]
29. Khan, N.A.; Razzaq, O.A.; Riaz, F.; Ahmadian, A.; Senu, N. Dynamics of fractional order nonlinear system: A realistic perception with neutrosophic fuzzy number and Allee effect. *J. Adv. Res.* **2021**, *32*, 109–118. [CrossRef] [PubMed]
30. Polat, G.G.; Özer, T. On group analysis of optimal control problems in economic growth models. *Discret. Contin. Dyn. Syst.-Ser. S* **2020**, *13*, 2853–2876.
31. Polat, G.; Özer, T. On Ramsey Dynamical Model and Closed-Form Solutions. *J. Nonlinear Math. Phys.* **2021**, *28*, 209–218. [CrossRef]
32. Tarasov, V.E.; Tarasova, V.V. Dynamic Keynesian model of economic growth with memory and lag. *Mathematics* **2019**, *7*, 178. [CrossRef]
33. Tarasov, V.E. Non-linear macroeconomic models of growth with memory. *Mathematics* **2020**, *8*, 2078. [CrossRef]
34. Traore, A.; Sene, N. Model of economic growth in the context of fractional derivative. *Alex. Eng. J.* **2020**, *59*, 4843–4850. [CrossRef]
35. Zhang, W.B. Banking and Money in an Extended Solow-Uzawa's Neoclassical Growth Model. *Stud. Bus. Econ.* **2021**, *16*, 221–243. [CrossRef]
36. Chen, Q.; Kumar, P.; Baskonus, H.M. Modeling and analysis of demand-supply dynamics with a collectability factor using delay differential equations in economic growth via the Caputo operator. *AIMS Math.* **2024**, *9*, 7471–7491. [CrossRef]
37. Akaev, A. Nonlinear differential equation of macroeconomic dynamics for long-term forecasting of economic development. *Appl. Math.* **2018**, *9*, 512–535. [CrossRef]
38. Buedo-Fernández, S.; Liz, E. On the stability properties of a delay differential neoclassical model of economic growth. *Electron. J. Qual. Theory Differ. Equ.* **2018**, *2018*, 1–14. [CrossRef]
39. Burgess, M.G.; Langendorf, R.E.; Moyer, J.D.; Dancer, A.; Hughes, B.B.; Tilman, D. Multidecadal dynamics project slow 21st-century economic growth and income convergence. *Commun. Earth Environ.* **2023**, *4*, 220. [CrossRef]
40. González-Parra, G.; Chen-Charpentier, B.; Arenas, A.J.; Díaz-Rodríguez, M. Mathematical modeling of physical capital diffusion using a spatial solow model: Application to smuggling in Venezuela. *Economies* **2022**, *10*, 164. [CrossRef]
41. Ming, H.; Wang, J.; Fečkan, M. The application of fractional calculus in Chinese economic growth models. *Mathematics* **2019**, *7*, 665. [CrossRef]
42. Tejado, I.; Pérez, E.; Valério, D. Fractional derivatives for economic growth modelling of the group of twenty: Application to prediction. *Mathematics* **2020**, *8*, 50. [CrossRef]
43. Combes, P.P.; Mayer, T.; Thisse, J.F.E.G. The integration of Regions and Nations. *Econ. Geogr.* **2010**, *10*, 255–275.
44. Annannab, H.; Surajo, A.Z.; Ahmad, F. Coal consumption and economic growth in Indonesia: An analysis of restricted structural var. *Econ. Bus. Account. Soc. Rev.* **2022**, *1*, 96–103.
45. Alim, M.B. Impact of Taxes and Technological Improvement for Economic Growth: English. *Tamansiswa Account. J. Int.* **2022**, *4*, 72–77. [CrossRef]
46. Chandra, K.; Sari, W.R.; Sriwulan, D.Y.; Adhimukti, M.R. Effect of Yield Spreads (State Bonds) on Economic Growth Performance in Indonesia. *J. Risk Financ. Manag.* **2023**, *16*, 175. [CrossRef]
47. Harnani, S.; Widarni, E.L.; Bawono, S. The The Role of Human Capital in Natural Sustainability and Economic Growth in Indonesia a Dynamic ARDL Approach: English. *Tamansiswa Account. J. Int.* **2022**, *5*, 28–35. [CrossRef]
48. Abdillah, K. Optimum government size and economic growth in Indonesia: ARDL model approach. *Ekuilibrium J. Ilm. Bid. Ilmu Ekon.* **2023**, *18*, 37–47. [CrossRef]
49. Ajnura, U.; Juliansyah, H. The Effect of Fluctuation World Oil Prices and the Rupiah Exchange Rate on Economic Growth in Indonesia. *J. Malikussaleh Public Econ.* **2021**, *4*, 38–44. [CrossRef]
50. Pertiwi, A.B.; Juwita, A.H.; Suryanto, S. Effects of Poverty, Income Inequality and Economic Growth to Environmental Quality Index (EQI) in 33 Province in Indonesia 2014–2019. *Ekuilibrium J. Ilm. Bid. Ilmu Ekon.* **2021**, *16*, 154–163. [CrossRef]
51. Elfaki, K.E.; Handoyo, R.D.; Ibrahim, K.H. The impact of industrialization, trade openness, financial development, and energy consumption on economic growth in Indonesia. *Economies* **2021**, *9*, 174. [CrossRef]
52. Rhamadhani, R.F.; Fanani, A. Optimizing the Role of Indonesia's Islamic Financial Industry: Empirical Analysis of Its Impact on Economic Growth. *JEKSYAH Islam. Econ. J.* **2023**, 3, 11–22. [CrossRef]
53. Elfaki, K.E.; Heriqbaldi, U. Analyzing the Moderating Role of Industrialization on the Environmental Kuznets Curve (EKC) in Indonesia: What Are the Contributions of Financial Development, Energy Consumption, and Economic Growth? *Sustainability* **2023**, *15*, 4270. [CrossRef]
54. Djulius, H. Foreign Direct Investment or External Debt and Domestic Saving: Which has Greater Impacts on Growth. *Etikonomi* **2018**, *17*, 37–44. [CrossRef]
55. Duja, B.; Supriyanto, H. The influence of GDP, interest rate, wage, inflation and exchange rate on residential property price in Indonesia. *Plan. Malays.* **2019**, *17*, 389–400. [CrossRef]
56. Fadli, F.; Hongbing, O.; Liu, Y. Earmarking Tax for Indonesia's Economic Growth through the Education and Health Sector in the Long and Short Term Period. *Bus. Econ. Res.* **2020**, *10*, 1–39. [CrossRef]

57. Fitriami, R.; Masbar, R.; Miksalmina, M. The Impact of Foreign Trade Policy on Economic Growth of Aceh Province, Indonesia. *Int. J. Financ. Econ. Bus.* **2020**, *1*, 109–117. [CrossRef]
58. Prabowo, B.H.; Drean, B. Green Finance and Green Economic Trade Off Economic and Environtment in Indonesia: English. *ASIAN Econ. Bus. Dev.* **2022**, *4*, 7–13. [CrossRef]
59. Adzimatinur, F.; Gloriman Manalu, V. The Effect of islamic financial inclusion on economic growth: A case study of islamic banking in indonesia. *Bp. Int. Res. Crit. Inst.-J.* **2021**, *4*, 976–985. [CrossRef]
60. Agusalim, L.; Pohan, F.S. Trade openness effect on income inequality: Empirical evidence from Indonesia. *Signifikan* **2018**, *7*, 1–14. [CrossRef]
61. Anggoro, A.C.P. Effect of Exports, Imports of Oil and Gas Products, Inflation, on Economic Growth. *Curr. Adv. Res. Sharia Financ. Econ. Worldw.* **2022**, *2*, 148–163. [CrossRef]
62. Bashir, A.; Thamrin, K.M.; Farhan, M.; Atiyatna, D.P. The causality between human capital, energy consumption, CO_2 emissions, and economic growth: Empirical evidence from Indonesia. *Int. J. Energy Econ. Policy* **2019**, *9*, 98–104.
63. Firdaus, E.N.; Septiani, Y. Effect analysis of inflation, exports and imports on economic growth in Indonesia. *J. Humanit. Soc. Sci. Bus.* **2022**, *2*, 32–46. [CrossRef]
64. Rao, T.S.; Rao, S.S.; Rao, C.R. (Eds.) *Time Series Analysis: Methods and Applications*; Elsevier: Amsterdam, The Netherlands, 2012; Volume 30.
65. Mills, T.C. *Time Series Econometrics: A Concise Introduction*; Springer: Berlin/Heidelberg, Germany, 2015.
66. Afandi, M.A.; Amin, M. Islamic bank financing and its effects on economic growth: A cross province analysis. *Signifikan J. Ilmu Ekon.* **2019**, *8*, 243–250. [CrossRef]
67. Asmarani, T.E.; Ningsih, E.A. Domestic credit and stock market impact on economic growth: A new evidence in Five asean countries. *Winners* **2022**, *23*, 95–102. [CrossRef]
68. Azizurrohman, M.; Hartarto, R.B.; Lin, Y.M.; Nahar, F.H. The Role of Foreign Tourists in Economic Growth: Evidence from Indonesia. *J. Ekon. Studi Pembang.* **2021**, *22*, 313–322. [CrossRef]
69. Gati, S.A. The Effect of Telecommunications Infrastructure on Inclusive Economic Growth in Indonesia 2011−2021. *Int. J. Innov. Technol. Soc. Sci.* **2023**, *2*, 1–12.
70. Asnawi, A.; Irfan, I.; Ramadhani, M.F.C. The Gap in Economic Growth from Foreign Investment and Domestic Investment across Provinces in Indonesia. *Electron. J. Educ. Soc. Econ. Technol.* **2020**, *1*, 34–38. [CrossRef]
71. Bechtel, G.G. Panel regression of arbitrarily distributed responses. *J. Data Sci.* **2009**, *7*, 255–266. [CrossRef]
72. Gonzales, J.T. Implications of AI innovation on economic growth: A panel data study. *J. Econ. Struct.* **2023**, *12*, 13. [CrossRef]
73. Al Shams, T.M.; Ashraf, A. Macroeconomic Indicators of Economic Growth using Panel Data: A Study from South Asian Countries. *ABC Res. Alert* **2023**, *11*, 9–20. [CrossRef]
74. Amaluddin, A. THE The Nexus Between Poverty, Education and Economic Growth in Indonesia. *Econ. Dev. Anal. J.* **2019**, *8*, 345–354. [CrossRef]
75. Erlando, A.; Riyanto, F.D.; Masakazu, S. Financial inclusion, economic growth, and poverty alleviation: Evidence from eastern Indonesia. *Heliyon* **2020**, *6*, e05235. [CrossRef]
76. Gao, J.; Peng, B.; Yan, Y. Time-Varying Vector Error-Correction Models: Estimation and Inference. *arXiv* **2023**, arXiv:2305.17829. [CrossRef]

MDPI AG
Grosspeteranlage 5
4052 Basel
Switzerland
Tel.: +41 61 683 77 34

Mathematics Editorial Office
E-mail: mathematics@mdpi.com
www.mdpi.com/journal/mathematics

www.ingramcontent.com/pod-product-compliance
Lightning Source LLC
LaVergne TN
LVHW072322090526
838202LV00019B/2332